ACCA

Taxation

(TX-UK)

Study Text

Finance Act 2020 for June 2021 to March 2022
examination sittings

British library cataloguing-in-publication data

A catalogue record for this book is available from the British Library.

Published by:

Kaplan Publishing UK
Unit 2 The Business Centre
Molly Millars Lane
Wokingham
Berkshire
RG41 2QZ

ISBN 978-1-78740-595-0

© Kaplan Financial Limited, 2020

Printed and bound in Great Britain

Acknowledgements

These materials are reviewed by the ACCA examining team. The objective of the review is to ensure that the material properly covers the syllabus and study guide outcomes, used by the examining team in setting the exams, in the appropriate breadth and depth. The review does not ensure that every eventuality, combination or application of examinable topics is addressed by the ACCA Approved Content. Nor does the review comprise a detailed technical check of the content as the Approved Content Provider has its own quality assurance processes in place in this respect.

We are grateful to the Association of Chartered Certified Accountants and the Chartered Institute of Management Accountants for permission to reproduce past examination questions. The answers have been prepared by Kaplan Publishing.

Contents

KAPLAN PUBLISHING

Introduction

How to use the Materials

These Kaplan Publishing learning materials have been carefully designed to make your learning experience as easy as possible and to give you the best chance of success in your examinations.

The product range contains a number of features to help you in the study process. They include:

(1)   Detailed study guide and syllabus objectives

(2)   Description of the examination

(3)   Study skills and revision guidance

(4)   Study text

(5)   Question practice

The sections on the study guide, the syllabus objectives, the examination and study skills should all be read before you commence your studies. They are designed to familiarise you with the nature and content of the examination and give you tips on how to best approach your learning.

The **Study Text** comprises the main learning materials and gives guidance as to the importance of topics and where other related resources can be found. Each chapter includes:

- The **learning objectives**, which have been carefully mapped to the examining body's own syllabus learning objectives or outcomes. You should use these to check you have a clear understanding of all the topics on which you might be assessed in the examination.

- The **chapter diagram** provides a visual reference for the content in the chapter, giving an overview of the topics and how they link together.

- The **content** for each topic area commences with a brief explanation or definition to put the topic into context before covering the topic in detail. You should follow your studying of the content with a review of the illustration/s. These are worked examples which will help you to understand better how to apply the content for the topic.

- **Test your understanding** sections provide an opportunity to assess your understanding of the key topics by applying what you have learned to short questions. Answers can be found at the back of each chapter.

- **Summary diagrams** complete each chapter to show the important links between topics and the overall content of the examination. These diagrams should be used to check that you have covered and understood the core topics before moving on.

- **Questions to practice** are provided at the back of the Study Text.

Quality and accuracy are of the utmost importance to us so if you spot an error in any of our products, please send an email to mykaplanreporting@kaplan.com with full details, or follow the link to the feedback form in MyKaplan.

Our Quality Coordinator will work with our technical team to verify the error and take action to ensure it is corrected in future editions.

Icon Explanations

 Definition – Key definitions that you will need to learn from the core content.

 Key point – Identifies topics that are key to success and are often examined.

 Supplementary reading – These sections will help to provide a deeper understanding of core areas. The supplementary reading is **NOT** optional reading. It is vital to provide you with the breadth of knowledge you will need to address the wide range of topics within your syllabus that could feature in an examination question. **Reference to this text is vital when self studying.**

 Helpful tutor tips – These sections give tips on the examinability of topics and whether information is provided in the tax rates and allowances in the examination.

 Test your understanding – Following key points and definitions are exercises which give the opportunity to assess the understanding of these core areas. Within the Study Text the answers to these exercises are at the end of the chapter; within the online version the answers can be hidden or shown on screen to enable repetition of exercises.

 Illustration – To help develop an understanding of topics the illustrative examples and the Test Your Understanding (TYU) exercises can be used.

 Progression – This symbol links the topics in the chapter to other relevant papers in the ACCA syllabus.

Online subscribers

Our online resources are designed to increase the flexibility of your learning materials and provide you with immediate feedback on how your studies are progressing.

If you are subscribed to our online resources you will find:

(1)   Online reference material: reproduces your Study Text online, giving you anytime, anywhere access.

(2)   Online testing: provides you with additional online objective testing so you can practice what you have learned further.

(3)   Online performance management: immediate access to your online testing results. Review your performance by key topics and chart your achievement through the course relative to your peer group.

Ask your local student experience staff if you are not already a subscriber and wish to join.

ACCA Performance Objectives

In order to become a member of the ACCA, as a trainee accountant you will need to demonstrate that you have achieved nine performance objectives. Performance objectives are indicators of effective performance and set the minimum standard of work that trainees are expected to achieve and demonstrate in the workplace. They are divided into key areas of knowledge which are closely linked to the exam syllabus.

There are five Essential performance objectives and a choice of fifteen Technical performance objectives which are divided into five areas.

The performance objectives which link to this exam are:

1   Ethics and professionalism (Essential)

2   Stakeholder relationship management (Essential)

3   Record and process transactions and events (Technical)

4   Prepare external financial reports (Technical)

5   Analyse and interpret financial reports (Technical)

The following link provides an in depth insight into all of the performance objectives:

https://www.accaglobal.com/content/dam/ACCA_Global/Students/per/PER-Performance-objectives-achieve.pdf

Progression

There are two elements of progression that we can measure: first how quickly students move through individual topics within a subject; and second how quickly they move from one course to the next. We know that there is an optimum for both, but it can vary from subject to subject and from student to student. However, using data and our experience of student performance over many years, we can make some generalisations.

A fixed period of study set out at the start of a course with key milestones is important. This can be within a subject, for example 'I will finish this topic by 30 June', or for overall achievement, such as 'I want to be qualified by the end of next year'.

Your qualification is cumulative, as earlier papers provide a foundation for your subsequent studies, so do not allow there to be too big a gap between one subject and another. We know that exams encourage techniques that lead to some degree of short term retention, the result being that you will simply forget much of what you have already learned unless it is refreshed (look up Ebbinghaus Forgetting Curve for more details on this). This makes it more difficult as you move from one subject to another: not only will you have to learn the new subject, you will also have to relearn all the underpinning knowledge as well. This is very inefficient and slows down your overall progression which makes it more likely you may not succeed at all.

In addition, delaying your studies slows your path to qualification which can have negative impacts on your career, postponing the opportunity to apply for higher level positions and therefore higher pay.

You can use the following diagram showing the whole structure of your qualification to help you keep track of your progress.

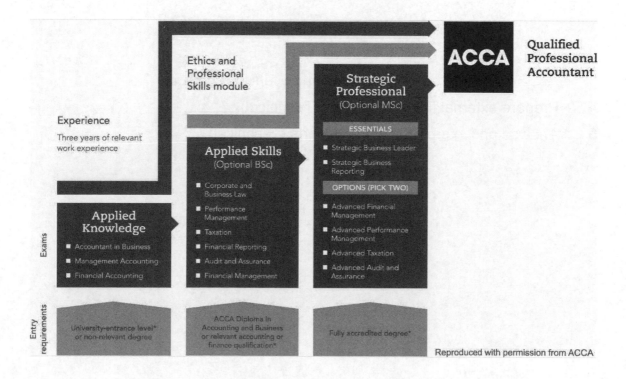

Reproduced with permission from ACCA

Syllabus

Examination background

The aim of ACCA **Taxation (TX-UK),** is to develop knowledge and skills relating to the tax system as applicable to individuals, single companies and groups of companies.

Objectives of the syllabus

- Explain the operation and scope of the tax system and the obligations of taxpayers and/or their agents and the implications of non-compliance.

- Explain and compute the income tax liabilities of individuals and the effect of national insurance contributions (NIC) on employees, employers and the self-employed.

- Explain and compute the chargeable gains arising on individuals.

- Explain and compute the inheritance tax liabilities of individuals.

- Explain and compute the corporation tax liabilities of individual companies and groups of companies.

- Explain and compute the effects of value added tax on incorporated and unincorporated businesses.

- Demonstrate employability and technology skills.

KAPLAN PUBLISHING

Core areas of the syllabus

- The UK tax system and its administration
- Income tax and NIC liabilities
- Chargeable gains for individuals
- Inheritance tax
- Corporation tax liabilities
- Value added tax.

Syllabus objectives

We have reproduced the ACCA's syllabus below, showing where the objectives are explored within this Study Text. Within the chapters, we have broken down the extensive information found in the syllabus into easily digestible and relevant sections, called Content Objectives. These correspond to the objectives at the beginning of each chapter.

Syllabus learning objective	Chapter reference
A THE UK TAX SYSTEM AND ITS ADMINISTRATION	
1 The overall function and purpose of taxation in a modern economy	
(a) Describe the purpose (economic, social, etc.) of taxation in a modern economy.[1]	1
(b) Explain the difference between direct and indirect taxation.[2]	1
(c) Identify the different types of capital and revenue tax.[1]	1
2 Principal sources of revenue law and practice	
(a) Describe the overall structure of the UK tax system.[1]	1
(b) State the different sources of revenue law.[1]	1
(c) Describe the organisation HM Revenue and Customs (HMRC) and its terms of reference.[1]	1
(d) Explain the difference between tax avoidance and tax evasion, and the purposes of the General Anti-Abuse Rule (GAAR).[1]	1
(e) Appreciate the interaction of the UK tax system with that of other tax jurisdictions.[2]	1
(f) Appreciate the need for double taxation agreements.[2]	1
(g) Explain the need for an ethical and professional approach.[2]	1

Syllabus learning objective	Chapter reference

Excluded topics:

- Specific anti-avoidance legislation.

3   The systems for self-assessment and the making of returns

(a)   Explain and apply the features of the self-assessment system as it applies to individuals.[2]   13

(b)   Explain and apply the features of the self-assessment system as it applies to companies, including the use of iXBRL.[2]   18

4   The time limits for the submission of information, claims and payment of tax, including payments on account

(a)   Recognise the time limits that apply to the filing of returns and the making of claims.[2]   13 & 18

(b)   Recognise the due dates for the payment of tax under the self-assessment system and compute payments on account and balancing payments/repayments for individuals.[2]   13

(c)   Explain how large companies are required to account for corporation tax on a quarterly basis and compute the quarterly instalment payments.[2]   18

(d)   List the information and records that taxpayers need to retain for tax purposes.[1]   13 & 18

Excluded topics:

- The payment of capital gains tax by annual instalments.

- The calculation of payments on account for disposals of residential property where there is more than one residential property disposal during a tax year.

- Simple assessments.

- Quarterly accounting by companies for income tax.

- Quarterly instalments for very large companies.

KAPLAN PUBLISHING

Syllabus learning objective	Chapter reference

5   The procedures relating to compliance checks, appeals and disputes

(a) Explain the circumstances in which HM Revenue & Customs can make a compliance check into a self-assessment tax return.[2]   13 & 18

(b) Explain the procedures for dealing with appeals and First and Upper Tier Tribunals.[2]   13 & 18

Excluded topics:

- Information powers.
- Pre-return compliance checks.
- Detailed procedures on the carrying out and completion of a compliance check.

6   Penalties for non-compliance

(a) Calculate late payment interest and state the penalties that can be charged.[2]   13 & 18

B   INCOME TAX AND NIC LIABILITIES

1   The scope of income tax

(a) Explain how the residence of an individual is determined.[1]   2

Excluded topics:

- The split year treatment where a person comes to the UK or leaves the UK.
- Foreign income, non-residents and double taxation relief.
- Income from trusts and settlements.

2   Income from employment

(a) Recognise the factors that determine whether an engagement is treated as employment or self-employment.[2]   5

(b) Recognise the basis of assessment for employment income.[2]   5

(c) Recognise the income assessable.[2]   5

Syllabus learning objective	Chapter reference

(d) Recognise the allowable deductions, including travelling expenses.[2] — 5

(e) Discuss the use of the statutory approved mileage allowances.[2] — 5

(f) Explain the PAYE system, how benefits can be payrolled, and the purpose of form P11D.[1] — 13

(g) Explain and compute the amount of benefits assessable.[2] — 5

(h) Recognise the circumstances in which real time reporting late filing penalties will be imposed on an employer and the amount of penalty which is charged.[2] — 13

Excluded topics:

- The calculation of a car benefit where emission figures are not available.

- The calculation of a car benefit where the car was registered before 6 April 2020.

- The calculation of a car benefit for non-hybrid cars with emissions below 50g/km.

- The reduced charge applicable to zero emission company vans.

- Tax free childcare scheme.

- Share and share option incentive schemes for employees.

- Payments on the termination of employment, and other lump sums received by employees.

- Optional remuneration arrangements.

3 Income from self-employment

(a) Recognise the basis of assessment for self-employment income.[2] — 7 & 9

(b) Describe and apply the badges of trade.[2] — 7

(c) Recognise the expenditure that is allowable in calculating the tax-adjusted trading profit.[2] — 7

(d) Explain and compute the assessable profits using the cash basis for small businesses.[2] — 7

	Syllabus learning objective	Chapter reference
(e)	Recognise the relief that can be obtained for pre-trading expenditure.[2]	7
(f)	Compute the assessable profits on commencement and on cessation.[2]	9
(g)	Recognise the factors that will influence the choice of accounting date.[2]	9
(h)	Capital allowances	
	(i) Define plant and machinery for capital allowances purposes.[1]	8
	(ii) Compute writing down allowances, first year allowances and the annual investment allowance.[2]	8
	(iii) Compute capital allowances for motor cars.[2]	8
	(iv) Compute balancing allowances and balancing charges.[2]	8
	(v) Compute structures and buildings allowances.	8
	(vi) Recognise the treatment of short-life assets.[2]	8
	(vii) Recognise the treatment of assets included in the special rate pool.[2]	8
(i)	Relief for trading losses	
	(i) Understand how trading losses can be carried forward.[2]	11
	(ii) Understand how trading losses can be claimed against total income and chargeable gains, and the restriction that can apply.[2]	11
	(iii) Explain and compute the relief for trading losses in the early years of trade.[1]	11
	(iv) Explain and compute terminal loss relief.[1]	11
	(v) Recognise the factors that will influence the choice of loss relief claim.[2]	11
(j)	Partnerships and limited liability partnerships	
	(i) Explain and compute how a partnership is assessed to tax.[2]	10
	(ii) Explain and compute the assessable profits for each partner following a change in the profit sharing ratio.[2]	10

(iii) Explain and compute the assessable profits for each partner following a change in the membership of the partnership.[2]   10

(iv) Describe the alternative loss relief claims that are available to partners.[1]   11

Excluded topics:

- Change of accounting date.

- Capital allowances for patents and research and development expenditure.

- Apportionment in order to determine the amount of annual investment allowance where a period of account spans 1 January 2021.

- Knowledge of the annual investment allowance limit of £200,000 applicable from 1 January 2021.

- Enterprise zones.

- Investment income of a partnership.

- The allocation of notional profits and losses for a partnership.

- Farmers averaging of profits.

- The averaging of profits for authors and creative artists.

- Loss relief following the incorporation of a business.

- Loss relief for shares in unquoted trading companies.

- The loss relief restriction that applies to the partners of a limited liability partnership.

- Trading allowance of £1,000.

- Non-deductible capital expenditure under the cash basis other than motor cars, land and buildings.

4   Property and investment income

(a) Compute property business profits.[2]   4

(b) Explain the treatment of furnished holiday lettings.[1]   4

(c) Understand rent-a-room relief.[1]   4

Syllabus learning objective		Chapter reference
(d)	Compute the amount assessable when a premium is received for the grant of a short lease.[2]	4
(e)	Understand and apply the restriction on property income finance costs.[2]	4
(f)	Understand how relief for a property business loss is given.[2]	4
(g)	Compute the tax payable on savings and dividends income.[2]	3
(h)	Recognise the treatment of individual savings accounts (ISAs) and other tax exempt investments.[1]	3
(i)	Understand how the accrued income scheme applies to UK Government securities (gilts).[1]	3

Excluded topics:

- Premiums for granting subleases.

- Junior ISAs.

- The additional ISA allowance for a surviving spouse or registered civil partner.

- Help-to-buy, innovative finance and lifetime ISAs.

- Savings income paid net of tax.

- The detailed rules for establishing whether higher or additional rate tax is applicable for the purposes of the savings income nil rate band.

- Property allowance of £1,000.

- Non-deductible capital expenditure under the cash basis other than motor cars, land and buildings.

- The cap in respect of the property income finance costs tax reducer.

- Carry forward of the property income finance costs tax reducer.

5   The comprehensive computation of taxable income and income tax liability

(a)	Prepare a basic income tax computation involving different types of income.[2]	2 & 3
(b)	Calculate the amount of personal allowance available.[2]	2

Excluded topics:

- Consideration of the most beneficial allocation of the personal allowance to different categories of income.

- The blind person's allowance and the married couple's allowance.

- Tax credits.

- Maintenance payments.

- The income of minor children.

6   National insurance contributions for employed and self-employed persons

Excluded topics:

- The calculation of directors' national insurance on a month-by-month basis.

- The offset of trading losses against non-trading income.

- The exemption from employer's class 1 NIC in respect of employees aged under 21 and apprentices aged under 25.

- Group aspects of the annual employment allowance.

7   The use of exemptions and reliefs in deferring and minimising income tax liabilities

(a)	Explain and compute the relief given for contributions to personal pension schemes, and to occupational pension schemes.[2]	6
(b)	Understand how a married couple or couple in a civil partnership can minimise their tax liabilities.[2]	3
(c)	Basic income tax planning.[2]	3, 9, 11

Excluded topics:

- The conditions that must be met in order for a pension scheme to obtain approval from HM Revenue & Customs.

- The anti-avoidance annual allowance limit of £4,000 for pension contributions (the tapering of the annual allowance down to a minimum of £4,000 is examinable).

- The threshold level of income below which tapering of the annual allowance does not apply.

- The enterprise investment scheme and the seed enterprise investment scheme.

- Venture capital trusts.

- Tax reduction scheme for gifts of pre-eminent objects.

C   CHARGEABLE GAINS FOR INDIVIDUALS

1   The scope of the taxation of capital gains.

(a)	Describe the scope of capital gains tax.[2]	19
(b)	Recognise those assets which are exempt.[1]	19

Excluded topics:

- Assets situated overseas and double taxation relief.

- Partnership capital gains.

Syllabus learning objective			Chapter reference

2 The basic principles of computing gains and losses.

    (a)   Compute and explain the treatment of capital gains.[2]   19

    (b)   Compute and explain the treatment of capital losses.[2]   19

    (c)   Understand the treatment of transfers between a married couple or between a couple in a civil partnership.[2]   20

    (d)   Understand the amount of allowable expenditure for a part disposal.[2]   20

    (e)   Recognise the treatment where an asset is damaged, lost or destroyed, and the implications of receiving insurance proceeds and reinvesting such proceeds.[2]   20

Excluded topics:

- Assets held at 31 March 1982.

- Small part disposals of land, and small capital sums received where an asset is damaged.

- Losses in the year of death.

- Relief for losses incurred on loans made to traders.

- Negligible value claims.

3 Gains and losses on the disposal of movable and immovable property

    (a)   Identify when chattels and wasting assets are exempt.[1]   20

    (b)   Compute the chargeable gain when a chattel or wasting asset is disposed of.[2]   20

    (c)   Calculate the chargeable gain when a principal private residence is disposed of.[2]   22

Excluded topics:

- The disposal of leases and the creation of sub-leases.

- The two year pre-occupation period exemption for private residence relief (PRR).

KAPLAN PUBLISHING

Excluded topics:

- The small part disposal rules applicable to rights issues, takeovers and reorganisations.

- Gilt-edged securities and qualifying corporate bonds other than the fact that they are exempt.

Excluded topics:

- Business asset disposal relief for associated disposals.

- Mixed use property.

- Expanded definition of the 5% shareholding condition for business asset disposal relief.

- Availability of business asset disposal relief where shareholding is diluted below the 5% qualifying threshold.

- Business asset disposal relief lifetime limit prior to 6 April 2020.

6   The use of exemptions and reliefs in deferring and minimising tax liabilities arising on the disposal of capital assets

(a)   Explain and apply capital gains tax reliefs

    (i)   rollover relief. [2]   22

    (ii)   holdover relief for the gift of business assets.[2]   22

(b)   Basic capital gains tax planning.[2]   19, 20, 22

Excluded topics:

- Incorporation relief.
- Reinvestment relief.

D   INHERITANCE TAX

1   The basic principles of computing transfers of value

(a)   Identify the persons chargeable.[2]   24

(b)   Understand and apply the meaning of transfer of value, chargeable transfer and potentially exempt transfer.[2]   24

(c)   Demonstrate the diminution in value principle.[2]   24

(d)   Demonstrate the seven year accumulation principle taking into account changes in the level of the nil rate band.[2]   24

Excluded topics:

- Pre 18 March 1986 lifetime transfers.
- Transfers of value by close companies.
- Domicile, deemed domicile, and non-UK domiciled individuals.
- Trusts.
- Excluded property.
- Related property.
- The tax implications of the location of assets.
- Gifts with reservation of benefit.
- Associated operations.

Syllabus learning objective	Chapter reference

2 The liabilities arising on chargeable lifetime transfers and on the death of an individual

(a)	Understand the tax implications of lifetime transfers and compute the relevant liabilities.[2]	24
(b)	Understand and compute the tax liability on a death estate.[2]	24
(c)	Understand and apply the transfer of any unused nil rate band between spouses.[2]	24
(d)	Understand and apply the residence nil rate band available when a residential property is inherited by direct descendants.[2]	24

Excluded topics:

- Specific rules for the valuation of assets (values will be provided).

- Business property relief.

- Agricultural property relief.

- Relief for the fall in value of lifetime gifts.

- Quick succession relief.

- Double tax relief.

- Post-death variation of wills and disclaimers of legacies.

- Grossing up on death.

- Post mortem reliefs.

- Double charges legislation.

- The reduced rate of inheritance tax payable on death when a proportion of a person's estate is bequeathed to charity.

- The tapered withdrawal of the residence nil rate band where the net value of the estate exceeds £2 million.

- The protection of the residence nil rate band where an individual downsizes to a less valuable property or where a property is disposed of.

- Nominating which property should qualify for the residence nil rate band where there is more than one residence.

Syllabus learning objective	Chapter reference

3 The use of exemptions in deferring and minimising inheritance tax liabilities

Excluded topics:

- Gifts to charities.
- Gifts to political parties.
- Gifts for national purposes.

4 Payment of inheritance tax

Excluded topics:

- Administration of inheritance tax other than listed above.
- The instalment option for the payment of tax.
- Interest and penalties.

E CORPORATION TAX LIABILITIES

1 The scope of corporation tax

Syllabus learning objective	Chapter reference

Excluded topics:

- Investment companies.
- Close companies.
- Companies in receivership or liquidation.
- Reorganisations.
- The purchase by a company of its own shares.
- Personal service companies.

2   Taxable total profits

(a)	Recognise the expenditure that is allowable in calculating the tax-adjusted trading profit.[2]	15
(b)	Recognise the relief which can be obtained for pre-trading expenditure.[1]	15
(c)	Compute capital allowances (as for income tax).[2]	15
(d)	Compute property business profits and understand how relief for a property business loss is given.[2]	15 & 16
(e)	Understand how trading losses can be carried forward.[2]	16
(f)	Understand how trading losses can be claimed against income of the current or previous accounting periods.[2]	16
(g)	Recognise the factors that will influence the choice of loss relief claim.[2]	16
(h)	Recognise and apply the treatment of interest paid and received under the loan relationship rules.[1]	15
(i)	Recognise and apply the treatment of qualifying charitable donations.[2]	15
(j)	Compute taxable total profits.[2]	14 & 15

Excluded topics:

- Research and development expenditure.
- Non-trading deficits on loan relationships.
- Relief for intangible assets.
- Patent box.
- Carried forward losses prior to 1 April 2017.
- Restriction on carried forward losses for companies with profits over £5 million.

Syllabus learning objective	Chapter reference

3 Chargeable gains for companies

(a) Compute and explain the treatment of chargeable gains.[2] — 23

(b) Explain and compute the indexation allowance available using a given indexation factor.[2] — 23

(c) Explain and compute the treatment of capital losses.[1] — 16 & 23

(d) Understand the treatment of disposals of shares by companies and apply the identification rules including the same day and nine day matching rules.[2] — 23

(e) Explain and apply the pooling provisions.[2] — 23

(f) Explain and apply the treatment of bonus issues, rights issues, takeovers and reorganisations.[2] — 23

(g) Explain and apply rollover relief.[2] — 23

Excluded topics:

- A detailed question on the pooling provisions as they apply to limited companies.
- Substantial shareholdings.
- Calculation of indexation factors.
- Restriction on carried forward capital losses for companies with chargeable gains over £5 million.

4 The comprehensive computation of corporation tax liability

(a) Compute the corporation tax liability.[2] — 14

Excluded topics:

- The tax rates applicable to periods prior to financial year 2017.
- Marginal relief.
- Franked investment income.

KAPLAN PUBLISHING

Syllabus learning objective		Chapter reference

2   The computation of VAT liabilities

(a)	Calculate the amount of VAT payable/recoverable.[2]	25
(b)	Understand how VAT is accounted for and administered.[2]	26
(c)	Recognise the tax point when goods or services are supplied.[2]	25
(d)	List the information that must be given on a VAT invoice.[1]	26
(e)	Explain and apply the principles regarding the valuation of supplies.[2]	25
(f)	Recognise the principal zero rated and exempt supplies.[1]	25
(g)	Recognise the circumstances in which input VAT is non-deductible.[2]	25
(h)	Recognise the relief that is available for impairment losses on trade debts.[2]	25
(i)	Understand the treatment of the sale of a business as a going concern.[2]	25
(j)	Understand when the default surcharge, a penalty for an incorrect VAT return, and default interest will be applied.[1]	26
(k)	Understand the treatment of imports, exports and trade within the European Union.[2]	26

Excluded topics:

- VAT periods where there is a change of VAT rate.

- Partial exemption.

- In respect of property and land: leases, do-it-yourself builders, and a landlord's option to tax.

- Penalties apart from those listed in the study guide.

- The reverse charge for building and construction services.

- Postponed accounting for VAT on imports.

Syllabus learning objective	Chapter reference

3   The effect of special schemes

(a)   Understand the operation of, and when it will be advantageous to use, the VAT special schemes

	Chapter reference
(i) cash accounting scheme.[2]	26
(ii) annual accounting scheme.[2]	26
(iii) flat rate scheme.[2]	26

Excluded topics:

*   The second-hand goods scheme.
*   The capital goods scheme.
*   The special scheme for retailers.

G   EMPLOYABILITY AND TECHNOLOGY SKILLS

1   Use computer technology to efficiently access and manipulate relevant information.

2   Work on relevant response options, using available functions and technology, as would be required in the workplace.

3   Navigate windows and computer screens to create and amend responses to exam requirements, using the appropriate tools.

4   Present data and information effectively using the appropriate tools.

The superscript numbers in square brackets indicate the intellectual depth at which the subject area could be assessed within the examination.

Level 1 (knowledge and comprehension) broadly equates to the Applied Knowledge level.

Level 2 (application and analysis) to the Applied Skills level.

Level 3 (synthesis and evaluation) to the Strategic Professional level.

However, lower level skills can continue to be assessed as you progress through each level.

The Examination

Examination format

The syllabus is assessed by a three-hour computer-based examination.

All questions are compulsory. The exam will contain both computational and discursive elements.

Some questions will adopt a scenario/case study approach.

Section A of the examination comprises 15 objective test (OT) questions of 2 marks each.

Section B of the examination comprises three objective test cases (OT cases), each of which includes five OT questions of 2 marks each.

Section C of the examination comprises one 10 mark and two 15 mark constructed response (long) questions.

The two 15 mark questions will focus on income tax (syllabus area B) and corporation tax (syllabus area E).

The section A OT questions, section B case OT questions and the other constructed response question in section C can cover any areas of the syllabus.

Examination tips

Spend time reading the examination carefully, paying particular attention to sections B and C, where questions will be based on longer scenarios than the 2 mark OTs in section A.

- **Divide the time** you spend on questions in proportion to the marks on offer.

- One suggestion **for this examination** is to allocate 1.8 minutes to each mark available (180 minutes/100 marks), so a 10 mark question should be completed in approximately 18 minutes.

TX is divided into three different sections, requiring the application of different skills to be successful.

KAPLAN PUBLISHING

Section A

Stick to the timing principle of 1.8 minutes per mark. This means that the 15 OT questions in Section A (30 marks) should take 54 minutes.

Work steadily. Rushing leads to careless mistakes and the OT questions are designed to include answers which result from careless mistakes.

If you don't know the answer, eliminate those options you know are incorrect and see if the answer becomes more obvious.

Remember that there is no negative marking for an incorrect answer. After you have eliminated the options that you know to be wrong, if you are still unsure, guess.

Practice section A questions can be found at the end of each chapter.

Section B

There is likely to be a significant amount of information to read through for each case. You should begin by reading the OT questions that relate to the case, so that when you read through the information for the first time, you know what it is that you are required to do.

Each OT question is worth two marks. Therefore you have 18 minutes (1.8 minutes per mark) to answer the five OT questions relating to each case. It is likely that all of the cases will take the same length of time to answer, although some of the OT questions within a case may be quicker than other OT questions within that same case.

Once you have read through the information, you should first answer any of the OT questions that do not require workings and can be quickly answered. You should then attempt the OT questions that require workings utilising the remaining time for that case.

Practice section B questions can be found in Chapter 27.

All of the tips for section A are equally applicable to each section B question.

Section C

The constructed response questions in section C will require a typed response rather than being OT questions. Therefore, different techniques need to be used to score well.

Unless you know exactly how to answer the question, spend some time planning your answer. Stick to the question and tailor your answer to what you are asked. Pay particular attention to the verbs in the question e.g. 'Calculate', 'State', 'Explain'.

If you **get completely stuck** with a question, leave it and return to it later.

If you do not understand what a question is asking, state your assumptions. Even if you do not answer in precisely the way the examining team hoped, you should be given some credit, provided that your assumptions are reasonable.

You should do everything you can to make things easy for the marker. The marker will find it easier to identify the points you have made if your answers are clear.

Computations: It is essential to include all your workings in your answers.

Many computational questions require the use of a standard format. Be sure you know these formats thoroughly before the examination and use the layouts that you see in the answers given in this Study Text and in model answers.

Adopt a logical approach and cross reference workings to the main computation to keep your answers tidy.

Practice section C style questions can be found as 'comprehensive examples' in most chapters and also in Chapter 27.

All sections

Do not skip parts of the syllabus. The TX exam has 33 different questions so the examination can cover a very broad selection of the syllabus each sitting.

Spend time learning the rules and definitions.

Practice plenty of questions to improve your ability to apply the techniques and perform the calculations.

Spend the last five minutes reading through your answers and making any additions or corrections.

Method of Examination

The TX examination is a computer-based examination (CBE).

OT questions in sections A and B of the CBE will be of **varying styles.** These styles include multiple choice, fill in the blank, pull down list, multiple response, hot area, and enhanced matching. A full explanation of these question types is included in the Kaplan Exam Kit FA2019.

The CBE will be 3 hours long. Students will have up to 10 minutes to familiarise themselves with the CBE system before starting the exam.

If you would like further information on sitting a CBE please contact either Kaplan, or the ACCA.

ACCA SUPPORT

For additional support with your studies please also refer to the ACCA Global website.

Study skills and revision guidance

This section aims to give guidance on how to study for your ACCA examinations and to give ideas on how to improve your existing study techniques.

Preparing to study

Set your objectives

Before starting to study decide what you want to achieve – the type of pass you wish to obtain. This will decide the level of commitment and time you need to dedicate to your studies.

Devise a study plan

Determine which times of the week you will study.

Split these times into sessions of at least one hour for study of new material. Any shorter periods could be used for revision or practice.

Put the times you plan to study onto a study plan for the weeks from now until the examination and set yourself targets for each period of study – in your sessions make sure you cover the course, course assignments and revision.

If you are studying for more than one examination at a time, try to vary your subjects as this can help you to keep interested and see subjects as part of wider knowledge.

When working through your course, compare your progress with your plan and, if necessary, re-plan your work (perhaps including extra sessions) or, if you are ahead, do some extra revision/practice questions.

Effective studying

Active reading

You are not expected to learn the text by rote, rather, you must understand what you are reading and be able to use it to pass the exam and develop good practice. A good technique to use is SQ3Rs – Survey, Question, Read, Recall, Review:

(1) **Survey the chapter** – look at the headings and read the introduction, summary and objectives, so as to get an overview of what the chapter deals with.

(2) **Question** – whilst undertaking the survey, ask yourself the questions that you hope the chapter will answer for you.

(3) **Read** through the chapter thoroughly, answering the questions and making sure you can meet the objectives. Attempt the exercises and activities in the text, and work through all the examples.

(4) **Recall** – at the end of each section and at the end of the chapter, try to recall the main ideas of the section/chapter without referring to the text. This is best done after a short break of a couple of minutes after the reading stage.

(5) **Review** – check that your recall notes are correct.

You may also find it helpful to re-read the chapter to try to see the topic(s) it deals with as a whole.

Note taking

Taking notes is a useful way of learning, but do not simply copy out the text. The notes must:

- be in your own words

- be concise

- cover the key points

- be well organised

- be modified as you study further chapters in this text or in related ones.

Trying to summarise a chapter without referring to the text can be a useful way of determining which areas you know and which you don't.

Three ways of taking notes:

(1) **Summarise the key points of a chapter.**

(2) **Make linear notes** – a list of headings, divided up with subheadings listing the key points. If you use linear notes, you can use different colours to highlight key points and keep topic areas together. Use plenty of space to make your notes easy to use.

(3) **Try a diagrammatic form** – the most common of which is a mind map. To make a mind map, put the main heading in the centre of the paper and put a circle around it. Then draw short lines radiating from this to the main sub-headings, which again have circles around them. Then continue the process from the sub-headings to sub-sub-headings, advantages, disadvantages, etc.

Highlighting and underlining

You may find it useful to underline or highlight key points in your Study Text – but do be selective. You may also wish to make notes in the margins.

KAPLAN PUBLISHING

Revision

The best approach to revision is to revise the course as you work through it. Also try to leave four to six weeks before the exam for final revision. Make sure you cover the whole syllabus and pay special attention to those areas where your knowledge is weak. Here are some recommendations:

Read through the text and your notes again and condense your notes into key phrases. It may help to put key revision points onto index cards to look at when you have a few minutes to spare.

Review any assignments you have completed and look at where you lost marks – put more work into those areas where you were weak.

Practise examination standard questions under timed conditions. If you are short of time, list the points that you would cover in your answer and then read the model answer, but do try to complete at least a few questions under examination conditions.

As you will be sitting the examination as a CBE, practice using the ACCA practice platform is important. Here you can access the specimen exam and past exam questions in the CBE layout, format and functionality that you will encounter in your real exam. It is very important that you practise as many questions as possible on the platform to familiarise yourself with how the software works.

Once you have completed questions in the practice platform your responses are saved, sections A and B will be marked automatically and you can self-mark section C using marking guides and sample answers.

Also, practise producing answer plans and comparing them to the model answer.

It is important to practise answering questions using the CBE software and to familiarise yourself with the CBE functionality, particularly the spreadsheet functions.

If you are stuck on a topic find somebody (a tutor) to explain it to you.

Read good newspapers and professional journals, especially ACCA's Student Accountant – this can give you an advantage in the examination.

Ensure you **know the structure of the examination** – how many questions and of what type you will be expected to answer. During your revision attempt all the different styles of questions you may be asked.

Further reading

You can find further reading and technical articles under the student section of ACCA's website.

TAX RATES AND ALLOWANCES

Supplementary instructions and tax rates and allowances given in the examination

1. **Calculations and workings need only be made to the nearest £.**

2. **All apportionments should be made to the nearest month.**

3. **All workings should be shown in section C.**

INCOME TAX

		Normal rates	Dividend rates
Basic rate	£1 – £37,500	20%	7.5%
Higher rate	£37,501 – £150,000	40%	32.5%
Additional rate	£150,001 and over	45%	38.1%
Savings income nil rate band	– Basic rate taxpayers		£1,000
	– Higher rate taxpayers		£500
Dividend nil rate band			£2,000

A starting rate of 0% applies to savings income where it falls within the first £5,000 of taxable income.

Personal allowance

Personal allowance	£12,500
Transferable amount	£1,250
Income limit	£100,000

Where adjusted net income is £125,000 or more, the personal allowance is reduced to zero.

Residence status

Days in UK	Previously resident	Not previously resident
Less than 16	Automatically not resident	Automatically not resident
16 to 45	Resident if 4 UK ties (or more)	Automatically not resident
46 to 90	Resident if 3 UK ties (or more)	Resident if 4 UK ties
91 to 120	Resident if 2 UK ties (or more)	Resident if 3 UK ties (or more)
121 to 182	Resident if 1 UK tie (or more)	Resident if 2 UK ties (or more)
183 or more	Automatically resident	Automatically resident

Child benefit income tax charge

Where income is between £50,000 and £60,000, the charge is 1% of the amount of child benefit received for every £100 of income over £50,000.

KAPLAN PUBLISHING

Car benefit percentage

The relevant base level of CO2 emissions is 55 grams per kilometre.

The percentage rates applying to petrol-powered motor cars (and diesel-powered motor cars meeting the RDE2 standard) with CO_2 emissions up to this level are:

51 grams to 54 grams per kilometre	13%
55 grams per kilometre	14%

A 0% percentage applies to electric-powered motor cars with zero CO_2 emissions.

For hybrid-electric motor cars with CO_2 emissions between 1 and 50 grams per kilometre, the electric range of a motor car is relevant:

Electric range

130 miles or more	0%
70 to 129 miles	3%
40 to 69 miles	6%
30 to 39 miles	10%
Less than 30 miles	12%

Car fuel benefit

The base figure for calculating the car fuel benefit is £24,500.

Company van benefits

The company van benefit scale charge is £3,490, and the van fuel benefit is £666.

Individual Savings Accounts (ISAs)

The overall investment limit is £20,000.

Property income

Basic rate restriction applies to 100% of finance costs relating to residential properties.

Pension scheme limits

Annual allowance	£40,000
Minimum allowance	£4,000
Income limit	£240,000

The maximum contribution which can qualify for tax relief without any earnings is £3,600.

Approved mileage allowances: cars

Up to 10,000 miles	45p
Over 10,000 miles	25p

Capital allowances: rates of allowance

Plant and machinery

Main pool	18%
Special rate pool	6%

Motor cars

New motor cars with CO_2 emissions up to 50 grams per kilometre	100%
CO_2 emissions between 51 and 110 grams per kilometre	18%
CO_2 emissions over 110 grams per kilometre	6%

Annual investment allowance

Rate of allowance	100%
Expenditure limit	£1,000,000

Commercial structures and buildings

Straight-line allowance	3%

Cash basis accounting

Revenue limit	£150,000

Cap on income tax reliefs

Unless otherwise restricted, reliefs are capped at the higher of £50,000 or 25% of income.

CORPORATION TAX

Rate of tax	– Financial year 2020	19%
	– Financial year 2019	19%
	– Financial year 2018	19%
Profit threshold		£1,500,000

VALUE ADDED TAX (VAT)

Standard rate	20%
Registration limit	£85,000
Deregistration limit	£83,000

INHERITANCE TAX: tax rates

Nil rate band		£325,000
Residence nil rate band		£175,000
Rate of tax on excess	– Lifetime rate	20%
	– Death rate	40%

Inheritance tax: taper relief

Years before death	Percentage reduction
More than 3 but less than 4 years	20%
More than 4 but less than 5 years	40%
More than 5 but less than 6 years	60%
More than 6 but less than 7 years	80%

CAPITAL GAINS TAX

		Normal rates	Residential property
Rates of tax	– Lower rate	10%	18%
	– Higher rate	20%	28%
Annual exempt amount			£12,300

Business asset disposal relief (formerly entrepreneurs' relief) and investors' relief

Lifetime limit	– business asset disposal relief	£1,000,000
	– investors' relief	£10,000,000
Rate of tax		10%

NATIONAL INSURANCE CONTRIBUTIONS

Class 1	Employee	£1 – £9,500 per year	Nil
		£9,501 – £50,000 per year	12%
		£50,001 and above per year	2%
Class 1	Employer	£1 – £8,788 per year	Nil
		£8,789 and above per year	13.8%
		Employment allowance	£4,000
Class 1A			13.8%
Class 2		£3.05 per week	
		Small profits threshold	£6,475
Class 4		£1 – £9,500 per year	Nil
		£9,501 – £50,000 per year	9%
		£50,001 and above per year	2%

RATES OF INTEREST (assumed)

Official rate of interest	2.25%
Rate of interest on underpaid tax	2.75%
Rate of interest on overpaid tax	0.50%

STANDARD PENALTIES FOR ERRORS

Taxpayer behaviour	Maximum penalty	Minimum penalty – unprompted disclosure	Minimum penalty – prompted disclosure
Deliberate and concealed	100%	30%	50%
Deliberate but not concealed	70%	20%	35%
Careless	30%	0%	15%

1

The UK tax system

Chapter learning objectives

Upon completion of this chapter you will be able to:

- describe the purpose (economic, social, etc.) of taxation in a modern economy

- explain the difference between direct and indirect taxation

- identify the different types of capital and revenue tax

- describe the overall structure of the UK tax system

- state the different sources of revenue law

- describe the organisation HM Revenue & Customs (HMRC) and its terms of reference

- explain the difference between tax avoidance and tax evasion, and the purposes of the General Anti-Abuse Rule (GAAR)

- appreciate the interaction of the UK tax system with that of other tax jurisdictions and the need for double taxation agreements

- explain the need for an ethical and professional approach.

PER

One of the PER performance objectives (PO1) is to always act in the wider public interest. You need to take into account all relevant information and use professional judgement, your personal values and scepticism to evaluate data and make decisions. You should identify right from wrong and escalate anything of concern. You also need to make sure that your skills, knowledge and behaviour are up-to-date and allow you to be effective in your role. Working through this chapter should help you understand how to demonstrate that objective.

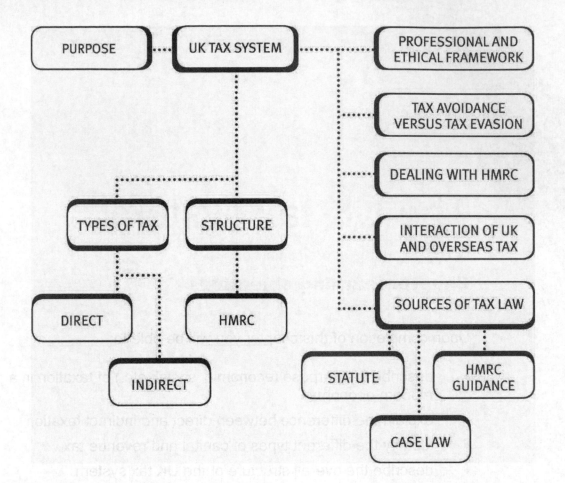

 Within the Financial Accounting unit, you had an introduction to VAT, this chapter will put VAT in context as an indirect tax and introduce direct taxes as well. This chapter also introduces you to professional ethics and the concept of money laundering which will feature in other papers you undertake such as Audit and Assurance and Corporate and Business Law.

Purpose of taxation

Economic

- The system of taxation and spending by government and its impact on the economy of a country as a whole.

- Taxation policies are used to influence many economic factors such as inflation, employment levels and imports/exports.

- They are also used to influence the behaviour of business and individuals.

The current UK tax system encourages:

(1) individual saving habits by offering tax incentives on savings accounts such as individual savings accounts (ISAs)

(2) charitable donations by offering tax relief e.g. through gift aid

(3) entrepreneurs and investors by offering tax relief for investments in specified schemes

The current UK tax system discourages:

(1) motoring by imposing fuel duties

(2) smoking and drinking alcohol by imposing significant taxes on cigarettes and alcoholic drinks

(3) environmental pollution by imposing a variety of taxes such as landfill tax, climate change levy and linking CO_2 emissions to the taxation of company cars.

- As government objectives change, taxation policies are altered.

Social justice

The type of taxation structure imposed has a direct impact on the accumulation and redistribution of wealth within a country.

The main taxation principles are listed below. The arguments for and against each of these are often the matter of significant political debate.

Progressive taxation

- As income rises, the proportion of tax raised also rises. For example: 20% up to £37,500 of taxable income and 40% up to £150,000 of taxable income.

- Income tax is an example of a progressive tax.

Regressive taxation

- As income rises the proportion of tax paid falls.

- For example, the tax on a litre of petrol is the same regardless of the level of income of the purchaser.

- This is a regressive tax as it represents a greater proportion of income for a low income earner than a high income earner.

Proportional taxation

- As income rises the proportion of tax remains constant. For example, 10% of all earnings regardless of the level.

Ad valorem principle

- A tax calculated as a percentage of the value of the item. For example, 20% VAT on most goods sold in the UK.

1 Types of tax

The UK tax system, administered by HM Revenue and Customs (HMRC), comprises a number of different taxes. The following taxes are examinable.

Income tax

- Payable by individuals on some of their earnings (e.g. self-employment and employment) and investment income.

National insurance contributions (NICs)

- Payable by individuals who are either employed or self-employed on their earnings.
- Also payable by businesses (e.g. sole trader, company) in relation to their employees.

Capital gains tax

- Payable by individuals on the disposal of certain types of capital assets.
- Capital assets include land, buildings and shares, and can also include smaller items such as antiques.

Inheritance tax

- Payable by executors on the value of the estate of a deceased person.
- Also payable in respect of certain gifts during an individual's lifetime.

Corporation tax

- Payable by companies on their income and gains.

Value added tax (VAT)

- Payable on the supply of goods and services by the final consumer.

 # 2 Direct versus indirect taxation

Direct taxation

- The taxpayer pays direct taxes directly to HMRC.
- Direct revenue taxes are based on income/profits and the more that is earned/received, the more tax is paid. Examples include income tax and corporation tax.
- Direct capital taxes are based on the value of assets disposed of either through sale, gift or inheritance. Examples include capital gains tax and inheritance tax.

Indirect taxation

- An indirect tax is collected from the taxpayer via an intermediary such as a retail shop.

- The intermediary then pays over the tax collected to HMRC.

- An example of an indirect tax is VAT. The consumer (taxpayer) pays VAT to the supplier (intermediary), who then pays it to HMRC.

3 Structure of the UK tax system

HM Revenue and Customs

- HMRC is the government department that controls and administers all areas of UK tax law.

- The purpose of HMRC is to:
  - make sure that the money is available to fund the UK's public services
  - help families and individuals with targeted financial support

- Heading up HMRC are the Commissioners whose main duties are:
  - to implement statute law
  - to oversee the process of UK tax administration.

- Staff who work for HMRC are known as Officers of Revenue and Customs.

- HMRC have offices located all over the UK, many of which have specialist functions such as dealing with international businesses or large companies.

- Most taxpayers will never deal directly with a local tax office as HMRC encourage taxpayers to file tax returns online, use their website www.hmrc.gov.uk to answer queries or telephone or email a number of specialist helplines (e.g. the self-assessment helpline).

- Taxpayers are encouraged to file their tax returns online and pay by electronic means.
  - Companies have to file returns and pay tax electronically.
  - Individual taxpayers can still send their returns and payments by post if they wish.

- Under self-assessment the responsibility for reporting the correct amount of taxable income and paying the correct amount of tax is delegated to the taxpayer to 'self-assess'.

- However, the Officers of Revenue and Customs can still be requested to do the calculation of tax payable based on the income reported for individual taxpayers (but not companies).

4 Sources of tax law

The basic rules of the UK tax system have been established from the following sources:

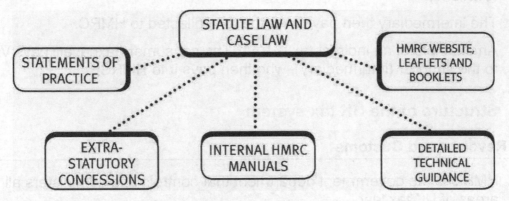

Sources of tax law

Statute law (tax legislation)

- This is law and therefore adherence is mandatory.

- Tax legislation is normally updated each year by one annual finance act that follows from the proposals made by the Chancellor of the Exchequer in his annual Budget statement.

- Statutory instruments are issued where detailed notes are required on an area of tax legislation.

Case law

- Case law refers to the decisions made in tax cases brought before the courts.

- Often the case challenges current tax legislation or argues a certain interpretation of the tax law should be applied.

- These rulings are binding and therefore provide guidance on the interpretation of tax legislation.

HMRC guidance

- As the tax legislation can be complex to understand and open to misinterpretation, further guidance is issued by HMRC in order to:

  - explain how to implement the law

  - give their interpretation of the law.

- The main types of guidance are listed below.

Statement of practice

- Provides HMRC's interpretation of tax law and often provides clarification or detail of how rules should be applied.

Extra-statutory concessions

- Extra-statutory concessions allow a relaxation of the strict letter of the law in certain circumstances. A concession is often given where undue hardship or anomalies would otherwise occur.

Internal HMRC manuals

- HMRC's own manuals, produced for their staff, give guidance on the interpretation of the law. They are also available to the public.

HMRC website, leaflets and booklets

- Aimed at the general public and provide explanations of various tax issues in non-technical language.

Detailed technical guidance

- HMRC issue Notices and Guidance Notes, aimed at tax agents and advisers, to explain tax issues in more technical detail than is normally required by the general public.

- HMRC Briefs provide detailed technical guidance on a specific tax issue that has arisen in the year.

5 Interaction of UK and overseas tax systems

Due to the differing tax systems in overseas countries, it is possible that income is taxed under two different systems.

Double taxation agreements

Agreements between most countries have been established to decide how a particular individual/company should be taxed. Some details of how these operate are given below.

Double taxation agreements

- These are known as bilateral double taxation treaties.

- Such treaties take precedence over domestic UK tax law and either:

    - exempt certain overseas income from tax in the UK, or

    - provide relief where tax is suffered in two countries on the same income.

- Where no such treaty exists, the UK system still allows for relief to be given where double tax is paid.

Double taxation relief (DTR) for individuals and companies is not examinable.

Influence of the European Union (EU)

- One of the aims of the EU is to remove trade barriers and distortions due to different economic and political policies imposed in different member states.

- Although EU members do not have to align their tax systems, members can agree to jointly enact specific laws, known as Directives.

- To date the most important of these have been agreements regarding VAT. EU members have aligned their VAT **policies** according to European legislation. They have not however aligned their **rates** of VAT.

- Many cases have been brought before the European Court of Justice regarding the discrimination of non-residents by the UK tax system, some of which have resulted in changes to UK tax law.

6 Tax avoidance versus tax evasion

The difference between tax avoidance and evasion is important due to the legal implications.

Tax evasion

- The term tax evasion summarises any action taken to avoid or reduce tax by illegal means.

- The main forms of tax evasion are:

  - suppressing information

    (e.g. failing to declare taxable income to HMRC)

  - submitting false information

    (e.g. claiming expenses that have not been incurred).

- Tax evasion is an illegal activity; and carries a risk of criminal prosecution (fines and/or imprisonment).

Tax avoidance

- Tax avoidance is using the taxation regime to one's own advantage by arranging your affairs to minimise your tax liability. This can also be referred to as tax planning.

- It is legal and does not entail misleading HMRC (e.g. making tax savings by investing in ISAs).

- The term is also used to describe tax schemes that utilise loopholes in the tax legislation.

Test your understanding 1

For each of the following explain whether it is an example of tax evasion or tax avoidance.

- Selling a capital asset in May 2021 instead of March 2021 to ensure that the gain is taxed in a later tax year.
- Altering a bill of £700 to read £7,000 so that a larger tax deduction is claimed on your tax return.
- Moving funds into an ISA account so that interest can be earned tax free.

- Specific tax avoidance schemes have been targeted by HMRC with anti-avoidance legislation to counter the tax advantages gained by the taxpayer.
- HMRC have also introduced:
  - disclosure obligations regarding anti-avoidance tax schemes requiring the declaration of the details of the scheme to HMRC
  - a General Anti-Abuse Rule (GAAR) to counter artificial and abusive schemes where arrangements (which cannot be regarded as a reasonable course of action) are put in place deliberately to avoid tax.

7 Professional and ethical guidance

The ACCA 'Professional Code of Ethics and Conduct' has already been covered in your earlier studies. A reminder of the key points is given below.

Fundamental principles

The ACCA expects its members to:
- adopt an ethical approach to work, employers and clients
- acknowledge their professional duty to society as a whole
- maintain an objective outlook, and
- provide professional, high standards of service, conduct and performance at all times.

To meet these expectations the ACCA 'Code of Ethics and Conduct' sets out five fundamental principles, which members should abide by:
- Objectivity
- Professional competence and due care
- Professional behaviour
- Integrity
- Confidentiality.

Remember: OPPIC

Objectivity (O)

- Members should not allow bias, conflicts of interest or the influence of others to override objectivity.

Professional competence and due care (P)

- Members have an ongoing duty to maintain professional knowledge and skills to ensure that a client/employer receives competent, professional service based on current developments.

- Members should be diligent and act in accordance with applicable technical and professional standards when providing professional services.

Professional behaviour (P)

- Members should refrain from any conduct that might bring discredit to the profession.

Integrity (I)

- Members should act in a straightforward and honest manner in all professional and business relationships.

Confidentiality (C)

- Members should respect the confidentiality of information acquired as a result of professional and business relationships and should not disclose any such information to third parties unless:

    – they have proper and specific authority, or

    – there is a legal or professional right or duty to disclose (e.g. money laundering).

- Confidential information acquired as a result of professional and business relationships, should not be used for the personal advantage of members or third parties.

Advise on taxation issues

- A person advising either a company or an individual on taxation issues has duties and responsibilities towards both his/her client, and HMRC.

- A member must never be knowingly involved in tax evasion.

- The distinction between acceptable tax planning and aggressive tax avoidance, whilst both legal, has been the subject of significant public debate in recent years.

- As a result the ACCA's ethical guidance states that members must not create, encourage or promote tax planning arrangements or structures that:

  - set out to achieve results that are contrary to the clear intention of Parliament in enacting relevant legislation and/or

  - are highly artificial or highly contrived and seek to exploit shortcomings within the relevant legislation.

Dealing with HMRC

It is important to ensure that information provided to HMRC is accurate and complete.

A member must not assist a client to plan or commit any offence.

If a member becomes aware that the client has committed a tax irregularity:

- they must discuss it with the client and ensure proper disclosure is made.

Examples would include:

- not declaring income that is taxable

- claiming reliefs to which they are not entitled

- not notifying HMRC where they have made a mistake giving rise to an underpayment of tax, or an increased repayment.

Where a client has made an error:

- it will be necessary to decide whether it was a genuine error or a deliberate or fraudulent act.

Once an error has been discovered:

- the member should explain to the client the requirement to notify HMRC as soon as possible, and the implications of their not doing so.

Should the client refuse to make a full and prompt disclosure to HMRC:

- the member must write and explain the potential consequences and,

- consider whether the amount is material, and if it is, whether they should continue to act for the client.

If the client still refuses to make a full disclosure, the member:

- should cease to act for the client.

- must then also write to HMRC informing them that they have ceased to act for the client, but without disclosing the reason why.

- must then consider their position under the Money Laundering Regulations.

Money Laundering Regulations

Money laundering is the term used for offences including benefiting from or concealing the proceeds of a crime.

All businesses within regulated sectors must appoint a Money Laundering Reporting Officer (MLRO) within the firm.

The MLRO will decide whether a transaction should be reported to the National Crime Agency (NCA).

Where a report is made the client should not be informed as this may amount to 'tipping off', which is an offence.

A report to NCA does not remove the requirement to disclose the information to HMRC.

Test your understanding 2

When you are checking a recent tax computation from HMRC you notice that they have made an error, which has resulted in your client receiving a larger repayment than should have been made.

What actions should you take?

Dishonest conduct of tax agents

- There is a civil penalty of up to £50,000 for dishonest conduct of tax agents.

- In cases where the penalty exceeds £5,000, HMRC may publish details of the penalised tax agent.

- With agreement of the Tax Tribunal (Chapter 13), HMRC can access the working papers of a dishonest agent.

8 Chapter summary

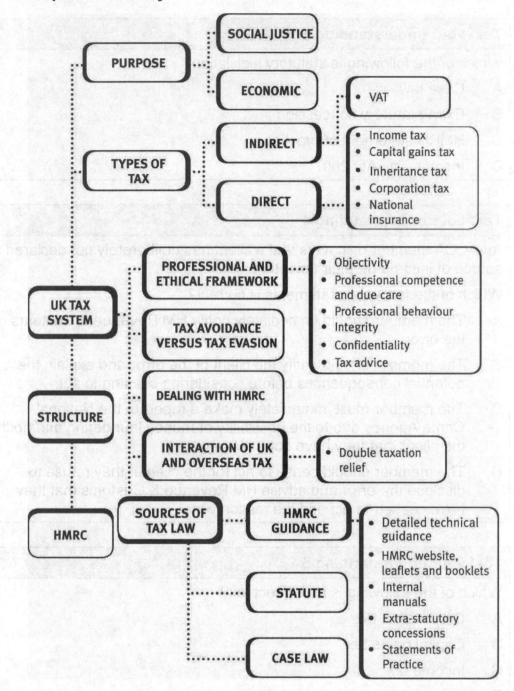

9 Practice objective test questions

Test your understanding 3

Which of the following is statutory legislation?

A   Case law

B   Extra-statutory concession

C   HMRC statement of practice

D   Income Tax Act 2007

Test your understanding 4

An ACCA member discovers that a client has deliberately not declared a source of income on their tax return.

Which of the following statements is correct?

A   The member should immediately notify HM Revenue & Customs of the error.

B   The member should notify the client of the error and explain the potential consequences before considering ceasing to act.

C   The member must immediately make a report to the National Crime Agency due to the possibility of money laundering and notify the client that they have done so.

D   The member should cease to act for the client if they refuse to disclose the error and advise HM Revenue & Customs that they have ceased to act and the reason why.

Test your understanding 5

Which of the following is an indirect tax?

A   Corporation tax

B   Capital gains tax

C   Income tax

D   Value added tax

Test your understanding 6

Which of the following taxes is NOT paid by a company?

A   Income tax

B   Corporation tax

C   National insurance contributions

D   Value added tax

Test your understanding answers

Test your understanding 1

Tax evasion or tax avoidance

- Changing the timing of the sale of an item so as to delay the tax charge is tax avoidance. Individuals may also do this to take advantage of capital gains tax allowances that are given each year.

- Altering paperwork is tax evasion – submitting false information.

- Moving funds into a tax-free ISA account is tax avoidance – minimising your tax liability within the law.

Test your understanding 2

HMRC error

The position should be reviewed carefully to confirm that an error has been made.

The client should be contacted for authority to disclose the error to HMRC. The client should be told the consequences of not disclosing the error, including the implications for interest and penalties.

If the client refuses to allow the disclosure it would be necessary to consider whether the amount is material, and if it is, whether you can continue to act for the client.

If it is decided that it is not appropriate to continue acting, the client must be informed in writing. HMRC should also be notified that you have ceased to act, but not the reason why.

It may be necessary to make a report to NCA under the Money Laundering Regulations.

Test your understanding 3

The correct answer is D.

Test your understanding 4

The correct answer is B.

A member cannot breach confidentiality by disclosing a client's error to HMRC without the client's permission.

A member should discuss any potential money laundering with their firm's Money Laundering Reporting Officer (MLRO), the MLRO will then decide whether a transaction should be reported to the National Crime Agency (NCA). The client should never be informed of any report made to the NCA as this may amount to 'tipping off', which is an offence.

Test your understanding 5

The correct answer is D.

Test your understanding 6

The correct answer is A.

Basic income tax computation

Chapter learning objectives

Upon completion of this chapter you will be able to:

- explain how the residence of an individual is determined

- prepare a basic income tax computation involving different types of income

- calculate the amount of personal allowance available

- understand the impact of the transferable amount of personal allowance for spouses and civil partners

- compute the amount of income tax payable

- understand the treatment of interest paid for a qualifying purposes

- understand the treatment of gift aid donations and charitable giving

- explain and compute the child benefit charge

- understand the treatment of property owned jointly by a married couple, or by a couple in a civil partnership.

PER

One of the PER performance objectives (PO15) is to prepare computations of taxable amounts and tax liabilities according to legal requirements. Working through this chapter should help you understand how to demonstrate that objective.

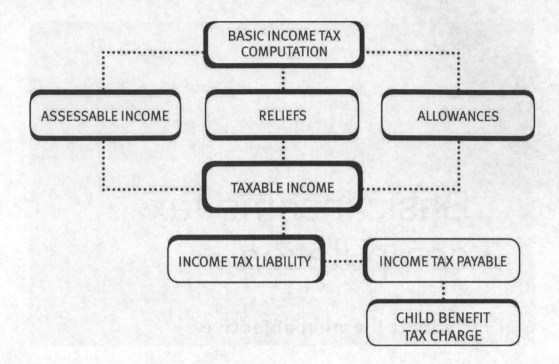

 The income tax computation and the detail behind it are explored further in the Advanced Taxation examination.

1 The principles of income tax

> ### Introduction
>
> This and the following nine chapters deal in detail with the way in which individuals, whether they are employed, self-employed or simply in receipt of investment income, are assessed to income tax.
>
> Income tax is an important topic as it will be the focus of one 15 mark question in section C of the examination. You can also expect income tax questions in both sections A and B of the examination.
>
> This chapter sets out the basis upon which individuals are assessed to income tax and how an individual's income tax liability is calculated.

Basis of assessment

Individuals are assessed to income tax on their income arising in a **tax year**.

- A tax year is the year ended on 5 April and is labelled by the calendar years it straddles.

- The year from 6 April 2020 to 5 April 2021, is referred to as the tax year 2020/21.

Personal allowance

Every taxpayer is entitled to a personal allowance (PA).

- The PA is an amount of tax free income that every taxpayer is entitled to each tax year.

- The amount is reduced, potentially to £Nil, for high income individuals.

- The personal allowance is dealt with in more detail in section 3.

Assessable persons

- All individuals, including children, are chargeable to income tax.

- Both spouses within a married couple are treated as separate individuals for the purposes of income tax.

The tax residency status of an individual determines how much income is assessed to UK tax.

- All persons resident for tax purposes in the UK are assessed to UK tax on their worldwide income.

The detail of how to determine an individual's residence for tax purposes is covered in section 9.

Married couples

There are special rules governing the allocation of income between spouses where assets are jointly owned:

- Generally, income generated from assets jointly owned is split 50:50 between spouses regardless of the actual percentage ownership.

- Election available:

  Where jointly owned assets are held other than in a 50:50 ratio, an election can be made to HM Revenue & Customs (HMRC) for the income to be taxed on the individual spouses according to their actual percentage ownership.

Civil partners (same-sex couples registered as a civil partnership) are treated in the same way as married couples.

Children

- Children under the age of 18 are taxable persons.

- However, their income typically falls short of their personal allowance in any tax year and therefore no tax liability actually arises on their income.

2 Taxable income

Basic pro forma

The first stage of the income tax computation is to prepare a short statement summarising all taxable income.

Any exempt income is excluded, but should be noted as exempt in your answer in the examination.

Income tax computation – 2020/21

	£
Trading income	X
Employment income	X
Property income	X
Pension income	X
Non-savings income	X
Savings income	
Building society interest	X
Bank interest	X
Dividends	X
Total income	X
Less: Reliefs	(X)
Net income	X
Less: Personal allowance (PA)	(X)
Taxable income	X

Classification of income

There are a number of different sources of income. For example:

- Income earned from employment and self-employment
- Income arising from the ownership of property
- Investment income (e.g. savings income and dividends)
- Income from pensions
- Income exempt from income tax.

It is important to classify each source of income correctly as the tax rules are different for each source.

It is also important to correctly classify each source as 'non-savings income', 'savings income' or 'dividend income' as they are taxed at different rates.

Non-savings income

Non-savings income comprises earned income and property income.

Earned income comprises:

- Trading income – the profit of a trade, profession or vocation of a self-employed individual (see Chapter 7).

- Employment income – earnings including salaries, bonuses and other benefits from an office or employment are assessed as employment income (see Chapter 5).

- Pension income – income from an occupational or personal pension fund.

Property income is typically rental income, but also includes other items such as the income element of a premium on granting a short lease (see Chapter 4).

Investment income

Sources of investment income include:

- Savings income – usually bank and building society interest (see Chapter 3).

- Dividend income (see Chapter 3).

Exempt income

The types of exempt income which may be tested in the examination are:

- Interest from National Savings and Investments ('NS&I') certificates

- Gaming, lottery and premium bonds winnings

- Income received from an individual savings account (ISA).

Reliefs

Reliefs are deducted from an individual's total income.

They include certain payments that an individual makes and certain losses that may be incurred by an individual (see section 6).

3 Personal allowance

Every taxpayer (including children) is entitled to a personal allowance (PA).

- The PA for the tax year 2020/21 is £12,500.

- In the TX examination the PA should always be deducted from the taxpayer's net income from the different sources of income in the following order:

  (1) Non-savings income

  (2) Savings income

  (3) Dividend income

- Surplus PA is lost.

- The PA cannot be set against capital gains.

- In certain circumstances, part of the PA can be transferred to a spouse or civil partner (see the marriage allowance in section 4).

 The PA is included in the tax rates and allowances provided to you in the examination.

 In certain situations it may be more beneficial to deduct the PA from the different sources of income in a different order to that set out above. However, this is not examinable in the TX exam.

Reduction of personal allowance – high income individuals

- The PA is gradually reduced for individuals with income in excess of £100,000.

- The reduction of the PA is based on the taxpayer's adjusted net income (ANI) which is calculated as follows:

	£
Net income	X
Less: Gross gift aid donations	(X)
Less: Gross personal pension contributions	(X)
Adjusted net income (ANI)	X

- Where the taxpayer's ANI exceeds £100,000, the PA is reduced by:

  – **50% × (ANI – £100,000)**

- If necessary, the reduced PA is rounded up to the nearest pound (although in the examination rounding up or down is acceptable).

- A taxpayer with ANI in excess of £125,000 will therefore be entitled to no PA at all, as the excess above £100,000 is twice the PA.

The income limit of £100,000 and the adjusted net income limit of £125,000 are included in the tax rates and allowances provided to you in the examination.

Illustration 1 – Reduction of personal allowance

Ethan received trading income of £110,000 in the tax year 2020/21. He also made gift aid donations of £4,000 (gross).

Compute Ethan's taxable income for the tax year 2020/21.

Solution

Income tax computation – 2020/21

	£
Trading income (Note)	110,000
Less: Adjusted PA (W)	(9,500)
Taxable income	100,500

Working: Adjusted PA

	£	£
Basic personal allowance		12,500
Net income (Note below)	110,000	
Less: Gross gift aid donation	(4,000)	
Adjusted net income	106,000	
Less: Income limit	(100,000)	
	6,000	
Reduction of PA (50% × £6,000)		(3,000)
Adjusted PA		9,500

Note: In this example, as there are no other sources of income and no reliefs; the trading income = total income = net income.

Test your understanding 1

Ellie received employment income of £125,000 in the tax year 2020/21. She also made gift aid donations of £16,000 (gross).

Compute Ellie's taxable income for the tax year 2020/21.

4 Income tax liability

The second stage of the income tax computation is to compute the income tax liability on the taxable income.

Different rates of tax apply dependent upon the type of income.

	£		£
Non-savings income	X	@ 20/40/45%	X
Savings income	X	@ 0/20/40/45%	X
Dividend income	X	@ 0/7.5/32.5/38.1%	X
Income tax liability			X

Rates of income tax – non-savings income

This chapter deals with the rates of income tax payable on 'non-savings income' i.e. trading income, employment income, pension income and property income.

The rates of income tax for the tax year 2020/21 for 'non-savings income' are as follows:

- a basic rate of 20% applies to the first £37,500 of taxable income

- a higher rate of 40% applies where taxable income falls in the range £37,501 to £150,000

- an additional rate of 45% applies to taxable income in excess of £150,000.

In summary the income tax rates for all sources of 'non-savings income' for the tax year 2020/21 are:

Level of income	Non-savings income
Basic rate band (first £37,500)	20%
Higher rate (£37,501 – £150,000)	40%
Additional rate (excess over £150,000)	45%

The income tax rates and thresholds are included in the tax rates and allowances provided to you in the examination.

The income tax liability is calculated on income in a strict order as follows:

(1) Non-savings income

(2) Savings income

(3) Dividend income

Special rates of tax apply to savings and dividend income and these are considered in detail in Chapter 3.

Approach to the income tax computation

(1) Calculate the individual's net income.

(2) Consider the reduction of the PA if ANI exceeds £100,000.

(3) Deduct the appropriate amount of PA to calculate the taxable income.

(4) Calculate the income tax liability bearing in mind the higher rate threshold of £37,500 and the additional rate threshold of £150,000 (see examples below).

Illustration 2 – Income tax liability

Amir has taxable trading income of £21,165 and employment income of £3,000 for the tax year 2020/21. He has no savings or dividend income.

Calculate Amir's income tax liability for the tax year 2020/21.

Solution

	£
Trading income	21,165
Employment income	3,000
Total income	24,165
Less: PA	(12,500)
Taxable income	11,665
Income tax liability (£11,665 × 20%)	2,333

Illustration 3 – Income tax liability

Tala has taxable trading income of £43,765 and employment income of £7,000 for the tax year 2020/21. She has no savings or dividend income.

Calculate Tala's income tax liability for the tax year 2020/21.

Solution

			£
Trading income			43,765
Employment income			7,000
			————
Total income			50,765
Less: PA			(12,500)
			————
Taxable income			38,265
			————

Income tax:	£		£
Basic rate	37,500	× 20%	7,500
Higher rate	765	× 40%	306
	————		
	38,265		
	————		
Income tax liability			7,806
			————

Illustration 4 – Income tax liability

Thomas has taxable trading income of £135,000 and employment income of £33,680 for the tax year 2020/21. He does not have any savings income or dividend income.

Calculate Thomas' income tax liability for the tax year 2020/21.

Solution

	£
Trading income	135,000
Employment income	33,680
	————
Total income	168,680
Less: Adjusted PA (Note)	(0)
	————
Taxable income	168,680
	————

Income tax:	£		£
Basic rate	37,500	× 20%	7,500
Higher rate	112,500	× 40%	45,000
Additional rate	18,680	× 45%	8,406
	————		
	168,680		
	————		
Income tax liability			60,906
			————

Note: In this example, as total income = net income = ANI, and this exceeds £125,000 (i.e. exceeds £100,000 plus double the PA), the PA is reduced to £Nil.

- The effective rate of tax on income between £100,000 and £125,000 is 60%. This is made up of:

  - higher rate income tax = 40%

  - lost PA (½ × 40%) = 20%

- Taxpayers at or near this margin may therefore wish to consider making additional gift aid or personal pension contributions in order to reduce their ANI below £100,000.

Illustration 5 – Reduction of personal allowance

Fernanda is employed on an annual salary of £100,000 in the tax year 2020/21.

How much additional income tax would Fernanda have paid if, in addition to her annual salary, she had received a taxable performance bonus of £25,000 during the tax year 2020/21?

Solution

Income tax computation 2020/21 – assuming no bonus

	£
Employment income	100,000
Less: PA (ANI ≤ £100,000)	(12,500)
Total income	87,500

Income tax:	£		£
Basic rate	37,500	× 20%	7,500
Higher rate	50,000	× 40%	20,000
	87,500		
Income tax liability			27,500

Income tax computation 2020/21 – with bonus of £25,000

	£
Employment income	125,000
Less: PA (ANI ≥ £125,000)	(0)
Total income	125,000

Income tax:	£		£
Basic rate	37,500	× 20%	7,500
Higher rate	87,500	× 40%	35,000
	125,000		
Income tax liability			42,500
Additional tax (£42,500 – £27,500) (Note)			15,000

Note: On an additional taxable income of £25,000, tax of £15,000 has been paid. This represents an effective tax rate of 60% (£15,000/£25,000). A quicker way to calculate the additional tax is:

	£
Higher rate tax on additional income (£25,000 × 40%)	10,000
Lost PA (£12,500 × 40%)	5,000
	15,000

Test your understanding 2

(1) Abdallah has income from self-employment of £16,336 and employment income of £2,500.

(2) Alice has income from self-employment of £37,335 and employment income of £21,000.

(3) Aya has income from self-employment of £238,780.

Assume that these taxpayers have no other income in the tax year 2020/21.

Calculate the income tax liabilities of Abdallah, Alice and Aya for the tax year 2020/21.

Marriage allowance (transferable amount)

The marriage allowance (MA) allows a spouse or civil partner to elect to transfer a fixed amount of the personal allowance to his/her spouse/civil partner.

The MA may also be referred to as the transferable amount of the PA.

The MA is available provided neither spouse (or civil partner) is a higher rate or additional rate taxpayer.

In practice, however, it will only be beneficial to make the election provided the transferor spouse (or civil partner) does not fully utilise his/her PA of £12,500 but the recipient spouse (or civil partner) does, so that their total income tax liability as a couple is reduced.

Electing for the MA allows the transfer:

- to the other spouse (or civil partner)

- of a fixed amount of PA (regardless of the amount of unused PA)

  = 10% × the individual personal allowance = £1,250 for 2020/21.

There is no provision for transferring more or less than this amount.

 The transferable amount of the PA of £1,250 is included in the tax rates and allowances provided to you in the examination.

The effect of the election is that the:

- transferring spouse's PA is reduced by the fixed amount of £1,250 (for 2020/21)

- the recipient spouse's income tax liability is reduced by a maximum of £250 (£1,250 MA × 20% basic rate (BR) income tax).

Note that:

- the relief is given as a deduction from the recipient's income tax liability

- the recipient's own PA is not increased

- the maximum benefit from the MA is £250

- if the recipient's income tax liability is less than £250, a tax repayment is not possible but the amount by which the transferor's PA is reduced remains £1,250

- at best the relief reduces the recipient's income tax liability to £Nil

- in the year of marriage the full allowance is available.

 Marriage allowance tax saving

If one spouse (or civil partner) has unused PA of ≥ £1,250:

- the maximum tax saving of £250 will be achieved, provided the recipient spouse has an income tax liability ≥ £250.

If one spouse (or civil partner) has unused PA of < £1,250:

- the fixed amount of £1,250 must still be transferred

- however, the transferring spouse will have to pay some tax, and

- the maximum total tax saving for the couple will be = (unused PA × BR income tax).

Illustration 6 – Marriage allowance

Kevin and Judy are married. Kevin is employed and has employment income of £35,500 per annum. Judy spends most of her time looking after their two children but works on a Saturday, and has employment income of £6,000. They do not have any other income.

Judy makes an election to transfer the marriage allowance to Kevin.

Calculate Kevin and Judy's income tax liabilities for the tax year 2020/21.

Solution

Income tax computation – 2020/21

	Kevin £	Judy £
Employment income = net income	35,500	6,000
Less: PA (Note)	(12,500)	(6,000)
Taxable income	23,000	0
Income tax liability (£23,000 × 20%)	4,600	0
Less: MA (£1,250 × 20%)	(250)	
Income tax liability	4,350	0

Note: Judy's personal allowance is reduced to £11,250 (£12,500 – £1,250). This is still more than her total income of £6,000 so she still has no income tax liability.

Test your understanding 3

Katie and Emily are civil partners. Katie is a basic rate taxpayer and her only source of income is trading income from self-employment. Emily is studying in the tax year 2020/21.

Emily makes an election to transfer the marriage allowance to Katie.

Calculate Katie and Emily's income tax liabilities for the tax year

2020/21 assuming they have the following amounts of income:

	Katie	Emily
(a)	£30,000	£0
(b)	£13,000	£0
(c)	£30,000	£11,800 from part time employment

To be effective for the tax year 2020/21, the election can be made:

- **in advance**
    - by 5 April 2021
    - the election will remain in force for future tax years, unless
    - the election is withdrawn, or
    - the conditions for relief are no longer met
- **in arrears**
    - by 5 April 2025

        (i.e. within 4 years of the end of the tax year)
    - in this case the election will only apply to the tax year 2020/21 in isolation.

5 Income tax payable

Employment income is received by an individual **after** income tax has been deducted.

The employer is required to deduct income tax from employment income, under the PAYE (Pay as You Earn) system and pay it to HMRC on behalf of the employee.

However, the employment income figure which must be included in the individual's income tax computation is the **gross** figure before PAYE has been deducted.

The individual's income tax liability therefore includes **income tax on the gross employment income**.

To avoid the double payment of tax by the employee, credit is given for the income tax already paid (PAYE) by deducting it from the income tax liability, as the final adjustment in the income tax computation.

Income tax payable is the income tax liability less any tax already deducted from taxable income i.e. PAYE.

Income tax payable is therefore the amount of tax still outstanding and due to be paid by the individual as follows:

	£
Income tax liability	X
Less: PAYE on employment income	(X)
Income tax payable	X

The income tax payable is collected via the self-assessment system (see Chapter 13).

In the event that the amount of tax already paid under PAYE is greater than the liability, a refund will be given via the self-assessment system (see Chapter 13).

 In summary:

- **Income tax liability:**
  - The total income tax due on the taxpayer's total gross income, after deducting reliefs and the personal allowance.

- **Income tax payable:**
  - The final tax bill to be paid via self-assessment after deducting, tax already paid on employment income (PAYE).

 In the examination, figures provided for employment income, salaries and bonuses will always be before tax has been deducted under PAYE, unless specifically stated otherwise.

Illustration 7 – Income tax payable

Akram has taxable trading income of £41,870 and gross employment income of £12,250 for the tax year 2020/21. He does not have any savings income or dividend income. PAYE of £80 was deducted from his employment income.

Calculate Akram's income tax payable for the tax year 2020/21.

Solution

Income tax computation – 2020/21

	£
Trading income	41,870
Employment income	12,250
	———
Total income	54,120
Less: PA	(12,500)
	———
Taxable income	41,620
	———

Income tax	£		£
Basic rate	37,500	× 20%	7,500
Higher rate	4,120	× 40%	1,648
	41,620		
Income tax liability			9,148
Less: PAYE			(80)
Income tax payable			9,068

Test your understanding 4

Waqar provides you with the following information for the tax year 2020/21:

Trading income	£23,000
Salary (gross)	£28,400

He has no other sources of income for the year, although he does notify you that he suffered £3,310 PAYE during the tax year 2020/21.

Calculate Waqar's income tax payable for the tax year 2020/21.

6 Reliefs against total income

Tax relief is available for certain payments made by an individual and for trading losses.

- Relief is available by deducting the payments/losses from total income, subject to a maximum amount of relief.

The only payments deductible from total income which are examinable at TX are certain qualifying interest payments (see below).

- Loss relief is covered in detail in Chapter 11.

- The amount of relief allowed to be deducted from total income is restricted. At TX, this restriction will only be examined in the context of loss relief. (see Chapter 11).

Qualifying interest payments

Relief is given for interest paid on loans incurred to finance expenditure for a qualifying purpose.

There are a number of qualifying purposes to which the loan must be applied. The only ones relevant to your examination are as follows:

- **Employees**

  - The purchase of plant or machinery by an employed person for use in his/her employment.

  - The purchase of shares in an employee-controlled trading company by a full-time employee.

- **Partners**

  - The purchase of a share in a partnership, or the contribution to a partnership of capital or a loan. The borrower must be a partner in the partnership.

  - The purchase of plant or machinery for use in the partnership, by a partner.

Relief is given by deducting the amount of interest **paid** in a tax year from total income.

Illustration 8 – Reliefs against total income

Anwar and Mila each have total income of £54,000 none of which is savings or dividend income.

They made the following payments during the tax year 2020/21.

- Anwar made interest payments during the year totalling £2,000 on his mortgage for his main private residence.

- Mila made interest payments of £2,000 on a loan to invest in a partnership in which she is a partner.

Calculate the income tax liability for Anwar and Mila for the tax year 2020/21.

Solution

Income tax computations – 2020/21

				Anwar £	Mila £
Total income				54,000	54,000
Less: Reliefs – Qualifying interest paid					(2,000)
Net income				54,000	52,000
Less: PA				(12,500)	(12,500)
Taxable income				41,500	39,500

	£	£		£	£
Income tax:					
Basic rate	37,500	37,500	× 20%	7,500	7,500
Higher rate	4,000	2,000	× 40%	1,600	800
	41,500	39,500			
Income tax liability				9,100	8,300

Note: Mortgage interest paid for a main private residence is not qualifying interest and therefore not deductible as a relief.

Test your understanding 5

Emmanuel provides the following information in respect of the tax year 2020/21:

Trading income	£26,000
Employment income (gross)	£29,950
Qualifying interest payment	£4,000

He notifies you that PAYE suffered was £3,620, for the tax year 2020/21.

Calculate Emmanuel's income tax payable for the tax year 2020/21.

7 Charitable giving

Tax relief is available for charitable giving, normally in one of two ways:

- Donations under the gift aid scheme

- Payroll giving under the payroll deduction scheme.

Donations under the gift aid scheme are covered below and the payroll deduction scheme is covered in Chapter 5.

In limited circumstances, tax relief is also available for charitable donations made by self-employed individuals by deduction from their trading profits. This is covered in Chapter 5.

Donations under the gift aid scheme

Taxpayers who wish to make gifts of money to charity can obtain tax relief under the gift aid scheme as follows:

- Donations made under the scheme attract relief at the donor's highest rate of tax.

- There are no minimum or maximum contribution limits, and gifts can either be one-off or a series of donations.

- The payments are made with basic rate tax deducted at source. Effectively providing basic rate tax relief (20%) at the time of payment.

- The basic rate tax is claimed by the charity from HMRC.

Therefore, if an individual wants a charity to receive £100:

- the individual pays the charity £80, and

- the charity claims £20 from HMRC.

Basic rate taxpayers – obtain the tax relief at the time of payment, by only paying 80% of the amount of the donation.

Higher and additional rate taxpayers – relief comes in two parts:

- 20% tax relief is granted at the time the payment is made, as above.

- Higher and additional rate relief is obtained by adding the **gross** amount of the donation to the basic and higher rate bands in the income tax liability calculation.

- The gross amount of the donation is calculated as:

  (amount paid by the individual to the charity × 100/80)

- The effect of extending the basic and higher rate bands is that income equivalent to the value of the gross donation is taxed at:

  – 20%, rather than 40% for a higher rate taxpayer or

  – if an additional rate taxpayer, at 20% rather than 45%.

This gives the further 20% (40% – 20%) tax relief that the higher rate taxpayer is entitled to, and a further 25% (45% – 20%) tax relief for the additional rate taxpayer.

Illustration 9 – Donations under gift aid scheme

Brenda has employment income of £55,000 each year and makes a payment of £3,600 to the RSPB under the gift aid scheme.

Calculate Brenda's income tax liability for the tax year 2020/21.

Solution

Income tax computation – 2020/21

	£
Employment income	55,000
Less: PA	(12,500)
Taxable income	42,500

Income tax:	£		£
Extended basic rate band (W)	42,000	× 20%	8,400
Higher rate	500	× 40%	200
	42,500		
Income tax liability			8,600

Working: Extended basic rate band

	£
Basic rate band	37,500
Plus: Gross gift aid donation (£3,600 × 100/80)	4,500
Extended basic rate band	42,000

Note: Although the higher rate band is also extended by £4,500, this has no effect on Brenda's tax liability as she is not an additional rate taxpayer.

Test your understanding 6

Twins Paul and Grace both have employment income of £54,345 a year. Grace makes a payment of £2,000 to a charity under the gift aid scheme.

Calculate the income tax liability for both Paul and Grace for the tax year 2020/21.

Test your understanding 7

Clare has taxable trading income of £156,000 and employment income of £12,000 for the tax year 2020/21. She does not have any savings income or dividend income. She makes gift aid payments to a charity of £47,000.

Calculate Clare's income tax liability for the tax year 2020/21.

8   Child benefit tax charge

Child benefit is a tax-free payment from the Government that can be claimed in respect of children.

However, a child benefit income tax charge arises where:

- an individual receives child benefit, and
- he/she, or
    - his/her spouse/civil partner, or
    - his/her partner, whom he/she is living with as if they were married or in a civil partnership

    has 'adjusted net income' of £50,000 or more.

'Adjusted net income' is calculated in the same way as for the restriction of the personal allowance for high income individuals.

The tax charge is as follows:

Income	Tax charge
Between £50,000 and £60,000	1% of child benefit for each £100 of income over £50,000
Over £60,000	The amount of child benefit received

 The thresholds and method of calculating the child benefit tax charge are included in the tax rates and allowances provided to you in the examination.

In calculating the tax charge both the appropriate percentage and the tax charge are rounded down to the nearest whole number.

The charge effectively removes the child benefit for high income individuals.

Where the charge applies the taxpayer must complete a tax return and the charge is collected through the self-assessment system (Chapter 13).

Child benefit claimants, or their partners, can avoid the tax charge if they choose not to claim child benefit.

 Where both partners have adjusted net income over £50,000, the charge is levied on the person with the higher income. However, at TX this scenario will not be examined.

 Illustration 10 – Child benefit tax charge

Patrick and Hayley are married with two children. Hayley received child benefit of £1,820 during the tax year 2020/21. Patrick has no income as he looks after the couple's children.

Hayley is employed with a salary of £54,000 per annum and has no other source of income. She paid £1,800 (net) to a registered charity under the gift aid scheme during the tax year 2020/21.

Calculate Hayley's income tax liability for the tax year 2020/21.

Solution

Income tax computation – 2020/21

			£
Employment income			54,000
Less: PA			(12,500)
Taxable income (all = 'non-savings income')			41,500
Income tax:	£		£
Extended basic rate band (W1)	39,750	× 20%	7,950
Higher rate	1,750	× 40%	700
	41,500		
Add: Child benefit charge (W2)			309
Income tax liability			8,959

Workings

(W1) Extension of basic rate band

	£
Current basic rate threshold	37,500
Add: Gross gift aid donation (£1,800 × 100/80)	2,250
Revised threshold	39,750

(W2) Child benefit tax charge

	£	£
Child benefit received		1,820
Total income – Net income	54,000	
Less: Gross gift aid donation (£1,800 × 100/80)	(2,250)	
Adjusted net income	51,750	
Less: Lower limit	(50,000)	
	1,750	

1% per £100 of £1,750 = 17.5% rounded down to 17%

	£
Child benefit charge = 17% of £1,820 (rounded down)	309

Test your understanding 8

Rizwan and Gisala live together with their son. Gisala received child benefit of £1,095 during the tax year 2020/21. Rizwan has no income in the tax year 2020/21.

Gisala runs a small nursery business and had taxable trading profits of £60,000 for the tax year 2020/21, and paid £2,000 to a charity under the gift aid scheme.

Calculate Gisala's income tax liability for the tax year 2020/21.

9 Tax status of an individual

The tax residency status of an individual determines how much income is assessed to UK tax.

All persons resident in the UK for tax purposes are assessed to UK tax on their worldwide income.

 Definition of residence

An individual is resident in the tax year if he/she:

- does not meet one of the **automatic non-UK residence tests**, and
- meets one of the **automatic UK residence tests**, or
- meets one or more of the **sufficient ties tests**.

 These rules are complex in practice; however the examining team have confirmed that the following simplified rules are to be applied in the TX examination.

Note that under these rules an individual is either UK resident or non-UK resident for the whole of a tax year.

Procedure to determine residence

Step 1	Check automatic non-UK residence tests
	• If satisfy one test = non-UK resident
	• If not = go to Step 2
Step 2	Check automatic UK residence tests
	• If satisfy one test = UK resident
	• If not = go to Step 3
Step 3	• Determine how many sufficient ties with the UK exist, and
	• How many days are spent in the UK in the tax year, then
	• Use tax tables to decide status

The order of the procedure is important because:

- it is possible for an individual to satisfy both one of the automatic non-UK residence tests and one of the automatic UK residence tests.

If this is the case:

- the non-UK residence test takes priority and the decision is made at Step 1
- there is no need to continue on to Step 2.

Automatic non-UK residency tests

An individual is automatically not UK resident if he/she is 'in the UK' **in the tax year** for **less than**:

- **16 days** or
- **46 days,** and has not been UK resident in any of the previous three tax years or
- **91 days,** and works full-time overseas.

Automatic UK residency tests

An individual is automatically UK resident if:

- he/she is in the UK for at least **183 days** in the **tax year** or
- his/her only home is in the UK or
- he/she works full-time in the UK.

Note that an individual is 'in the UK' if he/she is in the UK at midnight.

If the individual does not satisfy any of the automatic tests, his/her residency status is determined by:

- how many of the five 'sufficient ties tests' are satisfied, and
- the number of days spent in the UK.

Sufficient ties tests

To determine whether or not the individual is sufficiently connected to the UK to be considered UK resident, HMRC look at the following five ties:

		This tie with the UK exists if the individual:
(1)	Family	Has close family (a spouse/civil partner or minor children) in the UK
(2)	Accommodation	Has a house in the UK which is made use of during the tax year
(3)	Work	Does substantive work in the UK
(4)	Days in UK	Has spent more than 90 days in the UK in either, or both, of the previous two tax years
(5)	Country	Spends more time in the UK than in any other country in the tax year

Note that for an individual:

- leaving the UK (previously resident)

  i.e. UK resident for one or more of the previous three tax years:

  - **all five ties** are relevant to decide his/her residency status

- arriving in the UK (not previously resident)

  i.e. **not** UK resident for any of the previous three tax years:

  - only the **first four ties** are relevant (i.e. ignore country tie).

Individuals leaving the UK and arriving in the UK

To determine the residency status of the individual, consideration is given to:

- the automatic 'non-UK residency' and 'UK residency tests', and then if none of the automatic tests are met

- how many of the 'sufficient ties tests' are satisfied, together with

- the number of days spent in the UK

as shown in the table below.

Days in the UK	Previously resident	Not previously resident
Less than 16	Automatically **not** resident	Automatically **not** resident
16 to 45	Resident if 4 UK ties (or more)	Automatically **not** resident
46 to 90	Resident if 3 UK ties (or more)	Resident if 4 UK ties
91 to 120	Resident if 2 UK ties (or more)	Resident if 3 UK ties (or more)
121 to 182	Resident if 1 UK tie (or more)	Resident if 2 UK ties (or more)
183 or more	Automatically resident	Automatically resident

These rules make it more difficult for someone leaving the UK to lose UK residency status than it is for someone arriving in the UK to remain non-UK resident.

This table is included in the tax rates and allowances provided to you in the examination. No other information relating to residence is included in the tax rates and allowances.

Test your understanding 9

Explain whether or not the following individuals are resident in the UK in the tax year 2020/21.

(1) Dieter was born in Germany. He has lived in his home town in Germany until the tax year 2020/21 when he came to the UK to visit on 10 June 2020 until 18 January 2021.

(2) Simone was born in France. She has lived in her home town in France until the tax year 2020/21 when she came to the UK to visit for a month.

(3) Fred has always spent more than 300 days in the UK and has therefore been UK resident. He gave up work on 5 April 2020 and on 18 May 2020 he set off on a round the world holiday. He did not return to the UK until 6 April 2021.

Initially he spent 5 weeks in his second home in Portugal but then did not spend more than 10 days in any other country whilst he was away.

Whilst he was away he kept in touch with his wife and young children who remained in the family home in the UK.

(4)   Olga, a housewife, has previously visited the UK on holiday for 30 days in each of the last five years and was not UK resident in those years.

On 6 April 2020 she purchased a holiday cottage in the UK.

In the tax year 2020/21 she visited the UK for 80 days, staying in her UK home apart from the two weeks when she stayed with her 17 year old son who had come to study in the UK.

For the remainder of the year she lived in her home in Germany.

Summary of residence rules

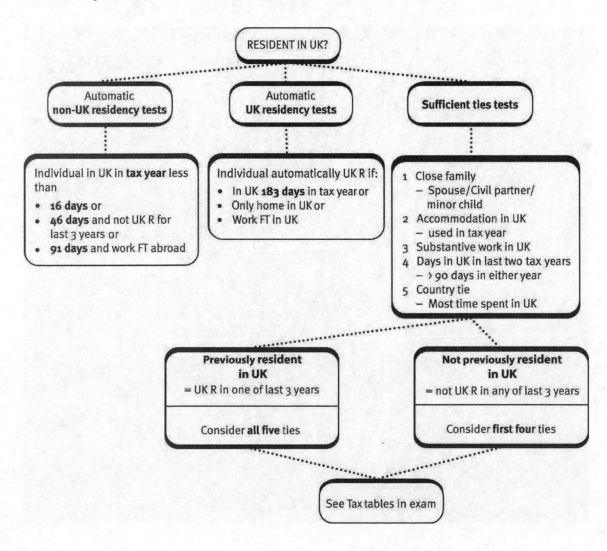

You need to be aware of the definition of residence and be able to apply it to scenarios in the TX examination that will require a written response. However, in income tax computational questions the individual will always be:

- resident in the UK, and

- therefore taxed on his or her worldwide income.

and you will therefore not be required to calculate tax liabilities for an individual who is not resident in the UK.

10 Chapter summary

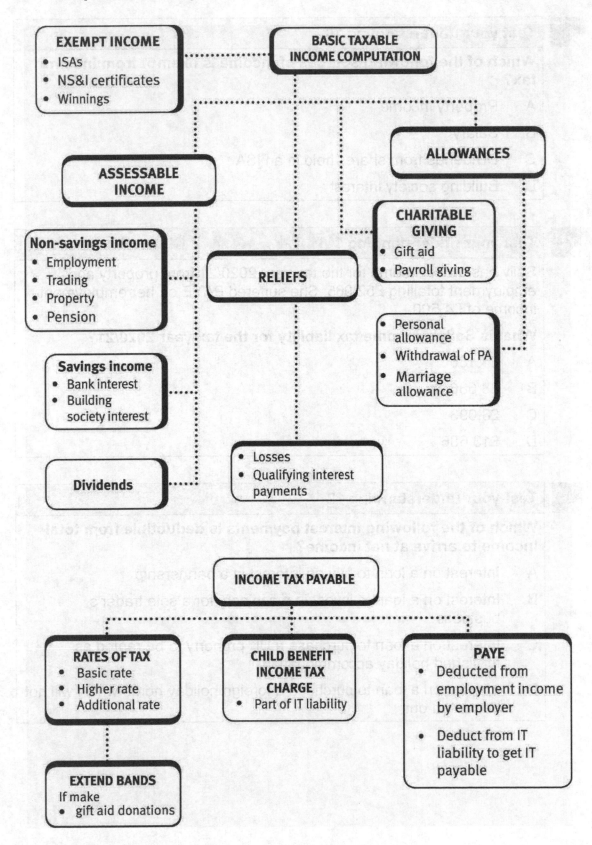

11 Practice objective test questions

Test your understanding 10

Which of the following sources of income is exempt from income tax?

A   Property income

B   Salary

C   Dividends from shares held in an ISA

D   Building society interest

Test your understanding 11

Sally has gross income for the tax year 2020/21 from property and employment totalling £52,965. She suffered PAYE on her employment income of £4,500.

What is Sally's income tax liability for the tax year 2020/21?

A   £4,186

B   £8,686

C   £8,093

D   £13,686

Test your understanding 12

Which of the following interest payments is deductible from total income to arrive at net income?

A   Interest on a loan to buy an interest in a partnership

B   Interest on a loan to invest in machinery for a sole trader's business

C   Interest on a loan to purchase a UK property to be rented as furnished holiday accommodation

D   Interest on a loan to purchase a foreign holiday home which will not be rented out

Test your understanding 13

Harry made gift aid donations to the NSPCC of £500 in the tax year 2020/21. This is the cash amount paid. His only income is employment income of £53,000.

What is his income tax liability for the tax year 2020/21?

A   £13,575

B   £8,700

C   £8,600

D   £8,575

Test your understanding 14

Yusuf had net income of £109,500 and paid a gift aid donation of £2,400 in the tax year 2020/21.

What is his personal allowance for the tax year 2020/21?

A   £0

B   £8,950

C   £9,250

D   £6,000

Test your understanding 15

Lucy and Ricardo have been married for 10 years. Lucy owns 75% of a rental home and Ricardo owns the other 25%. Rental income received from the property is £15,000 p.a. They have not made any elections in relation to the property.

How is this income taxed on the couple?

A   Lucy is taxed on the full £15,000 and Ricardo is not taxable

B   Lucy is taxed on £7,500 and Ricardo is taxed on £7,500

C   Lucy is taxed on £11,250 and Ricardo is taxed on £3,750

D   The income is not taxable

Test your understanding 16

Pierre was born in France. He has been working full time in the UK and been UK resident for tax purposes for the last five years. He plans to return to France in the tax year 2020/21.

Assuming he has two ties with the UK in the tax year 2020/21 what is the maximum number of days that Pierre could spend in the UK without being treated as UK resident in the tax year 2020/21?

A   91 days

B   90 days

C   120 days

D   121 days

Test your understanding answers

Ellie

Income tax computation – 2020/21

	£
Employment income (Note)	125,000
Less: Adjusted PA (W)	(8,000)
Taxable income	117,000

Working: Adjusted PA

	£	£
Basic personal allowance		12,500
Net income (Note)	125,000	
Less: Gross gift aid donations	(16,000)	
Adjusted net income	109,000	
Less: Income limit	(100,000)	
	9,000	
Reduction of PA (50% × £9,000)		(4,500)
Adjusted PA		8,000

Note: In this question, as there are no other sources of income and no reliefs; the employment income = total income = net income.

Test your understanding 2

Abdallah

Income tax computation – 2020/21

	£
Trading income	16,336
Employment income	2,500
Total income	18,836
Less: PA	(12,500)
Taxable income	6,336
Income tax liability (£6,336 × 20%)	1,267

Alice

Income tax computation – 2020/21

	£		£
Trading income			37,335
Employment income			21,000
Total income			58,335
Less: PA			(12,500)
Taxable income			45,835

Income tax			£
Basic rate	37,500	× 20%	7,500
Higher rate	8,335	× 40%	3,334
	45,835		
Income tax liability			10,834

Aya

Income tax computation – 2020/21

			£
Trading income/Total income			238,780
Less: PA (ANI ≥ £125,000)			(0)
Taxable income			238,780

Income tax	£		£
Basic rate	37,500	× 20%	7,500
Higher rate	112,500	× 40%	45,000
	150,000		
Additional rate	88,780	× 45%	39,951
	238,780		
Income tax liability			92,451

Note: In this example, as there is no other source of income and no reliefs; trading income = total income = net income = ANI. As ANI exceeds £125,000 (i.e. exceeds £100,000 plus double the PA), the PA is reduced to £Nil.

Test your understanding 3

(a) Income tax computation – 2020/21

	Katie £	Emily £
Trading income = net income	30,000	0
Less: PA	(12,500)	(0)
Taxable income	17,500	0
Income tax liability (£17,500 × 20%)	3,500	0
Less: MA (£1,250 × 20%)	(250)	
Income tax liability	3,250	0

Note: All of Emily's PA is unused. Maximum benefit of election = £250.

(b) Income tax computation – 2020/21

	Katie £	Emily £
Trading income = net income	13,000	0
Less: PA	(12,500)	(0)
Taxable income	500	0
Income tax liability (£500 × 20%)	100	0
Less: MA (£1,250 × 20%) restricted	(100)	
Income tax liability	0	0

Note: Emily's full PA is unused. Maximum benefit of election = restricted as Katie's income is not sufficient to obtain the full benefit.

(c) Income tax computation – 2020/21

	Katie £	Emily £
Trading/employment income = net income	30,000	11,800
Less: PA	(12,500)	(11,250)
Taxable income	17,500	550
Income tax liability (£17,500 × 20%)		
(£550 × 20%)	3,500	110
Less: MA (£1,250 × 20%)	(250)	
Income tax liability	3,250	110

Note: Only £700 of Emily's PA is unused, however if the election is made, the fixed amount of £1,250 must be transferred.

The couple's total income tax liability would be:

With the election £3,360 (£3,250 + £110)

Without the election £3,500 (£17,500 × 20%)

Tax saving from the election = £140 (£3,500 – £3,360)

Alternative calculation = (£700 unused PA × 20%) = £140

Test your understanding 4

Waqar

Income tax computation – 2020/21

	£
Trading income	23,000
Employment income	28,400
Total income	51,400
Less: PA	(12,500)
Taxable income	38,900

Income tax	£		£
Basic rate	37,500	× 20%	7,500
Higher rate	1,400	× 40%	560
	38,900		
Income tax liability			8,060
Less: PAYE			(3,310)
Income tax payable			4,750

Test your understanding 5

Emmanuel

Income tax computation – 2020/21

		£
Trading income		26,000
Employment income		29,950
		_____
Total income		55,950
Less: Reliefs – Qualifying interest		(4,000)
		_____
Net income		51,950
Less: PA		(12,500)
		_____
Taxable income		39,450
		_____

Income tax	£		£
Basic rate	37,500	× 20%	7,500
Higher rate	1,950	× 40%	780
	_____		
	39,450		
	_____		
Income tax liability			8,280
Less: PAYE			(3,620)
			_____
Income tax payable			4,660
			_____

Test your understanding 6

Paul and Grace

Income tax computation – 2020/21

					Paul	Grace
					£	£
Employment income					54,345	54,345
Less: PA					(12,500)	(12,500)
Total income					41,845	41,845
Income tax	£	£			£	£
	37,500	40,000	(W)	× 20%	7,500	8,000
	4,345	1,845		× 40%	1,738	738
	41,845	41,845				
Income tax liability					9,238	8,738

Despite having the same income, Grace's income tax liability is £500 lower than Paul's. This represents the additional 20% tax saving on the gross donation of £2,500 (£2,000 × 100/80) to the charity.

Working: Grace's extended basic rate band

	£
Basic rate band threshold	37,500
Plus: Gross gift aid donation (£2,000 × 100/80)	2,500
Extended basic rate band	40,000

Test your understanding 7

Clare

Income tax computation – 2020/21

	£
Trading income	156,000
Employment income	12,000
Total income	168,000
Less: Adjusted PA (W1)	(7,875)
Total income	160,125

Income tax	£		£
Basic rate (£37,500 + £58,750)	96,250	× 20%	19,250
Higher rate (£150,000 + £58,750 = £208,750)	63,875	× 40%	25,550
	160,125		
Income tax liability			44,800

Working: Adjusted personal allowance

	£	£
Basic personal allowance		12,500
Net income	168,000	
Less: Gross gift aid donation (£47,000 × 100/80)	(58,750)	
Adjusted net income	109,250	
Total income	(100,000)	
	9,250	
Reduction of PA (50% × £9,250)		(4,625)
Adjusted PA		7,875

Test your understanding 8

Gisala

Income tax computation – 2020/21

	£
Trading income	60,000
Less: PA	(12,500)
Total income	**47,500**

Income tax:

£	
40,000 × 20% (W1)	8,000
7,500 × 40%	3,000
47,500	

Add: Child benefit charge (W2)	821
Income tax liability	**11,821**

Workings

(W1)   Extension of basic rate band

	£
Current basic rate threshold	37,500
Add: Gross gift aid donation (£2,000 × 100/80)	2,500
Revised threshold	40,000

(W2) **Child benefit tax charge**

	£	£
Child benefit received		1,095
Total income – Net income	60,000	
Less: Gross gift aid donation (£2,000 × 100/80)	(2,500)	
Adjusted net income	57,500	
Less: Lower limit	(50,000)	
	7,500	

1% per £100 of £7,500 = 75%

Child benefit charge = 75% of £1,095 (rounded down)   821

Test your understanding 9

Residency status

(1) Dieter has been in the UK for 222 days in the tax year 2020/21, which is more than 183 days.

Accordingly, he will automatically be treated as **UK resident** in the tax year 2020/21.

(2) Simone has not been resident in the UK in any of the three previous tax years, and has been in the UK for less than 46 days in the tax year 2020/21.

Accordingly, she will automatically be treated as **not UK resident** in the tax year 2020/21.

(3) Fred spent 42 days in the UK in the tax year 2020/21.

– He has spent too many days in the UK to be automatically not resident (i.e. > 16 days as previously resident in UK).

– He is not automatically resident as he has not been in the UK for sufficient days, has an overseas home and has not had full-time work in the UK during the tax year 2020/21.

Fred is leaving the UK as he has been UK resident during the three previous tax years.

He was in the UK in the tax year 2020/21 for between 16 and 45 days and must therefore meet at least four of the UK ties tests to be deemed UK resident.

Fred meets the:

- close family tie

- accommodation tie (made use of a UK house)

- days in UK tie (spent more than 90 days in UK in both of previous two tax years), and

- country tie (spent more time in UK than any other country).

He is therefore UK resident in the tax year 2020/21.

(4) Olga has spent too many days in the UK in the tax year 2020/21 to be automatically considered non-UK resident (i.e. > 46 days) and although she has been in the UK for less than 91 days she does not work full time overseas.

She has not spent sufficient days in the UK and has a home in Germany therefore she is not automatically UK resident.

Olga has not been UK resident in any of the previous three tax years.

As she has spent between 46 and 90 days in the UK in the tax year 2020/21 she must have four UK ties to be considered UK resident.

Olga only meets two UK ties (close family and house in the UK) and so is not UK resident in the tax year 2020/21.

Test your understanding 10

The correct answer is C.

Income from an ISA is exempt.

Test your understanding 11

The correct answer is B.

B is the correct answer because a taxpayer's total income (same as net income in this case) must be reduced by the personal allowance of £12,500 to arrive at taxable income upon which income tax is calculated.

In addition, the calculation of a taxpayer's income tax liability is before the deduction of PAYE. The question asked for liability not payable.

The correct figure is arrived at as follows:

	£
Trading income	52,965
Less: PA	(12,500)
Total income	40,465

Income tax:

£	
37,500 × 20%	7,500
2,965 × 40%	1,186
40,465	
Income tax liability	8,686

Test your understanding 12

The correct answer is A.

Interest under B is deductible in arriving at tax adjusted trading profits for the business (see Chapter 7).

Interest under C is deductible in arriving at the assessable property income from the furnished holiday accommodation (see Chapter 4).

Interest under D is not eligible for any tax relief.

Test your understanding 13

The correct answer is D.

	£
Employment income (non-savings income)	53,000
Less: PA	(12,500)
Total income	40,500

Income tax:

£	
38,125 × 20% (W)	7,625
2,375 × 40%	950
40,500	
Income tax liability	8,575

Working: Extension of basic rate band

The basic rate band is extended by the gross gift aid donations

£37,500 + (£500 × 100/80) = £38,125

Test your understanding 14

The correct answer is C.

	£	£
Basic PA		12,500
Net income	109,500	
Less: Gross gift aid donation (£2,400 × 100/80)	(3,000)	
Adjusted net income	106,500	
Less: Income limit	(100,000)	
	6,500	
Reduction of PA (50% × £6,500)		(3,250)
Adjusted PA		9,250

Test your understanding 15

The correct answer is B.

Income received by a married couple on an asset held in joint names is automatically split 50:50, unless the couple elect, in which case, the split is based on the actual ownership of the asset.

Test your understanding 16

The correct answer is B.

Pierre has previously been resident in the UK and has two ties in the tax year 2020/21 with the UK. If he spends 91 to 120 days in the UK in the tax year 2020/21 he will be treated as UK resident. He therefore must spend a maximum of 90 days in the UK in the tax year 2020/21 to be treated as non-resident.

Investment income

Chapter learning objectives

Upon completion of this chapter you will be able to:

- compute the tax payable on savings and dividends income

- recognise the treatment of individual savings accounts (ISAs) and other tax exempt investments

- understand how the accrued income scheme applies to UK Government securities (gilts)

- prepare a basic income tax computation involving different types of income

- understand how a married couple or couple in a civil partnership can minimise their tax liabilities

- suggest basic tax planning.

One of the PER performance objectives (PO15) is to prepare computations of taxable amounts and tax liabilities according to legal requirements. Another objective (PO17) is to advise on mitigating and deferring liabilities through legitimate tax planning measures. Working through this chapter should help you understand how to demonstrate those objectives.

PER

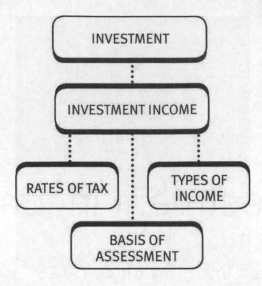

INVESTMENT

INVESTMENT INCOME

RATES OF TAX

TYPES OF INCOME

BASIS OF ASSESSMENT

Introduction

The primary source of income for most taxpayers is derived from earnings, either from employment or self-employment. However, some taxpayers also have investment income.

This chapter covers the taxation of income from investments in the form of savings and dividend income.

1 Savings income

The main types of savings income are bank and building society interest.

Other sources of savings income include:

- Interest from NS&I (National Savings and Investments) accounts, including income from NS&I investment accounts and NS&I direct saver accounts.

- Interest from gilt-edged securities, or gilts i.e. government bonds such as treasury stock and exchequer stock.

- Interest from quoted company loan stock.

Remember, income from NS&I certificates and premium bond winnings are exempt.

An individual is taxed on the amount of the savings income **received in a tax year**.

Rates of tax on savings

Savings income is normally taxed in the same way as 'non-savings income' at the basic, higher and additional rates of tax (20%, 40% and 45%).

- However, **a starting rate of tax of 0%** applies to all taxpayers where savings income falls into the first £5,000 of taxable income.

- In addition, basic rate and higher rate taxpayers are entitled to a **savings income nil rate band**.

- The savings income nil rate band is:

    – Basic rate taxpayer £1,000

    – Higher rate taxpayer £500

    – Additional rate taxpayer £Nil.

- In summary the rates of tax on savings income are:

	Normal rates
Basic rate (First £37,500) (Note)	20%
Higher rate (£37,501 – £150,000)	40%
Additional rate (£150,000 and over)	45%

Savings income nil rate band:

– Basic rate taxpayers	£1,000
– Higher rate taxpayers	£500

Note: A starting rate of 0% applies to savings income where it falls within the first £5,000 of taxable income.

 The rates of tax on savings income are shown in the tax rates and allowances provided in the examination.

Applying the appropriate rates of tax to savings income

Savings income is taxed as the next slice of income after 'non-savings income' (i.e. employment income, trading income, pension income and property income). Therefore the rates of tax applicable to savings income depend on the level of taxable 'non-savings income'. The procedure to follow is:

(1) Calculate income tax on 'non-savings income'.

(2) Apply the different rates of tax on savings income in the following order:

    (1) Starting rate

    (2) Savings income nil rate band

    (3) Normal rates (i.e. basic, higher and additional rates).

(1) Starting rate

This only applies in fairly limited situations i.e. where taxable 'non-savings income' is less than £5,000. If:

–   No taxable 'non-savings income' – the first £5,000 of taxable savings income is taxed at 0% (i.e. it is tax free)

–   Taxable 'non-savings income' below £5,000 – savings income falling into the rest of the first £5,000 is taxed at 0%

–   Taxable 'non-savings income' in excess of £5,000 – the 0% starting rate is not applicable.

(2) Savings income nil rate band

If there is further savings income to tax, consider the savings income nil rate band. If the taxpayer is:

–   A **basic rate taxpayer** – the next **£1,000** falls in the savings income nil rate band and is taxed at 0%

–   A **higher rate taxpayer** – the next **£500** falls in the savings income nil rate band and is taxed at 0%

–   An **additional rate taxpayer** i.e. taxable income is £150,000 or more – **not applicable**.

To determine whether the taxpayer is a basic, higher or additional rate taxpayer, ascertain the highest tax band that his/her taxable income falls within.

For example, a taxpayer with taxable income of £45,000 is a higher rate taxpayer as he has taxable income falling into the higher rate band of £37,500 to £150,000.

(3) Normal rates

If there is further savings income to tax, apply the normal savings rates as follows:

–   The basic rate of 20% applies to savings income falling within the basic rate band (BRB), i.e. the first £37,500 of taxable income.

–   The higher rate of 40% applies to savings income falling within the higher rate band (HRB), i.e. taxable income in the range £37,501 to £150,000.

–   The additional rate of 45% applies to savings income where taxable income exceeds £150,000.

Note that the BRB and HRB are first reduced by 'non-savings income' and savings income that has been taxed at the starting rate and the savings income nil rate.

The above procedure may seem complicated but if you use the columnar layout of the income tax computation (see below) it is relatively easy to determine which rates to apply.

Income tax computation

Where an individual has different sources of income, set up a computation (see below) using columns for each type of income to ensure that you:

- calculate the income tax liability on the different sources of income in the correct order, and

- apply the correct rates of income tax.

Income tax computation – 2020/21

	Non-savings income	Savings income	Dividends	Total
	£	£	£	£
Trading income	X			X
Employment income	X			X
Pension income	X			X
Property income	X			X
Savings income		X		X
Dividends			X	X
Total income	X	X	X	X
Less: Reliefs	(X)	(X)	(X)	(X)
Net income	X	X	X	X
Less: PA	(X)	(X)	(X)	(X)
Taxable income	X	X	X	X

Set off of reliefs and the personal allowance

Remember that in the TX examination the PA and reliefs are deducted from income in the following order:

(1) Non-savings income

(2) Savings income

(3) Dividend income.

Illustration 1 – Savings income rates of tax

Jane received bank interest of £3,000 during the tax year 2020/21.

Calculate Jane's income tax liability assuming she also had employment income in the tax year 2020/21 of:

(a) £11,000

(b) £15,200

(c) £29,000

Solution

Income tax computation – 2020/21

(a) **Employment income of £11,000**

	Non-savings income £	Savings income £	Total £
Employment income	11,000		11,000
Bank interest		3,000	3,000
	___	___	___
Total income	11,000	3,000	14,000
Less: PA (Note 1)	(11,000)	(1,500)	(12,500)
	___	___	___
Taxable income	0	1,500	1,500
	___	___	___

Income tax:	£		£
Savings income – starting rate (Note 2)	1,500	× 0%	0
	___		
	1,500		
			___
Income tax liability			0
			___

Notes:

(1) The PA is always offset first against non-savings income, then savings income and then dividend income.

(2) The starting rate applies as savings income falls within the first £5,000 of taxable income.

In the examination always indicate the rate at which income is taxed, even if the rate is 0%. This shows that you understand that the income is taxable and that you know how to apply the different rates.

(b) **Employment income of £15,200**

	Non-savings income	Savings income	Total
	£	£	£
Employment income	15,200		15,200
Bank interest		3,000	3,000
Total income	15,200	3,000	18,200
Less: PA	(12,500)		(12,500)
Taxable income	2,700	3,000	5,700

Income tax:			£		£
Non-savings income – basic rate		2,700	× 20%		540
Savings income – starting rate (Note 1)		2,300	× 0%		0
		5,000			
Savings income – nil rate (Note 2)		700	× 0%		0
		5,700			
Income tax liability					540

Notes:

(1) The starting rate applies to £2,300 of the savings income as it falls within the first £5,000 of taxable income.

(2) Jane is a basic rate taxpayer as her taxable income (£5,700) is less than £37,500. Her savings income nil rate band is therefore £1,000.

(c) Employment income of £29,000

	Non-savings income	Savings income	Total
	£	£	£
Employment income	29,000		29,000
Bank interest		3,000	3,000
	_____	_____	_____
Total income	29,000	3,000	32,000
Less: PA	(12,500)		(12,500)
	_____	_____	_____
Taxable income	16,500	3,000	19,500
	_____	_____	_____

Income tax:		£		£
Non-savings income – basic rate	16,500	× 20%		3,300
Savings income – nil rate (Note 2)	1,000	× 0%		0
Savings income – basic rate (Note 2)	2,000	× 20%		400
		_____		
		19,500		
		_____		
Income tax liability				3,700
				_____

Notes:

(1) The starting rate does not apply as savings income does not fall within the first £5,000 of taxable income.

(2) Jane is a basic rate taxpayer as her taxable income (£19,500) is less than £37,500. Her savings income nil rate band is therefore £1,000. The balance of her savings income of £2,000 (£3,000 – £1,000) is taxed at the basic rate.

Illustration 2 – Savings income rates of tax

Alonso received bank interest of £7,850 during the tax year 2020/21.

Calculate Alonso's income tax liability assuming he also had trading income in the tax year 2020/21 of:

(a) £43,000

(b) £53,000

(c) £145,000

Solution

(a) Trading income of £43,000

	Non-savings income £	Savings income £	Total £
Trading income	43,000		43,000
Bank interest		7,850	7,850
Total income	43,000	7,850	50,850
Less: PA	(12,500)		(12,500)
Taxable income	30,500	7,850	38,350

Income tax:		£		£
Non-savings income – basic rate	30,500 × 20%			6,100
Savings income – nil rate (Note 2)	500 × 0%			0
Savings income – basic rate (Note 3)	6,500 × 20%			1,300
		37,500		
Savings income – higher rate	850 × 40%			340
		38,350		
Income tax liability				7,740

Notes:

(1) The starting rate does not apply as savings income does not fall within the first £5,000 of taxable income.

(2) Alonso is a higher rate taxpayer as his taxable income (£38,350) falls in the band £37,501 to £150,000. His savings income nil rate band is therefore £500.

(3) The savings income taxed at the savings income nil rate uses up part of the basic rate band. The remaining basic rate band is therefore £6,500 (£37,500 – £30,500 – £500). The savings income falling in the basic rate band is taxed at 20% and the balance of £850 is taxed at the higher rate.

(b) **Trading income of £53,000**

	Non-savings income	Savings income	Total
	£	£	£
Trading income	53,000		53,000
Bank interest		7,850	7,850
Total income	53,000	7,850	60,850
Less: PA	(12,500)		(12,500)
Taxable income	40,500	7,850	48,350

Income tax:			£		£
Non-savings income – basic rate	37,500	× 20%			7,500
Non-savings income – higher rate	3,000	× 40%			1,200
Savings income – nil rate (Note 2)	500	× 0%			0
Savings income – higher rate	7,350	× 40%			2,940
	48,350				
Income tax liability					11,640

Notes:

(1) The starting rate does not apply as savings income does not fall within the first £5,000 of taxable income.

(2) Alonso is a higher rate taxpayer as his taxable income (£48,350) falls in the band £37,501 to £150,000. His savings income nil rate band is therefore £500. The balance of his savings income of £7,350 (£7,850 – £500) is taxed at the higher rate.

(c)   Trading income of £145,000

	Non-savings income	Savings income	Total
	£	£	£
Trading income	145,000		145,000
Bank interest		7,850	7,850
Total income	145,000	7,850	152,850
Less: PA	0		0
Taxable income	145,000	7,850	152,850

Income tax:			£	£
Non-savings income – basic rate	37,500	× 20%		7,500
Non-savings income – higher rate	107,500	× 40%		43,000
Savings income – higher rate (Note 3)	5,000	× 40%		2,000
	150,000			
Savings income – additional rate	2,850	× 45%		1,282
	152,850			
Income tax liability				53,782

Notes:

(1)   The personal allowance is abated to £Nil as total income exceeds £125,000.

(2)   The starting rate does not apply as savings income does not fall within the first £5,000 of taxable income.

(3)   Alonso is an additional rate taxpayer as his taxable income (£152,850) exceeds £150,000. His savings income nil rate band is therefore £Nil.

Test your understanding 1

Jamie received bank interest of £3,350 during the tax year 2020/21.

Calculate Jamie's income tax payable assuming he also had employment income and PAYE deductions in the tax year 2020/21 of:

(a)   £25,000 (PAYE £2,630)

(b)   £47,500 (PAYE £6,530)

(c)   £16,100 (PAYE £850)

Illustration 3 – Set off of reliefs and the personal allowance

Maria Luiza earned employment income of £13,085 and received building society interest of £7,500 in the tax year 2020/21. She paid qualifying interest of £100 during the year.

PAYE of £47 was deducted from her employment income.

Calculate the income tax payable by Maria Luiza.

Solution

Income tax computation – 2020/21

	Non-savings income £	Savings income £	Total £
Employment income	13,085		13,085
Building society interest		7,500	7,500
Total income	13,085	7,500	20,585
Less: Interest paid	(100)		(100)
Net income	12,985	7,500	20,485
Less: PA	(12,500)		(12,500)
Taxable income	485	7,500	7,985

Income tax:	£		£
Non-savings income – basic rate	485	× 20%	97
Savings income – starting rate	4,515	× 0%	0
	5,000		
Savings income – nil rate	1,000	× 0%	0
Savings income – basic rate	1,985	× 20%	397
	7,985		
Income tax liability			494
Less: PAYE			(47)
Income tax payable			447

Note: The starting rate band of £5,000 for savings income is firstly reduced by non-savings income before being applied to savings income.

For a basic rate taxpayer the savings income nil rate band is £1,000. The balance of the savings income is taxed at the basic rate of 20%.

2 Dividend income

Dividends received from a company are charged to income tax in the tax year in which they are **received**.

Rates of tax on dividends

- The first £2,000 of dividend income falls in the dividend nil rate band and is therefore tax free.

- The following rates of tax apply to any remaining dividend income

Dividends falling into the:	Dividend rates
Basic rate band (first £37,500)	7.5%
Higher rate (£37,501 – £150,000)	32.5%
Additional rate (over £150,000)	38.1%

 The rates of tax and thresholds applicable to dividends are included in the tax rates and allowances provided to you in the TX examination.

Applying the appropriate rates of tax to dividend income

Dividend income is taxed as the top slice of income (i.e. after non-savings income and savings income).

(1) The dividend nil rate band applies to the first £2,000 of dividend income.

    (1) Unlike the savings starting rate (which only applies in certain limited circumstances) and the savings income nil rate band (which depends on the tax position of the individual) the dividend nil rate band **always applies** to the first £2,000 of dividend income.

    (2) The dividend income taxed at the dividend nil rate reduces the available basic rate and higher rate bands when determining the rate of tax on the remaining dividend income.

(2) Any remaining dividend income is taxed at the special dividend rates set out above.

Illustration 4 – Dividend income

Jeremy earned employment income of £14,850 and received dividends of £4,500 in the tax year 2020/21. PAYE of £600 was deducted in respect of the employment income.

Calculate Jeremy's income tax payable for the tax year 2020/21.

Solution

Income tax computation – 2020/21

	Non-savings income	Dividend income	Total
	£	£	£
Employment income	14,850		14,850
Dividends		4,500	4,500
Total income	14,850	4,500	19,350
Less: PA (Note 1)	(12,500)		(12,500)
Taxable income	2,350	4,500	6,850

Income tax:		£		£
Non-savings income – basic rate		2,350	× 20%	470
Dividend income – nil rate (Note 2)		2,000	× 0%	0
Dividend income – basic rate (Note 3)		2,500	× 7.5%	187
				————
		6,850		
		————		
Income tax liability				657
Less: PAYE				(600)
				————
Income tax payable				57
				————

Notes:

(1) The PA is deducted from non-savings income in priority to dividend income.

(2) The dividends are treated as the highest part of Jeremy's income. The first £2,000 fall in the dividend nil rate band and are taxed at 0% (i.e. tax free).

(3) The remaining dividend income falls in the remaining basic rate band of £33,150 (£37,500 – £2,350 – £2,000) and is taxed at the dividend basic rate of 7.5%.

Illustration 5 – Dividend income

Imane earned employment income of £34,250 and received dividends of £17,500 in the tax year 2020/21. PAYE of £3,680 was paid in respect of her employment income.

Calculate Imane's income tax payable for the tax year 2020/21.

Solution

Income tax computation – 2020/21

	Non-savings income	Dividend income	Total
	£	£	£
Employment income	34,250		34,250
Dividends		17,500	17,500
	————	————	————
Total income	34,250	17,500	51,750
Less: PA	(12,500)		(12,500)
	————	————	————
Taxable income	21,750	17,500	39,250
	————	————	————

Income tax:	£		£
Non-savings income – basic rate	21,750	× 20%	4,350
Dividend income – nil rate (Note)	2,000	× 0%	0
Dividend income – basic rate	13,750	× 7.5%	1,031
	_____		
	37,500		
Dividend income – higher rate	1,750	× 32.5%	569
	_____		_____
	39,250		
	_____		
Income tax liability			5,950
Less: PAYE			(3,680)
			_____
Income tax payable			2,270
			_____

Note: The dividends are treated as the highest part of Imane's income. The first £2,000 of the dividends falls into the dividend nil rate band. £13,750 falls into the remaining basic rate band (£37,500 – £21,750 – £2,000 = £13,750) and is taxed at the dividend basic rate of 7.5% and the balance is taxed at the dividend higher rate.

Test your understanding 2

Emily has income in the tax year 2020/21 as follows:

Employment income	£45,100
Bank interest received	£2,000
Dividends received	£6,000

Calculate Emily's income tax liability for the tax year 2020/21.

Illustration 6 – Comprehensive scenarios

Mateo received dividend income of £1,500 and bank interest of £375 in the tax year 2020/21. He also has trading income. Assume his trading income in the tax year 2020/21 is as follows:

Situation	£
A	15,500
B	51,595
C	149,875

Calculate the income tax liability for each situation.

Solution

Situation A: Income tax computation – 2020/21

	Non-savings income	Savings income	Dividend income	Total
	£	£	£	£
Trading income	15,500			15,500
Bank interest		375		375
Dividends			1,500	1,500
	_____	_____	_____	_____
Total income	15,500	375	1,500	17,375
Less: PA	(12,500)			(12,500)
	_____	_____	_____	_____
Taxable income	3,000	375	1,500	4,875
	_____	_____	_____	_____

Income tax:			£
Non-savings income – basic rate	3,000	× 20%	600
Savings income – starting rate	375	× 0%	0
Dividend income – nil rate	1,500	× 0%	0
		_____	
		4,875	
		_____	
Income tax liability			600
			_____

Situation B: Income tax computation – 2020/21

	Non-savings income	Savings income	Dividend income	Total
	£	£	£	£
Trading income	51,595			51,595
Bank interest		375		375
Dividends			1,500	1,500
	_____	_____	_____	_____
Total income	51,595	375	1,500	53,470
Less: PA	(12,500)			(12,500)
	_____	_____	_____	_____
Taxable income	39,095	375	1,500	40,970
	_____	_____	_____	_____

Income tax:	£		£
Non-savings income – basic rate	37,500	× 20%	7,500
Non-savings income – higher rate	1,595	× 40%	638
	39,095		
Savings income – nil rate	375	× 0%	0
Dividend income – nil rate	1,500	× 0%	0
	40,970		
Income tax liability			8,138

Situation C: Income tax computation – 2020/21

	Non-savings income	Savings income	Dividend income	Total
	£	£	£	£
Trading income	149,875			149,875
Bank interest		375		375
Dividends			1,500	1,500
Total income	149,875	375	1,500	151,750
Less: Adjusted PA (Note 1)	(0)			(0)
Total income	149,875	375	1,500	151,750

Income tax:		£		£
Non-savings income – basic rate		37,500	× 20%	7,500
Non-savings income – higher rate		112,375	× 40%	44,950
		149,875		
Savings income – higher rate (Note 2)		125	× 40%	50
		150,000		
Savings income – additional rate		250	× 45%	112
Dividend income – nil rate band		1,500	× 0%	0
		151,750		
Income tax liability				52,612

Note:

1   As total income exceeds £100,000 by more than double the personal allowance, the PA is reduced to £Nil.

2   There is no savings income nil rate band as Gordon is an additional rate taxpayer.

Test your understanding 3

Susan has the following income and outgoings for the tax year 2020/21:

	£
Trading income	11,615
Employment income	13,500
Bank interest received	3,500
Dividend income received	2,000
Qualifying interest paid	1,000

PAYE of £330 was deducted from the employment income.

Calculate Susan's income tax payable for the tax year 2020/21.

Test your understanding 4

Alfie earned employment income of £187,450, and received bank interest of £18,750 and dividends of £12,000 in the tax year 2020/21.

Calculate Alfie's income tax liability for the tax year 2020/21.

3 Individual savings accounts

The objective of individual savings accounts (ISAs) is to enable the taxpayer to invest in an account that will create income that is **exempt** from tax.

ISA annual subscription limit

ISAs have an annual subscription limit for the tax year 2020/21 of £20,000 per person, which can be invested in a cash ISA and/or a stocks and shares ISA. There is no restriction on the proportion of the £20,000 limit that can be invested in the different types of ISA.

Note that spouses and civil partners each have their own limits.

The ISA limit is included in the tax rates and allowances provided to you in the TX examination.

Individual savings accounts

ISAs are the most common form of tax efficient investment. They can be opened by any individual aged 16 or over who is resident in the UK. However an individual must be aged 18 or over to open a stocks and shares ISA.

An ISA offers the following tax reliefs:

- Income (interest and dividends) is exempt from income tax.

- Disposals of investments within an ISA are exempt from capital gains tax.

There is no minimum holding period, so withdrawals can be made from the account at any time. The reinvestment of cash withdrawn from an ISA does not count towards the annual subscription limit of £20,000.

The main types of ISAs:

Cash ISAs

This includes bank and building society accounts, as well as those NS&I products where the income is not exempt from tax.

Stocks and shares ISAs

Investment is allowed in shares and securities listed on a stock exchange anywhere in the world.

Other ISAs such as the Help-to-buy ISA, the Innovative Finance ISA or the Lifetime ISA **are not examinable**.

ISAs and the income tax nil rate bands

The tax advantages of ISAs have been removed for many taxpayers by the introduction of the savings income nil rate band (SNRB) and the dividend nil rate band (DNRB):

Cash ISAs

- For many basic and higher rate taxpayers, the savings income nil rate band (SNRB) means investing in a cash ISA no longer provides a tax benefit. This is because their savings income is within the SNRB and is therefore taxed at 0%.

- ISAs will still be beneficial for additional rate taxpayers (who are not entitled to a SNRB) and all taxpayers whose SNRB is already fully utilised.

Stocks and shares ISAs

- For many individuals, the dividend nil rate band (DNRB) means that investing in a stocks and shares ISA no longer provides an income tax benefit. This is because their dividend income is within the DNRB and is therefore taxed at 0%.

- Stocks and shares ISAs will still be beneficial for taxpayers whose DNRB is already fully utilised.

- In addition, chargeable gains made within a stocks and shares ISA are exempt from capital gains tax (CGT) and these ISAs will therefore be advantageous to taxpayers who make chargeable gains in excess of the annual exempt amount. (see Chapter 19)

4 Accrued income

The accrued income scheme was introduced to prevent the practice of 'bond washing'.

Interest is normally paid on securities such as government bonds (gilts) and corporate bonds at regular intervals. As the interest payment date gets nearer, the capital value of the securities increases as any purchaser is buying the accrued income in addition to the underlying capital value.

When the securities are sold they are usually exempt from CGT so this element of growth relating to the interest, which is included in the sale proceeds, escapes tax.

Background – Bond washing

This scheme applies to marketable securities such as gilts and loan notes.

Interest is paid to the registered holder on a certain date. However, an individual who sells the security before that date will not receive the interest payment due on that date as by then it would no longer be owned by him. Part of the interest subsequently paid to the purchaser will relate to the vendor's period of ownership.

Therefore, the price the vendor receives for selling the security will be inflated to take account of the fact that the purchaser is due to receive the next interest payment.

The vendor has received a capital receipt in relation to the sale of the security, and as he will not receive interest income, there is no charge to income tax in respect of the increased selling price.

As gilts and loan notes are exempt from CGT, any gain arising on the disposal will also escape capital gains tax. Overall therefore, any interest due to be paid out and included in the selling price of the security will escape tax.

How the scheme operates

- Under the scheme, interest is deemed to accrue on a daily basis (but computations in the examination are calculated on a monthly basis unless the question says otherwise).

- The purchase price (or disposal price) of the security is apportioned between the income element and the capital element.

- The income element is assessed as interest income.

- The scheme does not apply unless the total nominal value of securities held by an individual exceeds £5,000 at some time during the tax year.

- The scheme does not apply if the securities are transferred on death.

Illustration 7 – Accrued income scheme

Ahmed sold £15,000 6% loan stock cum interest on 31 October 2020 for proceeds of £20,000. He originally acquired the loan stock on 1 May 2018. Interest is payable on 30 June and 31 December each year.

Calculate the amount assessed on Ahmed as interest income for 2020/21.

Solution

Interest income – 2020/21

	£
Interest received – 30 June 2020 (£15,000 × 6% × 6/12)	450
Accrued interest included in selling price of loan stock (from 1 July 2020 – 31 October 2020 (£15,000 × 6% × 4/12)	300
Total interest assessable to tax	750

Note: For CGT purposes the sale proceeds amount is £19,700 (£20,000 – £300). However, any gain arising is exempt as the loan stock is a qualifying corporate bond (QCB).

5 Married couples – planning opportunities

Spouses have their own personal allowance and income tax rate bands.

A married couple may save tax by making a marriage allowance election to transfer a fixed amount of the personal allowance from one spouse to the other.

In addition, a married couple can transfer income generating assets between them, at no tax cost, to minimise their joint tax liability.

Shared ownership can be transferred in order that both spouses receive dividend income. This will maximise the benefit of the dividend nil rate band. In total, the couple can receive £4,000 (2 × £2,000) of dividend income each year without suffering any tax.

These rules also apply to partners within a civil partnership.

Illustration 8 – Married couples – planning

Ting is married to Ning. She has employment income of £54,000 p.a. She has various bank accounts from which she receives interest of £5,625 each year.

Ning earns £20,000 trading profits from self-employment each year. He has no other income.

Calculate the couple's income tax liabilities for the tax year 2020/21 and advise how they could have saved tax by reorganising their investments.

Solution

Ting – Income tax computation – 2020/21

	Non-savings income	Savings income	Total
	£	£	£
Employment income	54,000		54,000
Bank interest		5,625	5,625
Total income	54,000	5,625	59,625
Less: PA	(12,500)		(12,500)
Taxable income	41,500	5,625	47,125

Income tax:			£		£
Non-savings income – basic rate		37,500	× 20%		7,500
Non-savings income – higher rate		4,000	× 40%		1,600
		41,500			
Savings income – nil rate		500	× 0%		0
Savings income – higher rate		5,125	× 40%		2,050
		47,125			
Income tax liability					11,150

Ning – Income tax computation – 2020/21

	Non-savings income £
Trading income	20,000
Less: PA	(12,500)
Total income	7,500
Income tax liability (£7,500 × 20%)	1,500

Tax saving advice

Ting is a higher rate taxpayer. She has a savings income nil rate band of £500 and mainly pays tax on her investment income at 40%. Ning, however, is a basic rate taxpayer, and has a savings income nil rate band of £1,000.

If the bank accounts were in Ning's name the first £1,000 of interest would be tax free and he would pay tax at 20% on the balance of £4,625. His tax liability on the interest would be £925 and the couple would save tax of £1,125 (i.e. £500 × 40% + £4,625 × 20%).

Alternatively Ting could invest up to £20,000 in an ISA. The interest would be tax free. If some of the bank account is in Ning's name he could also transfer up to £20,000 into an ISA.

6 Chapter summary

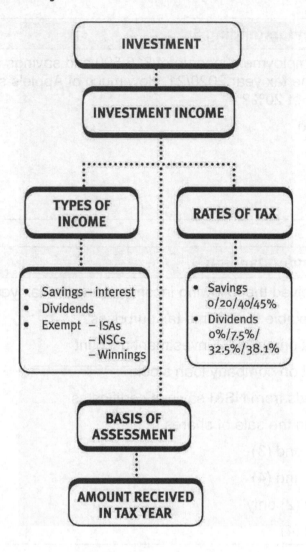

INVESTMENT

INVESTMENT INCOME

TYPES OF INCOME

RATES OF TAX

- Savings – interest
- Dividends
- Exempt – ISAs
   – NSCs
   – Winnings

- Savings 0/20/40/45%
- Dividends 0%/7.5%/ 32.5%/38.1%

BASIS OF ASSESSMENT

AMOUNT RECEIVED IN TAX YEAR

7 Practice objective test questions

Test your understanding 5

Apple has employment income of £16,500 and savings income of £10,000 in the tax year 2020/21. How much of Apple's savings income will be taxed at 20%?

A £10,000

B £4,000

C £8,000

D £9,000

Test your understanding 6

Reghan received the following income during the tax year 2020/21.

Which are taxable for income tax purposes?

(1) Interest on an NS&I investment account

(2) Interest on company loan stock

(3) Proceeds from NS&I savings certificates

(4) Profit on the sale of shares

A (1), (2) and (3)

B (1), (2) and (4)

C (1) and (2) only

D (3) and (4)

Test your understanding 7

The only income Aminata received during the tax year 2020/21 was dividends of £55,000.

What is Aminata income tax liability for the tax year 2020/21?

A £4,437

B £4,362

C £4,287

D £8,349

Test your understanding 8

Sasha's income for the tax year 2020/21 comprises a salary of £140,000 and dividends of £20,000. She is not entitled to a personal allowance.

How will her dividends be taxed?

A   All at 38.1%

B   £2,000 at 0% and £10,000 at 32.5% and £8,000 at 38.1%

C   £2,000 at 0% and £8,000 at 32.5% and £10,000 at 38.1%

D   £10,000 at 32.5% and £10,000 at 38.1%

Test your understanding answers

 Test your understanding 1

Jamie

(a) **Income tax computation – 2020/21**

	Non-savings income	Savings income	Total
	£	£	£
Employment income	25,000		25,000
Savings income		3,350	3,350
	———	———	———
Total income	25,000	3,350	28,350
Less: PA	(12,500)		(12,500)
	———	———	———
Taxable income	12,500	3,350	28,350
	———	———	———

Income tax:	£		£
Non-savings income – basic rate	12,500	× 20%	2,500
Savings income – nil rate	1,000	× 0%	0
Savings income – basic rate	2,350	× 20%	470
	———		
	15,850		
	———		
Income tax liability			2,970
Less: PAYE			(2,630)
			———
Income tax payable			340
			———

Note: The starting rate for savings income is not applicable as 'non- savings income' exceeds the £5,000 band limit. The savings income nil rate band is £1,000 as Jamie is a basic rate taxpayer (taxable income is less than £37,500). The remaining savings income falls in the basic rate band and is taxed at 20%.

(b) **Income tax computation – 2020/21**

	Non-savings income	Savings income	Total
	£	£	£
Employment income	47,500		47,500
Savings income		3,350	3,350
Total income	47,500	3,350	50,850
Less: PA	(12,500)		(12,500)
Taxable income	35,000	3,350	38,350

Income tax:			£		£
Non-savings income – basic rate	35,000	× 20%			7,000
Savings income – nil rate	500	× 0%			0
Savings income – basic rate	2,000	× 20%			400
	37,500				
Savings income – higher rate	850	× 40%			340
	38,350				

Income tax liability		7,740
Less: PAYE		(6,530)
Income tax payable		1,210

Note: In this situation, the starting rate for savings income is not applicable as non-savings income exceeds £5,000. Jamie is a higher rate taxpayer so his savings income nil rate band is £500.

(c) Income tax computation – 2020/21

	Non-savings income	Savings income	Total
	£	£	£
Employment income	16,100		16,100
Savings income		3,350	3,350
	———	———	———
Total income	16,100	3,350	19,450
Less: PA	(12,500)		(12,500)
	———	———	———
Taxable income	3,600	3,350	6,950
	———	———	———

Income tax:			£	£
Non-savings income – basic rate	3,600	× 20%		720
Savings income – starting rate	1,400	× 0%		0
	———			
	5,000			
Savings income – nil rate	1,000	× 0%		0
Savings income – basic rate	950	× 20%		190
	———			
	6,950			
	———			
Income tax liability				910
Less: PAYE				(850)
				———
Income tax payable				60
				———

Note: The starting rate band of £5,000 for savings income is firstly reduced by taxable non-savings income before being applied to savings income.

The savings income nil rate band is £1,000 as Jamie is a basic rate tax payer. The balance of the savings income is taxed at the basic rate of 20%.

Test your understanding 2

Emily

Income tax computation – 2020/21

	Non-savings income	Savings income	Dividend income	Total
	£	£	£	£
Employment income	45,100			45,100
Bank interest		2,000		2,000
Dividends			6,000	6,000
	–––––	–––––	–––––	–––––
Total income	45,100	2,000	6,000	53,100
Less: PA	(12,500)			(12,500)
	–––––	–––––	–––––	–––––
Taxable income	32,600	2,000	6,000	40,600
	–––––	–––––	–––––	–––––

Income tax:			£		£
Non-savings income – basic rate		32,600	× 20%		6,520
Savings income – nil rate (Note)		500	× 0%		0
Savings income – basic rate		1,500	× 20%		300
Dividend income – nil rate		2,000	× 0%		0
Dividend income – basic rate		900	× 7.5%		67
		–––––			
		37,500			
Dividend income – higher rate		3,100	× 32.5%		1,007
		–––––			
		40,600			
		–––––			
Income tax liability					7,894
					–––––

Note: Emily is a higher rate taxpayer as her taxable income (£40,600) exceeds the basic rate threshold of £37,500. She is therefore entitled to a savings income nil rate band of £500.

Test your understanding 3

Susan

Income tax computation – 2020/21

	Non-savings income	Savings income	Dividend income	Total
	£	£	£	£
Trading income	11,615			11,615
Employment income	13,500			13,500
Bank interest		3,500		3,500
Dividends			2,000	2,000
	———	———	———	———
Total income	25,115	3,500	2,000	30,615
Less Reliefs: Interest paid	(1,000)			(1,000)
	———	———	———	———
Net income	24,115	3,500	2,000	29,615
Less: PA	(12,500)			(12,500)
	———	———	———	———
Taxable income	11,615	3,500	2,000	17,115
	———	———	———	———

Income tax:		£		£
Non-savings income – basic rate	11,615	× 20%		2,323
Savings income – nil rate	1,000	× 0%		0
Savings income – basic rate	2,500	× 20%		500
Dividend income – nil rate	2,000	× 0%		0
	———			
	17,115			
	———			
Income tax liability				2,823
Less: PAYE				(330)
				———
Income tax payable				2,493
				———

Test your understanding 4

Alfie

Income tax computation – 2020/21

	Non-savings income	Savings income	Dividend income	Total
	£	£	£	£
Employment income	187,450			187,450
Bank interest		18,750		18,750
Dividends			12,000	12,000
Total income	187,450	18,750	12,000	218,200
Less: Adjusted PA (Note 1)	(0)			(0)
Taxable income	187,450	18,750	12,000	218,200

Income tax:		£		£
Non-savings income – basic rate	37,500	× 20%		7,500
Non-savings income – higher rate	112,500	× 40%		45,000
	150,000			
Non-savings income – additional rate	37,450	× 45%		16,852
	187,450			
Savings income – additional rate (Note 2)	18,750	× 45%		8,437
Dividend income – nil rate	2,000	× 0%		0
Dividend income – additional rate	10,000	× 38.1%		3,810
	218,200			
Income tax liability				81,599

Notes:

(1) As total income exceeds £100,000 by more than double the PA, the PA is reduced to £Nil.

(2) As Alfie is an additional rate taxpayer he is not entitled to a savings income nil rate band.

Test your understanding 5

Apple

The correct answer is C.

			£
Employment income			16,500
Savings income			10,000
			———
			26,500
Less: PA			(12,500)
			———
Taxable income			14,000
			———

Income tax:	£		£
Non-savings income – basic rate	4,000	× 20%	800
Savings income – starting rate	1,000	× 0%	0
	———		
	5,000		
Savings income – nil rate	1,000	× 0%	0
Savings income – basic rate	**8,000**	× 20%	1,600
	———		
	14,000		
	———		
Income tax liability			2,400
			———

Test your understanding 6

Reghan

The correct answer is C.

Proceeds from NS&I savings certificates are exempt income and profits on the sale of shares are subject to capital gains tax and not income tax.

Test your understanding 7

Aminata

The correct answer is C

	£
Dividend income	55,000
Less: PA	(12,500)
Taxable income	42,500

Income tax:			£
£			
2,000	× 0%		0
35,500	× 7.5%		2,662
———			
37,500			
5,000	× 32.5%		1,625
———			———
42,500			4,287

Test your understanding 8

Sasha

The correct answer is C

	£
Salary	140,000
Dividend income	20,000
Taxable income	160,000

The dividends will be taxed as follows:

£2,000 × 0%, £8,000 × 32.5% and £10,000 × 38.1%

Note: The remaining higher rate band is £10,000 (£150,000 – £140,000). The £2,000 dividend nil rate band uses part of the remaining HRB.

Property income

Chapter learning objectives

Upon completion of this chapter you will be able to:

- compute property business profits
- explain the treatment of furnished holiday lettings
- understand rent-a-room relief
- compute the amount assessable when a premium is received for the grant of a short lease
- understand and apply the restriction on property income finance costs
- understand how relief for a property business loss is given.

One of the PER performance objectives (PO15) is to prepare computations of taxable amounts and tax liabilities according to legal requirements. Working through this chapter should help you understand how to demonstrate that objective.

PER

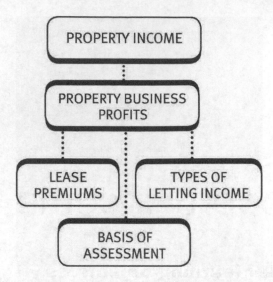

Introduction

The primary source of income for most taxpayers is derived from earnings, either from employment or self-employment. However, some taxpayers also have property income.

This chapter covers the taxation of property income in the form of rental income from properties, including furnished lets, as well as premiums received from the grant of short leases.

1   Property income

For the purposes of the examination, you are required to be able to deal with the following:

- Property business profits arising from the rental/lease of property.

- The premium received on the grant of a short lease.

- Profits arising from the commercial letting of furnished holiday accommodation.

- Rental income received from the rent-a-room scheme.

Property income – basis of assessment

- The property income assessed for an individual or partnership in a tax year is the **income less expenses actually arising in the tax year** i.e. for the tax year 2020/21 the net income arising in the period 6 April 2020 to 5 April 2021.

- The method used to calculate the assessable income arising in the tax year is **normally the cash basis** (i.e. accounted for when cash is received and paid) but is in certain circumstances the accruals basis.

- If the landlord lets more than one property, the assessable amount for each tax year is the aggregate of the net income from all properties (except furnished holiday lettings – see later).

The rules for property income received by a company are different and are covered in Chapter 15.

 The examining team have stated that 'in any examination question involving property income for **individuals or partnerships, the cash basis should be used** unless specifically stated to the contrary'.

Cash basis

- The cash basis is the default basis for **individuals and partnerships** to calculate assessable income from land and buildings each tax year. It is calculated as:

	£
Rental income **received**	X
Less: Related expenses **paid**	(X)
	―
Assessable income	X
	―

- The rental income and related expenses are assessable/deductible on a received/paid basis. Accordingly, the period to which the income/expense relates is irrelevant.

Property income – cash basis allowable deductions

The types of allowable expenses for property income are generally the same as those allowable under the normal rules for the assessment of trading income. These are discussed more fully in Chapter 7.

The main rules are as follows:

- The general rule is that to be allowable, the expenses must have been incurred **wholly** and **exclusively** for the **purposes of the property business**.

  This covers items such as:

  – insurance

  – agents fees and other management expenses

  – repairs

  – interest on a loan to acquire or improve a let **non-residential** property.

  However, there are special rules which apply to the financing costs of a let residential property (see below).

- Relief is available for any expenditure incurred before letting commenced, under the normal pre-trading expenditure rules (see Chapter 7).

- If property is occupied for part of the year by the owner, any expenses relating to private use are not an allowable expense.

- There are special rules which apply to capital expenditure incurred by an individual in a property business (see below).

Illustration 1 – Property income

Hembery owns a property that was let for the first time on 1 July 2020. The rent of £5,000 p.a. is paid quarterly in advance:

Hembery paid allowable expenses of £200 in December 2020 (related to redecoration following a burst pipe), and of £400 in May 2021 (related to repair work which was completed in March 2021).

Calculate Hembery's property income for the tax year 2020/21.

Solution

	£	£
Cash basis (Note 1)		
Rent received (Note 2)		5,000
Allowable expenses		
Redecoration	200	
Repairs (Note 3)	0	
		(200)
Property income		4,800

Notes:

(1) For an individual in the TX examination you should always assume that the cash basis applies to property income unless the question specifies otherwise.

(2) Hembery received four rent payments in the year to 5 April 2021. The rent for the quarter to 30 June 2021 was received in advance on 1 April 2021 and is therefore under the cash basis taxed in the tax year of receipt i.e. 2020/21.

(3) The repairs expense incurred during March 2021 will be deductible in the tax year 2021/22 when it is paid.

Financing costs – residential properties

Owners of residential property that live in their own property do not get tax relief for their mortgage costs.

Owners of buy-to-let residential properties however, have historically been entitled to claim a tax deduction for their finance costs. The costs were deducted from their assessable property income, thus giving tax relief at the highest marginal tax rate suffered by the taxpayer on non-savings income i.e. up to 45%.

As part of the government's overall housing strategy, from the tax year 2017/18 tax relief for the costs of financing residential property that is rented out, has been gradually reduced. As of the tax year 2020/21 tax relief for the full finance cost will be restricted to the basic rate of tax:

- Tax relief is given on costs at the basic rate (20%) by deduction from the taxpayer's final income tax liability.

 The basic rate restriction applicable to finance costs is given in the tax rates and allowances provided to you in the examination.

These special rules apply to loans to acquire, improve or repair a **residential** let property and also to acquire equipment or assets used for the residential letting business.

The finance costs restricted include interest payable as well as the incidental costs of obtaining the finance e.g. bank fees.

Note that these **rules do not apply to companies or qualifying furnished holiday accommodation** (see below) and that interest related to a non-residential property, such as a leased office or warehouse is fully deductible from rental income.

Illustration 2 – Financing costs

Adam owns a residential property that he lets out. During the tax year 2020/21 he received rent of £15,000 and paid the following expenses:

	£
Agent's fees	1,000
Insurance	1,500
Gardener's costs	1,300
Interest costs on loan to acquire property	7,500

During the tax year 2020/21 Adam also has trading income of £42,000 and bank interest income of £800.

Calculate Adam's income tax liability, after reliefs, for the tax year 2020/21.

Solution

	Non-savings income	Savings income	Total
	£	£	£
Trading income	42,000		42,000
Property income (W)	11,200		11,200
Bank interest		800	800
Total income	53,200	800	54,000
Less: PA	(12,500)		(12,500)
Taxable income	40,700	800	41,500

Income tax			£		£
Non-savings income – basic rate		37,500	× 20%		7,500
Non-savings income – higher rate		3,200	× 40%		1,280
		40,700			
Savings income – nil rate		500	× 0%		0
Savings income – higher rate		300	× 40%		120
		41,500			
					8,900
Less: Basic rate tax relief on property income interest (£7,500 × 20%)					(1,500)
Income tax liability					7,400

> **Working: Property income**
>
> | | £ | £ |
> |---|---|---|
> | Rent | | 15,000 |
> | Less: Allowable expenses | | |
> | Agent's fees | 1,000 | |
> | Insurance | 1,500 | |
> | Gardener's costs | 1,300 | |
> | Interest | 0 | |
> | | | (3,800) |
> | Property income | | 11,200 |

Capital expenditure

Under the **cash basis** there is generally no distinction between capital and revenue expenditure in respect of plant and machinery and equipment for tax purposes.

- Expenditure on plant and machinery (except cars) **used in a property business**, such as tools used for maintenance of the property or office equipment used for running the business is an **allowable deduction** from income when **paid**.

- However, this general rule does not apply to:

  – cars

  – assets provided for use in a **residential property** e.g. furniture, TV (but see replacement domestic items relief below).

- In addition, capital expenditure on land and buildings is not an allowable deduction, with the exception of some non-residential properties. In certain circumstances, non-residential buildings (not land) may be eligible for structures and buildings allowances (see Chapter 8).

  As capital expenditure on land and buildings is generally not allowable, it is important to distinguish between improvements (capital expenditure) and repairs (revenue expenditure).

  – Repairs expenditure is allowable.

  – Improvement expenditure is not allowable.

> ### Distinction between repairs and capital expenditure
>
> Caution is required where an item is in need of repair.
>
> Repair means the restoration of an asset by replacing subsidiary parts of the whole asset, for example, replacing roof tiles blown off in a storm. If significant improvements are made to the asset beyond its original condition this will be regarded as capital expenditure. For example, taking off the roof and building another storey.

Cars

- Capital allowances are available on the capital cost of the cars (see Chapter 8). In this case the actual motoring costs e.g. petrol, insurance are also deductible.

- Alternatively, HMRC's approved mileage allowances can be claimed instead of capital allowances and actual motoring costs.

  HMRC's approved mileage allowances are:

  First 10,000 miles p.a.   45p

  Over 10,000 miles p.a.   25p

  These approved mileage allowances are the same as those that can be used by employees and traders to calculate allowable motoring costs (see Chapters 5 and 7).

The HMRC approved mileage allowances are included in the tax rates and allowances provided to you in the examination.

Replacement domestic items relief

As stated expenditure on assets provided for use in a **residential property** e.g. furniture, TV is not allowable. In addition capital allowances are also not available.

However, for **furnished residential** lettings a special relief, **replacement domestic items relief** (also referred to as replacement furniture relief) is available.

- The relief allows a deduction for the replacement (i.e. not the original acquisition) of domestic items provided by the landlord.

- The allowable deduction is:
  replacement cost less any proceeds from the disposal of the original item

- The replacement cost allowed is limited to the cost of a similar item, excluding any improvement, but allowing for the modern equivalent. For example if a washing machine is replaced with a washer-dryer, only the cost of a replacement washing machine would qualify for relief.

- Domestic items are those acquired for domestic use for example, furniture, furnishings, household appliances (including white goods), carpets, curtains and kitchenware. However, 'fixtures' i.e. any plant and machinery that is fixed to a dwelling, including boilers and radiators are specifically excluded.

- This relief is not available to furnished holiday lettings (see section 3) and accommodation for which rent-a-room relief has been claimed (see section 4).

Illustration 3 – Property income

Amal owns a cottage that she lets out furnished at an annual rent of £3,600, payable monthly in advance.

She incurred the following expenditure:

May 2020	Replacement bedroom curtains	£150
May 2020	Replacement of one broken kitchen unit in a fitted kitchen with a unit of similar standard	£275
June 2020	Insurance for year from 5 July 2020 (previous year £420)	£480
November 2020	Dishwasher	£380
May 2021	Redecoration (work completed in March 2021)	£750

The tenant had vacated the property during June 2020, without having paid the rent due for June. Amal was unable to trace the defaulting tenant, but managed to let the property to new tenants from 1 July 2020. The new tenants paid a security deposit of £800 to Amal on 1 July 2020.

The old bedroom curtains had no disposal value. A dishwasher had not previously been provided in the property.

Amal drove 120 miles in her car in relation to the property business during the tax year 2020/21. Amal claims HMRC's approved mileage allowances.

Calculate the property income for the tax year 2020/21.

Solution

Property income – 2020/21

	£	£
Rent received (£3,600 × 11/12) (Note 1)		3,300
Expenses		
Replacement bedroom curtains (Note 2)	150	
Repair to kitchen units (Note 3)	275	
Insurance – cash basis	480	
Dishwasher – capital (Note 4)	0	
Redecoration – cash basis (Note 5)	0	
Mileage allowance (120 × £0.45)	54	
		(959)
Property income		2,341

Notes:

(1) Property income must be calculated using the cash basis unless the question specifically states otherwise. The rental income in relation to June was not received and as such it is not taxable. Security deposits are returned to the tenant, at the end of the lease, net of any recompense to the landlord for damages. They are therefore not taxable as income when received.

(2) A deduction is allowed for the replacement cost of domestic items in a residential property.

(3) The replacement of a kitchen unit in a fitted kitchen with one of a similar standard would normally be treated as allowable as a repair to the fitted kitchen.

(4) Expenditure on an asset provided for use in a residential property is not an allowable expense nor are capital allowances available. As the dishwasher is not a replacement there is also no relief under the replacement domestic items provisions.

(5) Under the cash basis a deduction will be allowed for the redecoration costs paid in May 2021 in the tax year 2021/22.

Test your understanding 1

Eastleigh acquired two residential properties on 1 June 2020 that were first let on 1 July 2020.

Property A is let unfurnished for an annual rent of £4,000, payable quarterly in advance. Eastleigh incurred the following expenditure in respect of this property.

20.6.20	Repairs to roof following a storm on 15 June	£1,600
29.6.20	Interest on loan to acquire property	£420
1.2.21	Repainting exterior	£845

Property B is let furnished for an annual rent of £5,000, payable quarterly in arrears. The tenants were late in paying the amount due on 31 March 2021 – this was not received until 15 April 2021.

Eastleigh incurred the following expenditure in respect of this property in the tax year 2020/21.

4.6.20	Letting expenses paid to agent	£40
5.6.20	Insurance for year ended 31.5.21	£585
30.6.20	Cost of furniture	£2,000
1.7.20	Cost of soft furnishings	£500

Calculate Eastleigh's property income for the tax year 2020/21.

Property income – Accruals basis

- An individual or partnership may opt to use the accruals basis and it must be used if property income receipts exceed £150,000. However, in the examination it should **only be used if the question specifies to do so**.

- Under the accruals basis the main difference is that rental income and related expenses are assessable/deductible on an accruals basis i.e. the **rent receivable** and the **expenses payable** in respect of the tax year.

- If a tenant leaves without paying outstanding rent, under the cash basis the outstanding amount is never taxed. Under the accruals basis the amount receivable is taxed but the outstanding amount owed can be deducted as an expense. This irrecoverable debt is referred to as an 'impairment loss' in the examination.

- The other main difference is that expenditure on plant and machinery **used in a property business**, such as tools used for maintenance of the property or office equipment used for running the business is not an **allowable deduction** from income. However, capital allowances are available instead (see Chapter 8).

- Other rules concerning allowable expenditure, including replacement domestic items relief and the restriction of finance costs for residential properties operate in the same way as for the cash basis.

Illustration 4 – Property income

Aubrey owns a property that was let for the first time on 1 July 2020. The rent of £5,000 p.a. is paid quarterly in advance:

Aubrey paid allowable expenses of £200 in December 2020 (related to redecoration following a burst pipe in November 2020), and £400 in May 2021 (related to repair work which was completed in March 2021).

Calculate Aubrey's property income, assuming he has elected to use the accruals basis, for the tax year 2020/21.

Solution

Accruals basis	£	£
Rent accrued (9/12 × £5,000) (Note 1)		3,750
Allowable expenses		
Redecoration	200	
Repairs (Note 2)	400	
	–––––	(600)
		–––––
Property income		3,150
		–––––

Notes:

(1) The rental income received on 1 April 2021 will not be assessed in the tax year 2020/21 as it relates to the quarter ended 30 June 2021. The date of receipt is irrelevant when using the accruals basis.

(2) As the work was completed in March 2021 under the accruals basis the expenditure is deductible in the tax year 2020/21, the period in which the work was undertaken, and not when the expenditure is paid.

Property business losses

If rental income is less than the allowable expenditure, a loss arises.

- If the landlord owns more than one property, the profits and losses on all the properties are aggregated to calculate the assessable income for the tax year. This effectively provides instant loss relief.

- If there is an overall loss on all properties, the property income assessment for the tax year is £Nil.

- Any unrelieved loss is carried forward indefinitely and offset against the first available future property business profits.

Illustration 5 – Property losses

Sheila owns three properties that were rented out. Her assessable income and allowable expenses for the two years to 5 April 2021 were

Property	1	2	3
	£	£	£
Income			
2019/20	1,200	450	3,150
2020/21	800	1,750	2,550
Expenses			
2019/20	1,850	600	2,800
2020/21	900	950	2,700

Calculate Sheila's property income/(loss) for the tax years 2019/20 and 2020/21.

Solution

Property	1	2	3	Total
	£	£	£	£
2019/20				
Income	1,200	450	3,150	4,800
Less: Expenses	(1,850)	(600)	(2,800)	(5,250)
Profit/(loss)	(650)	(150)	350	(450)
Property income				0
Loss carried forward				450
2020/21				
Income	800	1,750	2,550	5,100
Less: Expenses	(900)	(950)	(2,700)	(4,550)
Profit/(loss)	(100)	800	(150)	550
Less: Loss brought forward				(450)
Property income				100

Note: There is no need to calculate the profit/(loss) on each property separately. One computation amalgamating all income and expenses is all that is required.

For many years Hekla has owned six houses in Upland Avenue that are available for letting. The following details have been provided by the client:

Property number	21	23	25	38	40	67
	£	£	£	£	£	£
Rent receivable for the y/e 5.4.21	2,080	1,820	2,340	1,300	1,300	2,080
Insurance paid on 1 June 2020 annually in advance	280	220	340	150	150	140

The insurance premiums paid for the year ended 31 May 2020 were 5% lower than the above figures for all properties and were paid on 1 June 2019.

Hekla employs a gardener to look after all the properties, and pays him £1,200 a year. There are also accountancy charges of £480 a year; both of these costs are allocated equally to each property.

Numbers 23 and 40, had new tenancies in the year. The cost of advertising for tenants was £50, in respect of number 23 and £100 for number 40. The new tenant at number 23 took over immediately the old tenant moved out. Unfortunately, the old tenant at Number 40 defaulted on rent due before the new tenant moved in and rent of £350 included in the above rent receivable figure for the year was never paid.

During the year Hekla had to replace the carpets in number 40, at a cost of £800. During the year she also had to replace the crockery at number 21, at a cost of £100 and a replacement roof for number 25, cost her £8,600. No disposal proceeds were received in respect of any of the assets which were replaced.

Hekla has loans outstanding on each of the six properties and pays interest of £800 per year on each loan.

(a) **Explain how relief for a property business loss can be obtained.**

(b) **Calculate Hekla's property business loss for the tax year 2020/21.**

Solution

(a) **Relief for property business losses**

Where a taxpayer owns numerous properties, accounts will normally be prepared for each property for each tax year, resulting in either a profit or loss in each case. These are automatically offset against each other for the tax year to ascertain the property income or loss for the tax year.

However, it is not necessary to consider profits and losses on each property separately. For tax purposes the computation is drawn up to show the total rents, expenses, etc. for all the properties, instead of property by property, thereby giving automatic loss relief.

Where the aggregated total is a loss, this is carried forward indefinitely, to be offset against the first available future aggregate property income.

(b) **Property business loss – 2020/21**

	£	£
Rents received (Note 1)		
(£2,080 + £1,820 + £2,340 + £1,300 + £1,300 – £350 + £2,080)		10,570
Less: Expenses paid		
Insurance (Note 2)		
(£280 + £220 + £340 + £150 + £150 + £140)	1,280	
Gardener	1,200	
Accountancy	480	
Advertising (£50 + £100)	150	
Replaced domestic items (£800 + £100)	900	
Repairs (Note 3)	8,600	
		(12,610)
Property loss		(2,040)
Assessable property income		0

Notes:

(1) Property income must be calculated using the cash basis unless the question specifically states otherwise. The rental income of £350 was never received and as such it is not taxable.

(2) The insurance premiums are deductible when paid.

(3) The replacement roof is an allowable repair to the building.

(4) Basic rate income tax relief is given for the interest by reducing Hekla's income tax liability by £960 (£800 × 6 × 20%).

2 Premiums received on the grant of a short lease

Definitions

A **premium** is a lump sum payment made by the tenant to the landlord in consideration for the granting of a lease.

The **grant** of a lease is where the owner of a property gives the tenant the exclusive right to use the property for a fixed period of time.

A short lease is a lease for a period of less than or equal to 50 years.

Income tax treatment

- Part of the premium received in respect of the **granting** of a **short lease** is assessed on the landlord as property income in the tax year the lease is granted.

- The amount assessable as property income is:

	£
Premium	X
Less: Premium × 2% × (n – 1)	(X)
Property income	X

Where:

n = Length of lease = number of **complete** years (ignore part of a year).

Alternative calculation:

Property income = Premium × (51 – n)/50

These formulae are **not** included in the tax rates and allowances provided to you in the TX examination.

Illustration 7 – Premiums received on the grant of a short lease

Wakana granted a 21-year lease to Charles on 1 July 2020, for a premium of £10,500.

Calculate the amount assessable on Wakana as property income in the tax year 2020/21.

Solution

	£
Premium	10,500
Less: £10,500 × 2% × (21 – 1)	(4,200)
Property income	6,300

Alternative calculation:

Property income = £10,500 × (51 – 21)/50 = £6,300

Test your understanding 2

Albert granted an 18-year lease to Angeliki for £26,000, on 6 May 2020.

Calculate the amount assessable on Albert as property income for the tax year 2020/21.

3 Furnished holiday lettings

Profits arising from the commercial letting of furnished holiday accommodation (FHA) are still assessable as property income but are treated as though the profits arose from a single and separate trade.

As a result, separate records regarding these properties have to be kept because there are specific rules and reliefs that apply to such properties.

The **cash basis** is the **default** basis when calculating the property income assessable for the tax year.

Qualifying conditions

The letting will only be treated as FHA if it meets the following conditions:

- The property is let **furnished**.

- The letting is on a **commercial basis** with a view to the realisation of profits.

- It is **available** for commercial letting, to the public generally, as holiday accommodation for not less than **210 days** a year.

- The accommodation is **actually let** for at least **105 days** a year (excluding periods of 'long-term occupation' – see below).

  - Where a taxpayer owns more than one property, the 105 days test is satisfied if the average number of days for which the properties are let in the year is at least 105.

  - The property must not be let for periods of 'long-term occupation' in excess of 155 days in a year.

Long-term occupation is defined as a period of more than 31 consecutive days when the property is let to the same person.

It is possible for the property to be let to the same person for more than 31 days, however, when aggregating all such periods of longer term occupation (which could be a few periods of letting to different persons) the total must not exceed 155 days.

Tax treatment of furnished holiday lettings

Profits from commercially let FHA are assessable as property income. However, they are treated as arising from a separate trade carried on by the landlord, and are not pooled with other rental property.

The following advantages and reliefs are available:

- The profits are treated as relevant earnings for the purposes of tax relief for pension scheme contributions (see Chapter 6).

- Finance costs are fully deductible i.e. there is no basic rate tax relief restriction.

- Plant & Machinery

  Cash basis – a deduction is available on a paid basis for plant and machinery acquired **including furniture and furnishings**.

  Accruals basis – capital allowances are available in respect of plant and machinery **including furniture and furnishings**.

  Under both the cash and accruals bases these deductions apply instead of replacement of domestic items relief (see above).

- Capital gains tax rollover relief, gift relief and business asset disposal relief are available (see Chapter 22).

Any losses made in a qualifying UK FHA business may only be set against income from the same UK FHA business.

4 Rent-a-room relief

If an individual lets furnished accommodation in his or her main residence, and the income is liable to tax as property income, a special exemption applies.

As for other property income, the **cash basis** is the **default basis**, and should be used in the examination unless specifically stated to the contrary.

Gross annual rental receipts are £7,500 or less

- The income is exempt from tax.

- The individual's limit of £7,500 is reduced by half to £3,750 if, during a particular tax year, any other person(s) also received income from letting accommodation in the property while the property was the first person's main residence.

This rule allows a married couple taking in lodgers to either have all the rent paid to one spouse (who will then have the full limit of £7,500), or to have the rent divided between the spouses (and each spouse will then have a limit of £3,750).

 The rent-a-room relief limit is **not** included in the tax rates and allowances provided to you in the examination.

• An individual may elect to ignore the exemption for a particular year, for example, if a loss is incurred when taking account of expenses.

Gross annual rental receipts are more than £7,500

• The individual may choose between:

    – paying tax on the excess gross rent over £7,500

    – being taxed in the normal way on rental income i.e. profit from letting (rent less expenses less replacement furniture relief).

In summary, assess the lower of:

Method 1 – Normal assessment		Method 2 – Rent-a-room relief	
	£		£
Rental income received (or receivable)	X	Rental income received (or receivable)	X
Less: Expenses paid (or payable)	(X)	Less: Rent-a-room relief	(7,500)
Profit	X	Profit	X

 In deciding whether to elect for rent-a-room relief, the key question will therefore be whether or not expenses exceed £7,500.

5 Chapter summary

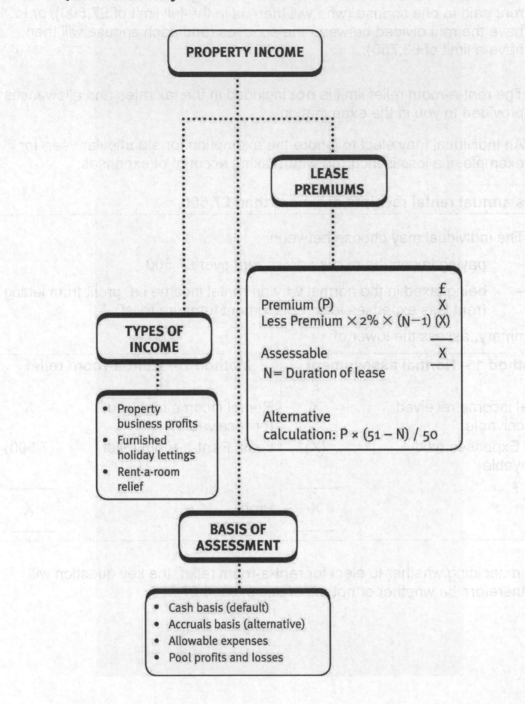

PROPERTY INCOME

LEASE PREMIUMS

	£
Premium (P)	X
Less Premium × 2% × (N−1)	(X)
Assessable	X

N = Duration of lease

Alternative calculation: P × (51 − N) / 50

TYPES OF INCOME

- Property business profits
- Furnished holiday lettings
- Rent-a-room relief

BASIS OF ASSESSMENT

- Cash basis (default)
- Accruals basis (alternative)
- Allowable expenses
- Pool profits and losses

6 Practice objective test questions

Test your understanding 3

Shanaya bought a house in January 2020 which she rented out furnished to students from 1 June 2020. She charged rent of £600 per month, payable in advance. In August 2020, she paid £900 for the windows in the house to be repainted, and £500 for replacement carpets.

What is the property business profit for Shanaya for the tax year 2020/21?

A   £4,600

B   £5,200

C   £6,100

D   £5,700

Test your understanding 4

Ganaraj granted a 45 year lease on a warehouse on 5 July 2020, charging a premium of £50,000 and an annual rent of £10,000 payable in advance.

What is his assessable property income for the tax year 2020/21?

A   £6,000

B   £10,000

C   £16,000

D   £13,500

Test your understanding 5

Percy rents out a home fully furnished. The house does not qualify as a furnished holiday letting. For the tax year 2020/21 his rental income and expenses are:

Interest on loan to acquire property	£460
Insurance	£600
New conservatory	£5,100
Replacement kitchen equipment	£200

How much can Percy claim as allowable expenses in calculating taxable property income in the tax year 2020/21?

A   £1,260

B   £800

C   £1,060

D   £5,900

Test your understanding 6

Maricel rents out a furnished room in her house at an annual rent of £8,050. Her household expenses in relation to the room are £450 (none of which are capital).

Assuming she elects the most beneficial basis of assessment, what is her assessable property income for the tax year 2020/21?

A   £100

B   £550

C   £7,600

D   £7,500

Test your understanding answers

Test your understanding 1

Eastleigh

Property business income – 2020/21

	£	£
Property A		
Rent received		4,000
Less: Roof repairs (pre-trading expenditure)	1,600	
Repainting exterior	845	
		(2,445)
Profit		1,555
Property B		
Rent received (£5,000/4) × 2		2,500
Less: Letting expenses	40	
Insurance (deductible in full on date paid)	585	
		(625)
Profit		1,875
Property income (£1,555 + £1,875)		3,430

Notes:

(1) Basic rate income tax relief is given on the interest cost by reducing Eastleigh's income tax liability by £84 (£420 × 20%).

(2) The original acquisition cost of domestic items such as furniture and soft furnishings is not an allowable deduction. Capital allowances are also not available for expenditure on assets acquired for use in a residential property.

Test your understanding 2

Albert

Property income – 2020/21

	£
Premium	26,000
Less: £26,000 × 2% × (18 – 1)	(8,840)
Property income	17,160

Alternative calculation = £26,000 × (51 – 18)/50 = £17,160

Test your understanding 3

Shanaya

The correct answer is B.

	£
Rent received (£600 × 11 months)	6,600
Less: Repainting windows	(900)
Less: Replacement carpets	(500)
Property business profit	5,200

Test your understanding 4

Ganaraj

The correct answer is C.

	£
Premium received	50,000
Less: 2% × (45 – 1) × £50,000	(44,000)
Premium assessable as rental income	6,000
Rent received	10,000
Assessable property income	16,000

Note. Always use the cash basis unless the question specifies otherwise.

Test your understanding 5

Percy

The correct answer is B.

All the expenses are allowable expenses apart from the conservatory which is disallowable capital expenditure and 25% of the interest cost. Allowable expenditure = £915 ((£460 × 25%) + £600 + £200)

Test your understanding 6

Maricel

The correct answer is B.

	£
Rent received	8,050
Less: Rent-a-room relief	(7,500)
	———
Assessable property income	550
	———

Since rent-a-room relief is greater than the tax allowable expenses this amount is deducted from the rent. It is not possible to deduct both the expenses and rent-a-room relief.

Employment income

Chapter learning objectives

Upon completion of this chapter you will be able to:

- recognise the factors that determine whether an engagement is treated as employment or self-employment

- recognise the basis of assessment for employment income

- recognise the income assessable

- recognise the allowable deductions including travelling expenses

- discuss the use of the statutory approved mileage allowances

- explain and compute the amount of benefits assessable.

PER

One of the PER performance objectives (PO15) is to prepare computations of taxable amounts and tax liabilities according to legal requirements. Working through this chapter should help you understand how to demonstrate that objective.

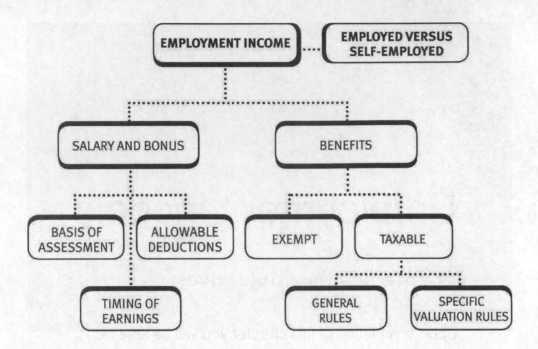

1 The scope of employment income

Employment or self-employment?

The distinction between employment and self-employment is fundamental:

- an employee is taxable under the employment income provisions

- self-employed person is assessed on the profits derived from his trade, profession or vocation, under the trading income provisions.

The following principles, laid down by statute and case law decisions, are important matters to be taken into account in deciding whether a person is employed or self-employed.

Nature of contract	Status
'of service'	employment
'for services'	self-employment

However, even in the absence of a written contract of service any of the following matters would corroborate the existence of such a contract, and, therefore, employment:

- **mutuality of obligations:** an obligation by the employer to offer work and an obligation by the employee to undertake the work offered. An employee would not normally be in a position to decline work when offered

- **control:** the employer controls the manner and method of the work

- **benefits:** the individual is entitled to benefits normally provided to employees such as sick pay and holiday pay

- **basis of payment:** the individual is committed to work a specified number of hours at certain fixed times, and is paid by the hour, week or month

- **length of engagement:** the engagement is for a long period of time

- **equipment:** the individual does not provide his own equipment

- **personal service:** the individual is obliged to work personally and exclusively for the employer, and cannot hire his own helpers

- **part and parcel of organisation:** the work performed by the individual is an integral part of the business of the employer, and not merely an accessory to it

- **financial risk:** the economic reality of self-employment is missing – namely the financial risk arising from not being paid an agreed, regular amount

- **sound management:** the individual cannot profit from sound management.

There is much case law on this area. However, note that an important case concerning a vision mixer who was engaged under a series of short-term contracts in the film industry, established the following fundamental points:

- it is necessary to look at the overall picture and to decide by examining a number of criteria, and

- no one factor is conclusive.

In this particular case, like many persons engaged in a profession or specialised vocation, he did not have all the trappings of a business, and did not supply his own equipment. However, the 'number of separate engagements' was held to be a key factor in the decision to treat him as self-employed.

2 Calculation of employment income

Pro forma – employment income computation

	£
Salary (see section 3)	X
Bonus/commission (see section 3)	X
Benefits (see sections 6, 8, 10 – 13)	X
Reimbursed expenses (see section 4)	X
Cash vouchers (see section 9)	X

Less: Allowable deductions (see section 4)

	£
– Expenses incurred wholly, exclusively and necessarily	(X)
– Contributions to employer's occupational pension scheme	(X)
– Subscriptions to professional bodies	(X)
– Charitable donations: payroll deduction scheme	(X)
– Travel and subsistence expenses	(X)
– Use of own car – mileage allowance (see section 5)	(X)
Employment income	X

3 Basis of assessment

Assessable earnings

- All directors and employees are assessed on the amount of earnings received in the tax year (the **receipts basis**).

- The term 'earnings' includes not only cash wages or salary, but also bonuses, commission, round sum allowances and benefits made available to the employee by the employer.

The date earnings are received

The date of receipt is the **earlier** of the following:

- Actual payment of, or on account of, earnings.

- Becoming entitled to such a payment.

In the case of directors, who are in a position to manipulate the timing of payments, there are extra rules.

They are deemed to receive earnings on the **earliest** of four dates; the two general rules set out above, and the following two rules:

- when sums on account of earnings are credited in the company's accounts

- where earnings are determined:

    - before the end of a period of account = the end of that period

    - after the end of a period of account = date the earnings are determined.

4 Deductibility of expenses from employment income

General rule

Expenditure is only deductible if it is incurred **wholly, exclusively** and **necessarily** in the **performance of duties**.

General rule for employment income expenses

- **In the performance of the duties**

  This aspect of the test means that there is no deduction for expenditure incurred beforehand, to gain the requisite knowledge or experience to do the work. So, for example, the cost of attending evening classes by a schoolteacher has been disallowed.

- **Necessarily**

  For expenditure to comply with this test, it must be an inherent requirement of the job, not something imposed by the employee's circumstances. Thus an employee who joins a golf club to meet clients could not deduct the cost of the membership. In other words, to be necessary expenditure, each and every person undertaking the duties would have to incur it.

- **Wholly and exclusively**

  To be deemed wholly and exclusively incurred, such expenditure must be made with the sole objective of performing the duties of the employment.

  Two examples show this distinction:

    - If an employee is required to wear clothes of a high standard for his or her employment and so purchases them, the expenditure is not deductible. The employee's clothes satisfy both professional and personal needs.

    - Expenditure on a home telephone can be partly deductible. Business calls are made 'wholly and exclusively' and so are deductible. But, for the same reason applied to the clothes, no part of the line rental for a home phone may be deducted.

Expenditure allowed by statute

A deduction for certain types of expenditure is specifically permitted by statute as follows:

- employee contributions to registered occupational pension schemes (within certain limits) (see Chapter 6)

- fees and subscriptions to professional bodies and learned societies, provided that the recipient is approved for the purpose by HMRC, and its activities are relevant to the individual's employment

- payments to charity made under a payroll deduction scheme, operated by an employer

- expenditure on travel and other business related expenses is deductible to the extent that it complies with very stringent rules

- capital allowances are available for plant and machinery necessarily provided by an employee for use in his or her duties.

 Capital allowances

Capital allowances are available where an employee uses his own computer for business use. Allowances are restricted to the proportion of business use (see Chapter 8).

Payroll deduction scheme

- Under the payroll deduction scheme an employee authorises his employer to make deductions from his salary and pay the amounts over to specified charities.

- There is no limit on the amount of donations that an employee can make under the scheme.

- The donations are deducted from the employee's gross pay before tax (PAYE) is applied to his taxable pay.

Travel expenditure

Travel expenses may be deducted only where they:

- are incurred necessarily in the performance of the duties of the employment, or

- are attributable to the necessary attendance at any place by the employee in the performance of his or her duties.

Relief is not given for the cost of journeys that are ordinary commuting or for the cost of private travel.

- Ordinary commuting is the journey made each day between home and a permanent workplace, or to a place which is essentially the same as the workplace (i.e. situated nearby).

- Private travel is a journey between home and any other place that is not for the purposes of work.

Travel expenditure

- Relief is available for travelling expenditure where an employee travels to visit a client. Where such travel is integral to the performance of the duties, it is allowable. This will include travel undertaken by commercial travellers and service engineers who move from place to place during the day.

- No relief is given for travelling between two separate employments. However, if an employee has more than one place where duties have to be performed for the same employer, then travelling expenses between them are allowable.

In addition, the following rules apply for travel to a temporary workplace:

- Relief is given where an employee travels directly from home to a temporary place of work.

- A temporary workplace is defined as one where an employee goes to perform a task of limited duration, or for a temporary purpose.

- A place of work will not be classed as a temporary workplace where an employee works there continuously for a period which lasts, or is expected to last, more than 24 months.

- Where an employee passes his or her normal permanent workplace on the way to a temporary workplace, relief will still be available provided the employee does not stop at the normal workplace, or any stop is incidental (e.g. to pick up some papers).

- Where an employee's business journey qualifies for relief, then the amount of relief is the full cost of that journey. There is no need to take account of any savings the employee makes by not having to make his or her normal commuting journey to work.

Reimbursement of employee's expenses by the employer

Where an employee is reimbursed expenses by the employer, the amount received is taxable income. However, an exemption applies where the employee would be able to claim a tax deduction for the business related expenses under the rules set out above e.g. business travel, professional subscriptions, expenses which fall within the wholly, exclusively and necessarily provisions.

Where an expense is partly allowable and partly disallowable, then the exemption can be applied to the allowable part. For example, where an employee's home telephone bill is fully reimbursed, the exemption can be applied to the business calls, but not to the private calls and the line rental.

Reimbursed expenses which are not exempt must be reported to HMRC using a form P11D and included on the employee's tax return.

Illustration 1 – Reimbursed expenses

Ada, is a marketing manager and is employed by Dale Ltd. During the tax year 2020/21 she incurred the following expenses in connection with her employment, all of which were reimbursed by Dale Ltd.

	£
Home phone	
– Line rental	100
– Business calls	85
Subscription to local gym	1,200
Subscription to The Chartered Institute of Marketing	600
Train fares to attend meeting at client premises	500

State the tax position of the reimbursed expenses and explain how they should be treated by Dale Ltd and Ada.

Solution

The reimbursement of expenses is taxable income unless Ada could claim a tax deduction for them. The following expenses are therefore exempt:

	£	
Home phone		
– Business calls	85	Wholly, exclusively and necessarily incurred in performance of duties
Subscription to The Chartered Institute of Marketing	600	Allowable professional subscription relevant to Ada's employment
Train fares to attend meetings at client premises	500	Allowable travel expenses

> The expenses can be reimbursed to Ada by Dale Ltd free of tax and without reporting them to HMRC.
>
> The home phone line rental and the subscription to the local gym are not incurred wholly, exclusively and necessarily in the performance of Ada's duties and do not fall within the other specifically allowable expenses e.g. travel. Dale Ltd must report the reimbursed expenses to HMRC on Ada's P11D and Ada must include taxable income on her 2020/21 tax return of £1,300.

5 Approved mileage allowance payments (AMAPs)

Allowable rates

Employees who use their own motor cars for business purposes are normally paid a mileage allowance by their employer.

HMRC approved mileage rates which are tax allowable are as follows:

First 10,000 miles p.a.	45p
Over 10,000 miles p.a.	25p

 The HMRC approved mileage rates are included in the tax rates and allowances provided to you in the examination.

- If the mileage allowance paid by the employer = the AMAP: No benefit arises

- Where payments made to the employee > the AMAP: Excess = assessed on the employee as a benefit

- Where the payment to the employee < the AMAP: Difference = allowable deduction from employee's employment income.

 Illustration 2 – Approved mileage allowance payments

An employee uses her own motor car for business travel. During the tax year 2020/21, she drove 13,000 miles on business. Her employer paid her 30p per mile.

Calculate the expense claim for the tax year 2020/21 that can be made to reduce taxable employment income.

Solution

The mileage allowance of £3,900 (13,000 at 30p) will be tax free, but in addition, the employee can make an expense claim as follows:

	£
10,000 miles at 45p	4,500
3,000 miles at 25p	750
Allowable amount	5,250
Less: Mileage allowance received	(3,900)
Expense claim	1,350

The £1,350 can be deducted in arriving at the individual's assessable employment income for the tax year 2020/21.

Test your understanding 1

Christos has travelled 12,000 business miles in the tax year 2020/21, in his own car. His employer pays him 42p per mile for each business mile.

(a) **Calculate how much of the mileage allowance is taxable.**

(b) **Explain how your answer would differ, if Christos's employer paid 35p per mile.**

The AMAP rates can also be used to calculate allowable motoring expenses in circumstances other than employment (e.g. mileage allowance deduction in relation to a property business (Chapter 4) and where fixed rate expenses are claimed by a self-employed trader (Chapter 7).

Test your understanding 2

Underwood is employed as an insurance salesman at a monthly salary of £950. In addition to his basic salary, he receives a bonus that is paid in May each year, and relates to the sales he achieved in the year to the previous 31 October.

His bonuses are as follows:

Bonus for year to:	Paid during:	£
31 October 2018	May 2019	1,920
31 October 2019	May 2020	1,260
31 October 2020	May 2021	2,700

Underwood made the following payments in respect of his employment in the tax year 2020/21.

	£
Contribution to occupational pension scheme	342
Subscription to Chartered Insurance Institute	100
Payroll deduction scheme (in favour of Oxfam)	200

Compute Underwood's assessable income from employment for the tax year 2020/21.

6 Employment benefits

In addition to salary, the term 'earnings' within the scope of income tax also covers benefits received by the employee.

Certain benefits however, are specifically exempt from tax

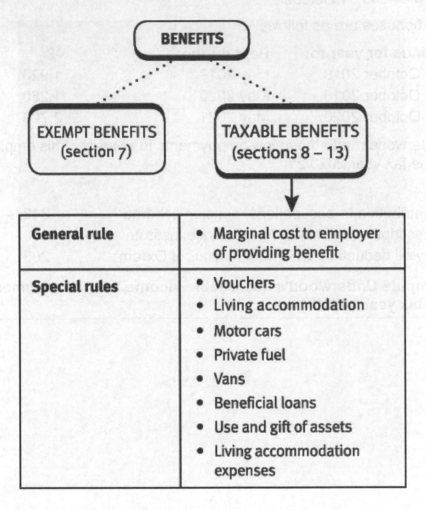

General rule	• Marginal cost to employer of providing benefit
Special rules	• Vouchers • Living accommodation • Motor cars • Private fuel • Vans • Beneficial loans • Use and gift of assets • Living accommodation expenses

Rules applicable to all benefits

There are two rules which must be applied in relation to **all** taxable benefits.

The taxable benefit will be:

- **reduced** by any contributions made by the employee towards the cost of the benefit (however, see exception in relation to private fuel).

- **time apportioned** if it was only available for part of the tax year.

7 Exempt benefits

There are a significant number of benefits that an employer can provide that do not attract a tax charge.

Of these the most commonly examined include:

- Trivial benefits (except vouchers) with a cost to the employer of no more than £50 per gift and which are not provided in recognition of services provided by the employee. This exemption applies to low value benefits given for non-work reasons, such as birthday gifts.

- Employer's contribution to a registered pension scheme.

- Subsidised on-site restaurant or canteen facilities, provided they are available for all employees.

- Provision of a car parking space at or near the place of work, including the reimbursement of the cost of such a parking place.

- Provision of one mobile telephone (including smart phones) for private use by an employee.

- Certain benefits aimed at encouraging employees to travel to work other than by private car. This exemption includes work buses, subsidies to public bus services, and the provision of bicycles and cycling safety equipment, provided they are available to employees generally.

- Christmas parties, annual dinner dances, etc. for staff generally, provided they are of modest cost (up to £150 p.a. per head). If the cost per head exceeds £150, the full cost of the annual event is taxable.

- Workplace nurseries for child care.

- Relocation and removal expenses up to £8,000.

- Expenses incurred by employees whilst away overnight on the employer's business, such as telephone calls home, laundry, etc. up to a maximum of UK £5 per night, overseas £10 per night.

- Home worker's additional household expenses of up to £6 per week can be paid tax free without the need for any supporting evidence. For higher amounts to be exempt, it is necessary to have supporting evidence that the payments are wholly in respect of **additional** household expenses incurred by the employee, in carrying out his duties at home.

- Loans with a beneficial interest rate, provided the loan is ≤ £10,000 throughout the tax year (see later).

- Provision of job-related accommodation (see later).

- Up to £500 per employee per tax year for recommended medical treatment to enable an employee to return to work.

Further exempt benefits

- Entertainment provided for an employee, by reason of his or her employment, by a genuine third party (e.g. a ticket or seat at a sporting or cultural event provided by a business contact or client, to generate goodwill).

- Gifts received, by reason of his or her employment, from genuine third parties, provided the cost from any one source does not exceed £250 in a tax year.

- Long service awards in kind (e.g. gold watches) to mark employment of 20 years or more are exempt up to a cost of £50 for each year of service.

- Provision of travel, accommodation and subsistence during public transport disruption caused by industrial action.

- Employer funded training. Where the expenses of training are paid for by the employer, no taxable benefit arises on the employee.

- Medical insurance for treatment and medical services where the need for treatment arises while abroad in the performance of employment duties.

- Security assets and services. Where a security asset or security service is provided by reason of employment, or where reimbursement is made for the cost of such measures.

- Recreational or sporting facilities available to employees generally and not to the general public, whether provided directly or by a voucher.

- Welfare counselling for employees provided the service is available to employees generally.

- Pension advice for employees. The first £500 in a tax year for pension advice either provided by the employer or as reimbursement of costs incurred by an employee. The support must be available to all employees or all employees of a certain category e.g. all employees nearing retirement.

- Employee liability insurance. Liability insurance is aimed at protecting an employee from a work-related liability.

- Provision by employers of eye care tests and/or corrective glasses for VDU use by their employees, provided they are made available to all employees.

- Awards of up to £25 under a staff suggestion scheme, which is available to all employees, for suggestions outside their duties. Higher awards may be justified if they reflect the financial importance of the suggestion to the business.

This is an extremely comprehensive list.

In reality, the TX examining team is likely to refer to one or two benefits within a question that you will be expected to identify as exempt.

Relocation and removal expenses

No taxable benefit arises on payment or reimbursement of removal expenses and benefits, provided that the following criteria are met:

- The expenses are incurred in connection with either:
  - a totally new employment
  - a new role with the existing employer, or
  - a change in the location at which the employee's duties are carried out.
- It is necessary to acquire a new residence as commuting would not be viable.
- The costs met or reimbursed must be qualifying expenses. These include costs of selling the first house, travel and subsistence when looking for a new house, removal expenses and interest on a bridging loan whilst the employee owns both homes.
- The expenditure must be incurred by the end of the tax year following the one in which the employment change occurred.

Recommended medical treatment

An exemption applies:

- for expenditure incurred by employers on recommended medical treatment
- by a health care professional
- for an employee assessed as unfit for work due to injury or ill health
- after a period of sickness absence of at least 28 consecutive days
- for the purpose of assisting the employee's return to work.

The exempt benefit amount is a maximum of **up to £500 per employee per tax year**.

8 Taxable benefits

General rule

The general rule is that the taxable amount of a benefit is:

- the **cost of providing** the benefit

- unless there are specific statutory rules for valuing a benefit.

Under case law, the 'cost of providing' the benefit has been held to mean the **additional or marginal** cost incurred by the employer – not a proportion of the total cost.

This principle is particularly relevant where employers provide in-house benefits, such as free tickets for employees of a bus company, or airline, or reduced fees for children of school teachers in a fee paying school.

Specific rules

There are specific rules for the following benefits:

- Vouchers and credit tokens (section 9)

- Living accommodation (section 10)

- Motor cars and vans (section 11)

- Private fuel (section 11)

- Beneficial loans (section 12)

- Assets provided to employees (section 13)

Note that:

- An employee is deemed to be provided with a benefit, not only when it is provided to him directly, but also when it is provided to a member of his family or household.

- To be taxed under these principles, a benefit must be provided to the employee, or a member of his family or household, by reason of his employment.

Reporting benefits

Non-cash taxable benefits provided to employees are normally reported to HMRC by the employer at the end of the tax year on form P11D. A copy of the form is given to the employee so that he can include the taxable benefit on his tax return.

Alternatively, the employer can apply to HMRC to tax the benefit through the PAYE system like other earnings. This is often referred to as 'payrolling' of benefits.

Payrolling of benefits

If the employer chooses to payroll a benefit, the employee will then pay tax on the benefit throughout the year under PAYE and is not required to report the benefit on his or her tax return.

The advantage of this for the employee is that the tax is collected on a real time basis, so there is less likelihood of underpayment.

However, it may result in a cash flow disadvantage, as the tax will be paid earlier.

If a benefit is payrolled, the employer is not required to include the benefit on a P11D, which could give cost savings due to a reduction in administration.

9 Vouchers and credit tokens

If an employee is provided with vouchers by his or her employer, e.g. department store vouchers, there is a taxable benefit. The value of the benefit is the cost to the employer of providing the voucher.

If an employee is provided with a 'credit token' e.g. a company credit card, the cost of the goods and services acquired is a taxable benefit for the employee, unless the purchases relate to expenses for which the employee could claim a tax deduction, e.g. business travel.

10 Living accommodation

Where an employee is provided with living accommodation as a result of his employment, the benefit is assessed as follows:

	Benefit arising
Basic charge	Higher of: • **Annual value of the property**, and • Rent paid by the employer, if any (only applicable if the property is rented on behalf of the employee).
Additional charge for expensive accommodation	(Cost of providing the accommodation – £75,000) × the appropriate percentage. Note that this is charged in addition to the basic charge and the formula is not provided in the examination.

Annual value

The annual value is assumed to be the rateable value of the property and represents the yearly rental income the property could be expected to yield. This figure will always be given to you in the examination.

Expensive living accommodation

An additional benefit arises where the 'cost of the accommodation' provided exceeds £75,000.

- The 'cost of providing the accommodation' is calculated as:

	£
Original cost (or market value – see below)	X
Add: Capital improvements prior to the start of the current tax year	X
Cost of providing accommodation	X

- The appropriate percentage is the official rate of interest (ORI) in force at the start of the tax year.

  For the tax year 2020/21, the ORI is 2.25% and will be provided in the tax rates and allowances in the examination.

- Where the employer acquired the accommodation more than **six years** before first providing it to the employee:

  Use the property's **market value when first provided** to the employee, rather than the original cost.

- Note that regardless of the market value, this additional benefit is only charged if the original cost + improvements completed before the start of the tax year > £75,000.

- The additional benefit cannot be charged where the accommodation is rented, rather than owned, by the employer.

The total living accommodation benefits are reduced to the extent that the accommodation is used wholly, exclusively and necessarily for business purposes.

Job-related accommodation

No benefit arises if the property is job-related accommodation (JRA).

 To qualify as JRA, the property must be provided:

- where it is necessary for the **proper performance** of the employee's duties (e.g. a caretaker on call outside normal working hours), or

- where it will enable the **better performance** of the employee's duties and, for that type of employment, it is **customary** for employers to provide living accommodation (e.g. managers of public houses), or

- where there is a special threat to the employee's security and he or she resides in the accommodation as part of special security arrangements (e.g. Prime Minister).

In the examination, you should assume that accommodation is not job-related unless there is anything in the question to suggest otherwise.

Exception for directors

A director can only claim one of the first two exemptions if:

- he or she has no material interest in the company (i.e. holds no more than 5% of the company's ordinary share capital), and

- he or she is a full-time working director or the company is a non-profit making organisation.

Illustration 3 – Living accommodation

Jack was provided with a house to live in by his employer in July 2019. It cost the employer £200,000 in June 2016 and has an annual value of £3,000. Assume the official rate of interest is 2.25%.

Calculate the taxable benefit for the tax year 2020/21 assuming the accommodation is not job-related.

Solution

	£	£
Basic charge:		
Higher of		
(1) annual value	3,000	
(2) rent paid by employer	0	
	———	3,000
Expensive living accommodation charge		
(£200,000 – £75,000) × 2.25%		2,813
		———
Taxable benefit		5,813
		———

Note: The official rate of interest will not normally be given in the question as it is included in the tax rates and allowances provided to you in the examination.

Illustration 4 – Living accommodation

Sachin lives in a house provided by his employer which cost £90,000, when it was acquired in June 2015.

Since this time the following improvements have taken place:

Date of expenditure:	Type of expenditure:	£
February 2016	Conservatory added	15,000
August 2018	Redecoration	2,000
July 2020	Garage extension	10,000

The house has an annual value of £1,700.

The market value of the house was as follows:

April 2020   £200,000

June 2020   £165,000

The accommodation is not job-related and Sachin pays a rent of £100 per month to his employer.

(a) **Calculate the amount assessable for the tax year 2020/21 in the following situations:**

  (1) **Sachin moved in during June 2020.**

  (2) **Sachin moved in during June 2020, but the property was actually acquired for £90,000 by his employer in June 2012.**

(b) **For each of the scenarios above and assuming Sachin remains in the property, with no further improvements than the ones referred to above, what will be the 'cost of providing the accommodation' for calculating the expensive accommodation charge for the tax year 2021/22?**

Solution

(a) **Taxable benefits for accommodation – 2020/21**

(1) **Property acquired – June 2015**

	£	£
Basic charge:		
Higher of		
(1) annual value	1,700	
(2) rent paid by employer	0	
	———	
		1,700
Expensive living accommodation charge (W1)		
(£105,000 – £75,000) × 2.25%		675
		———
		2,375
		———
Restriction for part-year occupation (June 2020 – March 2021) (10/12 × £2,375)		1,979
Less: Contributions paid by employee (10 months × £100)		(1,000)
		———
Taxable benefit		979
		———

(2) **Property acquired – June 2012**

	£	£
Basic charge:		
Higher of		
(1) annual value	1,700	
(2) rent paid by employer	0	
	———	
		1,700
Expensive living accommodation charge (W2)		
(£165,000 – £75,000) × 2.25%		2,025
		———
		3,725
		———
Restriction for part-year occupation (10/12 × £3,725)		3,104
Less: Contributions paid by employee (10 months × £100)		(1,000)
		———
Taxable benefit		2,104
		———

(b) **Cost of providing accommodation – 2021/22**

	Scenario (a)(1) £	Scenario (a)(2) £
Original cost + improvements (W1)	105,000	
Market value (W2)		165,000
(Garage extension (July 2020)	10,000	10,000
	115,000	175,000

Workings

(W1) Cost of providing accommodation – 2020/21

	£
Cost (June 2015)	90,000
Improvements	
Conservatory (Feb 2016)	15,000
Redecoration (Aug 2018) (Note 1)	0
Garage extension (July 2020) (Note 2)	0
Cost of providing accommodation	105,000

(W2) Market value

As Sachin has moved in more than 6 years after the employer acquired the property, the market value at the date the property was made available to Sachin (i.e. £165,000) is substituted for cost. The cost of the conservatory is already accounted for in the market value as at June 2020.

As in scenario (a)(1) the improvements that take place in the tax year 2020/21 do not come into the calculation until the following year.

Notes:

(1)   The redecoration does not represent capital expenditure and therefore is not included in the calculation.

(2)   Only those improvements up to the start of the tax year are included. As the garage extension does not take place until July 2020 it is not included in the calculation until the tax year 2021/22.

KAPLAN PUBLISHING

Test your understanding 3

Paolo lives in a company flat that cost his employer £105,000 in June 2015.

The annual value of the flat is £2,500 and Paolo pays his employer rent of £110 a month.

The accommodation is not job-related.

Calculate Paolo's taxable benefit for the tax year 2020/21.

Expenses connected with living accommodation

In addition to the benefit charges outlined above, assets (such as furniture) and expenses connected with living accommodation (such as lighting and heating) are also taxable on employees where the cost is met by their employer.

Assets (e.g. furniture) provided with the accommodation are taxed at 20% of cost each tax year (see section 13 below).

Job-related accommodation

Where the employee's accommodation is job-related, there is a limit on the living accommodation expenses benefit.

The limit applies to the following types of expense

- heating, lighting and cleaning

- repairing, maintaining or decorating the premises

- furniture and other goods normal for domestic occupation.

The taxable benefit for the expenses is limited to 10% of net earnings (i.e. employment income excluding this benefit for living accommodation).

Illustration 5 – Expenses connected with living accommodation

Fanta is a hotel manager and is provided with accommodation. Her salary is £25,000. She has other employment benefits of £500 and makes payments into her employer's registered occupational pension scheme of £2,000 p.a.

The accommodation has an annual value of £1,500 and cost her employer £90,000 four years ago (when she first occupied the accommodation). The accommodation contains furniture which cost the employer £10,000 four years ago. The employer pays all of her household bills totalling £1,000 per annum.

(a) Calculate the taxable benefit for the tax year 2020/21, assuming the accommodation is not job-related.

(b) Calculate the taxable benefit for the tax year 2020/21, assuming the accommodation is job-related.

Solution

(a) Taxable benefit – not job-related accommodation

	£
Basic charge – annual value	1,500
Expensive accommodation charge	
(£90,000 – £75,000) × 2.25%	338
Provision of services – furniture (20% × £10,000)	2,000
– household bills	1,000
Total benefit	4,838

Note: Be careful when calculating the accommodation benefit. Before starting to calculate consider all the factors that can impact the calculation (e.g. is it job-related, does it cost more than £75,000, is it owned or rented by the employer?)

(b) Taxable benefit – job-related accommodation

	£
Basic charge – N/A as job-related	0
Expensive accommodation charge – N/A as job-related	0
Provision of services – £3,000 (as for (a))	
Restricted to 10% × (£25,000 + £500 – £2,000)	2,350
Total benefit	2,350

If the accommodation is job-related, there is:

–   No basic charge.

–   No expensive accommodation charge.

–   The provision of services benefit is restricted to 10% of Fanta's net earnings.

11   Motor cars, private fuel and vans

Motor cars

Where a company car is available to the employee for private use a taxable benefit arises, calculated as follows:

	£
List price × appropriate %	X
Less: Employee contributions for the private use of the car	(X)
Taxable benefit	X

List price

The list price of a car is the **price when the car is first registered**.

- The price (including taxes) is the price published by the manufacturer for the car on the assumption that it is sold in the UK, as an individual sale in the retail market, on the day before the car's first registration.

  Note that the actual price paid for the car is not relevant. Consequently, employees of large companies cannot benefit from bulk discounts their employer might negotiate with car dealers.

- **Include** the value of **all accessories** and extras fitted at the time of issue, plus the cost of any added subsequently.

- **Reduced by** any **capital contributions** made by the employee towards the original purchase of the car, subject to a **maximum of £5,000**.

Note that capital contributions by an employee, which reduce the list price of the car, should not be confused with employee contributions towards the running costs for the private use of the car, which are deducted from the taxable car benefit.

Appropriate percentage – petrol and diesel-powered motor cars

The appropriate percentage depends on the CO_2 emissions of the car.

CO_2 emissions per km	Petrol car and diesel car meeting the RDE2 standard %	Diesel car not meeting RDE2 standard %
51 – 54 grams	13	17
55 grams	14	18
Each complete additional 5 grams emission above 55 grams	An additional 1% is added to the 14% or 18% up to a maximum of 37%	

Note that the appropriate percentage for a **diesel car is 4% higher** than for a petrol car, **unless** the diesel car meets the real driving emissions 2 (**RDE2**) **standard** (i.e. European standard for low nitrogen oxide emissions).

Appropriate percentage – electric-powered motor cars

A 0% percentage applies to electric-powered motor cars with zero CO_2 emissions.

Appropriate percentage – hybrid-electric motor cars

For hybrid-electric motor cars with CO_2 emissions between 1 and 50 grams per kilometre, the electric range of a motor car is relevant:

Electric range	%
130 miles or more	0
70 to 129 miles	3
40 to 69 miles	6
30 to 39 miles	10
Less than 30 miles	12

 The CO_2 percentages for petrol cars and diesel cars meeting the RDE2 standard are included in the tax rates and allowances provided to you in the examination. The 4% supplement for diesel cars not meeting the RDE2 standard and the maximum percentage of 37% are **not**.

Additional points to note

- The rules regarding to the appropriate percentage only apply to cars first registered on or after 6 April 2020. In the examination, questions will not state the registration date, but you should assume that all cars were registered after 6 April 2020.

- Where an employee changes his or her car during the tax year:
  - a separate calculation needs to be performed in respect of each car, with appropriate time apportionments.

- Where the car is unavailable for a period during the tax year (but was available both before and after, e.g. if it was under repair after a crash):
  - the benefit charge is proportionately reduced, however, the reduction applies only if the car was unavailable for a continuous period of at least 30 days.

- The car benefit takes into account all of the running expenses of the vehicle, so there is no additional benefit when the employer pays for insurance, road fund licence, maintenance etc.

- If a chauffeur is provided with the car:
  - this service constitutes an additional benefit.

- A separate benefit charge is made for private fuel (see below).

- When more than one car is made available simultaneously to an employee:
  - the benefit in respect of the second car is computed in exactly the same way as set out above.

Illustration 6 – Company car

Boris is provided with a petrol powered company car with CO_2 emissions of 145g/km.

Identify the % to be used in calculating the taxable benefit arising on the provision of the company car.

Explain the difference if:

(a) **The car was a diesel car which did not meet the RDE2 standard.**

(b) **The car was a diesel car meeting the RDE2 standard.**

Solution

	%
Basic % for petrol car	14
Plus: (145 – 55) = 90 ÷ 5	18
	───
Appropriate %	32
	───

(a) If the car was a diesel car, which did not meet the RDE2 standard, the % would be increased by 4% to 36%.

(b) If the car was a diesel car meeting the RDE2 standard, the % would be the same as for a petrol car i.e. 32%.

Note that if the CO_2 emissions of the car were 144g/km the starting point of the calculation would still be 140g/km as you always round down the g/km to the nearest full number divisible by 5.

Test your understanding 4

Louis is provided with a company car by his employer. The car has a carbon dioxide emission rate of:

(1) 132g/km.

(2) 187g/km.

(3) 62g/km.

(4) 53g/km

Calculate the appropriate percentage assuming the car runs on petrol or is a diesel car, which does not meet the RDE2 standard.

Pool cars

There is no taxable benefit if the car provided is a pool car.

To qualify as a pool car, **all** of the following conditions must be met during the tax year in question:

- The car must be used by more than one employee (and not usually by one employee to the exclusion of the others).

- It must not normally be kept overnight at or near the residence of any of the employees making use of it.

- Any private use by an employee must be merely incidental to his or her business use of it.

Illustration 7 – Company cars

During the tax year 2020/21 Fashionable plc provided the following employees with company motor cars:

(1) Marwa was provided with a diesel car, meeting the RDE2 standard, on 6 August 2020. The car had a list price when of £13,500 but Fashionable plc secured a discount and paid £12,500. The motor car has an official CO_2 emission rate of 107g/km.

(2) Betty was provided with a diesel powered company car throughout the tax year 2020/21. The car does not meet the RDE2 standard. . The motor car has a list price of £16,400 and an official CO_2 emission rate of 137g/km.

(3) Francisco was provided with a new petrol powered car throughout the tax year 2020/21. Francisco was required to contribute £3,000 towards the purchase cost. The motor car has a list price of £22,600 and an official CO_2 emission rate of 214g/km. Francisco paid the company £1,200 during the tax year 2020/21 for the private use of the motor car.

(4) Derek was provided with a hybrid-electric car throughout the tax year 2020/21. The car has a list price of £60,000. The official CO_2 emission rate of 39g/km and the electric range is 41 miles. Fashionable plc also paid for the road tax, insurance and maintenance on the car, which cost £1,600 during the tax year 2020/21.

(5) Eisha was provided with an electric-powered company car throughout the tax year 2020/21. The car has zero CO_2 emissions. The car had a list price of £17,000.

Calculate the car benefit taxable on each of the above employees of Fashionable plc in the tax year 2020/21.

Solution

	£
Marwa	
Benefit: (£13,500 × 24%) (W1)	3,240
Less: Reduction for non-availability (W2)	(1,080)
	___
Taxable benefit	2,160
	___
Betty	
Taxable benefit: (£16,400 × 34%) (W3)	5,576
	___
Francisco	
Benefit: (£19,600 × 37%) (W4)	7,252
Less: Payment for use of car (W5)	(1,200)
	___
Taxable benefit	6,052
	___
Derek	
Taxable benefit: (£60,000 × 6%) (W6)	3,600
	___
Eisha	
Taxable benefit (W7)	0
	___

Workings

(W1) The car benefit is based on the list price of the car. The price paid for the car by the company is not relevant.

Appropriate percentage

	%
Basic % for petrol cars and cars meeting the RDE2 standard	14
Plus: (105 – 55) = 50 ÷ 5	10
	___
	24
	___

The CO_2 emissions figure of 107 is rounded down to 105 so that it is divisible by 5. The car meets the RDE2 standard so the 4% diesel supplement does not apply and the minimum percentage is the same as for a petrol car i.e. 14%. The base % is increased in 1% steps for each 5g/km above the base level.

(W2) Reduction for non-availability

The car was not available for four months of the tax year 2020/21, so the benefit is reduced by £1,080 (£3,240 × 4/12).

Alternatively, the benefit can be time apportioned and calculated more quickly for the 8 months the car was available as follows:

(£13,500 × 24% × 8/12) = £2,160

(W3) Appropriate percentage

	%
Basic % for diesel car not meeting the RDE2 standard	18
Plus: (135 − 55) = 80 ÷ 5	16
	——
	34
	——

The CO_2 emissions figure of 137 is rounded down to 135 so that it is divisible by 5. The minimum percentage of 18% is increased in 1% steps for each 5g/km above the base level.

(W4) Francisco has contributed £3,000 towards the purchase price of the car. As this is less than £5,000, the capital contribution of £3,000 is deducted from the list price of the car upon which the benefit is calculated. The price on which the car benefit is calculated is £19,600 (£22,600 − £3,000).

The CO_2 emissions are above the base level of 50 g/km.

	%
Basic % for petrol car	14
Plus: (210 − 55) = 155 ÷ 5	31
	——
	45
	——
Restricted to	37
	——

(W5) The contributions by Francisco for the private use of the car reduce the taxable benefit.

(W6) CO_2 emissions are 39 g/km and the electric range is 41 miles, therefore the 6% rate applies. The benefit above covers the road tax, insurance and maintenance of the vehicle.

(W7) The CO_2 emissions are zero so a 0% rate applies and there is therefore no taxable benefit.

Test your understanding 5

Sue is provided with a petrol-powered car by her employer. The emission rate shown on the registration document is 141 grams of carbon dioxide per kilometre and the list price of the car is £16,000. During the tax year 2020/21, Sue drove 3,000 business miles and paid her employer £2,000 in respect of her private use of the car.

Prakash is provided with a diesel-powered car, which does not meet the RDE2 standard, by his employer. The list price of the car is £36,000. Prakash contributed £6,000 towards the cost of the car. During the tax year 2020/21, Paul drove 28,000 business miles. The emission rating of the car is 187g/km.

Calculate the benefit taxable on Sue and Paul for the tax year 2020/21.

Private fuel

In addition to the provision of a company car, some employees also have all (or part) of their fuel for private mileage paid for by their employer.

This is an entirely separate benefit from the provision of the car, and the rules are as follows:

- The benefit where fuel is provided for private motoring in a car provided by reason of a person's employment is also based on the CO_2 emissions of the car.

- The fuel benefit is calculated as:

  Base figure × appropriate percentage

  – The base figure for the tax year 2020/21 is **£24,500**.

  – The base figure is included in the tax rates and allowances provided to you in the examination.

- The CO_2 percentage used in the calculation of the car benefit is also used to calculate the fuel benefit charge.

  – The percentage will therefore range from 0% to 37%.

No benefit is charged in relation to any electricity provided for an electric or hybrid car.

Fuel provided for part of the tax year

It is not possible to opt in and out of the fuel benefit charge.

If, for example, fuel is provided from 6 April to 30 September 2020, then the fuel benefit for the tax year 2020/21 is only charged for six months as the provision of fuel has permanently ceased.

If fuel is provided from 6 April to 30 September 2020, and then again from 1 January to 5 April 2021, the fuel benefit is not reduced since the cessation was only temporary.

- No reduction is made to the fuel benefit for payments made by the employee:

    - **unless** the employee pays for **all fuel** used for private motoring.

    - in that case there would be no fuel benefit.

    This is the exception to the general rule that applies to all other benefits.

- The fuel benefit only applies to vehicles for which there is a car benefit charge. It does not therefore apply to pool cars or an employee's own car.

Illustration 8 – Private fuel

Continuing with the situations set out in Illustration 7 Fashionable plc.

Marwa was provided with fuel for private use between 6 August 2020 and 5 April 2021.

Betty was provided with fuel for private use between 6 April and 31 December 2020.

Francisco was provided with fuel for private use between 6 April 2020 and 5 April 2021. He paid Fashionable plc £600 during the tax year 2020/21, towards the cost of private fuel, although the actual cost of this fuel was £1,000.

Derek was provided with fuel for private use throughout the tax year 2020/21.

Eisha was not provided with fuel for private use.

Calculate the fuel benefit assessable on each of the above employees of Fashionable plc in the tax year 2020/21.

Solution

Marwa	£
Benefit: (£24,500 × 24%)	5,880
Less: Reduction for non-availability (W1)	(1,960)
Taxable benefit	3,952

Betty	
Benefit: (£24,500 × 34%)	8,330
Less: Reduction for non-availability (W2)	(2,083)
Taxable benefit	6,247

Francisco	£
Taxable benefit: (£24,500 × 37%) (W3)	9,065

Derek	
Taxable benefit: (£24,500 × 6%)	1,470

Workings

(W1) Reduction for non-availability:

The motor car was not available for four months of the tax year 2020/21, so the benefit is reduced by £1,960 (£5,880 × 4/12).

Alternatively the benefit can be time apportioned and calculated more quickly for the 8 months fuel was provided:

(£24,500 × 24% × 8/12) = £3,952

(W2) Reduction for non-availability:

Fuel was not available for three months of the tax year 2020/21, so the benefit is reduced by £2,083 (£8,330 × 3/12).

Alternatively the benefit is calculated as: (£24,500 × 34% × 9/12) = £6,247

(W3) There is no reduction for the contribution paid by Francisco towards the cost of private fuel, since he did not reimburse the full cost of the private fuel.

Test your understanding 6

Charles took up employment with Weavers Ltd on 1 July 2020. His remuneration package included a petrol driven car with a list price of £24,000. He took delivery of the car on 1 August 2020. The car has CO_2 emissions of 160g/km. As a condition of the car being made available to him for private motoring, Charles paid £100 per month for the car and £50 per month for petrol during the tax year 2020/21.

Weavers Ltd incurred the following expenses in connection with Charles's car:

Servicing	£450
Insurance	£980
Fuel (of which £1,150 was for business purposes)	£3,500
Maintenance	£640

Calculate Charles's taxable benefits for the tax year 2020/21 in connection with his private use of the car.

Test your understanding 7

Gita was employed as sales manager of Wilt Ltd from 1 August 2020 at a salary of £60,000 p.a. From 1 November 2020, the company provided her with a car, the list price of which was £15,000 and the emission rate was 119g/km. Up to 5 April 2021, she drove 6,000 miles of which 4,500 were for private purposes. The company paid for all running expenses.

Between 1 November 2020 and 31 January 2021, the company paid for all petrol usage including private use. Gita made a contribution to her employer of £15 per month towards the cost of the petrol for her private use. From 1 February 2021 her employer only paid for business use petrol.

Calculate Gita's taxable earnings for the tax year 2020/21.

Vans

The benefit rules for vans are different from those for cars.

- The taxable benefit for the private use of a van for the tax year 2020/21 is a flat rate scale charge of **£3,490 p.a.**

- No benefit arises where the private use of a van is **insignificant**.

  When determining the level of private use, journeys between home and work are ignored. This is not the case for cars.

- Proportionate reductions are made where the van is unavailable.

  Use the same definition for 'unavailable' as for cars.

- Where employees share the private use of the van, the scale charge is divided between the employees on a just and reasonable basis (e.g. by reference to the amount of private use).

- In addition a taxable benefit of **£666 p.a.** arises where fuel is provided for private mileage.

 The benefit figures in respect of vans and van fuel are included in the tax rates and allowances provided to you in the examination.

12 Beneficial loans

Beneficial loans are those made to an employee at a rate below the **official rate** of interest (ORI).

 The TX examining team will assume that the ORI is 2.25% throughout the tax year 2020/21. The ORI is included in the tax rates and allowances provided to you in the examination.

Employees are liable to a benefit charge on

	£
Interest that would be payable on the loan (had interest been charged at the official rate)	X
Less: Interest actually paid in respect of the tax year	(X)
Taxable benefit	X

- There are two methods of calculating the taxable benefit:

    - **The average (or simple) method** – this uses the average balance of the loan outstanding during the tax year.

      (Bal. outstanding at start of tax year + Bal. outstanding at end of tax year) × 1/2

      If the loan was taken out or repaid during the tax year:

      - that date is used instead of the beginning or end of the tax year, and

      - the resulting taxable benefit is time apportioned for the number of months it was available during the tax year.

    - **The precise (or accurate) method** – this calculates the benefit day by day on the balance actually outstanding.

    However, calculations in the examination should be on a monthly basis.

    Either the taxpayer or HMRC can decide that the precise method should be used.

The taxable benefit should be calculated using both methods in the examination unless the question states otherwise.

 An exemption applies for small loans where the total of all the employee's cheap or interest free loans (excluding loans which qualify for tax relief) is no more than £10,000, at any point in the tax year:

- no benefit arises.

- If an interest free or cheap loan is used for a purpose that fully qualifies for tax relief (e.g. loan to buy plant used wholly for employment):

  - no benefit arises.

- If all or part of a loan to an employee (whether or not made on low-interest or interest-free terms) is written off:

  - the amount written off is treated as a taxable benefit and charged to income tax.

 Illustration 9 – Beneficial loans

Daniel was granted a loan of £35,000 by his employer on 31 March 2020, to help finance the purchase of a yacht. Interest is payable on the loan at 1% p.a.

On 1 June 2020, Daniel repaid £5,000 and on 1 December 2020, he repaid a further £15,000. The remaining £15,000 was still outstanding on 5 April 2021.

Calculate the taxable benefit for the tax year 2020/21 using:

(a) **the average method**

(b) **the precise method.**

Solution

(a) **Average method**

	£	£
(£35,000 + £15,000) × 1/2 × 2.25%		563
Less: Interest paid		
6.4.20 – 31.5.20: (£35,000 × 1% × 2/12)	58	
1.6.20 – 30.11.20: (£30,000 × 1% × 6/12)	150	
1.12.20 – 5.4.21: (£15,000 × 1% × 4/12)	50	
		(258)
Taxable benefit		305

(b) **Precise method**

	£
6.4.20 – 31.5.20: (£35,000 × 2.25% × 2/12)	131
1.6.20 – 30.11.20: (£30,000 × 2.25% × 6/12)	338
1.12.20 – 5.4.21: (£15,000 × 2.25% × 4/12)	113
	——
	582
Less: Interest paid (as above)	(258)
	——
Taxable benefit	324
	——

In this situation HMRC could opt for the precise method, although they would probably accept £305 as the difference of £19 (£324 – £305) is not significant.

Test your understanding 8

Adin was loaned £15,000, interest free, by his employer on 6 April 2019. He repaid £4,000 on 6 September 2020.

Calculate the amount taxable on Adin in the tax year 2020/21.

Exemption for commercial loans

There is an exemption for loans made to employees on commercial terms by employers who lend to the general public (e.g. banks).

The exemption applies where:

- the loans are made by an employer whose business includes the lending of money

- loans are made to employees on the same terms and conditions as are available to members of the public

- a substantial number of loans on these terms are made to public customers.

13 Assets provided to employees

Private use of an asset provided by the employer

The general rule that applies to the provision of assets (other than cars, vans and accommodation) is that an employee is taxed on an annual benefit of:

20% of an asset's market value at the time it is first provided.

- Where the employer rents the asset made available to the employee instead of buying it, the employee is taxed on the **higher** of:

    - the rental paid by the employer, or

    - 20% of market value.

- The provision of one mobile phone to an employee is an exempt benefit. The above rules however, will apply to any additional mobile phones provided.

- These rules do not apply to cars, vans and living accommodation. As we have already seen special rules apply to the provision of these assets.

 Illustration 10 – Use of assets

Helen is provided with a computer by her employer for private use, which cost £800.

(a) **Calculate the annual taxable benefit arising on the employee.**

(b) **What if the employer rents the computer for £200 p.a.?**

Solution

(a) The benefit taxed as employment income is £160 (£800 × 20%).

   The benefit is assessed for **each** tax year in which it is provided (not just the one in which it was first made available).

(b) The taxable benefit will be the rent paid of £200 as this is higher than the benefit of £160 calculated under the general rule calculation.

Gifts of assets

If an employer purchases a new asset and gives it to an employee immediately, the employee is taxed on the cost to the employer.

Private use followed by gift of the asset

Where an asset is used by an employee and then subsequently given to that employee the taxable benefit that the employee is taxed on is the **higher** of:

	£	£
Asset market value (MV) when gifted		X
		—
Asset MV when **first made available** to the employee	X	
Less: The benefits taxed on the employee during the time he or she had the use of it, but did not own it	(X)	
	—	X
		—

The purpose of the special rule for gifts of used assets is to prevent employees gaining from gifts of assets that depreciate in value rapidly once they are used.

Where the asset being given to an employee is a used car, van or bicycle provided for journeys to work, the above rules do not apply. Instead, the taxable benefit is the market value at the date of transfer.

Illustration 11 – Use of assets

Brian's employer, X Ltd, purchased a dishwasher for his use on 1 June 2019, costing £600. On 6 April 2020, X Ltd gave the dishwasher to Brian (its market value then being £150).

(a)   **Calculate the benefit assessable on Brian for the gift of the dishwasher in the tax year 2020/21.**

(b)   **What would the assessable benefit be if Brian had paid X Ltd £100 for the dishwasher?**

Solution

(a)   **Gift of dishwasher**   £

Market value when first made available to Brian   600

Less: Benefit already assessed 2019/20

(£600 × 20% × 10/12) (Note)   (100)

Taxable benefit on gift: 2020/21   500

The taxable benefit is £500 since this is greater than the dishwasher's market value when given to Brian (£150).

(b)   **Sale of dishwasher to Brian for £100**   £

Benefit as calculated in (a) above   500

Less: Price paid   (100)

Taxable benefit on gift: 2020/21   400

Note: Where the benefit is provided for only part of a tax year, the benefit is reduced proportionately.

Test your understanding 9

A suit costing £300 was purchased for Habiba's use by her employer on 6 April 2019. On 6 August 2020, the suit was purchased by Habiba for £14, when the market value was £30.

Calculate the benefits assessable on Habiba for each of the tax years affected by the information above.

14 Comprehensive examples

 Illustration 12 – Employment benefits

Darcy is managing director of the Pemberley Trading Co Ltd. He is paid an annual salary of £36,000 and also bonuses based on the company's performance. Pemberley Trading Co Ltd's accounting year ends on 31 December each year and the bonuses are normally determined and paid on 31 May thereafter. In recent years bonuses have been:

	£
Year to 31 December 2018	4,000
Year to 31 December 2019	8,000
Year to 31 December 2020	4,000

Darcy has the use of a company car for private purposes. Its list price is £20,000. Running expenses, including diesel paid by the company for private and business purposes, were £2,600 in the year. The diesel car, which does not meet the RDE2 standard, has CO_2 emissions of 185g/km.

Compute Darcy's income tax liability for the tax year 2020/21.

Briefly give reasons for your treatment of items included or excluded, in arriving at his taxable income.

Solution

Darcy – Income tax computation – 2020/21

	£
Salary	36,000
Bonus (Note 1)	8,000
	44,000
Car benefit (£20,000 × 37%) (W)	7,400
Car fuel benefit (£24,500 × 37%) (Note 2)	9,065
Total income	60,465
Less: PA	(12,500)
Taxable income	47,965

Income tax:

	£		£
Basic rate	37,500	× 20%	7,500
Higher rate	10,465	× 40%	4,186
	47,965		
Income tax liability			11,686

Notes: Explanation of treatment

(1) Under the receipts basis for directors the bonus is treated as received, and therefore taxed, when it is determined. Thus the bonus determined in May 2020, is taxable in the tax year 2020/21.

(2) A fuel benefit is charged as Darcy is provided with fuel for private motoring.

Working: Car benefit percentage

	%
Basic % for diesel car which does not meet RDE2 standard	18
Plus: (185 – 55) = 130 ÷ 5	26
	44 Restricted to 37%

Test your understanding 10

Lily is a senior executive with Berkeley plc. In the tax year 2020/21 her employer made the following benefits available to her:

(1) A diesel car, meeting the RDE2 standard, from 6 October 2020. Its list price is £20,000 and its CO_2 emissions 149g/km. The company paid all running expenses including private diesel.

(2) She continued to have the use of a stereo system owned by the company which cost £2,000 two years ago and which is kept at her home.

(3) Berkeley plc has provided Lily with a television for her personal use since 6 April 2018 when it cost £1,200. On 6 April 2020 the television was sold to Lily for £225 when its market value was £375.

(4) Berkeley plc provided Lily with an interest-free loan of £30,000 on 1 January 2020. She repaid £10,000 of the loan on 30 June 2020. The loan is not used for a qualifying purpose.

(5) Lily was provided with a bouquet of flowers on her 50th birthday which cost the company £30.

In addition she was offered the choice of luncheon vouchers of £2 per day (for 200 working days) or free meals worth £3 per day in the company's canteen (for 200 working days). Meals are available free of charge to all other employees.

Assuming Lily made the most tax efficient choice in respect of the lunch facilities, calculate the total value for taxation purposes of the benefits she received for the tax year 2020/21.

Test your understanding 11

Basil is managing director of Boston plc. He is also a substantial shareholder in the company.

The company's accounts show the following information:

Years ended 30 April:	2019	2020	2021
	£	£	£
Salary, as managing director	13,620	43,560	44,100
Performance bonus	10,000	15,000	18,000

The performance bonus is determined and paid in the July following the accounting year end.

Basil has the use of a Porsche motor car with a list price of £34,000. The CO_2 emissions are 202g/km. All petrol and expenses were paid by the company. Basil drove a total of 18,000 miles in the tax year 2020/21, of which 10,000 were for private purposes.

He reimbursed the company £50 as a contribution towards the cost of private petrol.

Basil has also had the use of a company house since 6 April 2020, which has an annual value of £1,200 and which is provided rent free. The house had cost £90,000 in 2012 and its market value in April 2020 was £135,000.

The company pays private medical insurance for all its employees. Basil's share of the group premium was £320 for the tax year 2020/21. In June 2020 he needed to have treatment following a motor accident and the cost to the insurance company was £1,720.

In the tax year 2020/21 Basil was reimbursed £1,500 in respect of rail fares for business travelling in the UK.

Calculate Basil's employment income for the tax year 2020/21.

15 Chapter summary

```
                    ┌─────────────────────────┐
                    │   Employment benefits   │
                    └─────────────────────────┘
```

Exempt benefits

- Non-work benefits up to £50 per gift
- Employer's contribution to pension
- Pensions advice (up to £150)
- Subsidised canteen
- Car parking space
- Work buses, bicycles, subsidies for public transport
- One mobile phone per employee
- Work related training
- Sports and recreational facilities
- Staff parties (up to £150 p.a)
- Welfare counselling
- Workplace nurseries
- Home worker expenses (up to £6 per week or £26 per month)
- Job related accommodation
- Relocation expenses (up to £8,000)
- Overnight expenses (up to £5 per night in UK and £10 per night overseas)
- Employer liability insurance, death in service benefits and PHI
- Beneficial loans totalling ≤ £10,000
- Medical treatment up to £500 per year

Taxable benefits

- Valued at:
  - General rule: Cost to employer (in house benefits = marginal cost)
  - Specific rules for certain benefits
- Always:
  - deduct employee contributions (except private fuel)
  - time apportion if not available all year

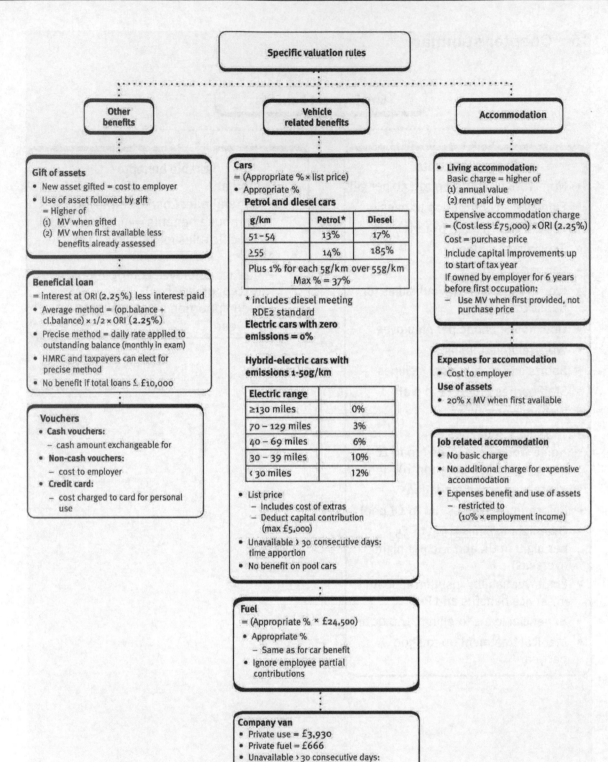

Specific valuation rules

Other benefits

Vehicle related benefits

Accommodation

Gift of assets
- New asset gifted = cost to employer
- Use of asset followed by gift
  = Higher of
  (1) MV when gifted
  (2) MV when first available less benefits already assessed

Beneficial loan
= interest at ORI (2.25%) less interest paid
- Average method = (op.balance + cl.balance) × 1/2 × ORI (2.25%)
- Precise method = daily rate applied to outstanding balance (monthly in exam)
- HMRC and taxpayers can elect for precise method
- No benefit if total loans ≤ £10,000

Vouchers
- **Cash vouchers:**
  - cash amount exchangeable for
- **Non-cash vouchers:**
  - cost to employer
- **Credit card:**
  - cost charged to card for personal use

Cars
= (Appropriate % × list price)
- Appropriate %

Petrol and diesel cars

g/km	Petrol*	Diesel
51–54	13%	17%
≥55	14%	185%
Plus 1% for each 5g/km over 55g/km Max % = 37%		

* includes diesel meeting RDE2 standard

Electric cars with zero emissions = 0%

Hybrid-electric cars with emissions 1–50g/km

Electric range	
≥130 miles	0%
70 – 129 miles	3%
40 – 69 miles	6%
30 – 39 miles	10%
< 30 miles	12%

- List price
  - Includes cost of extras
  - Deduct capital contribution (max £5,000)
- Unavailable > 30 consecutive days: time apportion
- No benefit on pool cars

Fuel
= (Appropriate % × £24,500)
- Appropriate %
  - Same as for car benefit
- Ignore employee partial contributions

Company van
- Private use = £3,930
- Private fuel = £666
- Unavailable > 30 consecutive days: time apportion

Living accommodation:
Basic charge = higher of
(1) annual value
(2) rent paid by employer
Expensive accommodation charge = (Cost less £75,000) × ORI (2.25%)
Cost = purchase price
Include capital improvements up to start of tax year
If owned by employer for 6 years before first occupation:
- Use MV when first provided, not purchase price

Expenses for accommodation
- Cost to employer

Use of assets
- 20% x MV when first available

Job related accommodation
- No basic charge
- No additional charge for expensive accommodation
- Expenses benefit and use of assets
  - restricted to (10% × employment income)

16 Practice objective test questions

Test your understanding 12

Shakera earns £45,000 p.a. as a graphic designer for Commercial Ltd, which prepares accounts to 31 March each year. For the last two years, Shakera has earned bonuses from her employer as follows:

	Date paid	£
Year ended 31 March 2020	1 June 2020	8,000
Year ended 31 March 2021	1 June 2021	11,000

In addition, Shakera incurs expenses in travelling to client's offices of £2,000 in the tax year 2020/21 which are not reimbursed by her employer.

What is Shakera's assessable employment income for the tax year 2020/21?

A £51,000

B £53,000

C £54,000

D £56,000

Test your understanding 13

Nazar is the finance director of a large company and incurred the following costs during the tax year 2020/21.

Which is deductible from his employment income?

A Subscription to the local health club where he frequently meets clients

B Travel between the two offices of his employer. He splits his time equally between the two centres

C Tips given to taxis drivers if he chooses to take a taxi home from work

D Cost of two new suits bought to impress clients

Test your understanding 14

Jacob was provided with a computer for private use on 1 October 2020. The market value of the computer when first provided was £4,300 and at 5 April 2021 the market value was £3,000.

What is the value of the taxable benefit in respect of this computer for the tax year 2020/21?

A £600

B £860

C £430

D £300

Test your understanding 15

Budget Ltd is an estate agency and provided the following benefits to a number of its employees during the tax year 2020/21.

Which one of the following is NOT assessable as employment income for the tax year 2020/21?

A Medical insurance provided to a key member of staff

B Free membership to the gym situated next door to the company headquarters

C A second mobile phone provided to the chief executive of the company

D An interest free loan of £6,000 made on 6 April 2020

Test your understanding 16

Carla was provided with a company car by her employer on 6 April 2020. The diesel car, which does not meet the RDE2 standard, has a list price of £35,000 and CO_2 emissions of 136g/km. Carla paid a contribution of £1,000 to her employer towards the initial purchase price of the car. Carla is not provided with fuel for private purposes.

What is the taxable benefit for Carla for the tax year 2020/21 in respect of the car?

A £10,200

B £11,560

C £10,900

D £9,500

Test your understanding 17

Leo was provided with a house to live in by his employer. The employer rented the house from a local landlord and paid rent of £32,000 p.a. Leo paid rent of £12,000 pa to his employer. The property has an annual value of £9,750 p.a.

What is the taxable benefit, assuming the accommodation is not job-related?

A   £9,750

B   £12,000

C   £20,000

D   £0

Test your understanding 18

Mika was provided with a company petrol driven van by his employer throughout the tax year 2020/21. Mika drives the van to work and back each day but uses his own car for all other private journeys. The van has a list price of £20,000 and CO_2 emissions of 115g/km.

What is the taxable benefit for Mika for the tax year 2020/21 in respect of the van?

A   £0

B   £3,490

C   £666

D   £5,200

Test your understanding answers

Test your understanding 1

Christos

(a)   Taxable amount

	£	£
Income (12,000 × 42p)		5,040
Less: Allowable expenses		
10,000 × 45p	4,500	
2,000 × 25p	500	
		(5,000)
Taxable amount		40

(b)   If employer paid 35p

If Christos's employer paid 35p per mile, the total income paid to Christos would be 12,000 × 35p = £4,200.

Christos could deduct the shortfall of £800 (£5,000 – £4,200) from his employment income, as an allowable expense.

Test your understanding 2

Underwood

	£
Basic salary (£950 × 12)	11,400
Bonus paid in May 2019 (receipts basis)	1,260
	12,660
Less: Allowable expenses	
Subscription	(100)
Pension contribution	(342)
Payroll deduction scheme	(200)
Assessable employment income	12,018

Test your understanding 3

Paolo

Taxable benefit for accommodation – 2020/21

	£
Basic charge – annual value (no rent paid by employer)	2,500
Expensive living accommodation charge ($£105,000 – £75,000$) × 2.25%	675
	3,175
Less: Contribution by employee (£110 × 12)	(1,320)
Taxable benefit	1,855

Test your understanding 4

Louis

CO₂ emissions		Petrol	Diesel
		%	%
132g/km	Basic %	14	18
	Plus: (130 – 55) × 1/5	15	15
		29	33
187g/km	Basic %	14	18
	Plus: (185 – 55) × 1/5	26	26
		40	44
	Restricted to maximum	37	37
62g/km	Basic %	14	18
	Plus: (60 – 55) × 1/5	1	1
		15	19
53g/km	Basic % (51 – 54g/km)	13	17

A 4% supplement applies to a diesel car that does not meet the RDE2 standard.

Test your understanding 5

Sue

	£
£16,000 × 31% (W)	4,960
Less: Contribution	(2,000)
Taxable benefit	2,960

Working: Appropriate %	%
Basic % for petrol car	14
Plus: (140 – 55) = 85 ÷ 5	17
	31

Prakash

Benefit (£31,000 × 37% (W))	£11,470

Working: Appropriate %	%
Basic % for diesel car not meeting RDE2 standard	18
Plus: (185 – 55) = 130 ÷ 5	26
	44 Restricted to 37%

Note that the amount of business mileage driven is not relevant to the calculation.

List price = (£36,000 – £5,000 maximum capital deduction) = £31,000

Test your understanding 6

Charles

	£
Car benefit: (£24,000 × 35% (W1) × 8/12 (W2))	5,600
Less: Employee contribution (£100 × 8 months)	(800)
	4,800
Fuel benefit: (£24,500 × 35% (W3) × 8/12 (W2))	5,717
Total taxable benefits	10,517

Workings

(W1) Appropriate %

	%
Basic % for petrol car	14
Plus: (160 − 55) = 105 ÷ 5	21
	35

(W2) Reduction for non-availability of car

Car first made available on 1 August 2020, therefore it has been available for 8 months.

(W3) Fuel benefit

The fuel benefit is calculated using the same percentage as the car benefit.

Charles cannot deduct the £50 per month paid towards his private petrol because he does not pay for all fuel used for private motoring.

Test your understanding 7

Gita

	£
Salary (£60,000 × 8/12)	40,000
Car benefit (£15,000 × 26% (W1) × 5/12)	1,625
Fuel benefit (£24,500 × 26% × 3/12 (W2))	1,593
Taxable earnings	43,218

Workings

(W1) Appropriate %

	%
Basic % for petrol	14
Plus: (115 – 55) = 60 ÷ 5	12
	26

The car has only been available for 5 months.

(W2) Private petrol was only provided for 3 months in the tax year 2020/21. The contribution towards the cost of private petrol does not reduce the fuel benefit, as the cost was not reimbursed in full.

Test your understanding 8

Adin

(a) Average method

	£
2.25% × ½ × (£15,000 + £11,000)	293
Less: Interest paid by employee	(0)
Taxable benefit	293

(b) Precise method

	£
6.4.20 – 5.9.20: (£15,000 × 2.25% × 5/12)	141
6.9.20 – 5.4.21: (£11,000 × 2.25% × 7/12)	144
	285

In this situation, whilst Adin can opt for the precise method it is likely he will accept an assessment of £293, as the difference is only £8 (£293 – £285).

Test your understanding 9

Habiba

	£	£
2019/20		
Annual value (20% × £300) – use benefit		60
		——
2020/21		
Annual value (20% × £300) × 4/12 – use benefit		20
Assessment upon gift, higher of:		
Suit's current market value	30	
	——	
Suit's original market value	300	
Less: Taxed in respect of use to date:		
2019/20	(60)	
2020/21	(20)	
	——	
	220	
	——	
Higher of above:	220	
Less: Price paid by employee	(14)	
	——	
	206	206
	——	——
Taxable benefit in 2020/21		226
		——

Note: Essentially, Habiba has received a £300 suit for £14 and been assessed on taxable income of £286 (£60 + £226).

Test your understanding 10

Lily

Taxable benefits – 2020/21

	£
Car (W1)	3,200
Fuel (W1)	3,920
Stereo system (20% × £2,000)	400
Television (W2)	495
Beneficial loan (W3)	507
Flowers – trivial benefit exemption	0
Lunch facility (W4)	0
Taxable benefits	**8,522**

Workings

(W1) Car and fuel benefit

	%
Base % for petrol cars and diesel cars meeting the RDE2 standard	14
Plus: (145 – 55) = 90 ÷ 5	18
	32

Car benefit = (32% × £20,000) = £6,400 for 12 months

The car was only available from 6 October 2020: (£6,400 × 6/12) = £3,200

Fuel benefit = (32% × £24,500 × 6/12) = £3,920

(W2) Television

Higher of:

(1) Original cost less benefits for use of television

£1,200 – (£240 + £240) £720

(2) Current market value £375

	£
Original cost less benefits assessed	720
Less: Amount paid to employer	(225)
Taxable benefit	**495**

(W3) Beneficial loan

	£
Average method	
(£30,000 + £20,000) × ½ × 2.25%	563
Precise method	
£30,000 × 3/12 (April/May/June) × 2.25%	169
£20,000 × 9/12 (July to March) × 2.25%	338
	507

Therefore Lily should elect for the precise method.

(W4) Lunch facilities

	£
Luncheon vouchers	
200 days × £2	400
Canteen (200 days × £3/day)	Exempt

Therefore Lily would have chosen the free meals in the canteen.

Test your understanding 11

Basil

Employment income – 2020/21

	£
Salary (1/12 × £43,560 + 11/12 × £44,100)	44,055
Performance bonus (received in July 2020)	15,000
Benefits:	
Car benefit (37% × £34,000) (W1)	12,580
Fuel benefit (37% × £24,500) (W1)	9,065
Living accommodation:	
Annual value	1,200
Expensive accommodation charge	
(£135,000 – £75,000) × 2.25% (Note)	1,350
Private medical insurance	320
Reimbursed business expenses – exempt	0
Employment income	83,570

Workings

(W1) Car and fuel percentage

	%	
Basic % for petrol car	14	
Plus: (200 − 55) = 145 ÷ 5	29	
	43	Restricted to 37%

There is no deduction for the reimbursement of part of the cost of the private petrol provided.

Note: The house was acquired by the employer more than six years before it was made available to the employee, therefore the market value at the date it was provided to Basil is used instead of the cost.

Test your understanding 12

The correct answer is A.

A is the correct answer because Shakera is taxed on her salary plus the bonus received during the tax year (i.e. the £8,000 bonus received in 2020/21), less the travel costs. The travel costs are deductible as they were incurred necessarily in the performance of the duties of her employment.

Test your understanding 13

The correct answer is B.

B is the correct answer because none of the other costs are incurred wholly, exclusively and necessarily for the purpose of employment. However, relief is given for travel between two places of work for the same employer.

Test your understanding 14

The correct answer is C.

The value of the taxable benefit is 20% of the market value when it was first provided. As the computer was not available until 1 October 2020, the benefit must be time apportioned. It is therefore calculated as follows:

(£4,300 × 20% × 6/12) = £430

Test your understanding 15

The correct answer is D.

D is the correct answer because all of the others are assessable benefits for 2020/21.

The loan is an exempt benefit as it is ≤ £10,000.

A second mobile phone is taxable, as are the provision of medical insurance and the payment of gym subscriptions.

Test your understanding 16

The correct answer is B.

The list price of £35,000 is reduced by Carla's capital contribution of £1,000.

The base % for a diesel car, that does not meet the RDE2 standard, is 18%.

The correct calculation is therefore:

List price (£35,000 – £1,000)	£34,000
Relevant %	
18% + [135 – 55 = 80/5 = 16%]	34%
Taxable benefit (£34,000 × 34%)	£11,560

Test your understanding 17

The correct answer is C.

C is the correct answer because Leo's assessable benefit is computed on the higher of:

- the annual value of the property (i.e. £9,750), or

- the rent paid by the employer (i.e. £32,000).

This figure is then reduced by any employee contribution (i.e. the rent paid by Leo).

The assessable benefit is therefore (£32,000 – £12,000) = £20,000.

Test your understanding 18

The correct answer is A.

A is the correct answer because there is no assessable benefit on a company van provided journeys from home to work represent the only private use of the van by the employee.

6

Pensions

Chapter learning objectives

Upon completion of this chapter you will be able to:

- explain and compute the relief given for contributions to personal pension schemes, and to occupational pension schemes.

PER

One of the PER performance objectives (PO15) is to prepare computations of taxable amounts and tax liabilities according to legal requirements. Another objective (PO17) is to advise on mitigating and deferring liabilities through legitimate tax planning measures. Working through this chapter should help you understand how to demonstrate those objectives.

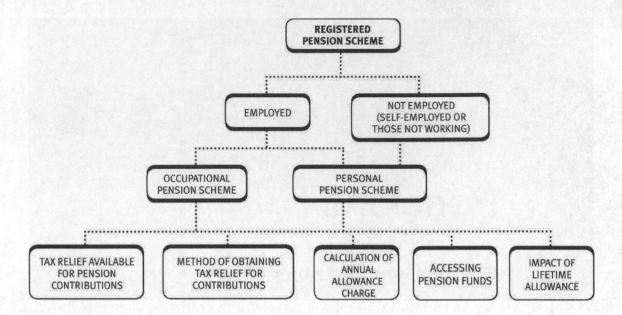

1 Types of registered pension schemes

An individual can set up an investment of funds to provide an income during his retirement in a tax efficient way by making payments into a registered pension scheme.

A pension scheme is a savings plan for retirement that enjoys special tax privileges, but only if the scheme is registered with HMRC.

Investing in a registered pension scheme is a long term investment and is very tax efficient for the following reasons:

- The individual obtains tax relief on the contributions made into the scheme.

- Where an employer contributes into the scheme, tax relief for the employer contributions is available without there being a taxable benefit for the employee.

- Registered pension scheme funds grow tax free as the scheme is exempt from income tax and capital gains tax.

- On retirement, some funds can be withdrawn as a tax free lump sum.

The two main types of registered pension scheme available are:

- Occupational pension schemes

- Personal pension schemes.

A self-employed or unemployed individual can only set up a personal pension scheme.

An employed individual may:

- join an occupational pension scheme provided by his employer (the employee may be automatically enrolled depending on the size of the employer), or

- choose not to join the employer's scheme and set up a personal pension scheme, or

- contribute into both his employer's occupational scheme and set up a personal pension scheme.

Occupational pension schemes

An occupational pension scheme is a scheme set up by an employer for the benefit of their employees.

Employers may use an insurance company to provide a pension scheme for its employees, or it may set up its own self-administered pension fund.

Contributions into occupational schemes may be made by the employer, and the employee.

Types of occupational pension schemes

Defined benefit scheme:

- the benefits obtained on retirement are linked to the level of earnings of the employee.

Money purchase scheme (or 'defined contribution' scheme):

- the benefits obtained depend upon the performance of the investments held by the pension fund.

Personal pension schemes

Personal pension schemes can be established by **any** individual:

- the employed
- the self-employed
- those not working (including children).

Contributions into personal pension schemes may be made by:

- the individual, and

- any third party on behalf of the individual (for example the employer, a spouse, parent or grandparent).

Personal pension schemes are usually money purchase schemes administered by financial institutions on behalf of the individual.

Overview of the tax relief rules for registered pension schemes

- The **amount** of tax relief available for pension contributions is the same regardless of whether the scheme is an occupational or personal pension scheme.

- The **method** of obtaining tax relief for the contributions is different depending on the scheme.

- Once the funds are invested in the scheme, all registered pension schemes are governed by the same rules.

2 Tax relief for pension contributions

The relief for contributions made by individuals

Tax relief is available for pension contributions if both:

- the pension scheme is a registered scheme

- the individual is resident in the UK and aged under 75.

Regardless of the level of earnings, an individual may make pension contributions of **any amount** into either:

- a pension scheme, or

- a number of different pension schemes.

However, **tax relief** is only available for up to a **maximum annual amount** each tax year.

Tax relief is available on contributions up to the **lower** of:

(1) Total gross pension contributions paid

(2) Maximum annual amount = **higher** of:

- £3,600

- 100% of the individual's 'relevant earnings', chargeable to income tax in the tax year.

Relevant earnings includes taxable trading profits, employment income and profits from furnished holiday lettings but not investment income.

- The maximum annual amount applies to the total gross contributions made into all schemes where:

- an employee contributes to both an occupational and a personal pension scheme, or

- an individual contributes into more than one personal pension scheme.

- An individual with no relevant earnings can still obtain tax relief on gross contributions of up to £3,600 p.a.

The maximum annual amount of £3,600 for an individual without earnings, is included in the tax rates and allowances provided to you in the examination.

Illustration 1 – Maximum tax relief for individuals

The following individuals made gross pension contributions into a personal pension scheme in the tax year 2020/21:

	Pension contributions (gross) £	Relevant earnings £
Karima	2,500	0
Nadia	6,000	0
Kenza	36,000	75,000
Yasmine	45,000	38,000

Explain the maximum amount of pension contribution for which tax relief is available for each individual in the tax year 2020/21.

Solution

	Tax relief	Explanation
Karima	£2,500	Relief = contributions made as they are below the maximum annual amount of £3,600 (higher of £3,600 and £Nil).
Nadia	£3,600	Contributions (£6,000) exceed the maximum annual amount (higher of £3,600 and £Nil). Relief = restricted to maximum annual amount of £3,600.
Kenza	£36,000	Relief = contributions made (£36,000) as they are below the maximum annual amount of £75,000 (higher of £3,600 and £75,000).
Yasmine	£38,000	Contributions (£45,000) exceed the maximum annual amount (higher of £3,600 and £38,000). Relief = restricted to the annual maximum amount of £38,000.

Summary

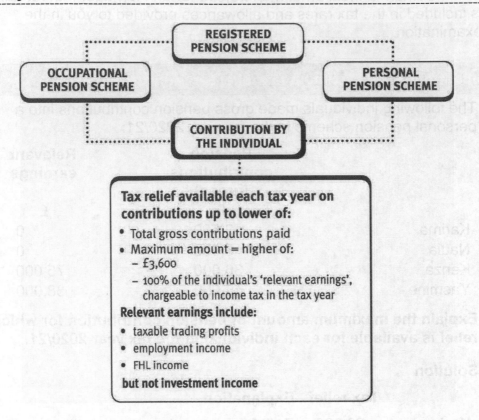

REGISTERED PENSION SCHEME

OCCUPATIONAL PENSION SCHEME

PERSONAL PENSION SCHEME

CONTRIBUTION BY THE INDIVIDUAL

Tax relief available each tax year on contributions up to lower of:
- Total gross contributions paid
- Maximum amount = higher of:
  - £3,600
  - 100% of the individual's 'relevant earnings', chargeable to income tax in the tax year

Relevant earnings include:
- taxable trading profits
- employment income
- FHL income

but not investment income

3 The method of obtaining tax relief for pension contributions

Personal pension schemes

The method of obtaining tax relief for contributions into a personal pension scheme (PPCs) is the same whether they are made by an employee, a self-employed individual or an individual who is not working.

Relief is given as follows:

Basic rate tax relief

- Basic rate tax relief is automatically given by deduction at source when contributions are paid, as an individual makes contributions net of the basic rate of income tax (20%).

- Contributions into a personal pension scheme benefit from basic rate tax relief, even if the taxpayer is paying tax at the starting rate, higher rate or not paying tax at all.

- HMRC pay the 20% tax relief to the personal pension scheme.

Higher and additional rate tax relief

Relief is obtained in two parts:

- Basic rate relief of 20% is given at source (as above).

- Further higher and additional rate relief is given by extending the basic and higher rate tax bands by the gross amount of pension contributions paid in the tax year (as for gift aid donations, see Chapter 2).

- This means that an amount of income equal to the gross pension contributions is removed from the charge to higher rate tax and is taxed at the basic rate instead, and the same amount is removed from the charge to additional rate tax and is taxed at the higher rate instead.

- For example, if an individual pays a contribution of £8,000 (net), this is equivalent to a gross contribution of £10,000 (£8,000 × 100/80).

- The individual's higher and additional rate thresholds are extended to £47,500 (£37,500 + £10,000), and £160,000 (£150,000 + £10,000).

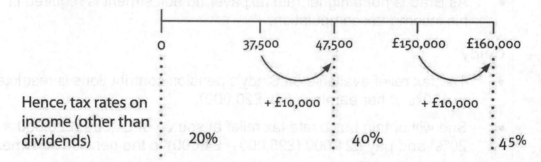

Hence, tax rates on income (other than dividends)

Illustration 2 – The method of obtaining relief for PPCs

The following individuals made gross pension contributions into a personal pension scheme in the tax year 2020/21.

	Pension contributions (gross) £	Trading profits £
Andy	5,000	0
Brad	5,000	20,000
Cindy	25,000	20,000
Don	40,000	95,000
Ed	60,000	25,000
Fran	30,000	195,000

They have no other sources of income.

Explain how tax relief for the pension contributions will be given in the tax year 2020/21 for each individual and calculate the income tax liability of Don, Ed and Fran for the tax year 2020/21. Ignore the annual allowance (see later).

Solution

Andy

- As Andy has no earnings he will obtain tax relief on a maximum gross amount of £3,600.

- He will obtain basic rate tax relief at source of £720 (£3,600 × 20%) and pay £4,280 (£5,000 – £720) to the pension scheme.

Brad

- Brad's pension contributions are less than his earnings for the year and he will therefore receive tax relief on the full amount of the contributions.

- He will obtain basic rate tax relief at source of £1,000 (£5,000 × 20%) and pay £4,000 (£5,000 – £1,000) to the pension scheme.

- As Brad is not a higher rate taxpayer no adjustment is required in his income tax computation.

Cindy

- The tax relief available on Cindy's pension contributions is restricted to 100% of her earnings (i.e. £20,000).

- She will obtain basic rate tax relief at source of £4,000 (£20,000 × 20%) and pay £21,000 (£25,000 – £4,000) to the pension scheme.

- As Cindy is not a higher rate taxpayer no adjustment is required in her income tax computation.

Don

- Don's pension contributions are less than his earnings; he will therefore receive tax relief on the full amount of the contributions.

- He will obtain basic rate tax relief at source of £8,000 (£40,000 × 20%) and pay £32,000 (£40,000 – £8,000) to the pension scheme.

- Higher rate tax relief will be given by extending the basic rate band by £40,000 from £37,500 to £77,500.

Don's income tax computation for the tax year 2020/21 will be:

	£		£
Trading profit			95,000
Less: PA			(12,500)
Taxable income			82,500
Basic rate	77,500	× 20%	15,500
Higher rate	5,000	× 40%	2,000
	82,500		
Income tax liability			17,500

Ed

- The tax relief available on Ed's pension contributions is restricted to 100% of his earnings (i.e. £25,000).

- He will obtain basic rate tax relief at source of £5,000 (£25,000 × 20%) and pay £55,000 (£60,000 – £5,000) to the scheme.

Ed's income tax computation for the tax year 2020/21 will be:

	£
Trading profit	25,000
Less: PA	(12,500)
Taxable income	12,500
Income tax (£12,500 × 20%)	2,500

Fran

- Fran's pension contributions are less than her earnings; she will therefore receive tax relief on the full amount of the contribution.

- She will obtain basic rate tax relief at source of £6,000 (£30,000 × 20%) and pay £24,000 (£30,000 – £6,000) to the pension scheme.

- Higher rate tax relief will be given by extending the basic rate band by £30,000 from £37,500 to £67,500.

- Additional rate tax relief will be given by extending the higher rate band by £30,000 from £150,000 to £180,000.

Fran's income tax computation for the tax year 2020/21 will be:

			£
Trading profit			195,000
Less: Adjusted PA (Note)			(0)
Taxable income			195,000

Income tax:	£		£
Basic rate	67,500	× 20%	13,500
Higher rate	112,500	× 40%	45,000
	180,000		
Additional rate	15,000	× 45%	6,750
	195,000		
Income tax liability			65,250

Note: In this example, trading income = total income = net income. ANI is net income less gross pension contributions (i.e. £195,000 – £30,000 = £165,000). As this exceeds £125,000 (more than £100,000 plus double the PA), the PA is reduced to £Nil. Note that the answer ignores the annual allowance (see later) as stated in the question.

Occupational pension schemes

Where employees make pension contributions into an occupational pension scheme, payments are made gross and tax relief is given at source by the employer through the PAYE system, as an allowable deduction against employment income.

Tax relief is given at basic, higher and additional rates of tax depending on the individual's level of income as follows:

- The employer will deduct the pension contribution from the individual's earned income, before calculating income tax under the PAYE system.

- Tax relief is therefore automatically given at source, at the employee's highest rate of tax.

Test your understanding 1

Carlos is employed by Lloyd Ltd on an annual salary of £80,000. He is a member of the company's occupational pension scheme.

Carlos pays 3% and Lloyd Ltd pays 5% of his salary into the scheme each year. He has no other income.

Calculate Carlos's income tax liability for the tax year 2020/21, showing how tax relief is obtained for his pension contributions.

Contributions made by employers into registered pension schemes

Contributions paid by an employer into a registered pension scheme are:

- tax deductible in calculating the employer's taxable trading profits, provided the contributions are paid for the purposes of the trade, and

- an exempt employment benefit for the employee, and

- added to the pension contributions paid by the employee on which tax relief is given to determine whether the annual allowance has been exceeded (see below).

Employer contributions – trading deduction

The deduction against the employer's trading profits for pension contributions is given in the accounting period in which the contribution is actually **paid**; the accounting treatment is not followed.

Therefore, in the adjustment to profit computation:

- **add back** any **amount charged** in the statement of profit or loss, and

- **deduct** the **amount paid** in the accounting period.

Annual allowance

There is no limit on the amount that may be paid into pension schemes by an individual, his employer or any other party.

However, as we have seen, **tax relief** for pension contributions made by an individual is restricted to the **maximum annual amount**.

In addition, if the total of all contributions (by the individual, their employer and third parties) on which tax relief has been obtained exceeds the **annual allowance (AA),** a tax charge is levied on the individual.

- The AA for a tax year is £40,000, but this can be increased by **bringing forward** any unused annual allowances from the **previous three tax years**.

- An unused AA can only be carried forward if the individual was a member of a registered pension scheme for that tax year, otherwise it is lost.

- The AA for the **current year is used first**, then the AA from earlier years, **starting with the earliest tax year** (i.e. on a FIFO basis).

 The annual allowance figure is included in the tax rates and allowances provided to you in the examination.

Illustration 3 – Calculation of annual allowance

Steve and Mike made gross personal pension contributions as follows:

	Steve	Mike
	£	£
2017/18	52,000	0
2018/19	25,000	15,000
2019/20	17,000	6,000

Steve has been a member of a registered pension scheme since the tax year 2010/11. Mike joined a registered pension scheme in the tax year 2018/19. Both have relevant earnings of £100,000 per annum.

State the maximum gross contribution that Steve and Mike could make in the tax year 2020/21 without incurring an annual allowance tax charge.

Solution

Steve – Unused allowances

	£
2017/18 Contributions in excess of £40,000	0
2018/19 (£40,000 – £25,000)	15,000
2019/20 (£40,000 – £17,000)	23,000
Total unused allowances b/f	38,000
Add: Allowance for 2020/21	40,000
Maximum gross contribution for 2020/21 to avoid charge	78,000

Mike – Unused allowances

	£
2017/18 Not member of registered pension scheme	0
2018/19 (£40,000 – £15,000)	25,000
2019/20 (£40,000 – £6,000)	34,000
Total unused allowances b/f	59,000
Add: Allowance for 2020/21	40,000
Maximum gross contribution for 2020/21 to avoid charge	99,000

Test your understanding 2

Ahmed has made the following gross contributions to his personal pension:

	£
2017/18	12,000
2018/19	26,000
2019/20	33,000
2020/21	58,000

He has relevant earnings of £100,000 each year.

State the amount of unused annual allowances to carry forward to the tax year 2021/22.

Calculation of annual allowance charge

Where the total of all contributions on which relief has been obtained exceeds the AA (including brought forward annual allowances) there is a tax charge on the excess.

The tax charge is calculated as if the excess is the individual's top slice of income (i.e. taxed last after all sources of income, including dividends) at non-savings rates.

The AA charge becomes part of the individual's total liability and is either paid through the self-assessment system or, in some cases, may be taken from the individual's pension fund.

Illustration 4 – Contributions in excess of the annual allowance

Sofia has been a self-employed interior designer for a number of years. In the tax year 2020/21 she had trading income of £105,000 and made a gross contribution of £90,000 into her personal pension scheme.

Sofia does not have any unused annual allowance brought forward.

Explain how tax relief will be obtained for the pension contribution made by Sofia and calculate her income tax liability for the tax year 2020/21.

Solution

Sofia can obtain tax relief for a pension contribution up a maximum of 100% of her earnings (i.e. £105,000 in the tax year 2020/21). She will therefore obtain relief on the gross contribution of £90,000.

Sofia will pay the pension contribution net of basic rate tax of £18,000 (£90,000 × 20%) and pay £72,000 (£90,000 – £18,000) into the pension scheme.

Higher rate relief is obtained by extending the basic rate band by £90,000 from £37,500 to £127,500.

However Sofia's gross contribution of £90,000 exceeds the AA of £40,000. She will therefore have an AA charge and be taxed on an additional £50,000 (£90,000 – £40,000) at her highest marginal rates of tax as though the AA was taxed after all of her income.

Sofia's income tax computation for the tax year 2020/21 will be:

			£
Trading income			105,000
Less: Personal allowance (Note)			(12,500)
Taxable income			92,500
Income tax liability	£		
Basic rate	92,500	× 20%	18,500
Annual allowance charge			
Basic rate	35,000	× 20%	7,000
	127,500		
Higher rate (£50,000 – £35,000)	15,000	× 40%	6,000
Income tax liability			31,500

Note: Sofia's ANI is less than £100,000 (i.e. £105,000 – £90,000) therefore there is no restriction of the PA.

Test your understanding 3

Marcus has been employed for many years, however he only become a member of a personal pension scheme in the tax year 2017/18.

In the tax year 2020/21 Marcus earned £100,000 and made a gross contribution of £86,000 into his personal pension scheme.

In March of the last 3 years Marcus made the following gross pension contributions:

	£
2017/18	17,000
2018/19	50,000
2019/20	34,000

Calculate Marcus' income tax liability for the tax year 2020/21.

Test your understanding 4

Zainab is a self-employed builder. Her trading income for the tax year 2020/21 is £115,000. Zainab's husband, Ali, has employment income from a part-time job of £13,500 p.a. and property income from an unfurnished flat of £20,000 p.a.

They also have a joint bank account on which they received interest of £5,000 in the tax year 2020/21.

During the year to 5 April 2021, Zainab paid £49,000 into her registered personal pension scheme. Zainab has contributed £38,000 (gross) into her personal pension in March each year for the last three years.

During the year to 5 April 2021, Ali paid £2,600 into his employer's registered occupational pension scheme and Ali's employer contributed a further £2,000.

Calculate how much of the pension contributions made by Zainab, Ali and Ali's employer in the tax year 2020/21 will obtain tax relief and explain how the tax relief will be obtained.

Restriction of annual allowance – high income individuals

- The annual allowance is gradually reduced for individuals with high income.

- The restriction applies to individuals with a 'threshold income' exceeding £200,000 and 'adjusted income' exceeding £240,000.

- However, the £200,000 threshold is not examinable in the TX examination.

- The restriction operates in a similar way to the reduction of the personal allowance for high earners.

- The annual allowance is reduced by:
  (Adjusted income – £240,000) × 50%.

- If necessary, the reduced AA is rounded up to the nearest pound (although in the examination rounding up or down is acceptable).

- The minimum that the annual allowance can be reduced to is £4,000.

- The calculation of 'adjusted income' is complicated in practice, but for TX purposes can be simplified as shown below.

	£
Net income (from the income tax computation)	X
Plus: Individual employee's occupational pension contributions	X
Employer's contributions to any scheme for that individual	X
Adjusted income	X

- If the 'adjusted income' exceeds £240,000 the annual allowance for the tax year is reduced.

- Where the annual allowance has been reduced for a high income individual, it is the reduced annual allowance which is compared to actual contributions in a tax year when determining if there is any unused annual allowance to carry forward.

 When an individual's adjusted income is £312,000 or more the annual allowance is reduced to £4,000.

 It is important to note that the term 'adjusted income' for annual allowance purposes is not the same as 'adjusted net income' for purposes of restricting the personal allowance.

When calculating the adjusted income for annual allowance purposes, there is no deduction for gross gift aid donations or the individual's gross personal pension contributions, and employer's pension contributions need to be added to net income.

 Illustration 5 – Annual allowance for high income individual

The following individuals have occupational pension schemes into which the following contributions were made during the tax year 2020/21.

	Employee's contributions	Employer's contributions	Taxable employment income
	£	£	£
Ann	30,000	5,000	200,000
Belinda	8,000	2,000	310,000
Carol	12,000	20,000	250,000

They have no other sources of income.

Calculate the annual allowance for the tax year 2020/21 for each individual assuming they have no unused allowances brought forward.

Solution

Ann

Ann's adjusted income is £235,000 (W). As this is less than £240,000 there is no restriction to her annual allowance of £40,000.

Working – Adjusted income

	£
Net income (employment income only)	200,000
Add: Employee's occupational pension contributions	30,000
Employer's pension contributions	5,000
	———
Adjusted income	235,000
	———

Belinda

Belinda's adjusted income is £320,000 (W1) therefore her annual allowance is restricted. As her adjusted income exceeds £312,000 the annual allowance is restricted to the minimum amount of £4,000 (W2).

Workings

(W1) Adjusted income

	£
Net income (employment income only)	310,000
Add: Employee's pension contributions	8,000
Employer's pension contributions	2,000
	———
Adjusted income	320,000
	———

(W2) Annual allowance

	£
Annual allowance – 2020/21	40,000
Less: 50% × (£320,000 – £240,000) = £40,000	
Maximum reduction	(36,000)
	———
Reduced AA	4,000
	———

Carol

Carol's adjusted income is £282,000 (W1) therefore her annual allowance is restricted to £19,000 (W2) for the tax year 2020/21.

Workings

(W1) **Adjusted income**

		£
Net income (employment income only)		250,000
Add	Employee's pension contributions	12,000
	Employer's pension contributions	20,000
Adjusted income		282,000

(W2) **Annual allowance**

	£
Annual allowance – 2020/21	40,000
Less: 50% × (£282,000 – £240,000)	(21,000)
Reduced AA	19,000

Test your understanding 5

Aksel is self-employed and has trading profits of £240,000 in the tax year 2020/21. He also has taxable savings income of £5,000 and made gross personal pension contributions of £40,000.

Ingrid is employed and has an annual salary of £290,000. She also has dividend income each year of £8,000. In the tax year 2020/21 she paid 10% of her salary into her employer's occupational pension scheme and her employer contributed 5% of her salary into the scheme.

Calculate the annual allowance for the tax year 2020/21 for each individual assuming they have no unused allowances brought forward.

4 Accessing the pension fund

Once invested, funds in a registered pension scheme are accumulated and can grow in value, tax free, as the scheme is:

- exempt from income tax in respect of any income earned from the assets invested

- exempt from capital gains tax in respect of any capital disposals made by the trustees over the life of the scheme.

The funds in the pension scheme cannot be accessed by the individual until he or she reaches pension age. Each pension scheme will have its own scheme rules regarding when an individual can access the scheme funds. However, the minimum pension age can never be below 55.

For those individuals in defined benefit schemes (principally occupational pension schemes, see above) the benefits on reaching pension age are linked to the level of earnings of the employee.

For those individuals in money purchase schemes (principally personal pension schemes, see above) the benefits on pension age are dependent on the amount of funds accumulated in the pension fund (i.e. contributions plus investment income/gains).

Individuals with money purchase schemes have complete flexibility in the way in which they can access the accumulated funds in their pension scheme when they reach pension age.

- They can withdraw 25% of the fund as a tax free lump sum.

- The balance (remaining 75%) of the fund can be accessed in a variety of ways (including purchasing an annuity), to suit the individual's circumstances, to provide income for the individual in their retirement.

Withdrawals from the balance of the fund are taxed as non-savings income in the tax year they are withdrawn at the normal rates of tax (i.e. 20%, 40% or 45%).

5 The lifetime allowance

Once invested, funds in a registered pension scheme are accumulated and can grow in value, tax free.

There is no restriction on the **total** contribution that an individual may make into a registered pension scheme. There is only a limit upon the annual contributions upon which **tax relief** is available.

In order to prevent wealthy individuals accumulating large sums in pension funds which can grow tax free, there is a maximum limit to the amount that an individual can accumulate in a pension scheme tax free, known as the 'lifetime allowance'.

The lifetime allowance is:

- £1,073,100 for the tax year 2020/21

- considered when a member becomes entitled to withdraw benefits out of the scheme (for example, when he or she becomes entitled to take an annuity and/or lump sum payment).

The lifetime allowance is not included in the tax rates and allowances provided to you in the examination.

If the value of the pension fund exceeds the lifetime allowance:

* an additional income tax charge arises on the excess fund value (i.e. the excess value above £1,073,100), when the individual withdraws funds from the scheme.

The detailed rules for the income tax charge are not examinable.

6 Chapter summary

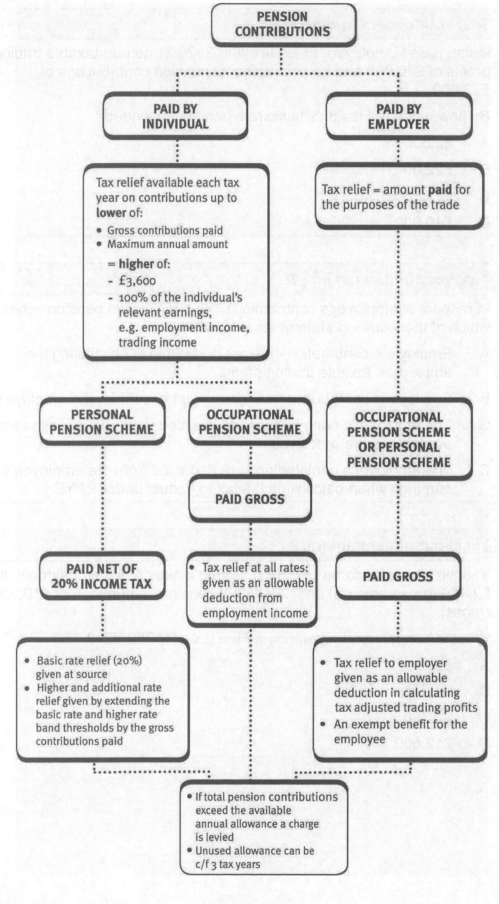

7 Practice objective test questions

Test your understanding 6

Isaiah is self-employed. In the tax year 2020/21 he had taxable trading profits of £70,000 and he paid personal pension contributions of £22,000.

By how much will Isaiah's basic rate band be extended?

A   £3,600

B   £22,000

C   £27,500

D   £40,000

Test your understanding 7

In respect of employer's contributions into a registered pension scheme, which of the following statements is incorrect?

A   Employer's contributions are tax deductible in calculating the employer's taxable trading profits

B   Employer's contributions are an exempt benefit for the employee

C   The employer's contributions are included in the annual allowance available to the employee

D   The employer's contributions are deducted from the employee's earnings when calculating the tax to deduct under PAYE

Test your understanding 8

Yasmin has net income of £119,500. She makes a gift aid payment of £2,400 (gross amount) and a personal pension contribution of £10,000 (gross).

What is her personal allowance for the tax year 2020/21?

A   £0

B   £8,950

C   £7,750

D   £12,500

Test your understanding 9

Hari earns £115,000 a year and has no other income. He pays personal pension contributions of £5,600 each year.

What is his personal allowance for the tax year 2020/21?

A   £5,000

B   £12,500

C   £7,800

D   £8,500

Test your understanding 10

Jasper has a personal pension scheme.

Which of the following can contribute to his pension scheme in the tax year 2020/21?

A   Jasper only

B   Jasper and his employer only

C   Jasper, his employer and Jasper's self-employed wife

D   Jasper and his self-employed wife only

Test your understanding 11

Zoila is employed part-time earning £2,500 per annum. She also receives property income from an unfurnished house of £25,000 per annum and dividend income of £10,000.

What is the maximum gross pension contribution Zoila can pay in the tax year 2020/21 and receive tax relief in full on her contribution?

A   £2,500

B   £3,600

C   £12,500

D   £27,500

Test your understanding answers

Test your understanding 1

Carlos

Income tax computation – 2020/21

	£
Salary	80,000
Less: Employee's pension contributions (3%)	(2,400)
Employment income	77,600
Less: PA	(12,500)
Taxable income	65,100

Income tax:	£		£
Basic rate	37,500	× 20%	7,500
Higher rate	27,600	× 40%	11,040
	65,100		
Income tax liability			18,540

Note: The employer's contribution into the pension scheme is an exempt employment benefit and is therefore not taxable income for Carlos.

Carlos's occupational pension scheme contributions have reduced his taxable income by £2,400 and thus the amount of tax that he has paid at the 40% rate. He has therefore obtained tax relief at 40% for his pension contributions.

Lloyd Ltd will deduct the £2,400 from the amount of taxable pay from which income tax is deducted through the PAYE system.

Test your understanding 2

Ahmed

	Allowance available £	Used 2020/21 £	Carried forward £
Allowance for 2020/21	40,000	(40,000)	0
Unused allowance b/f			
2017/18 (£40,000 – £12,000)	28,000	(18,000)	N/A
2018/19 (£40,000 – £26,000)	14,000		14,000
2019/20 (£40,000 – £33,000)	7,000		7,000
	89,000	(58,000)	21,000

Note: The allowance for the current tax year must be used first, then the unused allowance brought forward from the previous three years, starting with the earliest tax year.

The remaining allowance from 2017/18 of £10,000 (£28,000 – £18,000) cannot be carried forward to 2021/22 as it is more than three years ago.

Test your understanding 3

Marcus

- Marcus can obtain tax relief for a gross pension contribution of up to a maximum of 100% of his earnings (i.e. £100,000 in the tax year 2020/21).

- However, he only made a gross contribution of £86,000. Tax relief is therefore available on the full contribution of £86,000.

- Marcus will have paid the pension contribution net of basic rate tax of £17,200 (£86,000 × 20%) and paid £68,800 (£86,000 × 80%) into the pension scheme.

- Higher rate relief is obtained by extending the basic rate band threshold by £86,000 from £37,500 to £123,500.

- Marcus' unused annual allowances brought forward are as follows:

	£
2017/18 (£40,000 – £17,000)	23,000
2018/19 Contributions in excess of £40,000	
Uses part of 2017/18 allowance b/f (£50,000 – £40,000)	(10,000)
2019/20 (£40,000 – £34,000)	6,000
	———
	19,000
	———

- The gross contribution paid into the scheme on which tax relief has been given in the tax year 2020/21 of £86,000 exceeds the annual allowance available of £59,000 (£40,000 + £19,000 brought forward).

- Marcus will therefore be taxed on an additional £27,000 (£86,000 – £59,000) at his highest marginal rates of tax.

- There are no unused annual allowances prior to the tax year 2017/18 to offset against the excess contributions in the tax year 2018/19 as Marcus was not a member of a pension scheme prior to 2017/18.

Marcus' income tax computation for 2020/21 will be:

	£
Employment income	100,000
Less: Personal allowance	(12,500)
	———
Taxable income	87,500
	———

Income tax:	£		
Basic rate	87,500	× 20%	17,500
Annual allowance charge			
Basic rate	27,000	× 20%	5,400
			———
Income tax liability			22,900
			———

Note: Marcus' ANI is less than £100,000 (i.e. £100,000 – £86,000) therefore there is no restriction to the PA.

Test your understanding 4

Zainab

- Zainab can obtain tax relief for a pension contribution of up to a maximum of 100% of her earnings in the tax year 2020/21.

- Her earnings are her assessable trading profits for the tax year 2020/21 of £115,000.

- Investment income such as bank interest of £2,500 (£5,000 × 50% each) is not included as relevant earnings.

- Zainab will have paid the pension contribution net of basic rate tax of £12,250 (£49,000 × 20/80).

- The gross pension contribution is £61,250 (£49,000 × 100/80).

- As a higher rate taxpayer, higher rate tax relief is obtained by extending the basic rate band by £61,250 from £37,500 to £98,750.

Zainab's available annual allowance is:

	£
2017/18 (£40,000 – £38,000)	2,000
2018/19 (£40,000 – £38,000)	2,000
2019/20 (£40,000 – £38,000)	2,000
	———
Total unused allowances b/f	6,000
Add: Allowance for 2020/21	40,000
	———
Maximum gross contribution for 2020/21 to avoid charge	46,000
	———

Zainab's contributions exceed £46,000 by £15,250 (£61,250 – £46,000) and this amount will be taxed at 40% (Zainab's highest rate of tax). Therefore, an additional £6,100 of tax will be payable.

- Zainab's PA is still available in full as her net income is reduced by his gross PPCs of £61,250 to calculate ANI, which is clearly less than £100,000.

Ali

- Ali can obtain tax relief for a gross pension contribution of up to a maximum of the higher of £3,600 or 100% of his employment earnings in the tax year 2020/21 (i.e. £13,500).

- His gross pension contribution of £2,600 is less than £13,500, therefore he can obtain tax relief for all of the contribution paid.

- Ali's employer will deduct the gross contribution of £2,600 from his employment income before calculating his income tax liability under PAYE.

- Ali's employer's contributions of £2,000 are a tax free benefit.

Ali's employer

- Ali's employer will obtain tax relief for all of the £2,000 contribution made into the occupational pension scheme.

- Relief is given as an allowable deduction in the calculation of the employer's taxable trading profits.

Test your understanding 5

Aksel

Aksel's adjusted income is £245,000 (W1). As this is more than £240,000 his annual allowance is restricted to £37,500 (W2).

Workings

(W1) **Adjusted income**

	£
Trading profits	240,000
Savings income	5,000
Adjusted income	245,000

(W2) **Annual allowance**

	£
Annual allowance for the tax year 2020/21	40,000
Less: 50% × (£245,000 – £240,000)	(2,500)
Reduced AA	37,500

Ingrid

Ingrid's adjusted income is £312,500 (W1). As this is more than £312,000 her annual allowance is restricted to £4,000 (W2).

(W1) Adjusted income

	£
Salary	290,000
Less: Employee occupational pension contributions (£290,000 × 10%)	(29,000)
Employment income	261,000
Dividend income	8,000
Net income	269,000
Add: Employee and employer pension contributions (15% × £290,000)	43,500
Adjusted income	312,500

(W2) Annual allowance

	£
Annual allowance	40,000
Less: 50% × (£312,500 − £240,000) = £36,250	
Maximum reduction	(36,000)
Reduced AA	4,000

Test your understanding 6

The correct answer is C.

C is the correct answer because Isaiah is entitled to relief on the lower of his gross contributions £27,500 (£22,000 × 100/80) and the higher of £3,600 or his relevant earnings (£70,000).

Relief is therefore available for £27,500 and as a higher rate taxpayer his basic rate band will be extended by the gross contributions made of £27,500.

Test your understanding 7

The correct answer is D.

Contributions paid by an employer into a registered pension scheme are:

- tax deductible in calculating the employer's taxable trading profits, provided the contributions are paid for the purposes of the trade

- an exempt employment benefit for the employee

- added to the pension contributions paid by the employee to determine whether the annual allowance has been exceeded and an income tax charge is payable.

However, the contributions paid by the employer are not deducted in calculating the employee's income tax, only employee's contributions are deducted in this way.

Test your understanding 8

The correct answer is B.

	£	£
Basic PA		12,500
Adjusted net income		
(£119,500 – £10,000 – £2,400)	107,100	
Less: Limit	(100,000)	
	———	
	7,100	
	———	
Reduction of PA (50% × £7,100)		(3,550)
		———
Adjusted PA		8,950
		———

Test your understanding 9

The correct answer is D.

	£	£
Basic personal allowance		12,500
Net income	115,000	
Less: Gross personal pension contribution		
(£5,600 × 100/80)	(7,000)	
	108,000	
Less: Limit	(100,000)	
	8,000	
Reduction of PA (50% of £8,000)		(4,000)
Revised personal allowance		8,500

Test your understanding 10

The correct answer is C.

With a personal pension scheme the employer and any individual can contribute.

Test your understanding 11

The correct answer is B.

The maximum pension contribution which is eligible for tax relief is the **higher** of:

- **£3,600**

- 100% of the individual's **relevant earnings**, chargeable to income tax in the tax year.

Relevant earnings includes taxable trading profits, employment income and furnished holiday lettings, but not investment income (i.e. not property income from unfurnished lettings or dividend income).

Income from self-employment

Chapter learning objectives

Upon completion of this chapter you will be able to:

- recognise the basis of assessment for self-employment income

- describe and apply the badges of trade

- recognise the expenditure that is allowable in calculating the tax adjusted trading profit

- explain and compute the assessable profits using the cash basis for small businesses

- recognise the relief which can be obtained for pre-trading expenditure.

PER

One of the PER performance objectives (PO15) is to prepare computations of taxable amounts and tax liabilities according to legal requirements. Working through this chapter should help you understand how to demonstrate that objective.

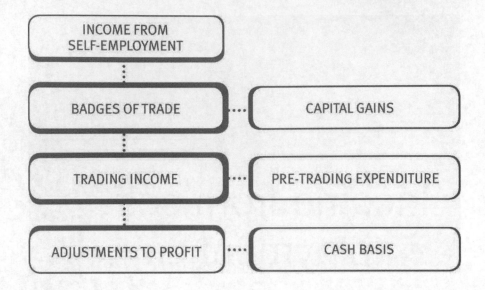

 The accounting profits of a company (drawn up in accordance with generally accepted accounting policy) will either generally determine the tax treatment of certain key items of revenue and expenditure, or will form the starting point from which the tax treatment will then depart - your knowledge gained in Financial Reporting of how to account for business transactions is therefore of fundamental importance when it comes to establishing the basis on which the profits are to be taxed.

1 Trading income

The profits of an unincorporated trader arising from a trade, profession or vocation are assessed as trading income.

Individuals with an unincorporated business are usually referred to as 'self-employed' or 'sole traders'.

Basis of assessment

The profits of an unincorporated business are assessed on a **current year basis (CYB)**.

This means the profits assessed in a tax year are those of the **twelve month period of account ending in that tax year**.

Test your understanding 1

A sole trader prepares his accounts for the year ended 31 December 2020.

In which tax year are the profits assessed?

The detailed basis of assessment rules are covered in more detail in Chapter 9.

2 Badges of trade

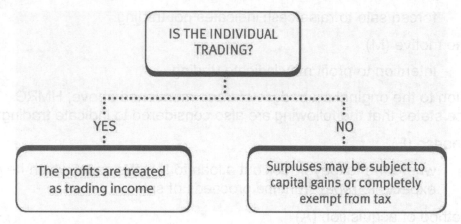

To determine whether an individual is trading, a number of tests, known as the 'badges of trade', are considered.

Nature of trade

'Trade includes any venture in the nature of trade.'

Although the above is the statutory definition of a trade, in practice it is not a very helpful one. What constitutes a trade has been reviewed numerous times by the courts and criteria have been developed and were set out by a Royal Commission. These criteria which should be considered are known as the 'badges of trade'.

The badges of trade which are used to determine if an activity is in the nature of a trade are as follows (and can be remembered by using two mnemonics 'SOFIRM', and 'FAST' as donated by the letters in the brackets below):

- The subject matter of the transaction (S).
  - are the goods of a type normally used for trading?
- The length of the period of ownership (O).
  - short period of ownership is more likely to indicate trading.
- The frequency of similar transactions by the same person (F).
  - frequent transactions indicate trading.
- Supplementary work, improvements and marketing (I).
  - work performed on goods to make them more marketable indicates trading.

- The circumstances/reason for the sale (R).

  - forced sale to raise cash indicates not trading.

- The motive (M).

  - intention to profit may indicate trading.

In addition to the original six badges of trade mentioned above, HMRC guidance states that the following are also considered to indicate trading:

- Finance (F)

  - where the taxpayer took out a loan to buy the asset which he or she expects to repay from the proceeds of sale.

- Method of acquisition (A)

  - where the taxpayer acquired the asset by way of purchase rather than receiving it as a gift or by inheritance.

- Existence of similar trading transactions (ST)

  - where the transactions are similar to those of an existing trade carried on by the taxpayer.

It is vital to appreciate that no one badge is decisive. In any set of circumstances some badges may indicate trading whilst others may not.

It is the overall impression, taking into account all relevant factors, that is important.

 Badges of trade

Subject matter of the transaction (S)

An asset is said to have been acquired for one of three reasons:

- an investment – capital in nature and not subject to income tax

- goods for private use of the individual (or family) – not subject to tax

- trade inventory – a trading transaction and subject to income tax.

Normally, to be considered an investment, goods must either be income producing (e.g. land or shares), or liable to be held for aesthetic reasons (e.g. works of art).

When an individual acquired 1,000,000 rolls of toilet paper and resold them at a profit, he was held not to have acquired them for private use, or as an investment and consequently was judged to have made a trading profit.

The length of the period of ownership (O)

As a general rule, the longer the period between acquisition and disposal, the more likely the transaction will not be treated as trading.

Care must be taken in applying this principle and in particular the nature of the asset has to be taken into account.

For instance, it would be necessary to hold land for far longer than quoted shares to obtain the benefit of this rule, since normally the market in land operates much more slowly than that in shares.

The frequency of similar transactions by the same person (F)

As in the toilet rolls case above, a single transaction may be regarded as trading. However, usually the more often similar transactions are entered into, the more likely they will be regarded as trading activities.

Again the nature of the assets involved is important:

- A taxpayer was held to be trading on the evidence of over 200 Stock Exchange sales and purchases over a period of three years.

- A taxpayer was engaged in buying the shares of mill-owning companies and then selling the assets of the companies (asset stripping). One transaction of this kind might have been regarded as capital, but when he had done the same thing four times, he was held to be trading.

Supplementary work, improvements and marketing (I)

For example, the purchase of brandy in bulk and subsequent blending and re-casking before resale was held to be a trade.

The circumstances/reason for the sale (R)

A 'forced sale' where an asset is sold as a consequence of unforeseen circumstances, such as a sudden need for funds, is unlikely to be treated as a trading activity.

The motive (M)

The more obvious an individual's intention to profit from a transaction the more likely it is that it will be viewed as trading.

For example, an individual purchased a large quantity of silver bullion as a hedge against the devaluation of sterling. The profit resulting from its resale was regarded as a trading profit, on the basis that the motive for the transaction was to make a profit in sterling terms.

It is important to appreciate, however, that the absence of a profit motive does not of itself preclude the transaction from being treated as trade.

Finance (F)

Where it is necessary to take out a loan to fund the purchase of an asset and it is expected that the loan will only be repaid when the asset is sold then this is an indication of trading.

An individual who took out a loan to acquire silver bullion at a high interest rate and in circumstances where it was clear that he would need to sell the asset in the short term to repay the loan was held to be trading.

Method of acquisition (A)

It is much harder to argue that a trade exists where an asset is acquired by gift or inheritance than if the taxpayer purchases it.

In such cases HMRC must demonstrate that before the sale of the asset the taxpayer had a change of intention such that the asset had become trading inventory (e.g. where land is developed for sale).

Existence of similar trading transactions (ST)

Where an individual undertakes a transaction that is related to his existing trade it is more difficult to argue that this is not a trading transaction than if the transaction was not so related.

Thus it is harder for a property developer to argue that a property was acquired for investment and not trading purposes than a butcher.

---

3 Adjusting the accounting profit

The net profit per the financial accounts and the taxable trading profit figure are rarely the same figure.

The main reason for this is that tax law does not allow a tax deduction for all expenses allowed in the accounts.

Therefore, a number of adjustments need to be made to the accounting profit shown in the statement of profit or loss in order to calculate the taxable trading profit (known as the **tax adjusted trading profit**).

Note that most traders must produce accounts for tax purposes using the **accruals basis** i.e. income receivable and expenses payable in respect of the accounting period. The rules below relate to the accruals basis.

In certain limited circumstances very small traders may choose to use the cash basis (see section 8).

Adjustments

There are four types of adjustment that need to be made to move from accounting profit to the tax adjusted trading profit as follows:

Reason for adjusting profits	Adjustment required
Expenditure which tax law prevents from being an allowable deduction may be charged in the statement of profit or loss	**Add** to accounting profit
Taxable trading income may not be included in the statement of profit or loss	**Add** to accounting profit
Expenditure that is deductible for tax purposes may not be charged in the statement of profit or loss	**Deduct** from accounting profit
Income may be included in the statement of profit or loss that is not taxable as trading income	**Deduct** from accounting profit

Remember that as you are starting from the accounting profit, you are adjusting for items which have already been accounted for, and are reversing what went through the statement of profit or loss.

Therefore, disallowed expenses already charged in the accounts are **added back** to the accounting profit.

Pro forma – Tax adjusted trading profit

	£	£
Net profit per accounts	X	
Add: Expenditure not allowed for taxation purposes	X	
Expenditure allowable for taxation purposes	0	
Taxable trading profit not credited in the accounts	X	
Less: Expenditure not charged in the accounts		
but allowable for taxation purposes		X
Income included in the accounts		
that is not taxable as trading profit		X
Capital allowances (see Chapter 8)		X
	X	Y
	(Y)	
Tax adjusted trading profit	X	

The above pro forma is a suggested pro forma that will help you to obtain full marks in these questions. Alternatively, you could present the working as a single column, as long as you show clearly which items you are adding and which you are deducting.

The TX examining team has confirmed that the question requirement will specify the figure to start the tax adjusted trading profit computation from. This will normally be the net profit figure from the statement of profit or loss. Adjustments should be listed in the order in which the items appear in the question.

In order to obtain full marks, in addition to the adjustments required, you should also show **all** items of expenditure which do **not** require any adjustment in your answer, and indicate by the use of a 0 that these items are allowable.

It is not necessary to add any explanatory notes to your answer, unless notes are specifically requested by the question.

Before considering the adjustments in detail, two important points need to be emphasised:

- We are only calculating the taxable **trading** profit here. The fact that an item of income (such as rental income) is excluded in calculating the tax adjusted trading profit, does not mean that it is not taxable. It just means that it is not taxable as **trading** income.

  As we saw in Chapter 4, rental income is taxable as property business income and comes into the income tax computation as a separate source of income.

- In deciding whether or not an adjustment is necessary, the principles of normal commercial accountancy will apply unless overridden by tax law (i.e. if an item is allowed for accounting; it is allowed for tax **unless** there is a provision in tax law requiring an adjustment).

4 Disallowable expenditure

Disallowable expenditure is the most common adjustment. The following are the main examples that you can expect to see in the examination.

Expenditure not incurred wholly and exclusively for trading purposes

 The general rule to follow in deciding whether expenditure is an allowable deduction from trading profits is that only expenditure incurred **wholly and exclusively for the purposes of the trade** is allowable.

Expenditure may be disallowed because:

- it is too remote from the purposes of the trade – the remoteness test

- it has more than one purpose and one of them is not trading – the duality principle.

 Remoteness test and duality principle

Remoteness test

Expenditure is regarded as being too remote from the trade when it is incurred in some capacity other than that of trading. For example, normal accountancy and compliance taxation fees are allowable, but the cost of any personal tax advice work is not.

Duality principle

- The duality principle is best illustrated by decided cases:

  - A self-employed trader was unable to eat lunch at home and claimed the extra cost of eating out as a tax allowable expense. It was held that the expenditure was not allowable. The duality of purpose lay in the fact that the taxpayer needed to eat to live, not just to work.

  - A self-employed barrister was refused a tax allowable expense for her expenditure on the black clothing necessary for court appearances. It was held that the expenditure had been for her personal as well as professional needs.

- Where expenditure has been incurred for both trading and non-trading purposes, a deduction can be claimed for the business use proportion, provided it can be separately identified. This is particularly relevant to expenditure on motor cars, where business and private mileage can be identified.

Appropriations

Appropriations are the withdrawal of funds from a business (i.e. profit extraction rather than expenses incurred in earning them) and, as such, are disallowed expenses. The most common examples are:

- interest paid to the owner on capital invested in the business.

- salary/drawings taken by a sole trader or partner.

- any private element of expenditure relating to the owner's motor car, telephone etc.

Illustration 1 – Motor expenses

Jim is a self-employed solicitor. During the year ended 31 December 2020, Jim drove a total of 20,000 miles and his motor expenses amounted to £10,800.

Each working day Jim drives from his home to his office, which is ten miles away. He works five days a week and 50 weeks a year.

Jim drove 1,500 miles on a holiday in August 2020, but for the rest of the year his wife's car was used for private journeys. Jim's wife owns her own car, and is not involved in Jim's business.

Calculate the amount of Jim's motor expenses that are allowable.

Solution

Jim's motor expenses are apportioned according to his proportion of business mileage to total mileage for the year.

Travel from home to work and back is classed as private mileage, so Jim's total private mileage is 6,500 miles ((10 miles × 5 days × 50 weeks × 2 journeys a day) + 1,500 holiday). His business mileage is therefore 13,500 miles (20,000 – 6,500).

Of the motor expenses, £7,290 (£10,800 × 13,500/20,000) is allowable and £3,510 (£10,800 × 6,500/20,000) is disallowed.

Excessive salary paid to a sole trader's family

- Business owners (especially sole traders) often employ their spouses or members of their families in their business.

- Any salary paid to the family of the owner of an unincorporated business is allowable provided it is not excessive. In other words, it must be remuneration at the commercial rate for the work performed. Any excessive salary payments are disallowed.

Test your understanding 2

Sheila is in business running her own advertising agency. Her husband Richard has given up work to look after their daughter who was born three years ago.

Until 2020 Sheila employed a part-time typist, who was paid £4,500 p.a. but the typist then left and Sheila could not find a suitable replacement. Richard therefore agreed to do Sheila's typing at home.

During the year ended 5 April 2021, Sheila paid Richard a salary of £10,000.

Explain the probable adjustment in calculating the tax adjusted trading profit for the year ended 5 April 2021.

Interest payable

- Interest on borrowings such as business account overdrafts, credit cards or hire purchase contracts, is an allowable trading expense calculated on an accruals basis.

- For unincorporated businesses, late payment interest charged by HMRC in respect of late paid income tax or capital gains tax is never allowable and likewise repayment interest paid by HMRC is not taxable.

Capital expenditure

- Expenditure on capital assets is not an allowable trading expense.

- Any expense in the form of depreciation, loss on sale of non-current assets or the amortisation of a lease is also disallowed.

- The distinction between revenue expenditure (allowable) and capital expenditure (disallowable) is not always clear cut. This is especially the case when deciding if expenditure is in respect of a repair to an asset (revenue expenditure) or is an improvement (capital expenditure).

Repair v Improvement

Whilst you are not required to know the legal cases from which the following decisions were reached, it is important to understand the legal principles behind case decisions regarding capital expenditure as this will help with examination questions:

- The cost of initial repairs in order to make an asset usable is disallowed.

  For example, a taxpayer failed to obtain a deduction for repair work on a newly bought ship, in order to make the ship seaworthy.

- The cost of initial repairs is allowed if the asset can be put into use before any repairs are carried out.

  For example, a taxpayer obtained a deduction for the cost of renovating newly acquired cinemas. The work was to make good normal wear and tear and the purchase price was not reduced to take account of the necessary repair work.

- The treatment of restoration costs is another disputed area. To be allowable, it needs to be proven that the restoration renews a subsidiary part of an asset, rather than replacing the entire asset.

  For example, the replacement of a factory chimney was held to be a repair to the factory.

  Where it is deemed as the renewal/replacement of a separate asset it is treated as disallowed capital expenditure.

  For example, the replacement of an old stand with a new one at a football club, was held to be expenditure on a new asset and thus capital expenditure.

- Capital expenditure on plant and machinery and structures and buildings is disallowed but may qualify for capital allowances.

  These are effectively a form of depreciation allowance for tax purposes. Capital allowances are covered in detail in Chapter 8.

Car leasing

- Rental and lease charges payable in respect of leased motor cars are allowable where the CO_2 emissions of the car are 110g/km or less.

- Where CO_2 emissions exceed 110g/km, 15% of the rental/lease charges are disallowed.

Illustration 2 – Car leasing

Ammanuel enters into a leasing contract for a motor car with CO_2 emissions of 128g/km, paying £8,000 p.a. in rental charges.

Calculate the amount of the rental charge that is disallowed.

Solution

Disallowable rental charge = (15% × £8,000) = £1,200

Subscriptions and donations

- Trade or professional subscriptions are normally deductible since they are made wholly and exclusively for the purposes of the trade.

- A charitable donation must meet three tests to be allowable.

  It must be:

  - wholly and exclusively for trading purposes (for example, promoting the business name)

  - local and reasonable in size in relation to the business making the donation, and

  - made to a registered charity.

- If the donation is disallowed but the payment was made to a charity, the taxpayer can instead claim relief under the gift aid provisions.

- Subscriptions and donations to political parties are disallowed.

- Non-charitable gifts are not allowable, except as set out below.

Entertaining and gifts

- Entertainment expenditure is disallowed.

- The only exception is for expenditure relating to employees, provided it is not incidental to the entertainment of others.

Gifts to employees

- Gifts to employees are normally treated as allowable for the employer.

- Care must be taken, however, as the gift may fall within the benefit rules and be assessed on the employee as employment income.

Gifts to customers

- Gifts to customers are only allowable if:

  - they cost less than £50 per recipient per year, and

  - the gift is not of food, drink, tobacco or vouchers exchangeable for goods, and

  - the gift carries a conspicuous advertisement of the business making the gift.

- The cost of a gift that does not meet these conditions is disallowed.

- If the total of gifts in the tax year exceeds £50, it is the full cost of the item that is disallowable, not just the excess.

- Gifts of business samples to advertise the goods to the public are allowable.

Legal and professional charges

In order to determine whether legal and professional charges are allowable, it is important to review the reasons for the business incurring the costs.

As a general principle, where expenditure is incurred for the purposes of the trade, the expenditure is allowable. Examples include:

- legal fees chasing trading debts

- charges incurred in defending the title to non-current assets.

Where expenditure is of a capital nature, it is disallowable. For example

- Fees associated with acquiring new non-current assets.

- There are the following exceptions:

  - Fees and other costs of obtaining long-term debt finance are allowable for a sole trader.

  - The cost of registering patents is allowable.

  - The expense of renewing a short lease (i.e. less than 50 years) is allowable, although the legal expenses incurred on the initial granting of the lease are not.

Impairment losses and allowances for trade receivables

The following are allowable items:

*   The write-off of a trade debt.

    Note that the recovery of a trade debt previously written-off is taxable.

*   An allowance for the irrecoverability or impairment of trade receivables, provided it is calculated in accordance with UK generally accepted accounting practice (UK GAAP) or International Financial Reporting Standards (IFRS® Standards).

    Note that the reduction in an allowance for trade receivables is taxable income.

The following items are disallowable

*   The write-off of a non-trade debt (e.g. a loan to a customer or a former employee).

Illustration 3 – Impaired debts and allowances for receivables

Catalina's statement of profit or loss for the year ended 30 June 2020 includes a figure for impaired debts of £300. This is made up as follows:

	£	£
Trade debts written-off		520
Loan to former employee written-off		280
Allowance for impaired receivables		
As at 1 July 2019	900	
As at 30 June 2020	700	
		(200)
Trade debts recovered		(400)
Loan to supplier written-off		250
Loan to a customer recovered		(150)
		300

The loan to supplier written-off relates to funds loaned to a supplier with cash flow problems. The loan to the customer recovered is in respect of a loan written-off two years ago.

Calculate the adjustment required in preparing Catalina's tax adjusted trading profit.

Solution

	£	£
Trade debts written-off	0	
Loan to former employee written-off	280	
Loan to supplier written-off	250	
Movement in allowance for impaired receivables		0
Trade debts recovered		0
Loan to customer recovered		150
	530	150
	(150)	
Amount to add back to profit	380	

To be allowed, debt write-offs must be in respect of normal trade debts. The recovery of such debts already written-off is taxable.

The write-off of other debts is not allowable when computing trading profit. Their recovery, after being written-off, is not taxable and will therefore not be included in the tax adjusted trading profit.

Amounts charged (or credited) to the statement of profit or loss in respect of allowances for impaired trade receivables are allowable deductions (or taxable) against trading profits.

Other items

Set out below is a list of some other items you may encounter and a brief description of how to treat them.

Type of expenditure	Treatment	Notes
Provisions for future costs, (e.g. provision for future warranty costs)	Allow	Provided they are calculated in accordance with UK GAAP or IFRS Standards and their estimation is sufficiently accurate
Compensation for loss of office paid to an employee	Allow	Only if for benefit of trade
Redundancy pay in excess of the statutory amount	Allow	On the cessation of trading the limit is 4 × the statutory amount
Counselling services for redundant employees	Allow	

Damages paid	Allow	Only if paid in connection with trade matter and is not a fine for breaking the law (see below)
Defalcations (e.g. theft/ fraud)	Allow	Only if by employee, not the business owner/director
Educational courses	Allow	Only if for trade purposes
Fines	Disallow	Unless parking fines incurred on business by employee, but not business owner/director
Payment that constitutes a criminal offence (e.g. bribe)	Disallow	
Pension contributions to registered pension scheme	Allow	If for employees – provided paid (not accrued) by the year end. Not allowable for business owner (see Chapter 6)
Premiums for insurance against an employee's death or illness	Allow	
Removal expenses	Allow	Provided not an expansionary move
Salaries accrued at year end	Allow	Provided paid not more than 9 months after year end

Test your understanding 3

For each item of expenditure state whether you need to adjust for tax purposes by adding an amount to the accounting profit.

Item of expenditure	Add back?
Drawings of the proprietor	
£45,000 salary paid to the proprietor's spouse. Typical market rate is estimated at £15,000	
Subscription to golf club where sole trader may meet/entertain clients	
Legal fees to acquire a short lease (7 years)	
Trade related NVQ training course for apprentice employee	

5 Other adjustments

Taxable trading income not included in the statement of profit or loss

This adjustment is normally only needed when a trader removes goods from the business for his or her own use.

- The trader is treated as making a sale to himself based on the selling price of the goods concerned.

- Note that this rule does not apply to the supply of services.

The adjustment required depends on the treatment in the accounts:

- if the trader has accounted for the removal of the goods, he will have already added back the cost element, therefore for tax purposes:
  - the profit element of the transaction needs to be added in the adjustment of profits computation

- if the trader has not accounted for the removal of the goods:
  - the full selling price must be added in the adjustment of profits computation.

Illustration 4 – Goods for own use

A car dealer removes a vehicle from the business for his own personal use. It had originally cost the business £10,000 and has a market value of £12,500. No entries have been made in the accounts to reflect this transaction, other than the original purchase.

Explain the adjustment, if any, that should be made to the accounts, for tax purposes, to reflect the above transaction.

Solution

The tax adjusted trading profit must reflect the transaction as if the owner has sold the vehicle to himself based on the selling price of the goods.

In determining the adjustment required, it is important to identify the entries made in the accounts to date. In this example, only the original cost has been recorded, therefore the adjustment is to add the market value £12,500 to the accounting profit.

If the removal of the vehicle had been accounted for i.e. by adding back the cost of the vehicle, only the profit element of £2,500 would need to be added to the accounting profit.

Illustration 5 – Goods for own use

A toy seller takes items with a cost price of £480 from inventory. No adjustment has been made in the accounts.

Explain the adjustment required if:

(a) **the normal mark-up on goods is 25%**

(b) **the profit margin is 25%.**

Solution

(a) The full selling price of £600 (£480 × 1.25) must be added back in the tax computation.

(b) The full selling price of £640 (£480 × 100/75) must be added back in the tax computation.

Note that 25% mark-up means that the profit is 25% of cost, whereas 25% profit margin means that profit is 25% of the selling price. It is important to distinguish between these to calculate the correct sales revenue figure.

Deductible expenditure not charged in the statement of profit or loss

- The most important item of deductible expenditure not charged in the statement of profit or loss is the figure for capital allowances. These are deductible as if they were a trading expense.

  Capital allowances are covered in detail in Chapter 8.

- In addition to this, other examples include:

  - allowable trading element of lease premiums paid on short leases

  - where a business owner uses his or her private residence partly for business purposes (e.g. uses a room in his or her private house as an office, the business portion of running expenses is allowable)

  - business calls from the private telephone of the sole trader

  - expenses that are wholly and exclusively for the trade that have been met from the private funds of the owner.

Short lease premiums

- When a landlord receives a premium for the grant of a short lease a proportion of the lease premium is charged to income tax as property income (see Chapter 4).

- Where a business pays a premium for a short lease, for premises used in the business, a proportion of the amount assessable on the landlord can be deducted in calculating the taxable trading profit.

  This will not be reflected in the accounts. However, the cost of the lease will be charged in the accounts in an annual amortisation charge.

The adjustments required for the lease are therefore as follows:

- Add back: the amortisation charged in the statement of profit or loss (disallowable as capital).

- Deduct: allowable proportion of the lease premium.

The allowable deduction for the trader is the property income element of the premium (see Chapter 4) spread evenly over the period of the lease.

Remember that the property income assessable on the landlord is calculated as:

P less (P × 2% × (n – 1)) or P × (51 – n)/50

Where P = total premium

n = duration of lease in years

Illustration 6 – Lease premium

Lawrie prepares accounts to 31 March. On 1 April 2020 he paid a premium of £25,200 for the grant of a 21 year lease on business premises.

Calculate the allowable deduction Lawrie can claim in his tax adjusted trading profit for the year to 31 March 2021.

Solution

	£
Premium	25,200
Less (£25,200 × 2% × (21 – 1))	(10,080)
	―――――
Amount assessed on landlord	15,120
	―――――

Alternative calculation: (£25,200 × ((51 – 21)/50)) = £15,120

The annual allowable trading deduction for Lawrie is therefore £720 (£15,120 × 1/21) each year.

If the premium had not been paid at the start of the accounting period, this deduction would be time apportioned for the y/e 31 March 2021.

Illustration 7 – Use of home for business

Florencia is in business as a central heating engineer. She uses one room of her five-room house as an office, and no adjustment has been made in her accounts for the year ended 5 April 2021, in respect of this.

Her household expenses relating to the year ended 5 April 2021, are:

	£
Utilities	1,100
Television repairs	50
Groceries	600
Mortgage interest on £20,000 mortgage	900

Calculate the amount Florencia can claim as an allowable deduction for her use of an office at home.

Solution

As Florencia uses one room out of five as an office, it is appropriate to allow one fifth of her expenses that relate to running the home.

Florencia's television repairs and groceries are all of a private nature and are therefore not deductible.

The total of the remaining items is £2,000 (£1,100 + £900).

Therefore, Florencia's allowable deduction for the use of the office is £400 (£2,000 × 1/5).

Income included in the statement of profit or loss that is not taxable trading income

There are three categories of income which need to be adjusted for:

- Capital receipts

  (which may be treated as chargeable gains – see Chapter 19).

  In addition, any profit on the sale of a capital asset should also be deducted in calculating the tax adjusted trading profit.

- Other forms of income (such as savings income, property income or dividends) must be deducted in arriving at the taxable trading profit.

  However, they may be subject to income tax by being included elsewhere in an individual's income tax computation.

- Income that is exempt from tax

  (such as interest received on overpaid income tax).

6 Relief for pre-trading expenditure

Any revenue expenditure, incurred in the **seven years** before a business commences to trade, which would have been allowable if the business was trading, is treated as an expense on the day that the business starts trading.

Illustration 8 – Relief for pre-trading expenditure

Able commenced trading on 1 April 2020. He had spent £6,000 in the previous six months advertising that he was about to start trading.

Explain how the expenditure of £6,000 on advertising is treated for tax purposes.

Solution

The £6,000 advertising expenditure is treated as a trading expense as if it had been incurred on 1 April 2020.

7 Comprehensive example

Test your understanding 4

On 1 June 2020 William, aged 38, commenced in self-employment running a retail clothing shop.

William's statement of profit or loss for the year ended 31 May 2021:

	£	£
Gross profit		139,880
Administration expenses:		
Depreciation	4,760	
Light and heat (Note 1)	1,525	
Motor expenses (Note 2)	4,720	
Repairs and renewals (Note 3)	5,660	
Rent and rates (Note 1)	3,900	
Professional fees (Note 4)	2,300	
Wages and salaries (Note 5)	83,825	
		(106,690)
Other operating expenses (Note 6)		(2,990)
Net profit		30,200

Notes:

(1) Private accommodation

William and his wife live in a flat that is situated above the clothing shop. Of the expenditure included in the statement of profit or loss for light, heat, rent and rates, 40% relates to the flat.

(2) Motor expenses

During the year ended 31 May 2021, William drove a total of 12,000 miles, of which 9,000 were for private journeys.

(3) Repairs and renewals

The figure of £5,660 for repairs and renewals includes £2,200 for decorating the clothing shop during May 2020, and £1,050 for decorating the private flat during June 2020. The building was in a usable state when it was purchased.

(4) Professional fees

	£
Accountancy	700
Legal fees in connection with the purchase of the shop	1,200
Debt collection	400
	2,300

Included in the figure for accountancy is £250 in respect of capital gains tax work.

(5) Wages and salaries

The figure of £83,825 for wages and salaries includes the annual salary of £15,500 paid to William's wife. She works in the clothing shop as a sales assistant. The other sales assistants doing the same job are paid an annual salary of £11,000.

(6) Other operating expenses

The figure of £2,990 for other operating expenses, includes £640 for gifts to customers of food hampers costing £40 each, £320 for gifts to customers of pens carrying an advertisement for the clothing shop costing £1.60 each, £100 for a donation to a national charity, and £40 for a donation to a local charity's fête. The fête's programme carried a free advertisement for the clothing shop.

(7) Goods for own use

During the year ended 31 May 2021, William took clothes out of the shop for his personal use without paying for them. The cost of these clothes was £460, and they had a selling price of £650. He has not made any adjustment in the accounts in respect of this.

> (8) **Plant and machinery**
>
> The capital allowances available for the year ended 31 May 2021 are £13,060.
>
> **Calculate William's tax adjusted trading profit for the year ended 31 May 2021.**
>
> **Your computation should commence with the net profit figure of £30,200 and should list all the items referred to in notes 1 to 8, indicating by the use of a zero (0) any items that do not require adjustment.**

8   Cash basis for small unincorporated businesses

Cash basis option for small businesses

Unincorporated businesses (i.e. sole traders and partnerships):

* can choose to calculate profits/losses on:
    - a cash basis (i.e. on the basis of **cash received and expenses paid** in the period of account), rather than
    - the normal accruals basis
* provided they have annual cash receipts of up to £150,000.

The cash basis option is not available to:

* companies, and
* limited liability partnerships (LLPs) (Chapter 10).

If an unincorporated business chooses the cash basis, it can continue to account on this basis until its annual cash receipts exceed £300,000.

 Note that the cash basis is optional and the detailed rules are complex, however, the TX examining team has confirmed that:

* only the level of detail in this section is examinable, and
* it should be assumed in all questions involving sole traders and partnerships that the **cash basis** does **not apply** unless it is specifically referred to in the question.

We looked at the cash basis for property income in Chapter 4. The main principles of the cash basis are applied in exactly the same way to property income and trading income. However, there are some minor differences in relation to capital expenditure and flat rate expenses deductions which apply to trading income.

Under the cash basis for trading income:

- the business accounts for cash receipts and payments in the period of account, i.e. the period for which the business prepares accounts.

- the business (like any other business) can prepare its accounts to any date in the year

- there is no distinction between capital and revenue expenditure in respect of plant, machinery and equipment for tax purposes, therefore:

  - purchases are allowable deductions when paid for, and

  - proceeds are treated as taxable cash receipts when an asset is sold

  - capital allowances remain available for expenditure on cars only; the capital cost is not an allowable deduction when paid

- in the TX examination, the flat rate expense deduction for motor car expenses is claimed (see below) instead of capital allowances (see Chapter 8)

- expenditure on buildings cannot be deducted when paid; structures and buildings allowances can be claimed in respect of qualifying expenditure (Chapter 8).

The key advantages of the cash basis are:

- simpler accounting requirements as there is no need to account for receivables, payables and inventory

- profit is not accounted for and taxed until it is realised and therefore cash is available to pay the associated tax liability.

However the main disadvantage is that:

- losses can only be carried forward to set against future trading profits, whereas under the accruals basis many more options for loss relief are available (Chapter 11).

Flat rate expense deduction option for any unincorporated business

Any unincorporated business (whether or not they are using the cash basis) can:

- opt to use flat rate expense adjustments

- to replace the calculation of actual costs incurred in respect of certain expenses.

 However, note that the TX examining team has confirmed that:

- flat rate expenses will only be examined where the business has chosen the cash basis, and

- if the cash basis applies, the use of flat rate expenses should be assumed to also apply.

The flat rate expense adjustments that are examinable are as follows:

Type of expense	Flat rate expense adjustment
Motoring expenses – capital costs and running costs (e.g. insurance, repairs, servicing and fuel)	Allowable deduction = amount using the AMAP rates of 45p and 25p per mile (Chapters 4 & 5) (i.e. same allowance as for property business and employed individual's use of own car)
Private use of part of a commercial building – private accommodation in a guest house or small hotel (e.g. a bed and breakfast)	Private use adjustment re household goods and services, rent, food and utilities = fixed amount based on the number of occupants Note that the private element of other expenses (e.g. mortgage interest and rates) must be adjusted for as normal

 In the TX examination, if the flat rate expense adjustment for private use of a commercial building is required, it will be provided within the question.

The AMAP rates are included in the tax rates and allowances provided to you in the examination.

Note: When you are asked to calculate taxable profit using the cash basis, you should begin your calculation with revenue received, and make any necessary deductions or additions to this figure. It is possible to calculate the correct answer by adjusting the net profit as you would under the accruals basis. However, this method is likely to be more time consuming and complicated.

Test your understanding 5

Rosemarie opened a bed and breakfast on 1 August 2020 and has prepared her first set of accounts to 5 April 2021.

Her accountant prepared her statement of profit or loss for the period ended 5 April 2021 as follows:

	Notes	£	£
Revenue	(1)		48,035
Less: Cost of sales (food and utilities)	(2)		(15,670)
			————
Gross profit			32,365
Depreciation	(3)	2,500	
Motor expenses	(4)	4,200	
Other expenses (all allowable)	(5)	14,500	
		————	(21,200)
			————
Net profit			11,165
			————

(1) Revenue includes £6,575 which is still receivable at 5 April 2021.

(2) Rosemarie paid for 80% of her purchases by 5 April 2021 and the remainder in June 2021. There is no closing inventory at 5 April 2021. Rosemarie lives with her husband at the bed and breakfast and £4,900 of the costs relate to their personal use.

(3) The depreciation charge relates to the fixtures, fittings and equipment bought in the period for £9,000 and a motor car purchased on 1 August 2020. Rosemarie purchased the motor car with CO_2 emissions of 108g/km for £9,600 and she uses the car 70% for business purposes.

(4) The motor expenses of £4,200 relate to Rosemarie's car and in the period she drove 11,000 business miles.

(5) The other expenses are all allowable for tax purposes, however Rosemarie paid for £460 of the expenses in June 2021.

The cash basis private use adjustment for two occupants in a business premises for 8 months is £4,000.

Calculate Rosemarie's tax adjusted trading profit for the year ended 5 April 2021 assuming:

(a) **She uses the normal accruals basis of accounting and claims capital allowances of £9,806 in respect of fixtures, fittings, equipment and the motor car acquired during the year.**

(b) **She uses the cash basis.**

9 Chapter summary

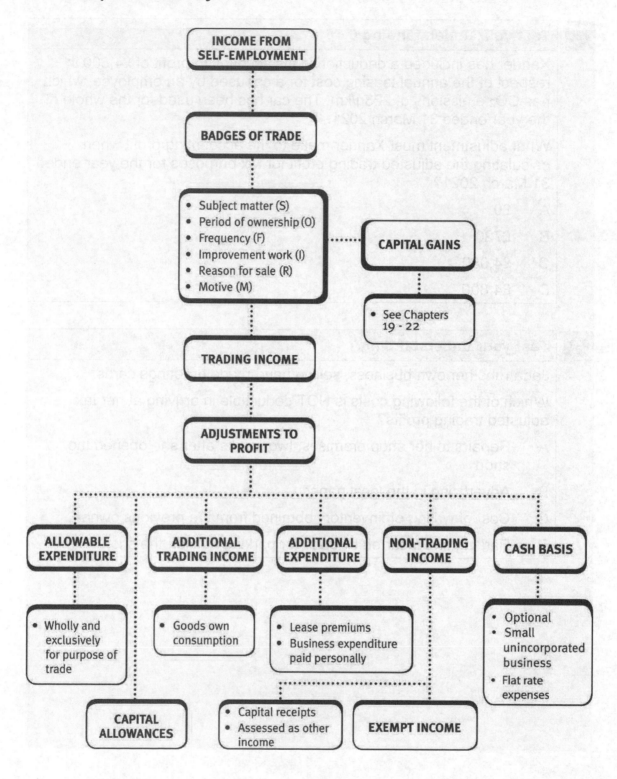

10 Practice objective test questions

Test your understanding 6

Xander has included a deduction in his accounting profit of £4,800 in respect of the annual leasing cost for a car used by an employee, which has CO_2 emissions of 223g/km. The car has been used for the whole of the year ended 31 March 2021.

What adjustment must Xander make to the accounting profit when calculating the adjusted trading profit for tax purposes for the year ended 31 March 2021?

A   £0

B   £720

C   £4,080

D   £4,800

Test your understanding 7

Jada runs her own business, selling hand-made greetings cards.

Which of the following costs is NOT deductible in arriving at her tax adjusted trading profits?

A   Repairs to her shop premises, two weeks after she opened the shop

B   Advertising in the local paper

C   Cost of writing off inventory obtained from the previous owner

D   Parking fine incurred by Jada for parking outside the shop

Test your understanding 8

Anya is a sole trader who operates a business as a wine merchant. Her accounts for the year ended 31 March 2021 include the following items

	£
Impaired trade debts written off	1,200
Subscription to Decanter magazine	500
Late payment interest in respect of the tax on the business profits for the year ended 31 March 2020	275
Legal fees in respect of the acquisition of a new shop	2,500

What amount is added back to the accounting profit in respect of the above items when calculating the adjusted trading profits for the year ended 31 March 2021?

A   £2,500

B   £2,775

C   £3,000

D   £4,475

Test your understanding 9

Which of the following receipts is not taxable as trading income?

A   Insurance proceeds for loss of trade

B   Impaired debt recovered

C   Repayment interest received on a tax repayment

D   Sales proceeds for selling inventory

Test your understanding 10

Fred starts to trade on 1 January 2021. He incurs the following expenditure in the 12 months before he starts to trade:

Rent for his business property £5,000.

A new suit so he can impress prospective customers £600.

Payment of £1,000 to an advertising agency for an advertising campaign to run through January 2021.

How much of this expenditure can Fred deduct for tax purposes in the year to 31 December 2021?

A   £0

B   £5,000

C   £6,000

D   £6,600

Test your understanding 11

Harry is a sole trader and has deducted the following items of expenditure in the statement of profit or loss for his most recent accounting period:

Depreciation	£2,000
Legal fees in acquiring a new ten-year lease on his business premises	£1,000
Entertainment of: staff	£2,800
clients	£4,300

How much should be added back to Harry's net profit to arrive at his tax adjusted trading profit?

A   £9,100

B   £10,100

C   £7,300

D   £6,300

Test your understanding answers

Test your understanding 1

Sole trader

The profits for the year ended 31 December 2020 are assessed in the tax year 2020/21.

Test your understanding 2

Sheila

Richard's salary of £10,000 appears to be excessive, and a disallowance of £5,500 (£10,000 – £4,500) is probably appropriate.

In practice the exact adjustment would depend on such matters as the nature of Richard's duties, and the hours that he works, as compared to the part-time typist.

Test your understanding 3

Item of expenditure	Add back?	Reason
Drawings of the proprietor	Add back	Appropriation of profit and therefore disallowed
£45,000 salary paid to the proprietor's spouse. Typical market rate is estimated at £15,000	Add back £30,000	HMRC will only allow that amount which represents a market rate
Subscription to golf club where sole trader may meet/entertain clients	Add back	Not wholly and exclusively for the purposes of the trade
Legal fees to acquire a short lease (7 years)	Add back	Legal fees incurred on the RENEWAL of a short lease only are allowed
Trade related NVQ training course for apprentice employee	No adjustment	Provided the course is for the purpose of the trade it is allowable

Test your understanding 4

William

Tax adjusted trading profit – year ended 31 May 2021

	£	£
Net profit as per accounts	30,200	
Add: Depreciation	4,760	
Light and heat (40% × £1,525)	610	
Motor expenses (9,000/12,000 × £4,720)	3,540	
Decorating clothing shop	0	
Decorating private flat	1,050	
Rent and rates (40% × £3,900)	1,560	
Accountancy	0	
Capital gains tax work	250	
Legal fees re purchase of new shop	1,200	
Debt collection	0	
Excessive remuneration to William's wife (£15,500 – £11,000)	4,500	
Gift of food hampers	640	
Gift of pens	0	
Donation to national charity	100	
Donation to local charity	0	
Goods own consumption	650	
Less: Capital allowances		13,060
	49,060	13,060
	(13,060)	
Tax adjusted trading profit	36,000	

Test your understanding 5

Rosemarie

(a) Normal accruals basis

	£
Net profit	11,165
Food and utilities	4,900
Depreciation	2,500
Motor expenses (£4,200 × 30%)	1,260
Other expenses	0
	19,825
Less: Capital allowances (per question) (Note 1)	(9,806)
Tax adjusted trading profit	10,019

Notes:

(1) In the examination you will be required to calculate the available capital allowances (see Chapter 8). Working 1 (W1) below sets out how the figure given in the question has been calculated. You may wish to revisit this once you have studied Chapter 8.

(2) The usual presentation of an adjustment of profits is produced above and must be used where accounts have been prepared and need adjustment.

However, an alternative method of calculating the same tax adjusted trading profit figure is to reproduce the accounts presentation but just deduct the expenses which are allowable, as opposed to adding back to net profit those that are not allowable.

This alternative presentation is given in (W3) as it provides a more direct comparison of the difference in the treatment when the cash basis is used.

(b) Cash basis

	£	£
Revenue (£48,035 – £6,575)		41,460
Less: Food and utilities (£15,670 × 80%)		(12,536)
Less: Expenses		
Depreciation (Note 1)	0	
Capital expenditure (Note 1)	9,000	
Motor expenses (W2) (Note 2)	4,750	
Other expenses (£14,500 – £460)	14,040	
		(27,790)
Add: Private use adjustment (Note 3)		4,000
Tax adjusted trading profit		5,134

Notes:

(1) Depreciation is not allowable under the cash basis. The cost of the fixtures and fittings is allowable when paid for. The cost of the car is not however allowable, capital allowances are available – but see Note 2.

(2) Where the flat rate mileage allowance is claimed, capital allowances are not available on the cost of the car. The TX examining team has stated that where the cash basis is used, you should assume that flat rate expenses will also be claimed.

(3) The private use adjustment of £4,000 relates to the private element of food and utility costs.

Workings

(W1) Capital allowances

	Main pool £	Private use car £		Allowances £
Additions:				
Car (CO$_2$ 108g/km)		9,600		
Fixtures and fittings	9,000			
AIA	(9,000)			9,000
		0		
WDA (18% × 8/12)		(1,152)	× 70%	806
TWDV c/f	0	8,448		
Capital allowances				9,806

(W2) Motor expenses – cash basis

	£
10,000 × 45p	4,500
1,000 × 25p	250
	———
	4,750
	———

(W3) Accruals basis – alternative presentation

	£	£
Revenue		48,035
Less: Food, utilities, etc. (£15,670 – £4,900)		(10,770)
		———
Gross profit		37,265
Less: Expenses		
Depreciation (Note 1)	0	
Motor expenses (£4,200 × 70%)	2,940	
Other expenses	14,500	
Capital allowances (per question)	9,806	
	———	(27,246)
		———
Tax adjusted trading profit		10,019
		———

Tutorial note:

This question is for tutorial purposes. In practice it is unlikely that a business would prepare accounts on an accruals basis if they intend to use the cash basis for tax purposes.

Indeed such businesses may not even need an accountant to prepare cash accounts.

Test your understanding 6

The correct answer is B.

Annual lease cost	£4,800
	———
Disallowable amount (15% × £4,800)	£720
	———

Test your understanding 7

The correct answer is D.

D is the correct answer because fines incurred by the owner of the business are not deductible.

Parking fines incurred by employees are generally deductible.

The other costs are deductible.

Test your understanding 8

The correct answer is B.

B is the correct answer because late payment interest is a personal liability of the owner of the business rather than the business itself, and is disallowable.

The legal fees in respect of the new shop are capital expenditure and also disallowed.

The write off of trade debts and subscribing to a trade related magazine are both allowable for tax purposes.

Test your understanding 9

The correct answer is C.

All the other items are taxable as trading income.

Test your understanding 10

The correct answer is C.

Expenditure which would be allowable once the business has commenced, is allowable if incurred in the 7 years before trading commences. The rent and advertising are allowable but the suit is a private expense.

Test your understanding 11

The correct answer is C.

Depreciation is not an allowable expense (usually being replaced by capital allowances); legal fees for acquiring (not renewing) short leases and entertainment of customers are also not allowable expenses for tax purposes. Staff entertaining is allowable.

Capital allowances

Chapter learning objectives

Upon completion of this chapter you will be able to:

- define plant and machinery for capital allowances purposes

- compute writing down allowances, first year allowances and the annual investment allowance

- compute capital allowances for motor cars

- compute balancing allowances and balancing charges

- compute structures and buildings allowances

- recognise the treatment of short life assets

- recognise the treatment of assets included in the special rate pool.

PER

One of the PER performance objectives (PO15) is to prepare computations of taxable amounts and tax liabilities according to legal requirements. Working through this chapter should help you understand how to demonstrate that objective.

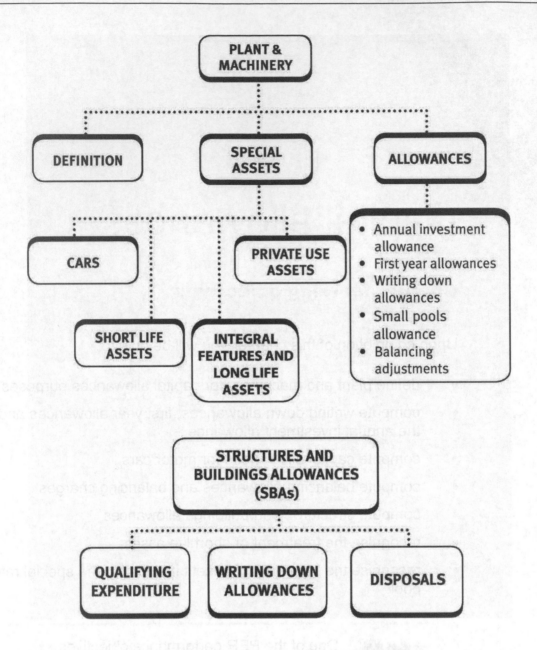

1 Capital allowances – plant and machinery

Purpose of capital allowances

Capital allowances are provided to give a business tax relief for capital expenditure on qualifying assets.

Remember that depreciation charged in the accounts is not allowable in computing tax adjusted trading profits; capital allowances are given instead.

This chapter details the capital allowances available for expenditure on plant and machinery followed by expenditure on qualifying structures and buildings.

Who may claim capital allowances?

Capital allowances are available to persons who buy **qualifying assets** i.e. plant and machinery for use in a trade or profession.

 In the TX examination, however, capital allowances are not available to unincorporated businesses that use the cash basis (see Chapter 7).

Qualifying expenditure

Capital allowances are given on the original cost of a capital asset and all subsequent qualifying expenditure of a capital nature (e.g. improvements).

Relief for capital allowances

Capital allowances are:

*   an allowable deduction in calculating the tax adjusted trading profit

*   calculated for a trader's period of account (i.e. the period for which they prepare accounts).

2 Meaning of plant and machinery

Definition

 'Machinery' has a commonly understood meaning. It includes all machines, computers, office equipment, etc.

The term 'plant' however, is not clearly defined in the tax legislation. HMRC has however codified some rules based on decided court cases and has specifically deemed certain types of expenditure to be plant and machinery.

Key principles

The key principle to apply in deciding the appropriate treatment of a capital purchase is to consider the function that the asset performs for the business:

Does the asset perform:	This means that the asset is:	Plant and machinery?
An active function	Apparatus with which the business is carried on	Yes
A passive function	The setting in which the business is carried on	No

Assets deemed to be plant

There are certain types of expenditure that, although not plant using the above key principle, are treated as plant by specific legislation.

These include:

- the cost of alterations to buildings needed for the installation of plant

- expenditure on acquiring computer software.

Assets deemed not to be plant

Statute also makes it clear that land, buildings and structures cannot be plant for capital allowance purposes. There is a separate allowance available for qualifying buildings and structures, detail is provided in section 12.

Summary

Determining what is and what is not plant can be difficult in practice.

In the examination the most common examples of plant and machinery are:

- computers and software

- machinery

- cars and lorries

- office furniture

- movable partitions

- air conditioning

- alterations of buildings needed to install plant and machinery.

Definition of plant and machinery

The original interpretation of plant and machinery was provided in the case of Yarmouth v France (1887). Plant was said to include:

'Whatever apparatus is used by a businessman for carrying on his business – not his stock-in-trade that he buys or makes for sale – but all goods and chattels, fixed or movable, live or dead, which he keeps for permanent employment in his business.'

This is a very far-reaching definition. It includes not only the obvious items of plant and machinery, but also such items as movable partitions, office furniture and carpets, heating systems, motor vehicles, computers, lifts and any expenditure incurred to enable the proper functioning of the item, such as reinforced floors or air conditioning systems for computers.

The courts' interpretation of 'plant'

The original definition of plant has been subsequently refined by the courts.

In particular, the key test that has been applied is a functional one. If the item is part of the setting or premises it is not plant, and thus no capital allowances are available, but if it fulfils a function it is plant.

The dividing line here is not always clear. Examples below show how the courts have reacted to claims for capital allowances:

- A canopy covering petrol pumps at a petrol station was held to be part of the setting and not plant and machinery (it did not assist in serving petrol to customers).

- False ceilings in a restaurant were held not to be plant (all they did was hide unsightly pipes).

- Swimming pools at a caravan park were held to be plant and machinery (the caravan park as a whole was the setting but the pool and its associated pumping and filtering equipment had an active role of providing leisure apparatus).

Buildings cannot be plant

Statutory provisions give detailed lists of items associated with buildings that are part of the building, and are deemed not to be plant, such as:

- walls, floors, ceilings, doors, windows and stairs

- mains services and systems of water, electricity and gas.

However the following may fall within the definition of a building but will still normally qualify as plant:

- electrical, cold water and gas systems provided mainly to meet the particular requirements of the trade, or to serve particular machinery used for the purposes of the trade

- space or water heating systems, systems of ventilation and air cooling, and any ceiling or floor comprised in such systems

- manufacturing or processing equipment, storage equipment, display equipment, counters, check outs and similar equipment

- cookers, washing machines, dishwashers, refrigerators and similar equipment

- wash basins, sinks, baths, showers, sanitary ware and similar equipment

- furniture and furnishings

- lifts, escalators and moving walkways
- sprinkler equipment and fire alarm systems
- movable partition walls
- decorative assets provided for the enjoyment of the public in a hotel, restaurant or similar trade
- advertising hoardings, signs and similar displays.

3 Calculating the allowances

The main pool (or general pool)

Generally expenditure on plant and machinery becomes part of a pool of expenditure upon which capital allowances are claimed. Normally capital allowances are not calculated on individual assets.

- Most items of plant and machinery purchased are included within the main pool (also known as the general pool).

- Some motor cars are also included in the main pool, namely:

  – New or second hand cars with CO_2 emissions between 51g/km and 110g/km

  – Second hand cars with CO_2 emissions of 50g/km or below

  The detailed rules relating to all types of car are in section 6.

- When an asset is acquired, the purchase price increases the value of the pool.

- When an asset is disposed of, the pool value is reduced by the lower of sale proceeds and original cost.

Certain items are not included in the main pool.

For unincorporated businesses, these are:

- new motor cars with CO_2 emissions of 50g/km and below or

- new or second hand cars with CO_2 emissions in excess of 110g/km

- assets that are used partly for private purposes by the owner of the business

- expenditure incurred on short life assets where an election to de-pool is made

- expenditure incurred on items that form part of the special rate pool.

These exceptions are dealt with later in this chapter.

The next few sections go through the different elements, and detailed rules, for calculating the allowances on different types of plant and machinery. A step-by-step approach is explained, building up to a full capital allowances pro forma which appears in section 11 of this chapter.

In all of the illustrations and test your understandings, a standard layout is adopted to build the bigger picture. It is very important that this standard layout is used for capital allowance computations in section C questions of the examination.

The annual investment allowance (AIA)

The annual investment allowance (AIA) is a 100% allowance for the first £1,000,000 of expenditure incurred by a business in a 12 month period on plant and machinery.

The key rules for the allowance are as follows:

*   available to **all** businesses

*   available on acquisitions of plant and machinery in the main pool and acquisitions of special rate pool items (see later)

*   **not** available on cars

*   limited to a maximum of £1,000,000 expenditure incurred in each 12 month period of account

*   for long and short periods of account the allowance is increased/reduced to reflect the length of the period

*   not available in the period of account in which the trade ceases (see section 5).

Where a business spends more than £1,000,000 in a 12 month period of account on assets qualifying for the AIA:

*   the expenditure above the £1,000,000 limit qualifies for writing down allowances (WDA) (see below).

Note also that:

*   taxpayers do not have to claim all/any of the AIA if they do not want to

*   any unused AIA cannot be carried forward or carried back, the benefit of the allowance is just lost.

 The AIA amount of £1,000,000 is included in the tax rates and allowances provided to you in the examination. The rate will decrease to £200,000 on 1 January 2021 but this will not be tested in the TX examination.

Illustration 1 – AIA

Matthew commenced trading on 1 January 2020. In his first year of trading he made the following purchases:

Plant and machinery	£1,060,000
Office furniture and equipment	£170,000
A new car with CO$_2$ emissions of 105g/km for his manager	£11,000

(a) **Calculate Matthew's AIA for the year ended 31 December 2020 and the balance on the main pool after deducting the AIA.**

(b) **Prepare the same calculations but this time assuming Matthew did not purchase the plant and machinery.**

Solution

(a) **Y/e 31 December 2020**

		Main pool
	£	£
Additions		
Not qualifying for AIA:		
Car (CO$_2$ between 51 – 110g/km)		11,000
Qualifying for AIA:		
Plant and machinery	1,060,000	
Office furniture and equipment	170,000	
	─────────	
	1,230,000	
AIA (Maximum)	(1,000,000)	
	─────────	230,000
		─────────
Balance after AIA (Note 1)		241,000
		─────────

(b) **If Matthew did not purchase the plant and machinery**

		Main pool
	£	£
Additions		
Not qualifying for AIA:		
Car (CO_2 between 51 – 110g/km)		11,000
Qualifying for AIA:		
Office furniture and equipment	170,000	
AIA (Note 2)	(170,000)	
		0
Balance after AIA (Note 1)		11,000

Notes:

(1) The balance after AIA on the main pool is eligible for a writing down allowance (WDA) (see below).

(2) The unused AIA of £830,000 (£1,000,000 – £170,000) is lost.

First year allowances (FYA) – low emission cars

The AIA is not available on cars, however a 100% first year allowance (FYA) is available on the purchase of new low emission cars.

A low emission car emits 50 or less grams per kilometre of carbon dioxide (i.e. CO_2 emissions ≤ 50g/km).

 The CO_2 emission limit and 100% allowance are included in the tax rates and allowances provided to you in the examination.

The 100% FYA is given as follows:

- In the period of acquisition, a 100% FYA is given instead of the WDA, (i.e. cannot have both the FYA and WDA on that expense in the first year).

- Unlike the AIA and WDA, the FYA is never time apportioned for periods of account greater or less than 12 months.

- The taxpayer does not have to claim all/any of the FYA.

- If the FYA is not claimed at all the WDA is available.

- However, if the FYA is only partially claimed the balance of cost goes into the main pool but is not entitled to any other allowance in that year.

- FYAs are not given in the final period of trading (see section 5).

- If the low emission car is not new (i.e. second hand) it is treated in the same way as a car with CO_2 emissions of between 51 – 110g/km.

As well as benefiting from full capital allowances in the year of purchase, low emission cars that are provided to employees as company cars result in lower taxable benefits and therefore lower income tax for the employee and lower class 1A NICs for the employer. Zero emission cars will have no taxable benefit at all. They are therefore very beneficial from a tax perspective.

See section 6 for more detail on other types of car.

Writing down allowances (WDA)

- An annual WDA of 18% is given on a reducing balance basis in the main pool.

- It is given on:

    - the unrelieved expenditure in the main pool brought forward at the beginning of the period of account (i.e. tax written down value) (TWDV), plus

    - any additions on which the AIA or FYA is not available, plus

    - any additions not covered by the AIA (i.e. exceeding the limit)

    - after taking account of disposals.

- The TWDV brought forward includes all prior expenditure, less allowances already claimed.

 The 18% WDA is included in the tax rates and allowances provided to you in the examination.

Computations

In the TX examination you will normally do computations for one period of account only. However, for tutorial purposes, the illustrations in this chapter may cover multiple accounting periods to enable you to practise the technique.

In all questions you should assume that the tax year 2020/21 rules apply throughout.

Illustration 2 – Writing down allowances

Calculate the total capital allowances available to Matthew in illustration 1 part (a).

Solution

y/e 31 December 2020	£	Main pool £	Allowances £
Additions:			
Not qualifying for AIA or FYA:			
Car (CO$_2$ between 51 – 110g/km)		11,000	
Qualifying for AIA:			
Plant and machinery	1,060,000		
Office furniture and equipment	170,000		
	1,230,000		
AIA (Maximum)	(1,000,000)		1,000,000
		230,000	
		241,000	
WDA (18% × £241,000)		(43,380)	43,380
TWDV c/f		197,620	
Total allowances			1,043,380

Illustration 3 – Writing down allowances

Grace commenced trading on 1 January 2020. Her trading profits, adjusted for tax purposes but before capital allowances, are as follows:

Year ended 31 December 2020	£1,520,770
Year ended 31 December 2021	£1,525,000

On 9 May 2020, she bought plant and machinery for £1,250,000, a second hand motor car with CO$_2$ emissions of 103g/km for £6,500 and a new motor car with CO$_2$ emissions of 42g/km for £13,600.

Calculate Grace's tax adjusted trading profit for both years.

Assume the tax year 2020/21 rules apply throughout.

Solution

Tax adjusted trading profit

	Adjusted trading profit	Capital allowances (W)	Tax adjusted trading profit
	£	£	£
y/e 31 December 2020	1,520,770	(1,059,770)	461,000
y/e 31 December 2021	1,525,000	(37,859)	1,487,141

Working: Capital allowances computation

		Main pool	Allowances
y/e 31 December 2020	£	£	£
Additions:			
Not qualifying for AIA or FYA:			
Car (CO$_2$ between 51 – 110g/km)		6,500	
Qualifying for AIA:			
Plant and machinery	1,250,000		
AIA	(1,000,000)		1,000,000
		250,000	
		256,500	
WDA (18% × £256,500)		(46,170)	46,170
Additions qualifying for FYA:			
New low emission car (CO$_2$ ≤ 50g/km)	13,600		
FYA (100%)	(13,600)		13,600
		0	
TWDV c/f		210,330	
Total allowances			1,059,770
y/e 31 December 2021			
WDA (18% × £210,330)		(37,859)	37,859
TWDV c/f		172,471	
Total allowances			37,859

Test your understanding 1

Ginevra commenced trading on 6 April 2020. Her trading profits, adjusted for tax purposes but before capital allowances, are as follows:

Year ended 5 April 2021	£1,595,740
Year ended 5 April 2022	£1,600,000

On 1 May 2020, Ginevra acquired plant and machinery for £1,203,000, a new motor car with CO_2 emissions of 108g/km for £10,000 and a new motor car with CO_2 emissions of 49g/km for £11,100.

Calculate Ginevra's tax adjusted trading profit for both years.

Assume the tax year 2020/21 rules apply throughout.

Short or long periods of account

- The AIA and WDAs are given for periods of account (i.e. the period for which a trader prepares accounts). The £1,000,000 AIA and the WDA percentage of 18% are based on a period of account of 12 months.

- Shorter or longer periods of account result in the allowances being reduced/increased to reflect the length of the period of account.

- If the period of account exceeds 18 months; it must be split into a 12 month period and a second period to deal with the remaining months.

- The most common occasion for a business not having a 12 month period of account is at the start of trading.

- Remember that FYAs are never adjusted to reflect the length of the period of account.

Illustration 4 – WDA: Long period of account

Googoosh commenced trading on 1 April 2019. He prepared accounts for the 14 month period ended 31 May 2020 and the year ended 31 May 2021.

On 1 June 2019, he bought plant and machinery for £1,100,000, a new motor car with CO_2 emissions of 106g/km for £19,800 and a new motor car with CO_2 emissions of 44g/km for £13,000.

Calculate his capital allowances for each of the periods of trading.

Assume the tax year 2020/21 rules apply throughout.

Solution

Capital allowances computation

14 m/e 31 May 2020	£	Main pool £	Allowances £
Additions:			
Not qualifying for AIA or FYA:			
Car (CO_2 between 51 – 110g/km)		19,800	
Qualifying for AIA:			
Plant and machinery	1,100,000		
AIA	(1,100,000)		1,100,000
	———	0	
		———	
		19,800	
WDA (18% × £19,800 × 14/12)		(4,158)	4,158
Additions qualifying for FYA:			
New low emission car (CO_2 ≤50 g/km)	13,000		
FYA (100%)	(13,000)		13,000
	———	0	
TWDV c/f		15,642	
		———	
Total allowances			1,117,158
			———
y/e 31 May 2021			
WDA (18% × £15,642)		(2,816)	2,816
TWDV c/f		12,826	
		———	———
Total allowances			2,816

Note: The AIA is increased to £1,166,667 (£1,000,000 × 14/12) to reflect the 14 month period of account and therefore all of the £1,100,000 expenditure in the period to 31 May 2019 is eligible for the allowance. The unused allowance is lost. Both the AIA and the WDA are proportionally increased to reflect the 14 month period.

Test your understanding 2

Graham commenced trading on 1 May 2020. He prepared accounts for the 4 month period ended 31 August 2020 and then the year ended 31 August 2021.

On 1 May 2020, he bought plant and machinery for £470,000, a used motor car with CO_2 emissions of 41g/km for £11,500 and a new motor car with CO_2 emissions of 44g/km for £16,500.

Calculate the capital allowances for each period of trading.

Assume the tax year 2020/21 rules apply throughout.

Length of ownership in the period of account

It is important to distinguish between the length of the period of account and the length of ownership of the asset during the period:

The WDA is applied proportionally according to the **length of the period of account**.

- The WDA is never restricted by reference to the length of ownership of an asset in the period of account.

- If a business prepares accounts for the year ended 31 March 2021, the same WDA is given whether an asset is purchased on 10 April 2020 or on 31 March 2021.

  The WDA is available provided the asset is owned on the last day of the period of account. The actual length of ownership of the asset during the period of account is not relevant.

4 Sale of plant and machinery

When an asset is sold or scrapped the following steps are taken

- The disposal value (lower of sale proceeds and original cost) is deducted from the total of:
  - the TWDV brought forward on the pool plus
  - Additions to the pool
    - additions not qualifying for either the AIA or FYA, and
    - additions qualifying for but not covered by AIA.
- The WDA for the year is then calculated on the remaining figure.

- If sale proceeds exceed the original cost of the asset:

  - the sale proceeds deducted from the pool are restricted to the original cost of the asset

  - note that any excess of sale proceeds over original cost may then be taxed as a chargeable gain (see later).

- Therefore, on a disposal, always deduct from the pool the lower of:

  - the sale proceeds, and

  - the original cost.

Illustration 5 – Sale of plant and machinery

Gustav prepares accounts to 31 May. In the year to 31 May 2021, the following transactions took place:

5 June 2020   Plant sold for £1,200 (purchased for £8,000)

3 September 2020   Plant purchased for £204,000

Compute the capital allowances for the year ended 31 May 2021, assuming that the TWDV on 1 June 2020 was £10,000.

Assume the tax year 2020/21 rules apply throughout.

Solution

Gustav – Capital allowances computation – y/e 31 May 2021

		Main pool	Allowances
	£	£	£
TWDV b/f		10,000	
Additions qualifying for AIA:			
Plant and machinery	204,000		
AIA	(204,000)		204,000
		0	
Disposal (lower of cost and SP)		(1,200)	
		8,800	
WDA (18% × £8,800)		(1,584)	1,584
TWDV c/f		7,216	
Total allowances			205,584

Test your understanding 3

Gloria has owned and run her own business for many years. She prepares accounts to 30 June each year. During the year ended 30 June 2021, the following transactions took place:

21 July 2020	Purchased a motor car with CO_2 emissions of 102g/km for £24,000.
14 August 2020	Sold a piece of plant for £12,400. She had paid £15,000 for this when she acquired it.
31 October 2020	Sold a van for £700. She had paid £600 for this when she acquired it.
19 November 2020	Purchased plant for £184,500.

The TWDV at 1 July 2020 was £21,000.

Compute the capital allowances for the year ended 30 June 2021.

Assume the tax year 2020/21 rules apply throughout.

Balancing charges

The basic idea underlying capital allowances is that the business will over time obtain relief for the actual net cost of an asset to the business (i.e. cost less sale proceeds (if any)).

Initially the asset is put into the pool at its original cost. If, on disposal of an asset in the pool, sale proceeds exceed the balance brought forward:

- the pool balance will become negative because too many allowances have been claimed in the past

- the negative amount = the excess allowances previously given

- these will be recovered and charged to tax by means of a balancing charge (BC)

- the BC reduces the capital allowances claim for the period

- if there is an overall net BC, it is added to the tax adjusted trading profit.

Test your understanding 4

Gun-woo has traded for many years as an ice cream manufacturer. He prepares accounts to 30 June and during the year ended 30 June 2021 he made the following transactions:

14 July 2020	Sold some machinery for £12,100 which originally cost £26,000.
30 August 2020	Purchased a new car with CO_2 emissions of 50g/km for £14,000.
16 March 2021	Purchased some equipment for £23,500.

The TWDV at 1 July 2020 was £11,000.

(a) **Calculate Gun-woo's capital allowances for the year ended 30 June 2021.**

(b) **Explain what would have happened had Gun-woo made no additions in the year.**

Assume the tax year 2020/21 rules apply throughout.

5 Cessation of trade

When the business is **permanently discontinued**, the AIA, WDA and FYA are not available in the final period of account. A normal capital allowance computation is therefore not prepared for the final period to the date of cessation. Instead the following steps should be followed:

(1) Add in any additions made in the final period.

(2) Do not calculate any AIAs, WDAs or FYAs.

(3) Deduct any disposals made in the final period and any sale proceeds on the ultimate disposal of plant and machinery.

(4) Calculate a **balancing charge** (BC) (as above) or **balancing allowance** (BA) (see below) as appropriate.

(5) There should not be any balances carried forward at the end of trade.

Balancing allowances

At cessation, if there is still a balance of unrelieved expenditure in the pool, a business can claim relief for the unrelieved balance by way of a balancing allowance (BA).

- This is the only time a BA will arise in the main pool (or special rate pool – see section 8).

- The BA is the excess of the pool balance at the end of the final period of account over the sale proceeds received on all disposals, including on the ultimate disposal of plant and machinery.

Test your understanding 5

Gene has previously prepared accounts to 31 March. He decided to cease to trade on 31 December 2020, after a period of ill health.

The following transactions have recently taken place:

21.2.2020   Plant sold for £320 (originally purchased for £2,000)

10.9.2020   Plant purchased for £4,000

On the completion of the sale of his business, Gene received £5,400 for his plant and machinery. No item was sold for more than its original cost.

The TWDV on 1 April 2019 was £9,000.

Compute the capital allowances for the year ended 31 March 2020, and the period ended 31 December 2020.

Assume the tax year 2020/21 rules apply throughout.

6 Motor cars

The treatment of motor cars depends on the CO_2 emissions as follows:

CO_2 emissions	Description	Treatment in capital allowances computation:
≤ 50g/km	Low emission	If purchased new: eligible for 100% FYA (see section 3) If second hand: treat as a standard emission car
51 – 110g/km	Standard emission	Included in main pool as an addition not qualifying for AIA or FYA
> 110g/km	High emission	Include in the special rate pool as an addition not qualifying for AIA or FYA (see section 8)

The FYA/WDA percentages applicable to different CO_2 emissions are included in the rates and allowances provided to you in the examination.

Note however that:

*   Motor cars with an element of private use by the owner of the business, regardless of their level of emissions, are treated separately (see section 7).

Remember that the AIA is not available on any type of car.

Illustration 6 – Motor cars

Glenda prepares accounts to 31 March. At 1 April 2019, the TWDV of the main pool was £21,200. The following transactions took place during the two years ended 31 March 2021:

25.4.19 Purchased a motor car with CO_2 emissions of 109g/km for £20,600

11.6.20 Purchased plant and machinery for £11,000

15.8.20 Sold equipment for £9,400 (originally purchased for £15,000)

Calculate the capital allowances for the two years to 31 March 2021. Assume the tax year 2020/21 rules apply throughout.

Solution

Capital allowances computations

	£	Main pool £	Allowances £
y/e 31 March 2020			
TWDV b/f		21,200	
Additions: Not qualifying for AIA or FYA:			
Car (CO_2 between 51 – 110g/km)		20,600	
		41,800	
WDA (18% × £41,800)		(7,524)	7,524
TWDV c/f		34,276	
Total allowances			7,524
y/e 31 March 2021			
Additions: Qualifying for AIA:			
Plant and machinery:	11,000		
AIA	(11,000)		11,000
		0	
Disposal (lower of cost and sales proceeds)		(9,400)	
		24,876	
WDA (18% × £24,876)		(4,478)	4,478
TWDV c/f		20,398	
Total allowances			15,478

Test your understanding 6

Glen prepares accounts to 31 December. At 1 January 2020, the TWDV of the main pool was £48,100.

Transactions during the year ended 31 December 2020 were:

10.5.20 Purchased plant for £1,003,300

25.6.20 Purchased two new cars, one with CO_2 emissions of 104g/km for £18,600 and one with CO_2 emissions of 47g/km for £13,000

18.11.20 Sold plant for £4,600 (originally purchased for £9,500)

Calculate the capital allowances for the year ended 31 December 2020.

7 Assets with private use by the owner of the business

Where an asset is **used by the owner of the business**, partly for business and partly for private purposes:

- only the business proportion of the available capital allowance is available as a tax deduction.

 The following rules must be followed when computing the allowances:

The cost of the privately used asset is not brought into the main pool, but must be the subject of a separate computation.

- The AIA, FYA or WDA on the asset is based on its full cost
  - but only the business proportion of any allowance is deductible in computing the taxable trading profit.
- Note that if applicable, the business can choose the expenditure against which the AIA is allocated.
- It will therefore be most beneficial for the AIA to be allocated against the main pool expenditure rather than any private use asset as only the business proportion of any AIA available can be claimed.
- However note that in the examination the assets most commonly used for private purposes are cars, which are not eligible for the AIA.
- Motor cars with private use are always treated separately
  - regardless of their CO_2 emissions.
- On disposal of the asset, a balancing adjustment is computed by comparing sale proceeds (SP) with the TWDV.

  There is a balancing charge (BC) if SP exceeds the TWDV, and a balancing allowance (BA) if SP is less than the TWDV.

- Having computed the balancing adjustment, the amount assessed or allowed is then reduced to the business proportion.

Note that these rules only apply if there is **private use by the owner** of the business.

Private use of an asset by an employee has no effect on the business's entitlement to capital allowances.

Illustration 7 – Assets with private use by the owner of the business

Gleb runs a business and prepares his accounts to 5 April. As at 6 April 2020, the TWDV in the main pool was £11,700. The following transactions took place in the year ended 5 April 2021:

- Purchased plant for £18,500

- Purchased a motor car with CO_2 emissions of 105g/km for £19,000

- Sold some machinery for £8,500 (originally purchased for £18,000)

- Purchased a motor car with CO_2 emissions of 103g/km for £9,400 (used 45% for private purposes by Gleb).

Calculate the capital allowances for the year ended 5 April 2021.

Solution

Capital allowances computation – y/e 5 April 2021

	Main pool	Private use car	Business use	Allowances
	£	£	£	£
TWDV b/f	11,700			
Additions: Not qualifying for AIA:				
Car (CO_2 between 51 – 110g/km)	19,000			
Private use car		9,400		
Additions: Qualifying for AIA:				
Plant and machinery	18,500			
AIA	(18,500)			18,500
	0			
Disposal (lower of cost and SP)	(8,500)			
	22,200	9,400		
WDA (18% × £22,200)	(3,996)			3,996
WDA (18% × £9,400) (Note)		(1,692)	× 55%	931
TWDV c/f	18,204	7,708		
Total allowances				23,427

Note: The TWDV of the private use car is reduced by the full amount of the WDA, but only the business use proportion of the allowance can be claimed (i.e. deducted from trading profits).

Test your understanding 7

Georgina runs a small business and prepares accounts to 31 March. At 1 April 2020, the TWDV in the main pool was £21,200. The following transactions took place during the year ended 31 March 2021:

10.5.20	Purchased plant for £6,600
25.6.20	Purchased a motor car with CO_2 emissions of 101g/km for £17,000
15.2.21	Sold some machinery for £9,400 (originally purchased for £12,000)
16.2.21	Purchased a motor car with CO_2 emissions of 102g/km for £10,600 (used 40% for private purposes by Georgina)
14.3.21	Purchased a new motor car with CO_2 emissions of 42g/km for £11,750

Calculate the capital allowances for the year ended 31 March 2021.

8 Special rate pool

The special rate pool is a pool of qualifying expenditure that operates in the same way as the main pool except that:

- the WDA is 6% for a 12 month period (rather than 18%).

The 6% WDA applicable to the special rate pool is included in the tax rates and allowances provided to you in the examination.

Qualifying expenditure

The special rate pool groups together expenditure incurred on the following types of asset:

- long life assets
- 'integral features' of a building or structure
- thermal insulation of a building
- high emission cars (with CO_2 emissions of > 110g/km).

Long life assets

Long life assets are defined as plant and machinery with:

- an expected working life of 25 years or more.
    - Examples of long life assets might include aircraft used by an airline and agricultural equipment used by a farm.
    - The 25 year working life is from the time that the asset is first brought into use, to the time that it ceases to be capable of being used. It is not sufficient to just look at the expected life in the hands of the current owner.

- a total cost of at least £100,000 (for a 12 month period)

Where the business spends less than £100,000 p.a. on long life assets, they are treated as normal additions to either the main or special rate pool, depending on the type of expenditure.

The following can never be classed as long life assets.

- Motor cars
- Plant and machinery situated in a building that is used as a retail shop, showroom, hotel or office.

Integral features of a building or structure and thermal insulation

'Integral features of a building or structure' include expenditure incurred on:

- electrical (including lighting) systems
- cold water systems
- space or water heating systems
- external solar shading
- powered systems of ventilation, air cooling or air purification
- lifts, escalators and moving walkways.

Thermal insulation in all business buildings (except residential buildings in a property business) is also included in the special rate pool.

High emission cars

Note that where a high emission car is privately used by the owner of the business, it is included in a separate column like other private use cars, but only receives a WDA of 6%.

The AIA in the special rate pool

- the AIA is available against all expenditure in this pool (except high emission cars), and
- the business can choose the expenditure against which the AIA is allocated.

It is most beneficial for the AIA to be allocated against expenditure in the following order:

(1) the special rate pool (as assets in the special rate pool are only eligible for 6% WDA, whereas main pool plant and machinery is eligible for 18% WDA).

(2) the main pool

(3) short life assets (see later)

(4) private use assets

Illustration 8 – Long life assets

Apple runs a manufacturing business and prepares her accounts to 31 December each year. As at 1 January 2020, the tax written down value in the main pool was £43,000.

In the year ended 31 December 2020 Apple incurred the following expenditure:

- Spent £1,008,000 on a new air conditioning system for the factory which is expected to last 30 years.

- Purchased a new computer and related software for £25,000 and £5,000 respectively.

- Spent £115,000 on a new packing machine. Apple also incurred £4,000 on alterations to the factory in order to accommodate the new machine.

- Purchased a new car with CO_2 emissions of 145g/km for £28,000.

In addition she sold machinery for £10,000 (original cost £60,000).

Calculate the capital allowances available to Apple for the year ended 31 December 2020.

Solution

Capital allowances computation – y/e 31 December 2020

	Main pool £	Special rate pool £	Allowances £
TWDV b/f			
Additions:	43,000	0	
Not qualifying for AIA or FYA:			
Car (CO$_2$ > 110g/km)		28,000	
Qualifying for AIA:			
Long life asset (Note 1)	1,008,000		
AIA (Max) (Note 2)	(1,000,000)		1,000,000
		8,000	
Computer and software	30,000		
Machine (Note 3)	119,000		
	149,000		
AIA (Note 2)	(0)		
	149,000		
Disposal (lower of cost and SP)	(10,000)		
	182,000	36,000	
WDA (18% × £182,000)	(32,760)		32,760
WDA (6% × £36,000)		(2,160)	2,160
TWDV c/f	149,240	33,840	
Total allowances			1,034,940

Notes:

(1) The air conditioning unit has an expected life of more than 25 years and is therefore a long life asset. As Apple has incurred more than £100,000 on such assets in the year the air conditioning unit is included in the special rate pool and WDAs are restricted to 6%.

(2) The AIA is allocated to the additions in the special rate pool in priority to the additions in the main pool. The maximum £1,000,000 is therefore all allocated to the special rate pool expenditure and there is no AIA available for the main pool expenditure.

(3) Software and the cost of altering buildings to accommodate plant are specifically deemed by statute to be items of plant and machinery.

9 The small pool WDA

Where the balance immediately before the calculation of the WDA:

- on the main and/or special rate pool
- is £1,000 or less

the balance can be claimed as a WDA and written off in that year.

Note that the **£1,000 limit** is for a **12 month period of account**.

It is therefore applied proportionally for long and short periods of account.

The claim is optional. However, the taxpayer will normally want to claim the maximum available and reduce the balance on the pool to £Nil.

Test your understanding 8

Angelina is in business as a sole trader and prepares accounts to 31 May each year.

During the year ending 31 May 2021 she purchased the following:

15 June 2020   Purchased new office furniture for £898,800.

2 July 2020   Purchased a new car (with CO_2 emissions of 154g/km) for £12,600 which Angelina will use 20% of the time for private purposes.

10 July 2020   Installed a new water heating system in her business premises at a cost of £40,000 and a new lighting system at a cost of £70,000.

In addition on 1 July 2020 she sold office equipment for £18,700 (original cost £28,000).

As at 1 June 2020 the TWDV on her main pool was £10,800, and on the special rate pool was £16,600.

Calculate Angelina's capital allowances for the year ended 31 May 2021.

Assume the tax year 2020/21 rules apply throughout.

10 Short life assets

The short life asset election exists to enable businesses to accelerate capital allowances on certain qualifying expenditure.

Qualifying expenditure

 For the purposes of the examination, qualifying expenditure is:

- all plant and machinery (with the exception of motor cars) which would normally go in the main pool

- where it is the intention to sell or scrap the item within eight years of the end of the period of account in which the asset is acquired.

Process for computation

If the election is made, the following steps must be taken:

Each short life asset is put in a separate column in the capital allowances computation.

- On disposal within eight years of the end of the period of account in which the asset was acquired:

  - a separate balancing allowance or balancing charge is calculated.

- The election (written application to HMRC) must be made to enable assets to be treated separately in the capital allowances computation as short life assets. This is known as de-pooling.

- The election must be made by the first anniversary of 31 January following the end of the tax year in which the period of account, which includes the acquisition, ends.

- If no disposal has taken place within eight years of the end of the period of account in which the acquisition took place:

  - the unrelieved balance is transferred to the main pool

  - the transfer takes place in the first period of account following the eight year anniversary.

- Note that the AIA is available against short life assets and the business can choose the expenditure against which the AIA is matched. However, if eligible for the AIA, there will be no expenditure left to 'de-pool' and the short life asset election will not be made.

If there is expenditure in excess of the maximum £1,000,000 of expenditure eligible for the AIA, it may be advantageous for the AIA to be allocated against the main pool expenditure rather than a short life asset and for the short life asset election to be made.

Expenditure in excess of the AIA that is de-pooled is eligible for WDAs.

- It will be advantageous to make the election if it is anticipated that a balancing allowance will arise within eight years following the period of account of acquisition.

Illustration 9 – Short life assets

Gina has traded for many years preparing accounts to 31 December each year. The TWDV on the main pool was £15,000 on 1 January 2020.

In May 2020, she acquired a new machine costing £10,000. She anticipated that the machine would last two years and she eventually sold it on 30 June 2022, for £1,750.

In August 2020, she acquired plant and machinery for £1,002,000.

Calculate the allowances available for the three years to 31 December 2022, illustrating whether or not an election to treat the new machine as a short life asset would be beneficial.

Assume the tax year 2020/21 rules apply throughout.

Solution

Gina – Capital allowances computation – without making a short life asset election

	£	Main pool £	Allowances £
y/e 31 December 2020			
TWDV b/f		15,000	
Additions: Qualifying for AIA:			
Plant and machinery (£1,002,000 + £10,000)	1,012,000		
AIA	(1,000,000)		1,000,000
	———	12,000	
		27,000	
WDA (18% × £27,000)		(4,860)	4,860
TWDV c/f		22,140	
Total allowances			1,004,860
y/e 31 December 2021			
WDA (18% × £22,140)		(3,985)	3,985
TWDV c/f		18,155	
Total allowances			3,985

y/e 31 December 2022

	£	£
Disposal (lower of cost and SP)	(1,750)	
	16,405	
WDA (18% × £16,405)	(2,953)	2,953
TWDV c/f	13,452	
Total allowances		2,953

Gina – Capital allowances computation – with a short life asset election

	Main pool	Short life asset	Allowances
	£	£	£
y/e 31 December 2020	15,000		
TWDV b/f			
Additions: Qualifying for AIA:			
Plant and machinery	1,002,000	10,000	
AIA	(1,000,000)	(0)	1,000,000
	2,000		
	17,000	10,000	
WDA (18% × £17,000/£10,000)	(3,060)	(1,800)	4,860
TWDV c/f	13,940	8,200	
Total allowances			1,004,860
y/e 31 December 2021			
WDA (18% × £13,940/£8,200)	(2,509)	(1,476)	3,985
TWDV c/f	11,431	6,724	
Total allowances			3,985

y/e 31 December 2022			
Disposal (lower of cost and SP)		(1,750)	
		———	
	11,431	4,974	
Balancing allowance		(4,974)	4,974
		———	
WDA (18% × £11,431)	(2,058)		2,058
	———		
TWDV c/f	9,373		
	———		———
Total allowances			7,032
			———

The total allowances claimed without making the election are £1,011,798 (£1,004,860 + £3,985 + £2,953). In the event Gina makes the election, the allowances available for the three years are £1,015,877 (£1,004,860 + £3,985 + £7,032).

Note that the election just accelerates the allowances available and only changes the timing of the allowances. The total allowances available will eventually be the same, however, without the election, it will take considerably longer to get the relief.

Therefore, if not covered by the AIA, it is recommended that the short life treatment is taken but only if it is expected that a balancing allowance can be accelerated. It is not advantageous to accelerate a balancing charge.

11 Summary of computational technique

- Capital allowances are an important element of the syllabus and are certain to appear in the examination, within at least one of the questions.

- To be successful answering these questions, it is vital to use a methodical approach to work through the information in the question.

- Always follow the approach to computational questions outlined below and always ensure that you answer the question using the following pro forma amended to reflect the particular circumstances of the question.

Approach to computational questions

(1) Read the information in the question and decide how many columns/pools you will require.

(2) Draft the layout and insert the TWDV b/f (does not apply in a new trade).

(3) Insert additions not eligible for the AIA or FYAs into the appropriate column taking particular care to allocate cars into the correct column according to CO_2 emissions.

(4) Insert additions eligible for the AIA in the first column, then allocate the AIA to the additions

 – remember to time apportion if the period of account is not 12 months

 – allocate the AIA to special rate pool additions in priority to additions in the main or single asset columns.

(5) Any special rate pool additions in excess of the AIA are added to the special rate pool to increase the balance available for 6% WDA.

Any main pool expenditure in excess of the AIA is added to the main pool to increase the balance qualifying for 18% WDA.

The same approach is taken for additions to single asset columns.

(6) Deal with any disposal by deducting the lower of cost and sale proceeds.

(7) Work out any balancing charge/balancing allowance for assets in individual pools.

Remember to adjust for any private use.

(8) Consider if the small pools WDA applies to the main pool and/or the special rate pool.

(9) Calculate the WDA on each of the pools at the appropriate rate (either 18% or 6%).

Remember to:

 – time apportion if the period of account is not 12 months

 – adjust for any private use by the owner if an unincorporated business.

(10) Insert additions eligible for FYAs (i.e. any new cars with emissions of 50g/km or less) which get 100% FYA.

Remember the FYA is never time apportioned.

(11) Calculate the TWDV to carry forward to the next period of account and total the allowances column.

(12) Deduct the total allowances from the tax adjusted trading profits.

Pro forma capital allowances computation

The following pro forma computation should be used for unincorporated businesses:

Pro forma capital allowances computation – unincorporated businesses

	Notes	Main pool £	Special rate pool £	Short life asset £	Private use asset (Note 2) £	Allowances £
TWDV b/f		X	X	X		
Additions:						
Not qualifying for AIA or FYA:	(1)					
Second hand cars (up to 50g/km)		X				
Cars (50 – 110g/km)		X				
Cars (over 110g/km)			X			
Car with private use					X	
Qualifying for AIA:						
Special rate pool expenditure	(3)		X			
AIA (Max £1,000,000 in total)			(X)			X
Transfer balance to special rate pool			X			
Plant and machinery		X				
AIA (Max £1,000,000 in total)		(X)				X
Transfer balance to main pool	(4)	X				
Disposals (lower of original cost and sale proceeds)		(X)	(X)	(X)	(X)	
		———	———	———	———	
		X	X	X	X	
BA/(BC)				X / (X)	X / (X)	X / (X)
Small pool WDA	(5)					
WDA at 18%		(X)				X
WDA at 6%			(X)			X
WDA at 6%/18% (depending on emissions)		0	(X)		(X) × BU%	X
Additions qualifying for FYAs:						
New low emission cars (up to 50g/km)		X				
Less: FYA at 100%		(X)				X
		———	———	———	———	
TWDV c/f		X	X	X	X	
Total allowances						X

Notes to the pro forma capital allowances computation

(1)   Cars are pooled according to their CO_2 emissions into either the main or special rate pool. New low emission cars receive 100% FYA.

(2)   Cars with private use are depooled regardless of their CO_2 emissions, and only the business proportion of allowances can be claimed. However, the CO_2 emissions are important in determining the rate of WDA available.

(3)   Allocate the AIA to the special rate pool expenditure in priority to main pool plant and machinery assets as a WDA of only 6% is available on the special rate pool as opposed to 18% available on main pool items.

(4)   Expenditure qualifying for AIA in the main pool which exceeds the level of AIA available, is eligible for a WDA of 18%.

(5)   Small pools WDA: can claim up to a maximum WDA of £1,000 but on the main pool and/or special rate pool only.

(6)   The taxpayer does not have to claim all or any of the AIA or WDA.

12   Structures and buildings allowance

Structures and buildings allowances (SBAs)

Where a business incurs expenditure on qualifying costs for new non-residential structures and buildings, or renovations or extensions to existing buildings on or after 29 October 2018, they will be eligible for SBAs. In the examination, questions will only be set where the building was constructed or renovated on or after 6 April 2020 (1 April 2020 for limited companies) and where relevant the construction date will be given. Where buildings are purchased (as opposed to newly constructed), it should be assumed that SBAs are not available unless stated otherwise. Relief is given as an annual straight line allowance of 3%.

The allowance can be claimed from the date the asset is brought into use in the trade or property letting business. It will therefore be time apportioned in the first period.

Expenditure qualifying for SBAs:

*   Buildings including offices, retail and wholesale premises, factories and warehouses and the cost of subsequent improvements.

*   Structures including roads, walls, bridges and tunnels.

Qualifying costs do not include land, legal fees or repairs and maintenance.

When an unused building is purchased from a builder or developer the qualifying cost is the price paid less the value of the land.

There is no pooling system for assets eligible for SBA, so they are kept separate from other assets that qualify for capital allowances. Any asset eligible for SBA will not be eligible for the AIA.

When an asset is sold any SBA claimed will increase the sale proceeds of the asset for chargeable gains purposes (see Chapter 19). There is no balancing adjustment made on sale. The buyer will take over the remaining allowances and, if necessary, allowances will be apportioned in the period of disposal.

Illustration 10 – Structures and buildings allowance

During the year ended 31 March 2021, Alejandro incurred the following expenditure on a new factory constructed to use in his business:

	£
Land	220,000
Levelling of land	9,000
Factory building	350,000
Planning permission	2,000

The factory was brought into use on 1 September 2020.

(a) **Calculate Alejandro's SBAs for the year ended 31 March 2021.**

(b) **Explain the SBA implications for Alejandro and the buyer if the building is sold for £750,000 on 1 December 2029. The buyer has a year end of 30 November.**

Solution

(a) **Qualifying expenditure**

	£
Levelling of land	9,000
Factory building	350,000
	———
Total qualifying expenditure	359,000
	———

The land cost and planning permission are not eligible for relief.

SBA	£
(£359,000 × 3%) × 7/12	6,283
	———

The allowance is calculated straight line from the date the building is brought into use in the business.

(b) **Sale of the building**

Alejandro (seller)

Allowances are available to the date of disposal for Alejandro. Allowances can be claimed for the eight months the factory was used in the business. The allowance for the year ended 31 March 2030 would be £7,180 (£359,000 × 3% × 8/12).

> ### Buyer
>
> The buyer takes over the balance of qualifying expenditure for the remaining useful life. The purchase price of £750,000 is irrelevant.
>
> The buyer can claim an allowance of £10,770 (£359,000 ×3%) in the year ended 30 November 2030 as the building is in use for the full period.

Test your understanding 9

Alysha had a new factory constructed during the year ended 31 March 2021. Alysha started to use the factory in her business on 1 May 2020.

The costs incurred in relation to the factory are:

Land	165,000
Factory building	244,000
Planning permission	1,700

Calculate the SBAs for the year ended 31 March 2021.

13 Comprehensive example – plant and machinery

Illustration 11 – Comprehensive example

Ashley runs a manufacturing business and prepares accounts to 31 December each year. During the year ending 31 December 2020 Ashley incurred the following expenditure:

1 May 2020	Spent £1,020,000 on a new air conditioning system for the factory which is expected to last 30 years.
1 June 2020	Purchased new machinery for £40,000.
3 June 2020	Purchased a new car with CO_2 emissions of 42g/km for £17,000.
15 July 2020	Purchased a new car with CO_2 emissions of 103g/km for £18,000.

In addition on 1 July 2020 Ashley sold an old machine for £10,000 (original cost £15,000).

As at 1 January 2020 the tax written down value on the main pool was £64,000.

Calculate Ashley's capital allowances for the year ended 31 December 2020.

Solution

Capital allowances computation – y/e 31 December 2020

	Main pool	Special rate pool	Allowances
	£	£	£	£
TWDV b/f		64,000		
Additions:				
Not qualifying for AIA or FYA:				
Car (CO$_2$ 51 – 110g/km)		18,000		
Qualifying for AIA:				
Long life asset	1,020,000			
AIA (Max)	(1,000,000)			1,000,000
			20,000	
Plant and machinery	40,000			
AIA (Max used)	(0)			
		40,000		
Disposal (lower of cost and SP)		(10,000)		
		112,000	20,000	
Balancing allowance				
WDA (18% × £112,000)		(20,160)		20,160
WDA (6% × £20,000)			(1,200)	1,200
Additions qualifying for FYA				
New car (CO$_2$ ≤ 50g/km)	17,000			
FYA (100%)	(17,000)			17,000
		0		
TWDV c/f		91,840	18,800	
Total allowance				1,038,360

Note: The AIA is allocated to the additions in the special rate pool (WDA 6%) in priority to the additions in the main pool (WDA 18%).

Test your understanding 10

On 1 May 2020, Gordon commenced in self-employment running a music recording studio. He prepared his first set of accounts for the three months to 31 July 2020.

The following information relates to the three months to 31 July 2020:

(1) The tax adjusted trading profit for the period is £349,340. This figure is before taking account of capital allowances.

(2) Gordon purchased the following assets:

		£
1 May 2020	Recording equipment	277,875
15 May 2020	Motor car with CO_2 emissions of 139g/km (used by Gordon – 60% business use)	15,800
20 June 2020	Motor car with CO_2 emissions of 108g/km (used by employee – 20% private use)	10,400
4 July 2020	Recording equipment (expected to be scrapped in 2 years)	3,250

Calculate Gordon's tax adjusted trading profit for the period ended 31 July 2020.

14 Chapter summary

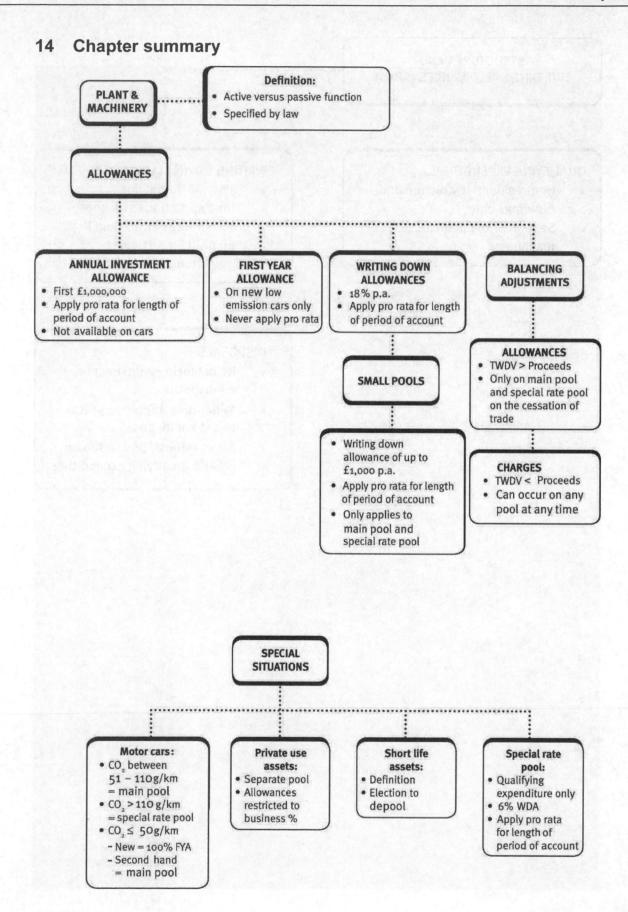

PLANT & MACHINERY

Definition:
- Active versus passive function
- Specified by law

ALLOWANCES

ANNUAL INVESTMENT ALLOWANCE
- First £1,000,000
- Apply pro rata for length of period of account
- Not available on cars

FIRST YEAR ALLOWANCE
- On new low emission cars only
- Never apply pro rata

WRITING DOWN ALLOWANCES
- 18% p.a.
- Apply pro rata for length of period of account

BALANCING ADJUSTMENTS

SMALL POOLS

ALLOWANCES
- TWDV > Proceeds
- Only on main pool and special rate pool on the cessation of trade

- Writing down allowance of up to £1,000 p.a.
- Apply pro rata for length of period of account
- Only applies to main pool and special rate pool

CHARGES
- TWDV < Proceeds
- Can occur on any pool at any time

SPECIAL SITUATIONS

Motor cars:
- CO_2 between 51 – 110 g/km = main pool
- CO_2 > 110 g/km = special rate pool
- CO_2 ≤ 50 g/km
  - New = 100% FYA
  - Second hand = main pool

Private use assets:
- Separate pool
- Allowances restricted to business %

Short life assets:
- Definition
- Election to depool

Special rate pool:
- Qualifying expenditure only
- 6% WDA
- Apply pro rata for length of period of account

STRUCTURES AND BUILDINGS ALLOWANCES (SBAs)

QUALIFYING EXPENDITURE
- Non-residential structure and buildings only
- Separate from plant and machinery

WRITING DOWN ALLOWANCES
- 3% p.a straight line
- Time apportioned for short accounting periods and if brought into use part way through period

DISPOSALS
- No balancing adjustments on disposal
- Seller time apportions SBAs to date of disposal
- Buyer claims SBAs based on seller's qualifying expenditure

15 Practice objective test questions

Test your understanding 11

Kelly runs a small business which she started on 1 May 2020. She prepared her first set of accounts for the nine months to 31 January 2021. On 1 June 2020, she purchased a car for £12,500 which she uses 30% for business purposes. The car has CO_2 emissions of 109g/km.

What are the capital allowances available to her for the nine month period ended 31 January 2021?

A £12,500

B £1,688

C £675

D £506

Test your understanding 12

Gideon draws up accounts to 30 June each year. On 5 August 2021 he sold a car for £17,560 which had originally been purchased on 1 September 2020 for £18,000. This car has CO_2 emissions of 180g/km.

On 1 July 2020 there was no balance on either the main or special rate pool.

For the year ended 30 June 2022, the sale of the car results in capital allowances of:

A £640 balancing charge

B £640 balancing allowance

C £2,800 balancing charge

D £2,800 balancing allowance

Test your understanding 13

Which one of the following would not qualify for capital allowances?

A Movable partitions in an office

B Swimming pools at a caravan park

C False ceilings in a restaurant installed to cover pipes

D Costs of altering factory to install new machinery

Test your understanding 14

Paul runs a small business as a hairdresser. He commenced trading on 1 July 2020 and prepared his first set of accounts for the nine months to 31 March 2021.

During this first period of account he purchased the following items:

Car   £8,000 (100% business use, CO_2 emissions
                                 147g/km)

 Plant & machinery   £15,000

What is Paul's maximum capital allowance claim for the nine months ended 31 March 2021?

A   £15,480

B   £15,360

C   £16,080

D   £23,000

Test your understanding answers

Test your understanding 1

Ginevra

Tax adjusted trading profit

	Adjusted profit	Capital allowances (W)	Tax adjusted trading profit
	£	£	£
y/e 5 April 2021	1,595,740	(1,049,440)	546,300
y/e 5 April 2022	1,600,000	(31,439)	1,568,561

Working: Capital allowances computations

		Main pool	Allowances
	£	£	£
y/e 5 April 2021			
Additions:			
Not qualifying for AIA or FYA:			
Car (CO_2 between 51 – 110g/km)		10,000	
Qualifying for AIA:			
Plant and machinery	1,203,000		
AIA	(1,000,000)		1,000,000
		203,000	
		213,000	
WDA (18% × £213,000)		(38,340)	38,340
Additions qualifying for FYA:			
New low emission car ($CO_2 \leq$ 50g/km)	11,100		
FYA (100%)	(11,100)		11,100
		0	
TWDV c/f		174,660	
Total allowances			1,049,440
y/e 5 April 2022			
WDA (18% × £174,660)		(31,439)	31,439
TWDV c/f		143,221	
Total allowances			31,439

Test your understanding 2

Graham

Capital allowances computations

	Main pool £	Allowances £
4 m/e 31 August 2020		
Additions:		
Not qualifying for AIA or FYA:		
Second-hand low emission car	11,500	
Qualifying for AIA:		
Plant and machinery	470,000	
AIA (note)	(333,333)	333,333
	136,667	
	148,167	
WDA (18% × £148,167 × 4/12)	(8,890)	8,890
Additions qualifying for FYA:		
New low emission car ($CO_2 \leq 50g/km$)	16,500	
FYA (100%) (note)	(16,500)	16,500
	0	
TWDV c/f	139,277	
Total allowances		358,723
y/e 31 August 2021		
WDA (18% × £139,277)	(25,070)	25,070
TWDV c/f	114,207	
Total allowances		25,070

Note: The maximum AIA is reduced to £333,333 (£1,000,000 × 4/12) to reflect the 4 month period of account.

The AIA and the WDA are reduced proportionally for the 4 month period. The FYA is never adjusted to reflect the length of the period of account.

Test your understanding 3

Gloria

Capital allowances computations – 30 June 2021

	Main pool	Allowances
	£	£	£
TWDV b/f		21,000	
Additions:			
Not qualifying for AIA or FYA:			
Car (51 – 110g/km)		24,000	
Qualifying for AIA:			
Plant and machinery	184,500		
AIA	(184,500)		184,500
	———	0	
		45,000	
Disposals (lower of cost and sale proceeds)			
Plant		(12,400)	
Van		(600)	
		———	
		32,000	
WDA (18% × £32,000)		(5,760)	5,760
		———	
TWDV c/f		26,240	
		———	
Total allowances			190,260
			———

Test your understanding 4

(a) **Gun-woo**

Capital allowances computations – 30 June 2021

	Main pool	Allowances
	£	£	£
TWDV b/f		11,000	
Additions qualifying for AIA:			
Plant and machinery	23,500		
AIA	(23,500)		23,500
	———	0	
Disposals			
(lower of SP and cost)		(12,100)	
		———	
		(1,100)	
Balancing charge (Note)		1,100	(1,100)
		———	
WDA		0	
Additions qualifying for FYA:			
New low emission car (CO$_2$ ≤ 50g/km)	14,000		
FYA	(14,000)		14,000
	———	0	
		———	———
			36,400
			———

Note: A balancing charge reduces the capital allowances claim in the period.

(b) **If Gun-woo had made no additions in the year**

No AIA or FYA would have been available and therefore a net balancing charge of £1,100 would arise.

This would be added to Gun-woo's tax adjusted trading profits for the year.

Test your understanding 5

Gene

Capital allowances computations

	Main pool £	Allowances £
Y/e 31 March 2020		
TWDV b/f	9,000	
Disposals (lower of cost and sale proceeds)	(320)	
	8,680	
WDA (18% × £8,680)	(1,562)	1,562
TWDV c/f	7,118	
Total allowances		1,562
Period ended 31 December 2020		
Additions:		
Not qualifying for AIA or FYA (Note 1)		
Plant and machinery	4,000	
	11,118	
Disposals (lower of cost and sale proceeds)	(5,400)	
	5,718	
Balancing allowance (Note 2)	(5,718)	5,718
Total allowances		5,718

Notes:

(1) There is no AIA, FYA or WDA available in the final period of account.

(2) A balancing allowance is treated as normal capital allowances, and is deducted from the tax adjusted trading profits.

Test your understanding 6

Glen

Capital allowances computation – y/e 31 December 2020

	Main pool	Allowances
	£	£	£
TWDV b/f		48,100	
Additions:			
Not qualifying for AIA or FYA:			
Car (CO_2 between 51 – 110g/km)		18,600	
Qualifying for AIA:			
Plant and machinery	1,003,300		
AIA	(1,000,000)		1,000,000
	———		
		3,300	
Disposal (lower of cost and SP)		(4,600)	
		———	
		65,400	
WDA (18% × £65,400)		(11,772)	11,772
Additions qualifying for FYA:			
New low emission car ($CO_2 \le$ 50g/km)	13,000		
FYA (100%)	(13,000)		13,000
	———	0	
		———	
TWDV c/f		53,628	
		———	
Total allowances			1,024,772
			———

Test your understanding 7

Georgina

Capital allowances computations – y/e 31 March 2021

	Main pool	Private use car (BU 60%)	Business use	Allowances
	£	£	£	£
TWDV b/f	21,200			
Additions:				
Not qualifying for AIA or FYA:				
Car (CO$_2$ between 51 – 110g/km)	17,000			
Private use car		10,600		
Qualifying for AIA:				
Plant and machinery	6,600			
AIA	(6,600)			6,600
	———	0		
Disposal (lower of cost and SP)	(9,400)			
	———	———		
	28,800	10,600		
WDA (18% × £28,800):	(5,184)			5,184
WDA (18% × £10,600)		(1,908)	× 60%	1,145
Additions: Qualifying for FYA				
New car (CO$_2$ ≤ 50g/km)	11,750			
FYA (100%)	(11,750)			11,750
	———	0		
	———	———		———
TWDV c/f	23,616	8,692		
	———	———		———
Total allowances				24,679
				———

Angelina

Capital allowances computations – 31 May 2021

	Main pool	Special rate pool	Private use Car (BU 80%)	Business use	Allowances
	£	£	£	£	£
TWDV b/f		10,800	16,600		
Additions:					
Not qualifying for AIA or FYA:					
Private use car – high emission				12,600	
Qualifying for AIA:					
Integral features (£40,000 + £70,000)	110,000				
AIA (Note)	(110,000)				110,000
Qualifying for AIA:					
Office furniture	898,800				
AIA (£1,000,000 – £110,000)	(890,000)				890,000
		8,800			
Disposal (lower of cost and SP)	(18,700)				
			16,600	12,600	
	900				
Small pool WDA	(900)				900
WDA (6% × £16,600)			(996)		996
WDA (6% × £12,600)				(756) × 80%	605
TWDV c/f	0	15,604	11,844		
Total allowances					1,002,501

Note: The AIA is allocated to the additions in the special rate pool (WDA 6%) in priority to the additions in the main pool (WDA 18%).

Test your understanding 9

Alysha

Y/e 31 March 2021

	£
Qualifying expenditure	
Factory	244,000

The cost of the land and the planning permission is not eligible for relief.

SBA	£
(£244,000 × 3%) × 11/12	6,710

The allowance is calculated straight line from the date the building is brought into use in the business.

Test your understanding 10

Gordon

Period ended 31 July 2020

	£
Adjusted profit	349,340
Less: Capital allowances (W1)	(252,010)
Tax adjusted trading profit	97,330

(W1) Capital allowances computation – p/e 31 July 2020

	Main pool	Short life asset	Private use car	Business use	Allowances
	£	£	£	£	£
Additions:					
Not qualifying for AIA or FYA:					
Car (CO_2 108g/km) (Note 1)	10,400				
Private use car ($CO_2 > 110$g/km)			15,800		
Qualifying for AIA:					
Equipment	277,875	3,250			
AIA (Max) (Note 2)	(250,000)	(0)			250,000
	———				
	27,875				
	38,275	3,250	15,800		
WDA (18% × 3/12)	(1,722)	(146)			1,868
WDA (6% × 3/12)			(237)	× 60%	142
	———	———	———		
TWDV c/f	36,553	3,104	15,563		
	———	———	———		
Total allowances					252,010
					———

Notes:

(1) Private use by an employee is not relevant. A separate private use asset column is only required where there is private use by the owner of the business.

(2) The AIA is time apportioned for the three month period. The maximum allowance is therefore £250,000 (£1,000,000 × 3/12). The AIA is allocated to the main pool plant and machinery in priority to the short life asset.

Test your understanding 11

The correct answer is D.

D is the correct answer. The car is not eligible for the AIA, but attracts a WDA at 18%, applied proportionally for the short 9 month accounting period and adjusted for private use, as follows:

9 months ended 31 January 2021

	Main pool	Business use (30%)	Allowances
	£		£
Addition – no AIA	12,500		
WDA (18% × 9/12)	(1,688)	× 30%	506

Test your understanding 12

The correct answer is A.

The capital allowances given are as follows:

	Special rate pool £
Y/e 30 June 2021	
TWDV b/f	0
Addition (high emission car)	18,000
WDA at 6%	(1,080)
	————
	16,920
Y/e 30 June 2022	
Disposal proceeds	(17,560)
	————
Balancing charge	(640)
	————

Test your understanding 13

The correct answer is C.

Test your understanding 14

The correct answer is B.

	Main pool £	Special rate pool £	Allowances £
Non-AIA assets – Car (CO_2 > 110g/km)		8,000	
Assets qualifying for AIA	15,000		
AIA	(15,000)		15,000
	————		
	0		
WDA (6% × 9/12)		(360)	360
		————	————
		7,640	15,360
		————	————

Sole traders: Basis of assessment

Chapter learning objectives

Upon completion of this chapter you will be able to:

- recognise the basis of assessment for self-employment income

- compute the assessable profits on commencement and on cessation

- recognise the factors that will influence the choice of accounting date.

One of the PER performance objectives (PO15) is to prepare computations of taxable amounts and tax liabilities according to legal requirements. Working through this chapter should help you understand how to demonstrate that objective.

PER

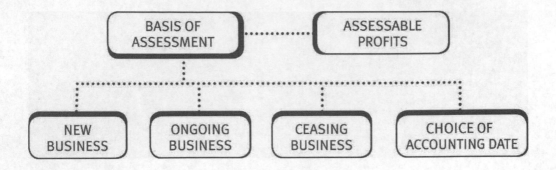

 The rules on how a sole trader is assessed in the opening years are very important and will be taken further in the ATX paper.

1 Introduction

Once the tax adjusted trading profit has been calculated for a period of account, it is important to identify in which tax year it is assessed.

- Income tax is charged for a tax year (also referred to as year of assessment) which runs from 6 April to the following 5 April.

- Since traders do not necessarily prepare their accounts to coincide with the tax year, there needs to be a system for attributing profits earned in a period of account to a particular tax year.

- The following basis of assessment rules apply regardless of whether the business uses the accruals basis or the cash basis for tax purposes.

The profit earning (or loss making) period of account that is attributed to a particular tax year is known as the 'basis period' for that tax year.

In the examination, where the apportionment of tax adjusted trading profits into different tax years is required, the apportionment should be performed on a monthly basis as shown in all the illustrations below.

2 Ongoing year rules

The basic rule is:

The profits for a tax year are the tax adjusted trading profits for the **12 month period of account ending in that tax year**.

This is sometimes referred to as the **current year basis** of assessment (or CYB for short).

Test your understanding 1

A sole trader has been operating for several years and prepares accounts to 31 December each year.

State which profits will be assessed in the 2020/21 tax year.

Test your understanding 2

Jerry prepares accounts to 30 September annually. His recent tax adjusted trading profits have been as follows:

	£
Year to 30 September 2019	20,000
Year to 30 September 2020	22,000

State in which tax years these profits will be assessed.

3 Opening year rules

Assuming a business starts to trade on 1 January 2020 and prepares accounts for calendar years, the first tax year it is trading in is 2019/20.

However, the first period of account will not end until 31 December 2020 and using the principle above this period will not be taxed until the tax year 2020/21.

In order to ensure that there is an assessment for each tax year that a business is trading, the following special provisions apply:

Tax year	Basis of assessment
First tax year (tax year in which trade starts)	From: Date of commencement To: following 5 April ('Actual basis')
Second tax year The period of account ending in the tax year is: (1) 12 months (2) less than 12 months (3) more than 12 months There is no period of account ending in the second tax year	 That period of account (CYB) The first 12 months of trade 12 months to the accounting date ending in the second tax year (i.e. the last 12 months of the long period of account) Actual profits in the second tax year: From: 6 April To: 5 April
Third tax year	12 months to the accounting date ending in the third tax year – normally CYB – if a long period of account = last 12 months of the long period
Fourth tax year onwards	Normal current year basis

Note that whichever scenario applies, from year 2 onwards the basis period will always be exactly 12 months long.

Illustration 1 – Opening year rules

Jenny commenced trading on 1 January 2020 and prepared her first set of accounts to 31 December that year. Her tax adjusted trading profits were £12,000 for the y/e 31 December 2020.

Explain which profits will be assessed in Jenny's first two tax years of trading.

Solution

First tax year – 2019/20

The profits assessed for 2019/20 will be the actual profits falling in the first tax year on a time apportioned basis.

Tax year	Basis period	Calculation	Assessable profits
2019/20	1.1.20 – 5.4.20	(3/12 × £12,000)	£3,000

Second tax year – 2020/21

In the second tax year there is a 12 month period of account ending in the tax year. The current year basis can therefore be applied.

Tax year	Basis period	Assessable profits
2020/21	CYB (y/e 31 December 2020)	£12,000

You will notice that in the two tax years above, the profits for the period 1 January to 5 April (£3,000) have been assessed twice. These are referred to as **overlap profits**.

Overlap profits

- Profits that are assessed in more than one tax year are known as the overlap profits.

- Overlap profits arise in every scenario at commencement of trade other than when the trader has a 31 March or 5 April year end.

- The overlap profits are carried forward and are normally deducted from the assessment for the tax year in which the business ceases.

- Whilst the trader will get relief for overlap profits, relief may not be obtained for many years if the business continues for a long while.

Test your understanding 3

Dimitrios started to trade on 1 September 2019 and prepared his first accounts for the year ended 31 August 2020. His tax adjusted trading profits were £18,000 in that year.

Calculate his assessable profits for the tax years 2019/20 and 2020/21. Identify the months that have been taxed more than once and the overlap profits.

Summary of opening year rules

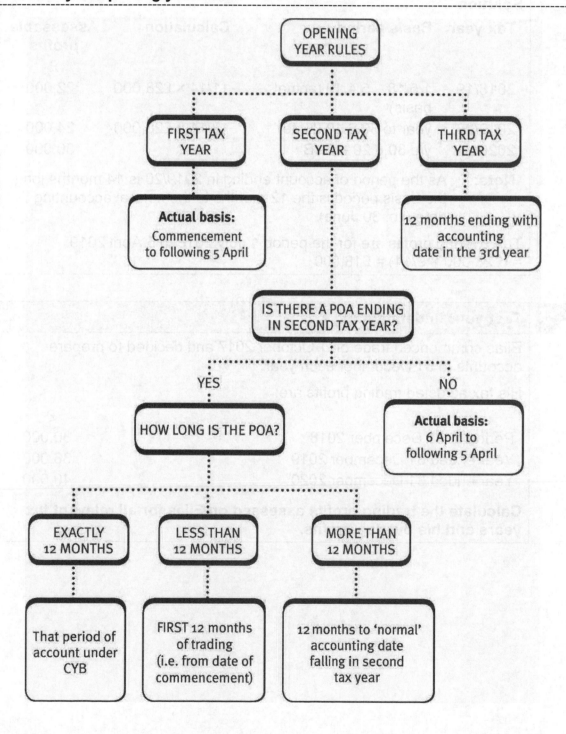

Illustration 2 – Opening year rules

Arthur commenced trading on 1 May 2018. He prepares accounts to 30 June each year. His tax adjusted trading profits were as follows:

Period ended 30 June 2019	£28,000
Year ended 30 June 2020	£30,000

Calculate Arthur's trading profit assessments for his first three tax years and his overlap profits.

Solution

Tax year	Basis period	Calculation	Assessable profits £
2018/19	1.5.18 – 5.4.19 (actual basis)	11/14 × £28,000	22,000
2019/20	year to 30.6.19 (Note)	12/14 × £28,000	24,000
2020/21	y/e 30.6.20 – CYB		30,000

Note: As the period of account ending in 2019/20 is 14 months long, the basis period is the 12 months to the normal accounting date (i.e. 30 June).

The overlap profits are for the period 1 July 2018 to 5 April 2019:
= (£28,000 × 9/14) = £18,000

Test your understanding 4

Elias commenced trade on 1 October 2017 and decided to prepare accounts to 31 December each year.

His tax adjusted trading profits are:

	£
Period to 31 December 2018	30,000
Year ended 31 December 2019	36,000
Year ended 31 December 2020	40,000

Calculate the trading profits assessed on Elias for all relevant tax years and his overlap profits.

Illustration 3 – Opening year rules

Pattie commenced trading on 1 September 2018. She prepared accounts to 30 June 2019 and annually thereafter.

Her tax adjusted trading profits for the first two periods were as follows:

Period ended 30 June 2019	£30,000
Year ended 30 June 2020	£48,000

Calculate Pattie's trading profit assessments for her first three tax years and her overlap profits.

Solution

Tax year	Basis period	Calculation	Assessable profits £
2018/19	1.9.18 – 5.4.19	(£30,000 × 7/10) (actual)	21,000
2019/20	1.9.18 – 31.8.19	£30,000 + (2/12 × £48,000) (Note)	38,000
2020/21	y/e 30.6.20 – CYB		48,000

Note: Because the accounting date ending in the second tax year is less than 12 months after the commencement of trading, the basis of assessment is the first 12 months of trading.

Overlap profits = £29,000:   £21,000 (1.9.18 to 5.4.19) and £8,000 (1.7.19 to 31.8.19: 2/12 × £48,000).

Test your understanding 5

Yassine commenced a new trade on 1 June 2017 and decided that his normal accounting date would be 30 April each year.

Given below are the tax adjusted trading profits since commencement:

Period to 30 April 2018	£11,000
Year ended 30 April 2019	£18,000
Year ended 30 April 2020	£22,000

Calculate the trading profits assessable on Yassine for all relevant tax years and his overlap profits.

Illustration 4 – Opening year rules

Cordelia commenced trading on 1 July 2018. She prepared accounts to 30 April 2020 and annually thereafter. Her tax adjusted trading profits for the first two periods were as follows:

Period ended 30 April 2020	£55,000
Year ended 30 April 2021	£32,000

Calculate Cordelia's trading profit assessments for her first four tax years and her overlap profits.

Solution

Tax year	Basis period	Calculation	Assessable profits £
2018/19	1.7.18 – 5.4.19	£55,000 × 9/22 (actual)	22,500
2019/20	6.4.19 – 5.4.20	£55,000 × 12/22 (Note 1)	30,000
2020/21	y/e 30.4.20	£55,000 × 12/22 (Note 2)	30,000
2021/22	y/e 30.4.21	CYB	32,000

Notes:

(1) Because there is no accounting date ending in the second tax year, the basis of assessment is the actual basis for the tax year from 6.4.19 to 5.4.20.

(2) In tax year three, the basis period is the profits of the 12 months ending with the accounting date in that year.

Overlap profits: £27,500 (1.5.19 to 5.4.20 = 11/22 × £55,000)

Test your understanding 6

Oumou commenced business on 1 January 2017 and prepared her first accounts for the period to 30 June 2018, and thereafter to 30 June in each year.

Her tax adjusted trading profits have been:

Period to 30 June 2018	£27,000
Year ended 30 June 2019	£30,000
Year ended 30 June 2020	£40,000

Calculate the trading profits assessed on Oumou for all relevant tax years and the overlap profits.

4   Closing year rules

- The objective in the final tax year is to ensure that any profits not previously assessed are assessed in that year.

- Any overlap profits from commencement are deducted from the assessment for the final tax year.

- To identify the basis period for the final tax year:

    - Identify the tax year in which the trade ceases. This is the last tax year that profits are assessed.

    - For the immediately preceding tax year, identify the assessment under normal CYB rules.

    - All profits after this period of account will not have been assessed and so fall into the assessment for the final tax year of trade.

    - Remember to deduct overlap profits in this final tax year.

Illustration 5 – Closing year rules

Michael ceased trading on 31 March 2021. His tax adjusted trading profits for the final three periods of trading are as follows:

Year ended 30 April 2019	£40,000
Year ended 30 April 2020	£42,000
Period ended 31 March 2021	£38,000

He has unrelieved overlap profits of £27,000.

Calculate Michael's final two trading profit assessments.

Solution

The final tax year of assessment is 2020/21 i.e. the tax year in which trade ceases.

		£
2019/20	Penultimate year:	
	CYB (Year to 30.4.19)	40,000
2020/21	Final year: all profits not yet assessed	
	(23 months from 1.5.19 – 31.3.21) (£42,000 + £38,000)	80,000
	Less: Overlap profits	(27,000)
	Final assessable amount	53,000

Test your understanding 7

Major, who has been trading for many years, ceased trading on 31 December 2020. Major prepared accounts to 30 June in each year.

The recent tax adjusted trading profits have been:

	£
Period to 31 December 2020	6,000
Year ended 30 June 2020	12,000
Year ended 30 June 2019	15,000
Year ended 30 June 2018	20,000
Year ended 30 June 2017	18,000

The overlap profits on commencement were £7,500.

Calculate the trading profits that will be assessed on Major for all tax years affected by the above accounts.

Test your understanding 8

Luka commenced to trade on 1 July 2015 and prepared his first accounts to 31 August 2016 and thereafter to 31 August annually. Luka ceased to trade on 31 December 2020.

Given below are the tax adjusted trading profits for all the relevant periods:

	£
Period ended 31 August 2016	10,500
Year ended 31 August 2017	18,000
Year ended 31 August 2018	22,500
Year ended 31 August 2019	31,500
Year ended 31 August 2020	27,000
Period ended 31 December 2020	8,400
	117,900

Compute the trading profits that will have been assessed on Luka for each tax year.

5 Choice of accounting date

There are various factors to consider when choosing an accounting date for a business:

- An accounting date of just after, rather than just before, 5 April (such as 30 April) will:

  - Ensure the maximum interval between earning profits and having to pay the related tax liability.

  - However, will result in increased overlap profits upon the commencement of trading. Although there is relief for overlap profits, there may be a long delay before relief is obtained.

  - Makes it easier to implement tax planning measures as there is a longer period over which to plan.

- Alternatively an accounting date of just before 5 April, such as 31 March, will:

  - Give the shortest interval between earning profits and having to pay the related tax liability.

  - However, there will be no overlap profits.

  - The shortest interval to implement tax planning measures.

6 Chapter summary

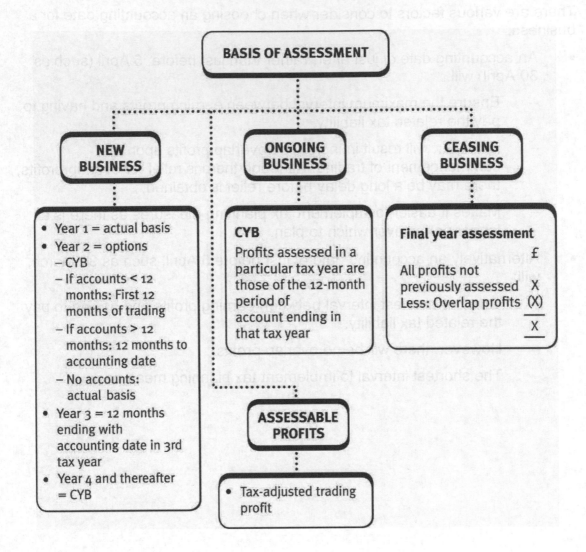

BASIS OF ASSESSMENT

NEW BUSINESS

- Year 1 = actual basis
- Year 2 = options
  - CYB
  - If accounts < 12 months: First 12 months of trading
  - If accounts > 12 months: 12 months to accounting date
  - No accounts: actual basis
- Year 3 = 12 months ending with accounting date in 3rd tax year
- Year 4 and thereafter = CYB

ONGOING BUSINESS

CYB
Profits assessed in a particular tax year are those of the 12-month period of account ending in that tax year

ASSESSABLE PROFITS

- Tax-adjusted trading profit

CEASING BUSINESS

Final year assessment

	£
All profits not previously assessed	X
Less: Overlap profits	(X)
	X

7 Practice objective test questions

Test your understanding 9

Robert has been a sole trader for many years preparing his accounts to 31 August each year. He ceased to trade on 31 January 2021. Robert's most recent adjusted profits for tax purposes have been:

Year ended 31 August 2019	£19,200
Year ended 31 August 2020	£16,800
5 months ended 31 January 2021	£8,400

He has overlap profits brought forward from commencement of trade amounting to £4,800.

What is Robert's taxable trading profit figure for the tax year 2020/21?

A   £25,200

B   £20,400

C   £16,800

D   £3,600

Test your understanding 10

Hardeep started to trade on 1 June 2021. His tax adjusted profits for the year ended 31 May 2022 are £50,000.

What is Hardeep's taxable trading profit for the tax year 2021/22?

A   £37,500

B   £41,667

C   £50,000

D   £45,833

Test your understanding 11

Xosé commenced trading on 1 February 2021 and prepared his first set of accounts to 30 June 2022.

The period for which his profits are assessed for the second tax year of trading is:

A   1 February 2021 to 5 April 2021

B   1 February 2021 to 31 January 2022

C   6 April 2021 to 5 April 2022

D   12 months ended 30 June 2022

Test your understanding 12

Richard has been a sole trader for many years preparing his accounts to 31 July each year. He ceased to trade on 31 December 2020.

Richard's most recent adjusted profits for tax purposes have been:

Year to 31 July 2019	£16,000
Year to 31 July 2020	£14,000
5 months to 31 December 2020	£7,000

He has unused overlap profits for earlier years amounting to £4,000.

What is Richard's tax adjusted trading profit figure for the tax year 2020/21?

A   £17,000

B   £14,000

C   £21,000

D   £3,000

Test your understanding 13

Cherry commenced business as a sole trader on 1 December 2019 and prepared her first set of accounts for the period ended 31 January 2021.

In the 14-month period ended 31 January 2021 her tax adjusted trading profit was £21,000.

Her second set of accounts will be for the year ended 31 January 2022 when the tax adjusted trading profits are expected to be £24,000.

What is Cherry's tax adjusted trading profit assessment for the tax year 2020/21?

A   £21,000

B   £18,000

C   £18,500

D   £24,000

Test your understanding 14

David commenced trading as a sole trader on 1 October 2019 and prepared accounts to 30 April each year.

David's results for his first two periods of account are as follows:

	£
Period to 30 April 2020	10,500
Year ended 30 April 2021	36,000

What is David's tax adjusted trading profit assessment for the tax year 2020/21?

A   £25,500

B   £9,000

C   £36,000

D   £28,500

Test your understanding answers

Test your understanding 1

Ongoing years

Assessable profits for the 2020/21 tax year will be based on the tax adjusted trading profits for the accounting year to 31 December 2020.

Test your understanding 2

Jerry

Tax year	Basis period	Assessable profits £
2019/20	Year to 30.9.19	20,000
2020/21	Year to 30.9.20	22,000

Test your understanding 3

Dimitrios

Tax year	Basis period	Assessable profits £
2019/20	1.9.19 – 5.4.20: Actual (£18,000 × 7/12)	10,500
2020/21	y/e 31 August 2020: CYB	18,000

The profits between 1 September 2019 and 5 April 2020 (7 months) are taxed in both tax years.

Overlap profits are therefore £10,500 (7/12 × £18,000).

Test your understanding 4

Elias

Tax year	Basis period	Assessable profits £
2017/18	1.10.17 – 5.4.18: Actual (6/15 × £30,000)	12,000
2018/19	1.1.18 – 31.12.18: 12 months ending on accounting date (12/15 × £30,000)	24,000
2019/20	y/e 31.12.19: CYB	36,000
2020/21	y/e 31.12.20: CYB	40,000

Overlap profits: 1.1.18 to 5.4.18 = (3/15 × £30,000) = £6,000

Test your understanding 5

Yassine

Tax year	Basis period	Assessable profits £
2017/18	1.6.17 – 5.4.18: Actual (10/11 × £11,000)	10,000
2018/19	1.6.17 – 31.5.18: First 12 months £11,000 + (1/12 × £18,000)	12,500
2019/20	y/e 30.4.19: CYB	18,000
2020/21	y/e 30.4.20: CYB	22,000

As the period of account ending in the second tax year is less than 12 months long, the basis period is the first 12 months of trading.

Overlap profits = £11,500

i.e. 1.6.17 to 5.4.18 (£10,000) and 1.5.18 to 31.5.18 (1/12 × £18,000).

Test your understanding 6

Oumou

Tax year	Basis period	Assessable profits £
2016/17	1.1.17 – 5.4.17: Actual (3/18 × £27,000)	4,500
2017/18	6.4.17 – 5.4.18: Actual (12/18 × £27,000) (Note)	18,000
2018/19	1.7.17 – 30.6.18: 12m to the accounting date (12/18 × £27,000)	18,000
2019/20	y/e 30.6.19: CYB	30,000
2020/21	y/e 30.6.20: CYB	40,000

Note: There is no period of account ending in the second tax year. The profits are therefore assessed on the actual basis.

Overlap profits: 1.7.17 – 5.4.18 = (9/18 × £27,000) = £13,500

Test your understanding 7

Major

Tax year	Basis period	Assessable profits £
2017/18	y/e 30.6.17: CYB	18,000
2018/19	y/e 30.6.18: CYB	20,000
2019/20	y/e 30.6.19: CYB	15,000
2020/21	1.7.19 – 31.12.20: Final – anything not yet taxed (£12,000 + £6,000 – £7,500)	10,500

The final tax year of assessment is the tax year 2020/21, the year in which trade ceases.

Test your understanding 8

Luka

Tax year	Basis period	Assessable profits £
2015/16	1.7.15 – 5.4.16: Actual (9/14 × £10,500)	6,750
2016/17	1.9.15 – 31.8.16: 12m to accounting date (12/14 × £10,500)	9,000
2017/18	y/e 31.8.17: CYB	18,000
2018/19	y/e 31.8.18: CYB	22,500
2019/20	y/e 31.8.19: CYB	31,500
2020/21	1.9.19 – 31.12.20: Final – anything not yet taxed (£27,000 + £8,400 – £5,250)	30,150
		117,900

Overlap profits: 1.9.15 to 5.4.16 = (7/14 × £10,500) = £5,250

Note that over the life of the business the total profits of £117,900 have been assessed to tax.

Test your understanding 9

The correct answer is B.

B is the correct answer because the business has ceased in the tax year 2020/21 and therefore the basis period is from the end of the basis period for the previous tax year until the date of cessation (i.e. the entire period not yet taxed).

The profits assessed in the tax year 2019/20 were the year ended 31 August 2019.

The profits assessable in the period to cessation are then reduced by overlap profits.

(£16,800 + £8,400) – £4,800 = £20,400

Test your understanding 10

The correct answer is B.

The profit assessed in the first tax year 2021/22 is the profit arising from 1 June 2021 to 5 April 2022 (i.e. 10/12 of £50,000).

Test your understanding 11

The correct answer is C.

C is the correct answer because Xosé commenced trading in the tax year 2020/21, the assessment for which is based on the profits for the period 1 February 2021 to 5 April 2021.

In the second tax year, 2021/22, there is no set of accounts ending in that year, and therefore Xosé is assessed on the basis of profits arising between 6 April 2021 and 5 April 2022.

The first set of accounts ends on 30 June 2022 which falls in the tax year 2022/23.

Test your understanding 12

The correct answer is A.

The business ceased in the tax year 2020/21 and therefore the basis period is the entire period covered by everything earned since the tax year 2019/20 assessment of £16,000. This amount is reduced by the unused overlap profit.

(£14,000 + £7,000) – £4,000   £17,000

Test your understanding 13

The correct answer is B.

2020/21 is the second tax year of Cherry's business. The accounting period ending in this tax year is longer than 12 months and the basis period is therefore the 12 months to the accounting date i.e. 12 months to 31 January 2021. Therefore (12/14 × £21,000) = £18,000.

Test your understanding 14

The correct answer is A.

2020/21 is the second tax year of trading.

Tax year	Basis of assessment	£
2020/21	First 12 months of trading (as the period of account ending in the tax year 2020/21 is less than 12 months long) (1 October 2019 – 30 September 2020) £10,500 + (£36,000 × 5/12)	25,500

Partnerships

Chapter learning objectives

Upon completion of this chapter you will be able to:

- explain and compute how a partnership is assessed to tax

- explain and compute the assessable profits for each partner following a change in the profit sharing ratio

- explain and compute the assessable profits for each partner following a change in the membership of the partnership.

PER

One of the PER performance objectives (PO15) is to prepare computations of taxable amounts and tax liabilities according to legal requirements. Working through this chapter should help you understand how to demonstrate that objective.

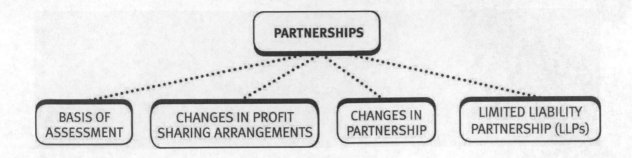

In Financial Accounting you learned how to account for partnerships. This chapter builds directly on that knowledge and focuses on the tax consequences of carrying on business in partnership with others. Many of the underlying principles in terms of the way profits are shared between the partners for accounts purposes also apply when it comes to tax.

1 Introduction

Definition

- A partnership is a body of persons carrying on business together with a view to profit.

Basis of assessment

- Each partner is taxed individually, despite the partnership being a single trading entity.

- Each partner is assessed on his share of the partnership profits as if he were a sole trader.

- To determine a partner's assessable profits:

  - firstly, the trading profits per the partnership accounts are adjusted for tax purposes as for a sole trader (see Chapter 7).

  - secondly, the tax adjusted trading profits of the partnership are allocated to the individual partners.

  - finally, the basis of assessment rules are applied to determine each partner's assessable profits in a tax year (see Chapter 9).

2 The allocation of profits and losses

The computation of partnership profits and losses

- The principles of computation of a partnership's tax adjusted trading profits are the same as those for a sole trader.

- Partners' salaries and interest on capital are not deductible expenses in the adjustment of profits computation, since these are merely an allocation of profit.

Note that the cash basis option and flat rate expenses are available to partnerships in the same way as sole traders. However, these topics will not be examined in relation to partnerships.

The allocation of the profit or loss

- The tax adjusted trading profit or loss is allocated (divided) between the partners according to their profit sharing arrangements for that period of account.

- Partners may be entitled to salaries (a fixed allocation of profit) and interest on capital.

- The balance of profits remaining after the allocation of any salaries or interest is allocated in the profit sharing ratio (PSR).

- Whether it is described as salary, interest on capital or profit share, the total allocated to a partner is assessable as trading profit.

Illustration 1 – The allocation of profits and losses

Phil and Dan have been in partnership for a number of years. The partnership agreement provides that each should take a salary of £25,000, 5% interest on capital balances at the start of the accounting period and then split the profit remaining 60:40 in Phil's favour.

Calculate the trading income assessable for each partner for the tax year 2020/21, if the tax adjusted trading profits for the year ended 30 September 2020, were £74,000.

Their respective capital balances at 1 October 2019, were

Phil	£75,000
Dan	£60,000

Solution

Year ended 30 September 2020	Total £	Phil £	Dan £
Salary	50,000	25,000	25,000
Interest on capital (£75,000/£60,000 × 5%)	6,750	3,750	3,000
	56,750	28,750	28,000
Balance (£74,000 – £56,750) (60:40)	17,250	10,350	6,900
Total allocation of partnership profits	74,000	39,100	34,900

The allocated profit represents each partner's share of the profits for this period of account.

Each partner's allocated share of the profit is then assessed to tax on the individual partners as trading profit using the basis of assessment rules for a sole trader.

Trading profit assessment – 2020/21

(CYB = Year ended 30 September 2020)

Phil	£39,100
Dan	£34,900

Test your understanding 1

Paul and Art have been in partnership for many years preparing accounts to 31 December each year.

The partnership agreement provides Paul with a salary of £3,000 and Art is entitled to 15% interest on his capital balance at the start of the period. His capital balance was £27,000 on 1 January 2020. Paul and Art agreed to split any remaining profits equally.

Calculate the trading income assessments for each partner for the tax year 2020/21, if in the year ended 31 December 2020, the tax adjusted trading profits were £30,000.

Partnership capital allowances

Capital allowances are calculated in the same way as for a sole trader.

- Capital allowances are deducted as an expense in calculating the tax adjusted trading profit or loss of the partnership. The profit allocated between the partners is therefore after deducting capital allowances.

- Individual partners cannot claim capital allowances on their own behalf.

- If assets are owned privately (such as motor cars):

    - The total cost of such assets are included in the partnership's capital allowances computation.

    - The maximum capital allowances available is calculated in the normal way.

    - The amount actually claimed is the business use proportion.

    - The capital allowances claimed are deducted as an expense prior to allocating the profit to each partner.

3 Changes in the profit sharing ratio

The profit sharing ratio may change for a number of reasons.

- The existing partners may decide to allocate profits in a different way. This may be as a result of a change in duties, seniority or simply by agreement of the parties concerned.

- The membership of a partnership may change as the result of the admission, death or retirement of a partner.

- Provided that there is at least one partner common to the business before and after the change, the partnership will automatically continue.

- Where there is a change in membership, the commencement or cessation basis of assessment rules apply to the individual partner who is joining or leaving the partnership only.

4 The effect of a change in the profit sharing ratio

If a partnership changes its basis of profit sharing during a period of account, then the period is split, with a different allocation of profits in the different parts.

Illustration 2 – The effect of a change in the profit sharing ratio

Rosalie and Logan are in partnership. Their tax adjusted trading profit for the year ended 30 September 2020, was £16,500.

Up to 30 June 2020, profits were shared between Rosalie and Logan 3:2, after paying annual salaries of £3,000 and £2,000 respectively.

From 1 July 2020, profits are shared between Rosalie and Logan 2:1, after paying annual salaries of £6,000 and £4,000 respectively.

Show the trading profit assessments for Rosalie and Logan for the tax year 2020/21.

Solution

	Total £	Rosalie £	Logan £
1.10.19 – 30.6.20			
Salaries (9/12)	3,750	2,250	1,500
Balance (3:2)	8,625	5,175	3,450
(Profits £16,500 × 9/12 = £12,375)	12,375		
1.7.20 – 30.9.20			
Salaries (3/12)	2,500	1,500	1,000
Balance (2:1)	1,625	1,083	542
(Profits £16,500 × 3/12 = £4,125)	4,125		
Total allocation of partnership profits	16,500	10,008	6,492

Trading income assessments – 2020/21

(CYB = Year ended 30 September 2020):

Rosalie	£10,008
Logan	£6,492

Test your understanding 2

John and Major have been in partnership for many years preparing accounts to 31 December.

Their original profit sharing arrangement provides for salaries of £4,500 and £3,000 p.a. for John and Major respectively and the balance in the ratio of 3:2 in John's favour.

From 1 July 2020, John received a salary of £9,000 p.a. and Major a salary of £6,000 p.a., with the balance shared in the ratio 2:1 in John's favour.

The recent tax adjusted trading profits for the accounting year ended 31 December 2020, are £24,800.

Show the division of profits for the year ended 31 December 2020 and the trading income assessments for each partner for the tax year 2020/21.

5 Commencement and cessation

Changes in membership

- The normal opening year and closing year basis of assessment rules apply upon commencement and cessation of a partnership.

- A change in the membership of the partnership will normally affect only the partner joining or leaving. The continuing partners are assessed on a CYB basis.

Commencement – New partner

The steps taken are:

- Identify the start date of the new partner.

- Allocate the profits between the old and new partner(s):
  - If the new start date is part way through the period of account, the allocation of profits is split between the two periods concerned.
  - If the new partner joins at the start of a new period of account, profits in the period are allocated throughout using the new PSR.

- Determine the assessable trading profits for the tax year:
  - For those partners common to the old and new partnership, there is no change in the method of calculating their assessable trading income and the normal CYB approach applies.
  - The partner joining must apply the opening year rules, as for the sole trader in Chapter 9. A partner is treated as commencing when he or she joins the partnership.
  - Each partner has his or her own overlap profits, available for overlap relief.

Illustration 3 – Commencement and cessation

Alex, Arsene and Jose have been in partnership for a number of years. Their recent results have been as follows:

	£
Year ended 30 September 2019	103,500
Year ended 30 September 2020	128,000

The relationship is often fractious and there have been a number of disputes over the years. In an attempt to improve the dynamics, on 1 January 2020, Rafa was admitted to the partnership.

Profits had been shared equally, after allocating salaries and interest on capital, prior to the admission of Rafa, as follows:

Partner	Salary £	Capital balance £	Interest on capital
Alex	15,000	100,000	5%
Arsene	12,000	80,000	5%
Jose	10,000	40,000	5%

Rafa's admission changed the profit sharing arrangements as follows:

Partner	Salary £	Capital balance £	Interest on capital	Profit share
Alex	20,000	100,000	5%	35%
Arsene	18,000	80,000	5%	30%
Jose	15,000	40,000	5%	25%
Rafa	10,000	0	n/a	10%

The projected result for the year ended 30 September 2021, is a tax adjusted profit of £140,000.

Calculate the assessable trading profit for each of the partners for the tax years 2019/20 to 2021/22.

Solution

Step 1: Allocate the tax adjusted trading profits for each period of account between the partners.

	Total £	Alex £	Arsene £	Jose £	Rafa £
Y/e 30.9.19					
Salary	37,000	15,000	12,000	10,000	
Interest at 5% on capital	11,000	5,000	4,000	2,000	
PSR	55,500	18,500	18,500	18,500	
Total	**103,500**	**38,500**	**34,500**	**30,500**	
Y/e 30.9.20					
1.10.19 – 31.12.19					
Salary (3/12)	9,250	3,750	3,000	2,500	
Interest at 5% (× 3/12)	2,750	1,250	1,000	500	
PSR	20,000	6,667	6,667	6,666	
(Profits £128,000 × 3/12 = £32,000)	32,000				
1.1.20 – 30.9.20					
Salary (9/12)	47,250	15,000	13,500	11,250	7,500
Interest at 5% (× 9/12)	8,250	3,750	3,000	1,500	0
PSR (35:30:25:10)	40,500	14,175	12,150	10,125	4,050
(Profits £128,000 × 9/12 = £96,000)	96,000				
Total	**128,000**	**44,592**	**39,317**	**32,541**	**11,550**
Y/e 30.9.21					
Salary	63,000	20,000	18,000	15,000	10,000
Interest at 5% on capital	11,000	5,000	4,000	2,000	0
PSR (35:30:25:10)	66,000	23,100	19,800	16,500	6,600
Total	**140,000**	**48,100**	**41,800**	**33,500**	**16,600**

Step 2: Compute each partner's assessable trading profits.

Alex, Arsene and Jose: are assessed on a CYB for each tax year.

Tax year	Basis period	Alex £	Arsene £	Jose £
2019/20	year ended 30.9.19	38,500	34,500	30,500
2020/21	year ended 30.9.20	44,592	39,317	32,541
2021/22	year ended 30.9.21	48,100	41,800	33,500

Rafa: is treated as commencing on 1 January 2020.

Tax year	Basis period	Assessable profits £
2019/20	1 January 2020 to 5 April 2020 (£11,550 × 3/9)	3,850
2020/21	First 12 months (£11,550 + (£16,600 × 3/12))	15,700
2021/22	Year ended 30 September 2021	16,600

He will carry forward overlap profits of £8,000 (£3,850 + £4,150).

Note: This question tests knowledge of a wide range of issues in relation to partnerships. It is very unlikely that such a wide range of issues would be tested in a single question in the examination.

Test your understanding 3

Able and Bertie have been in partnership since 1 July 2018 preparing accounts to 30 June each year. On 1 July 2020, Carol joined the partnership. Profits are shared equally.

The partnership's tax adjusted trading profits are as follows:

	£
Year ended 30 June 2019	10,000
Year ended 30 June 2020	13,500
Year ended 30 June 2021	18,000

Show the amounts assessed on the individual partners for the tax years 2018/19 to 2021/22.

Cessation – Partner leaving

The steps taken are:

- Identify the partner ceasing to be a member.

- Allocate the profits, remembering that if this is part way through the period of account it will affect the profit sharing ratio for that period of account and this will need to be calculated in two parts.

- For the partners continuing, use the normal CYB basis of assessment to determine the profits assessable for the tax year.

- For the partner ceasing, use the closing year rules and deduct any overlap profits he or she has available.

Illustration 4 – Commencement and cessation

Ball, Sphere, Globe and Bauble have been in partnership for a number of years, preparing accounts to 30 September each year.

The profit sharing arrangements have been as follows:

Partner	Annual salary £	Capital balance £	Interest on capital	Profit share
Ball	20,000	100,000	5%	35%
Sphere	18,000	80,000	5%	30%
Globe	15,000	40,000	5%	25%
Bauble	10,000	0	n/a	10%

Ball has decided to resign as a partner at the end of March 2021.

The existing salary and interest arrangements will remain in place, but the balance of the profit will then be split equally between the three remaining partners.

Profits for the year end 30 September 2020 and 2021 are expected to be £180,000 and £210,000 respectively.

Calculate the assessable trading profits of each partner for the tax years 2020/21 and 2021/22. Ball informs you he had £15,000 of overlap profits from commencement.

Solution

Allocation of profits

	Total £	Ball £	Sphere £	Globe £	Bauble £
Y/e 30.9.20					
Salary	63,000	20,000	18,000	15,000	10,000
Interest at 5% on capital	11,000	5,000	4,000	2,000	0
PSR (35:30:25:10)	106,000	37,100	31,800	26,500	10,600
Total	**180,000**	**62,100**	**53,800**	**43,500**	**20,600**
Y/e 30.9.21					
1.10.20 – 31.3.21					
Salary (6/12)	31,500	10,000	9,000	7,500	5,000
Interest at 5% (× 6/12)	5,500	2,500	2,000	1,000	0
PSR (35:30:25:10)	68,000	23,800	20,400	17,000	6,800
(Profits £210,000 × 6/12 = £105,000)	105,000				
1.4.21 – 30.9.21					
Salary (6/12)	21,500	0	9,000	7,500	5,000
Interest at 5% (6/12)	3,000	0	2,000	1,000	0
PSR (1:1:1)	80,500	0	26,834	26,833	26,833
(Profits £210,000 × 6/12 = £105,000)	105,000				
Total	**210,000**	**36,300**	**69,234**	**60,833**	**43,633**

Assessable trading profit

Sphere, Globe and Bauble will continue to be assessed on CYB:

Tax year	Basis period	Sphere £	Globe £	Bauble £
2020/21	year ended 30.9.20	53,800	43,500	20,600
2021/22	year ended 30.9.21	69,234	60,833	43,633

Ball will be treated as ceasing to trade on 31 March 2021 as follows:

Tax year	Basis period	Assessable profits £
2020/21	Year ended 30 September 2020	62,100
	Period ended 31 March 2021	36,300
		98,400
	Less: Overlap profits	(15,000)
	Assessable trading profit	83,400

Test your understanding 4

Continuing the TYU 3 above with Able, Bertie and Carol.

After suffering a period of ill health, Bertie plans to retire on 31 December 2021.

Profits for year ended 30 June 2022, are expected to be £24,000.

The profit sharing ratio will remain unchanged until Bertie retires. Thereafter it will be split 65:35 in Able's favour.

Calculate Bertie's revised trading income assessment for the tax year 2021/22 as a result of his retirement and Able and Carol's assessable trading income for the tax year 2022/23.

6 Limited liability partnerships (LLP)

An LLP is a special type of partnership where the amount that each partner contributes towards the partnership losses, debts and liabilities is limited by agreement.

The taxation implications of an LLP are as follows:

- It is generally taxed in the same way as all other partnerships.

- At TX, normal loss reliefs are available (see Chapter 11).

Note that the rules which may restrict the use of trading losses by LLPs are not examinable.

7 Chapter summary

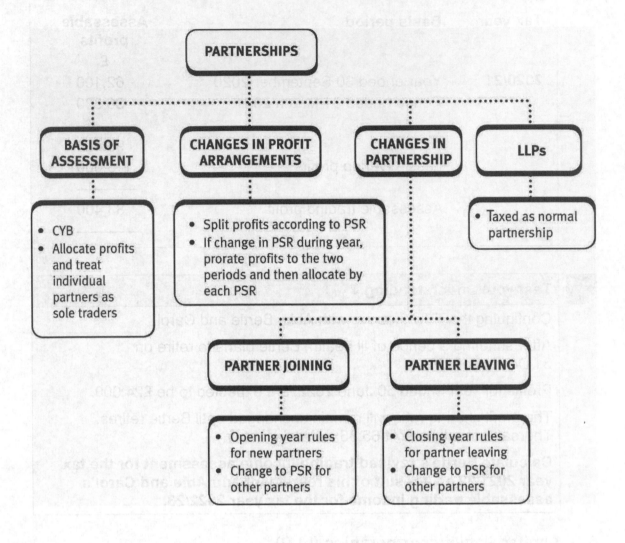

PARTNERSHIPS

BASIS OF ASSESSMENT
- CYB
- Allocate profits and treat individual partners as sole traders

CHANGES IN PROFIT ARRANGEMENTS
- Split profits according to PSR
- If change in PSR during year, prorate profits to the two periods and then allocate by each PSR

CHANGES IN PARTNERSHIP

LLPs
- Taxed as normal partnership

PARTNER JOINING
- Opening year rules for new partners
- Change to PSR for other partners

PARTNER LEAVING
- Closing year rules for partner leaving
- Change to PSR for other partners

8 Practice objective test questions

Test your understanding 5

Desmond and Elijah started trading on 6 April 2020. They agreed to split the profits equally.

Fatima joined the partnership on 6 January 2021, at which point the profit sharing arrangement was changed and Desmond, Elijah and Fatima agreed to share profits in the ratio 3:2:1.

The partnership made a tax adjusted trading profit for the year ended 5 April 2021 of £72,000.

What is Fatima's trading income assessment for the tax year 2020/21?

A   £18,000

B   £12,000

C   £6,000

D   £3,000

Test your understanding 6

Alan, Bob and Caroline have been in partnership since 1 April 2017. The partnership draws up accounts to 31 December each year.

On 1 November 2020, Alan retired from the partnership and the profit sharing arrangements were changed from that date onwards.

Which of the following statements is correct?

A   The partnership is deemed to cease on Alan's retirement and the partners will operate closing year rules to calculate their trading income assessments for the final tax year

B   The final tax year of trading for Alan, Bob and Caroline will be 2020/21

C   Bob and Caroline will have to operate the opening year rules to calculate their trading income assessments for the tax year 2020/21

D   Alan will operate the closing year rules in order to calculate his trading income assessment for the tax year 2020/21

Test your understanding 7

Chloe and Andrea are in partnership sharing profits 3:2 respectively after a salary of £15,000 per year to Andrea.

On 1 January 2021 the partners agree to share profits equally in the future with no salaries.

The tax adjusted trading profit for the year ended 30 June 2021 is £92,000.

What is Andrea's share of the profits for the year ended 30 June 2021?

A   £46,000

B   £41,400

C   £45,900

D   £50,400

Test your understanding 8

Sakeena and Bismah started trading on 1 June 2020. They agreed to split the profits evenly.

Bilal joined the partnership on 1 January 2021, at which point the profit sharing agreement was changed and Sakeena, Bismah and Bilal agreed to share profits in the ratio 4:1:1.

The partnership made a tax adjusted trading profit for the year ended 31 May 2021 of £60,000.

What is Bilal's tax adjusted trading profit assessment for the tax year 2020/21?

A   £2,500

B   £4,167

C   £10,000

D   £5,000

Test your understanding answers

Test your understanding 1

Paul and Art

Year ended 31 December 2020	Total £	Paul £	Art £
Salary	3,000	3,000	
Interest on capital (£27,000 × 15%)	4,050		4,050
	7,050		
Balance (£30,000 – £7,050) (50:50)	22,950	11,475	11,475
Allocation of partnership profits	30,000	14,475	15,525

Trading profit assessment for 2020/21

(CYB, Year ended 31 December 2020)

Paul	£14,475
Art	£15,525

Test your understanding 2

John and Major

	Total £	John £	Major £
1.1.20 – 30.6.20			
Salaries (6/12)	3,750	2,250	1,500
Balance (3:2)	8,650	5,190	3,460
(Profits £24,800 × 6/12 = £12,400)	12,400		
1.7.20 – 31.12.20			
Salaries (6/12)	7,500	4,500	3,000
Balance (2:1)	4,900	3,267	1,633
(Profits £24,800 × 6/12 = £12,400)	12,400		
Total allocation of partnership profits	24,800	15,207	9,593

Trading income assessments for the tax year 2020/21

(CYB Year ended 31 December 2020):

John	£15,207
Major	£9,593

Test your understanding 3

Able and Bertie

Step 1: Allocation of the tax adjusted trading profits.

	Total £	Able £	Bertie £	Carol £
Y/e 30.6.19	10,000	5,000	5,000	
Y/e 30.6.20	13,500	6,750	6,750	
Y/e 30.6.21	18,000	6,000	6,000	6,000

Step 2: Compute each partner's assessable trading profits.

Able and Bertie are both assessed as follows, based upon a commencement on 1 July 2018:

Tax year	Basis period	Assessable profits £
2018/19	1 July 2018 to 5 April 2019 (£5,000 × 9/12)	3,750
2019/20	Year ended 30 June 2019	5,000
2020/21	Year ended 30 June 2020	6,750
2021/22	Year ended 30 June 2021	6,000

They will each carry forward overlap profits of £3,750 in respect of the period 1 July 2018 to 5 April 2019.

Carol is treated as commencing on 1 July 2020, and is assessed on her share of the partnership profits as follows:

Tax year	Basis period	Assessable profits £
2020/21	1 July 2020 to 5 April 2021 (£6,000 × 9/12)	4,500
2021/22	Year ended 30 June 2021	6,000

She will carry forward overlap profits of £4,500 in respect of the period 1 July 2020 to 5 April 2021.

Test your understanding 4

Able, Bertie and Carol

Allocation of profits:

	Total £	Able £	Bertie £	Carol £
Y/e 30 June 2022				
1.7.21 – 31.12.21				
£24,000 × 6/12				
(1/3:1/3:1/3)	12,000	4,000	4,000	4,000
1.1.22 – 30.6.22				
£24,000 × 6/12 (65:35)	12,000	7,800	0	4,200
Total	24,000	11,800	4,000	8,200

Assessable trading profit:

Able and Carol will both be assessed on the current year basis:

Tax year	Basis period	Able £	Carol £
2022/23	Year ended 30 June 2022	11,800	8,200

Bertie will be treated as ceasing to trade on 31 December 2021. His final tax year of trade is 2021/22.

Tax year	Basis period	Assessable profits £
2021/22	Year ended 30 June 2021 (see TYU 3)	6,000
	Period ended 31 December 2021	4,000
		10,000
	Less: Overlap profits (see TYU 3)	(3,750)
	Assessable trading profit	6,250

Test your understanding 5

The correct answer is D.

	Total £	Desmond £	Elijah £	Fatima £
6 April 2020 – 5 January 2021 £72,000 × 9/12 – split evenly	54,000	27,000	27,000	
6 January 2021 – 5 April 2021 £72,000 × 3/12 – split 3:2:1	18,000	9,000	6,000	3,000

Fatima's trading income assessment for 2020/21 (her first tax year of trade) will be on the actual basis (i.e. 6 January 2021 to 5 April 2021) and is therefore £3,000.

Test your understanding 6

The correct answer is D.

D is the correct answer because the partnership continues despite Alan's resignation. Only Alan has to use the closing rules to calculate his trading income assessment for the tax year 2020/21, i.e. his final year.

Test your understanding 7

The correct answer is C.

	Total £	Chloe £	Andrea £
1 July 2020 to 31 December 2020 (profits £92,000 × 6/12 = £46,000)			
Salaries (6/12)	7,500	0	7,500
Balance (3:2)	38,500	23,100	15,400
	46,000	23,100	22,900
1 January 2021 to 30 June 2021 (profit £92,000 × 6/12 = £46,000)			
Balance (equal shares)	46,000	23,000	23,000
	92,000	46,100	45,900

KAPLAN PUBLISHING

Test your understanding 8

The correct answer is A.

Profit attributable to the period after Bilal joins the partnership (i.e. 5 months from 1 January 2021 to 31 May 2021):

($£60,000 \times 5/12$) = 25,000 × Bilal's partnership share (1/6) = £4,167

The assessment for 2020/21 (the first tax year of trading) is calculated using the actual basis (i.e. 1 January 2021 to 5 April 2021). Bilal's trading profit assessment for 2020/21 is therefore £2,500 (3/5 × £4,167).

Trading losses for individuals

Chapter learning objectives

Upon completion of this chapter you will be able to:

- understand how trading losses can be carried forward

- understand how trading losses can be claimed against total income and chargeable gains and the restriction that can apply

- explain and compute the relief for trading losses in the early years of a trade

- explain and compute terminal loss relief

- recognise the factors that will influence the choice of loss relief claim

- describe the alternative loss relief claims that are available to partners.

PER

One of the PER performance objectives (PO15) is to prepare computations of taxable amounts and tax liabilities according to legal requirements. Another objective (PO17) is to advise on mitigating and deferring liabilities through legitimate tax planning measures. Working through this chapter should help you understand how to demonstrate those objectives.

Sole traders may not always be profitable. In Financial Accounting and Financial Reporting you learn how to account for losses. In this chapter we explore the tax reliefs that are available to individuals for the trading losses they incur.

1 Introduction

Identifying a trading loss

A trading loss arises when the normal tax adjusted trading profit computation gives a negative result.

A trading loss can occur in two situations, as follows:

	£	£
Tax adjusted trading profit/(loss) before capital allowances	X	(X)
Less: Capital allowances	(X)	(X)
Trading loss	(X)	(X)

Note that capital allowances:

- are taken into account in calculating the amount of the trading loss available for relief, and

- can increase a tax adjusted trading loss, and

- can turn a tax adjusted trading profit into a trading loss.

Where a trading loss occurs:

- the individual's trading income assessment is £Nil

- a number of loss relief options are available to obtain relief for the loss.

Tax year of loss

The tax year of the loss is the tax year in which the loss making period ends.

For example: a loss for the year ended 31 December 2020 arises in the tax year 2020/21. Therefore, the tax year of the loss is 2020/21.

Loss relief options

The main reliefs available for a trading loss are as follows:

- Carry forward against future trading profits (section 3)
- Relief against total income (section 4)
- Opening year loss relief against total income (section 6)
- Terminal loss relief against previous trading profits (section 7).

2 Loss relief options in ongoing years

If an individual makes a trading loss in the ongoing years of a business, he or she initially has to decide whether to claim relief against total income or carry forward all of the loss.

The choices can be summarised as follows:

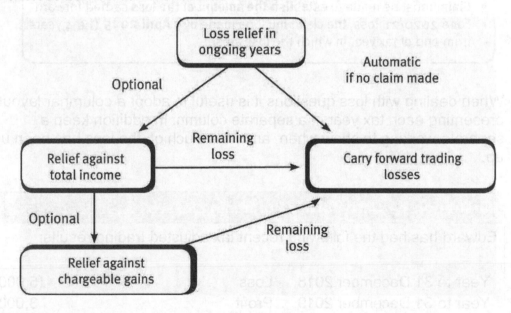

Where a claim against total income is made:

- any remaining loss is automatically carried forward

unless the individual then makes a claim to:

- set the loss against chargeable gains.

Note that a claim against gains can only be made after a claim against total income, in the same tax year, has been made.

3 Carry forward of trading losses

Principles of the relief

The key rules are as follows:

```
Carry forward trading losses
```

- **Automatic relief**
- **Carry forward** against
  - **First available**
  - **Trading profits**
  - Of the **same trade**
- Can carry forward indefinitely
- But **must set off maximum amount** possible each year, no partial offset allowed
- If no specific claim made:
  - carry all loss forward
- If specific claim made (i.e. against total income or chargeable gains):
  - carry forward remaining unrelieved loss
- Claim must be made to **establish the amount of the loss** carried forward
- For a 2020/21 loss, the claim must be made by **5 April 2025** (i.e 4 years from end of tax year in which the loss arose)

When dealing with loss questions it is useful to adopt a columnar layout, presenting each tax year in a separate column. In addition keep a separate working to show when, and how much of, the loss has been used up.

Illustration 1 – Carry forward of trading losses

Edward has had the following recent tax adjusted trading results:

		£
Year to 31 December 2018	Loss	(5,000)
Year to 31 December 2019	Profit	3,000
Year to 31 December 2020	Profit	10,000

Assuming that Edward wishes to carry the loss forward, calculate his assessable trading profits for the tax years 2018/19 to 2020/21 inclusive.

Solution

	2018/19 £	2019/20 £	2020/21 £
Trading income (Note)	0	3,000	10,000
Less: Loss relief b/f (W)	0	(3,000)	(2,000)
Net trading income	0	0	8,000

Working – Loss memorandum

	£
Trading loss – year to 31 December 2018	5,000
Less: Used in 2019/20	(3,000)
Less: Used in 2020/21	(2,000)
Loss carried forward to 2021/22	0

Note: The trading income assessment in the tax year of the loss (2018/19) is £Nil.

In the examination **never** put the loss in the income tax computation, **always** show trading income assessment as £Nil.

In addition, always show the amount of the loss in a separate loss working.

Test your understanding 1

Kamila has been trading for many years as a retailer. Her recent tax adjusted trading results are as follows:

		£
Year to 31 August 2018	Loss	(9,000)
Year to 31 August 2019	Profit	6,000
Year to 31 August 2020	Profit	19,000

Kamila has had no other sources of income.

Calculate Kamila's assessable trading income for the tax years 2018/19 to 2020/21, assuming she carries the loss forward.

Carry forward loss relief is useful as:

- the taxpayer gets the potential of an unrestricted period over which to utilise the available loss

  - providing that he continues to trade, and

  - makes subsequent future profits from the same trade.

However, there are a number of disadvantages to carrying losses forward:

- In a prolonged difficult trading period for a business, relief may take a long time to materialise.

- Obtaining relief in a latter period is less advantageous from a perspective of cash flow and time value of money.

- There is no certainty about the levels of future trading profits and whether it will be possible to utilise the loss.

Due to the number of disadvantages of carry forward relief, taxpayers are likely to consider the alternative loss reliefs available.

4 Loss relief against total income

A taxpayer making a loss in the tax year 2020/21 has the option to make a claim against **total income**.

Relief against total income is **optional** but if claimed it permits the taxpayer to relieve trading losses against the **total income** of the:

- tax year of the loss, **and/or**

- previous tax year.

A claim may be made in:

- either year in isolation, or

- both years, in any order.

For example: A loss for the year ended 31 December 2020 arises in the tax year 2020/21.

Therefore, the tax year of the loss is 2020/21 and the loss can be set against total income in:

- 2020/21, and/or

- 2019/20.

Illustration 2 – Loss relief against total income

Abbas's recent tax adjusted trading results are as follows:

		£
Year to 31 December 2019	Profit	10,000
Year to 31 December 2020	Loss	(6,000)
Year to 31 December 2021	Profit	12,000

Explain how Abbas can utilise the loss arising in the y/e 31 December 2020 assuming he claims to offset it against his total income.

Solution

The loss of £6,000 arises in the tax year 2020/21.

Loss relief is available against total income in 2020/21 and/or 2019/20.

Obtaining relief for the loss

Due to the wording 'and/or', and the fact that a claim can be made in any order, the taxpayer has five key options to consider:

(1) set against total income of the tax year of the loss, then set against total income of the previous tax year, or

(2) set against total income of the previous tax year, then set against total income of the current tax year, or

(3) set against total income of the tax year of the loss only

(4) set against total income of the previous tax year only

(5) make no claim and carry all of the loss forward.

In the case of the first four options, any unrelieved loss is carried forward automatically.

 However, a key point to note is that if relief against total income is claimed, the taxpayer must set off the **maximum amount possible** for a given year; a partial claim is not allowed.

Other points to note:

- The personal allowance is deducted from net income (i.e. total income after deducting reliefs). Therefore, a claim for loss relief against total income may result in the personal allowance being wasted.

- The savings income nil rate band and dividend nil rate band could also be wasted if a claim is made to use the loss against total income.

- A claim must be made within one year of 31 January following the end of the tax year of loss.

  For a 2020/21 loss the claim must be made by 31 January 2023.

- A taxpayer may have losses for two consecutive tax years and wish to relieve both against total income.

  In these circumstances the total income of a tax year is relieved by the loss of that year, in priority to the loss carried back from the following tax year.

Illustration 3 – Loss against total income

Rose's recent tax adjusted trading results are as follows:

		£
Year ended 31 July 2018	Profit	18,000
Year ended 31 July 2019	Loss	(43,200)
Year ended 31 July 2020	Profit	13,000
Year ended 31 July 2021	Profit	15,000

Rose's other income each year is £12,000.

Show Rose's net income for all tax years affected assuming:

(a) **No claim is made against total income for the trading loss.**

(b) **Claims against total income are made to obtain relief for the loss as early as possible.**

Solution

(a) **No relief against total income** – If no claim is made against total income, the trading loss of the tax year 2019/20 is carried forward against future trading profits.

	2018/19 £	2019/20 £	2020/21 £	2021/22 £
Trading profits	18,000	0	13,000	15,000
Less: Loss relief b/f	–	–	(13,000)	(15,000)
	18,000	0	0	0
Other income	12,000	12,000	12,000	12,000
Total income	30,000	12,000	12,000	12,000

Working – Loss memorandum

	£
Loss in y/e 31 July 2019	43,200
Less: Used in 2020/21	(13,000)
Less: Used in 2021/22	(15,000)
Loss relief carry forward to 2022/23	15,200

(b) **Claims against total income** – The loss of the tax year 2019/20 can be claimed against total income for 2018/19 and/or 2019/20. Any balance is carried forward. As relief is to be claimed for the loss as early as possible a claim will be made against total income for both 2018/19 and 2019/20.

	2018/19 £	2019/20 £	2020/21 £	2021/22 £
Trading income	18,000	0	13,000	15,000
Less: Loss relief b/f	–	–	(1,200)	–
	18,000	0	11,800	15,000
Other income	12,000	12,000	12,000	12,000
Total income	30,000	12,000	23,800	27,000
Less: Loss relief	(30,000)	(12,000)	–	–
Net income	0	0	23,800	27,000

Working – Loss memorandum

	£
Loss in y/e 31 July 2019 (i.e. 2019/20)	43,200
Less: Used in 2018/19	(30,000)
Less: Used in 2019/20	(12,000)
Loss to carry forward	1,200
Less: Used in 2020/21	(1,200)
Loss to carry forward	0

Test your understanding 2

Adrian's recent trading results have been:

		£
Year ended 31 December 2019	Profit	34,000
Year ended 31 December 2020	Loss	(48,000)
Year ended 31 December 2021	Profit	6,800

Adrian had other income as follows:

Tax year	£
2019/20	5,000
2020/21	6,000
2021/22	13,000

Calculate the taxable income for the tax years 2019/20 to 2021/22 inclusive, assuming that Adrian makes claims against total income to the extent that they are beneficial. State the amount of the remaining loss, if any.

Assume the tax rates and allowances for the tax year 2020/21 continue in the future.

5 Relief of trading losses against chargeable gains

If any loss remains after a claim against total income, a taxpayer can make a claim against chargeable gains.

Relief against chargeable gains is **optional** but if claimed it permits the taxpayer to relieve trading losses against the **chargeable gains** in the same tax years as a claim against total income, i.e. in the:

- tax year of the loss, and/or

- previous tax year.

A claim may be made in:

- either year in isolation, or

- both years, in any order.

The relief operates as follows:

- A trader is permitted to set unrelieved trading losses against chargeable gains, provided the maximum possible amount is offset against total income of the tax year in question first.

- There is no need to make a claim against total income for the previous tax year, but relief against chargeable gains is only granted if the maximum amount of loss is offset against total income in the same tax year first i.e. total income reduced to nil if no restrictions apply.

- If claimed, the unrelieved trading loss, is treated as a current year capital loss (see Chapter 19).

- The loss is deducted before both the CGT annual exempt amount and any capital losses brought forward as follows:

	£
Chargeable gains in year	X
Less: Capital losses in year	(X)
	X
Less: Trading loss relief (subject to the maximum amount)	(X)
Less: AEA	(12,300)
Net chargeable gains before brought forward losses	X

 A key point to note is that if a claim is made against chargeable gains, the taxpayer must set off the **maximum amount** possible for a given year; a partial claim is not allowed.

The maximum amount of loss relief under these rules is the **lower** of:

- the remaining loss, or

- chargeable gains in the tax year **after** the deduction of current year capital losses **and** brought forward capital losses.

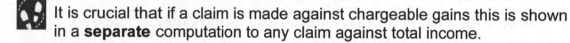 It is crucial that if a claim is made against chargeable gains this is shown in a **separate** computation to any claim against total income.

Other points to note:

- The annual exempt amount is deducted after this relief, therefore a claim may result in wasting the annual exempt amount.

- A claim is required in the same time period as for a claim against total income (i.e. within one year of 31 January following the end of the tax year of loss).

  For a 2020/21 loss the claim must be made by 31 January 2023.

- Relief against chargeable gains normally saves tax at 10% or 20% (see Chapter 19).

Test your understanding 3

Charlotte made a trading profit of £3,000 in the year ended 31 December 2020 and a trading loss of £14,000 the following year.

She has other income of £4,500 in the 2020/21 tax year and also realised chargeable gains of £26,000 and capital losses of £5,000 in that tax year.

Calculate the amounts that remain in charge to tax for the tax year 2020/21, assuming that Charlotte claims loss relief against both total income and chargeable gains for that tax year, but makes no claims in respect of any other tax year.

The procedure for dealing with questions involving losses

As seen in the previous examples and test your understandings, the following procedure should be adopted when answering questions:

(1) Determine the tax adjusted profits and losses after capital allowances for each accounting period.

(2) Determine when losses arise and therefore when loss relief is available (i.e. in which tax years).

(3) Set up a pro forma income tax computation for each tax year side by side and leave spaces for the loss set off to be inserted later.

(4) Set up a loss memo working for each loss to show how it is utilised.

(5) If more than one loss – consider in chronological order.

(6) Consider each option – be prepared to explain the options, the consequences of making a claim, the advantages and disadvantages.

(7) Set off losses according to the requirements of the question, or in the most beneficial way if it is a tax planning question.

6 Relief for trading losses in the opening years

The options available in the opening years of trade are exactly the same as those available to an ongoing business, with one extra option to carry back losses three years against total income.

The choices can be summarised as follows:

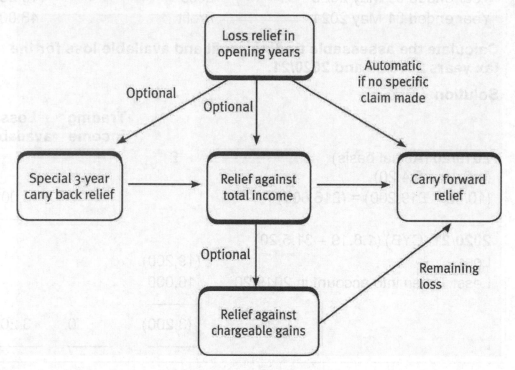

If an individual makes a trading loss in the opening years, he or she has to decide whether to claim normal relief against total income, special opening year loss relief or carry forward the loss.

However before a particular loss relief can be claimed it is necessary to determine the loss arising in each tax year.

Calculation of loss in opening years

The normal opening year basis of assessment rules apply regardless of whether the individual makes a profit or loss.

However in calculating a loss in the opening years note that:

- It is vital to remember that a loss may only be relieved once.

- There is no such thing as overlap losses.

- If a loss is included in the computation in more than one tax year, then the amount taken into account in the first tax year cannot also be included in the second tax year.

Illustration 4 – Loss relief against total income in opening years			

Geraldine started trading on 1 June 2019. Her results, as adjusted for tax purposes, are:

		£
Year ended 31 May 2020	Loss	(19,200)
Year ended 31 May 2021	Profit	48,000

Calculate the assessable trading profit and available loss for the tax years 2019/20 and 2020/21.

Solution

	£	Trading income £	Loss available £
2019/20 (Actual basis) (1.6.19 – 5.4.20) (10/12 × £19,200) = (£16,000)		0	16,000
2020/21 (CYB) (1.6.19 – 31.5.20)			
Loss	(19,200)		
Less: Taken into account in 2019/20	16,000		
	(3,200)	0	3,200

Test your understanding 4			

Sakura started trading on 1 May 2019. The results of her initial periods of trading were as follows:

		£
Year ended 30 April 2020	Loss	(36,000)
Year ended 30 April 2021	Profit	30,000
Year ended 30 April 2022	Profit	35,000

Calculate Sakura's assessable trading profit and available loss for each tax year affected by the above results.

Special opening year loss relief

As an alternative to, or in addition to, a claim against total income the taxpayer can make a special opening year loss relief claim.

The relief operates as follows:

> **Special opening year relief against total income**
>
> - Optional claim
> - Applies to loss arising in any of **first 4 tax years** of trading
> - If claimed, set loss against
>   - **total income**
>   - **in 3 tax years** before tax year of loss
>   - on a FIFO basis (i.e. earliest year first)
> - There is no need for the trade to have been carried on in the earlier years
> - **One claim** covers all 3 years
> - For example:
>   Loss in y/e 31.12.20 (2020/21) will be set off in:
>   1. 2017/18
>   2. 2018/19
>   3. 2019/20
> - If claimed
>   - Must set off **maximum amount possible**
>   - Cannot restrict set-off to preserve the personal allowance
>   - Therefore, the benefit of the personal allowance may be wasted if a claim is made
> - For 2020/21 loss, the claim must be made by 31 January 2023

Illustration 5 – Relief for trading losses in opening years

Caroline started her business on 1 July 2019. Her trading results, as adjusted for tax purposes, for the first two years are as follows:

		£
Year ended 30 June 2020	Loss	(12,000)
Year ended 30 June 2021	Profit	5,465

Before becoming self-employed, Caroline had been employed as a dressmaker. Her remuneration from this employment, which ceased on 30 September 2018, was:

2018/19	£7,300
2017/18	£13,490
2016/17	£16,200

Caroline has other income of £4,850 p.a.

Calculate the taxable income for all tax years after claiming special opening year loss relief.

Assume the tax rates and allowances for the tax year 2020/21 apply throughout.

Solution

Taxable income computations

	2016/17 £	2017/18 £	2018/19 £	2019/20 £
Employment income	16,200	13,490	7,300	0
Other income	4,850	4,850	4,850	4,850
Total income	21,050	18,340	12,150	4,850
Less: Loss relief (W)	(9,000)	(3,000)	–	–
Net income	12,050	15,340	12,150	4,850
Less: PA	(12,500)	(12,500)	(12,500)	(12,500)
Taxable income	0	2,840	0	0

	2020/21 £	2021/22 £
Trading profit (W)	0	5,465
Other income	4,850	4,850
Total income	4,850	10,315
Less: PA	(12,500)	(12,500)
Taxable income	0	0

Notes:

(1) When there is a loss in consecutive years, deal with the loss of the first tax year first.

(2) Under the special opening year loss relief rules, the loss from the tax year 2019/20 of £9,000 is set firstly against total income for the tax year 2016/17. Any loss remaining would have been set automatically against total income of 2017/18 and finally against total income of 2018/19.

(3) The loss of the tax year 2020/21 of £3,000 is set firstly against total income of the tax year 2017/18 before relieving 2018/19 and 2019/20 (had any loss remained).

(4) Where opening year losses are carried back before the commencement of trade, they are usually set against previous other income e.g. employment income. This is possible because there is no requirement in the legislation that the trade be carried on in the earlier year for which a claim is made.

Workings: New business – assessments/available loss

Tax year	Basis period	Available loss £	Assessable profits £
2019/20	1.7.19 – 5.4.20 (9/12 × £12,000)	9,000	0
2020/21	y/e 30.6.20 (£12,000 – £9,000)	3,000	0
2021/22	y/e 30.6.21		5,465

Test your understanding 5

Lance started a business on 1 June 2020. His taxable trade profits are:

		£
11 months to 30 April 2021	Loss	(28,480)
Year ended 30 April 2022	Profit	35,000

Prior to commencing in business Lance had been employed.

His employment income for the tax years 2017/18, 2018/19 and 2019/20 was £23,660, £5,564 and £6,120 respectively. In addition he has savings income amounting to £1,700 each year.

Show how Lance will obtain relief for the loss if he makes a claim for special opening year loss relief.

7 Terminal loss relief

The options available in the closing years of trade are exactly the same as those available to an ongoing business, except that:

- the option to carry forward losses is not available as there will be no further trading profits once the trade ceases

- an extra option of terminal loss relief is available.

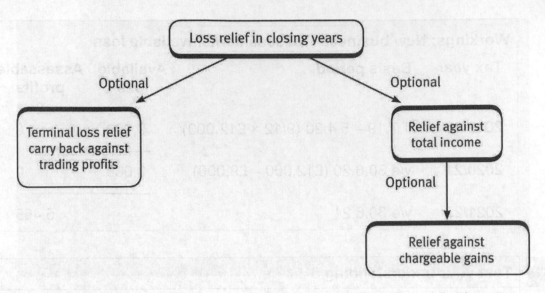

If an individual makes a trading loss in the closing years, he or she has to decide whether to claim relief against total income (and then possibly offset against gains) or claim terminal loss relief against trading profits.

Terminal loss relief

The relief operates as follows:

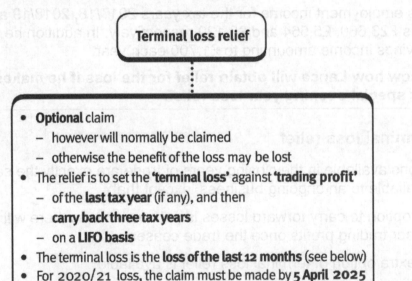

- **Optional** claim
  - however will normally be claimed
  - otherwise the benefit of the loss may be lost
- The relief is to set the **'terminal loss'** against **'trading profit'**
  - of the **last tax year** (if any), and then
  - **carry back three tax years**
  - on a **LIFO basis**
- The terminal loss is the **loss of the last 12 months** (see below)
- For 2020/21 loss, the claim must be made by **5 April 2025** (i.e. within 4 years of the end of the last tax year of trading)

The terminal loss is the loss of the **last 12 months of trading** and is calculated as follows:

	£
6 April before cessation to the date of cessation	
(1) Actual trading loss in this period (ignore if a profit)	X
(2) Overlap profits not yet relieved	X
12 months before cessation to 5 April before cessation	
(3) Actual trading loss in this period (ignore if a profit)	X
Terminal loss	X

Note that it is not compulsory to make a claim against total income before claiming terminal loss relief.

However, where losses included in the above terminal loss calculation have already been relieved under another claim (i.e. against total income or chargeable gains), the amount of the terminal loss must be reduced.

Test your understanding 6

Yves ceased trading on 30 June 2020. His final period of trade was the nine months to 30 June 2020 and beforehand he prepared accounts annually to 30 September.

His tax adjusted trading results are as follows:

		£
Nine months to 30.6.20	Loss	(7,200)
Year to 30.9.19	Profit	100
Year to 30.9.18	Profit	7,300
Year to 30.9.17	Profit	7,500

There was overlap profits of £1,800 brought forward.

Yves had no other sources of income.

Calculate the terminal loss available to Yves and show how relief may be obtained for it.

8 Maximum deduction from total income

There is a limit on the amount of relief that can be deducted when a claim is made against total income.

The **maximum deduction** from total income is the **greater of**:

*   £50,000, or
*   25% of adjusted total income.

Adjusted total income (ATI) for the TX examination is calculated as follows:

	£
Total income	X
Less: Gross personal pension contributions	(X)
Adjusted total income	X

Note that the restriction will be £50,000 unless the individual's ATI exceeds £200,000 (£200,000 × 25% = £50,000).

The limit applies to trading losses set against:

*   current year total income, and
*   the prior year **if** set against income other than profits of the same trade.

It does not apply where the trading loss is set against profits from the same trade of an earlier year. Note that in this instance, trading losses are set against trading income from the same trade before income from other sources.

Any trade loss that cannot be set off against total income is carried forward against future trade profits from the same trade.

As the reliefs against total income are 'all or nothing', it is possible that this restriction of the amount of the loss allowed to be deducted could be beneficial and prevent the wastage of the personal allowance.

Test your understanding 7

Sheetal is a sole trader and has adjusted trading results as follows:

Year ended 30 November 2019	£64,000
Year ended 30 November 2020	(£127,800)

She has savings income of £63,000 each year but no other income.

She makes gross personal pension scheme contributions of £5,725 each year.

Sheetal wishes to offset the trading loss against her total income for the tax years 2020/21 and then 2019/20.

Calculate Sheetal's taxable income for the tax years 2019/20 and 2020/21. Assume that the rates and allowances for the tax year 2020/21 apply throughout.

9 Choice of loss reliefs

Utilising loss relief

When planning relief for trading losses, careful consideration needs to be given to the personal circumstances of the individual.

Tax advice should aim to satisfy the following goals of a taxpayer:

- Obtain tax relief at the highest marginal rate of tax.

- Obtain relief as soon as possible.

- Ensure the taxpayer's PA, savings income nil rate band and dividend nil rate band are not wasted, if possible.

It may not be possible to satisfy all of these aims, for example:

- in order to get a higher rate of relief, the taxpayer may have to waste his or her PA

- carrying losses forward may give a higher rate of relief, but the cash flow implications of claiming relief now rather than waiting for relief, may be more important to the taxpayer.

The specific circumstances faced by the taxpayer will help to determine which of these is most important.

Factors to consider

In understanding the position of the taxpayer, it is important to understand the comparative features of the various reliefs.

Income relieved	Timing of relief	Flexibility
Total income – normal claim (possibly also chargeable gains relief)	Current and/or previous tax year	Either, neither or both tax years (in either order). All or nothing. Maximum restriction may apply.
Total income – special opening years claim	Preceding three tax years on a FIFO basis	Only in opening years. All or nothing. Can be used with a normal claim against total income. Maximum restriction may apply.
Future trading profit	As soon as possible in future	None.

Trading profit – terminal loss claim	Current and then preceding three tax years on a LIFO basis	Only on cessation. All or nothing. Can be used with a normal claim against total income.

Choice of loss relief

Although the reliefs against total income (normal relief and special opening year relief) obtain relief more quickly than relief by carry forward, they frequently involve loss of the personal allowance, savings income nil rate band and dividend nil rate band.

However, for a large loss that will eliminate several years' modest trading profits, there is no point in choosing to carry forward a loss if there is no non-trading income in those future years to obtain relief for personal allowances. All that will have happened is that future personal allowances rather than current ones will be wasted.

The taxpayer can choose when to claim relief against total income, that is, in the tax year of the loss; or the preceding year, as the legislation does not dictate that either takes priority.

If neither a current nor a previous year claim against total income appears appropriate, look at the chargeable gains position.

Where the taxpayer has made a large chargeable gain, a claim against it may be appropriate. Since the claim can only be made once total income for the year is reduced as far as possible, it will generally involve wasting at least one year's personal allowance.

However, at all times be mindful of the maximum restriction rules and the rate of tax relief available as the taxpayer's primary aim is usually to save as much tax as possible.

10 Partnership losses

The allocation of trading losses

Trading losses are allocated between partners in exactly the same way as trading profits.

Loss relief claims available

Claims available to partners are the same as those for sole traders.

- A partner joining a partnership may be entitled to claim opening year loss relief, where a loss is incurred in the first four tax years of his membership of the partnership.

  This relief would not be available to the existing partners.

- A partner leaving the partnership may be entitled to claim for terminal loss relief.

  Again, this relief would not be available to the partners remaining in the partnership.

Test your understanding 8

Diane, Lynne and John are in partnership preparing their accounts to 5 April. During the tax year 2020/21, John left the partnership and Helen joined in his place.

For the year ended 5 April 2021, the partnership made a tax adjusted trading loss of £40,000.

State the loss relief claims that are available to the partners.

Illustration 6 – Partnership loss

Jake and Milo have been in partnership together since 2005, but ceased trading on 30 September 2020. Profits and losses have always been shared 40% to Jake and 60% to Milo.

The tax adjusted trading profits and losses for the final four years before allocation between the partners are as follows:

		£
2017/18	Profit – y/e 30.9.17	21,000
2018/19	Profit – y/e 30.9.18	22,500
2019/20	Profit – y/e 30.9.19	19,000
2020/21	Loss – y/e 30.9.20	(65,000)

Jake is single and has no other income or outgoings.

Milo is single and also has no other income or outgoings apart from bank interest of £4,350 received on 1 December 2020 from investing a recent inheritance. He has a chargeable gain of £35,000 for the tax year 2020/21 in respect of the disposal of an asset on 18 July 2020.

Assume that the rates and allowances for the tax year 2020/21 apply to all years and that capital gains tax is payable at 10%.

Ignore relief for overlap profits.

(a) **Advise the partners of the possible ways of relieving the partnership loss for the tax year 2020/21.**

(b) **Advise the partners as to which loss relief claims would be the most beneficial.**

(c) **After taking into account the advice in (b), calculate the partners' taxable income for the tax years 2017/18 to 2020/21. Show Milo's tax saving under each of the options considered in part (b).**

Solution

(a) **Options for relieving loss**

There are two possible ways to relieve the partnership loss:

(1) A claim can be made against total income for the tax years 2020/21 and/or 2019/20.

Subject to this claim being made, it would then be possible to claim against chargeable gains of the same tax year.

(2) Terminal loss relief can be claimed.

The tax adjusted trading profits and loss are split between the partners:

	Jake 40%	Milo 60%
	£	£
2017/18	8,400	12,600
2018/19	9,000	13,500
2019/20	7,600	11,400
2020/21	(26,000)	(39,000)

(b) **Most beneficial relief**

The most beneficial loss relief claim available to Jake is a terminal loss claim, as he has no other income or gains.

Milo could also make a terminal loss claim, but this would waste most of his personal allowances for several years.

It is more beneficial for Milo to make a claim against his total income of £4,350 for the tax year 2020/21, which wastes his personal allowance in that year, but then allows a claim against his chargeable gain of £35,300 for the tax year 2020/21.

(c) **Jake – Taxable income**

	2017/18	2018/19	2019/20	2020/21
	£	£	£	£
Trading profit	8,400	9,000	7,600	0
Less: Terminal loss (Note)	(8,400)	(9,000)	(7,600)	(0)
Net income	0	0	0	0
Less: PA (restricted)	–	–	–	–
Taxable income	0	0	0	0

Note: In this instance there is no need to do a separate terminal loss calculation as there are no overlap profits and the final accounts have been prepared for the final 12 months of trading.

The remaining loss of £1,000 (£26,000 – £7,600 – £9,000 – £8,400) is wasted as there are no future profits from the same trade to carry forward against and Jake has no other income or gains in the tax years 2020/21 or 2019/20.

Milo – Taxable income

	2017/18 £	2018/19 £	2019/20 £	2020/21 £
Trading profit	12,600	13,500	11,400	0
Bank interest	–	–	–	4,350
Total income	12,600	13,500	11,400	4,350
Less: Loss relief	–	–	–	(4,350)
Net income	12,600	13,500	11,400	0
Less: PA	(12,500)	(12,500)	(12,500)	–
Taxable income	100	1,000	0	0

Assuming that tax year 2019/20 rates apply throughout, claiming terminal loss relief would save income tax of:

(£100 + £1,000) = £1,100 × 20% = £220

Claiming relief against total income and then chargeable gains in the tax year 2019/20 would save:

	£
Income tax – income would be covered by PA	0
Capital gains tax (£23,000 (W) × 10%)	2,300
Total tax saving	2,300

Working: Taxable gain without loss relief

	£
Chargeable gain	35,300
Less: Annual exempt amount	(12,300)
Taxable gain	23,000

Loss relief available is £34,650 (£39,000 – £4,350 used against total income).

The loss is offset before the deduction of the annual exempt amount (AEA). Thus the remaining loss of £34,650 is fully utilised, most of the AEA is wasted, and tax is saved on taxable gains of £23,000.

For further information regarding the calculation of tax on chargeable gains see Chapter 19.

11   Chapter summary

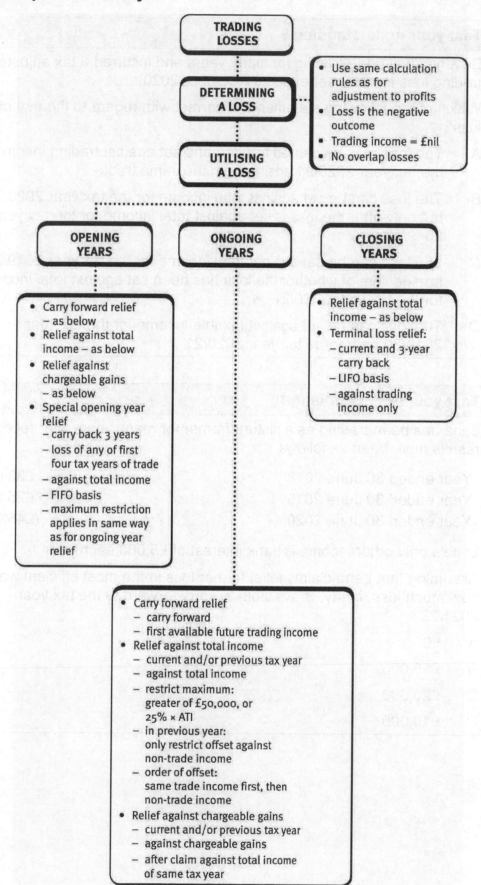

12 Practice objective test questions

Test your understanding 9

Beverley has been trading for many years and incurred a tax adjusted trading loss for the year ended 31 October 2020.

Which of the following statements is correct with regard to the use of the loss?

A   The loss may be carried forward and set against trading income for the tax year 2020/21 arising from the same trade

B   The loss can be set against total income for the tax year 2020/21, but only after the loss is set against total income for the tax year 2019/20

C   The loss can be set against total income for the tax year 2019/20, irrespective of whether the loss has been set against total income for the tax year 2020/21

D   The loss can be set against taxable income for the tax year 2019/20 and/or the tax year 2020/21

Test your understanding 10

Lena has been trading as a picture framer for many years. Her recent results have been as follows:

Year ended 30 June 2018	£30,000
Year ended 30 June 2019	£25,000
Year ended 30 June 2020	(£45,000)

Lena's only other income is bank interest of £5,000 each year.

Assuming that Lena claims relief for her loss in the most efficient way, how much loss, if any, is available to carry forward to the tax year 2021/22?

A   £0

B   £15,000

C   £20,000

D   £10,000

Test your understanding 11

Which of the following statements about trading losses is true?

A   A trade loss can only be carried forward for a maximum of two years.

B   A trade loss carried forward must be deducted from future profits of the same trade.

C   A claim against total income must be made for the tax year of loss first before carrying it back to the previous tax year.

D   When a loss is deducted from total income it can be restricted to allow the personal allowance to be relieved in full.

Test your understanding answers

Test your understanding 1

Kamila

	2018/19 £	2019/20 £	2020/21 £
Trading income	0	6,000	19,000
Less: Loss relief b/f (W)	0	(6,000)	(3,000)
Net trading income	0	0	16,000

Working – Loss memorandum

	£
Trading loss – year to 31 August 2018	9,000
Less: Used in 2019/20	(6,000)
Less: Used in 2020/21	(3,000)
Loss carried forward to 2021/22	0

Test your understanding 2

Adrian

Year of the loss = 2020/21

Relief against total income in: 2020/21 and/or 2019/20.

	2019/20 £	2020/21 £	2021/22 £
Trading income	34,000	0	6,800
Less: Loss relief b/f (W)	–	–	(6,800)
	34,000	0	0
Other income	5,000	6,000	13,000
Total income	39,000	6,000	13,000
Less: Loss relief (W)	(39,000)	–	–
Net income	0	6,000	13,000
Less: PA (Note)	0	(6,000)	(12,500)
Taxable income	0	0	500

Working – Loss memorandum

	£
2020/21 – loss of y/e 31.12.20	48,000
Less: Used in 2019/20	(39,000)
	———
Loss carried forward	9,000
Less: Used in 2021/22	(6,800)
	———
Loss carried forward to 2022/23	2,200
	———

Note: A claim for relief against total income in the tax year 2020/21 is not beneficial as the income is already covered by the PA. Therefore if a claim is made in this year it would needlessly utilise the loss, waste the PA for that year and save no tax.

However, a claim in the tax year 2019/20 will achieve a tax saving and will obtain relief for the loss as soon as possible. The PA in that year is wasted, however relief sooner rather than later is preferable to carrying forward a loss and waiting for the relief.

The best course of action will depend on the personal circumstances of each case but as a general principle there is no point in claiming relief against total income where the PA already covers all or most of the total income.

Test your understanding 3

Charlotte

Income tax computation – 2020/21

	£
Trading income (y/e 31.12.20)	3,000
Other income	4,500
	———
Total income	7,500
Less: Loss relief	(7,500)
	———
Net income	0
	———

Chargeable gains computation – 2020/21

	£
Chargeable gains	26,000
Less: Capital losses – current year	(5,000)
Net chargeable gains	21,000
Less: Trading loss relief (W)	(6,500)
Net chargeable gains before annual exempt amount	14,500

Note: As a result of the claims, Charlotte' personal allowance is wasted. However, a claim against chargeable gains cannot be made unless a claim against total income in the same tax year is made first.

Working – Loss memorandum

	£
Loss for year ending 31 December 2021	14,000
Less: Used in 2020/21 against total income	(7,500)
	6,500
Less: Used in 2020/21 against chargeable gains	(6,500)
Loss carried forward	0

Test your understanding 4

Sakura

		Trading income	Loss available
		£	£
2019/20 (Actual basis)			
1.5.19 – 5.4.20			
11/12 × (£36,000) = (£33,000)		0	33,000
2020/21 (CYB)	£		
Year ended 30 April 2020	36,000		
Less: Used in 2019/20 (Note)	(33,000)		
	(3,000)	0	3,000

2021/22 (CYB)

Year ended 30 April 2021	30,000	0

2022/23 (CYB)

Year ended 30 April 2022	35,000	0

Note: The loss allocated to 2019/20 cannot also be treated as a loss in 2020/21.

Test your understanding 5

Lance

	Loss available £	Trading profit £
2020/21 (1 June 2020 – 5 April 2021) (10/11 × £28,480 loss)	25,891	0
2021/22 First 12 months trading (1 June 2020 – 31 May 2021) £28,480 loss (– loss 25,891 allocated to 2019/20) + (1/12 × 35,000)		328
2022/23 CYB (Year ended 30 April 2022)		35,000

Note: 2020/21 is the tax year of the loss. Therefore, the loss of £25,891 is set off against total income of the tax year 2017/18 first, then 2018/19, and finally 2019/20.

	2017/18 £	2018/19 £	2019/20 £
Trading income	0	0	0
Employment income	23,660	5,564	6,120
Savings income	1,700	1,700	1,700
Total income	25,360	7,264	7,820
Less: Loss relief	(25,360)	(531)	–
Net income	0	6,733	7,820

Working – Loss memorandum

	£
Trading loss 2020/21	25,891
Less: Used in 2017/18	(25,360)
Less: Used in 2018/19	(531)
	—
	0
	—

Test your understanding 6

Yves

	2017/18 £		2018/19 £		2019/20 £	2020/21 £
Trading profit	7,500		7,300		100	0
Less: TLR (W2) (3)	(1,575)	(2)	(7,300)	(1)	(100)	0
	—		—		—	—
Revised trading profit	5,925		0		0	0
	—		—		—	—

Workings

(W1) Calculation of terminal loss

	£
6.4.20 to 30.6.20: Actual loss (3/9 × £7,200)	2,400
1.7.19 to 5.4.20: Actual loss (6/9 × £7,200) – (3/12 × £100)	4,775
Overlap profits	1,800
	—
Terminal loss	8,975
	—

(W2) Terminal loss relief (TLR)

The terminal loss is relieved on a LIFO basis in the final tax year and the previous three years, against the trading profits.

Test your understanding 7

Sheetal

Loss relief offset

	2019/20 £	2020/21 £
Trade profits	64,000	0
Savings income	63,000	63,000
Total income	127,000	63,000
Less: Loss relief		
Current year claim (restricted) (W1)		(50,000)
Carry back claim:		
– no restriction where losses set against profits from same trade	(64,000)	
– balance of loss is set against other income (not restricted as < £50,000)	(13,800)	
Net income	49,200	13,000
Less: Personal allowance	(12,500)	(12,500)
Taxable income	36,700	500

Note: The restriction in the tax year 2020/21 is useful as it prevents the wastage of Sheetal's personal allowance.

Workings

(W1) Maximum loss relief for 2020/21

	£
Total income	63,000
Less: Gross personal pension contributions	(5,725)
Adjusted total income (ATI)	57,275
25% thereof	14,319

Maximum set off is £50,000 as that is greater than £14,319

(W2) Loss memorandum

	£
Loss for 2020/21 (year ended 30 November 2020)	127,800
Used 2020/21	(50,000)
Used 2019/20 against profits from the same trade	(64,000)
Used 2019/20 against other income (within maximum £50,000)	(13,800)
Loss carried forward	0

Note: If the trading loss was £165,000, the amount used against other income in the tax year 2019/20 would be restricted to £50,000.

Test your understanding 8

Diane, Lynne and John

All the partners are entitled to relief against total income, as well as the option to extend the relief against chargeable gains.

All the partners except John are entitled to carry forward loss relief.

John is entitled to terminal loss relief since he has ceased trading.

Helen is entitled to claim special opening years relief since she has commenced trading.

Diane and Lynne are not entitled to terminal loss relief or special opening year loss relief.

Test your understanding 9

Beverley

The correct answer is C.

C is the correct answer because the trading loss can be:

- Carried forward and set against future trading profits, but the loss is incurred in the tax year 2020/21 and will therefore be available to carry forward to the tax year 2021/22.

- The loss can be set against total income (not taxable income) of the tax years 2020/21 and/or 2019/20. There is no need for the claim for the tax year 2019/20 to be made before that of the tax year 2020/21.

Test your understanding 10

The correct answer is B.

B is the correct answer because Lena should make a claim to offset the loss in the tax year 2019/20, but not in the tax year 2020/21 when her income is covered by the personal allowance.

Lena cannot offset the loss against the year ended 30 June 2018, which is taxable in the tax year 2018/19. The loss is utilised as shown below:

	2019/20 £	2020/21 £
Trading profits	25,000	0
Bank interest	5,000	5,000
	30,000	5,000
Less: loss claim	(30,000)	–
	0	5,000
Less: PA	Wasted	(5,000)
Taxable income	0	0

	£
Loss arising in 2020/21	(45,000)
Utilised in 2019/20	30,000
Loss available to c/f to 2021/22	(15,000)

Test your understanding 11

The correct answer is B.

A is false because there is no limit on the time that a loss can be carried forward.

C is false because a claim against total income can be made for the tax year of loss and/or the previous tax year in any order.

D is false because a loss claimed against total income is deducted before the personal allowance and the offset cannot be restricted to preserve the personal allowance.

National insurance

Chapter learning objectives

Upon completion of this chapter you will be able to:

- explain and compute national insurance contributions payable:

  (i)   Class 1 and 1A NIC

  (ii)   Class 2 and 4 NIC

- understand the annual employment allowance.

One of the PER performance objectives (PO15) is to prepare computations of taxable amounts and tax liabilities according to legal requirements. Working through this chapter should help you understand how to demonstrate that objective.

PER

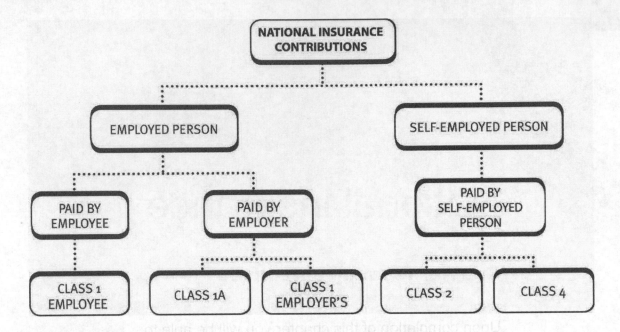

1   Classes of national insurance contributions

The amount of national insurance contributions (NICs) a person pays and the payment of contributions depend on the class of contribution.

The main classes and persons who are liable are as follows:

Class of contribution	Basis of assessment	Person liable
Class 1 employee	A percentage based contribution levied on employee earnings in excess of the **employee** threshold for the tax year 2020/21 of £9,500	Employee
Class 1 employer's	A percentage based contribution levied on employee earnings in excess of the **employer's** threshold for the tax year 2020/21 of £8,788	Employer
Class 1A	A percentage based contribution levied on taxable employment benefits provided to employees	Employer
Class 2	A flat rate weekly contribution	Self-employed
Class 4	A percentage based contribution levied on tax adjusted trading profits in excess of the lower profits threshold £9,500 for the tax year 2020/21	Self-employed

Illustration 1 – Classes of NICs

Catalina has been self-employed for many years. She employs a full-time salesman and six part-time employees. Catalina' tax adjusted trading profits for the tax year 2020/21 are £86,000.

The salesman earns a salary of £14,000 p.a. and is provided with a company car. The remaining members of staff earn £3,000 p.a.

Explain which classes of NICs are payable by Catalina.

Solution

Catalina will pay:

(1)   Flat rate class 2 contributions in respect of her self-employed business.

(2)   Class 4 contributions in respect of her self-employed business based on her tax adjusted trading profits as they are in excess of £9,500.

(3)   Employer's class 1 contributions as Catalina is an employer. The contributions are based on the salesman's salary of £14,000 as his earnings are in excess of £8,788.

(4)   Class 1A contributions based on the assessable employment benefit arising from the provision of a company car to the salesman.

Notes:

(1)   No NICs are payable in respect of the remaining six part-time staff members as they each earn less than £8,788 p.a.

(2)   The salesman is liable to pay employee class 1 contributions based on his salary of £14,000.

Illustration 2 – Classes of NICs

Stephen works for Camberley Cars Ltd on a part-time basis earning a salary of £19,000 p.a. He is provided with a company car; petrol for both business and private mileage; and a place is provided for his daughter at the company's workplace nursery while he is working for them.

Stephen also runs a small bed and breakfast business from his home. In the year to 31 March 2021 his tax adjusted trading profit from the business is £10,300.

Explain which classes of NICs are payable by Stephen and Camberley Cars Ltd in respect of the tax year 2020/21.

Solution

Stephen will pay:

(1) Employee class 1 contributions based on his salary from Camberley Cars Ltd of £19,000 as his earnings are in excess of £9,500.

(2) Flat rate class 2 contributions in respect of his bed and breakfast business.

(3) Class 4 contributions in respect of his bed and breakfast business based on his tax adjusted trading profits as they are in excess of £9,500.

Camberley Cars Ltd will pay:

(1) Employer's class 1 contributions based on Stephen's salary of £19,000 as his earnings are in excess of £8,788.

(2) Class 1A contributions based on the assessable employment benefit arising from the provision of a company car and private petrol to Stephen.

Note: Class 1A contributions are not payable in respect of the provision of a nursery place as it is an exempt benefit.

2 NICs payable in respect of employees

The following NICs are payable in respect of employees:

- Class 1 employee contributions
- Class 1 employer's contributions
- Class 1A contributions.

Class 1 employee and employer's NICs

Both the class 1 contribution paid by the employee and the class 1 contribution paid by the employer are a percentage based contribution levied on the 'gross earnings' of the employee in excess of the earnings threshold. The earnings threshold for the tax year 2020/21 is £9,500 for employees and £8,788 for employers.

 The definition of earnings for class 1 NIC purposes

'Earnings' for the purpose of class 1 NICs consists of:

- **any** remuneration derived from the employment, which is
- paid in **cash** or assets which are readily convertible into cash.

The calculation of class 1 NICs is based on:

gross earnings with no allowable deductions

(i.e. earnings before deductions that are allowable for income tax purposes, such as employee occupational pension scheme contributions and subscriptions to professional bodies).

Gross earnings **include**:

- wages, salary, overtime pay, commission or bonuses
- sick pay, including statutory sick pay
- tips and gratuities paid or allocated by the employer
- reimbursement of the cost of travel between home and work
- vouchers (exchangeable for cash or non-cash items, such as goods).

Gross earnings **do not include**:

- exempt employment benefits (e.g. employer contributions into a pension scheme, a mobile phone, etc.) (see Chapter 5)
- most taxable **non-cash benefits** except remuneration received in the form of financial instruments, readily convertible assets and non-cash vouchers (see above)
- tips directly received from customers
- mileage allowance received from the employer provided it does not exceed the HMRC approved mileage allowance rate of 45p per mile (the excess above 45p per mile is subject to class 1 NICs). The allowance does not decrease to 25p after 10,000 miles as for income tax. As a result, the amount assessed to income tax can be different from the amount subject to national insurance
- expenses paid for or reimbursed by the employer for which an income tax deduction would be available e.g. employment related travel and subsistence costs.

Note that dividends are not subject to NICs, even if they are drawn by a director/shareholder in place of a monthly salary.

Illustration 3 – Definition of class 1 earnings

Lia and Ariel are employed by Garden Gnomes Ltd and both pay into the company's occupational pension scheme. Their remuneration for the tax year 2020/21 is as follows:

	Lia	Ariel
	£	£
Salary	30,000	55,000
Bonus	0	4,000
Car benefit	0	3,950
Employer's pension contribution	2,300	4,575
Employee's pension contribution	1,650	3,800

Calculate Lia and Ariel's gross earnings for class 1 NIC purposes.

Solution

	Lia	Ariel
	£	£
Salary	30,000	55,000
Bonus	0	4,000
Gross earnings for class 1 NICs	30,000	59,000

Notes:

(1) The employer's pension contributions are excluded as they are an exempt benefit.

(2) The employee's pension contributions are ignored as these are not deductible in calculating earnings for NIC purposes.

(3) The car benefit is excluded as it is a non-cash benefit which will be assessed to class 1A NICs, not class 1.

Relevant employees

Class 1 contributions are payable where the individual:

- is employed in the UK, and

- is aged 16 or over, and

- has earnings in excess of the earnings threshold (£9,500 for employees and £8,788 for employers for 2020/21).

Class 1 employee contributions

Class 1 employee contributions are also known as primary contributions and are payable by employees:

- aged 16 or over until
- attaining state pension age.

 State pension age

> Up to 5 April 2010 the state pension age was 65 for men and 60 for women.
>
> Between 2010 and 2018 the state pension age for women gradually increased to 65 and from 2018 onwards the state pension ages for both men and women are further increasing.
>
> Knowledge of the detailed rules over this transitional period is not required.

The employer is responsible for calculating the amount of class 1 employee NICs due and deducting the contributions from the employee's wages.

Note that class 1 employee contributions:

- are not an allowable deduction for the purposes of calculating the individual employee's personal income tax liability
- do not represent a cost to the business of the employer, as they are ultimately paid by the employee. Therefore, they are not a deductible expense when calculating the employer's tax adjusted trading profits.

Calculating class 1 employee contributions

Employee contributions are normally calculated by reference to an employee's earnings period:

- if paid weekly, the contributions are calculated on a weekly basis
- if paid monthly, the contributions are calculated on a monthly basis.

 In the examination, the class 1 NIC thresholds are always shown on an annual basis and class 1 NIC calculations should therefore be performed on an annual basis unless you are clearly told otherwise.

The employee contributions payable are calculated as:

- 12% on gross earnings between £9,500 and £50,000
- 2% on gross earnings in excess of £50,000.

 The class 1 employee rates and thresholds are included in the tax rates and allowances provided to you in the examination.

Earnings period

The annual earnings thresholds can be used to calculate the rate of class 1 NICs payable where the employee's earnings do not fluctuate during the year.

However, where an employee's earnings fluctuate during the year:

- the calculations must be performed on an earnings period basis
- the annual thresholds are divided into weekly or monthly thresholds.

For example, the monthly upper threshold would be £4,167 (£50,000 × 1/12).

Class 1 employer's contributions

Class 1 employer's contributions, also known as secondary contributions are payable by employers in respect of employees:

- aged 16 or over
- until the employee ceases employment.

 There is no upper age limit for employer's contributions, the employer is liable even if the employee's age exceeds state pension age.

Employer's contributions are an additional cost of employment and are a deductible expense when calculating the employer's tax adjusted trading profits.

 The exemptions from class 1 employer's NIC for employee's aged under 21 and apprentices aged under 25 are not examinable.

Calculating class 1 employer's contributions

Employer's contributions are calculated by reference to an employee's earnings period.

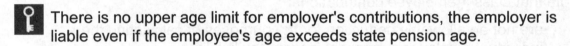 In the examination, class 1 NIC calculations should be performed on an annual basis unless you are clearly told otherwise.

Employer's contributions are calculated as:

- 13.8% on all gross earnings above £8,788.

Note that there is:

- no upper earnings threshold
- no change in the rate of NICs payable for employer's contributions.

Illustration 4 – Class 1 NICs

Millie is employed by Blue Forge Ltd and is paid an annual salary of £49,000. Millie is also provided with the following taxable benefits:

	£
Company car	5,000
Vouchers for the local gym	2,000

Calculate Millie's and Blue Forge Ltd's class 1 NIC liability due for the tax year 2020/21.

Solution

Class 1 NICs are due on annual earnings of £51,000 (salary £49,000 and vouchers £2,000). The company car is a non-cash benefit and is therefore not subject to class 1 NICs.

	£
Millie's class 1 employee's NICs	
(£50,000 – £9,500) × 12%	4,860
(£51,000 – £50,000) × 2%	20
	———
	4,880
	———
Blue Forge Ltd's class 1 employer's NICs	
(£51,000 – £8,788) × 13.8%	5,826
	———

Test your understanding 1

Alex is paid £10,850 per year and Betty is paid £52,000 per year.

Calculate the employee's and the employer's class 1 NIC liability for the tax year 2020/21.

Company directors

Special rules apply to company directors to prevent the avoidance of NICs by paying low weekly or monthly salaries, and then taking a large bonus in a single week or month.

Therefore, when an employee is a company director, his class 1 NICs are calculated as if he had an annual earnings period, regardless of how he is paid (e.g. monthly, weekly).

Payment of class 1 contributions

The administration and payment of class 1 NICs is carried out by the employer as follows:

- The employer is responsible for calculating the amount of class 1 employee and employer's contributions at each pay date.

- Employee contributions are deducted from the employee's wages or salary by the employer and paid to HMRC on the employee's behalf.

- The total employee and employer's contributions are payable by the employer to HMRC, along with income tax deducted from the employees under PAYE.

- The payment is due on the 19th of each month (i.e. due not later than 14 days after the end of each PAYE month).

- However, most businesses pay electronically and are allowed an extra 3 days to pay. Therefore the payment is **normally due on the 22nd of each month**. The electronic pay day should be used in the examination.

- The specific payment rules for very small employers and those not paying electronically are covered in detail in Chapter 13.

NIC employment allowance

Employers are able to claim up to £4,000 relief p.a. from their class 1 employer's NIC payments.

Note that the allowance:

- cannot be used against any other classes of NICs (e.g. class 1A)

- is claimed through the real time information (RTI) PAYE system (see Chapter 13)

- is not available to companies where a director is the sole employee

- is only available to employers with total class 1 employer's contributions <£100,000 in the previous tax year.

Information regarding the prior year's class 1 employer's NICs will be provided in the examination question where required.

The £4,000 allowance is included in the tax rates and allowances provided to you in the examination.

Class 1A NICs

Employers are required to pay class 1A contributions on taxable benefits provided to employees.

No class 1A contributions are payable in respect of:

- exempt benefits (i.e. those benefits which are exempt from income tax (see Chapter 5)).

- benefits already treated as earnings and assessed to class 1 NICs, such as remuneration received in the form of non-cash vouchers (see above).

The contributions are calculated as:

- 13.8% on the value of the taxable benefits.

Class 1A contributions are an additional cost of employment and are a deductible expense when calculating the employer's tax adjusted trading profits.

 Illustration 5 – Class 1A NICs

Simon is employed by Dutton Ltd at an annual salary of £53,000.

He was provided with a company car throughout the tax year 2020/21 that had a list price of £15,000. The car has CO_2 emissions of 133g/km. Petrol for both business and private mileage is provided by his employer.

Calculate the employee's and the employer's class 1 and class 1A NIC liabilities due for the tax year 2020/21 in respect of Simon. Ignore the employment allowance.

Solution

(a) **Class 1 NICs**

	£
Employee class 1 NICs	
(£50,000 – £9,500) × 12% (maximum)	4,860
(£53,000 – £50,000) × 2%	60
	4,900
Employer's class 1 NICs	
(£53,000 – £8,788) × 13.8%	6,101

(b) **Class 1A NICs**

Simon's taxable benefits for class 1A purposes are as follows:

	£
Company motor car	
13% + ((130 − 50) × 1/5) = 29% × £15,000	4,350
Private fuel provided by company (29% × £24,500)	7,105
	———
Taxable benefits for class 1A	11,455
	———
Employer's class 1A NICs (£11,455 × 13.8%)	1,581
	———

Note: The employment allowance is deducted from the total class 1 employer's NICs, not from the liability relating to one individual.

Test your understanding 2

Blessing is paid £25,000 per year and had taxable benefits for the tax year 2020/21 of:

	£
Company motor car	5,250
Private fuel provided by company	4,200
Beneficial loan	2,600
Vouchers to be used at the local department store	250

The company also provided Blessing with a mobile phone, which cost £135.

Contributions into her personal pension scheme were as follows:

Employer's contribution	£2,540
Employee's contribution	£1,380

Calculate the employee's and the employer's class 1 and class 1A NIC liabilities for the tax year 2020/21 in respect of Blessing. Ignore the employment allowance.

Payment of class 1A contributions

Class 1A contributions are payable to HMRC by 19 July following the end of the tax year (i.e. by 19 July 2021 for the tax year 2020/21).

However, most businesses pay electronically and therefore pay by **22 July following the end of the tax year**. The electronic pay day should be used in the examination.

Summary

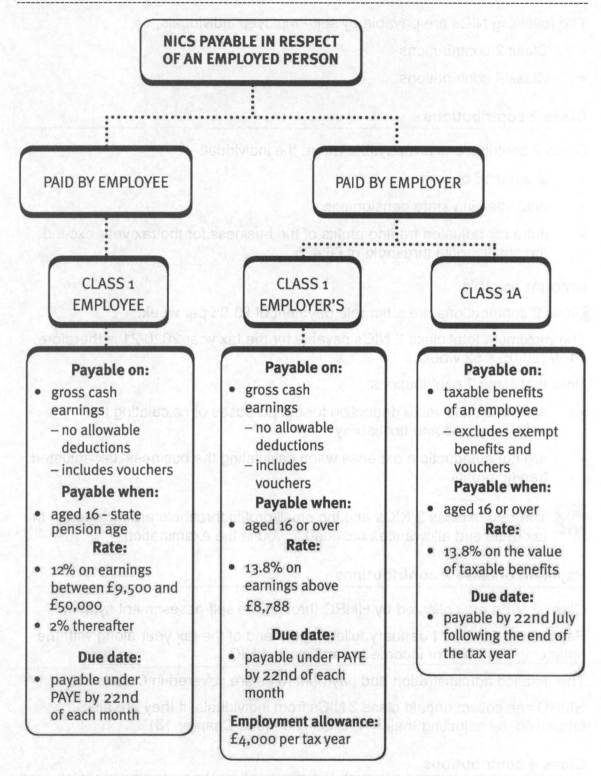

NICS PAYABLE IN RESPECT OF AN EMPLOYED PERSON

PAID BY EMPLOYEE

PAID BY EMPLOYER

CLASS 1 EMPLOYEE

CLASS 1 EMPLOYER'S

CLASS 1A

Payable on:
- gross cash earnings
  - no allowable deductions
  - includes vouchers

Payable when:
- aged 16 – state pension age

Rate:
- 12% on earnings between £9,500 and £50,000
- 2% thereafter

Due date:
- payable under PAYE by 22nd of each month

Payable on:
- gross cash earnings
  - no allowable deductions
  - includes vouchers

Payable when:
- aged 16 or over

Rate:
- 13.8% on earnings above £8,788

Due date:
- payable under PAYE by 22nd of each month

Employment allowance: £4,000 per tax year

Payable on:
- taxable benefits of an employee
  - excludes exempt benefits and vouchers

Payable when:
- aged 16 or over

Rate:
- 13.8% on the value of taxable benefits

Due date:
- payable by 22nd July following the end of the tax year

3 NICs payable in respect of self-employed individuals

The following NICs are payable by self-employed individuals:

- Class 2 contributions
- Class 4 contributions.

Class 2 contributions

Class 2 contributions are payable where the individual:

- is aged 16 or over
- until attaining state pension age
- if the tax adjusted trading profits of the business for the tax year exceed the small profits threshold of £6,475.

Amount payable

Class 2 contributions are a flat rate payment of £3.05 per week.

The maximum total class 2 NICs payable for the tax year 2020/21 is therefore £159 (£3.05 × 52 weeks).

Note that class 2 contributions:

- are not an allowable deduction for the purposes of calculating the individual's income tax liability
- are not a deductible expense when calculating the business' tax adjusted trading profits.

 The rate of class 2 NICs and the small profits threshold are included in the tax rates and allowances provided to you in the examination.

Payment of class 2 contributions

Class 2 NICs are collected by HMRC through the self-assessment system.

Payment is due by 31 January following the end of the tax year along with the balancing payment for income tax and class 4 NIC.

The detailed administration and payment rules are covered in Chapter 13.

HMRC can collect unpaid class 2 NICs from individuals, if they are also employed, by adjusting their PAYE tax code (see Chapter 13).

Class 4 contributions

In addition to class 2 NICs, a self-employed individual may also be liable to class 4 NICs.

Class 4 contributions are payable by self-employed individuals who:

- at the start of the tax year, are aged 16 or over.

They continue to pay **until**:

* the end of the tax year in which they reach state pension age.

Class 4 NICs are a percentage based contribution levied on the 'profits' of the individual in excess of £9,500 for the tax year 2020/21.

Note that class 4 contributions:

* are not an allowable deduction for the purposes of calculating the individual's income tax liability

* are not a deductible expense when calculating the business' tax adjusted trading profits.

 The definition of profits

'Profits' for the purposes of class 4 NICs consists of:

* the tax adjusted trading profits of the individual that are assessed for income tax after deducting trading losses (if any).

This definition of profits also applies for class 2 NIC purposes (see earlier).

Note that 'profits' for class 2 and class 4 NICs are **before** deducting the individual's personal allowance that is available for income tax purposes.

If the individual has more than one business, the aggregate of all profits from all self-employed occupations are used to calculate the class 4 NIC liability.

Calculating class 4 NICs

The contributions payable are calculated as:

* 9% on profits between £9,500 and £50,000.

* 2% on profits in excess of £50,000.

 The rate and thresholds for class 4 NICs are included in the tax rates and allowances provided to you in the examination.

Illustration 6 – Class 4 NICs

James has been trading as a self-employed painter and decorator since 2001. His tax adjusted trading profits for the tax year 2020/21 are £62,000 and he has trading losses brought forward of £10,000.

His wife, Poppy, is a part-time mobile hairdresser. Her tax adjusted trading profits for the tax year 2020/21 are £10,560.

Calculate the class 4 NICs payable by James and Poppy for the tax year 2020/21.

Solution

James	**£**
Tax adjusted trading profits	62,000
Less: Trading losses brought forward	(10,000)
Profits for class 4 purposes	52,000
Class 4 NICs	**£**
(£50,000 – £9,500) × 9% (maximum)	3,645
(£52,000 – £50,000) × 2%	40
	3,685
Poppy	
(£10,560 – £9,500) × 9%	95

 Test your understanding 3

Jackie is a self-employed builder who has been in business for many years and prepares accounts to 31 March each year.

Her tax adjusted trading profit for the year ended 31 March 2021 is £56,850.

Calculate Jackie's class 2 and class 4 NIC liabilities for the tax year 2020/21.

Payment of class 4 contributions

Class 4 contributions are paid to HMRC at the same time as the individual's income tax payments.

Income tax and class 4 NICs due are collected by HMRC through the self-assessment system.

The detailed administration and payment rules are covered in Chapter 13.

Summary

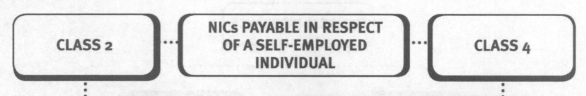

```
┌──────────────┐     ┌─────────────────────┐     ┌──────────────┐
│              │     │  NICs PAYABLE IN    │     │              │
│   CLASS 2    │ ··· │  RESPECT OF A       │ ··· │   CLASS 4    │
│              │     │  SELF-EMPLOYED      │     │              │
│              │     │  INDIVIDUAL         │     │              │
└──────────────┘     └─────────────────────┘     └──────────────┘
```

Class 2

Payable when:

- aged 16 – state pension age

Rate:

- fixed rate £3.05 per week

Due date:

- payable on 31 January following the end of the tax year under self-assessment

Class 4

Payable on:

- tax adjusted trading profits after trading losses

Payable when:

- aged 16 - state pension age at the start of the tax year

Rate:

- 9% on profits between £9,500 and £50,000
- 2% thereafter

Due date:

- payable with income tax due under self assessment

4 Total NICs payable by a self-employed individual

A self-employed individual pays:

- both class 2 and class 4 NICs in respect of his trading profits.

In addition, if self-employed individuals employ staff, they will also be required to account for:

- class 1 employee, class 1 employer's and class 1A NICs in respect of earnings and benefits provided to employees.

 An examination scenario focusing on a sole trader could therefore involve consideration of all of these classes of NIC.

 Test your understanding 4

Diane has been a self-employed computer consultant for many years. Her tax adjusted trading profits for the tax year 2020/21 are £52,500.

Diane employs one employee, a full-time personal assistant, at a salary of £38,300 p.a. She also provides the assistant with a diesel-engine company car, which has a list price of £13,500 and CO_2 emissions of 114g/km. Diane pays for the assistant's private and business fuel.

Diane's class 1 employer's liability was £3680 in the previous tax year.

Calculate the total NICs that Diane must account for to HMRC in respect of the tax year 2020/21.

5 Chapter summary

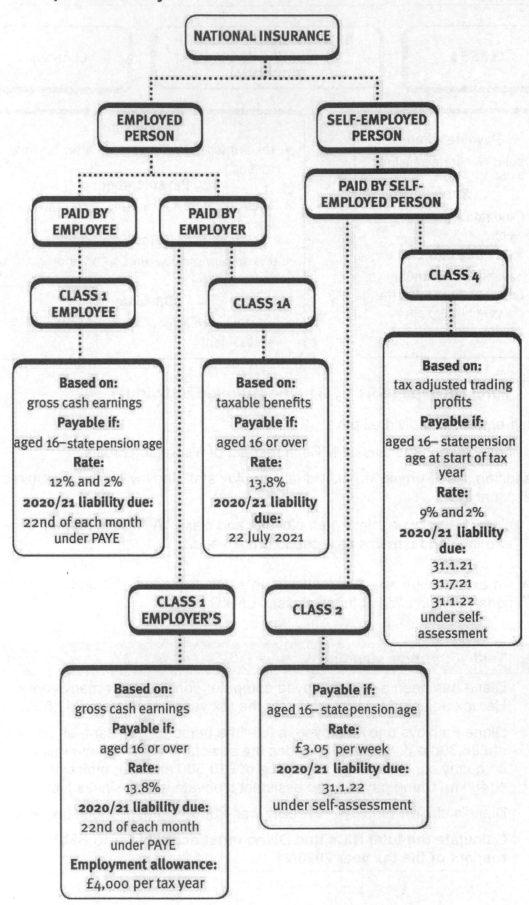

6 Practice objective test questions

Test your understanding 5

Keith is an employee of K Ltd. Keith receives cash earnings of £31,400 and a car benefit valued at £5,800 in the tax year 2020/21.

What amount of class 1 employee national insurance contributions (NIC) does Keith suffer in respect of the tax year 2020/21?

A   £2,628

B   £3,324

C   £3,768

D   £4,464

Test your understanding 6

Anastasia is self-employed and runs her own business as a caterer. She employs Patrice who is paid £15,000 p.a.

What classes of national insurance contributions is Anastasia liable to pay in respect of her business?

A   Class 2 only

B   Class 4 only

C   Class 2 and class 4 only

D   Class 2, class 4 and class 1 employer's contributions

Test your understanding 7

Atharv is employed and received the following from his employer for the tax year 2020/21.

	£
Salary	35,000
Employer pension contributions	3,250
A company car – assessable benefit	3,570

In addition, Atharv incurred business travel expenses of £400, which were not reimbursed by his employer.

Atharv's earnings for the purpose of calculating his class 1 national insurance contributions are:

A   £35,000

B   £38,250

C   £34,600

D   £38,570

Test your understanding 8

Jess is employed by A Ltd and earns a salary of £50,000 per year. In addition, Jess receives taxable non-cash benefits of £3,000 every year.

What are A Ltd's class 1 employer's national insurance contributions for the tax year 2020/21?

A   £6,101

B   £6,900

C   £4,945

D   £5,687

Test your understanding answers

Test your understanding 1

	£
Alex	
Employee's class 1 NICs (£10,850 – £9,500) × 12%	162
Employer's class 1 NICs (£10,850 – £8,788) × 13.8%	285
Betty	
Employee's class 1 NICs	
(£50,000 – £9,500) × 12% (maximum)	4,860
(£52,000 – £50,000) × 2%	40
	4,900
Employer's class 1 NICs (£52,000 – £8,788) × 13.8%	5,963

Test your understanding 2

Blessing

Class 1 NICs

	£
Salary	25,000
Vouchers	250
Cash earnings for class 1 NICs	25,250
Employee's class 1 NICs (£25,250 – £9,500) × 12%	1,890
Employer's class 1 NICs (£25,250 – £8,788) × 13.8%	2,272

Notes:

(1) The provision of one mobile phone per employee, and employer pension contributions, are excluded as they are exempt benefits.

(2) The employee pension contributions are not allowable deductions in calculating earnings for NIC purposes.

(3) The car, fuel and beneficial loan benefits are excluded as they are non-cash benefits, which are assessed to class 1A NICs, not class 1.

Class 1A NICs	£
Company motor car	5,250
Private fuel provided by company	4,200
Beneficial loan	2,600
Taxable benefits for class 1A	12,050
Employer's class 1A NICs (£12,050 × 13.8%)	1,663

Note: The employment allowance is deducted from the total class 1 employer's NICs, not from the liability relating to one individual.

Test your understanding 3

Jackie

	£159
Class 2 NICs (£3.05 × 52 weeks)	£159

Class 4 NICs	£
(£50,000 – £9,500) × 9% (maximum)	3,645
(£56,850 – £50,000) × 2%	137
	3,782

Test your understanding 4

Diane

(1) Flat rate class 2 contributions in respect of the business.

Class 2 NICs

(£3.05 × 52 weeks)   £159
                                                                    ───────

(2) Class 4 contributions in respect of the business based on tax adjusted trading profits as they are in excess of £9,500.

Class 4 NICs	£
(£50,000 – £9,500) × 9% (maximum)	3,645
(£52,500 – £50,000) × 2%	50
	───────
	3,695
	───────

(3) Class 1 employer's contributions as Diane is an employer, based on her personal assistant's salary of £38,300.

Employer's class 1 NICs	£
(£38,300 – £8,788) × 13.8%	4,073
Less: Employment allowance	(4,000)
	───────
Class 1 employer's contributions payable	73
	───────

Note: The employment allowance is £4,000 per tax year and reduces employer's class 1 NIC payable to HMRC. As the personal assistant is the only employee it is deducted from the employer's class 1 liability on the employee's earnings.

(4) Class 1A contributions based on the benefit arising from the provision of a company car to the personal assistant.

Company motor car	£
17% + ((110 – 50) × 1/5) = 29% × £13,500	3,915
Private fuel provided (29% × £24,500)	7,105
	───────
Taxable benefits for Class 1A	11,020
	───────

Employer's class 1A NICs	
(£11,020 × 13.8%)	1,521
	───────

(5) Employee class 1 contributions are levied on the personal assistant. However, it is Diane's responsibility to deduct the NICs from the assistant's salary and pay them to HMRC along with the employer's class 1 contributions on the 22nd of each month (Note).

Employee's class 1 NICs

(£38,300 – £9,500) × 12%	£3,456

Summary	£
Class 2	159
Class 4	3,695
Employer's class 1	73
Class 1A	1,521
Diane's total liability	5,448
Employee's class 1	3,456
Total amount Diane must account for to HMRC	8,904

Note: In the examination quote the electronic pay date as most businesses pay electronically.

Test your understanding 5

The correct answer is A.

Class 1 employee contributions: (£31,400 – £9,500) × 12% = £2,628

Benefits are not liable to class 1 contributions. They are liable to class 1A which is payable by the employer.

Test your understanding 6

The correct answer is D.

D is the correct answer because Anastasia is liable to pay:

- Class 2 contributions
- Class 4 contributions and
- Class 1 employer's contribution as a result of employing Patrice.

Test your understanding 7

The correct answer is A.

A is the correct answer because class 1 employee contributions are not payable on either exempt benefits (the employer pension contributions) or taxable benefits, (i.e. the company car).

No deduction is made for allowable expenses in arriving at the earnings figure.

Test your understanding 8

The correct answer is D.

Employer's class 1 national insurance contributions (NIC) are calculated on cash earnings, but not benefits. The first £8,788 is exempt and the remainder is charged at 13.8%.

The NIC is therefore: (£50,000 – £8,788) × 13.8%	£5,687

Tax administration for individuals

Chapter learning objectives

Upon completion of this chapter you will be able to:

- explain and apply the features of the self-assessment system as it applies to individuals

- recognise the time limits that apply to the filing of returns and the making of claims

- recognise the due dates for the payment of tax under the self-assessment system, and compute payments on account and balancing payments/repayments for individuals

- list the information and records that taxpayers need to retain for tax purposes

- explain the circumstances in which HM Revenue & Customs can make a compliance check into a self-assessment tax return

- explain the procedures for dealing with appeals and First and Upper Tier Tribunals

- calculate late payment interest and state the penalties that can be charged

- explain the PAYE system, how benefits can be payrolled, and the purpose of form P11D

- recognise the circumstances in which real time reporting late filing penalties will be imposed on an employer and the amount of penalty which is charged.

PER

One of the PER performance objectives (PO16) is to make sure that individuals and entities comply with their tax obligations – on time, and in the spirit and letter of the law. Working through this chapter should help you understand how to demonstrate that objective.

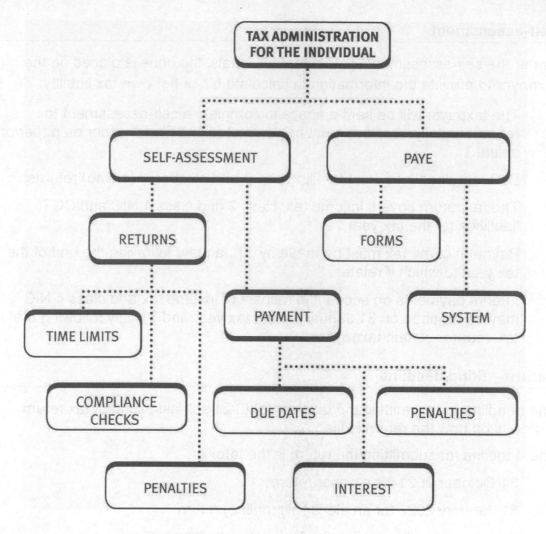

1 Personal tax administration

The collection of income tax

Employees have their income tax and national insurance liabilities on their employment income, and in some cases on small amounts of other income, collected at source through the PAYE system.

Self-assessment is the system for the collection of tax, which is not deducted through the PAYE system.

Therefore, employees with more complicated tax affairs and other taxpayers (e.g. the self-employed) will normally be required to submit details of their taxable income and gains annually in a tax return, so that their tax liability can be calculated and collected through the self-assessment system.

Self-assessment

Under the self-assessment system for individuals, the onus is placed on the taxpayer to provide the information to calculate his or her own tax liability:

- The taxpayer will be sent a notice to complete a self-assessment tax return annually. A return must be completed and filed – either on paper or online.

- Different deadlines exist for filing paper and electronic (online) returns.

- The tax return covers income tax, class 2 and class 4 NIC and CGT liabilities for the tax year.

- Payment of the tax must be made by 31 January following the end of the tax year to which it relates.

- Interim payments on account in respect of income tax and class 4 NIC may be required on 31 January in the tax year and 31 July following the tax year for certain taxpayers.

Return – filing deadline

The deadline for submitting the tax year 2020/21 self-assessment tax return depends on how the return is filed.

The deadline for submitting the return is the **later** of:

- 31 October 2021 for a paper return

- 31 January 2022 for an electronic (online) return

- three months after the issue of the notice to file a return.

The 31 January following the end of the tax year is known as the **'filing date'**, regardless of whether the return is filed on paper or electronically.

This must be distinguished from the date on which the return is actually filed/submitted, which is the 'actual filing date'.

Content of tax return

The taxpayer completes the main tax return form (SA100) to give basic details including his or her name, address and certain types of investment income.

The taxpayer should then complete relevant supplementary pages to tell HMRC about all of his or her income and gains relating to the tax year. For example, income from employment, income from property, or capital gains.

If the taxpayer is completing his or her tax return online, these supplementary pages can be added as necessary. If the taxpayer is completing a paper tax return, the supplementary pages needed should be requested at the same time as the main tax return.

Self-employed people: Should complete the self-employment supplementary pages.

Employees: Generally pay their tax liability under PAYE and often a self-assessment tax return will not be required as there is no further tax liability. However, if they receive other taxable income that is not fully taxed through the PAYE system, they will need to complete a tax return.

Partnerships: Although partners are dealt with individually, a partnership return is required to aid self-assessment on the individual partners. This gives details of the partners, includes a partnership statement detailing the partnership's tax adjusted trading profit and shows how this is allocated between the partners.

Return – calculation of tax

- Where a return is filed electronically:

  - a calculation of the tax liability is automatically provided as part of the online filing process.

- Where a paper return is submitted:

  - HMRC will calculate the tax liability on behalf of the taxpayer, provided the return is submitted by the 31 October deadline. The taxpayer also has the option of calculating the tax himself.

  - the calculation by HMRC is treated as a self-assessment on behalf of the taxpayer.

- Where HMRC calculates the tax it makes no judgement of the accuracy of the figures included in the return, but merely calculates the tax liability based on the information submitted.

- HMRC normally communicate with the taxpayer by issuing a statement of account, which is a reminder of amounts owing to HMRC.

Statement of account

The statement of account sets out:

- the tax charges

- any charges of interest or penalties (see later)

- any payments already made by the taxpayer.

Amendments to the return

Either party may amend the return:

- HMRC may correct any obvious errors or mistakes within **nine months** of the date that the return is filed with them.

  These would include arithmetical errors or errors of principle. However, this does not mean that HMRC has necessarily accepted the return as accurate.

- The taxpayer can amend the return within **12 months** of the 31 January filing date. For the tax year 2020/21, amendments must therefore be made by 31 January 2023.

  Note that the deadline is the same regardless of whether the return is filed on paper or electronically.

If an error is discovered at a later date then the taxpayer can make a claim for overpayment relief (see later) to recover any tax overpaid.

Notification of chargeability

Self-assessment places the responsibility on the taxpayer to notify HMRC of all taxable income, therefore:

- Taxpayers who do not receive a notice to file a return are required to notify HMRC if they have income or chargeable gains on which tax is due.

- The time limit for notifying HMRC of chargeability is six months from the end of the tax year in which the liability arises (i.e. 5 October 2021 for the tax year 2020/21).

- Notification is not necessary if there is no actual tax liability. For example, if the income or capital gain is covered by allowances or exemptions.

- A standard penalty may arise for failure to notify chargeability (see section 7).

Penalty for failure to submit a return

HMRC can impose fixed penalties and tax geared penalties for the failure to submit a return, depending on the length of the delay.

See section 7 for the detail on the penalties that can be imposed.

Determination of tax due if no return is filed

Where a self-assessment tax return is not filed by the filing date, HMRC may determine the amount of tax due. The impact of this is:

- The determination is treated as a self-assessment by the taxpayer.

- The determination can only be replaced by the actual self-assessment when it is submitted by the taxpayer (i.e. the submission of a tax return).

- There is no appeal against a determination, which therefore encourages the taxpayer to displace it with the actual self-assessment.

A determination can be made at any time within **three years** of the filing date (i.e. by 31 January 2025 for 2020/21 tax return).

Records

Taxpayers are required to keep and preserve records necessary to make a correct and complete return.

Taxpayers with a business

For a business (including the letting of property), the records that must be kept include:

- all receipts and expenses

- all goods purchased and sold

- all supporting documents relating to the transactions of the business, such as accounts, books, contracts, vouchers and receipts.

These taxpayers (i.e. the self-employed), must keep all their records (not just those relating to the business) until five years after the 31 January filing date.

For the tax year 2020/21 records must therefore be retained until 31 January 2027.

Other taxpayers

Other taxpayers are likely to have fewer records, but should keep evidence of income received such as dividend vouchers, P60s, copies of P11Ds and bank statements.

The records for these taxpayers must be retained until the **later** of:

- 12 months after the 31 January filing date (31 January 2023 for the tax year 2020/21)

- the date on which a compliance check into the return is completed (see section 5)

- the date on which it becomes impossible for a compliance check to be started.

Penalty for not keeping records

A penalty may be charged for failure to keep or retain adequate records.

The maximum penalty is only likely to be imposed in the most serious cases such as where a taxpayer deliberately destroys his records in order to obstruct an HMRC compliance check.

See section 7 for the detail on the penalties which can be imposed.

2 Payment of tax

A taxpayer is required to settle liabilities by 31 January following the end of the tax year for:

- income tax
- class 2 national insurance
- class 4 national insurance
- capital gains.

For the tax year 2020/21 this is by 31 January 2022.

Payments on account

For certain taxpayers, payments on account (POAs) may also be required.

If the taxpayer had an income tax liability in the previous tax year in excess of any tax deducted at source, a POA is normally required for the following year.

The exceptions to this are if:

- the total tax liability (i.e. income tax plus class 4 NIC) less PAYE for the previous tax year is less than £1,000, or
- more than 80% of the total tax liability (i.e. income tax plus class 4 NICs) for the previous tax year was met by deduction of tax at source.

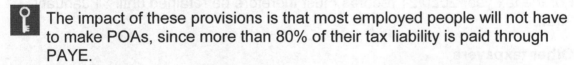 The impact of these provisions is that most employed people will not have to make POAs, since more than 80% of their tax liability is paid through PAYE.

Due dates

For those taxpayers who are required to make POAs, the payment dates for the tax year 2020/21 are:

- first POA – 31 January 2021
- second POA – 31 July 2021.

Any remaining liability is then settled on the 31 January 2022 due date.

POAs are only required for:

- income tax, and
- class 4 national insurance contributions (NICs).

No POAs are ever required for capital gains tax or class 2 NICs.

There are temporary Covid-19 tax deferral options available regarding the second self-assessment payment on account due on 31 July 2020. However, for any question relating to this payment, you should assume that the taxpayer has not deferred any payments.

Calculation of POAs

POAs are calculated using the previous tax year's 'relevant amount'. Therefore the POAs for the tax year 2020/21 are based on the 'relevant amount' for the tax year 2019/20.

 The 'relevant amount' is calculated as:

	£
Total tax liability for the year (income tax and class 4 NICs)	X
Less: PAYE	(X)
Relevant amount	X

Note: No POAs are required if there is no 'relevant amount' in the previous year. Therefore, for example, a taxpayer who commences self-employment on 1 May 2020 will not have to make POAs for the tax year 2020/21, since he or she will not have a 'relevant amount' for the tax year 2019/20.

Illustration 1 – Payment of tax

Roderick is required to make payments on account of his tax liability for the tax year 2020/21. His income tax liability for the tax year 2019/20 was £5,100. Of this, £1,250 was collected via PAYE.

Calculate Roderick's POAs for the tax year 2020/21.

Solution

The relevant amount for the previous year is £3,850 (£5,100 − £1,250).

As this exceeds £1,000 and exceeds 20% of the total tax liability (20% × £5,100 = £1,020), POAs are required.

The amounts payable as POAs are based on an **equal** division of the 'relevant amount' for the previous year, hence (£3,850 × 1/2) = £1,925.

Roderick is required to make two POAs of £1,925 on 31 January 2021 and 31 July 2021.

Test your understanding 1

Ahmed's tax liability for the tax year 2019/20 was as follows:

	£
Income tax	9,400
Less: PAYE	(2,100)
	7,300
Class 2 NIC	153
Class 4 NIC	700
CGT	3,347
Total tax liability	11,500

Calculate Ahmed's POAs for the tax year 2020/21.

Claims to reduce POAs

- A taxpayer can claim to reduce POAs, at any time before 31 January following the tax year, if he expects the actual income tax and class 4 NIC liability (net of PAYE) for the tax year 2020/21 to be lower than the tax year 2019/20.

- The claim must state the grounds for making the claim.

Following a claim:

- The POAs will be reduced.

- Each POA will be for half the reduced amount, unless the taxpayer claims that there is no tax liability at all.

- If POAs based on the prior year figures are paid before the claim, then HMRC will refund the overpayment.

Incorrect claims to reduce POAs

A taxpayer should only claim to reduce POAs if the tax liability (net of PAYE) for the current year is expected to be less than the POAs based on the previous year's 'relevant amount'.

In the event that the claim is incorrect and the actual tax liability for the current year turns out to be higher than the reduced POAs, then the following consequences arise:

- Interest will be charged on the tax underpaid.

- A penalty may be charged if a taxpayer fraudulently or negligently claims to reduce POAs. See section 7 for the detail on penalties which can be imposed.

- A penalty will not be sought in cases of innocent error. The aim is to penalise taxpayers who claim large reductions in payments on account without any foundation to the claim.

Balancing payments

The balancing payment is due on 31 January following the tax year.

For the tax year 2020/21 this is 31 January 2022.

The balancing payment is calculated as:

	£	£
Total tax liability for the year		X
(Income tax, class 2 NIC, class 4 NIC and CGT)		
Less: PAYE	X	
Less: POAs	X	
	——	(X)
		——
Balancing payment		X
		——

- It is possible that a balancing repayment will be due, in which case HMRC will repay the amount of tax overpaid.

- Where the amount of tax due changes as a result of an amendment to the self-assessment (by either the taxpayer or HMRC), any additional tax due must be paid within 30 days of the notice of amendment if this is later than the normal due date.

Illustration 2 – Payment of tax

Continuing the example of Roderick from above. You now learn that his final liability for the tax year 2020/21 is £7,629. Of this amount, £1,635 has been collected via the PAYE system.

State the total amount payable by Roderick on 31 January 2022 and what the payment relates to.

Solution

The payment made on 31 January 2022 will comprise two parts:

- the balancing payment for the tax year 2020/21

- the first POA for the tax year 2021/22.

The balancing payment for the tax year 2020/21 is based on the final liability for the tax year 2020/21 less PAYE and the POAs already made.

	£
2020/21 – IT liability	7,629
Less: PAYE	(1,635)
Less: POAs	(3,850)
Balancing payment	2,144

The first POA for 2021/22 will be 50% of the 'relevant amount' for 2020/21.

	£
2020/21 – IT liability	7,629
Less: PAYE	(1,635)
Relevant amount	5,994

The first POA is (£5,994 × 1/2) = £2,997

Summary:

	£
Balancing payment – 2020/21	2,144
First POA – 2021/22	2,997
Total payable by 31 January 2022	5,141

Test your understanding 2

Ebba's tax payable for the tax year 2020/21 is as follows:

	£
Income tax	10,800
Less: PAYE	(2,500)
	8,300
Class 2 NIC	156
Class 4 NIC	800
CGT	4,444
Total tax payable	13,700

She made POAs of £8,000 in respect of the tax year 2020/21.

Identify the balancing payment due for the tax year 2020/21, the first POA for the tax year 2021/22 and state the payment date for both.

3 Interest and penalties

There are two types of interest:

- Late payment interest
  - calculated at 2.75% p.a.

- Repayment interest
  - calculated at 0.5% p.a.

 The late payment and repayment interest rates are included in the tax rates and allowances provided to you in the examination.

Late payment interest

Interest is automatically charged if **any** tax is paid late.

Interest can arise in respect of:

- payments on account
- balancing payments
- any tax payable following an amendment to a self-assessment
- any tax payable following a discovery assessment.

All interest is charged on a daily basis

- from: the date the tax was due to be paid
- to: the date of payment.

 In the examination calculations are performed to the nearest month and £ unless indicated otherwise in the question.

 Illustration 3 – Interest

A taxpayer pays his POAs for the tax year 2020/21 on 31 March 2021 and 31 August 2021. The balancing payment is paid on 30 April 2022.

Identify the payments on which interest will be charged and state the period for which interest will be charged.

Solution

Interest will be charged as follows:

- first POA: from 31 January 2021 to 31 March 2021 – 2 months
- second POA: from 31 July 2021 to 31 August 2021 – 1 month
- balancing payment: from 31 January 2022 to 30 April 2022 – 3 months.

Test your understanding 3

Rodney was due to make the following payments of tax for the tax year 2020/21.

Due Date	Payment	Actual date of payment
31 January 2021	£2,100	28 February 2021
31 July 2021	£2,100	31 August 2021
31 January 2022	£1,500	31 March 2022

Identify the periods for which interest will be charged.

Calculate, to the nearest month and pound, the amount of interest payable.

Interest on incorrect claims to reduce POAs

- Interest is charged where an excessive claim is made to reduce POAs.

- The charge is based on the difference between the amounts actually paid and the amounts that should have been paid.

  The amount that should have been paid is the lower of:

  - the original POAs based on the 'relevant amount' for the previous tax year

  - 50% of the final tax liability (excluding CGT and class 2 NIC, net of PAYE) for the current tax year.

Illustration 4 – Interest

A taxpayer's relevant amount for the tax year 2019/20 is £5,000 (POAs for the tax year 2020/21 are therefore £2,500), but a claim is made to reduce the POAs to £1,000 each. These payments are made on time.

Subsequently the taxpayer calculates the actual tax liability (net of PAYE) for the tax year 2020/21 to be £4,500. The correct balancing payment (i.e. £4,500 – £2,000 = £2,500) is paid on 31 January 2022.

Identify the amounts on which interest will be charged and state the period(s) for which interest will be charged.

Solution

POAs should have been reduced to £2,250 (£4,500 × 1/2) rather than £1,000. Interest will therefore be charged as follows:

- on £1,250 from 31 January 2021 to 31 January 2022

- on £1,250 from 31 July 2021 to 31 January 2022

Illustration 5 – Interest

Helena's POAs for the tax year 2020/21 based on her income tax liability for the tax year 2019/20 were £4,500 each. However, Helena made a claim to reduce these amounts to £3,500.

She made her POAs for the tax year 2020/21 as follows:

Payment	£	Date
First POA	3,500	29 January 2021
Second POA	3,500	31 August 2021

Helena's actual liability for the tax year 2020/21 was as follows:

Income tax liability (net of PAYE)	£10,000
Capital gains tax	£2,500

Helena paid the balance of the tax due £5,500 on 28 February 2022.

Identify the amounts on which interest will be charged and state the period(s) for which interest will be charged.

Solution

POAs should not have been reduced as Helena's tax liability for the tax year 2020/21 (£10,000) is greater than the relevant amount for the tax year 2019/20 (£9,000). Therefore the amount that should have been paid, on each of the due dates was £4,500.

First POA:

£3,500 is paid on time.

Interest charge therefore only levied on £1,000 that should also have been paid.

Levied for the period 31 January 2021 to 28 February 2022.

Second POA:

£3,500, as well as being the wrong amount, was also paid late.

On £3,500, interest charged 31 July 2021 to 31 August 2021.

On the additional £1,000 not paid, interest levied for the period 31 July 2021 to 28 February 2022.

On balancing payment:

Income tax of £9,000 (£4,500 × 2) has been dealt with above, so it is only the remaining £1,000 that will incur an interest charge, from 31 January 2022 to 28 February 2022.

Capital gains tax of £2,500 incurs interest from 31 January 2022 to 28 February 2022.

Repayment interest

Interest may be paid by HMRC on any overpayment of tax.

If applicable, interest runs:

- from: the later of:
  - the date the tax was due, or
  - the date HMRC actually received the tax
- to: the date of repayment.

Where interest is paid, it is only paid on the amount of tax that should have been paid (i.e. deliberate overpayments do not attract interest).

Penalties for late payments

Late payment interest is not a penalty, since it merely aims to compensate for the advantage of paying late.

Therefore, to further encourage payment of tax by the due date, penalties can also be imposed by HMRC where income tax, class 2 NIC, class 4 NIC or CGT is paid late.

 Penalties do not apply to POAs.

Penalties are calculated as follows:

Tax paid (Note)	Penalty (% of tax due)
More than 1 month late	5%
More than 6 months late	Additional 5%
More than 12 months late	Additional 5%

 Technically the penalties apply if tax is paid more than 30 days late, 5 months and 30 days late and 11 months and 30 days late, but the TX examining team article gives these time limits to the nearest month and it is acceptable to do so in the examination.

HMRC have the discretion to reduce a penalty in special circumstances, for example if it is considered that the penalty would be inappropriate or disproportionate. However, the inability to pay will not be classified as special circumstances.

For details of other penalties relating to self-assessment, see section 7.

Illustration 6 – Interest and penalties

A taxpayer's balancing payment due for the tax year 2020/21 is £5,000. Only £1,200 of this was paid on 31 January 2022.

Set out the interest and penalties that will be payable and state the implication of continued non-payment of the liability.

Solution

Interest

Interest will be charged on £3,800 from 31 January 2022 to the date of payment.

Penalties

A penalty of £190 (£3,800 at 5%) will be due if the tax of £3,800 is not paid by 28 February 2022 (i.e. one month after due date).

A further penalty of £190 will be due if the tax is not paid by 31 July 2022, and again if the tax is not paid by 31 January 2023.

 Test your understanding 4

Rowena's tax payable (after PAYE but before POAs) for the tax year 2020/21 is:

Income tax	£6,000
Capital gains tax	£3,000

POAs of £4,000 in total were made on the relevant dates. The balance of the tax due was paid as follows:

Income tax	28 February 2022
Capital gains tax	31 March 2022

Calculate the interest and penalties due on a monthly basis.

4 Claims

- A claim for a relief, allowance or repayment can be made to HMRC, usually via the tax return.

- The amount of the claim must be quantified at the time that the claim is made. For example, if loss relief is claimed, then the amount of the loss must be stated.

Claims for earlier years

Certain claims will relate to earlier years. The most obvious example of this is the claiming of loss relief for earlier years.

The basic rule is that such a claim is:

*   established in the later year

*   calculated based on the tax liability of the earlier year.

The tax liability for the earlier year is not adjusted. Instead, the tax reduction resulting from the claim is set off against the tax liability for the later year. The logic is that it avoids re-opening assessments for earlier years.

Alternatively if a separate claim is made HMRC will refund the tax due.

As the claim is only quantified by reference to the earlier year, POAs that are based on the relevant amount for the earlier year, do not change.

Illustration 7 – Claims for earlier years

A taxpayer's relevant amount for the tax year 2019/20 is £4,400. In the tax year 2020/21 the taxpayer makes a trading loss of £1,000, and makes a claim to offset this against his total income of the tax year 2019/20.

Explain how the taxpayer will receive the tax refund arising as a result of the relief for the loss arising in the tax year 2020/21.

Solution

The taxpayer's POAs for the tax year 2020/21 are £2,200 (£4,400 × 1/2), and these will not change as a result of the loss relief claim.

The tax refund due will be calculated at the taxpayer's marginal income tax rate(s) for the tax year 2019/20.

The tax refund due will either be set off against the tax liability for the tax year 2020/21, thereby affecting the balancing payment on 31 January 2022, or if there is insufficient tax left owing, HMRC will make a refund.

Claims for overpayment relief

Where an assessment is excessive due to an error or mistake in a return, the taxpayer can claim relief. The claim must be made within four years of the end of the tax year concerned.

For the tax year 2020/21 the claim must be made by 5 April 2025.

A claim can be made in respect of errors made, and mistakes arising from not understanding the law.

5   Compliance checks

- HMRC have the right to enquire into the completeness and accuracy of any self-assessment tax return under their compliance check powers.

- HMRC must give written notice before commencing a compliance check (also known as an enquiry).

- The written notice must be issued within 12 months of the date the return is filed with HMRC. Once this deadline is passed, the taxpayer can normally consider the self-assessment for that year as final.

- The information requested by HMRC should be limited to that connected with the return.

- An appeal can be made against the request.

- The compliance check (enquiry) ends when HMRC gives written notice that it has been completed. The notice will state the outcome of the enquiry.

- The taxpayer has 30 days to appeal against any amendments by HMRC. The appeal must be in writing.

Compliance check procedure – further details

The compliance check may be made as a result of any of the following:

- a suspicion that income is undeclared

- deductions being incorrectly claimed

- other information in HMRC's possession

- being part of a random review process.

Additional points:

- HMRC do not have to state a reason for the compliance check and are unlikely to do so.

- a compliance check can be made even if HMRC calculated the taxpayer's tax liability.

HMRC can demand that the taxpayer produces any or all of the following:

- documents

- accounts

- other written particulars

- full answers to specific questions.

A closure notice must include either:

- confirmation that no amendments are required

- HMRC's amendments to the self-assessment.

> ### Discovery assessment
>
> HMRC must normally begin compliance checks into a self-assessment return within 12 months of the date the return is filed, however a discovery assessment can be raised at a later date to prevent the loss of tax.
>
> The use of a discovery assessment is restricted where a self-assessment has already been made.
>
> - Unless the loss of tax was brought about carelessly or deliberately by the taxpayer, a discovery assessment cannot be raised where full disclosure was made in the return, even if this is found to be incorrect.
>
> - HMRC will only accept that full disclosure has been made if any contentious items have been clearly brought to their attention – perhaps in a covering letter or in the 'white space' on the tax return.
>
> - Information contained in the attached accounts will not constitute full disclosure if its significance is not emphasised.
>
> - Only a taxpayer who makes full disclosure in the tax return has absolute finality 12 months after the date the return is filed.
>
> The time limit for issuing a discovery assessment is:
>
> | | Time from end of tax year | For 2020/21 |
> |---|---|---|
> | Basic time limit | Four years | 5 April 2025 |
> | Careless error | Six years | 5 April 2027 |
> | Deliberate error | Twenty years | 5 April 2041 |
>
> A discovery assessment may be appealed against.

6   Appeals

Taxpayers can appeal against a decision made by HMRC, but they must do so within 30 days of the disputed decision.

Most appeals are then settled amicably by discussion between the taxpayer and HMRC.

However, if the taxpayer is not satisfied with the outcome of the discussions, he or she can proceed in one of two ways:

- request that his or her case is reviewed by another HMRC officer, or

- have his or her case referred to an independent Tax Tribunal.

If the taxpayer opts to have his or her case reviewed but disagrees with the outcome, he or she can still send an appeal to the Tax Tribunal.

The taxpayer must also apply to postpone all or part of the tax charged. Otherwise he or she will have to pay the disputed amount.

Tax Tribunals

The Tax Tribunal is an independent body where cases are heard by independently appointed tax judges and/or panel members.

There are two tiers (layers) of the Tax Tribunal system:

- First-tier Tribunal, and
- Upper Tribunal.

Tax Tribunals

First-tier Tribunal

The First-tier Tribunal is the first tribunal for most issues. It deals with:

- *Default paper cases:* simple appeals, (e.g. against a fixed penalty) – will usually be disposed of without a hearing provided both sides agree.

- *Basic cases:* straightforward appeals involving a minimal exchange of paperwork in advance of a short hearing.

- *Standard cases:* appeals involving more detailed consideration of issues and a more formal hearing.

- *Complex cases:* some complex appeals may be heard by the First-tier however they will usually be heard by the Upper Tribunal.

If the dispute is not resolved at the First-tier level then the appeal can go to the Upper Tribunal.

Upper Tribunal

The Upper Tribunal mainly, but not exclusively, reviews and decides appeals from the First-tier Tribunal on a point of law.

In addition, it also deals with complex cases requiring detailed specialist knowledge and a formal hearing – e.g. involving long or complicated issues, points of principle and large financial amounts.

Hearings are held in public and decisions are published.

A decision of the Upper Tribunal may be appealed to the Court of Appeal. However, the grounds of appeal must always relate to a point of law.

7 Penalties

Standard penalties

HMRC has standardised penalties across taxes for different offences.

The standard penalty applies to two key areas:

- submission of incorrect returns – all taxes

- failure to notify liability to tax – income tax, CGT, corporation tax, VAT and NIC.

The penalty is calculated as a percentage of 'potential lost revenue' which is generally the tax unpaid as a result of the error or failure to notify.

Taxpayer behaviour	Maximum penalty (% of revenue lost)
Genuine mistake (for incorrect returns only)	No Penalty
Careless/Failure to take reasonable care	30%
Deliberate but no concealment	70%
Deliberate with concealment	100%

An incorrect return:

- must result in an understatement of the taxpayer's liability, and

- no reasonable steps have been taken to notify HMRC of the error.

- Includes:

    - deliberately supplying false information

    - deliberately withholding information

    - inflating a loss and/or claims for allowances and reliefs

    - inflating a tax repayment claim

    - submitting incorrect accounts in relation to a liability.

If there is more than one error in a return, a separate penalty can be charged for each error.

Failure to notify liability to tax applies where:

- the taxpayer has a liability to tax, and notification is required

- but notification of chargeability is not made to HMRC.

Note from the penalty table above that where a taxpayer makes a genuine mistake in submitting a return then no standard penalty is charged in respect of the incorrect return. However, this does not apply in the case of failure to notify chargeability. A 30% standard penalty applies where the failure to notify is not deliberate, regardless of whether this was a genuine mistake. Higher penalties apply for deliberate failures, as set out above.

The maximum penalties can be reduced where:

- the taxpayer informs HMRC of the error (i.e. makes a disclosure), and
- co-operates with HMRC to establish the amount of tax unpaid
- with larger reductions given for unprompted disclosure.

There are minimum penalties that vary based on:

- behaviour
- whether disclosure was prompted or unprompted.

An unprompted disclosure is where a taxpayer:

- makes a disclosure
- when he or she has no reason to believe that HMRC have, or are about to, discover the error.

An unprompted disclosure of a careless error can reduce the penalty to 0%.

A taxpayer can appeal to the First-tier Tribunal against:

- a penalty being charged, and
- the amount of the penalty.

Penalties for late filing of returns

Standardised penalties are also being introduced for the late filing of tax returns in phases. However, for TX, in the 2021 sittings, these rules apply for individuals only.

Date return is filed	Penalty
- after due date	- £100 fixed penalty
- 3 months late	- Daily penalties of £10 per day (maximum 90 days), in addition to £100 fixed penalty
- 6 months late	- 5% of tax due (minimum £300), plus above penalties
- more than 12 months after due date where withholding information was:	The above penalties plus:
– not deliberate	- Additional 5% of tax due (minimum £300)
– deliberate but no concealment	- 70% of tax due (minimum £300)
– deliberate with concealment	- 100% of tax due (minimum £300)

The tax geared penalties for submitting a return more than 12 months late can be reduced by prompted/unprompted disclosure.

Penalties for late payment of tax

Covered in section 3 of this chapter.

Other penalties

Offence	Penalty
Penalty for fraud or negligence on claiming reduced payments on account	<table><tr><td></td><td>£</td></tr><tr><td>POAs should have paid</td><td>X</td></tr><tr><td>Less: POAs actually paid</td><td>(X)</td></tr><tr><td></td><td>X</td></tr></table>
Failure to keep and retain required records	Up to £3,000 per tax year

8 The PAYE system

Pay as you earn (PAYE) is the system used for collecting income tax and national insurance at source from the earnings paid to employees.

- All payments of earnings assessable as employment income are subject to deduction of tax under the PAYE system.

- All employers making payments of earnings are required to deduct the appropriate amount of tax from each payment (or repay over-deductions) by using payroll software.

- The aim of the system is for the tax deducted from payments to date to correspond with the correct proportion to date of the total tax liability (after allowances and reliefs) of the employee for the tax year.

- Non-cash taxable benefits provided to employees are normally reported to HMRC by the employer at the end of the tax year on form P11D. Alternatively, the employer can apply to HMRC to tax the benefit through the PAYE system like other earnings.

Coding notice

To enable the employer to match the tax collected with the particular tax affairs of the individual taxpayer, HMRC issues a tax coding.

The system enables different amounts of tax to be collected from different taxpayers according to their personal circumstances.

Coding notice

- From the information supplied either in his or her tax return, each employee is sent a coding notice that sets out the total reliefs and allowances available to him for the year.

- The last digit is removed to arrive at the code number shown. Thus, allowances of £12,500 become 1250.

- The employer is also notified of the code number.

- Using this code number the employer can calculate the correct amount of tax each week or month.

- Most code numbers issued to the employer carry a suffix of which the most usual is L. The letter L denotes that just the ordinary personal allowance of £12,500 has been given.

- These letters are added in order to simplify the revision of codes, e.g. when the personal allowance is increased from one tax year to the next, all code numbers with the suffix L can easily be increased by the employer, so that PAYE can continue to operate effectively.

- Some code numbers carry a K prefix. This indicates that the deductions, such as benefits, to be made from allowances actually exceed the allowances. The code number is effectively 'negative'.

- Where an employee has not been allocated a code number (perhaps because the individual was previously self-employed), the employer must deduct tax under PAYE in accordance with an emergency code that reflects only the personal allowance (i.e. Code 1250L). This code is applied until the correct code number is supplied by HMRC.

- PAYE can also be used to collect/repay small amounts of tax under or over paid in respect of previous tax years and also to collect tax on small amounts of other income such as bank interest.

Tax code calculation

Allowances	£	Deductions	£
Personal allowance	X	Benefits	X
Allowable expenses	X	Adjustment for underpaid tax (must be less than £3,000)	X
Adjustment for overpaid tax	X	Other income	X
Total allowances	X	Total deductions	X

The tax code is:

(Total allowances less total deductions) × 1/10

The answer is then rounded down to the nearest whole number.

Calculation of deductions

PAYE is calculated using payroll software, or by a separate payroll provider.

The tax is calculated for any given pay week or month on a cumulative basis (i.e. the tax for, say month five, is the difference between the cumulative total tax due at the end of month five compared with the cumulative total due at the end of month four).

Payments to HMRC

Employers are generally required to make monthly payments of income tax and NIC to HMRC as follows:

- The income tax and NIC that the employer deducts during each tax month is due for payment to HMRC not later than 14 days after the tax month ends.

  A tax month runs from the sixth of a month to the 5th of the following month. Therefore the payment due date is the 19th of each month.

- However, employers with 250 or more employees must make their monthly PAYE payments electronically on the 22nd of each month.

- Employers with less than 250 employees may make their monthly PAYE payments by cheque or electronically. However, as most employers now pay electronically the electronic pay day (22nd) should be used in the examination.

- Employers whose average monthly payments of PAYE and NICs are less than £1,500 in total are allowed to make quarterly, rather than monthly, payments. Payments are due by the 22nd of the month following the quarters ending 5 July, 5 October, 5 January and 5 April.

Real time information (RTI)

Employers are required to submit income tax and NIC information to HMRC electronically when or before employees are paid each week or month. A year end summary of all the tax and NICs deducted will be provided with the final RTI submission for the tax year.

HMRC will charge penalties for late submission of RTI returns.

Penalties are charged on a monthly basis, where a RTI submission is made late.

No penalty is charged for the first late submission in the tax year. However, subsequent failures in the same tax year result in a penalty based on the number of employees as follows:

Number of employees	Monthly penalty £
1 – 9	100
10 – 49	200
50 – 249	300
250 or more	400

If the submission is more than 3 months late, an additional penalty of 5% of the tax and national insurance which should have been reported is charged.

9 Key PAYE forms

Specific forms are issued for use in certain circumstances to ensure all appropriate information is gathered and to simplify the process.

The key forms that you are required to know are:

Form	Purpose of use	Timing
P45	Provided to employee when he or she leaves	Ongoing with staffing changes
P60	Year end summary	Provided to employee by 31 May following tax year
P11 D	Summary of benefits	Provided by 6 July following tax year

 Procedures on leaving or joining

Procedure to be adopted when an employee leaves

When an employee leaves an employment the PAYE system is interrupted. A form P45 must be completed for each employee immediately after he or she leaves employment in order that either:

- a new employer can carry on making PAYE deductions using the appropriate code and cumulative totals from the last employment

- the employee can claim a tax repayment.

The employer notifies HMRC by entering the employee's leaving date on the first RTI submission submitted after he or she leaves.

Procedure to be adopted when an employee joins

The operation of the PAYE system depends upon having a tax code for each employee. The form P45 details his or her tax code, pay to date and tax to date and will allow the new employer to operate PAYE for the employee's pay.

Where form P45 cannot be produced the employee has to provide sufficient information to enable the employer to work out what tax code to use, so that the appropriate amount of tax can be deducted.

End-of-year procedure

P60 certificate of pay and tax deducted

Not later than 31 May the employer must send form P60 to each employee, to enable them to complete the employment pages of their self-assessment tax return. The form shows:

- Employee's national insurance number
- Employer's name and address
- Employee's name and address
- Total earnings for the year
- Final PAYE code
- Total income tax deducted for the year
- Total NIC for the year.

10 Chapter summary

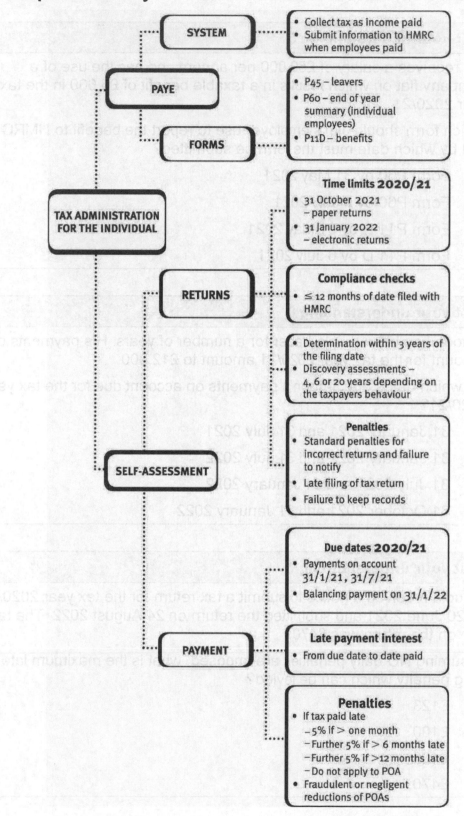

SYSTEM
- Collect tax as income paid
- Submit information to HMRC when employees paid

PAYE

FORMS
- P45 – leavers
- P60 – end of year summary (individual employees)
- P11D – benefits

TAX ADMINISTRATION FOR THE INDIVIDUAL

Time limits 2020/21
- 31 October 2021 – paper returns
- 31 January 2022 – electronic returns

RETURNS

Compliance checks
- ≤ 12 months of date filed with HMRC

- Determination within 3 years of the filing date
- Discovery assessments – 4, 6 or 20 years depending on the taxpayers behaviour

Penalties
- Standard penalties for incorrect returns and failure to notify
- Late filing of tax return
- Failure to keep records

SELF-ASSESSMENT

Due dates 2020/21
- Payments on account 31/1/21, 31/7/21
- Balancing payment on 31/1/22

Late payment interest
- From due date to date paid

PAYMENT

Penalties
- If tax paid late
  - 5% if > one month
  - Further 5% if > 6 months late
  - Further 5% if >12 months late
  - Do not apply to POA
- Fraudulent or negligent reductions of POAs

11 Practice objective test questions

Test your understanding 5

Jim receives a salary of £50,000 per annum and has the use of a company flat on which results in a taxable benefit of £5,600 in the tax year 2020/21.

Which form should Jim's employer use to report the benefit to HMRC and by which date must the form be submitted?

A   Form P60 by 31 May 2021

B   Form P60 by 6 July 2021

C   Form P11 D by 31 May 2021

D   Form P11 D by 6 July 2021

Test your understanding 6

Ji-hoon has been a sole trader for a number of years. His payments on account for the tax year 2020/21 amount to £12,000.

On which dates are Ji-hoon's payments on account due for the tax year 2020/21?

A   31 January 2021 and 31 July 2021

B   31 January 2022 and 31 July 2022

C   31 July 2021 and 31 January 2022

D   31 October 2021 and 31 January 2022

Test your understanding 7

Claudia received a notice to submit a tax return for the tax year 2020/21 on 20 June 2021 and submitted the return on 24 August 2022. The tax due on the return was £470.

Assuming NO daily penalties are imposed, what is the maximum late filing penalty which can be levied?

A   £123

B   £100

C   £400

D   £470

Test your understanding 8

Kaleel is required to make payments on account of his tax liability. For the tax year 2019/20, his income tax liability was £22,440, of which £2,400 was collected under PAYE. He estimates that his income tax payable for the tax year 2020/21 will be £26,400.

What is the amount of the first payment on account that Kaleel should make on 31 January 2021 in respect of his income tax liability for the tax year 2020/21?

Ignore national insurance.

A £10,020

B £11,220

C £12,000

D £13,200

Test your understanding 9

Which of the following statements is incorrect?

A Business records relating to the tax year 2020/21 do not need to be retained after 31 January 2023

B A taxpayer who submits a tax return 2 months late may receive a penalty of £100

C An electronic tax return for the tax year 2020/21 should normally be filed by 31 January 2022

D A taxpayer who submits his 2020/21 tax return electronically on 13 January 2022 has until 31 January 2023 to amend his return

Test your understanding 10

A taxpayer who does not normally receive a tax return must notify HMRC of any chargeability for the tax year 2020/21 by which date?

A 30 September 2021

B 5 October 2021

C 31 October 2021

D 31 December 2021

Test your understanding 11

If a taxpayer is not satisfied with a decision made by HMRC he or she can have the case referred to:

(1)   The Tax Tribunal

(2)   Another officer of HMRC

(3)   The Court of Appeal

A   All of them

B   (1) only

C   (2) only

D   (1) and (2) only

Test your understanding answers

Test your understanding 1

Ahmed

The relevant amount is £8,000 (£7,300 + £700).

As this exceeds £1,000 and exceeds 20% of the total tax liability (20% × (£9,400 + £700) = £2,020)), POAs are required.

POAs for the tax year 2020/21 are due as follows:

31 January 2021 (£7,300 + £700 = £8,000 × 1/2)	£4,000
31 July 2021	£4,000

Note: No POAs of capital gains tax or class 2 NIC are ever required so they are ignored in the calculations.

Test your understanding 2

Ebba

	£
Total tax payable	13,700
Less: POAs	(8,000)
Balancing payment 2020/21	5,700

The balancing payment comprises:

	£
Income tax and class 4 NIC (£8,300 + £800 – £8,000)	1,100
Class 2 NIC	156
CGT	4,444
Balancing payment	5,700

The first POA for the tax year 2021/22 will be 50% of the 'relevant amount' using the tax year 2020/21 position.

	£
2020/21 – IT payable (after deducting PAYE)	8,300
Class 4 NIC	800
Relevant amount	9,100

The first POA is (£9,100 × 1/2) = £4,550

Summary:

	£
Balancing payment – 2020/21	5,700
First POA – 2021/22	4,550
Total payable by 31 January 2022	10,250

Test your understanding 3

Rodney

Periods on which interest is charged:

On first POA	31 January 2021 – 28 February 2021	1 month
On second POA	31 July 2021 – 31 August 2021	1 month
On final payment	31 January 2022 – 31 March 2022	2 months

Interest payable:

On first POA	$(£2,100 \times 2.75\% \times 1/12) = £5$
On second POA	$(£2,100 \times 2.75\% \times 1/12) = £5$
On final payment	$(£1,500 \times 2.75\% \times 2/12) = £7$

Note: The rate of interest (2.75%) is included in the tax rates and allowances provided to you in the examination.

Test your understanding 4

Rowena

The relevant date for balancing payments is 31 January 2022.

No POAs are ever required for CGT.

The amounts due were therefore as follows:

31 January 2022	Income tax (£6,000 – £4,000)	£2,000
	Capital gains tax	£3,000

Interest will run as follows:

Income tax	£2,000 from 31 January 2022 to 28 February 2022, $(1/12 \times 2.75\% \times £2,000) = £5$
CGT	£3,000 from 31 January 2022 to 31 March 2022, $(2/12 \times 2.75\% \times £3,000) = £14$

In addition a penalty is due on the CGT (as it was more than one month late) of 5% of £3,000 = £150.

There is no penalty in respect of the late payment of income tax as it was paid within one month.

Total interest and penalties payable = (£4 + £13 + £150) = £167.

The penalty may be reduced if HMRC accept there were special circumstances.

Test your understanding 5

The correct answer is D.

Test your understanding 6

The correct answer is A.

Test your understanding 7

The correct answer is C.

The return for the tax year 2020/21 was due on 31 January 2022 and was therefore submitted more than six months late. A fixed penalty of £100 is imposed plus a further 5% of tax due. As 5% of £470 is less than the minimum penalty of £300, the minimum will be imposed instead.

The total penalties will therefore be £400 (£100 + £300).

Test your understanding 8

The correct answer is A.

A is the correct answer because of the following calculation:

	£
2019/20 – income tax liability	22,440
Less: PAYE	(2,400)
Income tax payable under self-assessment	20,040
Payment on account for 2020/21 (£20,040 × 1/2)	10,020

Test your understanding 9

The correct answer is A.

Business records for 2020/21 must be kept until 5 years after the filing date (i.e. 31 January 2027).

The other statements are true.

Test your understanding 10

The correct answer is B.

Test your understanding 11

The correct answer is D.

Introduction to corporation tax

Chapter learning objectives

Upon completion of this chapter you will be able to:

- define the terms 'period of account', 'accounting period', and 'financial year'

- recognise when an accounting period starts and when an accounting period finishes

- explain how the residence of a company is determined

- compute taxable total profits

- compute the corporation tax liability.

One of the PER performance objectives (PO15) is to prepare computations of taxable amounts and tax liabilities according to legal requirements. Working through this chapter should help you understand how to demonstrate that objective.

PER

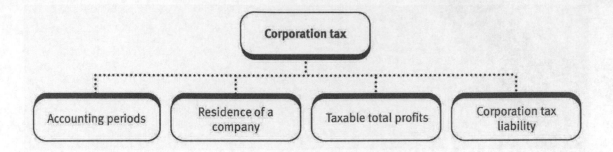

 You will have learnt how to produce financial statements in your Financial Accounting and Financial Reporting papers. In this unit we look at how the profits generated are taxed.

Introduction

Corporation tax is an important topic as it will be the focus of a 15 mark question in section C in the examination. You should also expect to be tested on this area in both sections A and B of your TX examination as well.

UK resident companies are assessed to corporation tax on their worldwide income and chargeable gains arising in an accounting period.

This and the following four chapters and Chapter 23 deal with the way in which companies are assessed to corporation tax. This first introductory chapter sets out the basis of assessment and explains how a company's corporation tax liability is calculated.

1 Basis of assessment

- Corporation tax is assessed on a company's taxable total profits arising in an accounting period.

- The accounting period is not necessarily the same period as the company's set of accounts (period of account).

It is important when dealing with corporation tax to understand the terms 'period of account' and 'accounting period'.

Period of account

 A period of account is any period for which a company prepares accounts. It is usually 12 months in length, but may be shorter or longer than this.

Accounting period

 An accounting period (AP) is the period for which a charge to corporation tax is made. It is **never longer than 12 months**.

2 Accounting periods

When does an AP start?

An AP starts:

- when a company starts to trade (or receives income chargeable to corporation tax), and

- when the previous accounting period ends.

When does an AP end?

The main situations where an AP ends are:

- twelve months after the beginning of the accounting period

- the end of the company's period of account, and

- the date the company begins or ceases to trade.

Long periods of account

For corporation tax purposes, an AP can never exceed 12 months.

Therefore, if a company prepares accounts for a period of more than 12 months, there are two accounting periods for tax purposes.

The long period of account is divided into APs as follows:

- First AP: first 12 months of long period

- Second AP: the balance of the long period.

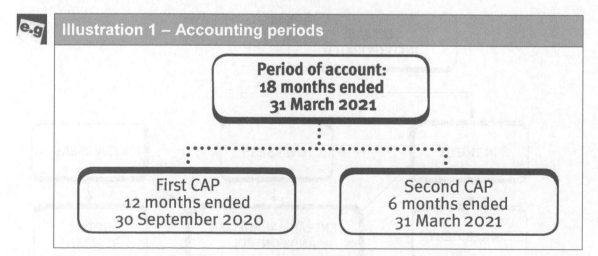

Illustration 1 – Accounting periods

Period of account: 18 months ended 31 March 2021

First CAP 12 months ended 30 September 2020

Second CAP 6 months ended 31 March 2021

A corporation tax computation is prepared for each AP. See Chapter 15 for the method of allocating the accounting profits between the two APs.

Choice of accounting date

A company can choose any accounting date, however there are certain tax advantages to having an accounting date of 31 March:

- Being aligned with the financial year makes it easier for a company to calculate its corporation tax liability, since the same reliefs and legislation will apply throughout the accounting period (see section 5 below).

- For owner-managed companies, alignment with the income tax year (the odd five days can be ignored) makes it easier to calculate the most tax efficient method of extracting profits from the company for the individual owners.

3 The tax residence of a company

Companies **resident** in the UK are chargeable to corporation tax on:

- all profits (i.e. income and chargeable gains) **wherever they arise** (i.e. on worldwide income and gains).

It is therefore important to correctly determine where a company is resident.

 Determining residence

A company is UK resident if it is:

- **incorporated** in the UK, or

- incorporated elsewhere, but is **centrally managed and controlled** in the UK.

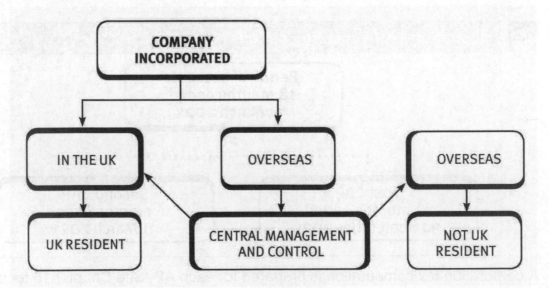

A company that is incorporated in the UK is resident in the UK regardless of where it is centrally managed and controlled.

Illustration 2 – The tax residence of a company

X Ltd is incorporated in the UK. The directors hold monthly board meetings overseas when major policy decisions are made.

Y Ltd is incorporated overseas. The directors hold frequent board meetings in the UK, which is where the directors are based.

Z Ltd is incorporated overseas. The directors hold weekly meetings overseas, but have quarterly meetings in the UK because this is where the non-executive directors are based.

Explain for each company whether they will be treated as UK resident.

Solution

- X Ltd is resident in the UK. If a company is incorporated in the UK it is irrelevant where meetings are held and decisions are made.

- Y Ltd would probably be treated as resident in the UK for corporation tax purposes. Although not incorporated in the UK, it would appear that the company is centrally managed and controlled from the UK.

- Z Ltd would probably not be treated as resident in the UK. The company is not incorporated in the UK, and it appears to be centrally managed and controlled from overseas.

Test your understanding 1

Mill Ltd is incorporated in France but holds all its board meetings in Germany. Its directors live in the UK most of the year.

Marble Ltd is incorporated in Italy but holds its monthly board meetings in London. Other interim board meetings are held in Italy, where some of the directors are based. Most of the directors are based in the UK.

Lamb Ltd is incorporated in the UK. Board meetings are held in France.

Explain for each of the above companies whether they will be treated as resident in the UK for corporation tax purposes.

4 Taxable total profits

- A company's taxable total profits for an accounting period are total profits from all sources, less qualifying charitable donations (QCDs).

- A company's total profits are:
  - worldwide income (excluding dividends) **plus**
  - net chargeable gains.

- The pro forma below sets out the different sources of income included in total profits

- **Taxable total profits (TTP) = Total profits – Qualifying charitable donations**

Layout of a corporation tax computation

Company name

Corporation tax computation for the year ended 31 March 2021

	£
Tax adjusted trading profit	X
Interest income	X
Property income	X
Miscellaneous income	X
Chargeable gains	X
	—
Total profits	X
Less: Qualifying charitable donations (QCD)	(X)
	—
Taxable total profits (TTP)	X
	—

Tax adjusted trading profit

- Assesses all trading income net of trading expenditure.

- See Chapter 15 for detail.

Interest income

- Assesses all interest receivable net of some interest payable.

- See Chapter 15 for more detail.

Property income

- Assesses the profit (or loss) from letting furnished or unfurnished property and is calculated on the accruals basis.

- See Chapter 15 for more detail.

Miscellaneous income

- Patent royalties receivable in respect of non-trade related patents would be included here.

Dividends

- Dividends received from UK and overseas companies are exempt from corporation tax and are therefore **excluded** from the TTP computation. Only UK dividends are examinable in the TX examination.

Chargeable gains/losses

- Corporation tax is also charged on any chargeable gains that arise on chargeable disposals made by the company during an accounting period.

- Chargeable gains for companies are covered in detail in Chapter 23.

 It is essential to understand that companies pay **corporation tax** on their chargeable gains, not capital gains tax.

Qualifying charitable donations

- All donations to charity by a company (except those allowed as a trading expense) are an allowable deduction from total profits in a corporation tax computation.

- The relief is referred to as 'qualifying charitable donations (QCD) relief'.

- All charitable donations by a company are paid gross.

- Note that the tax treatment of donations to charity made by a company is different from that applied to payments made by an individual (see Chapter 15 for more detail).

 Illustration 3 – Taxable total profits

Westmorland Ltd has the following income and outgoings for the year ending 31 March 2021.

	£
Tax adjusted trading profit	1,456,500
Property income	25,000
Interest receivable	10,000
Chargeable gains	35,000
Dividends from UK companies	14,400
Qualifying charitable donation	(10,000)

Compute the taxable total profits for the y/e 31 March 2021.

Solution

Taxable total profits – y/e 31 March 2021

	£
Tax adjusted trading profit	1,456,500
Property income	25,000
Interest receivable	10,000
Chargeable gains	35,000
Total profits	1,526,500
Less: QCD relief	(10,000)
TTP	1,516,500

Notes:

1   Dividends received are not included when calculating taxable total profits as they are exempt from corporation tax.

2   All charitable donations are allowable deductions from total profits and are paid gross.

Test your understanding 2

Cumberland Ltd has the following income and outgoings for the year ended 30 September 2020.

	£
Tax adjusted trading profit	81,500
Property income	1,300
Interest receivable	2,200
Chargeable gains	3,000
Dividends from UK companies	4,400
Qualifying charitable donation paid	1,000

Compute the taxable total profits for the y/e 30 September 2020.

5 The corporation tax liability

The company's corporation tax liability is calculated by applying the appropriate rate of corporation tax to the company's taxable total profits.

Financial year

- The rate of corporation tax is fixed by reference to financial years.

- A financial year runs from 1 April to the following 31 March and is identified by the calendar year in which it begins.

- The year commencing 1 April 2020 and ending on 31 March 2021 is the Financial Year 2020 (FY2020).

 Financial years should not be confused with tax years for income tax, which run from 6 April to the following 5 April.

- The rate of corporation tax applicable to FY2020 is 19%

- The rate of corporation tax applicable to FY2019 and FY2018 is also 19%.

 The rates of corporation tax are included in the tax rates and allowances provided to you in the examination.

Test your understanding 3

Z Ltd has taxable total profits of £148,000 in the y/e 31 March 2021.

Calculate Z Ltd's corporation tax liability for the y/e 31 March 2021.

Test your understanding 4

Sycamore Ltd has the following results for the y/e 31 March 2021:

Tax adjusted trading profit	£320,000
Chargeable gain	£10,000
Dividends received from UK companies	£18,000

Calculate Sycamore Ltd's corporation tax liability for the year ended 31 March 2021.

Accounting periods straddling 31 March

Where a company's accounting period falls into two financial years in which the tax rates are the same, there is no need to calculate the corporation tax liability for each financial year separately.

Illustration 4 – Accounting periods straddling 31 March

Flute Ltd had taxable total profits of £400,000 in the year ended 30 September 2020.

Calculate Flute Ltd's corporation tax liability for the year ended 30 September 2020.

Solution

Flute Ltd corporation tax liability – y/e 30 September 2020

The company's CAP straddles 31 March 2020. The first six months (1 October 2019 to 31 March 2020) fall into FY2019 and the second six months (1 April 2020 to 30 September 2020) fall into FY2020.

The rate of tax is 19% for both financial years and therefore the corporation tax liability can be calculated by simply applying the tax rate to the taxable total profits.

	£
£400,000 × 19%	76,000

6 Chapter summary

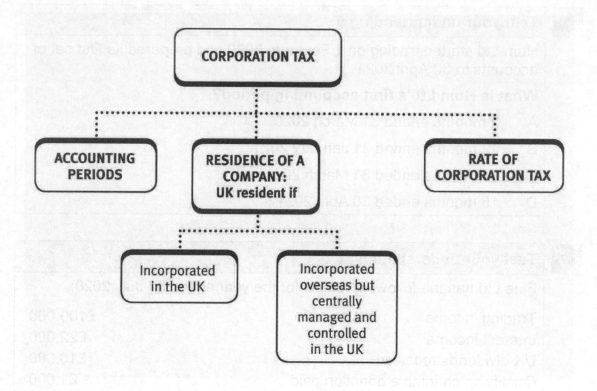

7 Practice objective test questions

Test your understanding 5

Hum Ltd started trading on 1 February 2020 and prepared its first set of accounts to 30 April 2021.

What is Hum Ltd's first accounting period?

A   2 months ended 31 March 2020

B   12 months ended 31 January 2021

C   14 months ended 31 March 2021

D   15 months ended 30 April 2021

Test your understanding 6

Fine Ltd has the following results for the year ended 31 July 2020:

Trading income	£100,000
Interest income	£22,000
UK dividends received	£10,000
Qualifying charitable donation paid	£1,000

What are the taxable total profits of Fine Ltd for the year ended 31 July 2020?

A   123,000

B   121,000

C   133,000

D   131,000

Test your understanding 7

Cardwell Ltd prepared its first set of accounts for the 9 months to 31 March 2021.

Cardwell Ltd had a tax adjusted trading profit of £120,000, chargeable gains of £20,000, property income of £10,000 and dividends received of £25,000 in this 9 month period.

What is the corporation tax liability of Cardwell Ltd for the 9 months ended 31 March 2021?

A   £33,250

B   £28,500

C   £21,375

D   £24,700

Test your understanding answers

Test your understanding 1

Mill Ltd

- Mill Ltd would not be treated as resident in the UK. The company is not incorporated in the UK, and it appears to be centrally managed and controlled from overseas. The rules in each of the overseas countries in question would have to be reviewed to determine whether Mill Ltd is considered resident in those countries.

- Marble Ltd would probably be treated as resident in the UK for corporation tax purposes. Although not incorporated in the UK, it would appear that the company is centrally managed and controlled from the UK as its monthly board meetings are held in London and the majority of directors are based here.

- Lamb Ltd is resident in the UK as it is incorporated in the UK. It is therefore irrelevant where meetings are held and decisions are made.

Test your understanding 2

Cumberland Ltd

Taxable total profits – y/e 30 September 2020

	£
Tax adjusted trading profit	81,500
Property income	1,300
Interest receivable	2,200
Chargeable gains	3,000
Total profits	88,000
Less: QCDs	(1,000)
TTP	87,000

Note: The UK dividends are exempt from UK corporation tax.

Test your understanding 3

Z Ltd

Z Ltd's accounting period (y/e 31 March 2021) falls entirely in FY2020 and therefore the tax rate for FY2020 of 19% is applied to the company's TTP.

Corporation tax liability (£148,000 × 19%) = £28,120.

Test your understanding 4

Sycamore Ltd

Corporation tax computation – y/e 31 March 2021

	£
Tax adjusted trading profit	320,000
Chargeable gain	10,000
TTP	330,000
Corporation tax (£330,000 × 19%)	62,700

Notes:

1   Dividends received are exempt from corporation tax and are therefore not included in the TTP computation.

2   The company's accounting period falls entirely in FY2020 and therefore the FY2020 tax rate of 19% is applied to the TTP.

Test your understanding 5

The correct answer is B.

B is the correct answer because the long period of account is divided into two accounting periods, the first for the 12 months ended 31 January 2021 and the second for the remaining 3 months to 30 April 2021.

KAPLAN PUBLISHING

Test your understanding 6

The correct answer is B.

Fine Ltd

TTP calculation – y/e 31 July 2020

	£
Trading income	100,000
Interest income	22,000
Less: QCD	(1,000)
TTP	121,000

Note: Dividends received are exempt from corporation tax and are therefore excluded from TTP.

Test your understanding 7

The correct answer is B.

	£
Tax adjusted trading profit	120,000
Chargeable gains	20,000
Property income	10,000
Taxable total profits	150,000

	£
Corporation tax liability	
(£150,000 × 19%)	28,500

Dividends received are exempt from corporation tax and are therefore not included in taxable total profits.

Taxable total profits

Chapter learning objectives

Upon completion of this chapter you will be able to:

- recognise the expenditure that is allowable in calculating the tax adjusted trading profit

- recognise the relief which can be obtained for pre-trading expenditure

- compute capital allowances (as for income tax)

- compute property business profits and understand how relief for a property business loss is given

- recognise and apply the treatment of interest paid and received under the loan relationship rules

- recognise and apply the treatment of qualifying charitable donations

- compute taxable total profits.

PER

One of the PER performance objectives (PO15) is to prepare computations of taxable amounts and tax liabilities according to legal requirements. Working through this chapter should help you understand how to demonstrate that objective.

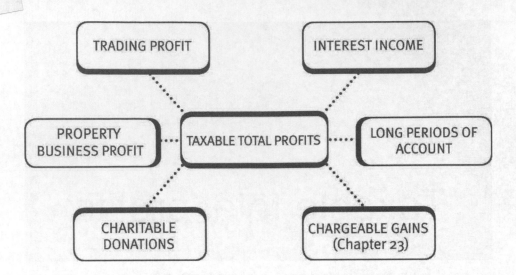

1 Taxable total profits

Companies pay corporation tax on their taxable total profits for an accounting period.

As illustrated in Chapter 14, taxable total profits is calculated as follows:

	£
Tax adjusted trading profit (section 2)	X
Interest income (section 3)	X
Property income (section 4)	X
Miscellaneous income (see below)	X
Chargeable gains (Chapter 23)	X
Total profits	X
Less: Qualifying charitable donations (QCD) (section 5)	(X)
Taxable total profits	X

Miscellaneous income (e.g. patent royalties re: non-trade patents) is obscure and is unlikely to appear in the TX examination.

This and the following chapters show in detail how each item within taxable total profits is calculated.

2   Trading profit

In Chapter 7 we studied how to adjust a sole trader's trading profit for tax purposes. The rules for companies are very similar.

For reference, a summary of the main adjustments is given below:

- Disallow expenditure which is not wholly and exclusively for the purposes of the trade
- Disallow entertaining (except entertaining staff)
- Disallow expenditure on capital items
- Adjust for leased high emission cars (CO_2 > 110g/km)
- Adjust for gifts to customers
- Disallow depreciation
- Adjust for profits/losses on disposal of capital items
- Add back charitable donations (unless small and local)
- Adjust for non-trading income.

All the above rules apply for companies.

 However, there are a number of key differences which apply when computing the taxable trading profits for a company.

Differences relating to companies

The main differences are in relation to:

- private use adjustments
- interest payable/receivable
- dividends payable
- capital allowances.

In addition the accruals basis must always be used by a company to prepare its accounts for tax purposes.

 Key differences

Private use adjustments – there are no private use restrictions for companies:

- Any private expenses of a director or employee of a company are fully allowable, when calculating the tax adjusted trading profit.
- Any private use of assets by a director or employee of the company is ignored in the capital allowances calculation. There is no restriction for private usage.

The director or employee may however suffer income tax on the private use as an employment benefit (Chapter 5).

Interest payable/receivable – Companies have special rules which cover interest payments and interest income. These are known as the loan relationship rules.

The detail of the rules is covered in section 3.

Dividends payable – Dividends payable by a company are an appropriation of profit and are not allowable as a trading expense.

Illustration 1 – Trading profit

The statement of profit or loss of Hart Ltd shows the following for the year ended 31 December 2020:

	£	£
Gross profit from trading		280,000
Rental income		2,850
		———
		282,850
Less: Expenses:		
Rent and rates	10,950	
Depreciation	6,730	
Entertaining and gifts (Note 1)	7,420	
Delivery costs	2,890	
Motor expenses (Note 2)	5,480	
Miscellaneous (Note 3)	12,000	
	———	
		(45,470)
		———
Profit before tax		237,380
		———

Notes:

(1) Entertaining and gifts comprise:

	£
Gifts to customers (Christmas champagne: cost £25 per customer)	1,500
Staff Christmas party	3,430
Client Christmas party	2,490

(2) Motor expenses represent costs for the director's car. He uses the car 60% for private use.

(3) Miscellaneous includes a fine of £3,500 for a breach of health and safety regulations.

Calculate the tax adjusted trading profit before capital allowances for Hart Ltd, for the year ended 31 December 2020.

Your computation should commence with the profit before tax figure of £237,380 and should list all the items referred to in notes 1 to 3, indicating by the use of a zero (0) any items that do not require adjustment.

Solution

Adjustment of profits – y/e 31 December 2020

	£	£
Profit per accounts	237,380	
Rental income		2,850
Rent and rates	0	
Depreciation	6,730	
Gifts to customers: Drink (Note 1)	1,500	
Staff Christmas party	0	
Client entertaining	2,490	
Delivery costs	0	
Motor expenses (Note 2)	0	
Health and safety fine (Note 3)	3,500	
	————	————
	251,600	2,850
	(2,850)	————
	————	
Adjusted trading profit (before capital allowances)	248,750	
	————	

Notes:

(1)   Gifts to customers are disallowed unless they amount to £50 or less per customer during the year and display a conspicuous advert for the business. Gifts of food or drink or tobacco are disallowed irrespective of their cost.

(2)   No adjustment is required for the private use motor expenses of the director. These are fully deductible when calculating tax adjusted trading profits for a company. The director will be taxed on the benefit of private use as an employment benefit.

(3)   As for a sole trader, fines (with the exception of parking fines incurred by employees on business) are disallowable expenditure.

It is important to use a zero where no adjustment is necessary as above in order to obtain the maximum marks (as shown in Chapter 7).

The notes above would not be required in the examination unless specifically asked for. They are provided here for tutorial purposes only.

Test your understanding 1

Corn Ltd runs a small printing business and the managing director wishes to know the amount of the company's tax adjusted trading profit for the year ended 31 December 2020.

You are presented with the following statement of profit or loss for Corn Ltd, for the year ended 31 December 2020.

	£	£
Gross profit from trading		21,270
Profit on sale of business premises (Note 1)		1,750
		———
		23,020
Advertising	760	
Depreciation	2,381	
Light and heat	372	
Miscellaneous expenses (Note 2)	342	
Motor car expenses (Note 3)	555	
Rates	1,057	
Repairs and renewals (Note 4)	2,480	
Staff wages (Note 5)	12,124	
Telephone	351	
	———	
		(20,422)
		———
Profit before tax		2,598

Notes:

(1) The profit on the sale of premises relates to the sale of a small freehold industrial unit in which the company stored paper, before building the extension (see Note 4).

(2) Miscellaneous expenses is made up as follows:

	£
Subscription to Printers' association	40
Contribution to a national charity	45
Gifts to customers:	
• Calendars costing £7.50 each and bearing the company's name	75
• Two food hampers bearing the company's name	95
Other allowable expenses	87
	———
	342
	———

> (3)   A director uses the motor car 75% for business purposes and 25% for private purposes.
>
> (4)   Repairs and renewals comprise the following expenditure:
>
> | | £ |
> |---|---:|
> | Redecorating administration offices | 833 |
> | Building extension to enlarge paper store | 1,647 |
> | | ----- |
> | | 2,480 |
> | | ----- |
>
> (5)   Staff wages includes an amount of £182 for a staff Christmas lunch.
>
> **Calculate Corn Ltd's tax adjusted trading profit before capital allowances for the year ended 31 December 2020.**
>
> **Your computation should commence with the profit before tax figure of £2,598 and should list all the items referred to in notes 1 to 5, indicating by the use of a zero (0) any items that do not require adjustment.**

Capital allowances

Chapter 8 covered the main principles of calculating capital allowances (including SBAs) for sole traders.

 The same rules apply for companies, but in addition, the following points should be noted when calculating capital allowances for companies:

Maximum AIA

- The maximum AIA for a 12 month accounting period is £1,000,000, the same as for a sole trader.

 The AIA amount of £1,000,000 is included in the tax rates and allowances provided to you in the examination.

Short accounting period

- Allowances are given for **accounting periods** by reference to acquisitions and disposals in that accounting period.

- As for sole traders, if the accounting period is less than 12 months:

  - the AIA and the WDA are proportionately reduced.

  - but FYAs are always given in full. They are never reduced for a short accounting period.

Long accounting period

- Unlike sole traders, where a company has a long period of account:

  - there are two accounting periods (APs) for corporation tax purposes

  - two capital allowances computations are required; one for each of these APs

  - the first AP is 12 months in length

  - the second AP is a short accounting period, therefore the rules above should be followed when calculating the capital allowances for this period.

Private use adjustments

- There are no private use adjustments in a company's capital allowances computation where company assets are used by directors or employees.

Illustration 2 – Trading profit

Build Ltd prepares accounts to 31 March. The company's tax written down value at 1 April 2020 on the main pool was £23,500.

In the two years ended 31 March 2022, the following capital transactions took place:

Year ended 31 March 2021

1 November 2020   Purchased plant costing £13,260.

10 November 2020 Sold two lorries (purchased for £8,450 each) for £2,500 each. Purchased two replacement lorries for £5,250 each.

Year ended 31 March 2022

1 November 2021   Purchased a motor car with CO_2 emissions of 109g/km for £7,500. The car will be used by the MD 25% of the time for private purposes.

1 December 2021   Sold a machine for £12,000 (cost £18,600).

Compute the capital allowances available to Build Ltd for the years ended 31 March 2021 and 31 March 2022.

Assume the FY2020 rules apply throughout.

Solution

	Main pool	Allowances
y/e 31 March 2021	£	£
TWDV b/f	23,500	
Qualifying for AIA		
Plant and machinery	13,260	
Lorries (£5,250 × 2)	10,500	
	———	
	23,760	
AIA	(23,760)	23,760
	———	
	0	
Disposal proceeds	(5,000)	
	———	
	18,500	
WDA (18%)	(3,330)	3,330
	———	
TWDV c/f	15,170	
	———	
Total allowances		27,090
		———
y/e 31 March 2022		
Not qualifying for AIA or FYA:		
Car (Note)	7,500	
Disposal proceeds	(12,000)	
	———	
	10,670	
WDA (18%)	(1,921)	1,921
	———	
TWDV c/f	8,749	
	———	
Total allowances		1,921
		———

Note: Private use of the car by the MD is not relevant for companies. Full capital allowances are available.

Test your understanding 2

Ellingham Ltd is a UK resident company that manufactures aeroplane components. The company has always prepared accounts to 31 December in each year and has now decided to change its accounts preparation date to 31 March, after having prepared accounts to 31 December 2019.

On 1 January 2020, the TWDVs of plant and machinery were as follows:

	£
Main pool	149,280
Short life asset (acquired May 2018)	13,440

The following assets were purchased during the 15 m/e 31 March 2021.

		£
11 April 2020	Heating system	12,800
5 June 2020	Equipment	1,000,800
22 September 2020	Motor car (CO$_2$ emissions 109g/km)	11,760
18 November 2020	Van	7,200
11 December 2020	New motor car (CO$_2$ emissions 44g/km)	12,200

Ellingham Ltd made the following sales

15 August 2020	Lorry	(14,160)
12 September 2020	Short-life asset	(5,520)

The lorry sold on 15 August 2020 for £14,160 originally cost £21,600.

Compute the capital allowances for the 15 m/e 31 March 2021.

Pre-trading expenditure

The rules for pre-trading expenditure are the same for companies and sole traders (see Chapter 7) and are as follows:

- Any revenue expenditure incurred in the seven years before a company commences to trade, which would have been allowable if the company was trading, is treated as an expense, on the day that the company starts trading.

- Any capital expenditure is treated as if bought on the first day, when the trade commences. Any capital allowances will be claimed in the first capital allowances computation.

3   Interest income – loan relationship rules

 All income and expenses related to the borrowing and lending of money are dealt with under the loan relationship rules.

Expenses related to borrowing money	**Income received from lending money**
• interest paid on overdrafts, bank loans, corporate loan notes • other costs such as arrangement fees, and other incidental costs incurred in raising loan finance	• interest income (including interest from bank deposits, loans, government stocks and corporate loan notes)

In addition, the cost of writing down an impaired debt arising from the lending of money is an allowable expense under the loan relationship rules.

Trade v non-trade purposes

In order to apply the loan relationship rules correctly, all interest paid/received must first be identified as either 'trading' or 'non-trading'.

	Interest receivable	Interest payable
Trade purpose	N/A (note)	• on a loan taken out to purchase plant and machinery for the trade • on a loan taken out to purchase property used for trading purposes e.g. office, warehouse, factory • on a loan or overdraft to fund daily operations (i.e. working capital) • on loan notes to fund trading operations

Non-trade purpose	• interest received on bank accounts • interest receivable on investments such as gilts and loan notes	• on a loan to purchase a commercially let property (where the rent would be taxable as property business income – see section 4) • on a loan to acquire shares of another company

Note: Generally, all interest received by a company is non-trade interest, unless it is a company's trade to lend money (e.g. a bank, which is not likely to be the case in the examination).

 In the TX examination you will be expected to be able to identify whether loan interest payable is for trading or for non-trading purposes.

Interest income

- Interest receivable should be deducted when calculating adjusted trading profits and included in the TTP computation as interest income.

- Interest received and receivable is usually credited in the company accounts on an accruals basis. As interest receivable is taxed on an accruals basis, the figure included in the accounts is the figure which is taxed as interest income.

Interest paid

- Interest paid and payable on borrowings for a trading purpose is deductible as a trading expense.

- Interest payable on borrowings for a non-trading purpose is:

  - added back to trading profit

  - deducted from interest income in the TTP computation.

 • In certain specific circumstances companies are required to deduct income tax from payments of interest. However, for the purposes of the TX examination all interest paid by a company is paid gross (i.e. without the deduction of income tax).

Impaired debts

- The write off of impaired trade debts (i.e. trade receivables) is an allowable deduction from trading profits and the recovery of trade debts previously written off is taxable trading income.

- The write off of impaired non-trade debts (e.g. loan to a customer or a former employee) is an allowable deduction from interest income. The write off must be added back when calculating the tax adjusted trading profit and deducted from interest income in the calculation of TTP.

Assessment in taxable total profits

- All interest paid by a company is deductible on the accruals basis.

- As the company accounts are also prepared on the accruals basis, the figure included in the accounts is also the figure used for tax purposes.

- If only cash payments/receipts are provided, these must be adjusted for opening and closing accruals of interest payable/receivable.

- Where interest income exceeds non-trade related interest payable

  - the net income is assessed as interest income in taxable total profits.

 • The situation where non-trade related interest payable exceeds interest income is not examinable.

Illustration 3 – Interest income – loan relationship rules

Trinity Ltd, a clothing manufacturer, received bank interest of £2,800, on 14 December 2020 and paid loan note interest of £19,500 to other companies, on 26 September 2020.

The loan notes were issued in January 2020, to raise finance for the purchase of a new packing machine and is therefore a trade related loan.

The company prepares accounts to 31 December each year. Accrued loan note interest payable at 31 December 2020 was £9,000. There was no interest receivable at either 31 December 2019 or 31 December 2020.

Explain how the bank and loan note interest will be treated in the corporation tax computation for the year to 31 December 2020.

Solution

Bank interest receivable

The bank interest receivable in the period will be taxable as non-trading interest income.

As there was no interest receivable at the beginning or end of the year, the taxable interest income will be the amount received of £2,800.

Loan note interest payable

The loan note interest paid relates to finance raised for the purposes of the trade (i.e. to purchase new machinery). It is therefore allowed as a trading expense.

The interest will be recorded in the accounts on the accruals basis (i.e. interest payable of £28,500) (£19,500 paid + £9,000 accrued). No adjustment will therefore be required for tax purposes.

Illustration 4 – Interest income – loan relationship rules

PQR Ltd prepares its accounts to 31 December.

The company issued £100,000 of 12% loan notes on 1 May 2020. The proceeds of the issue were used to purchase a new factory, which is a trade related loan.

Explain how the interest on the loan notes is treated for tax purposes for the year ended 31 December 2020.

Solution

The loan note interest paid relates to financing for the purposes of the trade (i.e. to purchase a new factory). It is therefore allowed as a trading expense.

For the year ended 31 December 2020, PQR Ltd will be entitled to a deduction against trading profits of £8,000 (£100,000 at 12% × 8/12).

Provided this amount is included in the accounts, no adjustment will be necessary when calculating the tax adjusted trading profit.

The amount of loan note interest actually paid is irrelevant as interest payable is deductible on the accruals basis.

Test your understanding 3

The profit before tax of Smith Ltd per the statement of profit or loss for the year ended 31 December 2020, is £105,940, which includes:

	£
Depreciation	9,750
Loan note interest payable (on trade related loan)	12,760
Bank interest payable	6,590
Bank interest receivable	15,860

Notes:

1   Bank interest receivable includes an accrual of £2,340 as at 31 December 2020 and £1,210, as at 31 December 2019. There were no accruals in respect of the loan note or bank interest payable at either the beginning or the end of the year.

2   The bank interest is payable on a loan to purchase an investment property, which is a non-trade related loan.

3   The company's capital allowances for the year are £11,800.

Calculate Smith Ltd's taxable total profits for the year ended 31 December 2020, clearly showing the different types of income.

Summary – interest payable/receivable

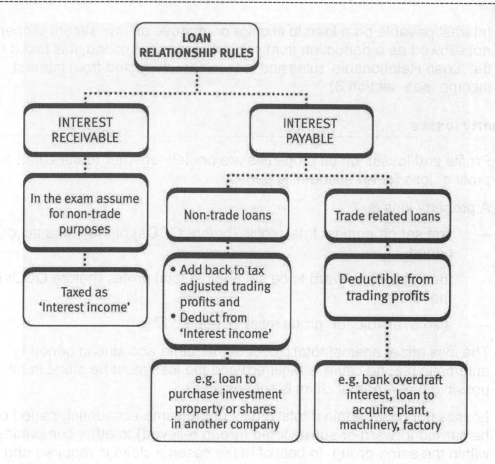

4 Property income

A trading company may hold property for investment purposes or have premises which are rented out, as they are surplus to the company's current trading requirements.

Treatment for companies

The income from these properties is assessed as property business income, calculated basically in the same way as for sole traders:

- Allowable expenses are those associated with the normal running and upkeep of the property (generally revenue expenses, like property maintenance, repairs, insurance and irrecoverable debts).

However, there are a few differences in the way that companies are assessed on their property income as follows:

- Property income is **always** taxed on the **accruals basis**.

- The company is assessed on the property income arising in the accounting period (not the tax year as for individuals).

- The treatment of interest payable.

- The treatment of property losses.

Interest on a loan to buy a property

 Interest payable on a loan to acquire or improve an investment property, is not allowed as a deduction from property income. Instead, it is taxed under the 'Loan Relationship' rules and is therefore deducted from interest income (see section 3).

Property losses

- Profits and losses on all properties are pooled together to obtain an overall profit or loss for an accounting period.

- A property loss is:
  - first set off against total profits (before QCDs) of the same accounting period
  - then carried forward to be set against total profits (before QCDs) in the future
  - also available for 'group relief' (Chapter 17).

- The loss offset against total profits of the same accounting period is automatic (i.e. no claim is required) and the loss must be offset in full if possible (i.e. a partial claim is not possible).

- Losses not offset against total profits of the same accounting period can be carried forward or surrendered (group relieved) to other companies within the same group. In both of these cases a claim is required and the amount of the loss offset can be specified.

- A claim to carry a property loss forward and offset against total profits of a future period must be made within two years of the end of the accounting period in which the loss is relieved.

- A property loss can never be carried back to previous accounting periods.

Lease premiums

Where a company receives a premium for the grant of a lease, an element of the premium is taxed as property income, in the same way as for sole traders (see Chapter 4), in the accounting period in which it is received.

Illustration 5 – Property income

Speed Ltd prepared accounts for the year ended 31 March 2021. During the year the company received a premium of £12,000 on the grant of a seven year lease.

The building was rented out from 1 September 2020, for £6,000 p.a. It lay empty until this date. Rent is received quarterly in advance.

Calculate the property income for the year ended 31 March 2021.

Solution

	£
Premium (W)	10,560
Rent receivable (£6,000 × 7/12) (Note)	3,500
Total property income	14,060

Note. Property income for a company is always calculated using the accruals basis

Working: Assessment of premium

	£
Premium	12,000
Less: 2% × (7 – 1) × £12,000	(1,440)
	10,560

Alternative calculation: £12,000 × (51 – 7)/50 = £10,560

Test your understanding 4

Tasman Ltd is a UK resident trading company. The company lets out two warehouses that are surplus to requirements.

The company's results regarding property income for the year ended 31 March 2021, are as follows:

- The first warehouse was empty from 1 April to 31 August 2020. On 1 September 2020 the company granted a seven year lease and received a premium of £47,000 and the annual rent of £10,500.

- The second warehouse was let until 31 January 2021, at an annual rent of £11,200. On that date the tenant left owing three months' rent, which the company is not able to recover. The roof of the warehouse was repaired at a cost of £7,200, during March 2021.

Calculate the property income for the year ended 31 March 2021.

5 Qualifying charitable donations (QCDs)

- All donations to charity by companies are allowable:

  - if a small local donation; as a trading expense

  - all other donations (whether under gift aid or not); as an allowable deduction from total profits.

- All charitable donations made by companies are paid gross.

- The amount **paid** in the accounting period is deducted from total profits.

- If the QCDs paid exceed the total profits of the company:

  - no relief for the excess is given

    (i.e. it cannot be carried forward or carried back)

  - unless the company is part of a 75% group, in which case, group relief may be available (see Chapter 17).

 The tax treatment of charitable donations for individuals is different to the treatment for companies.

For **individuals:**

- a small local donation; is deductible as a trading expense (see Chapter 7), or

- if made under the gift aid scheme (see Chapter 2).

  - gift aid payments are paid net of basic rate tax.

  - tax relief is given by extending the basic and higher rate tax bands by the gross amount of the gift aid paid in the tax year.

6 Comprehensive example

Test your understanding 5

Geronimo Ltd is a UK resident company that manufactures motorcycles. The company's summarised statement of profit or loss for the year ended 31 March 2021 is as follows:

	£	£
Gross profit		921,540
Operating expenses:		
Impaired debts (Note 1)	22,360	
Depreciation	83,320	
Gifts and donations (Note 2)	2,850	
Professional fees (Note 3)	14,900	
Staff party (Note 4)	7,200	
Repairs and renewals (Note 5)	42,310	
Other expenses (all allowable)	111,820	
	————	(284,760)
Operating profit		636,780
Income from investments		
Bank interest (Note 6)	2,800	
Loan interest (Note 7)	22,000	
Dividends (Note 8)	36,000	
	————	60,800
		————
		697,580
Interest payable (Note 9)		(45,000)
		————
Profit before taxation		652,580
		————

Notes

1 Impaired debts

	£
Trade debts written off	19,890
Loan to customer written off	600
Increase in allowance for trade debtors	1,870
	————
	22,360
	————

2   Gifts and donations

	£
Donation to a national charity	1,800
Donation to local charity (Geronimo Ltd received free advertising in the charity's magazine)	50
Gifts to customers (food hampers costing £40 each)	1,000
	2,850

3   Professional fees

	£
Accountancy and audit fee	4,100
Legal fees re the renewal of a 20 year property lease	2,400
Legal fees in connection with the issue of loan notes (see Note 9)	8,400
	14,900

4   Staff party

The staff party, for employees only, cost £200 a head.

5   Repairs and renewals

The figure of £42,310 for repairs includes £6,200 for replacing part of a wall that was knocked down by a lorry, and £12,200 for an extension to the office building. The extension was constructed on 15 October 2020 and brought into use on 1 January 2021.

6   Bank interest received

The bank interest was received on 31 March 2021. The bank deposits are held for non-trading purposes.

7   Loan interest received

The figure for loan interest received is calculated as follows:

	£
Accrued at 1 April 2020	(5,500)
Received 30 June 2020	11,000
Received 31 December 2020	11,000
Accrued at 31 March 2021	5,500
	22,000

The loan was made for non-trading purposes.

8   Dividends received

The dividends were received from other UK companies.

9 **Interest payable**

Geronimo Ltd raised funding through loan notes on 1 May 2020. The loan was used for trading purposes. Interest of £30,000 was paid on 31 October 2020, and £15,000 was accrued at 31 March 2021.

10 **Plant and machinery**

On 1 April 2020 the tax written down value of the main pool of plant and machinery was £66,000. There were no purchases or sales of plant and machinery during the year ended 31 March 2021.

(a) **Calculate Geronimo Ltd's tax adjusted trading profit for the year ended 31 March 2021.**

Your computation should commence with the profit before taxation figure of £652,580 and should list all the items referred to in Notes 1 to 10, indicating by the use of a zero (0) any items that do not require adjustment.

(b) **Calculate the corporation tax payable by Geronimo Ltd for the year ended 31 March 2021.**

7 Long periods of account

Where a company has a period of account of more than 12 months, it must be split into two accounting periods (APs) as follows:

- First 12 months.

- Remainder of the period of account.

There are rules to determine how to allocate taxable profits between these two accounting periods.

Allocation of taxable profits

Profits	Method of allocation
Trading profits before capital allowances	Adjust profit for period of account for tax purposes and then apportion on a time basis.
Capital allowances	Separate calculation for each accounting period. AIA and WDAs are restricted if accounting period is less than 12 months.
Property income	Calculate accrued amount for each AP separately.
Interest income	If the information to apply the strict accruals basis is not available; time apportion.
Chargeable gains	Taxed in the accounting period in which disposal takes place.
Qualifying charitable donations (QCDs)	Deducted from profits of the accounting period in which donations are paid.

Having allocated profits and QCDs to the two separate APs:

- two separate corporation tax computations are prepared
- with two separate payment dates.

<table>
<tr><td colspan="2">**Illustration 6 – Long periods of account**</td></tr>
</table>

Oak Ltd prepared accounts for the 15 months to 30 June 2021, with the following results:

	£
Trading profit (adjusted for tax purposes before capital allowances)	882,955
Bank interest (received 30 September 2020)	22,000
Property income	10,000
Chargeable gain (asset disposed of 1 June 2021)	16,000
Charitable donation (paid 1 January 2021)	24,000
Bank interest (income) accrued was as follows:	
At 1 April 2020	5,200
At 31 March 2021	4,100
At 30 June 2021	9,780

The company bought plant costing £220,000 for use in its trade on 28 August 2020. The TWDV on the main pool on 1 April 2020 is £37,000.

Calculate Oak Ltd's taxable total profits for the accounting periods in the 15 month period to 30 June 2021.

Assume the FY2020 rates and allowances apply throughout.

Solution

Oak Ltd – Taxable total profits

	y/e 31.3.2021 £	3 m/e 30.6.2021 £
Trading profit (12:3)	706,364	176,591
Less: Capital allowances (W)	(226,660)	(1,365)
Tax adjusted trading profit	479,704	175,226
Interest income		
(£22,000 – £5,200 + £4,100)	20,900	
(£9,780 – £4,100)		5,680
Property income (12:3)	8,000	2,000
Chargeable gain	0	16,000
Total profits	508,604	198,906
Less: QCD relief	(24,000)	
TTP	484,604	198,906

Working: Capital allowances computation

		Main pool	Allowances
	£	£	£
y/e 31 March 2021			
TWDV b/f		37,000	
Plant and machinery	220,000		
AIA	(220,000)		220,000
		0	
		37,000	
WDA (18%)		(6,660)	6,660
TWDV c/f		30,340	
Total allowances			226,660

	Main pool	Allowances
3 m/e 30 June 2021		
	£	£
TWDV b/f	30,340	
WDA (18% × 3/12)	(1,365)	1,365
TWDV c/f	28,975	
Total allowances		1,365

Test your understanding 6

Ash Ltd prepared accounts for the 17 month period to 31 May 2021, with results as follows:

	£
Trading profit (adjusted for tax purposes but before capital allowances)	1,949,614
Bank interest (received 31 August 2020)	11,540
Property income	25,500
Chargeable gain (asset disposed of 1 November 2020)	12,995
Charitable donations (paid 1 October 2020)	16,500
Bank interest (income) accrued was as follows:	
At 1 January 2020	7,400
At 31 December 2020	5,600
At 31 May 2021	10,540

The company bought plant costing £1,040,000, for use in its trade on 1 September 2020. The tax written down value on the main pool on 1 January 2020 is £45,000.

Calculate Ash Ltd's taxable total profits for the accounting periods in the 17 month period to 31 May 2021.

8 Chapter summary

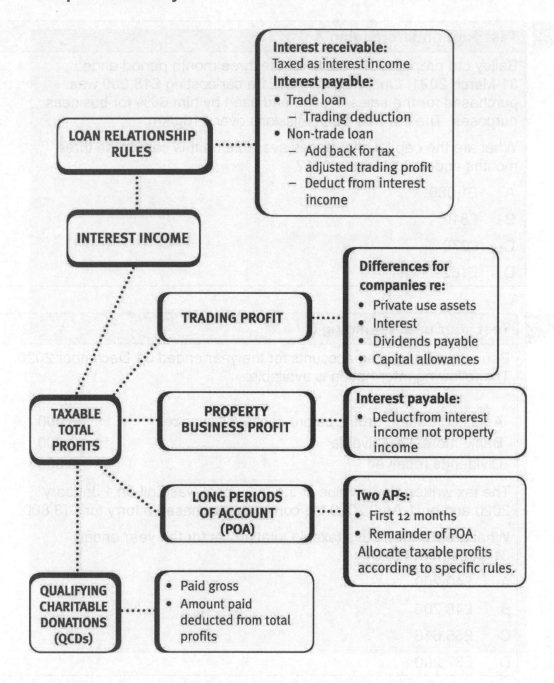

LOAN RELATIONSHIP RULES

Interest receivable:
Taxed as interest income
Interest payable:
- Trade loan
  - Trading deduction
- Non-trade loan
  - Add back for tax adjusted trading profit
  - Deduct from interest income

INTEREST INCOME

TRADING PROFIT

Differences for companies re:
- Private use assets
- Interest
- Dividends payable
- Capital allowances

TAXABLE TOTAL PROFITS

PROPERTY BUSINESS PROFIT

Interest payable:
- Deduct from interest income not property income

LONG PERIODS OF ACCOUNT (POA)

Two APs:
- First 12 months
- Remainder of POA
Allocate taxable profits according to specific rules.

QUALIFYING CHARITABLE DONATIONS (QCDs)
- Paid gross
- Amount paid deducted from total profits

9 Practice objective test questions

Test your understanding 7

Bailey Ltd prepared accounts for the three month period ended 31 March 2021. On 1 February 2021 a car costing £18,000 was purchased for the sales director and used by him 60% for business purposes. The car has CO_2 emissions over 110g/km.

What are the capital allowances available on this car for the three months ended 31 March 2021?

A   £1,080

B   £810

C   £270

D   £162

Test your understanding 8

Bennett Ltd prepared accounts for the year ended 31 December 2020. The following information is available:

	£
Adjusted trading profits before capital allowances	56,000
Bank interest receivable	3,000
Dividends received	8,000

The tax written down value of the main pool was £nil on 1 January 2020 and on 1 April 2020 the company purchased a lorry for £18,800.

What are Bennett Ltd's taxable total profits for the year ended 31 December 2020?

A   £40,200

B   £48,200

C   £55,616

D   £37,200

Test your understanding 9

Smith and Jones Ltd had the following results for the year ended 31 March 2021:

	£
Tax adjusted trading profit before capital allowances	330,000
Chargeable gains	9,000

The tax written down value on the main pool as at 1 April 2020 was £57,778.

There were no additions or disposals of plant and machinery during the year.

What is the company's taxable total profit for the year ended 31 March 2021?

A   £319,600

B   £339,000

C   £281,222

D   £328,600

Test your understanding 10

X Ltd has included a deduction in its accounting profit of £3,200 in respect of the annual leasing cost for a car, which has CO_2 emissions of 135g/km.

The car has been used for the whole of the 12 month period ended 31 March 2021.

When calculating the adjusted profit for tax purposes, what adjustment must be made to the accounting profit in the statement of profit or loss in respect of the leasing cost in the year ended 31 March 2021?

A   £480 deduction

B   £480 add back

C   £0

D   £2,720 add back

Test your understanding 11

A company has the following expenses in its statement of profit or loss:

Legal fees for the purchase of a new building	£800
Legal fees for defending an action for faulty goods	£1,500
Christmas party for staff (the company has 20 employees)	£3,200
Bank fee for arranging a trade related long term loan	£1,000

How much must be added back to the company's accounting profit when calculating the tax adjusted trading profit?

A £2,300

B £800

C £3,200

D £1,800

Test your understanding answers

 Test your understanding 1

Corn Ltd

Tax adjusted trading profit – y/e 31 December 2019

	£	£
Profit before tax	2,598	
Profit on sale of business premises		1,750
Advertising	0	
Depreciation	2,381	
Light and heat	0	
Subscription to Printers' association	0	
Charitable donation (Note 1)	45	
Gifts to customers:		
Calendars	0	
Food hampers (Note 2)	95	
Motor expenses (Note 3)	0	
Rates	0	
Redecorating administration offices	0	
Repairs – building extension (capital)	1,647	
Staff wages (Note 4)	0	
Telephone	0	
	6,766	1,750
	(1,750)	
Adjusted trading profit (before capital allowances)	5,016	

Notes:

1 Charitable donations to a national charity made by a company are disallowed as trading expenditure but are deductible when calculating TTP.

2 Gifts to customers are disallowed, unless they amount to £50 or less per customer during the year and display a conspicuous advert for the business. Gifts of food or drink or tobacco are disallowed irrespective of their cost.

3 Motor car expenses are all allowable for the company, although the director will be taxed on the private use of the car as an employment benefit.

4 The expenditure on the Christmas lunch is an allowable deduction for the employer.

It is important to show a zero if no adjustment is required as shown above (and in Chapter 7) in order to obtain maximum marks. The notes above would not normally be required in the examination and are for tutorial purposes.

Test your understanding 2

Ellingham Ltd

The 15 month period is split into two accounting periods:

1. First 12 months: 12 m/e 31 December 2020
2. Balance period: 3 m/e 31 March 2021

Capital allowances computation

	Main Pool	Short life asset	Special rate pool	Allowances
	£	£	£	£	£
y/e 31 December 2020					
TWDV b/f		149,280	13,440		
Additions:					
Not qualifying for AIA or FYA:					
Car (CO$_2$ ≤ 110g/km)		11,760			
Qualifying for AIA (special rate pool):					
Heating system	12,800				
AIA	(12,800)				12,800
			0		
Qualifying for AIA (main pool):					
Equipment	1,000,800				
Van	7,200				
	1,008,000				
AIA (Note)	(987,200)				987,200
		20,800			
Disposal proceeds		(14,160)	(5,520)		
		167,680	7,920	0	
Balancing allowance			(7,920)		7,920
WDA (18%)		(30,182)			30,182
WDA (6%)				(0)	
Low emission car	12,200				
FYA (100%)	(12,200)				12,200
		0			
TWDV c/f		137,498		0	
Total allowances					1,050,302

Note: The AIA is allocated to the additions in the special rate pool (WDA 6%) in priority to the addition in the main pool (WDA 18%).

3 m/e 31 March 2021		Main Pool	Allowances
	£	£	£
TWDV b/f		137,498	
Additions:			
WDA (18% × 3/12)		(6,187)	6,187
TWDV c/f		131,311	
Total allowances			6,187

Test your understanding 3

Smith Ltd – Taxable total profits – y/e 31 December 2020

	£	£	£
Profit per accounts		105,940	
Non-trading interest payable		6,590	
Depreciation		9,750	
Non-trading interest receivable			15,860
Capital allowances			11,800
		122,280	27,660
		(27,660)	
Tax adjusted trading profit		94,620	
Interest income:			
Non-trading interest receivable	15,860		
Non-trading interest payable	(6,590)		
		9,270	
TTP		103,890	

Test your understanding 4

Tasman Ltd

Property income – y/e 31 March 2021

	£	£
Rent receivable		
(7/12 × £10,500)		6,125
(10/12 × £11,200)		9,333
Premium	47,000	
Less: 2% × (7 – 1) × £47,000	(5,640)	
		41,360
		56,818
Less: Allowable expenses		
Irrecoverable debt (3/12 × £11,200)		(2,800)
Roof repairs		(7,200)
Property income		46,818

Note: There is no need to calculate individual profits or losses for each property. Profit and losses are pooled to obtain total property income.

Alternative calculation for assessment on the premium:

£47,000 × (51 – 7)/50 = £41,360

Test your understanding 5

Geronimo Ltd

(a) Tax adjusted trading profit – y/e 31 March 2021

	£	£
Profit before tax	652,580	
Trade debts written off	0	
Loan to customer (Note 1)	600	
Increase in allowance for trade debtors	0	
Depreciation	83,320	
Donation to national charity (Note 2)	1,800	
Donation to local charity	0	
Gifts to customers (food disallowed)	1,000	
Accountancy and audit fees	0	
Legal fees re renewal of short lease (Note 3)	0	
Legal fees re issue of loan notes (Note 4)	0	
Staff party (Note 5)	0	
Replacing part of a wall (Note 6)	0	
Extension to office building (Note 7)	12,200	
Bank interest		2,800
Loan interest		22,000
Dividends		36,000
Interest payable (Note 8)	0	
Capital allowances – P&M (£66,000 × 18%)		11,880
Capital allowances – SBAs (Note 7) (£12,200 × 3% × 3/12)		92
	751,500	72,772
	(72,772)	
Tax adjusted trading profit	678,728	

Notes:

1   The loan to a customer is for non-trade purposes (money lending is not the company's trade). The write off of the loan is therefore not an allowable deduction in calculating taxable trading profits. The write off is allowable against interest income under the loan relationship rules.

2 The donation to the national charity is deducted in the corporation tax computation from total profits and is therefore added back in calculating trading profits.

3 Costs of renewing a short lease (< 50 years) are allowable.

4 The legal fees in connection with the issue of the loan notes are incurred in respect of a trading loan relationship and are therefore deductible as a trading expense.

5 The individual employees will be assessed to income tax on the cost of the party (as it exceeds £150 per head) as a benefit of employment. However, all of the costs of providing the staff party are allowable for the company for corporation tax purposes.

6 The replacement of the wall is allowable since the whole structure is not being replaced.

7 The cost of the extension to the office building is not allowable, being capital in nature. Structures and buildings allowances (SBAs) can be claimed on the expenditure as it was incurred on the construction of a building used in a business on or after 29 October 2018. The allowance is time apportioned in this accounting period, as the building was not brought into use until 1 January 2021.

8 Interest on the loan notes used for trading purposes is deductible in calculating the taxable trading profit on an accruals basis.

(b) **Geronimo Ltd**

Corporation tax computation – y/e 31 March 2021

	£	£
Trading profit		678,728
Interest income – Bank interest	2,800	
– Loan interest	22,000	
– Customer loan written off	(600)	
		24,200
Total profits		702,928
Less: QCDs		(1,800)
TTP		701,128

Corporation tax liability

	£
FY2020	
Corporation tax payable (£701,128 × 19%)	133,214

Test your understanding 6

Ash Ltd

Taxable total profits

	y/e 31.12.20	5 m/e 31.5.21
	£	£
Trading profit (12:5)	1,376,198	573,416
Less: Capital allowances (W)	(1,015,300)	(5,228)
Trading income	360,898	568,188
Interest income		
(£11,540 – £7,400 + £5,600)	9,740	
(£10,540 – £5,600)		4,940
Property income (12:5)	18,000	7,500
Chargeable gain	12,995	0
Total profits	401,633	580,628
Less: QCD relief	(16,500)	0
TTP	385,133	580,628

Working: Capital allowances computation

	Main pool	Allowances
	£	£	£
y/e 31 December 2020			
TWDV b/f		45,000	
Additions:			
Qualifying for AIA:			
Plant and machinery	1,040,000		
AIA (max)	(1,000,000)		1,000,000
		40,000	
		85,000	
WDA (18%)		(15,300)	15,300
TWDV (c/f)		69,700	
Total allowances			1,015,300

5 m/e 31 May 2021		
WDA (18% × 5/12)	(5,228)	5,228
TWDV c/f	64,472	
Total allowances		5,228

Test your understanding 7

Bailey Ltd

The correct answer is C.

C is the correct answer because for corporation tax purposes, there is no adjustment to capital allowances as a result of private use of assets by employees. The allowances are computed as follows:

3 months ended 31 March 2021	£
Car with high emissions	18,000
WDA at 6% × 3/12	(270)

Test your understanding 8

Bennett Ltd

The correct answer is A.

	£
Adjusted trading profits	56,000
Less: Capital allowances (AIA)	(18,800)
Tax adjusted trading profit	37,200
Bank interest receivable	3,000
Taxable total profits	40,200

Note: Dividends received are not subject to corporation tax.

Test your understanding 9

Smith and Jones Ltd

The correct answer is D.

Year ended 31 March 2021

	£
Tax adjusted trading profit	330,000
Less: CAs (£57,778 × 18%)	(10,400)
Trading profit	319,600
Chargeable gains	9,000
Taxable total profits	328,600

Test your understanding 10

X Ltd

The correct answer is B.

(£3,200 × 15%) = £480 add back

15% of car leasing costs are disallowed if CO_2 emissions exceed 110g/km. As £3,200 has been deducted in the accounts the disallowable amount of £480 must be added back.

Test your understanding 11

The correct answer is B.

The legal fees for the purchase of a new building are capital in nature and therefore not deductible from trading profits.

The legal fees for defending an action for faulty goods are a trade related revenue expense and therefore a deductible trading expense.

Staff entertainment is fully allowable, although there may be a taxable benefit for the employee if the cost exceeds £150 per head.

The bank fee on a trade related loan is a trading expense under the loan relationship rules.

Losses for companies

Chapter learning objectives

Upon completion of this chapter you will be able to:

- understand how relief for a property business loss is given
- understand how trading losses can be carried forward
- understand how trading losses can be claimed against income of the current or previous accounting periods
- recognise the factors that will influence the choice of loss relief claim
- explain and compute the treatment of capital losses.

One of the PER performance objectives (PO15) is to prepare computations of taxable amounts and tax liabilities according to legal requirements. Working through this chapter should help you understand how to demonstrate that objective.

PER

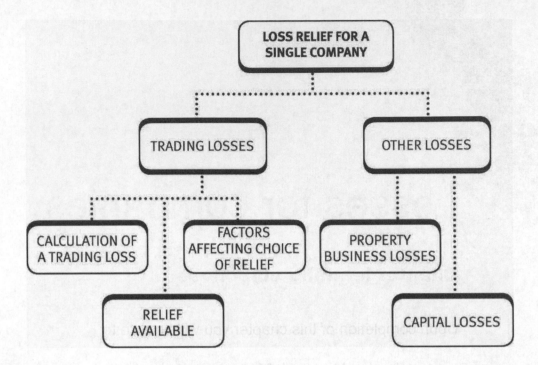

 Companies may not always be profitable – in both Financial Accounting and Financial Reporting (FR) you learn how to account for losses. A loss can also arise for tax purposes – you need an appreciation of the consequences of generating a loss from a wider financial perspective including its impact in terms of accounts recognition (FR) and budgetary and cash flow considerations.

Introduction

This chapter covers the rules for loss reliefs available to a single company. The following losses are dealt with:

- Trading losses (sections 1 to 3).
- Property business losses (section 4).
- Capital losses (section 5).

1 Trading losses

Calculation of a trading loss

- Trading losses are computed in the same way as tax adjusted trading profits:

	£
Tax adjusted net profit/(loss)	X/(X)
Less: Capital allowances	(X)
Adjusted trading loss	(X)

If a company has made an adjusted trading loss, the tax adjusted trading profit shown in the TTP computation for that period is £Nil.

 Illustration 1 – Trading losses

Carlos Ltd had the following results for its year ended 31 August 2020:

	£	£
Gross profit		30,000
Less: Expenditure		
Depreciation	5,000	
Allowable costs	12,000	
		(17,000)
Net profit per accounts		13,000

The capital allowances for the year amount to £21,000.

(a) **Calculate the tax adjusted trading loss for the year ended 31 August 2020.**

(b) **Calculate the tax adjusted trading loss for the year ended 31 August 2020 assuming the facts are the same except that the company made a net loss per the accounts of £10,000.**

Solution

(a) **Tax adjusted trading loss – y/e 31 August 2020**

	£
Net profit per accounts	13,000
Add: Depreciation	5,000
	18,000
Less: Capital allowances	(21,000)
Tax adjusted trading loss	(3,000)
Tax adjusted trading profit included in TTP	0

(b) **Tax adjusted trading loss**

	£
Net loss per accounts	(10,000)
Add: Depreciation	5,000
	(5,000)
Less: Capital allowances	(21,000)
Tax adjusted trading loss	(26,000)
Tax adjusted trading profit included in TTP	0

Relief for trading losses

There are four ways in which a company can offset trading losses:

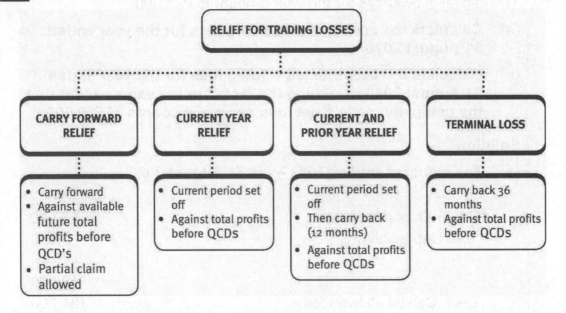

Carry forward loss relief

The key features of this relief are:

- The loss is carried forward for offset in future accounting periods.

- The loss is set against **total profits before qualifying charitable donations (QCDs)**.

- It is possible to restrict the amount of loss relieved

- The loss can be carried forward indefinitely.

- There is no need to make a current year or a prior year claim first.

- A claim must be made within two years of the end of the accounting period **in which the loss is relieved**.

Carry forward loss relief

- The loss can be carried forward and set off against future total profits before QCDs.

- Losses can be carried forward:

  - After a current year claim only.

  - After a current year and prior year claim.

  - If no current or carry back claims are made.

Illustration 2 – Trading losses

Poppy Ltd has a current year tax adjusted trading loss of £35,000, for the year ended 31 October 2020.

The company's projected tax adjusted trading profits are as follows:

	£
Year ended 31 October 2021	14,000
Year ended 31 October 2022	6,500
Year ended 31 October 2023	15,600

Poppy Ltd also has property income of £5,000 each year.

Calculate Poppy Ltd's taxable total profits for the four years ended 31 October 2023, assuming that the loss for the year ended 31 October 2020 is carried forward and a claim is made to relieve as much of the loss as possible in each of the future periods.

Solution

Year ended 31 October	2020	2021	2022	2023
	£	£	£	£
Tax adjusted trading profit	0	14,000	6,500	15,600
Property income	5,000	5,000	5,000	5,000
Total profits	5,000	19,000	11,500	20,600
Less: Loss relief b/f	0	(19,000)	(11,500)	(4,500)
TTP	5,000	0	0	16,100

Working – loss memorandum	
	£
Loss – y/e 31.10.20	35,000
Used in – y/e 31.10.21	(19,000)
y/e 31.10.22	(11,500)
y/e 31.10.23	(4,500)
	———
Carry forward to y/e 31.10.24	0
	———

Current year relief

If a current year loss relief claim is made, trading losses are set off against:

- total profits before deduction of QCDs
- of the same accounting period.

A current year claim must be made:

- for the whole loss; a partial claim is not allowed.
- within two years of the end of the loss making accounting period.

Illustration 3 – Trading losses

Sage Ltd had the following results for the year ended 31 March 2021

	£
Tax adjusted trading loss	(40,000)
Property income	10,000
Chargeable gain	50,000
Qualifying charitable donation	(10,000)

(a) **Show how the trading loss could be relieved with a current year claim.**

(b) **Show how your answer to (a) would be different if the tax adjusted trading loss was £60,000.**

(c) **Explain how your answer to (b) would be different if in the year ended 31 March 2021 the trading profit was £nil and the company had a £60,000 trading loss brought forward from the previous accounting period.**

Solution

(a) **Taxable total profits computation – y/e 31 March 2021**

	£
Tax adjusted trading profit	0
Property income	10,000
Chargeable gain	50,000
Total profits	60,000
Less: Loss relief – current year	(40,000)
Less: QCD relief	(10,000)
TTP	10,000

Loss memorandum

Year ended 31 March 2021	40,000
Less: Used in current period	(40,000)
Loss carried forward	0

(b) **Taxable total profits computation – y/e 31 March 2021**

	£
Total profits (as before)	60,000
Less: Loss relief – current year	(60,000)
TTP	0
QCD wasted	(10,000)

As the loss is set off before the deduction of QCDs, the QCDs have become excess (i.e. not used), as there are insufficient profits after the loss relief against which to offset them. An important principle of a current period claim is that no restriction in the amount of loss set off is permitted.

It is **not** possible to restrict the loss relief to (£50,000), to relieve the QCD of (£10,000), and find an alternative use for the remaining (£10,000) loss.

Excess QCDs cannot be carried forward or back and are therefore wasted unless the company is a member of a group (Chapter 17).

> (c) If the trading loss of £60,000 was brought forward from the previous year a claim to offset the loss against total profits of the year ended 31 March 2021 could be restricted to £50,000 in order to avoid wasting QCDs. The ability to restrict the amount of loss offset in a brought forward loss relief claim is an important feature which distinguishes it from current year and prior year carry back claims.

Carry back relief

Any trading loss remaining after a current year claim can be carried back.

Under carry back loss relief, trading losses are set off against:

- total profits (before deduction of QCDs)
- of the previous 12 months
- on a LIFO (last in first out) basis.

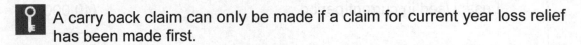 A carry back claim can only be made if a claim for current year loss relief has been made first.

The carry back claim:

- is optional
- must be made within two years of the end of the loss making accounting period.

Trading losses – pro forma computation

Assume the loss arises in 2020	2019	2020	2021
	£	£	£
Tax adjusted trading profit	X	0	X
Other income	X	X	X
Chargeable gains	X	X	X
Total profits	X	X	X
Less: Loss relief			
– Current year		(X)	
– 12 month carry back	(X)		
– Loss relief c/f			(X)
	0	0	X
Less: QCD relief	Wasted	Wasted	(X)
Taxable total profits	0	0	X

Illustration 4 – Trading losses

Marjoram Ltd has the following results:

Year ended 31 March	2019 £	2020 £	2021 £
Tax adjusted trading profit/(loss)	11,000	9,000	(45,000)
Bank interest receivable	500	500	500
Chargeable gain	0	0	4,000
Qualifying charitable donations	(250)	(250)	(250)

Calculate the taxable total profits for all periods affected, assuming that loss relief is taken as soon as possible.

Solution

Marjoram Ltd – Corporation tax computations

Year ended 31 March	2019 £	2020 £	2021 £
Tax adjusted trading profit	11,000	9,000	0
Interest income	500	500	500
Chargeable gain	0	0	4,000
Total profits	11,500	9,500	4,500
Less: Loss relief (W)			
– Current year			(4,500)
– 12 month carry back		(9,500)	
	11,500	0	0
Less: QCD relief	(250)	Wasted	Wasted
TTP	11,250	0	0

Working – loss memorandum

	£
Loss for the y/e 31 March 2021	45,000
Less: Used in current year – y/e 31.3.21	(4,500)
Less: Used in 12 month carry back – y/e 31.3.20	(9,500)
Loss carried forward	31,000

Note: The y/e 31 March 2019 is not effected, as the loss cannot be carried back that far.

The QCDs in the years ended 31 March 2020 and 2021 are wasted.

Loss making period of less than 12 months

The length of the loss making period is not important:

- Full relief is given against the current period total profits.

- The remaining loss can be carried back in full in the normal way.

Test your understanding 1

Mint Ltd has the following results:

	y/e 31.3.19 £	y/e 31.3.20 £	9 m/e 31.12.20 £	y/e 31.12.21 £
Tax adjusted trading profit/(loss)	30,000	15,000	(100,000)	40,000
Interest income	3,000	5,000	10,000	10,000
Chargeable gain	10,000	0	40,000	0
Qualifying charitable donations	(1,000)	(1,000)	(1,000)	(1,000)

Calculate the taxable total profits, for all of the accounting periods shown above, clearly indicating how you would deal with the trading loss, to obtain relief as soon as possible.

Short accounting periods prior to year of loss

If the accounting period preceding the period of the loss is less than 12 months:

- The total profits of the accounting period that falls partly into the 12 month carry back period must be time apportioned.

- The loss can only be offset against the total profits which fall within the 12 month carry back period.

- Remember, the loss is offset on a LIFO basis (i.e. against the later accounting period first).

Illustration 5 – Trading losses

Star plc's recent results are as follows:

	y/e 31.12.18 £	5 m/e 31.5.19 £	y/e 31.5.20 £
Tax adjusted trading profit/(loss)	24,000	10,000	(50,000)
Interest income	3,500	2,000	6,000

Calculate the taxable total profits for all periods assuming the trading loss is relieved as early as possible.

Solution

	y/e 31.12.18 £	5 m/e 31.5.19 £	y/e 31.5.20 £
Tax adjusted trading profit/(loss)	24,000	10,000	0
Interest income	3,500	2,000	6,000
Total profits	27,500	12,000	6,000
Less: Loss relief			
– Current year			(6,000)
– 12 month carry back	(16,042)	(12,000)	
TTP	11,458	0	0

Loss memorandum

	£
Trading loss y/e 31.5.20	50,000
Less: Used in current year claim – y/e 31.5.20	(6,000)
	44,000
Less: Used in 12 month carry back	
– 5 m/e 31.5.19	(12,000)
	32,000
– y/e 31.12.18	
Lower of:	
(i) Total profits × 7/12 = (7/12 × £27,500) = £16,042	
(ii) Remaining loss = £32,000	(16,042)
Loss remaining to carry forward	15,958

Test your understanding 2

Catalyst Ltd has been trading for many years with the following results:

	y/e 31.3.19 £	9 m/e 31.12.19 £	y/e 31.12.20 £	y/e 31.12.21 £
Tax adjusted trading profit/(loss) before capital allowances	33,000	16,500	(75,000)	31,000
Capital allowances	(5,400)	(4,050)	(6,550)	(5,000)
Interest income	1,200	1,300	1,400	1,600
Qualifying charitable donations paid	0	(3,000)	(3,000)	(8,000)

(a)   **Calculate the tax adjusted trading profits/losses after capital allowances for all of the above accounting periods.**

(b)   **Assuming that Catalyst Ltd claims relief for its trading loss as early as possible, calculate the company's taxable total profits for all of the above accounting periods.**

Your answer should show the amount of unrelieved losses as at 31 December 2021.

2   Terminal loss relief

When a company incurs a trading loss during the **final 12 months of trading**, it is possible to make a carry back claim:

- set against **total profits** (before QCDs)

- of the **three years** preceding the loss making period (not 12 months)

- on a **LIFO basis**.

However, the company must first claim to set the trading loss against total profits (before QCDs) of the accounting period of the loss.

Where the company has prepared accounts for a period other than 12 months during the three years preceding the loss making period:

- apportionment will be necessary in the same way as for a normal carry back claim

- so that losses are only carried back against the proportion of profits falling within the three year period.

Test your understanding 3

Brown Ltd has been trading for many years. The company prepared its annual accounts to 31 March, each year, but changed its accounting date to 31 December in 2019. The company ceased trading on 31 December 2020.

	y/e 31.3.17 £	y/e 31.3.18 £	y/e 31.3.19 £	9 m/e 31.12.19 £	y/e 31.12.20 £
Tax adjusted trading profit	450,000	87,000	240,000	45,000	0
Bank interest income	9,000	3,000	6,000	1,500	1,500
Chargeable gain	7,500	–	–	–	–
Qualifying charitable donations	(30,000)	(30,000)	(30,000)	(30,000)	(30,000)

In the year ended 31 December 2020, Brown Ltd made a tax adjusted trading loss of £525,000.

Calculate Brown Ltd's taxable total profits, for all of the above accounting periods, assuming terminal loss relief is claimed for the trading loss arising in the year ended 31 December 2020.

3 Choice of loss relief

Factors that influence choice of loss relief

Where there is a choice of loss reliefs available, the following factors will influence the loss relief chosen:

- Tax saving
- Cash flow
- Wastage of relief for QCDs.

Tax saving

The company will want to save (or obtain a refund at) the highest possible rate of tax. The tax saved is calculated by reference to the accounting period in which the loss is offset (not the accounting period in which the loss arose).

As the tax rate in FY2018, FY2019 and FY2020 is 19% the tax saving will be the same regardless of which of these financial years a loss is offset. There may, however, be a difference if QCDs are paid in one year and not another (see below).

Generally the tax saved from offsetting a loss in an accounting period is the loss multiplied by 19%. However, this will not be the case if the loss relief results in wasted QCDs (see below).

Cash flow

A company's cash flow position may affect its choice of loss relief.

Note that when a loss is carried back, it will result in a repayment of corporation tax, whereas carrying losses forward will only result in a reduction of a future tax liability.

Loss of relief for QCDs

Unrelieved QCDs cannot be carried forward and relieved against future tax adjusted trading profits. It may therefore be beneficial to restrict the amount of a loss offset against total profits in a loss carry forward claim to ensure there are sufficient profits to offset the QCDs.

Remember though that the amount of a current year and prior year loss carry back claim cannot be restricted and so these may result in the wastage of QCDs.

Illustration 6 – Choice of loss relief

Minor Ltd has the following results:

Year ended 31 March	2020	2021
	£	£
Tax adjusted trading profit/(loss)	(20,000)	16,000
Bank interest receivable	20,000	0
Chargeable gain	0	4,000
Qualifying charitable donations	(2,000)	

Calculate the tax saved assuming the trading loss in the year ended 31 March 2020 is:

(i)   **Offset in the year ended 31 March 2020**

(ii) **Offset in the year ended 31 March 2021.**

Solution

Minor Ltd – Corporation tax computations

(i) Loss offset in the year ended 31 March 2020

	Without loss relief £	With loss relief £
Tax adjusted trading profit	0	0
Interest income	20,000	20,000
Total profits	20,000	20,000
Less: Loss relief (W)		
– Current year		(20,000)
	20,000	0
Less: QCD relief	(2,000)	Wasted
TTP	18,000	0
Tax payable £18,000 × 19%	3,420	0

The whole of the loss has been used and tax of £3,420 has been saved. The loss is offset before the QCDs resulting in the QCDs being wasted and £2,000 of the loss being used which does not result in any tax saving.

(ii) Loss offset in the year ended 31 March 2021

	Without loss relief £	With loss relief £
Tax adjusted trading profit	16,000	16,000
Chargeable gain	4,000	4,000
Total profits	20,000	20,000
Less: Loss relief (W)		
– Losses brought forward		(20,000)
TTP	20,000	0
Tax payable £20,000 × 19%	3,800	0

The whole of the loss has been used and tax of £3,800 has been saved.

Approach to questions

Loss questions will often give you taxable total profits information for a company for a number of years. This may initially appear daunting.

However, the following step by step approach will provide you with a logical way to attempt the question and ensure that you offset the losses correctly.

Step 1: Write out the skeleton TTP pro forma remembering to leave space for loss relief claims and laying out the years side by side.

Step 2: Fill in the pro forma with the TTP information provided, ignoring loss relief. In the year of the loss, the tax adjusted trading profit is £Nil.

Step 3: Keep a separate working for the 'trading loss'. Update the working as the loss is relieved.

Step 4: Consider the loss relief options available.

- Where there is more than one loss to offset:

    - Deal with the earliest loss first.

- If a question states relief is to be obtained as 'early as possible' or 'in order to maximise the tax saving', the order of set off is:

    - Current year claim followed by a carry back claim to the previous 12 months (or 36 months for a terminal loss).

    - Carry forward any remaining loss and offset against future total profits.

- If a question asks you to identify the options available and the tax savings for each option, consider in turn the three options:

    - Carry forward only

    - Current year claim and then carry forward any excess

    - Current year claim, followed by a carry back claim and then carry forward any excess.

- Identify the amount of tax saving, the loss of relief for QCDs and cash flow implications under each option and conclude as to which option is preferable.

Step 5: Work out the revised TTP after the appropriate loss reliefs.

Test your understanding 4

Loser Ltd prepares its accounts to 30 September. The company's recent results have been as follows:

	y/e 30.9.19 £	y/e 30.9.20 £	y/e 30.9.21 £
Tax adjusted trading profit/(loss)	200,000	(180,000)	200,000
Interest income	7,000	5,000	6,000
QCDs	(2,000)	(2,000)	(2,000)

Advise Loser Ltd of the loss relief options available for the trading loss arising in the year 30 September 2020 and calculate the amount of tax saved for each option.

Assume that the tax rate for FY2020 continues into the future.

Summary of trading loss reliefs

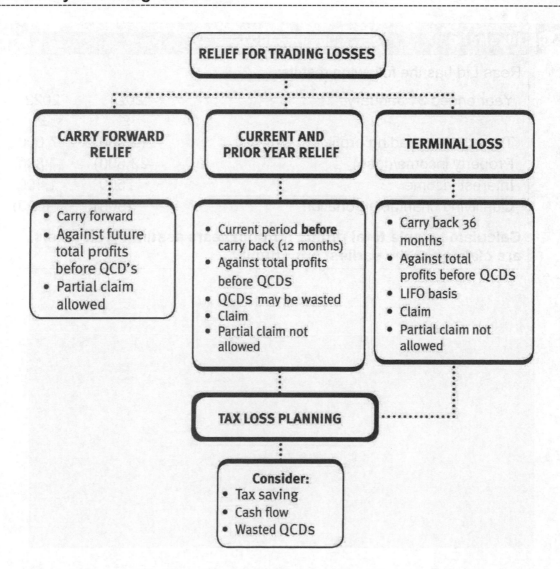

4 Property business losses

Property business losses are:

- automatically offset (i.e. mandatory) against **total profits (before QCDs)** for the current period.

- any excess can be carried forward and offset against future **total profits (before QCDs)** of the company.

Note that:

- A claim to carry forward a loss and offset it against total profits of a future period must be made within two years of the end of the accounting period in which the loss is relieved.

- There is no carry back facility for property business losses.

- Partial loss claims are not allowed when offsetting the loss in the current period but are allowed for losses brought forward from earlier periods.

- If applicable, property business losses are set off before trading losses.

Illustration 7 – Property business losses

Reas Ltd has the following results:

Year ended 31 January:	2021	2022
	£	£
Tax adjusted trading profit	12,000	7,000
Property income/(loss)	(22,600)	800
Interest income	500	1,400
Qualifying charitable donation	(500)	(500)

Calculate taxable total profits for both years assuming all reliefs are claimed at the earliest opportunity.

Solution

Year ended 31 January:

	2021 £	2022 £
Tax adjusted trading profit	12,000	7,000
Property income	0	800
Interest income	500	1,400
Total profits	12,500	9,200
Less: Property business loss (W)	(12,500)	0
	0	9,200
Less: Loss relief b/f	0	(8,700)
QCD relief	Wasted	(500)
TTP	0	0

Working: Property business loss

	£
Loss in y/e 31 January 2021	22,600
Less: Used in current period – y/e 31 January 2021	(12,500)
	10,100
Less: Used in carry forward – y/e 31 January 2022	(8,700)
Unrelieved loss carried forward	1,400

Note: The current year offset against total profits is mandatory and cannot be restricted to preserve relief for the QCDs. The remaining losses can be carried forward. A carried forward loss is also offset against total profits (before QCDs) but the amount can be specified to preserve relief for the QCDs.

Test your understanding 5

Comfy Ltd has the following results:

Year ended 31 December:	2018 £	2019 £	2020 £
Tax adjusted trading profit/(loss)	12,450	(14,500)	4,000
Property income/(loss)	2,000	1,800	(500)
Interest income	1,000	600	1,000
Qualifying charitable donation	(400)	(400)	(400)

Calculate taxable total profits for all three years assuming all reliefs are claimed at the earliest opportunity.

5 Capital losses

A capital loss incurred in an accounting period is:

- relieved against any chargeable gains arising in the same accounting period.

- Any excess losses are then carried forward for relief against gains arising in future accounting periods.

Note that:

- Relief is automatic – no claim is required.

- A capital loss may never be carried back and relieved against chargeable gains for earlier periods.

- Capital losses can only be set against gains, they may not be set against the company's income.

- Partial claims are not allowed.

Illustration 8 – Capital losses

Rose Ltd has the following results:

Year ended 31 March:	2020 £	2021 £
Tax adjusted trading profit/(loss)	(34,000)	18,000
Interest income	6,000	9,000
Capital loss	(2,000)	
Chargeable gains		7,000

Calculate the taxable total profits for the two accounting periods assuming that the trading loss is carried forward and a claim is made to offset it against the year ended 31 March 2021.

Show any unrelieved losses carried forward at 1 April 2021.

Solution

Trading losses carried forward can be relieved against total profits. Partial claims can be made.

Capital losses can only be set against current or future chargeable gains and are automatically offset against the first available gains before considering relief for the trading loss brought forward. This is beneficial for the company, as relief for the capital loss is more restrictive than relief for the trading loss.

Rose Ltd

Taxable total profit computations

Year ended 31 March	2020	2021
	£	£
Tax adjusted trading profit	0	18,000
Interest income	6,000	9,000
Chargeable gains (£7,000 – £2,000)	0	5,000
	——	——
Total profits	6,000	32,000
Less: Loss relief b/f	0	(32,000)
	——	——
TTP	6,000	0
	——	——
Trading loss brought forward at 1 April 2021 (£34,000 – £32,000)		2,000
		——

Test your understanding 6

Coriander Ltd started to trade on 1 January 2020 and has the following results:

Year ended 31 December:	2020	2021	2022
	£	£	£
Tax adjusted trading profit/(loss)	37,450	(81,550)	20,000
Interest income	1,300	1,400	1,600
Chargeable gain/(loss)	(6,000)	0	13,000
Qualifying charitable donations	(3,000)	(3,000)	(3,000)

Calculate taxable total profits for all relevant periods assuming loss relief is claimed as early as possible.

6 Comprehensive example

Test your understanding 7

Eagle Ltd is a UK resident company that manufactures components. The company's results for the year ended 31 December 2020 are:

	£
Trading loss (as adjusted for taxation but before taking account of capital allowances) (Note 1)	(263,112)
Income from property (Note 2)	56,950
Profit on disposal of shares (Note 3)	141,517
Qualifying charitable donation (QCD) (Note 4)	(3,000)

Notes:

1 **Plant and machinery**

On 1 January 2020 the TWDV on the main pool was £64,700. Some machinery was sold on 15 February 2020 for £12,400 (original cost £18,000).

The following assets were purchased during the year:

20 October 2020	Lorry	£32,400
15 December 2020	Equipment	£13,040
18 December 2020	Motor car (CO$_2$ emissions 106g/km)	£11,300

2 **Income from property**

Eagle Ltd lets out two warehouses that are surplus to requirements.

The first warehouse was empty from 1 January to 31 March 2020, but was let from 1 April 2020. On that date the company received a premium of £50,000 for the grant of an eight year lease, and the annual rent of £12,600 which is payable in advance.

The second warehouse was let until 30 September 2020 at an annual rent of £8,400. On that date the tenant left owing three months' rent which the company is not able to recover. The roof was repaired at a cost of £6,700 during November 2020.

3 **Profit on disposal of shares**

The profit on disposal of shares relates to a 1% shareholding in a UK company that was sold on 22 December 2020 for £254,317.

The shareholding was purchased on 5 September 2007 for £112,800.

A chargeable gain of £97,525 arises on this disposal.

4 **Qualifying charitable donation**

The donation to charity was to Asthma UK (a national charity).

<table>
<tr><td>5</td><td colspan="3">Other information</td></tr>
</table>

Eagle Ltd's results for the year ended 30 June 2019 and the six month period ended 31 December 2019 were as follows:

	y/e 30.6.19 £	p/e 31.12.19 £
Tax adjusted trading profit	137,900	52,000
Property business profit/(loss)	(4,600)	18,700
Chargeable gain/(allowable loss)	(8,900)	18,200
QCDs	(2,300)	(2,600)

(a) **Calculate Eagle Ltd's tax adjusted trading loss for the year ended 31 December 2020.**

(b) **Assuming that Eagle Ltd claims relief for its trading loss as early as possible, calculate the company's taxable total profits for the three accounting periods ended 31 December 2020.**

Your answer should show the amount of unrelieved trading losses as at 31 December 2020.

(c) **Describe the alternative ways in which Eagle Ltd could have relieved the trading loss for the year ended 31 December 2020.**

7 Chapter summary

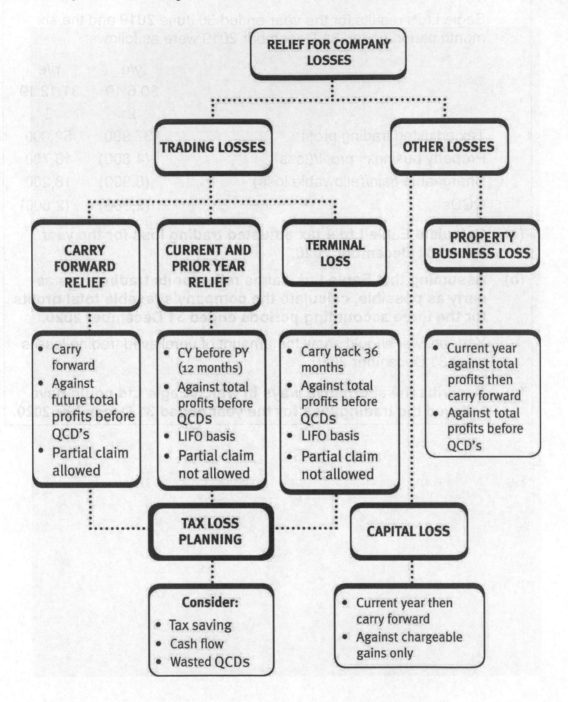

8 Practice objective test questions

Test your understanding 8

Bath Ltd has the following results for its first two years of trading:

Year ended 31 March	2020	2021
	£	£
Adjusted trading profit/(loss)	100,000	(240,000)
Bank interest receivable	4,000	6,000
Qualifying charitable donation	(2,000)	(1,000)

Assuming Bath Ltd uses its loss as early as possible, what is the trading loss carried forward to the year ended 31 March 2022?

A £234,000

B £136,000

C £133,000

D £130,000

Test your understanding 9

Dartmouth Ltd realised a trading loss of £140,000 in the year ended 31 March 2021. The loss is carried back against total profits for the year ended 31 March 2020.

By what date must a claim in respect of these losses be made?

A 31 March 2025

B 31 March 2022

C 31 March 2023

D 31 March 2024

Test your understanding 10

Davies Limited has the following results:

Year ended	31.03.20	31.03.21
	£	£
Tax adjusted trading profit/(loss)	25,000	(60,000)
Chargeable gain	6,000	3,000
Qualifying charitable donations	(3,000)	(1,000)

Assuming that Davies Limited uses its losses as early as possible, what is the trading loss available to carry forward at the year ended 31 March 2021?

A   £26,000

B   £29,000

C   £57,000

D   £30,000

Test your understanding 11

Which of the following statements is incorrect in respect of a loss incurred by a company?

A   A property business loss carried forward can only be offset against the first available future property income.

B   A trading loss carried forward can be offset against total profits.

C   A capital loss is offset against chargeable gains of the current accounting period with any excess being carried forward and offset against chargeable gains of future accounting periods.

D   A current year trading loss can be offset against the company's other income and chargeable gains of the current accounting period.

Test your understanding answers

Test your understanding 1

Mint Ltd

Taxable total profit computations

	y/e 31.3.19 £	y/e 31.3.20 £	9 m/e 31.12.20 £	y/e 31.12.21 £
Tax adjusted trading profit	30,000	15,000	0	40,000
Interest income	3,000	5,000	10,000	10,000
Chargeable gain	10,000	0	40,000	0
Total profits	43,000	20,000	50,000	50,000
Less: Loss relief (W)				
– Current period			(50,000)	
– 12 month carry back		(20,000)		
	43,000	0	0	50,000
Less: Loss relief b/f (W)				(30,000)
Less: QCD relief	(1,000)	Wasted	Wasted	(1,000)
TTP	42,000	0	0	19,000

Working – loss memorandum

	£
Loss in 9 months to 31 December 2020	100,000
Less: Used in current period – 9 m/e 31.12.20	(50,000)
Used in 12 month carry back – y/e 31.3.20	(20,000)
Carried forward	30,000
Used in y/e 31.12.21	(30,000)
	0

Note: The length of the loss making period is not important. The current period and 12 month carry back is unrestricted in amount.

Losses cannot be carried back to the y/e 31 March 2019.

Test your understanding 2

Catalyst Ltd

(a) **Tax-adjusted trading profits/losses after capital allowances**

	12 m/e 31.3.19 £	9 m/e 31.12.19 £	12 m/e 31.12.20 £	12 m/e 31.12.21 £
Adjusted profits	33,000	16,500	(75,000)	31,000
Less: CAs	(5,400)	(4,050)	(6,550)	(5,000)
Tax adjusted trading profit/ (loss)	27,600	12,450	(81,550)	26,000

(b) **Taxable total profit computations**

	12 m/e 31.3.19 £	9 m/e 31.12.19 £	12 m/e 31.12.20 £	12 m/e 31.12.21 £
Trading profits	27,600	12,450	0	26,000
Interest income	1,200	1,300	1,400	1,600
Total profits	28,800	13,750	1,400	27,600
Less: Loss relief				
– Current year			(1,400)	
– 12 month carry back	(7,200)	(13,750)		
	21,600	0	0	27,600
Less: Loss relief b/f				(19,600)
QCD relief	0	wasted	wasted	(8,000)
TTP	21,600	0	0	0

Note: Unrelieved trading loss available to carry forward at 31 December 2021 is £39,600 (W2).

Tax adjusted trading loss available and its utilisation

	£
Tax adjusted trading loss available (part (a))	81,550
Less: Used in current year claim – y/e 31.12.20	(1,400)
	80,150
Less: Used in 12 month carry back	
– 9 months (p/e 31.12.19)	(13,750)
	66,400
– Three months only (y/e 31.3.19)	
Maximum (3/12 × £28,800)	(7,200)
Available to carry forward	59,200
Less: Used against future total profit (y/e 31.12.21)	
restricted to avoid wasting QCDs	(19,600)
Loss carried forward at 31.12.21	39,600

Test your understanding 3

Brown Ltd

Taxable total profit computations

	y/e 31.3.17 £	y/e 31.3.18 £	y/e 31.3.19 £	9m/e 31.12.19 £	y/e 31.12.20 £
Tax adjusted trading profit	450,000	87,000	240,000	45,000	0
Interest income	9,000	3,000	6,000	1,500	1,500
Chargeable gain	7,500	0	0	0	0
Total profits	466,500	90,000	246,000	46,500	1,500
Less: Loss relief					
– Current year					(1,500)
– Terminal loss	(116,625)	(90,000)	(246,000)	(46,500)	
	349,875	0	0	0	0
Less: QCD relief	(30,000)	Wasted	Wasted	Wasted	Wasted
TTP	319,875	0	0	0	0

Loss memorandum

	£
Tax adjusted trading loss of final 12 months of trading	525,000
Less: Used in current year – y/e 31.12.20	(1,500)
	523,500
Less: Used in terminal loss carry back (LIFO):	
9 months to 31.12.19	(46,500)
12 months to 31.3.19	(246,000)
12 months to 31.3.18	(90,000)
3 months of y/e 31.3.17 (3/12 × £466,500)	(116,625)
Balance of loss = lost	24,375

Test your understanding 4

Loser Ltd has the following options regarding the trading loss arising in the year to 30 September 2020:

1   **Carry forward to offset against future total profits before QCDs**

   The loss can be fully offset in the year ended 30 September 2021. As this will leave sufficient total profits to relieve the QCDs there is no advantage to restricting the amount of the loss offset. The accounting period for the year ended 30 September 2021 falls in FY2020 and FY2021. The tax rate in both these years is 19% and the tax saved is £34,200 (£180,000 × 19%).

2   **Current year claim and then carry forward any excess**

   The loss is offset against total profits (before QCDs). In the current year the loss offset cannot be restricted and so £5,000 of the loss will be offset in the year ended 30 September 2020. The balance of the loss of £175,000 can be fully offset in the following year and as in option 1 above there is no advantage to restricting the amount offset.

   The QCDs paid in the year ended 30 September 2020 will be wasted and the tax saved is £570 (19% × (£5,000 − £2,000)).

   The tax saved in the year ended 30 September 2021 is £33,250 (£175,000 × 19%).

   The total saved from this option is £33,820 (£570 + £33,250).

3   **Current year claim, followed by a carry back claim and then carry forward any excess**

   As in option 2 £5,000 of the loss will be offset in the year ended 30 September 2020. The balance of the loss of £175,000 will be carried back to the previous year. There are no remaining losses to carry forward.

   The tax saved in the year ended 30 September 2020 is £570 (as (2) above). Again, the QCDs are wasted.

   The accounting period for the year ended 30 September 2019 falls in FY2018 (6 months) and FY2019 (6 months). The tax rate in both these years is 19% and the tax saved is £33,250 (£175,000 × 19%).

   The total saved from this option is £33,820 (£570 + £33,250).

   Conclusion

   Option 1 will therefore save the most tax.

Test your understanding 5

Comfy Ltd

Taxable total profit computations

Year ended 31 December:	2018	2019	2020
	£	£	£
Tax adjusted trading profit	12,450	0	4,000
Property income	2,000	1,800	0
Interest income	1,000	600	1,000
Total profits	15,450	2,400	5,000
Less: Property business loss (W2)			(500)
Less: Loss relief			
– Current year (W1)		(2,400)	
– 12 month carry back	(12,100)		
	3,350	0	4,500
Less: QCD relief	(400)	Wasted	(400)
TTP	2,950	0	4,100

Workings

(W1) Trading loss

	£
Trading loss – y/e 31.12.19	14,500
Less: Used in current year – y/e 31.12.19	(2,400)
Used in 12 month carry back – 31.12.18	(12,100)
Carry forward at 31 December 2019	0

(W2) Property business loss

	£
Loss in y/e 31 December 2020	500
Less: Used in current year – y/e 31 December 2020	(500)
Carry forward at 31 December 2020	0

Test your understanding 6

Coriander Ltd

Taxable total profit computations

Year ended 31 December:	2020 £	2021 £	2022 £
Tax adjusted trading profit	37,450	0	20,000
Interest income	1,300	1,400	1,600
Chargeable gains (£13,000 – £6,000 b/f)	0	0	7,000
Total profits	38,750	1,400	28,600
Less: Loss relief			
– Current year		(1,400)	
– 12 month carry back	(38,750)		
	0	0	28,600
Less: Loss relief b/f			(25,600)
QCDs	Wasted	Wasted	(3,000)
TTP	0	0	0
QCDs = unrelieved	3,000	3,000	

Loss memorandum

	£
Loss in y/e 31 December 2021	81,550
Less: Used in current period	(1,400)
Less: Used in 12 month carry back	
– y/e 31 December 2020	(38,750)
Loss relief to carry forward	41,400
Less: Used in y/e 31 December 2022 (Note)	(25,600)
Carry forward at 31 December 2022	15,800

Note: The loss carry forward claim is restricted to preserve relief for the QCDs.

Test your understanding 7

Eagle Ltd

(a) **Tax adjusted trading loss for the y/e 31 December 2020**

	£
Trading loss before capital allowances	(263,112)
Capital allowances	
– Plant and machinery (W)	(56,888)
Tax adjusted trading loss	(320,000)

Working: Capital allowances computation

	Main pool	Allowances
	£	£
£		
TWDV b/f	64,700	
Additions:		
No AIA or FYA:		
Car	11,300	
With AIA:		
Lorry	32,400	
Equipment	13,040	
	45,440	
AIA	(45,440)	45,440
Disposal	(12,400)	
	63,600	
WDA (18%)	(11,448)	11,448
TWDV c/f	52,152	
Total allowances		56,888

(b) **Corporation tax computations**

Period ended:	30.6.19	31.12.19	31.12.20
	£	£	£
Tax adjusted trading profit	137,900	52,000	0
Property income (W1)	0	18,700	49,950
Chargeable gains (W3) (Note 1)	0	9,300	97,525
Total profits	137,900	80,000	147,475
Less: Property loss (W2) (Note 2)	(4,600)	0	0
	133,300	80,000	147,475
Less: Loss relief			
– Current year (W3)			(147,475)
– 12 month carry back (W4)	(66,650)	(80,000)	
	66,650	0	0
Less: QCD relief (Note 3)	(2,300)	Wasted	Wasted
TTP	64,350	0	0

Notes:

1 The chargeable gain for the year ended 31 December 2020 is given in the question and so no workings were required.

2 A property business loss is set off automatically against total profits of the same period and takes priority over relief for trading losses.

3 All charitable donations made by a company are tax deductible as Qualifying Charitable Donations (QCDs) from total profits, after loss relief.

Workings:

(W1) The property income for the y/e 31 December 2020:

	£
Premium received	50,000
Less: £50,000 × 2% × (8 – 1)	(7,000)
	———
(see alternative calculation)	43,000
Rent receivable	
– Warehouse 1 (£12,600 × 9/12)	9,450
– Warehouse 2 (£8,400 × 9/12)	6,300
– Irrecoverable debt (£8,400 × 3/12)	(2,100)
	———
	56,650
Repairs to roof	(6,700)
	———
Property income	49,950
	———

Alternative calculation of assessment on premium received

= P × (51 – n)/50 = £50,000 × (51 – 8)/50 = £43,000

(W2) **Property business loss**

The property business loss in the year ended 30 June 2019 is set off against total income of that period in priority to utilising the trading loss carried back.

(W3) **Loss relief**

	£
Loss in y/e 31.12.20	320,000
Less: Used in current year	(147,475)
Used in 12 month carry back – p/e 31.12.19	(80,000)
	———
	92,525
y/e 30.6.19 (restricted) Max (£133,300 × 6/12)	(66,650)
	———
Loss available to carry forward	25,875
	———

Note: The QCDs paid in the periods ending 31 December 2019 and 2020 are unrelieved.

(c) **Alternative ways to relieve loss**

The claim against current and prior year total profits need not be made. The total loss could be carried forward against future total profits.

The claim could be restricted to just a current year claim in the year ended 31 December 2020 and no carry back. The balance of the loss could be carried forward against future total profits.

Test your understanding 8

The correct answer is D.

The loss is set off against total profits in the current year and then total profits in the preceding 12 months.

A current year claim must be made before a carry back claim, as follows:

	£
Trading loss	(240,000)
Utilised: Current year offset	6,000
Carry back claim	104,000
	———
Available to carry forward	(130,000)
	———

Test your understanding 9

The correct answer is C.

C is the correct answer because a claim to carry back the loss must be made within two years of the end of the accounting period in which the loss arose.

Test your understanding 10

The correct answer is A.

Offset against current period and preceding 12 months provides the earliest relief.

The company must set the loss against total profits (which includes chargeable gains but is before deducting qualifying charitable donations) arising in the current year first, and then carry back the remaining loss to the previous 12 months.

Any unrelieved qualifying charitable donations are lost.

The remaining loss can be carried forward and is:

(£60,000 – £3,000 – £25,000 – £6,000) = £26,000

Test your understanding 11

The correct answer is A.

A property business loss carried forward is offset against total profits if a claim is made to relieve the loss in a future period.

Groups of companies

Chapter learning objectives

Upon completion of this chapter you will be able to:

- define a 75% group, and recognise the reliefs that are available to members of such a group

- define a 75% chargeable gains group, and recognise the reliefs that are available to members of such a group.

PER

One of the PER performance objectives (PO15) is to prepare computations of taxable amounts and tax liabilities according to legal requirements. Another objective (PO17) is to advise on mitigating and deferring liabilities through legitimate tax planning measures. Working through this chapter should help you understand how to demonstrate those objectives.

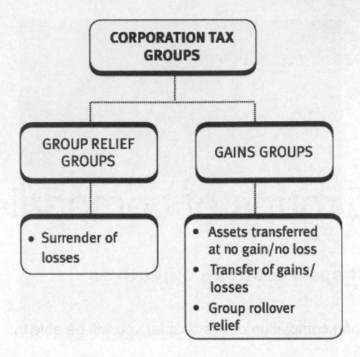

 The application of tax rules surrounding a loss group and a gains group is introduced in TX and will be explored in greater depth in ATX.

Introduction

This chapter deals with the tax position of groups of companies (i.e. where a company controls another company).

For corporation tax purposes, each company within the group is treated as a separate entity and is required to submit its own tax return, based on its individual results.

Being a member of a group however, has certain corporation tax implications.

This chapter sets out the corporation tax implications of:

- groups for group relief purposes

- capital gains groups.

1 Group relief group

Group loss relief is available to members of a 75% group relief group.

Losses of one member of the group can be surrendered to other group companies, to utilise against their own taxable total profits.

 Definition of a 75% group relief group

- Two companies are members of a 75% group relief group where:

  - one company is the 75% subsidiary of the other, or

  - both companies are 75% subsidiaries of a third company.

- A company (the parent company) has a 75% subsidiary if:

  - it owns, directly or indirectly, at least 75% of its ordinary share capital, and

  - it has the right to 75% or more of its distributable profits, and

  - it has the right to 75% or more of its net assets on a winding up.

- For sub-subsidiaries to be in a group, the parent company must have an effective interest in the sub-subsidiary of at least 75%.

- Groups can be created through companies resident overseas.

- However, for the purposes of the TX examination, the companies actually claiming/surrendering group relief must be resident in the UK.

Illustration 1 – 75% group relief group

The following information relates to the Holding Ltd group:

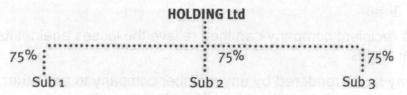

State which companies form a group for group relief purposes.

Solution

Holding Ltd (the parent company) has a 75% direct holding in Sub 1, Sub 2 and Sub 3 and therefore, all four companies are part of a 75% group for group relief purposes.

Illustration 2 – 75% group relief group

Beef Ltd owns 75% of Lamb Ltd. Lamb Ltd owns 75% of Bacon Ltd.

State which companies form a group for group relief purposes.

Solution

Beef Ltd and Lamb Ltd form a group as Beef Ltd directly owns 75% of Lamb Ltd.

Bacon Ltd does not belong to the same group relief group as Beef Ltd, as Beef Ltd only indirectly owns (75% × 75%) = 56.25%.

However, as Lamb Ltd directly owns 75% of Bacon Ltd, they form a separate group relief group.

Therefore, there are two group relief groups:

- Beef Ltd and Lamb Ltd.

- Lamb Ltd and Bacon Ltd.

Test your understanding 1

Toast Ltd owns:

- 75% of Honey Ltd.
- 100% of Marmalade Ltd.
- 65% of Jam Ltd.

Honey Ltd owns 75% of Butter Ltd.

Marmalade Ltd owns 75% of Crumpet Ltd.

State which companies form a group for group relief purposes.

Implications of being in a group relief group

Where a group of companies form a group relief group:

- Losses of one group company may be surrendered to other companies in the group.

- The recipient company can then relieve the losses against its own taxable total profits.

A loss may be surrendered by any member company to any other member of the same group, provided they are UK resident.

Illustration 3 – 75% group relief group

Birmingham Ltd and Sheffield Ltd are both UK resident companies.

State which companies form a group for group relief purposes and between which companies losses can be transferred.

Solution

Birmingham Ltd and Sheffield Ltd are in a 75% group relief group, as both companies are 75% subsidiaries of Holland Ltd. Remember, that non-UK resident companies can be used to establish a group relief group.

Birmingham Ltd and Sheffield Ltd can therefore transfer losses between each other (i.e. Birmingham Ltd to Sheffield Ltd or vice versa).

Losses cannot be transferred to or from Holland Ltd, as the company is resident outside of the UK.

Test your understanding 2

GROUP 1	GROUP 2
HOLDING Ltd	HOLDING Ltd
90% ⦙	80% ⦙
Sub 1 Ltd	Sub 1 Ltd
90% ⦙	80% ⦙
Sub 2 Ltd	Sub 2 Ltd

From the above structures, identify which companies form a group for group relief purposes and between which companies losses can be transferred, assuming they are all UK resident.

Mechanics of group relief

- Companies which form part of the same group relief group can transfer losses between each other.

- The surrendering company is the company that surrenders its loss.

- The claimant company is the company to which the loss is surrendered.

- The losses which may be surrendered are:

  - **trading losses**

    - current period

    - brought forward trading losses to the extent that they cannot be used against the surrendering company's own total profits

  - **unrelieved** QCDs

  - **unrelieved** property business losses

    - current period and brought forward losses.

- QCDs and property losses are only 'unrelieved' if they exceed any other income and gains **before** the deduction of any losses (current year, brought forward or carried back).

- Unrelieved QCDs are treated as surrendered before unrelieved property business losses.

- Capital losses cannot be surrendered to group companies under these rules (i.e. cannot be 'group relieved'). See section 2 for the transfer of capital losses.

The percentage holding in a company is only relevant for determining whether companies are in a group relief group. It is not relevant in determining the amount of group relief available. Thus, a 75% subsidiary company can surrender 100% of its available losses to another member of the group.

The surrendering company

- The surrendering company may surrender **any amount** of its **current** period trading losses, unrelieved QCDs and unrelieved property business losses.

- **Brought forward** trading and property losses can be surrendered to the extent that the surrendering company is unable to use the loss.

- There is no requirement for the surrendering company to actually claim to relieve a trading loss against its own profits first.

Illustration 4 – 75% group relief group

Mountain Ltd owns 100% of the share capital of a number of profitable UK resident companies. All companies prepare accounts to 31 March.

Mountain Ltd's results for the year ended 31 March 2021 are as follows:

	£
Trading loss	(130,000)
Interest income	2,300
Property business loss	(15,000)
Qualifying charitable donations	(4,000)
Capital loss	(12,000)

In addition Mountain Ltd has unrelieved trading losses brought forward at 1 April 2020 of £50,000.

What is the maximum amount of loss that Mountain Ltd can surrender to its 100% subsidiaries, using group relief, for the year to 31 March 2021?

Solution

The maximum amount of loss that Mountain Ltd can surrender using group relief is calculated as follows:

	£	£
Trading loss – current period		(130,000)
Excess property business loss and QCDs and trading loss b/f:		
Trading loss b/f	(50,000)	
Property business loss	(15,000)	
Qualifying charitable donations	(4,000)	
Less: Interest income	2,300	
		(66,700)
Maximum group relief		(196,700)

- Current year losses can be surrendered in full.

- Only excess property business losses, QCDs and trading losses b/f can be surrendered. So these losses are reduced by the amount of other income, in this case interest income.

- Capital losses cannot be surrendered under the group relief provisions.

The claimant company

- Offsets the group relieved losses against taxable total profits of its corresponding accounting period.

- The surrendering company may surrender any amount of its eligible losses. However, the maximum group loss relief that can be accepted by the claimant company is:

	£
Total profits	X
Less: Losses brought forward (full amount)	(X)
Less: Current year losses	(X)
Less: QCD relief	(X)
Maximum group loss relief that can be accepted	X

- Note that the maximum group loss relief that can be accepted by the claimant company is its taxable total profits, assuming that losses brought forward and current year losses are offset first and for the maximum amount.

  This is regardless of the fact that the company may not actually make a claim to offset current year trading losses and the amount of a claim to offset brought forward trading losses and property business losses may be made for a specified amount.

- Group relief is deducted from TTP (i.e. **after** QCDs) in the claimant company's corporation tax computation.

Claim for group relief

The claim for group relief:

- is made by the claimant company on its corporation tax return

- within two years of the end of its AP

- but requires a notice of consent from the surrendering company.

Test your understanding 3

Red Ltd has trading losses for the year to 31 December 2020, of £65,000. It has brought forward trading losses of £12,000. Red Ltd has no other income or gains in the current or prior year.

Red Ltd owns 85% of Pink Ltd.

Pink Ltd has tax adjusted trading profits of £85,000, for the year to 31 December 2020. It has brought forward trading losses of £35,000 and brought forward capital losses of £5,000.

Show the maximum amount of group relief available in the year to 31 December 2020 and state the amount of any unrelieved losses.

Corresponding accounting periods

Losses surrendered by group relief, must be set against the claimant company's profits of a 'corresponding' accounting period as follows:

- A corresponding accounting period is any accounting period falling wholly or partly within the surrendering company's accounting period.

- Where the companies do not have coterminous (same) year ends, the available profits and losses must be time apportioned, to find the relevant amounts falling within the corresponding accounting period.

- In this situation, the maximum 'loss' that can be surrendered = lower of:

		£
(a)	'loss' in the surrendering (loss making) company for the corresponding accounting period, and	X
(b)	'taxable total profits' in the claimant company for the corresponding accounting period	X

Illustration 5 – 75% group relief group

Cup Ltd is a wholly owned subsidiary of Sugar Ltd.

Sugar Ltd incurs a trading loss of £27,000, in its nine month accounting period to 31 March 2021.

The taxable total profits of Cup Ltd are £24,000 and £38,000 for the 12 month accounting periods to 30 September 2020 and 2021 respectively.

State the maximum amount of group relief which Cup Ltd can claim from Sugar Ltd, in each of the two accounting periods to 30 September 2021.

Solution

As the companies have non-coterminous year ends, firstly identify the corresponding accounting periods:

- 9 m/e 31.3.21 and y/e 30.9.20:

  The corresponding accounting period is 1 July 2020 to 30 September 2020 (i.e. three months).

- 9 m/e 31.3.21 and y/e 30.9.21:

  The corresponding accounting period is 1 October 2020 to 31 March 2021 (i.e. six months).

Cup Ltd can therefore claim the following group relief:

AP to 30.9.20

Sugar Ltd	can surrender	3/9 × £27,000 loss	£9,000
Cup Ltd	can claim	3/12 × £24,000	£6,000

Therefore maximum loss claim is £6,000.

AP to 30.9.21

Sugar Ltd	can surrender	6/9 × £27,000 loss	£18,000
Cup Ltd	can claim	6/12 × £38,000	£19,000

Therefore maximum loss claim is £18,000.

Note that after these current year group relief claims, Sugar Ltd would have £3,000 (£27,000 – £6,000 – £18,000) of loss carried forward as at 1 April 2021.

It may be possible to claim group relief for this loss carried forward against Cup Ltd's taxable total profits for the period 1 April 2021 to 30 September 2021, if any loss remains after offsetting against Sugar Ltd's profits for the following period.

Test your understanding 4

White Ltd and Black Ltd are in a group relief group and had the following recent results:

	£
White Ltd – trading loss for the y/e 30 June 2021	(24,000)
Black Ltd – taxable total profits:	
Y/e 30 September 2020	36,000
Y/e 30 September 2021	20,000

Explain the amount of group relief Black Ltd can claim from White Ltd, for each of the two accounting periods ended September 2021.

Companies joining/leaving the 75% group

If a company joins or leaves a group, group relief is only available for the 'corresponding accounting period' (i.e. when both companies have been a member of the same group).

The profits and losses are therefore time apportioned (as above) to calculate the maximum group relief available.

However, an alternative method of allocating the loss can be used, with the agreement of HMRC, where it would be unjust or unreasonable to use time apportionment.

You should always use time apportionment in the examination.

Payment for group relief

If the claimant company pays the surrendering company for the group relief, the payment is ignored for corporation tax purposes:

- it is not tax allowable in the claimant company's computation, and
- it is not taxable income in the surrendering company's computation.

Tax loss planning

The following points should be considered, when deciding how to offset a trading loss which arises within a 75% group relief group company:

- Whether the loss should be surrendered.
- Order of surrender.

Choosing whether to surrender

A group member with a loss has the choice of:

- making a claim against its own profits, and/or
- surrendering some/all of the loss to another group member.

Remember that:

- Unlike utilising current year losses against a company's own profits (which is **'all or nothing'**), group relief is very flexible.
- It is possible to specify the amount of loss to be surrendered within a group – which can be **any amount up to the maximum amount**.
- The surrendering company may surrender **some** of its losses using group relief and utilise the rest against its own profits.
- If it has paid QCDs, it should ensure that losses retained will reduce total profits before deduction of QCDs to the amount of any QCDs paid. This will allow the QCDs to be deducted in full without any corporation tax becoming due.

- If the surrendering company was profitable in the previous period, it may be beneficial to retain enough losses to make a carry back claim. The carry back claim will generate a refund of corporation tax already paid. However, in order to make a prior year claim, an 'all or nothing' current year claim must first be made, which may waste QCDs in the current year.

- As a current year claim against the company's own profits is 'all or nothing' it is important that the optimum group relief surrender is made first, leaving the desired amount of loss available against the company's own profits.

Illustration 6 – 75% group relief group

A Ltd has two wholly owned subsidiaries, B Ltd and C Ltd.

The group companies have the following results for the year ended 31 March 2021.

	A Ltd £	B Ltd £	C Ltd £
Trading profit/loss	(100,000)	20,000	83,000
Interest income	10,000	2,000	5,000
Qualifying charitable donations	0	(22,000)	(3,000)

A Ltd is not expected to return its trading operations to profitability until the year ended 31 March 2024. A Ltd does not expect significant gains or other income in the near future. A Ltd's total profits for the year ended 31 March 2020 were £20,000 before deduction of a QCD of £5,000.

Calculate the corporation tax payable by each of these companies for the year ended 31 March 2021:

(a) **if no elections are made to utilise A Ltd's loss**

(b) **if elections are made to utilise A Ltd's loss in the most beneficial manner.**

Solution

(a) **if no elections made to utilise A Ltd's loss**

	A Ltd £	B Ltd £	C Ltd £
Trading profit	0	20,000	83,000
Interest income	10,000	2,000	5,000
Total profits	10,000	22,000	88,000
Less: QCDs	0	(22,000)	(3,000)
TTP	10,000	0	85,000
Corporation tax liability (£10,000/£85,000 × 19%)	1,900	0	16,150

(b) **if elections are made to utilise A Ltd's loss in the most beneficial manner**

In order to utilise its loss, A Ltd has the following options:

- A current year claim against total profits followed by a carry back claim in A Ltd
- Carry the loss forward against total profits
- Group relief (current year or carry forward) to B Ltd or C Ltd.

The most beneficial use of the loss would be for A Ltd to make a current year claim against total profits followed by a prior year claim against total profits. This would save tax at 19% and would also generate a refund of tax paid in respect of the prior year, which would be advantageous for cash flow purposes.

However, if these 'all or nothing' claims are made first, the profits in the prior year (year ended 31 March 2020) will be reduced to nil, resulting in the QCD made that year being wasted. Therefore current year group relief claims should be made first, leaving sufficient loss to offset the current year and prior year profits of A Ltd without losing the benefit of QCD relief.

Carrying the loss forward would be less beneficial than the other options as profits are not expected until the year ended 31 March 2024 and no significant gains or other income is anticipated. Although this would save corporation tax in the future, it is not beneficial for cash flow, and it is not certain that profits will arise in A Ltd as soon as expected.

Year ended 31 March 2021:

	A Ltd £	B Ltd £	C Ltd £
Trading profit/loss	0	20,000	83,000
Interest income	10,000	2,000	5,000
	10,000	22,000	88,000
Less: Current year loss relief	(10,000)	0	0
Total profits	0	22,000	88,000
Less: QCDs	0	(22,000)	(3,000)
TTP before group relief	0	0	85,000
Less: Group relief (working)		0	(75,000)
TTP after group relief	0	0	10,000
Corporation tax liability (£10,000 × 19%)	0	0	1,900

Year ended 31 March 2020:

	A Ltd £
Total profits	20,000
Less: Prior year loss relief	(15,000)
Total profits after loss relief	5,000
Less: QCDs	(5,000)
TTP	0
Corporation tax liability	0

Note: By offsetting £15,000 of loss against total profits in year ended 31 March 2020 a refund of £2,850 (£15,000 × 19%) is generated.

Loss memorandum

	£
Loss in A Ltd year ended 31 March 2021	100,000
Less: Group relief to C Ltd	(75,000)
Less: Used in current period by A Ltd	(10,000)
Less: Used in 12 month carry back	
– y/e 31 March 2020	(15,000)
Carry forward at 31 March 2021	0

Working: maximum group relief to yield optimum current and prior year claims in A Ltd.

	£
Loss available in A Ltd year ended 31 March 2021	100,000
Loss needed to reduce A Ltd current year profits to nil	(10,000)
Loss needed to reduce A Ltd prior year profits to amount of QCD relief available (£20,000 – £5,000)	(15,000)
Loss available for group relief	75,000

Note: Group relief should be allocated to C Ltd. The total profit in B Ltd is reduced to nil by qualifying charitable donations and therefore no corporation tax will be saved if losses are surrendered to B Ltd.

The group relief claim saves corporation tax for the group of £14,250 (£75,000 × 19%).

Test your understanding 5

A Ltd is the parent company of a group of four companies. The relationships between the companies in the group, are shown in the diagram below:

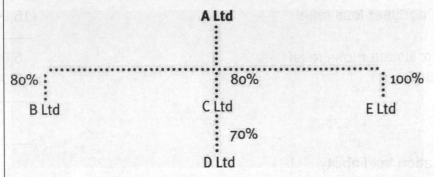

All of the companies are UK resident except for E Ltd, which is resident overseas and all its trading activities are conducted outside the UK.

All of the companies have an accounting year ended 31 March 2021 and their income/(losses) for this year, were as follows:

	Tax adjusted trading profit/(loss)	Interest income	Qualifying charitable donations
	£	£	£
A Ltd	100,000	–	–
B Ltd	50,000	15,000	(20,000)
C Ltd	(110,000)	12,000	–
D Ltd	(25,000)	–	–
E Ltd	15,000	–	(5,000)

C Ltd total profits for the year ended 31 March 2020 were £20,000. C Ltd is not expected to return to profitability for at least 5 years and interest income is expected to remain at a low level.

The directors of C Ltd are concerned about cash flow and would like to use the losses to generate a refund of corporation tax.

On the assumption that the most beneficial use is made by the group of any trading losses, compute the corporation tax payable by each UK resident company in respect of the above results.

2 75% capital gains group

Special capital gains advantages are available to members of a capital gains group. They enable:

- assets to be transferred tax efficiently around the group

- the efficient use of capital losses within the group

- the advantages of rollover relief (see below) to be maximised.

Definition of a 75% capital gains group

- • A capital gains group comprises the parent company and its 75% subsidiaries and also, the 75% subsidiaries of the first subsidiaries and so on.

- • The parent company must have an effective interest of over 50%, in ALL companies.

- • A company which is a 75% subsidiary, cannot itself be a 'parent company' and form a separate gains group.

- • While applying the 75% test, the shares held by overseas companies can be taken into account. Non-UK resident companies, however, cannot take advantage of the special reliefs available to UK resident members.

- • The 75% requirement only applies to the ownership of the ordinary share capital.

It is important to note that the definition of a gains group is different from that for a group relief group. It is essential to learn the different definitions.

Test your understanding 6

The A Ltd group consists of the following companies:

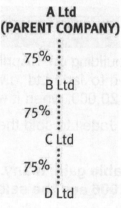

A Ltd
(PARENT COMPANY)
75%
B Ltd
75%
C Ltd
75%
D Ltd

(a) **State which companies form a capital gains group.**

(b) **State which companies form a group relief group.**

Implications of being in a 75% capital gains group

The reliefs that are available to members of a 75% capital gains group are:

1 Assets are transferred at no gain/no loss.

2 Chargeable gains and allowable capital losses can be transferred around the group.

3 Rollover relief is available on a group basis.

Transfer of assets within a group

- The detailed rules on chargeable gains for companies are covered in Chapter 23. However, broadly a chargeable gain for a company is calculated as:

  – proceeds less original cost less indexation allowance to the date of disposal or December 2017 if earlier.

  Indexation allowance is calculated by applying the relevant indexation factor to the original cost. You might like to revisit this section once you have studied Chapter 23.

- Assets transferred within a gains group are automatically transferred at no gain/no loss (i.e. without a chargeable gain or allowable loss arising).

- The transfer is deemed to take place at a price that does not give rise to a gain or a loss (i.e. original cost plus indexation allowance to the date of the transfer or December 2017 if earlier).

- The transferor's deemed proceeds figure is also the deemed cost of the acquiring company.

- No claim is made – the treatment is automatic and mandatory.

- When the acquiring company sells the asset outside of the gains group, a chargeable gain/allowable loss arises on the disposal in the normal way.

Illustration 7 – Inter group transfer then sale outside group

Green Ltd acquired a building on 1 April 1996, for £100,000. The building was transferred to Jade Ltd, a wholly owned subsidiary, on 1 October 2006, for £120,000, when it was worth £180,000.

On 1 December 2020, Jade Ltd sold the building outside of the group for £350,000.

Calculate the chargeable gain, if any, arising on the transfer of the building in October 2006 and the sale of the building in December 2020.

Assume the indexation factors are as follows:

April 1996 to October 2006	0.313
April 1996 to December 2017	0.822
October 2006 to December 2017	0.388
April 1996 to December 2020	0.962
October 2006 to December 2020	0.494

Solution

Transfer of building – October 2006

The transfer from Green Ltd to Jade Ltd, takes place at such a price that gives Green Ltd, no gain and no loss as follows:

	£
Cost	100,000
Plus: IA (April 1996 to October 2006)	
0.313 × £100,000	31,300
	────
Deemed proceeds	131,300
	────

Sale of building – December 2020

When Jade Ltd sells the building outside the group, its cost is deemed to be £131,300:

	£
Sale proceeds	350,000
Less: Deemed cost	(131,300)
	────
Unindexed gain	218,700
Less: IA (Oct 2006 to Dec 2017) (IA frozen at Dec 2017)	
0.388 × £131,300	(50,944)
	────
Chargeable gain	167,756
	────

The gain is chargeable on Jade Ltd, the company selling the building.

Illustration 8 – Inter group transfer and sale outside group

Orange Ltd acquired a factory on 1 June 1998, for £80,000. The factory was transferred to Amber Ltd, a wholly owned subsidiary, on 1 September 2010, for £115,000, when it was worth £160,000.

On 21 November 2020, Amber Ltd sold the factory outside the group for £385,000.

Calculate the chargeable gain, if any, arising in September 2010 and November 2020.

Assume the following indexation factors:

June 1998 to September 2010	0.379
September 2010 to December 2017	0.234
June 1998 to December 2017	0.702
June 1998 to November 2020	0.827
September 2010 to November 2020	0.325

> **Solution**
>
> **Transfer of factory – September 2010**
>
> The transfer from Orange Ltd to Amber Ltd, takes place at such a price as gives Orange Ltd no gain and no loss as follows:
>
> | | £ |
> |---|---:|
> | Cost | 80,000 |
> | Plus: IA (June 1998 to September 2010) | |
> | 0.379 × £80,000 | 30,320 |
> | | ——— |
> | Deemed proceeds | 110,320 |
> | | ——— |
>
> **Sale of factory – November 2020**
>
> When Amber Ltd sells the factory outside the group, its cost is deemed to be £110,320:
>
> | | £ |
> |---|---:|
> | Sale proceeds | 385,000 |
> | Less: Deemed cost | (110,320) |
> | | ——— |
> | Unindexed gain | 274,680 |
> | Less: IA (Sept 2010 to Dec 2017) (Note) | |
> | 0.234 × £110,320 | (25,815) |
> | | ——— |
> | Chargeable gain | 248,865 |
> | | ——— |
>
> The gain is chargeable in Amber Ltd, the company selling the factory.
>
> **Note:** Indexation allowance is frozen at December 2017.

Transfer of chargeable gains and allowable losses

As shown above, assets can be transferred around a capital gains group with no tax cost (i.e. assets are transferred at no gain/no loss).

A company will typically transfer an asset in this way if the other group company wants to use the asset in its business.

Transferring an asset to another group company with a capital loss, immediately before the asset is sold outside of the group at a gain, would also enable the offset of group capital losses and gains to be maximised.

However, it is also possible to elect to transfer current period chargeable gains/allowable losses within a group without physically transferring the asset.

Election to transfer chargeable gains and allowable losses

 Members of capital gains groups can make a **joint election** to transfer chargeable gains or allowable losses to any other company in the group.

As a result, a group can plan to maximise the use of its capital losses as early as possible by matching chargeable gains with capital losses without having to make an actual transfer of an asset.

The joint election:

- is available provided both companies are members of the gains group at the time the gain or loss arose

- must be made within 2 years of the end of the accounting period, in which the gain or loss arose

- must specify in which company in the group the gain or loss is to be treated for tax purposes, as arising.

 Remember, that only **current year** chargeable gains or allowable losses can be transferred, not brought forward losses.

Benefits of the joint transfer election

- As no actual transfer of assets is taking place within the gains group, there will be savings in legal and administrative costs.

- The two year time limit for making the election, means that tax planning can be undertaken retrospectively.

- An election can specify the amount of gain or loss to be transferred (i.e. it does not need to be the whole chargeable gain/allowable loss arising on a disposal). This gives increased flexibility with tax planning.

> **Illustration 9 – 75% capital gains group**
>
> Red Ltd has brought forward capital losses of £60,000.
>
> Its 100% subsidiary Blue Ltd, disposed of an asset on 15 June 2020, that resulted in a chargeable gain of £55,000.
>
> Both companies prepare accounts to 31 March.
>
> **Explain how Red Ltd and Blue Ltd can make an election to minimise the tax payable for the year ended 31 March 2021.**

Solution

The two companies can make a joint election to transfer Blue Ltd's gain to Red Ltd.

The election must be made by 31 March 2023 (i.e. two years after the year ended 31 March 2021). There is no need for the asset to actually be transferred from Blue Ltd to Red Ltd before the disposal.

Red Ltd can then set off its capital losses brought forward against the chargeable gain arising on the disposal outside of the group.

Note that Red Ltd cannot transfer its capital losses to Blue Ltd as capital losses brought forward cannot be transferred around the group.

Test your understanding 7

In the accounting period to 31 March 2021, Alpha Ltd disposed of a chargeable asset which resulted in a chargeable gain of £90,000.

Alpha Ltd has a 80% subsidiary, Beta Ltd.

In the accounting period to 31 March 2021, Beta Ltd disposed of a chargeable asset, which resulted in a capital loss of £65,000.

Alpha Ltd and Beta Ltd are both UK resident companies.

Show how the tax liabilities of the Alpha Ltd group may be minimised.

Explain whether your advice would change if Beta Ltd also had £20,000 capital losses brought forward.

Group rollover relief

Rollover relief (ROR) is covered in detail in Chapters 22 and 23.

- Companies within a 75% gains group, are treated as if they form a single trade, for the purposes of ROR.

- ROR can therefore be claimed, where:

  – one company within a gains group, disposes of an eligible asset and makes a chargeable gain, and

  – another company within the same gains group, acquires a replacement eligible asset.

Illustration 10 – 75% capital gains group

Cheese Ltd sold a factory for £600,000, in the year ended 31 December 2020. The original cost of the factory was £200,000 and the relevant indexation allowance was £65,000.

Cheese Ltd owns 75% of Ham Ltd.

Ham Ltd bought a warehouse costing £750,000, in the year ended 31 December 2021.

(a) Calculate the chargeable gain arising on the sale of the factory assuming all available reliefs are taken.

(b) Calculate the base cost of the warehouse.

Solution

(a) **Gain on sale of factory for Cheese Ltd**

	£
Proceeds	600,000
Less: Cost	(200,000)
	———
Unindexed gain	400,000
Less: IA	(65,000)
	———
Indexed gain	335,000
Less: ROR	(335,000)
	———
Chargeable gain	0
	———

Note: Full ROR is available, as all proceeds were reinvested by a member of the gains group, within the required time limit.

(b) **Base cost of the warehouse for Ham Ltd**

	£
Original cost	750,000
Less: ROR	(335,000)
	———
Base cost	415,000
	———

3 Chapter summary

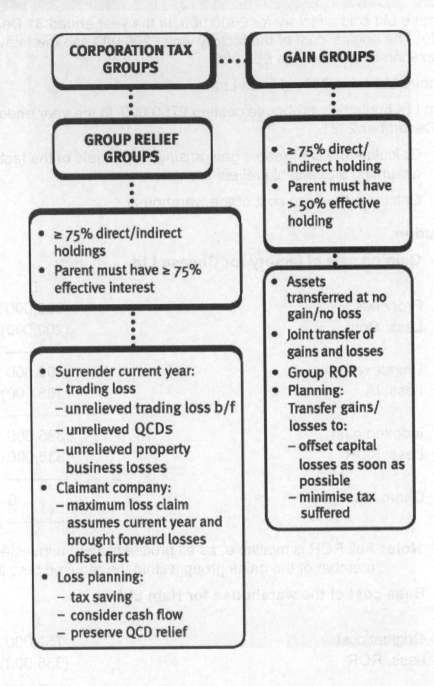

CORPORATION TAX GROUPS ···· **GAIN GROUPS**

GAIN GROUPS
- ≥ 75% direct/ indirect holding
- Parent must have > 50% effective holding

- Assets transferred at no gain/no loss
- Joint transfer of gains and losses
- Group ROR
- Planning: Transfer gains/ losses to:
  - offset capital losses as soon as possible
  - minimise tax suffered

GROUP RELIEF GROUPS

- ≥ 75% direct/indirect holdings
- Parent must have ≥ 75% effective interest

- Surrender current year:
  - trading loss
  - unrelieved trading loss b/f
  - unrelieved QCDs
  - unrelieved property business losses
- Claimant company:
  - maximum loss claim assumes current year and brought forward losses offset first
- Loss planning:
  - tax saving
  - consider cash flow
  - preserve QCD relief

KAPLAN PUBLISHING

4 Practice objective test questions

Test your understanding 8

Advanced Ltd has the following interests in its subsidiaries:

60% in Elementary Ltd

90% in Intermediate Ltd

Intermediate Ltd has a subsidiary, Standard Ltd, in which it owns 80% of the issued share capital.

All companies are profitable with the exception of Advanced Ltd, which made a trading loss.

To which company(ies) can Advanced Ltd surrender its loss?

A   Intermediate Ltd only

B   Intermediate Ltd and Standard Ltd only

C   Elementary Ltd and Intermediate Ltd only

D   Elementary Ltd, Intermediate Ltd and Standard Ltd

Test your understanding 9

Desire Ltd has the following losses for the year ended 31 October 2020:

Trading loss	£23,000
Capital loss	£11,000
Unrelieved qualifying charitable donations	£8,500

What is the maximum loss that can be surrendered for group relief?

A   £23,000

B   £31,500

C   £42,500

D   £34,000

Test your understanding 10

Broccoli Ltd has the following income/(losses) for the year ended 31 March 2021:

Trading loss	(£80,000)
Capital loss	(£20,000)
Property income	£15,000

Broccoli Ltd has a trading loss of £18,000 brought forward from the year ended 31 March 2020.

Cauliflower Ltd is in a 75% loss relief group with Broccoli Ltd. Cauliflower Ltd has TTP of £85,000 for the year ended 31 March 2021.

What is the maximum loss that can be surrendered to Cauliflower Ltd for group relief?

A   £98,000

B   £85,000

C   £118,000

D   £83,000

Test your understanding 11

Orchid Ltd owns 80% of Rose Ltd and 65% of Lily Ltd.

Orchid Ltd bought a building for £20,000 and sold it to Rose Ltd for £32,000 when its market value was £36,000.

Two years later, Rose Ltd sold the building to Lily Ltd when its market value was £40,000.

Ignoring indexation allowance, and assuming no elections are made, what chargeable gains would arise on each company?

A   Orchid Ltd gain =   £12,000   Rose Ltd gain =   £8,000
B   Orchid Ltd gain =   £0   Rose Ltd gain =   £0
C   Orchid Ltd gain =   £16,000   Rose Ltd gain =   £4,000
D   Orchid Ltd gain =   £0   Rose Ltd gain =   £20,000

Test your understanding answers

Test your understanding 1

Toast Ltd

Toast Ltd and all its direct 75% holdings:

- Honey Ltd.
- Marmalade Ltd.

Toast Ltd only owns 65% of Jam Ltd, therefore, Jam Ltd does not form part of the group relief group.

Also include any 75% indirect holdings of Toast Ltd:

- Crumpet Ltd
  Toast Ltd indirectly holds (100% × 75%) = 75% of Crumpet Ltd).

Note: Butter Ltd is not included, as Toast Ltd only indirectly holds (75% × 75% = 56.25%).

Honey Ltd owns 75% of Butter Ltd, so they will form a second group relief group.

Therefore, there are two group relief groups:

- Toast Ltd, Honey Ltd, Marmalade Ltd and Crumpet Ltd.
- Honey Ltd and Butter Ltd.

Test your understanding 2

Group 1	**Group 2**
Holding Ltd (H), Sub 1 (S1) and Sub 2 (S2) are within a 75% group relief group.	Holding Ltd (H) and Sub 1 are within a 75% group relief group; Sub 1 and Sub 2 are within another 75% group relief group.
The direct shareholding links between the group are all 75% and over.	Holding Ltd and Sub 2 are **not** within a 75% group relief group **because** H's effective holding in Sub 2, is only 64% (80% × 80%).
In addition, Holding Ltd has an indirect shareholding in Sub 2 Ltd, of over 75% (90% × 90% = 81%).	
Losses can be transferred from:	**Losses can be transferred between:**
H to S1 and S2	H to S1 or S1 to H
S2 to S1 and H	S1 to S2 or S2 to S1
S1 to H and S2.	**but** not from H to S2 or S2 to H.

Test your understanding 3

Red Ltd

Maximum group relief, the lower of:

• Loss of Red Ltd (£65,000 + £12,000) (Note)	£77,000
• Maximum claim by Pink Ltd (W)	£50,000

Therefore, Red Ltd can group relieve £50,000 of its trading losses, to Pink Ltd.

Note: The trading loss b/f cannot be utilised by Red Ltd therefore it is available to surrender.

Working: Maximum loss that can be accepted

	£
Tax adjusted trading profits	85,000
Less: Trading losses b/f	(35,000)
	——————
Maximum claim by Pink Ltd	50,000

Unrelieved losses

Red Ltd:

Assuming maximum group relief is claimed Red Ltd will have £27,000 of trading losses unrelieved. As the company has no other income or gains in the current or prior year the losses will be carried forward. They can be set against Red Ltd's total profits in future years, or possibly surrendered as group relief.

Pink Ltd:

Pink Ltd could fully utilise the brought forward trading losses of £35,000 to reduce its taxable total profits to £50,000. These profits could then be reduced to £nil by making the maximum group relief claim of £50,000, as set out above. This would leave no unrelieved losses to carry forward.

Alternatively, Pink Ltd could claim to offset only part of the losses brought forward in the year to 31 December 2020 and/or carry the balance of the unutilised losses forward. However, for cash flow reasons, given that the losses could be fully relieved in the year ended 31 December 2020 this is unlikely.

The company's brought forward capital losses, will be carried forward and used against the first chargeable gains of the company.

Test your understanding 4

White Ltd and Black Ltd

Firstly, identify the corresponding accounting period:

- Y/e 30.9.20 and y/e 30.6.21:

  The corresponding accounting period is 1 July 2020 to 30 September 2020 (i.e. three months).

- Y/e 30.9.21 and y/e 30.6.21

The corresponding accounting period is 1 October 2020 to 30 June 2021 (i.e. nine months).

Black Ltd can therefore claim the following group relief:

y/e 30 September 2020

			£
Black Ltd	can claim	(£36,000 × 3/12)	9,000
White Ltd	can surrender	(£24,000 × 3/12)	(6,000)

Black Ltd can claim group relief of £6,000 against its profits, for the y/e 30 September 2020.

y/e 30 September 2021

			£
Black Ltd	can claim	(£20,000 × 9/12)	15,000
White Ltd	can surrender	(£24,000 × 9/12)	(18,000)

Black Ltd can claim group relief of £15,000, against its profits for the y/e 30 September 2021.

Note that after these current year group relief claims, White Ltd would have £3,000 (£24,000 – £6,000 – £15,000) of loss carried forward as at 1 July 2021.

It may be possible to claim group relief for this loss carried forward against Black Ltd's taxable total profits for the period 1 July 2021 to 30 September 2021, if any loss remains after offsetting against White Ltd's profits for the year ended 30 June 2022.

Test your understanding 5

Group relief group

A Ltd, B Ltd and C Ltd form a group of companies for group relief purposes.

D Ltd is not a group member, as it is not a 75% subsidiary of A Ltd.

E Ltd is non-UK resident and therefore, cannot participate in a group relief claim.

In order to utilise its loss, C Ltd has the following options:

- A current year claim against total income followed by a carry back claim in C Ltd

- Carry the loss forward against total profits

- Group relief to A Ltd or B Ltd.

The most beneficial use of the loss would be for C Ltd to make a current year claim against total profits followed by a prior year claim against total profits. This would generate a refund of tax paid in respect of the prior year, which would be advantageous for cash flow purposes. The remaining loss can be offset via group relief to reduce corporation tax due in the current year.

Carrying the loss forward would be less beneficial than the other options as trading profits are not expected for at least 5 years and other income is expected to be low. Although this would save corporation tax in the future, it is not beneficial for cash flow, and it is not certain that profits will arise in C Ltd as soon as expected.

Corporation tax computations – y/e 31 March 2021

	A Ltd £	B Ltd £	C Ltd £	D Ltd £
Tax adjusted trading profit	100,000	50,000	0	0
Interest income	0	15,000	12,000	0
Total profits	100,000	65,000	12,000	0
Less: Loss relief (W1)				
– Current year claim			(12,000)	
Less: Qualifying charitable donations	0	(20,000)	0	0
TTP before group relief	100,000	45,000	0	0
Less: Group relief (W2)	(78,000)			
TTP after group relief	22,000	45,000	0	0
CT @ 19%	4,180	8,550	0	0

Note: The trading loss of D Ltd (£25,000) can only be carried forward in D Ltd for set off against future total profits as it is not a member of the group relief group.

Test your understanding 6

A Ltd group

Gains group

- A Ltd, B Ltd and C Ltd are in a gains group, as there is 75% ownership at each level and A Ltd (the parent) owns more than 50% (75% × 75% = 56.25%) in C Ltd.

- A Ltd does not own more than 50% of D Ltd (75% × 75% × 75% = 42.19%) and therefore D Ltd does not form part of the gains group.

- C Ltd and D Ltd, cannot form a separate gains group, as C Ltd is part of the A Ltd gains group and cannot therefore, be a 'parent' company and form a separate gains group.

Group relief group

There are three group relief groups:

- A Ltd and B Ltd.

- B Ltd and C Ltd.

- C Ltd and D Ltd.

Remember that for a group relief group the parent company (A Ltd) must have an effective interest in all companies of at least 75%.

Test your understanding 7

Alpha Ltd

As the two companies satisfy the criteria of a gains group, they can make a joint election to either:

- transfer Beta Ltd's allowable capital loss of £65,000 to Alpha Ltd, or

- transfer Alpha Ltd's chargeable gain of £90,000 to Beta Ltd.

In both instances, the capital loss will be set off against the chargeable gain, resulting in a net chargeable gain of £25,000, chargeable to corporation tax.

In the first example the net chargeable gain of £25,000 would be taxed in Alpha Ltd and in the second example it would be taxed in Beta Ltd.

The time limit for making the election is 31 March 2023 (i.e. within two years from 31 March 2021).

If Beta Ltd also had £20,000 capital losses brought forward

- The advice concerning the transfer of the chargeable gain or allowable loss above is still valid.

- However, as the brought forward capital loss cannot be transferred, it would be preferable to ensure that at least net gains of £20,000 out of the £25,000 arise in Beta Ltd so that the capital losses brought forward can be utilised.

Test your understanding 8

The correct answer is A.

Losses can be surrendered between:

- Advanced Ltd and Intermediate Ltd

  (as Advanced Ltd has a 90% (≥ 75%) direct interest)

Losses cannot be surrendered between:

- Advanced Ltd and Standard Ltd

  (as Advanced Ltd has a 72% (< 75%) indirect interest)

- Advanced Ltd and Elementary Ltd

  (as Advanced Ltd has a 60% (< 75%) direct interest)

Test your understanding 9

The correct answer is B.

Capital losses cannot be group relieved.

Unrelieved qualifying charitable donations can be group relieved along with trading losses.

Note: A separate election can be made to transfer current year capital losses to another group company, but they cannot be group relieved.

Test your understanding 10

The correct answer is D.

Capital losses cannot be group relieved.

The current period trading loss can be surrendered in full.

Brought forward trading losses can only be surrendered to the extent that the surrendering company cannot use them. Broccoli could offset the brought forward loss against its property income of £15,000. Therefore, this is deducted to determine the loss available for group relief.

	£
Current year trading loss	80,000
Excess trading losses b/f (£18,000 – £15,000)	3,000
Loss available for group relief	83,000

Broccoli Ltd can surrender a maximum amount of £83,000 as this is lower than Cauliflower Ltd's TTP of £85,000.

Note: A separate election can be made to transfer current year capital losses to another group company, but they cannot be group relieved.

Test your understanding 11

The correct answer is D.

Sale from Orchid Ltd to Rose Ltd = within a 75% group, therefore a no gain/no loss transaction.

Ignoring indexation allowance, the asset is transferred to Rose Ltd at Cost = £20,000.

Sale from Rose Ltd to Lily Ltd = outside the 75% group, therefore a chargeable gain arises:

	£
Sale proceeds (Market value)	40,000
Less: Base cost of asset to Rose Ltd	(20,000)
Chargeable gain (ignoring IA)	20,000

The gain is taxed on Rose Ltd, the company selling the asset outside of the 75% group (unless a separate election is made to transfer the gain to another group company or group rollover relief can defer the gain).

Tax administration for a company

Chapter learning objectives

Upon completion of this chapter you will be able to:

- explain and apply the features of the self-assessment system as it applies to companies, including the use of iXBRL

- recognise the time limits that apply to the filing of returns and the making of claims

- explain how large companies are required to account for corporation tax on a quarterly basis and compute the quarterly instalment payments

- list the information and records that taxpayers need to retain for tax purposes

- explain the circumstances in which HM Revenue and Customs can make a compliance check into a self-assessment tax return

- explain the procedures for dealing with appeals and First and Upper Tier Tribunals

- calculate late payment interest and state the penalties that can be charged.

PER

One of the PER performance objectives (PO16) is to make sure that individuals and entities comply with their tax obligations – on time, and in the spirit and letter of the law. Working through this chapter should help you understand how to demonstrate that objective.

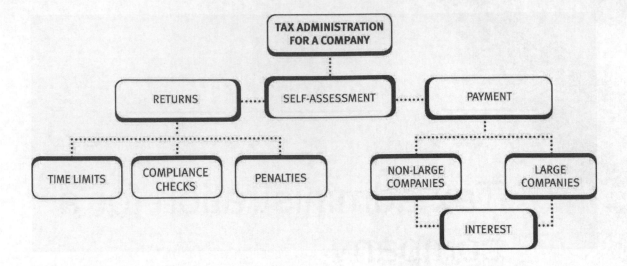

1 The self-assessment system for companies

As for individuals, self-assessment applies for corporate taxpayers. Responsibility rests with the company to:

- calculate its own corporation tax liability for each accounting period

- submit a self-assessment corporation tax return **within 12 months** after the end of the period of account

- pay any corporation tax due **within nine months and one day** after the end of the accounting period.

Given the timing of the due date for payment of tax, in practice, many companies will aim to complete the self-assessment tax return prior to the nine month deadline for paying the corporation tax.

Large companies have a different payment date (see later).

The self-assessment tax return

The self-assessment tax return must be submitted by the later of:

- **12 months** after the end of the period of account, and

- **three months** after the issue of the notice to file a return.

The return must:

- contain all information required to calculate the company's taxable total profits

- include a self-assessment of the amount of corporation tax payable for that accounting period

- be submitted online.

A company has to submit a copy of its financial accounts together with the self-assessment tax return.

All companies must file self-assessment returns and copies of accounts electronically using 'Inline eXtensible Business Reporting Language' (iXBRL). iXBRL is the global standard for exchanging business information in an electronic format and tags the accounts so they can be read by a computer.

HMRC provide free online filing software applications for companies with straightforward tax affairs that automatically produces and submits a self-assessment return with accounts and computations in the required iXBRL format, as well as calculating the tax liability.

For other companies, commercial software applications and services enable the submission of the tax return in one of three ways:

1   Integrated software applications – automatically inserts iXBRL tags to data and produces iXBRL accounts and/or computations.

2   Managed tagging services – provided by agents whereby the company outsources the process of iXBRL tagging to convert non-iXBRL accounts and computations into the required format.

3   Conversion software applications – allows the company to apply appropriate iXBRL tags to each item of data itself to convert the accounts and computation into the required format.

iXBRL

The items to be tagged are those which appear in 'taxonomies'. HMRC has published minimum tagging lists for UK GAAP, UK IFRS and corporation tax computation taxonomies.

Making claims

Any claims must be included in the self-assessment tax return.

A claim for a relief, allowance or repayment must be quantified at the time that the claim is made. For example, if loss relief is claimed, then the amount of the loss must be stated.

Notification of chargeability

A company coming within the scope of corporation tax for the first time must notify HMRC when its first accounting period begins, **within three months** of the start of its first accounting period.

Companies that do not receive a notice to file a tax return are required to notify HMRC if they have income or chargeable gains on which tax is due.

The time limit for notifying HMRC of chargeability is **12 months** from the end of the accounting period in which the liability arises.

A standard penalty may be imposed for failure to notify HMRC of chargeability (see section 6).

Penalties for failure to submit a return

HMRC can impose fixed penalties and tax geared penalties for the failure to submit a return, depending on the length of the delay in submitting the return.

See section 6 for details of the penalties that can be imposed.

Determination assessments

To prevent companies deliberately delaying the submission of the return HMRC may determine the amount of corporation tax due by issuing a determination assessment.

- The determination assessment is treated as a self-assessment by the company, and is replaced by the actual self-assessment when it is submitted by the company.

- There is no appeal against a determination assessment. Instead, the company must displace it with the actual self-assessment return.

- A determination assessment can be raised at any time **within three years** of the filing date (i.e. four years from the end of the period of account).

Records

Companies are required to keep and preserve records necessary to make a correct and complete return.

The records that must be kept include records of:

- all receipts and expenses

- all goods purchased and sold

- all supporting documents relating to the transactions of the business, such as accounts, books, contracts, vouchers and receipts.

The records must be retained until the later of:

- six years after the end of the accounting period

- the date on which a compliance check into the return is completed

- the date on which it becomes impossible for a compliance check to be started.

A penalty may be charged for failure to keep or retain adequate records.

The maximum penalty is only likely to be imposed in the most serious cases, such as where a company deliberately destroys its records in order to obstruct an HMRC compliance check.

See section 6 for the detail of penalties that can be imposed.

2 Tax returns – amendments and errors

Either the company or HMRC may make amendments to a return:

- HMRC may correct any obvious errors or mistakes **within nine months** of the date that the return is filed with them. For example, they will correct arithmetical errors or errors of principle. This type of correction does not mean that HMRC has accepted the return as accurate.

- A company can amend the return **within 12 months** of the filing date. For a AP ending on 31 March 2021, the filing date is 31 March 2022, and the company has until 31 March 2023 to make any amendments.

- If an error is discovered at a later date, then the company can make a claim for overpayment relief to recover any corporation tax overpaid.

Claims for overpayment relief

Where an assessment is excessive due to an error or mistake in a return, the company can claim relief. A claim can be made in respect of errors made, and mistakes arising from not understanding the law.

The claim must be made **within four years** of the end of the accounting period to which it relates.

3 Due dates for payment

The payment date for corporation tax depends on the size of the company:

- For companies which are not 'large'
    - the due date is **nine months and one day** after the end of the accounting period.

- For 'large' companies
    - the liability is settled by **quarterly instalment payments**.

All companies must pay their corporation tax electronically.

 Very large companies (i.e. those with augmented profits above £20 million) have different quarterly instalment payment dates from large companies. These payment dates are **not examinable**.

4 Quarterly instalment payments for large companies

Large companies do not have the benefit of paying corporation tax nine months after the end of the accounting period. Instead, large companies must pay their tax by instalments, starting during the accounting period.

Definition of a large company

The key points here are:

- For TX purposes a large company is one whose augmented profits for the accounting period in question are more than £1.5 million.

- The £1.5 million threshold is time apportioned for short accounting periods, and is divided by the total number of related 51% group companies (see below).

The threshold of £1.5 million is included within the tax rates and allowances provided to you in the examination.

Companies that become large during an accounting period do not have to make instalment payments provided:

- their augmented profits for the accounting period do not exceed £10 million, and

- they were not a large company for the previous accounting period.

Augmented profits

To determine if a company is large, its augmented profit are compared with the £1.5 million threshold. Augmented profits are calculated as follows:

	£
Taxable total profits (TTP)	X
Plus: Dividends received from non-group companies	X
Augmented profits	X

Dividends received

Although dividends received from UK companies are exempt from corporation tax, they can have an impact on whether a company is large and therefore whether corporation tax needs to be paid by instalments.

- Dividends received are added to TTP in order to arrive at the augmented profits figure.

- However, dividends from related 51% group companies are not included.

Corporation tax is always calculated on a company's TTP, not its augmented profits.

Test your understanding 1

Zachary Ltd has taxable total profits of £1.4 million in the year ended 31 March 2021. The company also received a dividend of £103,000 from another UK company in which it holds 5% of the shares. Zachary Ltd was a large company in the year ended 31 March 2020.

Calculate Zachary Ltd's augmented profits for the year ended 31 March 2021 and explain if the company will be required to pay corporation tax by instalments.

Groups of companies

The £1.5 million and £10 million thresholds are reduced if a company has any related 51% group companies.

However, instalments are never due if a company's corporation tax liability is below £10,000.

The thresholds are divided by the number of related 51% group companies. Two companies are related 51% group companies if:

- One is a 51% subsidiary of the another, or

- Both are 51% subsidiaries of a third company.

A 51% subsidiary is one where more than 50% of the ordinary share capital is directly or indirectly owned.

Dormant companies are excluded from being 51% group companies. Overseas companies are included if the 51% test is met.

The number of 51% companies in a group for an AP is determined at the end of the previous AP.

Therefore:

- Companies that join the 51% group during the accounting period are deemed to be part of the group from the beginning of the **following accounting period**.

- Companies that leave the 51% group during the accounting period are deemed to still be part of the group until the end of the **current accounting period**.

If two companies are over 50% owned by an individual they are not 51% group companies. Companies can only be linked through a corporate parent company.

Illustration 1 – 51% group companies

The Stationery group has the following structure:

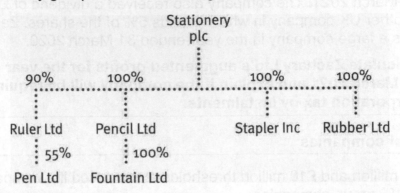

Rubber Ltd is dormant throughout the year ended 31 March 2021. Fountain Ltd was purchased on 1 January 2021. Stapler Inc is incorporated in the United States.

Explain which companies are related 51% group companies of Stationery plc and calculate the augmented profit threshold that will apply for the purposes of determining whether Stationery plc is required to pay corporation tax by instalments for the year ended 31 March 2021.

Solution

For the year ended 31 March 2021 Stationery plc has 3 related 51% group companies – Ruler, Pencil and Stapler.

The augmented profit threshold used to decide if Stationery plc is large is therefore divided by 4 (i.e. Stationery plc plus its 3 related 51% group companies). Therefore if Stationery plc's augmented profits exceed £375,000 (£1,500,000/4) it will be a large company for the purposes of paying its corporation tax liability for the year ended 31 March 2021.

Pen is not a 51% subsidiary of Stationery as Stationery only owns 49.5% (90% × 55%) of Pen. Pen is a 51% group company of Ruler.

Fountain is deemed not to be a 51% group member for the year ended 31 March 2021 as it was purchased during the year. It will be included from 1 April 2021.

Stapler is a 51% group company even though it is incorporated overseas.

Rubber is excluded from being a 51% group company as it is dormant throughout the accounting period.

Test your understanding 2

The Flower group has the following structure:

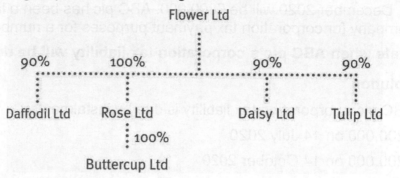

Daisy Ltd is incorporated outside of the UK. 90% of Tulip Ltd was purchased on 1 August 2019.

Daffodil Ltd is dormant throughout the year ended 31 March 2021.

State how many companies are in a 51% group with Flower Ltd in the year ended 31 March 2021, and calculate the augmented profit threshold for corporation tax payment purposes.

Instalment dates

Four quarterly instalments are due

- by the 14th day

- in months 7, 10, 13 and 16 following the **start** of the accounting period.

Note that the first two instalments are therefore paid **during** the AP.

Basis of payment

Instalments are based on the expected corporation tax liability for the **current** accounting period. It is, therefore, necessary for companies to produce an accurate forecast of their current period tax liability.

Interest will be charged or paid (see below) based on the **actual** corporation tax due per the final tax return.

Companies will normally be able to obtain a refund, if they subsequently find that instalments have been overpaid.

Illustration 2 – Quarterly instalment payments for large companies

ABC plc estimates that its corporation tax liability for the year ended 31 December 2020 will be £800,000. ABC plc has been a large company for corporation tax payment purposes for a number of years.

State when ABC plc's corporation tax liability will be due.

Solution

ABC plc's corporation tax liability is due by instalments:

£200,000 on 14 July 2020

£200,000 on 14 October 2020

£200,000 on 14 January 2021

£200,000 on 14 April 2021

Test your understanding 3

XYZ Ltd has an expected corporation tax liability of £2,000,000 for the year ended 31 March 2021. XYZ Ltd has been a large company for corporation tax purposes for a number of years.

State when XYZ Ltd's corporation tax liability for the year ended 31 March 2021 will be due.

Special rules apply where the accounting period is less than 12 months.

Short accounting periods

Where the accounting period is less than 12 months:

- First instalment due by:

  14th day of 7th month after the start of the AP (as normal)

- Subsequent instalments are due at 3 monthly intervals thereafter, until the date of the last instalment (see below) is reached.

- Last instalment due by:

  14th day of 4th month after the end of the accounting period.

- For an accounting period of 3 months or less applying the above instalment rules would result in the date of the first instalment being later than the last instalment. Therefore, in this situation the full tax due for the accounting period is due on the date of the last instalment, i.e. 14th day of 4th month after the end of the accounting period.

- The amount of each instalment:

  = (estimated CT liability for AP) × (n/length of AP)

  Where n = 3 months for a full quarterly instalment

  But n = 2 or 1 for the last instalment if the period since the previous instalment is less than 3 months.

Illustration 3 – Short accounting periods

Assume ABC plc in illustration 2 prepared accounts for the 8 months ended 31 December 2020 and that its corporation tax liability is £800,000.

Show when ABC plc's corporation tax liability will be due.

Solution

ABC plc's corporation tax liability will be due by instalments as follows:

Due date		Paying	Amount £
14.11.20	(14th day of 7th month after start of AP)	3/8 × £800,000	300,000
14.2.21	(three months later)	3/8 × £800,000	300,000
14.4.21	(14th day of 4th month after end of AP)	2/8 × £800,000	200,000
			———
		8 months	800,000
			———

5 Interest

There are two key types of interest:

- Late payment interest
  - calculated at 2.75% p.a.

- Repayment interest
  - calculated at 0.5% p.a.

 The interest rates will be provided in the tax rates and allowances section of the examination.

Late payment interest

Interest is automatically charged if corporation tax is paid late.

Interest runs:

- **from:** the normal due date
- **to:** the date of payment.

Interest paid to HMRC on corporation tax paid late is a deductible expense from interest income.

> ## Test your understanding 4
>
> Able Ltd prepares accounts to 31 March.
>
> The company has a corporation tax liability of £75,000, for the year ended 31 March 2021. Able Ltd paid £25,000 of its corporation tax liability on 1 January 2022, but did not pay the balance of £50,000 until 15 March 2022.
>
> **Explain the period that interest will run on the late payment of corporation tax. Assume Able Ltd is not a large company.**

Repayment interest

Interest is paid by HMRC on any overpayment of corporation tax.

Where interest is due, the interest runs:

- **from:** the later of:
  - the due date
  - the date of actual payment
- **to:** the date of repayment.

Interest paid by HMRC on overpayments of corporation tax is taxable interest income.

6 Penalties

In addition to interest on the late payment of tax, HMRC can impose penalties.

Standard penalty

HMRC has standardised penalties across taxes for the submission of incorrect returns and failure to notify liability to tax. The rules are explained in Chapter 13.

The penalty is calculated as a percentage of 'potential lost revenue' which is generally the tax unpaid. The percentage charged can be reduced where the taxpayer makes a disclosure and co-operates with HMRC to establish the amount of tax unpaid.

Other penalties

Offence	Penalty
Late filing of corporation tax return: • within 3 months of filing date • more than 3 months after filing date Additional penalties: • 6 – 12 months after filing date • More than 12 months after filing date	• Fixed penalty = £100 (Note) • Fixed penalty increased to £200 (Note) • Additional 10% of tax outstanding 6 months after filing date • Additional penalty increased to 20% **Note:** Fixed penalties rise to £500 and £1,000 if persistently filed late (i.e. return for 2 preceding periods also late)
Failure to keep and retain records	Up to £3,000 per accounting period

Illustration 4 – Self-assessment for companies

Late Ltd submitted its self-assessment return for the year ended 31 March 2021, on 30 November 2022. The corporation tax due of £50,000 was paid on the same day. Late Ltd has submitted its previous tax returns on time.

State the penalties that are due as a result of the late submission of the tax return.

Solution

The tax return should have been submitted by 31 March 2022, and so it is eight months late.

The fixed penalty is therefore £200, and the tax geared penalty is £5,000 (£50,000 at 10%).

Test your understanding 5

Everlate Ltd submitted its corporation tax return for the year ended 28 February 2021, on 30 September 2022. This is the fifth consecutive occasion the company has submitted its return late.

The corporation tax liability for the year was £100,000 which was paid when the return was submitted.

State the penalties that are due as a result of the late submission of the tax return.

7 Compliance checks into returns

HMRC have the right to enquire into the completeness and accuracy of any self-assessment tax return and issue discovery assessments under their compliance check powers. The procedures and rules are similar to those for individuals.

Compliance checks

The compliance check (enquiry) may be made as a result of any of the following:

- suspicion that income is undeclared
- suspicion that deductions are being incorrectly claimed
- other information in HMRC's possession
- being part of a random review process.

Additional points:

- HMRC do not have to state a reason for the compliance check and are unlikely to do so.
- HMRC must give **written notice** before commencing a compliance check by the following dates:

If return filed:	Notice must be issued within 12 months of:
On time	the actual delivery of the tax return to HMRC
Late	the 31 January, 30 April, 31 July or 31 October next following the actual date of delivery of the tax return to HMRC

- Once this deadline is passed, the company can normally consider the self-assessment for that accounting period as final.

Compliance check procedure

HMRC can demand that the company produce any or all of the following:

- documents
- accounts
- other written particulars
- full answers to specific questions.

The information requested should be limited to that connected with the return.

- The company has 30 days to comply with the request. An appeal can be made against the request.
- The compliance check ends when HMRC give written notice that it has been completed.
- The notice will state the outcome of the compliance check and HMRC's amendments to the self-assessment.
- Refer to Chapter 13 for details about appeal procedures.
- The company then has 30 days to appeal, in writing, against HMRC's amendment.

Discovery assessments

HMRC has the capacity to raise additional assessments, referred to as discovery assessments. The key points are:

- The use of a discovery assessment is restricted where a self-assessment return has already been made. However, although compliance checks must normally begin **within 12 months** of the actual submission date, a discovery assessment can be raised at a later date to prevent the loss of corporation tax.

- Unless the loss of corporation tax was brought about carelessly or deliberately by the company, a discovery assessment cannot be raised where full disclosure was made in the return, even if this is found to be incorrect.

- HMRC will only accept that full disclosure has been made if any contentious items have been clearly brought to their attention – perhaps in a covering letter.

- Only a company that makes full disclosure in the self-assessment tax return, therefore, has absolute finality 12 months after the actual submission date.

- The time limit for making a discovery assessment is:

	Time from the end of the AP
Basic time limit	four years
Careless error	six years
Deliberate error	twenty years

- A discovery assessment may be appealed against.

8 Chapter summary

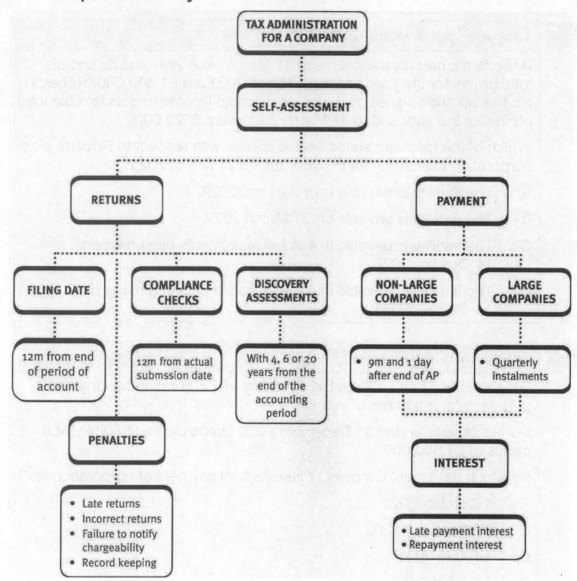

9   Practice objective test questions

Test your understanding 6

Roberts plc prepares accounts to 31 March each year and its taxable total profits for the year ended 31 March 2021 are £1,800,000. Roberts plc has no subsidiaries, receives no dividend income and its taxable total profits for the year ended 31 March 2020 were £920,000.

Which of the following statements is correct with respect to Roberts plc's corporation tax liability for the year ended 31 March 2021?

A   The liability is payable on 1 January 2022

B   The liability is payable on 31 March 2022

C   The liability is payable in 4 equal instalments beginning on 14 October 2020

D   The liability is payable in 4 equal instalments beginning on 14 October 2021

Test your understanding 7

Grape plc has been a large UK company for corporation tax payment purposes for a number of years.

During its year ended 31 December 2020 Grape plc had taxable total profits of £1,600,000.

By which date must Grape plc make its final payment of corporation tax?

A   1 October 2021

B   31 December 2021

C   14 April 2021

D   14 July 2021

Test your understanding 8

ABC Ltd has taxable total profits of £800,000 and prepares accounts to 31 December every year. ABC Ltd has no related 51 % group companies.

By which dates must ABC Ltd file its tax return and pay its corporation tax for the accounting period ended 31 December 2020?

	Return date	Tax payable date
A	31 January 2022	31 January 2022
B	31 December 2021	1 October 2021
C	31 January 2022	30 September 2021
D	31 December 2021	31 January 2022

Test your understanding 9

Which of the following statements is/are true?

1   Only companies with revenue of £100,000 or more are required to file returns and pay corporation tax electronically.

2   All companies must file their accounts using iXBRL.

3   iXBRL stands for inline eXtended Blank Reports Limits.

A   (1) and (2)

B   (1) only

C   (2) only

D   None of them

Test your understanding answers

Test your understanding 1

Zachary Ltd

Augmented profits – y/e 31 March 2021

	£
TTP	1,400,000
Plus: Dividends received	103,000
Augmented profits	1,503,000

The dividends are received from a company which is not a related 51% group company and are therefore included in the calculation of augmented profits.

Augmented profits exceed £1.5 million. Therefore, Zachary Ltd is a large company for corporation tax purposes. As Zachary Ltd was also a large company in the previous period, the corporation tax for the period must be paid by instalments.

Test your understanding 2

Flower Ltd is in a 51% group with:

- Rose (51% subsidiary)
- Buttercup (Flower Ltd indirectly owns >50%)
- Daisy (even though it is incorporated overseas), and
- Tulip (purchased prior to the start of the AP).

Daffodil Ltd is not a 51% group company as it is dormant throughout the year ended 31 March 2021.

There are therefore 5 related 51% group companies in Flower Ltd's group.

The augmented profit threshold used to decide if these companies are large for the purposes of corporation tax is £300,000 (£1,500,000/5). Therefore if any of the group companies' augmented profits exceed £300,000 they will be required to make instalment payments.

Test your understanding 3

XYZ Ltd

XYZ Ltd's corporation tax liability is due by instalments as follows:

£500,000 on 14 October 2020

£500,000 on 14 January 2021

£500,000 on 14 April 2021

£500,000 on 14 July 2021

Test your understanding 4

Able Ltd

Interest at the rate of 2.75% p.a. will run from the due date of 1 January 2022 to the date of payment (15 March 2022), on the underpayment of corporation tax of £50,000.

Test your understanding 5

Everlate Ltd

The tax return should have been submitted by 28 February 2022, and so it is seven months late.

The fixed penalty is therefore £1,000 (as the return is more than three months late and Everlate Ltd is a persistent offender).

The tax geared penalty is £10,000 (£100,000 at 10%).

Test your understanding 6

The correct answer is A.

Roberts plc is a large company for the year ended 31 March 2021. Therefore instalments payments would normally be expected.

However, Roberts plc was not large in the previous accounting period and therefore (given its profits do not exceed £10m) it will not have to pay instalments for the year ended 31 March 2021.

Roberts plc's corporation tax liability will be payable by 9 months and 1 day after the end of the accounting period (i.e. by 1 January 2022).

Test your understanding 7

The correct answer is C.

Grape plc is a large company and must therefore pay its tax in instalments. The last instalment is due three months and 14 days from the end of the accounting period.

Test your understanding 8

The correct answer is B.

The return must be submitted within 12 months of the end of the accounting period and the tax paid nine months and one day after the end of the accounting period.

Test your understanding 9

The correct answer is C.

All companies are required to file their returns electronically and file their accounts using iXBRL. This stands for inline eXtensible Business Reporting Language.

Computation of gains and tax payable

Chapter learning objectives

Upon completion of this chapter you will be able to:

- describe the scope of capital gains tax
- recognise those assets which are exempt
- compute and explain the treatment of capital gains
- compute and explain the treatment of capital losses
- compute the amount of capital gains tax payable
- basic capital gains tax planning.

PER

One of the PER performance objectives (PO15) is to prepare computations of taxable amounts and tax liabilities according to legal requirements. Another objective (PO17) is to advise on mitigating and deferring tax liabilities through legitimate tax planning measures. Working through this chapter should help you understand how to demonstrate those objectives.

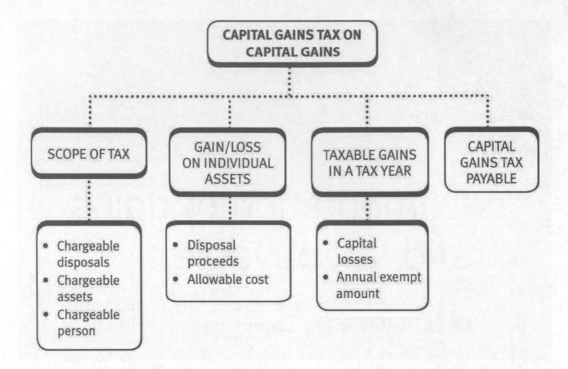

 Introduction

This and the following three chapters deal with the way in which **individuals** are subject to tax on their capital gains.

The taxation of capital gains is an important topic. You should expect to be tested on this area in both sections A and B of your TX examination. Capital gains could also be the focus of the 10 mark question in section C.

1 Scope of capital gains tax

Capital gains tax (CGT) is charged on gains arising on **chargeable persons** making **chargeable disposals** of **chargeable assets**.

Chargeable persons

Chargeable persons include individuals and companies.

In these CGT chapters we are concerned with disposals by individuals.

- Individuals who are UK resident in the tax year in which the disposal takes place are subject to capital gains tax on their gains.

 - UK resident individuals are subject to UK CGT on all disposals of chargeable assets, regardless of where in the world the assets are situated.

- Non-UK residents only pay UK CGT on the disposal of interests in UK land. However, this is not examinable.

Definition of residence

The definition of residence for CGT is the same as for income tax purposes (see Chapter 2). This definition could be tested in an income tax or a CGT question in the examination.

Chargeable disposal

Chargeable disposal	Exempt disposal

The following are treated as chargeable disposals:
 	
1   sale or gift of the whole or part of an asset
 	
2   exchange of an asset
 	
3   loss or total destruction of an asset
 	
4   receipts of a capital sum derived from an asset, for example:
 	
  •   compensation received for damage to an asset
 	
  •   receipts for the surrender of rights to an asset.
	Exempt disposals include:
	
	1 disposals as a result of the death of an individual
	
	2 gifts to charities.

Chargeable assets

Note that exempt assets (below) are outside the scope of CGT and therefore:

- gains are not taxable

- losses are not allowable.

 The TX examining team usually includes the disposal of an exempt asset in the examination. Therefore, make sure you have learnt the key exempt assets and do not be tempted in the examination to waste time doing unnecessary calculations on these assets. To gain marks in the examination for an exempt asset you must state that it is exempt so that the marker knows you understand this point (section C questions only).

Chargeable assets	Exempt assets
All forms of capital assets, wherever situated, are chargeable assets. Common examples include: • Freehold land and buildings • Goodwill • Unquoted shares • Quoted shares • Certain types of chattels – Chapter 20 **Note:** Chattels are tangible movable assets (e.g. furniture, plant and machinery).	Exempt assets include: • Motor vehicles (including vintage cars) • Main residence • Cash • Certain types of chattels – Chapter 20 • Investments held within an ISA • Qualifying corporate bonds (QCBs) • Gilt-edged securities • NS&I certificates • Foreign currency for private use • Receivables • Trading inventory • Prizes and betting winnings.

Test your understanding 1

Which of the following disposals may give rise to a chargeable gain?

• Sale of shares in an unquoted trading company.

• Damage to an insured building caused by a fire.

• Sale of 13% Treasury stock 2021.

• Exchange, with a friend, of a house, which was not his main residence, for an apartment.

• Sale of a motor car to brother at less than market value.

• Gift of UK shares by an individual who is not resident in the UK.

2 Calculation of capital gain/loss on individual disposals

An individual is subject to CGT on the total **taxable gains** arising on the disposal of all assets in a tax year.

The following steps are carried out to compute the capital gains tax payable by an individual for a tax year:

Step 1 Calculate the chargeable gain/allowable loss arising on the disposal of each chargeable asset separately

Step 2 Calculate the net chargeable gains arising in the tax year = (chargeable gains less allowable losses)

Step 3 Deduct the annual exempt amount

Step 4 Deduct capital losses brought forward = taxable gains

Step 5 Calculate the CGT payable for the tax year.

Pro forma – individual

Step 1: For each disposal by an individual calculate the chargeable gain/allowable loss as follows:

	£	£
Disposal proceeds		X
Less: Allowable selling costs		(X)
		—
Net disposal proceeds		X
Less: Allowable expenditure		
Cost of acquisition	X	
Incidental costs of acquisition	X	
Additional (capital) enhancement expenditure	X	
	—	(X)
		—
Chargeable gain/(allowable loss)		X/(X)
		—

Net disposal proceeds

- The disposal proceeds used in the computation is normally the sale proceeds received.

- Incidental costs arising on disposal are deducted from the gross proceeds (e.g. auctioneer's fees, estate agent fees).

- However, market value is substituted for actual gross proceeds received where:

    – the deal was not made at arm's length (e.g. a gift)

    – the law assumes that it was not made at arm's length (e.g. transfers between connected parties).

- At TX, an individual is 'connected' with close relatives (i.e. parents, siblings and children).

Allowable expenditure

The types of expenditure that rank as allowable deductions are:

- cost of acquisition (e.g. purchase cost)

- expenditure on enhancing the value of the asset (improvement expenditure)

- expenditure incurred to establish, preserve or defend the taxpayer's title to the asset

- incidental costs arising on the acquisition of the asset.

Where an individual acquires an asset as a gift (or from a sale for less than market value):

- the cost of acquisition = market value of the asset at the date of the gift (or sale at undervaluation).

Where an individual inherits an asset on death:

- the cost of acquisition = market value of the asset at the date of the death (i.e. probate value).

Illustration 1 – Calculation of net chargeable gains

Sergei sold an antique vase for £12,000 and a painting for £20,000 during the tax year. He incurred auctioneer's fees of 1% of the proceeds. He acquired the assets for £13,000 and £7,000, respectively.

Calculate the net chargeable gain arising.

Solution

Vase

	£	£
Sale proceeds	12,000	
Less: Allowable selling costs (1% auctioneer's fees)	(120)	
	———	
Net sale proceeds	11,880	
Less: Allowable expenditure		
Cost of acquisition	(13,000)	
	———	
Allowable loss		(1,120)

Painting

Sale proceeds	20,000
Less: Allowable selling costs (1% auctioneer's fees)	(200)
	———
Net sale proceeds	19,800
Less: Allowable expenditure	
Cost of acquisition	(7,000)
	———
Chargeable gain	12,800
	———
Net chargeable gains	11,680
	———

Test your understanding 2

On 1 August 2020, Margaret sold a holiday villa to her sister for £25,000. Its market value at that date was £100,000.

Margaret had acquired the villa on 1 June 2005 for £20,000 and had paid legal fees on acquisition of £500. On 1 May 2010, she had added a conservatory at a cost of £10,000.

Calculate the chargeable gain arising on the sale of the villa.

Test your understanding 3

Puteri sold a holiday cottage for £75,000 on 13 August 2020. It cost £53,500 in May 2007 and was extended in September 2011 at a cost of £16,000. The estate agent and solicitor fees for the purchase totalled £2,300 and for the sale totalled £5,400.

She also sold her grandmother's engagement ring for £12,000 in August 2020. She had inherited the ring on the death of her grandmother in August 2013 when the ring was valued at £9,000.

Calculate the net chargeable gain arising in the tax year 2020/21.

3 Calculation of CGT payable

An individual pays capital gains tax on the total taxable gains arising on the disposal of all assets in a tax year.

The following pro forma covers Steps 3 to 5 in the procedure to calculate the CGT payable by an individual.

Pro forma capital gains tax payable computation – 2020/21

	£
Net chargeable gains for the tax year	X
Less: Annual exempt amount (2020/21)	(12,300)
	——
	X
Less: Capital losses brought forward (see later)	(X)
	——
Taxable gains	X
	——
CGT liability (taxable gains × appropriate tax rate)	X
Less: Payment on account re residential property disposals	(X)
	——
CGT payable	X
	——

Annual exempt amount

Every individual is entitled to an annual exempt amount (AEA) for each tax year.

- For 2020/21, the AEA is £12,300.

- The AEA is deducted from net chargeable gains for the tax year i.e. after current year capital losses but before capital losses brought forward.

- If an individual's net chargeable gains after current year capital losses for the tax year are:

  - £12,300 or less; he or she is not chargeable to tax

  - in excess of £12,300; he or she is chargeable to tax on the excess (unless these are covered by capital losses brought forward).

- If the AEA is not utilised in a particular tax year, then it is wasted. It cannot be carried forward or backward to another tax year.

 For the purpose of the examination:

Chargeable gain(s) means the gain(s) **before deducting the annual exempt amount and any brought forward capital losses**.

Taxable gain(s) means the gain(s) **after deducting the annual exempt amount and any brought forward capital losses**.

Capital losses

Current year capital losses

Capital losses arising on assets in the current tax year are set off:

- against chargeable gains arising in the same tax year
- to the maximum possible extent, (i.e. they cannot be restricted to avoid wasting all or part of the AEA).

Any unrelieved/unused capital losses are carried forward to offset against chargeable gains in future years.

Brought forward capital losses

Brought forward capital losses are offset against the first available net chargeable gains after the AEA. Any remaining brought forward losses are carried forward for future offset against future chargeable gains.

 Illustration 2 – Calculation of taxable gains in the tax year

Tom and Jerry made chargeable gains and allowable losses for the tax years 2019/20 and 2020/21 as set out below.

	Tom £	Jerry £
2019/20		
Chargeable gains	12,000	4,000
Allowable losses	8,000	7,000
2020/21		
Chargeable gains	14,900	14,300
Allowable losses	2,000	1,000

Calculate the taxable gains for Tom and Jerry for the tax years 2019/20 and 2020/21 and the amount of any losses carried forward.

Solution

Tom – 2019/20

	£
Chargeable gains	12,000
Less: Allowable losses – current year	(8,000)
Net chargeable gains	4,000

Net chargeable gains are covered by the AEA. There are no losses to carry forward to the tax year 2019/20.

Tom – 2020/21

	£
Chargeable gains	14,900
Less: Allowable losses – current year	(2,000)
Net chargeable gains	12,900
Less: AEA	(12,300)
Taxable gains	600

Tom is taxed on gains of £600 in 2020/21

Jerry – 2019/20

	£
Chargeable gains	4,000
Less: Allowable losses – current year	(4,000)
Net chargeable gains	0

Jerry is unable to use his 2019/20 AEA since his gains are all covered by current year losses. He has losses of £3,000 (£7,000 – £4,000) to carry forward to the tax year 2020/21.

Jerry – 2020/21

	£
Chargeable gains	14,300
Less: Allowable losses – current year	(1,000)
Less: AEA	(12,300)
	1,000
Less: Losses brought forward (2019/20)	(1,000)
Taxable gains	0

Jerry used £1,000 of his losses brought forward. He still has losses of £2,000 (£3,000 – £1,000) to carry forward against future net chargeable gains after the AEA.

> ### Test your understanding 4
>
> Gigi and Zayn made chargeable gains and allowable losses for the tax years 2019/20 and 2020/21 as set out below.
>
> | | Gigi | Zayn |
> |---|---|---|
> | **2019/20** | £ | £ |
> | Chargeable gains | 15,000 | 5,000 |
> | Allowable losses | 10,000 | 9,000 |
> | **2020/21** | | |
> | Chargeable gains | 23,800 | 15,300 |
> | Allowable losses | 10,700 | 2,200 |
>
> **Calculate the taxable gains for Gigi and Zayn for the tax years 2019/20 and 2020/21 and the amount of any losses carried forward at the end of 2020/21.**
>
> **Assume the 2020/21 rates and allowances apply throughout.**

Computation of CGT payable

CGT is payable on the taxable gains arising in a tax year as follows:

- The rate of CGT is dependent upon the amount of a taxpayer's total taxable income (i.e. after deduction of the personal allowance) and the type of assets disposed of.

- Taxable gains are taxed **after** taxable income (i.e. as the top slice), but do **not** combine income and gains in one computation (see key point below).

- Generally, where taxable gains fall into the basic rate band, CGT is at 10%.

- Generally, to the extent that any gains (or any part of gains) exceed the basic rate band, they are taxed at 20%.

- Higher rates of CGT apply to certain residential property.

- If the basic rate band is extended due to gift aid donations or personal pension contributions, the extended basic rate band is also used to establish the rate of CGT.

- Any unused income tax personal allowance cannot be used to reduce taxable gains.

 If an examination question requires calculation of income tax and CGT, two separate calculations **must** be prepared; one for income tax, and one for CGT.

Rates of CGT

CGT is paid at the normal rates, unless the gain arises on the disposal of a residential property.

	Normal rate	Residential property rates
Falling in basic rate band	10%	18%
In excess of basic rate band	20%	28%

In practice, a taxpayer's main residential property (i.e. his or her home) will be exempt from CGT under the private residence relief rules (PRR) (see Chapter 22). However, where the gain on the disposal of a residential property is not fully exempt (e.g. on an investment property which is let out) it is taxed at the higher rates.

Offset of AEA and capital losses

Taxpayers can offset the AEA and capital losses against whichever gains they choose. In order to maximise the reliefs they should be offset firstly against residential property gains, as they are taxable at higher rates than other gains.

The unused basic rate may also be used in the most beneficial way. The tax saving is the same regardless of the gains against which it is used (as switching gains taxed at 28% to 18% or switching gains taxed at 20% to 10% produces the same result). In your materials the unused basic rate band is firstly offset against other gains

UK residential property disposals

Disposals of UK residential property made on or after 6 April 2020 must be reported to HMRC within 30 days of completion, along with a payment on account of the relevant CGT liability.

The rate of CGT is determined using an estimate of the individual's income at the point of the disposal, i.e. estimating how much of the BRB will be remaining. In questions involving the calculation of the tax due, an indication of whether the taxpayer is basic or higher rate or an estimate of the income will be provided.

Brought forward losses, current year capital losses realised prior to the residential property disposal and the AEA may be offset against the gain when calculating the tax due. Any losses incurred subsequently are ignored.

There is no need to submit a return if there is no CGT due, for example if the gain is covered by the AEA, private residence relief or sold at a loss.

All disposals made during a tax year (including any residential property disposals) are included in the final tax return. Any payment on account made is deducted from the CGT liability to reach the final amount of CGT payable. The amount paid may be provided or you may be required to calculate it.

If a repayment is due it will be claimed on the CGT return.

Calculations of payments on account on multiple residential property disposals are not examinable.

Illustration 3 – Calculation of CGT payable

In the tax year 2020/21 Jane realised the following chargeable gains:

	£
Residential property	40,600
Antique table	20,000

Jane has taxable income of £28,500 in the tax year 2020/21.

Jane estimated the CGT due & made a payment on account of £7,860.

Calculate Jane's capital gains tax liability for the tax year 2020/21.

Solution

	Total	Other gains	Residential property
	£	£	£
Residential property	40,600		40,600
Antique table	20,000	20,000	
Total gains	60,600	20,000	40,600
Less: AEA	(12,300)		(12,300)
Taxable gains	48,300	20,000	28,300

	£		£
9,000 × 10% (W) (Other)			900
11,000 × 20% (Other)			2,200
28,300 × 28% (Residential)			7,924
	48,300		
Capital gains tax liability			11,024
Less: Payment on account re residential property			(7,860)
CGT payable			3,164

Working:

Jane's unused basic rate is £9,000 (£37,500 – £28,500).

Test your understanding 5

In the tax year 2020/21 Jacob realised the following chargeable gains:

	£
Residential property	16,600
Necklace	20,000
Land	10,000

Jacob expected to be a higher rate taxpayer when the residential property disposal was made. His only income was employment income of £44,000 and he paid contributions of £4,000 into his personal pension scheme during the tax year 2020/21.

Calculate Jacob's capital gains tax payable for the tax year 2020/21.

4 Payment of CGT

CGT is due as follows.

- On 31 January following the tax year (i.e. 31 January 2022 for 2020/21).
- Payments on account for UK residential property are deducted from the final liability.

Test your understanding 6

Eevi sold a commercial investment property on 1 July 2020 for £650,300. She had acquired the building for £80,000 in June 2003 and had extended it at a cost of £30,000 in June 2005.

Eevi also disposed of a painting on 1 September 2020 for £20,000, incurring auctioneer's fees of 1%. She had acquired the painting for £35,000 in April 2005.

Eevi had capital losses brought forward of £15,300.

Eevi's only source of income in the tax year 2020/21 is trading income of £40,000.

Calculate Eevi's capital gains tax payable for the tax year 2020/21 and state the due date for payment.

5 CGT planning opportunities

Delaying disposals until the following tax year

Tax saving

- If the AEA has already been utilised in a particular tax year, delaying the disposal of an asset until the following year will:

    - allow the offset of the later year's AEA against any gain arising

    - thereby saving tax on a further £12,300.

- If the individual is a basic rate taxpayer, and taxable income is lower in a subsequent tax year, delaying the disposal would mean that:

    - more of the basic rate band would be available, and

    - therefore more of the resulting taxable gain could be taxed at 10% (or 18% for residential property).

Cash flow advantage

- Gains realised on disposals up to and including 5 April 2021 are assessable in the tax year 2020/21 and the associated CGT is payable by 31 January 2022.

- If disposals later in the tax year can be delayed until 6 April 2021 or later:

    - the gain is realised in the tax year 2021/22, and

    - any CGT is payable one year later, by 31 January 2023.

Selling assets in tranches

Where assets can be split and sold piecemeal (e.g. shares), selling them in tranches in different tax years can allow the use of more than one AEA and result in a lower total taxable gain overall.

6 Chapter summary

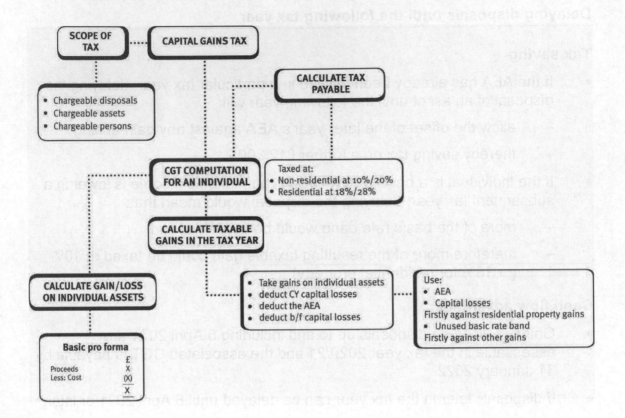

7 Practice objective test questions

Test your understanding 7

On 23 April 2020, Ander sold a commercial investment property for £174,000, before agent's fees of 2%. He had purchased the property on 5 June 2012 for £129,600. The seller incurred fees in June 2012 of £2,400.

What is the value of the chargeable gain arising on this disposal?

A   £38,520

B   £40,920

C   £42,000

D   £44,400

Test your understanding 8

Owen has the following chargeable gains and losses for the tax years 2019/20 and 2020/21.

	2019/20	2020/21
	£	£
Chargeable gains	10,000	14,000
Capital losses	(21,600)	(1,600)

What loss, if any, is available to carry forward to 2021/22?

A   £21,500

B   £11,500

C   £100

D   £0

Test your understanding 9

In August 2020, Robbie sold a residential investment property for £750,000 which he purchased in April 2002 for £125,000. In June 2007 the property was extended at a cost of £30,000. In November 2013 the property was redecorated at a cost of £5,000.

What is Robbie's chargeable gain arising on the disposal?

A   £595,000

B   £625,000

C   £590,000

D   £620,000

Test your understanding 10

Which of the following are exempt from capital gains tax for an individual?

1   Premium bond prize

2   Qualifying corporate bonds (QCBs)

3   Gilt-edged securities

4   Receipts of compensation for damaged assets

5   Goodwill

A   1, 2 and 5

B   2, 3 and 4

C   1, 2 and 3

D   1, 3 and 5

Test your understanding 11

In the tax year 2020/21 Paul had a chargeable gain (before the annual exempt amount) of £51,000. It all arose on non-residential property. His taxable income is £22,000.

How much capital gains tax is payable by Paul for the tax year 2020/21?

A   £7,740

B   £3,870

C   £9,286

D   £6,190

Test your understanding answers

Test your understanding 1

Not chargeable	Chargeable disposal
Sale of 13% Treasury stock 2021 (gilt-edged security – exempt asset)	Sale of shares in an unquoted trading company
Sale of a motor car to brother at less than market value (motor vehicle – exempt asset)	Damage to an insured building, caused by fire
Gift of UK shares by an individual who is not resident in the UK (not a chargeable individual)	Exchange, with a friend, of a house, which was not his main residence, for an apartment

Test your understanding 2

Margaret

	£	£
Market value (Note 1)		100,000
Less: Allowable expenditure		
Cost of acquisition	20,000	
Incidental costs of acquisition – legal fees	500	
Enhancement expenditure (Note 2)	10,000	
	———	(30,500)
		———
Chargeable gain		69,500
		———

Notes:

1   Market value is substituted for actual proceeds as the sale was to a connected person (Margaret's sister) and is therefore deemed to not be an 'arm's length transaction'.

2   The conservatory is allowable expenditure as it enhanced the value of the villa.

Test your understanding 3

Puteri

Cottage	£	£
Sale proceeds	75,000	
Less: Allowable selling costs	(5,400)	
Net sale proceeds	69,600	
Less: Allowable expenditure		
Cost of acquisition	(53,500)	
Incidental costs of acquisition	(2,300)	
Extension	(16,000)	
Allowable loss		(2,200)
Ring		
Sale proceeds	12,000	
Less: Probate value	(9,000)	
Chargeable gain		3,000
Net chargeable gain		800

Test your understanding 4

Gigi

2019/20

	£
Chargeable gains	15,000
Less: Allowable losses – current year	(10,000)
Net chargeable gains	5,000

Net chargeable gains are covered by the AEA. There are no losses to carry forward to the tax year 2020/21.

2020/21	£
Chargeable gains	23,800
Less: Allowable losses – current year	(10,700)
Net chargeable gains	13,100
Less: AEA	(12,300)
Taxable gains	800

Gigi is taxed on gains of £800 in the tax year 2020/21.

Zayn

2019/20	£
Chargeable gains	5,000
Less: Allowable losses – current year	(5,000)
Net chargeable gains	0

Zayn is unable to use his 2019/20 AEA since his gains are all covered by current year losses. He has losses of £4,000 (£9,000 – £5,000) to carry forward to the tax year 2020/21.

2020/21	£
Chargeable gains	15,300
Less: Allowable losses – current year	(2,200)
Less: AEA	(12,300)
	800
Less: Losses brought forward (2019/20)	(800)
Taxable gains	0

Zayn used £800 of his losses brought forward, to reduce his chargeable gains to £0. He still has losses of £3,200 (£4,000 – £800) to carry forward against future net chargeable gains.

Test your understanding 5

Jacob

	Total	Other gains	Residential property
	£	£	£
Residential property	16,600		16,600
Necklace	20,000	20,000	
Land	10,000	10,000	
	———	———	———
Total gains	46,600	30,000	16,600
Less: AEA	(12,300)	–	(12,300)
	———	———	———
Taxable gains	34,300	30,000	4,300
	———	———	———

£	
11,000 × 10% (W1) (Other)	1,100
19,000 × 20% (Other)	3,800
4,300 × 28% (Residential)	1,204
———	
34,300	
———	

Capital gains tax liability	6,104
Less: Payment on account re residential property (W2)	(1,204)
	———
CGT payable	4,900
	———

Working:

1   Jacob's taxable income is £31,500 (£44,000 – £12,500).

His basic rate band is increased by the gross personal pension contributions and is £42,500 (£37,500 + (£4,000 × 100/80)).

His unused basic rate is £11,000 (£42,500 – £31,500).

2   The payment on account was calculated assuming Jacob was a higher rate taxpayer:

(£16,600 – £12,300) × 28% = £1,204

Test your understanding 6

Eevi

Capital gains tax computation – 2020/21

	£	£
Commercial property		
Sale proceeds	650,300	
Less: Allowable expenditure		
Cost of acquisition	(80,000)	
Enhancement expenditure	(30,000)	
	———	
Chargeable gain		540,300
Painting		
Sale proceeds	20,000	
Less: Allowable selling costs	(200)	
	———	
Net sale proceeds	19,800	
Less: Allowable expenditure		
Cost of acquisition	(35,000)	
	———	
Allowable loss		(15,200)
Less: AEA		(12,300)
		———
		512,800
Less: Capital losses brought forward		(15,300)
		———
Taxable gains		497,500
		———

£	
10,000 × 10% (W)	1,000
487,500 × 20%	97,500
———	
497,500	
———	
Capital gains tax payable	98,500
	———
Due date of payment	31 January 2022

Working:

Taxable income = (£40,000 − £12,500 PA) = £27,500

Basic rate band remaining = (£37,500 − £27,500) = £10,000

Test your understanding 7

The correct answer is B.

	£
Proceeds	174,000
Less: Incidental costs of disposal	(3,480)
	170,520
Less: Cost	(129,600)
Chargeable gain	40,920

Note: The fees of £2,400 were incurred by the seller, not Ander.

Test your understanding 8

The correct answer is B.

	2019/20 £	2020/21 £
Chargeable gains	10,000	14,000
Less: Capital losses – current year	(10,000)	(1,600)
Less: Annual exempt amount	–	(12,300)
	0	100
Less: Capital losses – b/f	–	(100)
Taxable gains	0	0

	£
2019/20 loss	(21,600)
Utilised 2019/20	10,000
	(11,600)
Utilised 2020/21	100
Carried forward	(11,500)

Test your understanding 9

The correct answer is A.

	£
Proceeds	750,000
Less: Cost	(125,000)
Enhancement	(30,000)
Unindexed gain	595,000

Note: Redecoration is revenue expenditure and does not qualify as a capital improvement.

Test your understanding 10

The correct answer is C.

Only the compensation for damaged assets and goodwill are subject to capital gains tax.

Test your understanding 11

The correct answer is D.

	£
Non-residential property	51,000
Less: AEA	(12,300)
Taxable gains	38,700

£	
15,500 × 10% (W) (Other)	1,550
23,200 × 20% (Other)	4,640
38,700	
Capital gains tax liability	6,190

Working:

Paul's unused basic rate is £15,500 (£37,500 − £22,000).

Computation of gains: Special rules

Chapter learning objectives

Upon completion of this chapter you will be able to:

- understand the treatment of transfers between a husband and wife or between a couple in a civil partnership

- understand the amount of allowable expenditure for a part disposal

- recognise the treatment where an asset is damaged, lost or destroyed, and the implications of receiving insurance proceeds and reinvesting such proceeds

- identify when chattels and wasting assets are exempt

- compute the chargeable gain when a chattel or a wasting asset is disposed of

- basic capital gains tax planning.

PER

One of the PER performance objectives (PO15) is to prepare computations of taxable amounts and tax liabilities according to legal requirements. Another objective (PO17) is to advise on mitigating and deferring tax liabilities through legitimate tax planning measures. Working through this chapter should help you understand how to demonstrate those objectives.

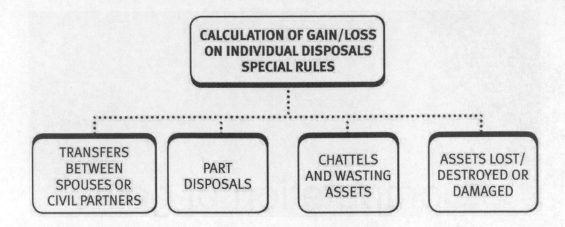

 Introduction

The basic pro forma for calculating gains on the disposal of assets is adapted by special rules in the following circumstances:

- transfers between spouses or civil partners

- part disposals

- chattels and wasting assets

- assets lost or destroyed

- damaged assets.

1 Transfers between spouses or civil partners

 Where an asset is transferred between spouses or civil partners:

- no gain or loss arises on the transfer

- any actual proceeds are ignored

- the transferor is deemed to dispose of the asset at its acquisition cost

- the deemed proceeds of the transferor are treated as the deemed acquisition cost of the transferee (i.e. the recipient spouse acquires the asset at its original acquisition cost).

However note that these rules only apply whilst the spouses or civil partners are living together (i.e. not separated).

Illustration 1 – Transfers between spouses and civil partners

David purchased some jewellery in August 2002 for £50,000. In July 2020 he gave it to his wife Victoria when it was worth £200,000.

Calculate the deemed sale proceeds of David's disposal and state Victoria's deemed acquisition cost.

Solution

David is deemed to have transferred the asset at its acquisition cost so that no gain or loss arises on the transfer.

The deemed proceeds are therefore £50,000 and Victoria's deemed acquisition cost is the same as David's deemed proceeds (i.e. £50,000).

Subsequent disposal by transferee

On a subsequent disposal of the transferred asset by the transferee, the deemed acquisition cost (often referred to as the base cost of the asset) is the original acquisition cost to the first spouse.

Illustration 2 – Subsequent disposal

Fernanda acquired a holiday cottage for £29,175 on 1 September 1994 and transferred it to her husband, Luiz, on 31 August 2015. Luiz sold the cottage to a third party on 31 January 2021 for £42,000.

Compute the chargeable gain on Luiz's disposal in January 2021.

Solution

	£
Sale proceeds	42,000
Less: Deemed acquisition cost (Base cost)	(29,175)
Chargeable gain	12,825

Test your understanding 1

John acquired a warehouse as an investment for £100,000 on 1 September 2001. On 1 May 2015 he gave the warehouse to his wife, Tania, when it was worth £300,000. Tania sold the warehouse for £350,300 on 1 July 2020.

Tania had no other capital disposals in the tax year 2020/21, but has capital losses brought forward of £11,800. Her taxable income for the tax year 2020/21 is £45,000.

Calculate Tania's capital gains tax payable in the tax year 2020/21.

Planning opportunities

Married couples and civil partners can transfer assets between them at no tax cost (i.e. the assets are transferred at no gain/no loss). This provides opportunities to minimise their total capital gains tax liability.

They can transfer assets between them to maximise the use of:

- each individual's annual exempt amount
- each individual's basic rate band, and
- capital losses.

Illustration 3 – Planning opportunities

Tereza, who is married to Kerry, made three chargeable disposals in the tax year 2020/21, as follows:

Asset 1	Chargeable gain	£10,900
Asset 2	Chargeable gain	£19,600
Asset 3	Chargeable gain	£49,000

None of the gains were in respect of residential property.

Tereza's only income for the year is a trading profit of £45,000, whilst Kerry has no taxable income.

(a) **Calculate Tereza's CGT payable for the tax year 2020/21.**

(b) **Advise how tax savings could have been made by the couple, and calculate the revised CGT payable by the couple assuming they had taken your advice.**

Solution

(a) **Tereza's CGT payable – 2020/21**

	£
Asset 1	10,900
Asset 2	19,600
Asset 3	49,000
	———
Total chargeable gains	79,500
Less: AEA	(12,300)
	———
Taxable gains	67,200
	———

	£		£
Basic rate (W)	5,000	× 10%	500
Higher rate	62,200	× 20%	12,440
	67,200		
Capital gains tax payable			12,940

Working: Taxable income = (£45,000 – £12,500) = £32,500
Remaining BR band = (£37,500 – £32,500) = £5,000

Note: The question stated Tereza's trading income rather than her taxable income and therefore her taxable income must be calculated to determine the remaining basic rate band.

(b) **Advice**

As a married couple, Kerry and Tereza can transfer assets between themselves at no gain/no loss (i.e. at no tax cost).

Accordingly, they should transfer assets between themselves to ensure that they both use their AEAs and basic rate bands.

If Tereza had transferred Asset 3 to Kerry, then the gain on the asset would be reduced by her AEA of £12,300 and taxed at 10%.

Tereza's revised CGT payable for the year is as follows:

	£
Asset 1	10,900
Asset 2	19,600
	30,500
Less: AEA	(12,300)
Taxable gain	18,200

	£		£
Basic rate (W as before)	5,000	× 10%	500
Higher rate	13,200	× 20%	2,640
	18,200		
Capital gains tax liability			3,140

Kerry's CGT payable would be:	£
Asset 3	49,000
Less: AEA	(12,300)
Taxable gain	36,700

	£		£
Basic rate	36,700	× 10%	3,670
	36,700		
Capital gains tax liability			3,670
Total CGT payable (£3,140 + £3,670)			6,810
Tax saving (£12,940 – £6,810)			6,130
Alternative tax saving calculation:			
Use of Kerry's AEA (£12,300 × 20%)			2,460
Use of Kerry's basic rate band (£36,700 × (20% – 10%))			3,670
			6,130

2 Part disposals

When there is a part disposal of an asset, we need to identify how much of the original cost of the asset relates to the part of the asset disposed of.

- The allowable expenditure of the part of the asset disposed of is calculated using the following formula:

  Cost × A/(A + B)

  Where: A = Value of the part disposed of

  B = Market value of the remainder at the time of the part disposal.

- The allowable expenditure, calculated using the formula, is then used in the basic capital gains tax computation as normal.

Incidental costs of acquisition or enhancement expenditure, relating to:

- solely the part of the asset being disposed of = deducted in full in the chargeable gain calculation

- the whole asset (rather than just the part being disposed of) = apportioned in the same way as cost (i.e. A/A+B).

Illustration 4 – Part disposal

Yayha acquired 20 hectares of land in March 2005 for £6,000. On 1 June 2020, he disposed of 8 hectares for £8,000. The value of the remaining 12 hectares at this date was £15,000.

On 1 July 2020, Yayha sold the remainder of the land for £18,000.

Calculate the chargeable gains arising on the disposals of land in the tax year 2020/21.

Solution

1 June 2020 disposal

	£
Sale proceeds	8,000
Less: Deemed cost of part disposed of	
£6,000 × £8,000/(£8,000 + £15,000)	(2,087)
Chargeable gain	5,913

Note that the number of hectares owned and sold is irrelevant in calculating the cost of the land disposed of. **Always** use the (A/A + B) formula, which uses the **value** of the asset disposed of and retained.

1 July 2020 disposal

	£
Sale proceeds	18,000
Less: Deemed cost of the remainder	
((£6,000 – £2,087 (above))	(3,913)
Chargeable gain	14,087

Test your understanding 2

Jacob bought 10 hectares of land for £8,000 in August 2009. He sold 3 hectares of the land for £20,000 in January 2021. At that time the remaining land was worth £60,000.

In May 2011, Jacob spent £3,000 levelling the 3 hectares of land sold in January 2021.

In March 2021 Jacob sold the remaining hectares for £75,600.

Jacob's employment income for the tax year 2020/21 is £30,440. He has no other income.

Calculate the chargeable gains arising on the two disposals of land and the capital gains tax payable for the tax year 2020/21. State the due date of payment.

Test your understanding 3

Gemma a bought a commercial investment property in May 2007 for £50,000. On 1 July 2013 she disposed of part of the land attached to the property for £40,000. The value of the property and the remaining land at this date was £100,000.

Gemma paid legal fees of £4,500 in relation to the purchase of the investment property and the land.

On 1 August 2020 Gemma sold the property and remaining land for £200,600.

Gemma's taxable income for the tax year 2020/21 is £52,000.

Calculate the capital gains tax payable for the tax year 2020/21.

3 Chattels and wasting assets

It is important to be able to identify a chattel and a wasting asset as there are special rules for calculating the gain or loss arising on them.

Chattels

Chattels are defined as tangible movable property (e.g. a picture or table). Note that the asset must be:

- movable – therefore a building is not a chattel
- tangible – therefore shares are not chattels.

Wasting assets

A wasting asset is an asset with a predictable life not exceeding 50 years.

Chattels may be wasting or non-wasting as follows.

	Wasting chattels	**Non-wasting chattels**
Expected life	Not exceeding 50 years	More than 50 years
Examples	Greyhound	Antiques
	Boat	Jewellery
	Plant and machinery	Paintings
	Racehorse	

Plant and machinery are deemed to have a useful life of less than 50 years and are therefore **always** wasting chattels (but see below).

Chattels – exempt disposals

Certain disposals of chattels are exempt from capital gains tax as follows.

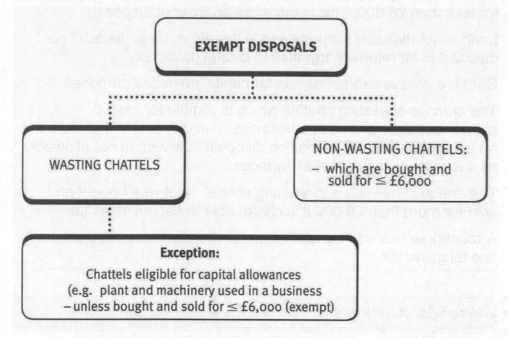

Illustration 5 – Chattels

Hana has made the following disposals in the tax year 2020/21.

1. A painting was sold in July 2020 for £5,600. She originally bought it in February 1997 for £3,500.

2. A piece of land, which she bought in April 2012 for £2,000 (as an investment), was sold in September 2020 for £5,000.

3. She sold a vintage car for £25,000 in November 2020 that had originally cost £5,500 in June 2006.

4. She bought a movable crane for £20,000 in August 1999, which she used in her haulage business. She sold the crane for £10,000 in January 2021.

5. An antique vase was sold in August 2020 for £10,000. It originally cost £8,000 in April 2007.

6. In October 2020 she sold her half share in a racehorse for £5,000, which she had acquired in June 2008 for £4,000.

For each of the above transactions, state whether they are chattels (wasting or non-wasting) and whether they will be subject to capital gains tax.

Solution

1   The painting is a non-wasting chattel which was bought and sold for less than £6,000. This is therefore an exempt disposal.

2   Land is not movable property and is therefore not a chattel. The disposal is therefore chargeable to capital gains tax.

3   Cars are always exempt assets for capital gains tax purposes.

4   The crane is a wasting chattel, which is eligible for capital allowances as it is used in a business. The disposal is therefore not an exempt disposal. The loss on disposal however, is not allowable as it is relieved via capital allowances.

5   The antique vase is a non-wasting chattel. As it was bought and sold for more than £6,000 it is chargeable to capital gains tax.

6   A racehorse is a wasting chattel and is therefore exempt from capital gains tax.

Test your understanding 4

Which of the following disposals are exempt from, and which are chargeable to, capital gains tax?

1   Gift of a necklace which was bought for £4,000. Its market value at the date of the gift was £7,000.

2   Sale of shares in a quoted trading company for £2,000 which were bought for £1,000.

3   Sale of a motor car, for £5,000, which was used for business purposes. It was acquired for £6,000.

4   Sale of a boat for £20,000, which was acquired for £15,000.

5   Sale of a painting for £5,000, which was acquired for £1,000.

6   Sale of a greyhound for £10,000, which was acquired for £5,000.

Non-wasting chattels

When a non-wasting chattel is disposed of the following rules apply:

(1)   asset bought **and** sold for £6,000 or less = exempt

(2)   asset bought and sold for more than £6,000 = the chargeable gain is computed in the normal way

(3)   asset either bought or sold for £6,000 or less = special rules apply:

- **Sold at a gain**

    Calculate the chargeable gain as normal but the gain cannot exceed a maximum of:

    5/3 × (gross disposal consideration – £6,000)

- **Sold at a loss**

Gross sale proceeds are deemed to be £6,000.

The above rules are referred to as **the £6,000 rule** and can be summarised in the table below.

	Cost	
	£6,000 or less	**More than 6,000**
Sale proceeds: **£6,000 or less**	Exempt	Allowable loss but gross proceeds are deemed = £6,000
More than £6,000	Taxed on lower of: • Normal calculation. • 5/3 × (gross proceeds – £6,000)	Normal CGT computation

Illustration 6 – Non-wasting chattel

Andrew sold a picture on 1 February 2021 for £6,600. He had acquired it on 1 March 2011 for £3,200.

Calculate the chargeable gain arising on the disposal.

Solution

As the picture is a non-wasting chattel, that was sold for more than £6,000, the disposal is not an exempt disposal.

	£
Sale proceeds	6,600
Less: Cost	(3,200)
Chargeable gain	3,400

Gain cannot exceed: 5/3 × (£6,600 – £6,000) = £1,000 so the chargeable gain is £1,000.

Illustration 7 – Non-wasting chattel

Hasan bought an antique table for £6,500 in September 2008 and sold it for £5,600 in December 2020. He incurred £250 to advertise it for sale.

Calculate the allowable loss arising, if any.

Solution

This is a disposal of a non-wasting chattel that cost more than £6,000 but which was sold for less than £6,000. The disposal is not an exempt disposal but the allowable loss is restricted as follows:

		£
Deemed gross sale proceeds		6,000
Less: Expenses of sale		(250)
Cost		(6,500)
		———
Allowable loss		(750)
		———

Test your understanding 5

Marjory bought two antique tables in March 1992 for £1,000 each. She sold them both in October 2020 for £6,400 and £13,600 respectively.

Calculate the chargeable gains arising on the disposal of the two antique tables.

Test your understanding 6

Brian bought a picture in April 1990 for £10,400 plus purchase costs of £100. The market for the artist's work slumped and Brian sold the picture on 27 June 2020 for £500, less disposal costs of £50.

Calculate the allowable loss on disposal of the picture.

Test your understanding 7

During January 2021, Leyla sold four paintings, which she had acquired in May 2007. Details were as follows.

Painting	Cost	Proceeds
	£	£
1	2,000	7,000
2	8,000	4,500
3	3,000	5,500
4	7,000	9,500

Calculate Leyla's net chargeable gains for the tax year 2020/21.

Chattels – summary

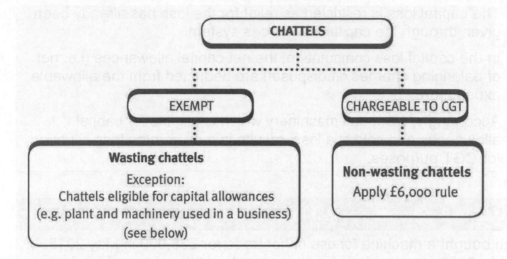

Wasting assets

Wasting assets (i.e. predictable life of 50 years or less) can be split into the following categories:

- Chattels not eligible for capital allowances = exempt from CGT.
- Chattels eligible for capital allowances.
- Other wasting assets.

Chattels eligible for capital allowances

For example, plant and machinery that has been used for the purposes of a trade.

Where capital allowances have been claimed on an asset, in the gain/loss computation we must take into account the tax relief already given for the net cost of the asset in the capital allowances computation.

Accordingly the following rules apply:

- **Sold at a gain**

   Calculate the gain as normal, applying the £6,000 rule if applicable. Any capital allowances given over the life of the asset will have been clawed back with a balancing charge on disposal.

- **Sold at a loss**

    The capital loss is restricted as relief for the loss has already been given through the capital allowances system.

    In the capital loss computation, the net capital allowances (i.e. net of balancing charges on disposal) are deducted from the allowable expenditure.

    Accordingly, plant and machinery which is eligible for capital allowances and sold at a loss, results in a no gain/no loss situation for CGT purposes.

Illustration 8 – Plant and machinery - Sarah

Sarah bought a machine for use in her trade for £35,000 in May 2013. In October 2020 she decided to replace it and sold the old machine for £40,000.

Calculate the chargeable gain arising on the disposal in October 2020.

Solution

The asset was sold at a gain. The capital gain is therefore calculated as normal.

	£
Sale proceeds	40,000
Less: Cost	(35,000)
	———
Chargeable gain	5,000
	———

Illustration 9 – Plant and machinery – Murad

Murad bought a machine for use in his trade for £35,000 in April 2009. In October 2020 he decided to replace it and sold the old machine for £26,500.

Calculate the chargeable gain or allowable loss arising.

Solution

Murad has sold the machine for a real loss of £8,500 (£35,000 – £26,500). He is compensated for this loss through the capital allowances system (i.e. he receives net capital allowances of £8,500 in respect of the machine).

The capital loss computation is therefore adjusted to reflect the relief for the loss already given through capital allowances as follows:

	£	£
Sale proceeds		26,500
Less: Cost	35,000	
Less: Net capital allowances	(8,500)	
	———	(26,500)
		———
Allowable loss		0
		———

Other wasting assets

This category covers wasting assets that are not chattels as they are not tangible and/or not movable (e.g. a copyright). The allowable expenditure on these assets is deemed to waste away over the life of the asset on a straight line basis.

Consequently, when a disposal is made:

- the allowable expenditure is restricted to take account of the asset's natural fall in value

- the asset's fall in value is deemed to occur on a straight line basis over its predictable useful life

- the allowable cost is calculated as:

$$\text{Cost} \times \frac{\text{Remaining life at disposal}}{\text{Estimated useful life}}$$

Illustration 10 – Other wasting assets – Ian

On 1 February 2011 Ian bought a wasting asset (that is not a chattel) at a cost of £24,000. It had an estimated useful life of 30 years. He sold the asset for £38,000 on 1 February 2021.

Calculate the chargeable gain or allowable loss arising.

Solution

	£
Sale proceeds	38,000
Less: Allowable element of acquisition cost (W)	(16,000)
	———
Chargeable gain	22,000
	———

Working: Allowable element of acquisition cost

Remaining life at disposal = 20 years

Estimated useful life = 30 years

Allowable cost = £24,000 × 20/30 = £16,000

Test your understanding 8

On 1 March 2016 Jan bought a wasting asset (which is not a chattel) at a cost of £19,000. It had an estimated useful life of 40 years. She sold the asset for £30,000 on 1 March 2021.

Calculate the chargeable gain or allowable loss arising.

Wasting assets – summary

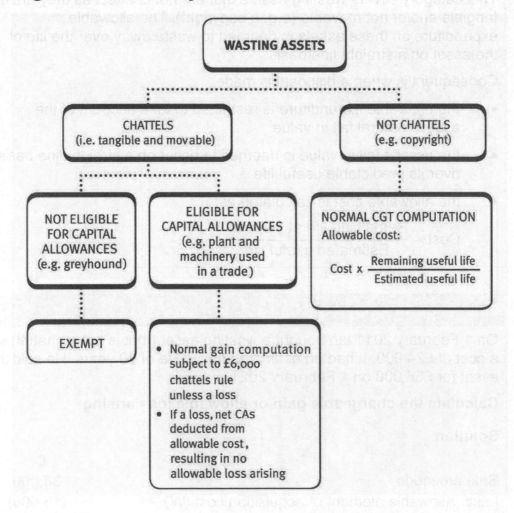

4 Assets lost or destroyed or damaged

A capital transaction usually has two parties, a buyer and a seller.

However, when an asset is damaged, destroyed or lost and the asset's owner receives compensation (either from the perpetrator or an insurance company) the position is different. The owner has received a capital sum without disposing of the asset and the payer has received nothing in return. Consequently, a special set of rules is required.

The rules vary according to whether:

- the asset has been completely lost/destroyed or merely damaged

- the owner has replaced or restored the asset.

Asset lost or destroyed

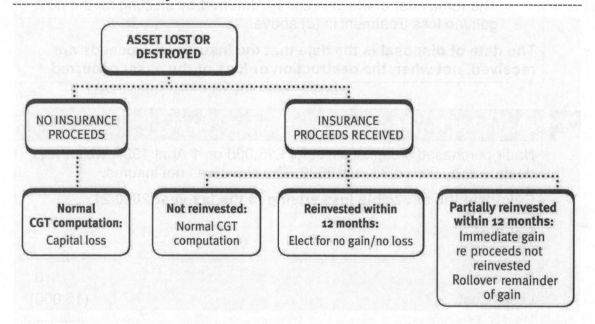

Assets lost or destroyed

There is a deemed disposal for capital gains tax purposes as follows:

(a) **No insurance proceeds**

Compute a capital loss using the normal CGT computation:

– Disposal proceeds are £Nil.

– Deduction of the allowable expenditure will create a loss.

(b) **Insurance proceeds received – no replacement of asset**

Chargeable gain/loss is computed using the normal CGT computation pro forma.

(c) **Insurance proceeds received – asset replaced within 12 months**

The taxpayer can claim that the destruction/loss of the asset is treated as a no gain/no loss disposal (as for transfers between spouses/civil partners).

If the insurance proceeds are greater than the deemed disposal proceeds under the no gain/no loss computation, the excess is deducted from the replacement asset's allowable cost.

(d) **Insurance proceeds received – partially used to replace asset within 12 months**

There is an immediate chargeable gain in respect of the excess proceeds that are not reinvested in the replacement asset.

The remainder of the gain can be deferred by electing for the no gain/no loss treatment in (c) above.

The date of disposal is the date that the insurance proceeds are received, not when the destruction or loss of the asset occurred.

Illustration 11 – Assets lost or destroyed – Nadir

Nadir purchased a capital asset for £15,000 on 1 April 1997, which was destroyed by fire on 31 July 2020. The asset was not insured.

Calculate the allowable loss arising in the tax year 2020/21.

Solution

	£
Proceeds	0
Less: Cost	(15,000)
Allowable loss	(15,000)

Illustration 12 – Assets lost or destroyed – Padma

Padma purchased an antique table for £35,000 on 1 May 1999, which was destroyed by fire on 30 June 2020. She received insurance proceeds of £50,000 on 1 September 2020. She did not replace the table.

Calculate the chargeable gain arising in the tax year 2020/21.

Solution

	£
Insurance proceeds	50,000
Less: Cost	(35,000)
Chargeable gain	15,000

Illustration 13 – Assets lost or destroyed – Silvio

Silvio purchased a painting for £57,000 on 1 June 2000 which was destroyed in a fire on 31 July 2020. He received insurance proceeds of £50,000 on 1 September 2020. He did not replace the painting.

Calculate the allowable loss arising in the tax year 2020/21.

Solution

	£
Insurance proceeds	50,000
Less: Cost	(57,000)
Allowable loss	(7,000)

Illustration 14 – Assets lost or destroyed – Bill

Bill purchased an asset for £25,000 on 1 October 1997, which was destroyed by fire on 30 September 2020. He received compensation of £35,000 from his insurance company on 1 January 2021. He purchased a replacement asset for £40,000 on 1 February 2021.

Assuming that Bill claims the loss by fire to be a no gain/no loss disposal, calculate the allowable expenditure (base cost) of the replacement asset.

Solution

	£	£
Cost of replacement asset		40,000
Less: Compensation	35,000	
Less: Deemed disposal proceeds of old asset (W)	(25,000)	
		(10,000)
Replacement asset base cost		30,000

Working – deemed disposal proceeds

Since the disposal of the old asset is assumed to be on a no gain/no loss basis. The disposal proceeds are the allowable cost of the asset.

Allowable cost = Deemed disposal proceeds   £25,000

Illustration 15 – Assets lost or destroyed – Belinda

Belinda purchased an antique necklace for £21,140 on 1 October 2003, which she lost on 30 June 2015. She received compensation of £45,000 from her insurance company on 1 October 2015 and purchased a replacement necklace for £50,000 on 1 November 2015.

She sold the replacement necklace for £65,000 on 1 March 2021.

Assuming that Belinda claims the loss of the necklace to be a no gain/no loss disposal, calculate the chargeable gain arising on the sale of the replacement necklace on 1 March 2021.

Solution

	£
Sale proceeds	65,000
Less: Cost (W)	(26,140)
Chargeable gain	38,860

Working – Replacement asset base cost

	£	£
Cost of replacement necklace		50,000
Less: Insurance proceeds	45,000	
Less: Deemed disposal proceeds of lost necklace		
= Base cost	(21,140)	
		(23,860)
Replacement asset base cost		26,140

Illustration 16 – Asset lost or destroyed – Esa

Esa purchased a holiday cottage for £83,040 on 4 May 2008, which was destroyed in a hurricane on 27 October 2019. He received insurance proceeds of £113,000 on 5 June 2020 and purchased a replacement holiday apartment for £103,440.

Assuming that Esa claims to defer the gain arising from the insurance proceeds, calculate any gain arising in the tax year 2020/21 and state the base cost of the replacement apartment.

Solution

	£
Insurance proceeds	113,000
Less: Cost	(83,040)
	─────
	29,960
Gain deferred (balancing figure)	(20,400)
	─────
Chargeable gain (proceeds not reinvested)	
((£113,000 – £103,440)	9,560
	─────
Base cost of holiday apartment:	
Purchase price	103,440
Less: Deferred gain	(20,400)
	─────
	83,040
	─────

Asset damaged

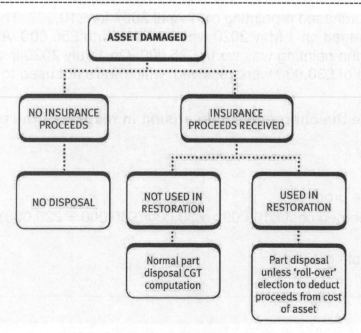

Asset damaged

There are no implications for capital gains tax purposes unless compensation (e.g. insurance proceeds) is received.

Where an asset is damaged and compensation is received there is a part disposal for capital gains tax purposes.

The allowable cost is calculated using the normal part disposal formula:

Cost × A/A + B

Where: A = Compensation received

B = Market value of the remainder at the time of the part disposal (i.e. value in its damaged condition).

The computation is varied depending on how the insurance proceeds are applied.

(a) **Proceeds not used in restoration work**

Normal part disposal capital gains computation is used. The value of the part retained is the value of the asset in its damaged condition.

(b) **Proceeds fully used in restoration work**

Where all of the insurance proceeds are used in restoring the asset the taxpayer may claim to deduct the proceeds from the cost of the asset rather than be treated as having made a part disposal of the asset.

This is a form of rollover relief (see Chapter 22).

Illustration 17 – Asset damaged – Sasha

Sasha purchased a painting on 1 April 2007 for £10,000. The painting was damaged on 1 May 2020 when it was worth £50,000. After the damage the painting was worth £25,000. On 1 July 2020 insurance proceeds of £30,000 were received, which were not used to restore the painting.

Calculate the chargeable gain arising in respect of the painting.

Solution

	£
Insurance proceeds	30,000
Less: Deemed cost £10,000 × £30,000/(£30,000 + £25,000)	(5,455)
Chargeable gain	24,545

Illustration 18 – Asset damaged – Amy

Amy purchased a painting on 1 April 2007 for £10,000. The painting was damaged on 1 May 2020 when it was worth £50,000. After the damage the painting was worth £40,000. On 1 July 2020 insurance proceeds of £8,000 were received. All of the proceeds were used immediately to restore the painting.

Assuming Amy elects for the insurance proceeds to be rolled over against the cost of the painting, calculate the revised base cost for CGT purposes of the painting after it has been restored.

Solution

There is no part disposal and the revised base cost of the painting is:

	£
Original cost	10,000
Plus: Restoration expenditure	8,000
Less: Insurance proceeds	(8,000)
Revised base cost	10,000

Note that when the amount spent on restoring the asset is the same as the insurance proceeds then the revised base cost is the same as the original cost.

Illustration 19 – Asset damaged – Sari

Sari purchased a commercial investment property on 1 May 2009 for £200,000. In June 2020 it was damaged by fire. On 1 August 2020 insurance proceeds of £100,000 were received. On 1 September 2020 £110,000 was spent on restoring the property. After the restoration the property was worth £500,000.

Assuming Sari elects for the insurance proceeds to be rolled over against the cost of the property calculate the revised base cost for CGT purposes of the property after it has been restored.

Solution

As the proceeds are fully used in restoration and the 'rollover' election is made, there is no part disposal and the revised base cost is:

	£
Original cost	200,000
Plus: Restoration expenditure	110,000
Less: Insurance proceeds	(100,000)
Revised base cost	210,000

5 Chapter summary

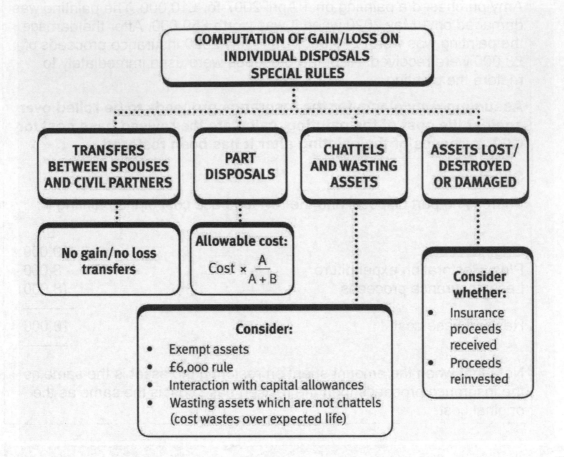

6   Practice objective test questions

Test your understanding 9

Denis bought 20 hectares of land on 13 September 2019 for £30,000. On 22 November 2020, Denis sold 10 hectares for £60,000 and the market value of the remaining land at that time was £15,000.

What is Denis' chargeable gain arising on the disposal of the land in November 2020?

A   £30,000

B   £24,000

C   £45,000

D   £36,000

Test your understanding 10

Laticia makes the following capital disposals in the tax year 2020/21:

1   A machine, which she used for business purposes, that was purchased for £8,000 and sold for £10,000.

2   A greyhound which was purchased for £7,000 and sold for £15,000.

3   A painting that was purchased for £4,000 and sold for £7,500.

4   Land that was purchased for £1,000 and sold for £5,200.

Which of these capital disposals are chargeable to capital gains tax?

A   1, 2 and 3

B   1 and 4 only

C   3 and 4 only

D   1, 3 and 4

Test your understanding 11

Nikhil purchased a valuable painting which was destroyed in a fire. He received compensation from his insurance company but did not purchase a replacement.

The transaction is treated as follows:

A   No gain arises as there is no disposal

B   The transaction is treated as a disposal at no gain/no loss

C   The value of the insurance proceeds received are treated as a chargeable gain

D   A gain/loss is computed using the normal chargeable gains rules

Test your understanding 12

Gaynor sold an antique vase for £7,800 in July 2020, incurring an auctioneer's fee of 1% of the gross sales value. She bought the vase in December 2011 for £2,300.

What is Gaynor's chargeable gain?

A   Nothing, the transaction is exempt from capital gains tax

B   £5,422

C   £5,500

D   £3,000

Test your understanding answers

Test your understanding 1

Tania

Capital gains tax computation – 2020/21

	£
Disposal proceeds	350,300
Less: Deemed acquisition cost	(100,000)
Chargeable gain	250,300
Less: AEA	(12,300)
Less: Capital losses b/f	(11,800)
Taxable gains	226,200
Capital gains tax payable (£226,200 × 20%)	45,240

Note: Tania's deemed acquisition cost is equal to the deemed proceeds on the transfer from her husband, John. This is equal to his acquisition cost.

Since Tania's taxable income exceeds the basic rate band she is taxed on all her non-residential property gains at 20%.

Test your understanding 2

Jacob

Disposal in January 2021	£	£
Sale proceeds		20,000
Less: Deemed cost of part disposed of		
£8,000 × £20,000/(£20,000 + £60,000)		(2,000)
Enhancement (levelling)		(3,000)
		15,000
Disposal in March 2021		
Sales proceeds	75,600	
Less: Deemed cost of remainder		
(£8,000 – £2,000)	(6,000)	
		69,600
Total chargeable gains		84,600
Less: AEA		(12,300)
Taxable gains		72,300

	£		
Basic rate (W)	19,560	× 10%	1,956
Higher rate	52,740	× 20%	10,548
	72,300		
Capital gains tax liability			12,504
Due date			31.1.2022

Working: Remaining BR band

The question stated Jacob's employment income rather than his taxable income and therefore his taxable income must be calculated to determine the remaining basic rate band.

Taxable income = (£30,440 – £12,500) = £17,940
Remaining BR band = (£37,500 – £17,940) = £19,560.

Test your understanding 3

Gemma

Disposal of the remainder – 2020/21

	£
Sale proceeds	200,600
Less: Deemed cost of remainder (£50,000 – £14,286) (W)	(35,714)
Incidental cost of acquisition (£4,500 – £1,286) (W)	(3,214)
Chargeable gain	161,672
Less: AEA	(12,300)
Taxable gain	149,372
Capital gains tax (£149,372 × 20%) (Note)	29,874

Note: Gemma has no basic rate band remaining, therefore the gains are taxed at 20%.

Working: Allowable expenditure

The allowable expenditure in relation to the part disposal of the land on 1 July 2013 was:

$$£50,000 \times \frac{£40,000}{(£40,000 + £100,000)} = £14,286$$

The allowable incidental costs of acquisition in relation to the part disposal of the land on 1 July 2013 were:

$$£4,500 \times \frac{£40,000}{(£40,000 + £100,000)} = £1,286$$

Test your understanding 4

Exempt disposals	Chargeable disposals
3 Motor car – exempt asset	1 Necklace (deemed proceeds £7,000). Non-wasting chattel not sold and bought for ≤ £6,000
4 Boat – wasting chattel	
5 Painting – non-wasting chattel bought and sold for ≤ £6,000	2 Shares – not chattels (not tangible property)
6 Greyhound – wasting chattel	

Test your understanding 5

Marjory

	Table A £	Table B £
Sale proceeds	6,400	13,600
Less: Cost	(1,000)	(1,000)
Chargeable gains	5,400	12,600
Gains cannot exceed:		
5/3 × (sale proceeds – £6,000)	667	12,667
Decision = take the lower gain	667	12,600

Note: Both tables are chattels and were bought for less than £6,000 and sold for more than £6,000; therefore the 5/3 rule needs to be considered.

Test your understanding 6

Brian

	£
Deemed gross sale proceeds	6,000
Less: Selling costs	(50)
Net sale proceeds	5,950
Less: Cost (including acquisition expenses)	(10,500)
Allowable loss	(4,550)

Note: It is the gross sale proceeds before deducting selling costs that are deemed to be £6,000. The £500 actual sale proceeds received are ignored.

Test your understanding 7

Leyla

Net chargeable gains – 2020/21

Painting	1	2	4
	£	£	£
Sale proceeds	7,000		9,500
Deemed proceeds		6,000	
Less: Cost	(2,000)	(8,000)	(7,000)
Chargeable gain/(allowable loss)	5,000	(2,000)	2,500
Gain cannot exceed			
5/3 × (£7,000 – £6,000)	1,667		

Net chargeable gains (£1,667 – £2,000 + £2,500) = £2,167

Note: Painting 3 is exempt as the cost and proceeds are both less than £6,000.

Test your understanding 8

Jan

	£
Sale proceeds	30,000
Allowable element of acquisition cost (W)	(16,625)
Chargeable gain	13,375

Working: Allowable element of acquisition cost

Remaining life at disposal = 35 years

Estimated useful life = 40 years

Allowable cost = £19,000 × 35/40 = £16,625

Test your understanding 9

Denis

The correct answer is D.

	£
Proceeds	60,000
Less: Cost	
$£30,000 \times \dfrac{60,000}{(60,000 + 15,000)}$	(24,000)
Chargeable gain	36,000

Test your understanding 10

Laticia

The correct answer is D.

A The machine, although a wasting asset, is chargeable as it qualifies for capital allowances.

B The greyhound is a wasting chattel and therefore exempt.

C The painting is a non-wasting chattel and was sold for more than £6,000. The gain will be restricted using the 5/3 rule, however it is still chargeable.

D The land, although bought and sold for less than £6,000 is not movable property and therefore not a chattel.

Test your understanding 11

Nikhil

The correct answer is D.

D is the correct answer because there is a disposal. If the proceeds are not used to replace the asset, then a normal gain/loss is computed.

Test your understanding 12

Gaynor

The correct answer is D.

The asset qualifies as a chattel, but is not a wasting chattel, and therefore is not exempt.

As the chattel has been sold for more than £6,000 but purchased for less than £6,000, the eventual gain should be restricted to 5/3 × (gross sale proceeds – £6,000), as follows:

	£
Gross sale proceeds	7,800
Less: Auctioneer's fee	(78)
Less: Allowable costs	(2,300)
Capital gain	5,422

Restricted to: 5/3 × (£7,800 – £6,000) = £3,000

CGT: Shares and securities for individuals

Chapter learning objectives

Upon completion of this chapter you will be able to:

- recognise the value of quoted shares where they are disposed of by way of a gift

- explain and apply the identification rules as they apply to individuals including the same day and 30 day matching rules

- explain and apply the pooling provisions

- explain and apply the treatment of bonus issues, rights issues, takeovers and reorganisations

- identify the exemption available for gilt-edged securities and qualifying corporate bonds.

One of the PER performance objectives (PO15) is to prepare computations of taxable amounts and tax liabilities according to legal requirements. Working through this chapter should help you understand how to demonstrate that objective.

PER

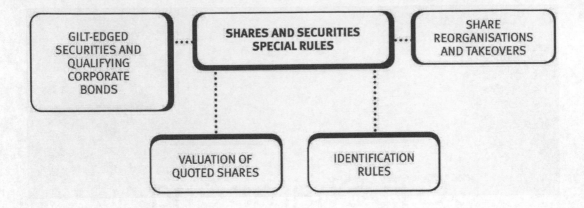

 You will have learned about the issue of shares by a company and the impact of a bonus and rights issue from an accounting perspective in Financial Accounting. In this chapter we will look at the impact on individuals when they look to dispose of a shareholding, either for cash or as part of a takeover transaction.

Introduction

The basic chargeable gain computation is used as normal on a disposal of shares or securities. However, because shares in the same company are indistinguishable from each other there are special rules to identify the allowable cost.

This chapter covers the rules as they apply to disposals by an individual.

1 Government securities and qualifying corporate bonds

All shares and securities disposed of by an individual are subject to capital gains tax except for the following, which are exempt:

- listed government securities (gilt-edged securities or gilts)
- qualifying corporate bonds (e.g. company loan notes)
- shares held in an Individual Savings Account (ISA).

Definition of a qualifying corporate bond

A qualifying corporate bond (QCB) is one that:

(a) represents a normal commercial loan

(b) is expressed in sterling and has no provision for either conversion into, or redemption in, any other currency, and

(c) was issued after 13 March 1984 or was acquired by the disposer after that date (whenever it was issued).

Test your understanding 1

Which of the following shares and securities are exempt assets for CGT purposes when disposed of by an individual?

1   £1 ordinary shares in the unquoted property development company, Sealand Ltd.

2   10½% Exchequer Stock 2022.

3   10% preference shares in the quoted trading company, Ace plc.

4   6% loan note issued by Amble plc in 2014.

2   Valuation of quoted shares

On a sale of shares between unconnected parties, the actual proceeds are used in the capital gains computation.

However, it is necessary to identify the market value of quoted shares when shares are either:

* gifted

* transferred to a connected party.

For capital gains tax purposes, their market value is determined by taking the mid-price (i.e. average) of the prices quoted in the Stock Exchange Daily Official List on the disposal date.

Illustration 1 – Valuation of quoted shares

The shares in XYZ plc are quoted in the Stock Exchange Daily Official List at 230p – 270p.

If a disposal of XYZ plc shares were made on that day to a connected party, what would their value be for CGT purposes?

Solution

The value of XYZ plc shares is 250p, being the:

Average of the two quoted prices
(270p + 230p) × ½   250p
                                                                        ‾‾‾‾

Test your understanding 2

The shares in Sawyer plc are quoted in the Stock Exchange Daily Official List at 460p – 540p.

If a gift of Sawyer plc shares were made on that day, what would their value be for CGT purposes?

3 Identification rules

It is necessary to have identification (or matching) rules to determine which shares have been disposed of as:

- Shares and securities that are bought in a particular company of the same class are not distinguishable from one another.

- Each time shares are bought in any quoted company the price paid may be different.

- They enable you to decide which shares have been sold and to work out the allowable cost to use in the capital gains computation.

Identification rules for disposals by individuals

When shares are disposed of they are matched against shares acquired of the same class in the following order:

- Same day as the date of disposal.

- Within **following** 30 days.

- The share pool (shares acquired before the date of disposal are pooled together).

 Shares acquired within the following 30 days

It may appear strange that a disposal is matched with acquisitions following the date of sale. The reason for this is to counter a practice known as 'bed and breakfasting'.

Without this 30 day matching rule, shares could be sold at the close of business one day and then bought back at the opening of business the next day. A gain or loss would be established without making a genuine disposal of the shares.

This was useful for an individual to establish:

- a capital loss (e.g. in the same tax year that he or she has chargeable gains), or

- a capital gain to use his or her AEA, if it had not been used already, and effectively reacquire the same shares with a higher base cost for future disposals.

The 30 day matching rule makes the practice of 'bed and breakfasting' much more difficult, since the subsequent reacquisition of shares cannot take place within 30 days.

Illustration 2 – Identification rules

Frederic had the following transactions in the shares of DEF plc, a quoted company.

			£
1 June 2003	Bought	4,000 shares for	8,000
30 July 2007	Bought	1,800 shares for	9,750
30 April 2012	Bought	500 shares for	4,000
20 May 2017	Bought	1,000 shares for	8,500
15 March 2021	Sold	3,500 shares for	36,000
28 March 2021	Bought	800 shares for	6,400

Identify with which acquisitions the shares sold on 15 March 2021 will be matched.

Solution

	Number of shares
Shares sold	3,500
1 Shares acquired on same day	(0)
2 Shares acquired in following 30 days	
28 March 2021	(800)
	2,700
3 Share pool	
(Shares pre 15 March 2021))	
1 June 2003	4,000
30 July 2007	1,800
30 April 2012	500
20 May 2017	1,000
	7,300

The disposal from the share pool is therefore 2,700 out of 7,300 shares

	(2,700)
	0

The share pool

For an individual, the share pool contains shares in the same company, of the same class purchased before the date of disposal.

- The share pool simply keeps a record of the number of shares acquired and sold and the cost of those shares.

- When shares are disposed of out of the share pool, the appropriate proportion of the cost which relates to the shares disposed of is calculated. The shares are disposed of at their average cost.

  Thus if there are 6,000 shares in the pool with a cost of £8,000 and 2,000 shares are disposed of:

  - the cost of the shares removed is £2,667 ((2,000/6,000) × £8,000).

4 Calculating the gain/loss on the disposal of shares

Once the identification rules have been used to identify which shares have been disposed of, the cost of those shares is used in the normal chargeable gains computation.

Illustration 3 – Calculating the gain/loss on the disposal of shares

Frances sold 11,000 ordinary shares in Hastings Co plc, a quoted company, on 18 December 2020 for £50,000. She had bought ordinary shares in the company on the following dates.

	Number of shares	Cost £
6 April 2005	8,000	7,450
12 December 2013	4,000	5,500
10 January 2021	2,000	6,000

Calculate the chargeable gain arising on the disposal of shares.

Solution

Capital gains computation – 2020/21

Stage 1   Use identification rules to identify the shares disposed of

	Number
Shares sold	11,000
1 Acquired on same day	(0)
2 Acquired in following 30 days: 10 January 2021	(2,000)
	9,000
3 Share pool (9,000 out of 12,000 shares)	(9,000)
	0

Stage 2   Calculate the chargeable gain arising on each of the individual parcels of shares disposed of

(a) **Shares acquired on 10 January 2021**   £
    Sale proceeds (2,000/11,000 × £50,000)   9,091
    Less: Acquisition cost   (6,000)

    Chargeable gain   3,091

(b) **Shares in the share pool**   £
    Sale proceeds (9,000/11,000 × £50,000)   40,909
    Less: Acquisition cost (W)   (9,713)

    Chargeable gain   31,196

    Total chargeable gains   34,287

Working: Share pool

	Number	**Cost**
		£
Acquisition – 6 April 2005	8,000	7,450
Acquisition – 12 December 2013	4,000	5,500
	12,000	12,950
Disposal – 18 December 2020 (9,000/12,000) × £12,950 (Note)	(9,000)	(9,713)
Balance carried forward	3,000	3,237

Note: The 'average cost' method is used to calculate the cost removed from the share pool on the disposal.

Test your understanding 3

Zoe purchased 2,000 shares in XYZ Ltd on 16 April 2002 for £10,000.

In addition she acquired 1,500 shares in the company on 30 April 2016 for £18,000, and 500 shares on 31 May 2016 for £7,000. On 10 February 2021, Zoe bought a further 200 shares in XYZ Ltd for £3,600.

Zoe sold 3,500 shares in XYZ Ltd on 31 January 2021 for £70,000.

Calculate Zoe's chargeable gain on the disposal of shares.

5 Bonus issues and rights issues

Bonus issues

A bonus issue is the distribution of free shares to shareholders based on their existing shareholding.

For capital gains tax purposes they are treated as follows:

- For the purposes of the share identification rules the bonus shares acquired are included in the share pool at nil cost.

- The bonus shares are not treated as a separate holding of shares.

 Illustration 4 – Bonus issues

Blackburn had the following transactions in the shares of Gray Ltd:

January 2016	Purchased 3,500 shares for £7,350
May 2016	Purchased 500 shares for £1,750
June 2017	Bonus issue of one for five
September 2020	Sold 2,600 shares for £10,400

Calculate the chargeable gain arising on the disposal.

Solution

	£
Sale proceeds	10,400
Less: Cost (Working)	(4,929)
Chargeable gain	5,471

Working: Share pool

		Number	Cost £
January 2016	Purchase	3,500	7,350
May 2016	Purchase	500	1,750
		4,000	9,100
June 2017	Bonus issue (1:5)	800	0
		4,800	9,100
September 2020 Sale (2,600/4,800) × £9,100		(2,600)	(4,929)
Balance c/f		2,200	4,171

Test your understanding 4

Odval had the following transactions in Black plc shares:

January 2012	Purchased 3,000 shares for £6,000
May 2016	Bonus issue of one for three
June 2017	Purchased 500 shares for £1,500
February 2021	Sold 3,000 shares for £12,000

Calculate the chargeable gain arising on the disposal.

Rights issues

A rights issue is the offer of new shares to existing shareholders only, in proportion to their existing shareholding, usually at a price below the current market price.

Rights issues are similar in concept to bonus issues, however because money is paid for the new shares there are additional factors to consider:

- As for bonus issues, for the purposes of the share identification rules the rights shares acquired are included in the share pool.

- For the purposes of TX the number and cost of shares are included in the pool, in the same way as a normal purchase.

Illustration 5 – Rights issue

Carmichael had the following transactions in Rudderham Ltd shares:

January 2015	Purchased 2,700 shares for £5,400
May 2016	Purchased 600 shares for £1,500
June 2017	Took up 1 for 3 rights issue at £2.30 per share
August 2020	Sold 4,000 shares for £14,000

Calculate the chargeable gain on the disposal.

Solution

	£
Sale proceeds	14,000
Less: Cost (Working)	(8,573)
Chargeable gain	5,427

Working: Share pool		Number	Cost £
January 2015	Purchase	2,700	5,400
May 2016	Purchase	600	1,500
		3,300	6,900
June 2017	Rights issue (1:3) @ £2.30 per share	1,100	2,530
		4,400	9,430
August 2020	Sale (4,000/4,400) × £9,430	(4,000)	(8,573)
Balance c/f		400	857

Test your understanding 5

Victor had the following transactions in the ordinary shares of Victorious Vulcanising plc, a quoted company:

April 2007	Purchased 1,000 shares for £11,000
September 2019	Rights issue of 1 for 2 at £6 each
August 2020	Sold 1,200 shares for £46,000

Calculate Victor's chargeable gain on the sale of shares.

6 Reorganisations and takeovers

Definitions

A reorganisation involves the exchange of existing shares in a company for other shares of another class in the same company.

A takeover occurs when one company acquires the shares in another company either in exchange for shares in itself, cash, or a mixture of both.

Consideration: shares for shares

Where the consideration for the reorganisation or takeover only involves the issue of shares in the acquiring company, the tax consequences are:

- No CGT is charged at the time of the reorganisation/takeover.
- The cost of the original shares becomes the cost of the new shares.

- Where the shareholder receives more than one type of share in exchange for the original shares, the cost of the original shares is allocated to the new shares by reference to the market values of the various new shares on the first day of dealing in them.

This treatment is **automatic**.

Illustration 6 – Reorganisations and takeovers

Emina purchased 2,000 ordinary shares in Blue plc for £5,000 in June 2009. In July 2016, Blue plc underwent a reorganisation and Emina received two 'A' ordinary shares in exchange for each of her ordinary shares.

In December 2020, Emina sold all of her holding of 'A' ordinary shares for £8,000.

Calculate the chargeable gain arising on the disposal.

Solution

	£
Sale proceeds	8,000
Less: Cost (Note)	(5,000)
	———
Chargeable gain	3,000
	———

Note: The cost of the original ordinary shares (£5,000) becomes the cost of the new 'A' ordinary shares.

Illustration 7 – Reorganisations and takeovers

In July 2020, Craig sold his entire holding of ordinary shares in Corus plc for £75,000. Craig had originally purchased 20,000 £1 ordinary shares in BNB plc at a cost of £20,000 in April 2008.

In July 2011, BNB plc was taken over by Corus plc. Craig received one ordinary 50p share and one 50p 6% preference share in Corus plc for each ordinary share he held in BNB plc.

Immediately after the takeover the values of these new shares were quoted as:

50p ordinary share	£1.80 each
50p preference shares	£0.80 each

Compute the chargeable gain arising on the disposal.

Solution

	£
Sale proceeds	75,000
Less: Allocated acquisition cost (W)	(13,846)
Chargeable gain	61,154

Working: Acquisition cost

Following the takeover in July 2011 of BNB plc by Corus plc, Craig now owns the following shares in Corus plc as per the terms of the takeover:

	Total MV	Original cost
	£	£
20,000 50p ordinary shares @ £1.80	36,000	13,846
20,000 50p preference shares @ £0.80	16,000	6,154
	52,000	20,000

Allocate the original cost incurred in April 2008 to the shares now owned in July 2011, using the normal average cost method.

(£36,000/£52,000) × £20,000 = £13,846

(£16,000/£52,000) × £20,000 = £6,154

Test your understanding 6

In June 2016, Marie purchased 2,000 ordinary shares in Black Ltd for £5,000. In July 2017 Black Ltd was taken over by Red plc, and Marie received 2 ordinary shares and 1 preference share in Red plc for each ordinary share in Black Ltd.

Immediately after the takeover the ordinary shares in Red plc were valued at £2 and the preference shares in Red plc were valued at £1.

In December 2020, Marie sold all her holding of ordinary shares in Red plc for £11,000.

Calculate the chargeable gain arising on the disposal.

Takeovers: consideration in cash and shares

If the consideration for the takeover includes a cash element:

- there is a part disposal of the original shares

- a gain arises on the cash element of the consideration on the date the cash is received.

Cash proceeds – part disposal computation

In these circumstances the part of the cost of the original holding apportioned to the cash is calculated as:

$$\frac{\text{Cash received}}{\text{Cash received} + \text{M.V. of new shares}} \times \text{Cost of original shares}$$

Illustration 8 – Reorganisations and takeovers

Patrick bought 10,000 shares in Target plc in May 2011 for £20,000. On 3 November 2020, the entire share capital of Target plc was acquired by Bidder plc. Target plc shareholders received 2 Bidder plc shares and £0.50 cash for each share held. Bidder plc shares were quoted at £1.25.

Calculate the chargeable gain as a result of the takeover in November 2020.

Solution

The total consideration provided by Bidder plc is:

	MV £	Cost £
Shares (10,000 × 2 × £1.25)	25,000	16,667
Cash (10,000 × 1 × £0.50)	5,000	3,333
	30,000	20,000

As Patrick has received part of the consideration in cash he has made a part disposal of the original shares.

	£
Disposal proceeds (cash)	5,000
Less: Deemed cost (£5,000/£30,000) × £20,000	(3,333)
Chargeable gain	1,667

Patrick's allowable cost on the future disposal of his shares in Bidder plc will be £16,667.

Test your understanding 7

Paula bought 25,000 shares in Tiny plc in May 2012 for £20,000. On 3 October 2020 the entire share capital of Tiny plc was acquired by Big plc. Tiny plc shareholders received 2 Big plc shares and £1.20 cash for each share held. Big plc shares were quoted at £1.75.

Calculate the chargeable gain as a result of the takeover in October 2020 and state the allowable cost of Paula's shares in Big plc.

7 Chapter summary

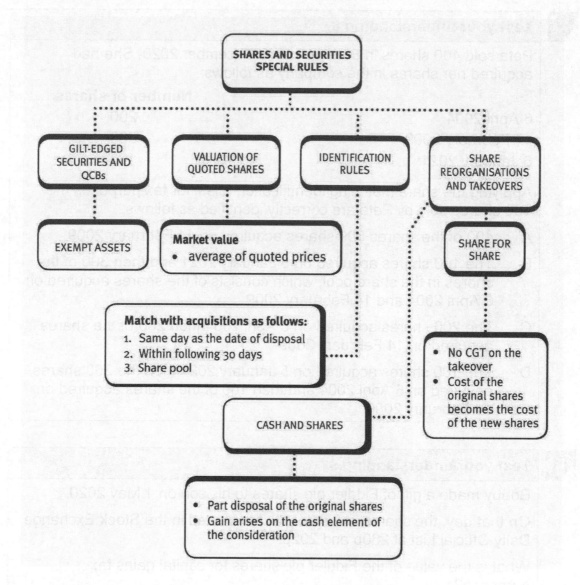

SHARES AND SECURITIES SPECIAL RULES

GILT-EDGED SECURITIES AND QCBs

VALUATION OF QUOTED SHARES

IDENTIFICATION RULES

SHARE REORGANISATIONS AND TAKEOVERS

EXEMPT ASSETS

Market value
- average of quoted prices

SHARE FOR SHARE

Match with acquisitions as follows:
1. Same day as the date of disposal
2. Within following 30 days
3. Share pool

- No CGT on the takeover
- Cost of the original shares becomes the cost of the new shares

CASH AND SHARES

- Part disposal of the original shares
- Gain arises on the cash element of the consideration

8 Practice objective test questions

Test your understanding 8

Peta sold 400 shares in Blue plc on 13 December 2020. She had acquired her shares in the company as follows:

	Number of shares
6 April 2004	200
14 February 2009	500
5 January 2021	100

Applying the share matching/identification rules, for tax purposes the 400 shares sold by Peta are correctly identified as follows:

A   400 of the shares 500 shares acquired on 14 February 2009

B   The 100 shares acquired on 5 January 2021 and then 300 of the shares in the share pool, which consists of the shares acquired on 6 April 2004 and 14 February 2009

C   The 200 shares acquired on 6 April 2004 then 200 of the shares acquired on 14 February 2009

D   The 100 shares acquired on 5 January 2021 then the 200 shares acquired on 6 April 2004 and then 100 of the shares acquired on 14 February 2009

Test your understanding 9

Bobby made a gift of Fiddler plc shares to his son on 1 May 2020.

On that day, the shares in Fiddler plc are quoted in the Stock Exchange Daily Official List at 260p and 292p.

What is the value of the Fiddler plc shares for capital gains tax purposes?

A   276p

B   268p

C   260p

D   292p

Test your understanding 10

Polina sold 1,000 shares in XY plc on 14 May 2020 for £7,400. Her other dealings in these shares were as follows:

12 January 2020	Purchased 1,000 shares	£5,100
20 May 2020	Purchased 1,500 shares	£10,000

What is Polina's chargeable gain on the disposal of his XY plc shares?

A £2,300

B £1,360

C £733

D £6,667

Test your understanding answers

Test your understanding 1

Exempt shares and securities

10½% Exchequer Stock 2022 is a government security and the 6% loan note is a qualifying corporate bond. Both of these are exempt assets for CGT purposes.

Test your understanding 2

Sawyer plc

The value of the shares in Sawyer plc would be the average of the two quoted prices on the date of disposal:

= (540p + 460p) × 1/2 = 500p

The value is therefore 500p or £5.00 per share.

Test your understanding 3

Zoe

(a) **Match with acquisitions within following 30 days (10 February 2021) (200 shares)**

	£
Sale proceeds (£70,000 × 200/3,500)	4,000
Less: Purchase price	(3,600)
Chargeable gain	400

(b) **Match with acquisitions in the share pool (balance of 3,300 shares)**

	£
Sale proceeds (£70,000 × 3,300/3,500)	66,000
Less: Purchase price (W)	(28,875)
Chargeable gain	37,125
Total chargeable gains (£400 + £37,125)	37,525

Working – Share pool

		Number	Cost £
Acquisitions			
16.4.02		2,000	10,000
30.4.16		1,500	18,000
31.5.16		500	7,000
		4,000	35,000
Sale 31.1.21 (£35,000 × (3,300/4,000))		(3,300)	(28,875)
Balance carried forward		700	6,125

Test your understanding 4

Odval

	£
Sale proceeds	12,000
Less: Cost (Working)	(5,000)
Chargeable gain	7,000

Working: Share pool

		Number	Cost £
January 2012	Purchase	3,000	6,000
May 2016	Bonus issue (1:3)	1,000	0
June 2017	Purchase	500	1,500
		4,500	7,500
February 2021	Sale	(3,000)	(5,000)
Balance c/f		1,500	2,500

Test your understanding 5

Victor

		£
Sale proceeds		46,000
Less: Cost (Working)		(11,200)
Chargeable gain		34,800

Working:

Share pool

		Number	Cost £
April 2007	Purchase	1,000	11,000
September 2019	Rights issue (1:2) @ £6 per share	500	3,000
		1,500	14,000
August 2020	Sale (1,200/1,500) × £14,000	(1,200)	(11,200)
Balance c/f		300	2,800

Test your understanding 6

Marie

Chargeable gains computation – 2020/21

	£
Sale proceeds	11,000
Less: Cost (W)	(4,000)
Chargeable gain	7,000

Working – Cost of ordinary shares in Red plc

	MV £	Cost £
Marie received		
4,000 ordinary shares, valued at (4,000 × £2)	8,000	4,000
2,000 preference shares, valued at (2,000 × £1)	2,000	1,000
	10,000	5,000

Notes:

Cost attributable to the ordinary shares is calculated as:
(£8,000/£10,000 × £5,000) = £4,000

The cost of the preference shares of £1,000 (£2,000/£10,000 × £5,000) is carried forward until those shares are disposed of.

Test your understanding 7

Paula

The total consideration provided by Big plc is:

	MV £	Cost £
Shares (25,000 × 2 × £1.75)	87,500	14,894
Cash (25,000 × 1 × £1.20)	30,000	5,106
	117,500	20,000

Paula has made a part disposal on 3 October 2020 in relation to the cash consideration.

	£
Disposal proceeds (cash)	30,000
Less: Original cost (£30,000/£117,500 × £20,000)	(5,106)
Chargeable gain	24,894

Paula's allowable cost on the future disposal of her shares in Big plc will be £14,894.

Test your understanding 8

The correct answer is B.

The share identification rules match shares in the following order:

- Shares acquired on the same day as the disposal – not applicable here.

- Shares acquired in the following 30 days
  - 100 shares acquired on 5 January 2021.

- Shares in the share pool
  - 300 of the shares acquired on 6 April 2004 and 14 February 2009.

Test your understanding 9

The correct answer is A.

Shares are valued at the average of the two quoted prices.

(292 + 260)/2 = 276p

Test your understanding 10

The correct answer is C.

The disposal on 14 May 2020 is matched with shares purchased in the next 30 days.

	£
Proceeds	7,400
Less: Cost (1,000/1,500 × £10,000)	(6,667)
Gain	733

CGT: Reliefs for individuals

Chapter learning objectives

Upon completion of this chapter you will be able to:

- calculate the chargeable gain when a private residence is disposed of

- explain and apply business asset disposal relief

- explain and apply investors' relief

- explain and apply capital gains tax reliefs:

    (i) rollover relief

    (ii) holdover relief for the gift of business assets

- basic capital gains tax planning.

PER

One of the PER performance objectives (PO15) is to prepare computations of taxable amounts and tax liabilities according to legal requirements. Another objective (PO17) is to advise on mitigating and deferring tax liabilities through legitimate tax planning measures. Working through this chapter should help you understand how to demonstrate those objectives.

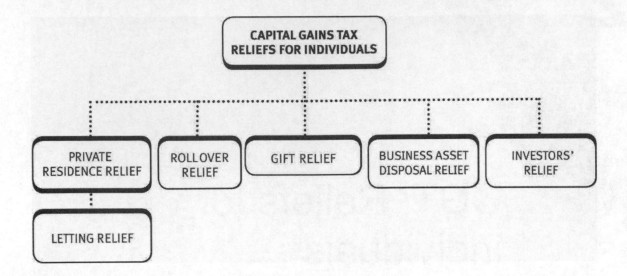

 The availability of CGT reliefs to mitigate an individual's chargeable gains is introduced in this chapter and will be explored further in ATX.

Introduction

In certain situations, the tax payable on the disposal of an asset may be reduced or a gain may be delayed by claiming capital gains tax reliefs.

The main reliefs available to individuals are as follows.

	Relief	Available on the:
Non-business assets	Private residence relief	disposal of an individual's private residence
	Letting relief	disposal of private residence after letting
Business assets	Business asset disposal relief	disposal of certain business assets
	Rollover relief	sale of and reinvestment in certain business assets
	Gift relief	gift of certain business assets
	Investors' relief	disposal of certain shares

1 Private residence relief (PRR)

PRR applies when an individual disposes of:

- a dwelling house (including normally up to half a hectare of adjoining land)
- which has at some time during their ownership been their only or main private residence.

The relief

The relief applies where the main residence has been occupied for either the whole or part of the period of ownership.

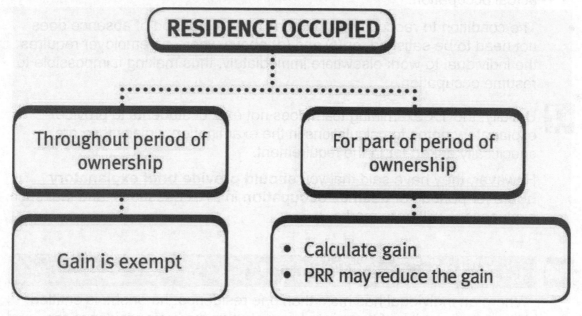

Calculating the relief

Where there has been a period of absence from the main residence the procedure is:

- Calculate the gain on the disposal of the property.
- Compute the total period of ownership.
- Calculate the periods of occupation (see below).
- Calculate the PRR as follows:

    Gain × (Periods of occupation/Total period of ownership)

- Deduct the PRR from the gain on the property.

Periods of occupation

The period of occupation includes periods of both actual occupation and deemed occupation.

Periods of deemed occupation are:

(a) the last nine months of ownership (always exempt, unconditionally)

(b) up to three years of absence for any reason

(c) any period spent living overseas due to employment

(d) up to four years of absence as a result of working elsewhere in the UK (employed or self-employed).

Note that:

• The absences in (b) to (d) must be preceded and followed by a period of actual occupation.

• The condition to reoccupy the property after the period of absence does not need to be satisfied for (c) and (d) above where an employer requires the individual to work elsewhere immediately, thus making it impossible to resume occupation.

 Usually, the TX examining team does not expect students to provide explanatory notes to calculations in the examination, unless they are specifically asked for in the requirement.

However, they have said that you **should provide brief explanatory notes** for periods of **deemed occupation** in PRR questions, and that such explanations will earn marks.

Ownership of more than one residence

Where an individual has more than one residence, he or she is entitled to nominate which of them is to be treated as the main residence for capital gains tax purposes by notifying HMRC in writing.

The election must be made within two years of acquiring an additional residence, otherwise it is open to HMRC, as a question of fact, to decide which residence is the main residence.

Illustration 1 – Private residence relief

On 1 May 1993 Karim purchased a house in Southampton for £25,000. He occupied the house as follows:

	Months
Lived in the house	14
Lived in a rental property in Southampton	27
Employed overseas	12
Lived with relatives	4
Lived in the house	161
Lived in a rental property in Newcastle	115

Karim remained in the rental property in Newcastle until he sold his Southampton house on 1 February 2021 for £95,000.

Calculate the chargeable gain after reliefs, if any, arising on the disposal of the house on 1 February 2021.

Solution

	£
Sale proceeds	95,000
Less: Cost	(25,000)
	———
	70,000
Less: PRR (W)	(47,718)
	———
Chargeable gain after reliefs	22,282
	———

Working – Chargeable and exempt periods of ownership

	Total	Exempt	Chargeable
Lived in house (actual occupation)	14	14	–
Lived in Southampton rental (absent – any reason)	27	27	–
Employed overseas (absent – employed abroad)	12	12	–
Lived with relatives (absent – any reason)	4	4	–
Lived in house (actual occupation)	161	161	–
Lived in Newcastle rental (absent – see note)	106	–	106
Lived in Newcastle rental (final 9 months)	9	9	–
Number of months	333	227	106

Total period of ownership (106 + 227) = 333 months.

Exempt element of gain = (£70,000 × 227/333) = £47,718.

Notes:

1 After Karim left his residence to live in Newcastle he never returned. Consequently the exemption for the remaining 5 months (36 months – 27 months – 4 months) for 'any reason' is not available as there is not actual occupation both before and after the period of absence.

2 In contrast, the final nine months of ownership is always exempt unconditionally, there is no such restriction.

Remember that where a chargeable gain arises on a residential property, such as when a main residence is not fully covered by PRR, then the gain is chargeable at the higher rates of CGT of 18% or 28% depending on the level of the taxpayer's taxable income.

Test your understanding 1

Andrea bought a house on 1 January 1999 and sold it on 30 September 2020 making a gain of £189,000.

She occupied the house as follows:

	Months
Lived in the house	24
Employed overseas	78
Travelled the world	66
Lived in the house	93

Andrea made no other disposals in the tax year 2020/21 and had taxable income of £30,500.

Calculate Andrea's capital gains tax liability for the tax year 2020/21 assuming all available reliefs are claimed.

Business use

Where a house, or part of it, is used wholly and exclusively for business purposes, this part loses its PRR and becomes taxable.

It should be noted that:

- The taxpayer cannot benefit from the rules of deemed occupation for any part of the property used for business purposes.

- However, where part of the property was used for business purposes but was also at any time used as the taxpayer's main residence, the exemption for the last nine months applies to the whole property.

- The nine month exemption does not however apply to any part of the property used for business purposes **throughout** the whole period of ownership.

Illustration 2 – Private residence relief

On 30 June 2020 Alex sold his house for £125,000, resulting in a capital gain of £70,000. The house had been purchased on 1 July 2006, and one of the five rooms had always been used for business purposes.

Calculate the chargeable gain after reliefs arising on the disposal of the house.

Solution

Alex owned the house for 14 years and used 1/5th of the house (one of the five rooms) for business purposes. The nine month exemption does not apply to the part of the property used for business purposes as it has never been used at any time for private purposes.

The chargeable gain is therefore: (£70,000 × 1/5) = £14,000

Alternative approach:

	£
Chargeable gain before reliefs	70,000
Less: PRR (£70,000 × 4/5)	(56,000)
Chargeable gain after reliefs	14,000

Test your understanding 2

On 30 September 2020 Hessa sold her house for £150,000, resulting in a chargeable gain before reliefs of £60,000. The house had been purchased on 1 October 2011, and one of the seven rooms had always been used for business purposes.

Calculate the chargeable gain after reliefs arising on the disposal of the house.

In the TX examination, whilst you will be expected to calculate a chargeable gain after reliefs for a private residence that has also been used for commercial purposes, you will not be expected to calculate the capital gains tax liability for such a mixed use property.

Letting relief

Letting relief is available where an individual's main residence is let out for residential use.

It applies when the owner lets part of the property whilst still occupying the remainder. However, if the owner has one lodger who lives as a member of the owner's family, sharing the accommodation and taking meals with them, then full PRR will be available and letting relief will not be considered.

Letting relief does not apply to let property that is not the owner's main residence (e.g. buy-to-let properties).

Letting relief is the lowest of:

- £40,000
- the amount of the gain exempted by the normal PRR rules
- the part of the gain (still in charge) attributable to the letting period.

Illustration 3 – Letting relief

Nicholas bought a house in Luton on 1 June 1994. He occupied the house as follows:

	Months
Lived in the house	12
Travelled the world	84
Lived in the house	217

Nicholas rented out one quarter of his house in the final period of occupation. The tenant did not share any living space with Nicholas. He sold the house on 1 July 2020 realising a chargeable gain before reliefs of £209,730.

Calculate the chargeable gain after reliefs arising on the sale of the house.

Solution

	£
Chargeable gain before reliefs	209,730
Less: PRR (W1)	(142,724)
	————
Chargeable gain after reliefs	67,006
Less: Letting relief (W2)	(34,843)
	————
Chargeable gain after reliefs	32,163
	————

Workings

1 **PRR**

	Total	Exempt	Chargeable
Lived in house	12		
Actual occupation		12	
Travelled the world	84		
3 years – any reason		36	
Rest of period – chargeable			48
Lived in house	217		
Last 9 months		9	
Rest of period			
– 3/4 actual occupation		156	
– 1/4 let			52
	313	213	100

PRR = (£209,730 × 213/313) = £142,724

Letting relief

One quarter of the house was let in the final chargeable period and therefore, letting relief is available for this period.

Letting relief = lowest of:

(1) Maximum = £40,000

(2) PRR = £142,724

(3) Gain on letting (£209,730 × 52/313) = £34,843   £34,843

An alternative working for the gain on letting is (£67,006 × 52/100) = £34,843. This uses the gain after PRR and only the chargeable months. Either method would be acceptable in the exam.

Test your understanding 3

On 30 September 2020, Eleni made a gift of a house to her grandson, Kostas. The house had been bought by Eleni on 1 September 2007 for £45,000, and was extended at a cost of £10,600 during June 2008. A market value of £140,000 at 30 September 2020 had been agreed by HMRC.

Eleni occupied the house as her main residence until 30 September 2016, a period of 109 months. During this period, Eleni rented out one third of the house for 96 months. The tenant did not share any living space with Eleni.

Eleni then went to live with her sister for the remaining 48 months, until 30 September 2020.

Calculate the chargeable gain after reliefs arising on the gift.

Summary

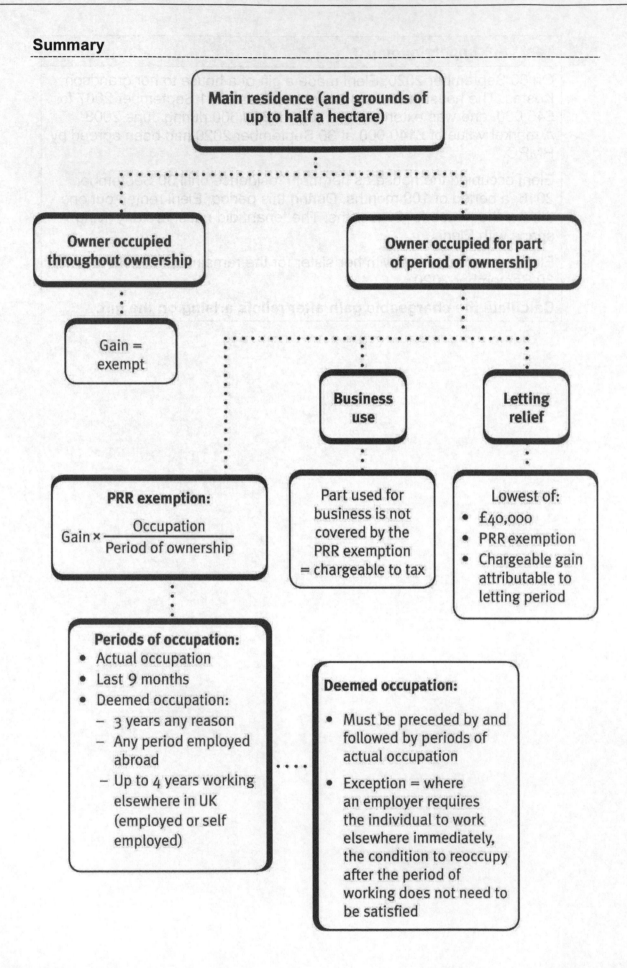

Main residence (and grounds of up to half a hectare)

Owner occupied throughout ownership

Gain = exempt

Owner occupied for part of period of ownership

Business use

Letting relief

PRR exemption:

$$\text{Gain} \times \frac{\text{Occupation}}{\text{Period of ownership}}$$

Part used for business is not covered by the PRR exemption = chargeable to tax

Lowest of:
- £40,000
- PRR exemption
- Chargeable gain attributable to letting period

Periods of occupation:
- Actual occupation
- Last 9 months
- Deemed occupation:
  - 3 years any reason
  - Any period employed abroad
  - Up to 4 years working elsewhere in UK (employed or self employed)

Deemed occupation:

- Must be preceded by and followed by periods of actual occupation

- Exception = where an employer requires the individual to work elsewhere immediately, the condition to reoccupy after the period of working does not need to be satisfied

2 Business asset disposal relief

The rate of tax on business disposals which qualify for business asset disposal relief (BADR) is 10%.

The relief operates as follows:

- The first £1 million of gains on 'qualifying business disposals' is taxed at 10%, regardless of the level of the taxpayer's income.

- Any gains above the £1 million limit are taxed at the usual rate depending on the individual's taxable income.

- Gains qualifying for BADR are set against any unused basic rate band (BRB) before non-qualifying gains.

- The 10% CGT rate is calculated after the deduction of:
  - allowable losses, and
  - the AEA.

- However, the taxpayer can choose to set losses (other than any losses on assets that are part of the disposal of the business) and the AEA against non-qualifying gains first, in order to maximise the relief.

- It is therefore helpful to keep gains which qualify for BADR separate from those which do not qualify.

The relief must be claimed within 12 months of the 31 January following the end of the tax year in which the disposal is made.

For disposals in the tax year 2020/21, the relief must be claimed by 31 January 2023.

The £1 million limit is a lifetime limit which is diminished each time a claim for the relief is made.

Qualifying business disposals

The relief applies to the disposal of:

- the whole or substantial part of a business carried on by the individual either alone or in partnership

- assets of the individual's or partnership's trading business that has **now ceased**

- shares **provided**:
  - the shares are in the individual's 'personal trading company', **and**
  - the individual is an employee of the company (part-time or full-time).

For the purposes of the TX examination an individual's 'personal trading company' is one in which the individual:

- owns at least 5% of the ordinary shares

- which carry at least 5% of the voting rights.

Note that:

- the disposal of an individual business asset used for the purposes of a continuing trade does not qualify. There must be a disposal of the whole of the trading business or a substantial part (meaning part of the business which is capable of separate operation). The sale of an asset in isolation does not qualify.

- Where the disposal is a disposal of assets (i.e. not shares), relief is not available on gains arising from the disposal of those assets held for investment purposes.

- There is no requirement to restrict the gain qualifying for relief on shares by reference to any non-business assets held by the company.

- There are no minimum working hours for an employee to qualify.

Qualifying ownership period

In the case of the disposal of a business it must have been owned by the individual making the disposal in the two years prior to the disposal.

In the case of shares the individual must have been an employee of the company and the company must have been their personal trading company for at least two years prior to the disposal.

Where the disposal is an asset of the individual's or partnership's trading business that has now ceased, the business must have been owned for at least two years prior to the date of cessation and the disposal must also take place within three years of the cessation of trade.

Illustration 4 – Business asset disposal relief

In the tax year 2020/21, Katie sold her trading business which she set up in 2008 and realised the following gains and losses:

	£
Factory	275,000
Goodwill	330,000
Warehouse	(100,000)
Commercial investment property	200,300

Katie also sold her shares in an unquoted trading company and realised a gain of £400,000. She owned 25% of the ordinary shares of the company, which she purchased ten years ago. She has worked for the company on a part time basis for the last three years.

Katie has not made any other capital disposals in the tax year 2020/21, but she has capital losses brought forward of £7,800. She has never claimed any BADR in the past.

Her only source of income is a trading profit of £43,650.

Calculate Katie's capital gains tax payable for the tax year 2020/21.

Solution

	Qualifying for BADR £	Not qualifying for BADR £
Sale of investment property (Note 1)		200,300
Sale of trading business:		
Factory	275,000	
Goodwill	330,000	
Warehouse (Note 2):	(100,000)	
	―――――	
	505,000	
Sale of trading company shares	400,000	
	―――――	―――――
	905,000	200,300
Less: AEA (Note 3)	(0)	(12,300)
Less: Capital losses b/f (Note 3)	(0)	(7,800)
	―――――	―――――
Taxable gains	905,000	180,200
	―――――	―――――
Capital gains tax:		
Qualifying gains (£905,000 × 10%)		90,500
Non-qualifying gains (£180,200 × 20%) (Note 4)		36,040
		―――――
		126,540

Notes:

1   Despite being part of the sale of the whole business, the gain on the investment property does not qualify for BADR as it is held for investment and not business purposes. The property is non-residential and the gain is therefore taxed at normal rates (10% and 20%).

2   The net chargeable gains on the disposal of an unincorporated business qualify for BADR (i.e. the gains after netting off losses arising on the disposal of the business, but excluding investment assets).

3   Capital losses and the AEA are first set against gains not qualifying for BADR.

4   The gains qualifying for BADR are deemed to utilise the BR band first. Katie's trading income is £43,650, so her taxable income is £31,150 (£43,650 – £12,500) and her remaining BR band is £6,350 (£37,500 – £31,150). This is set against gains qualifying for BADR of £905,000. The remaining gains are therefore taxed at 20%.

Note that there is no need to calculate the remaining BR band because even if Katie had no taxable income, the gains qualifying for BADR are > £37,500, therefore the non-qualifying gains must be taxed at 20%.

Illustration 5 – Business asset disposal relief

Luka disposed of a business in November 2020, realising a net chargeable gain of £660,000. He had started the business in January 2012 and has used all the chargeable assets for business use throughout the period of ownership.

He has previously claimed BADR for qualifying gains of £400,000.

He also disposed of a holiday home in February 2021, realising a chargeable gain of £21,200. The home had never been his main residence.

Luka had taxable income of £40,000 in the tax year 2020/21.

Calculate Luka's capital gains tax payable for the tax year 2020/21.

Solution

Luka – 2020/21

	Qualifying for BADR £	Not qualifying for BADR £
Sale of holiday home		21,200
Sale of trading business	660,000	
Less: AEA (Note 1)	0	(12,300)
Taxable gains	660,000	8,900

Capital gains tax:

Qualifying gains (£600,000 × 10%) (W)	60,000
(£60,000 × 20%) (Note 2 and 3)	12,000
Non-qualifying gains (£8,900 × 28%) (Note 3)	2,492
	74,492

Working: Qualifying gains in 2020/21

	£
Lifetime limit	1,000,000
Claims prior to 2020/21	(400,000)
Qualifying gains in 2020/21	600,000

Notes:

1. The AEA is set against gains not qualifying for BADR.

2. Luka has a BADR lifetime limit of £1 million. He has already claimed relief for £400,000, therefore he has £600,000 of the limit remaining. After the first £600,000 of gains qualifying for BADR have been taxed at 10%, any remaining qualifying gains are taxed at the appropriate rate depending on the taxpayer's level of income.

3. Luka's taxable income is £40,000, therefore the BRB is no longer available. All other gains are therefore taxed at the higher rates of 20% for the remaining gain on the business and 28% for the residential property.

Test your understanding 4

In the tax year 2020/21 Paul sold shares in Dual Ltd, an unquoted trading company, and realised a gain of £43,000. Paul has worked for Dual Ltd for eight years and has owned 10% of the ordinary shares of the company for the last five years.

Paul set up a trading business in 2015 and in the tax year 2020/21 he sold a warehouse used in the business, realising a gain of £246,000.

Paul's trading profit was £38,000 in the tax year 2020/21. He did not have any other taxable income.

In the tax year 2021/22 Paul sold the rest of the business and realised the following gains:

Factory	£649,500
Goodwill	£13,000

Paul also sold an antique table in the tax year 2021/22 and realised a chargeable gain of £6,225.

His trading profit in the tax year 2021/22 was £51,350, and prior to the tax year 2020/21 Paul has claimed BADR of £350,000.

Calculate Paul's CGT payable for the tax years 2020/21 and 2021/22.

Assume that the AEA and rates for the tax year 2020/21 continue in the future.

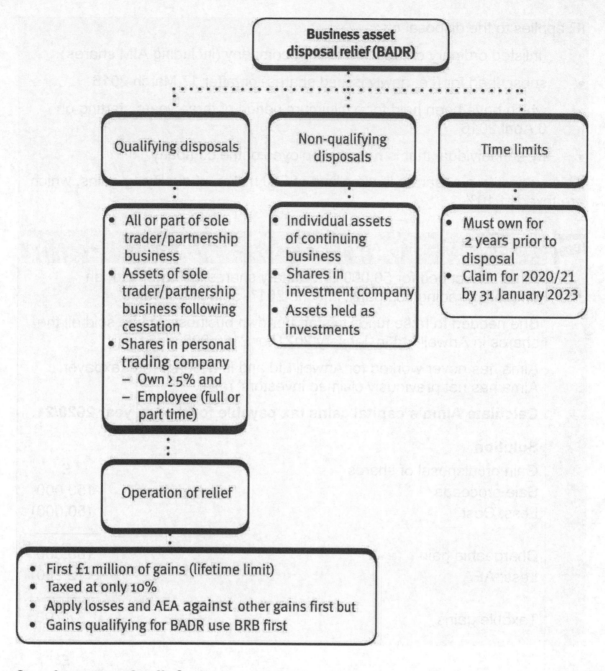

Business asset disposal relief (BADR)

Qualifying disposals

- All or part of sole trader/partnership business
- Assets of sole trader/partnership business following cessation
- Shares in personal trading company
  - Own ≥ 5% and
  - Employee (full or part time)

Operation of relief

- First £1 million of gains (lifetime limit)
- Taxed at only 10%
- Apply losses and AEA against other gains first but
- Gains qualifying for BADR use BRB first

Non-qualifying disposals

- Individual assets of continuing business
- Shares in investment company
- Assets held as investments

Time limits

- Must own for 2 years prior to disposal
- Claim for 2020/21 by 31 January 2023

3 Investors' relief

BADR is only available on a disposal of shares if the shares are in the individual's personal trading company (i.e. the individual holds 5% of the shares) and the individual is also an officer or employee of the company.

Investors' relief (IR) extends the benefits of BADR to certain investors who do not meet the conditions for BADR.

IR applies to the disposal of:

- unlisted ordinary shares in a trading company (including AIM shares)

- subscribed for (i.e. newly issued shares) on/after 17 March 2016

- which have been held for a minimum period of three years starting on 6 April 2016

- by an individual that is **not** an employee of the company.

IR is subject to a separate lifetime limit of £10 million of qualifying gains, which are taxed at 10%.

 Illustration 6 – Investors relief

Alma subscribed for 50,000 £1 ordinary shares in Artwell Ltd, an unquoted trading company, in June 2017, at their par value.

She needed to raise funds to start her own business so she sold all the shares in Artwell Ltd in January 2021 for £150,000.

Alma has never worked for Artwell Ltd and is a higher rate taxpayer. Alma has not previously claimed investors' relief.

Calculate Alma's capital gains tax payable for the tax year 2020/21.

Solution

Gain on disposal of shares	£
Sale proceeds	150,000
Less: Cost	(50,000)
	_____
Chargeable gain	100,000
Less: AEA	(12,300)
	_____
Taxable gains	87,700
	_____
	£
Capital gains tax:	
Qualifying gains for IR (£87,700 × 10%)	8,770
	_____

Alma can claim investors' relief on the sale as she subscribed for shares, in an unlisted trading company, after 17 March 2016 and has held them for more than 3 years after 6 April 2016. Additionally, she has never worked for Artwell Ltd.

Test your understanding 5

Dwight subscribed for 95,000 £1 ordinary shares in Dart Ltd, at par value, on 1 November 2017.

Dwight purchased a 6% shareholding in Beta Ltd in June 2018 for £40,000.

In December 2020 Dwight sold the shares in Dart Ltd for £150,000 and the shares in Beta Ltd for £60,300.

Both companies are unquoted trading companies and Dwight has never worked for either company.

Dwight has not previously claimed investors' relief or business asset disposal relief and had taxable income of £60,000 in 2020/21.

Calculate Dwight's CGT liability for 2020/21.

4 Replacement of business asset relief (Rollover relief)

Rollover relief (ROR) allows the gain arising on the disposal of a qualifying business asset to be rolled over (i.e. deferred) when the sale proceeds are reinvested in a replacement qualifying business asset.

The relief is available to both individuals and companies.

The relief

The relief operates as follows:

- The gain arising on the disposal of the qualifying business asset is deducted from (rolled over against) the acquisition cost of the replacement asset.

- Provided the net sale proceeds are fully reinvested, no tax is payable at the time of the disposal.

- ROR effectively increases the gain arising on the disposal of the replacement asset, as its base cost is reduced by the amount of deferred gain.

- Gains may be 'rolled over' a number of times such that a tax liability will only arise when there is a disposal without replacement.

- When the deferred gain crystallises, it is taxed at the appropriate CGT rate applicable at that time (not the rate applicable at the time of the deferral).

- The relief is not automatic, it must be claimed.

- An individual must claim the relief within 4 years of the later of the end of the tax year in which the:

  - disposal is made, and

  - replacement asset is acquired.

- A disposal in the tax year 2020/21 which is reinvested in a new asset in the tax year 2021/22 requires a claim by 5 April 2026.

Illustration 7 – Rollover relief

Anaya purchased an asset qualifying for ROR in January 2004 for £160,000. In August 2020, she sold the asset for £180,000 and spent £200,000 in November 2020 on a new qualifying asset.

Calculate the chargeable gain arising on the disposal of the asset assuming that ROR is claimed.

Calculate the base cost of the new asset acquired.

Solution

Gain on disposal of asset

	£
Sale proceeds	180,000
Less: Cost	(160,000)
	20,000
Less: ROR (deferred gain)	(20,000)
Chargeable gain	0

Base cost of new asset

	£
Acquisition cost	200,000
Less: ROR (deferred gain)	(20,000)
Revised base cost	180,000

Conditions

Where a **qualifying business** asset is sold at a gain, the taxpayer may roll over the gain provided the net sale proceeds are reinvested in a replacement qualifying business asset acquired within the **qualifying time period**, and brought into business use when it is acquired.

Qualifying business assets

 The main categories of assets qualifying for ROR on a disposal by an individual are:

- goodwill
- land and buildings
- fixed plant and machinery (i.e. not movable).

Both the old and the replacement assets must be qualifying business assets which are used in the trade.

Qualifying time period

The replacement assets must be acquired within a period:

- beginning **one** year before, and
- ending **three** years after the date of sale of the old asset.

Illustration 8 – Rollover relief

Jenna purchased a warehouse in February 2010 for £170,000. In July 2020, she sold the warehouse for £300,000. She used the warehouse for the purposes of her trade throughout the period of ownership.

In December 2022 Jenna bought a new warehouse for £360,000 for the purposes of her trade. She plans to sell the warehouse in January 2024 for £550,000.

Calculate the chargeable gains arising on the two sales assuming rollover relief is claimed.

Solution

First warehouse – July 2020 – 2020/21

	£
Sale proceeds	300,000
Less: Cost	(170,000)
	————
	130,000
Less: ROR (Note)	(130,000)
	————
Chargeable gain	0
	————

Note: The full gain of £130,000 can be rolled over (i.e. deferred) as:

- the asset disposed of is a qualifying business asset
- the replacement asset is a qualifying business asset
- the reinvestment has been made in December 2022 (i.e. within the qualifying period of July 2019 to July 2023)
- the amount reinvested exceeds the sale proceeds received (i.e. purchase price of new warehouse of £360,000 exceeds the sale proceeds of £300,000).

Second warehouse – January 2024 – 2023/24

	£	£
Sale proceeds		550,000
Less: Base Cost		
Cost	360,000	
Less: ROR	(130,000)	
	————	(230,000)
		————
Chargeable gain		320,000
		————

Note: This gain can also be rolled over (i.e. deferred) if a qualifying replacement asset is purchased in the qualifying time period.

However, assuming the gain is not rolled over, it will be taxed in the tax year 2023/24 at 10% or 20% depending on the level of taxable income in that tax year.

The gain does not qualify for BADR as this is the disposal of an individual asset used for the purposes of a continuing business. The business itself is not being disposed of.

Test your understanding 6

Feng acquired a freehold commercial building in April 2002. In May 2005 he sold the building for £100,000 and realised a gain of £56,360. In August 2006, he bought another freehold commercial building for £140,000 and this was sold in November 2020 for £380,000.

All of the buildings were used for the purposes of a trade by Feng.

Calculate the chargeable gain that arises in the tax year 2020/21, assuming rollover relief was claimed on the sale of the first building.

Partial reinvestment of proceeds

Full ROR is only available when all of the net sale proceeds from the sale of the old asset are reinvested.

Where there is partial reinvestment of the proceeds, part of the gain is chargeable at the time of the disposal.

The gain that is **chargeable** (cannot be rolled over) is the **lower** of:

- the amount of the proceeds **not** reinvested
- the full gain.

Test your understanding 7

Sherifa bought a factory in September 2004 and in December 2020, wishing to move to a more convenient location, She sold the factory for £750,000. The cost of the factory was £635,000.

Sherifa moved into a rented factory until March 2021 when she purchased and moved into a new factory.

Calculate the amount of the gain which is chargeable, if any, on the sale of the original factory and calculate the base cost of the new factory assuming the new factory was purchased for:

(a) **£700,000, or**

(b) **£550,000**

Non-business use

Full ROR is only available where the old asset being replaced was used entirely for trade purposes throughout the trader's period of ownership.

Where this condition is not met, ROR is still available but it is scaled down in proportion to the non-trade use.

Illustration 9 – Rollover relief

Robert acquired a freehold commercial building in April 2002 for £65,500. He only used 60% of the freehold building for the purposes of his trade. The building was sold in November 2020 for £162,000.

A replacement building was acquired in January 2020 for £180,000 and this was used 100% for trade purposes by Robert.

The replacement building was sold for £250,000 in May 2021.

Calculate the gain rolled over and the chargeable gains arising on the disposals in November 2020 and May 2021.

Solution

First building – November 2020 – 2020/21

	£
Sale proceeds	162,000
Less: Cost	(65,500)
Chargeable gain before reliefs	96,500

Note: The asset disposed of is a qualifying business asset for ROR purposes, but as only 60% of the building has been used for trade purposes, the gain eligible for ROR must be restricted to 60%.

	Business portion £	Non-business portion £
Split of chargeable gain (60%:40%)	57,900	38,600
Less: ROR (Note)	(57,900)	(n/a)
Chargeable gain	0	38,600

Note:
- the replacement asset is a qualifying business asset, used 100% for the purposes of the trade.

- the reinvestment has been made in January 2020 (i.e. within the qualifying period of November 2019 to November 2023).

- the amount reinvested for the purposes of the trade (i.e. purchase price of new building of £180,000) exceeds the sale proceeds received on the first building relating to the trade use of the building (i.e. £162,000 × 60% = £97,200).

- therefore ROR is available on all of the business portion of the gain.

Sale of replacement building – May 2021 – 2021/22

	£	£
Sale proceeds		250,000
Less: Base Cost		
Cost	180,000	
Less: ROR	(57,900)	
		(122,100)
Chargeable gain		127,900

Note: Assuming there is no replacement of this asset and the rates of CGT remain unchanged, the gains in the tax years 2020/21 and 2021/22 will be taxed at 10% or 20% depending on the level of taxable income in those years.

The gains do not qualify for BADR as the disposal of an individual asset used for the purposes of a continuing business does not qualify. The business itself is not being disposed of.

Test your understanding 8

Hadley purchased a factory in November 1995 and not needing all the space, he let out 15% of it.

In August 2020 he sold the factory for £560,000 and realised a capital gain of £45,000.

In October 2020 Hadley bought another factory, for £500,000, which he used 100% for business purposes. He claimed ROR.

(a) **Calculate the chargeable gain arising on the disposal in August 2020.**

(b) **Calculate the base cost of the new factory.**

Depreciating assets

ROR is modified where the new asset is a depreciating asset:

- If the replacement asset acquired is a depreciating asset, the gain cannot be rolled over. Instead, it is deferred until the earliest of the following three events:

  - Disposal of replacement asset.

  - The replacement asset ceases to be used for the purposes of the trade.

  - Ten years from the date of acquisition of the replacement asset.

- The deferred gain is not deducted from the cost of the replacement asset.

- The deferred gain is just 'frozen' and becomes chargeable on the earliest of the three events above.

- When the deferred gain crystallises, it is taxed at the appropriate CGT rate applicable at that time (not the rate applicable at the time of the deferral).

- If prior to the deferred gain crystallising, a non-depreciating asset is bought, then the original deferred gain can now be rolled over.

A depreciating asset is a wasting asset (i.e. with a predictable life of 50 years or less), or an asset that will become a wasting asset within ten years.

The only depreciating assets that you need to be aware of for the purposes of the TX examination are:

- Fixed plant and machinery

- Leasehold property with ≤ 60 years remaining on the lease.

Illustration 10 – Depreciating assets

Lily purchased a freehold factory in June 1992 for £250,000. In May 2019 she sold it for £420,000 and in June 2019 bought fixed plant and machinery for £450,000. In March 2021, Lily sold the fixed plant and machinery for £475,000.

Calculate the chargeable gains arising in the tax years 2019/20 and 2020/21 assuming Lily claims ROR relief where possible.

Solution

Freehold factory – May 2019 – 2019/20

	£
Sale proceeds	420,000
Less: Cost	(250,000)
	170,000
Less: Deferred gain (see Note)	(170,000)
Chargeable gain	0

Note:
- the asset disposed of is a qualifying business asset

- the replacement asset is a qualifying business asset, but is a depreciating asset (fixed plant and machinery)

- the reinvestment has been made in June 2019 (i.e. within the qualifying period of May 2018 to May 2022)

- the amount reinvested (i.e. purchase price of new plant and machinery of £450,000) exceeds the sale proceeds received on the factory of £420,000

- therefore all of the gain can be deferred, but the deferred gain is not deducted from the base cost of the plant and machinery

- the gain of £170,000 is frozen and becomes chargeable on the earliest of:

    - the sale of the fixed plant and machinery (March 2021)

    - the date the plant and machinery ceases to be used in the trade (presumably March 2021)

    - ten years from the acquisition of the plant and machinery (June 2029).

Sale of plant and machinery – March 2021 – 2020/21

	£
Sale proceeds	475,000
Less: Cost	(450,000)
Capital gain on plant and machinery	25,000
Deferred gain becomes chargeable	170,000
Chargeable gains	195,000

Note: Assuming there is no replacement of this asset the gains in 2020/21 will be taxed at 10% or 20% depending on the level of taxable income in that year.

The gains do not qualify for BADR as this is the disposal of an individual asset used for the purposes of a continuing business. The business itself is not being disposed of.

Test your understanding 9

Amir purchased a freehold factory in May 1994 and in May 2008 he sold it for £350,000 realising a capital gain of £150,000. In July 2010 Amir bought fixed plant and machinery for £400,000. In March 2022 Amir sold the fixed plant and machinery for £500,000.

Calculate the chargeable gains arising in respect of the sale of the freehold factory and the fixed plant and machinery, assuming Amir claims ROR where possible.

Clearly identify in which tax year the gains arise.

Summary

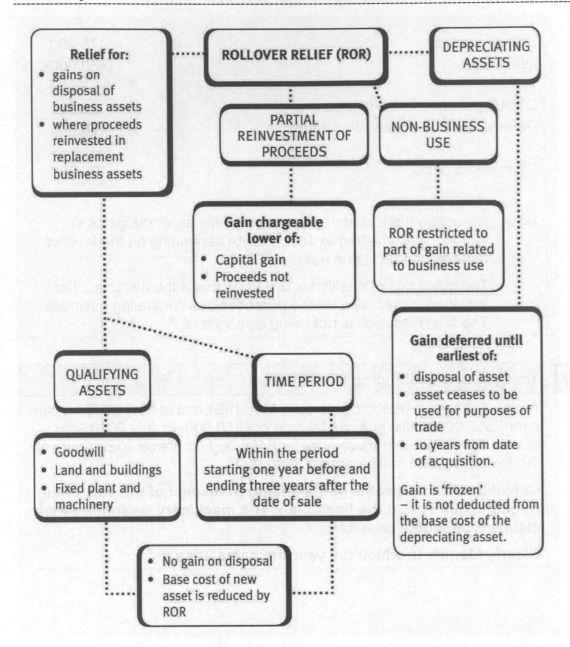

Relief for:
- gains on disposal of business assets
- where proceeds reinvested in replacement business assets

ROLLOVER RELIEF (ROR)

DEPRECIATING ASSETS

PARTIAL REINVESTMENT OF PROCEEDS

NON-BUSINESS USE

Gain chargeable lower of:
- Capital gain
- Proceeds not reinvested

ROR restricted to part of gain related to business use

QUALIFYING ASSETS

TIME PERIOD

Gain deferred until earliest of:
- disposal of asset
- asset ceases to be used for purposes of trade
- 10 years from date of acquisition.

Gain is 'frozen' – it is not deducted from the base cost of the depreciating asset.

- Goodwill
- Land and buildings
- Fixed plant and machinery

Within the period starting one year before and ending three years after the date of sale

- No gain on disposal
- Base cost of new asset is reduced by ROR

5 Gift of business assets – holdover relief (gift relief)

The gift of an asset is a chargeable disposal, which gives rise to a capital gains tax liability for the donor. However, the donor has not received any funds with which to pay the tax.

Gift relief (GR) allows the gain arising on the gift of qualifying business assets to be held over (i.e. deferred) until the asset is eventually sold by the donee.

The relief however is only available for:

- qualifying business assets

- gifts by individuals.

The relief

The relief operates as follows:

Donor	Donee
• Normal capital gain is calculated using market value as proceeds • The gain is not chargeable on the donor; it is deferred against the base cost of the asset acquired by the donee	• Acquisition cost = deemed to be market value at the date of gift • Base cost = Acquisition cost less the gain deferred by the donor

- Both the donor and the donee must make a joint claim for the relief.

- For 2020/21 gifts, the claim must be made by 5 April 2025, (i.e. within four years from the end of the tax year in which the gift was made).

On the subsequent sale of the asset by the donee:

- the base cost is compared with the sale proceeds received to calculate the chargeable gain.

- the chargeable gain is taxed at the appropriate rate of CGT applicable when the donee disposes of the asset.

- assuming the rates of CGT remain unchanged, the gain will be taxed at:

    - 10% if the disposal qualifies for BADR from the donee's point of view, or

    - usual rates depending on the level of the donee's taxable income in the year of disposal and the type of asset.

Illustration 11 – Gift relief

Advik bought a business asset for £25,000 in August 2011. In August 2020 he gave it to Oti, when its market value was £40,000. Advik and Oti have made an election to holdover any gain arising.

Show Advik's capital gains tax position on the gift to Oti and calculate Oti's base cost in the asset.

Solution

Advik's CGT position

Gift to Oti – August 2020

	£
Market value of asset	40,000
Less: Cost	(25,000)
	15,000
Less: GR	(15,000)
Chargeable gain	0

Oti's base cost

Oti has allowable expenditure to set against a future disposal, calculated as follows:

	£
Market value of asset acquired	40,000
Less: GR	(15,000)
Base cost	25,000

Qualifying assets

The relief is only available where there is a gift of a qualifying asset.

The following are the main categories of qualifying asset.

- Assets used in the trade of:
  - the donor (i.e. where he or she is a sole trader)
  - the donor's personal company (this extends the relief to assets owned by the individual but used in the company owned by him or her directly for trading purposes).
- Unquoted shares and securities of any trading company.
- Quoted shares or securities of the individual donor's personal trading company.

A company qualifies as an individual's personal trading company if at least 5% of the voting rights are owned by the individual.

However, unlike BADR, there is no minimum holding period and no requirement for the individual to work for the company to qualify for GR.

Rate of CGT – tax planning

The outright gift of a qualifying asset results in:

* no chargeable gain arising on the donor at the time of the gift

* a higher gain arising on the donee on the subsequent disposal of the asset by the donee

* which is taxed at the appropriate rate depending on:

    – the availability of the donee's AEA,

    – the availability of BADR or IR from the donee's point of view or, if not available,

    – the level of the donee's taxable income in that tax year.

However, claiming GR is optional, and if it is not claimed:

* the gain arising at the time of the gift is assessed on the donor

* which is taxed at the appropriate rate depending on the same factors from the donor's perspective.

Consequently:

* the donor may **choose not to claim** GR in order to:

    – crystallise a gain and utilise their AEA, and/or

    – claim BADR or IR

    – so that the gain is taxed at 0% or 10% now rather than potentially at a higher rate later.

This may be advantageous if:

* the donor qualifies for BADR or IR now but the donee will not qualify for BADR or IR when he or she subsequently disposes of the asset (for example if he or she would not satisfy the employment condition for BADR or the subscription condition for IR)

* the donor has no other gains and therefore the AEA is available, and/or is a basic rate taxpayer whereas the donee is likely to be a higher rate taxpayer when the asset is disposed of.

Note that the donor and donee are independent persons and thus in the above two situations the donor may be more concerned about his or her tax liability on the gift than the donee's liability on the ultimate disposal.

Sales at an undervalue

The relief applies not just to outright gifts but also to sales for less than market value (i.e. where there is an element of gift).

For sales at an undervalue the relief is modified as follows:

- Any proceeds received that exceed the **original cost** of the asset gifted are chargeable to CGT on the donor at the date of the gift.

- The rest of the gain may be deferred (held over).

The chargeable gain arising on the donor will be taxed at the appropriate rate depending on the same factors mentioned above.

Illustration 12 – Gift relief

Ronald bought a warehouse on 4 July 2009 for £20,000. He gave the warehouse to his son, Regan, on 1 September 2011 when the market value was £52,000. Ronald and Regan made a joint election to holdover any gain arising. Regan sold the warehouse on 18 December 2020 for £95,000.

(a) **Calculate the gain 'held over' and the chargeable gain arising on the eventual disposal by Regan in the tax year 2020/21.**

(b) **Calculate the gain eligible for GR and the base cost for Regan, assuming the same facts as above, but Regan pays his father on 1 September 2011:**

    (i)   **£28,000 or**

    (ii) **£18,000.**

Solution

(a) **Ronald – Capital gains computation – 2011/12**

	£
Deemed disposal proceeds (MV at date of gift)	52,000
Less: Acquisition cost	(20,000)
	32,000
Less: GR	(32,000)
Chargeable gain	0

As Ronald and Regan have made a joint election, all of the gain of £32,000 can be 'held over' (i.e. deferred) from Ronald to Regan.

Therefore there would be no chargeable gain on Ronald in the tax year 2011/12.

Regan – Capital gains computation – 2020/21

	£	£
Sale proceeds		95,000
Less Base cost:		
MV at date of gift	52,000	
Less: Gain held over from Ronald	(32,000)	
	———	(20,000)
		———
Chargeable gain		75,000
		———

Note: This gain will be taxed at 10% or 20% depending on the level of Regan's taxable income in that year. The gain does not qualify for BADR. This is because this is the gift of an individual asset, not the disposal of a whole or substantial part of a business.

(b) **Sale at undervaluation**

(i) **Ronald – Capital gains computation – 2011/12**

	£	£
Deemed disposal proceeds (MV at date of gift)		52,000
Less: Acquisition cost		(20,000)
		———
Potential gain (as before)		32,000
Actual proceeds	28,000	
Less: Original cost	(20,000)	
	———	
Excess proceeds over cost chargeable now		8,000
Less: Gain eligible to be held over		(24,000)
		———
Chargeable gain		8,000
		———

This gain was taxed on Ronald at the rate of CGT applicable in 2011/12.

Regan – Base cost (for future disposal)

	£
Deemed acquisition cost (MV at date of gift)	52,000
Less: Gain held over from Ronald	(24,000)
	———
Base cost	28,000
	———

(ii) Ronald – Capital gains computation – 2011/12

	£
Deemed disposal proceeds (MV at date of gift)	52,000
Less: Acquisition cost	(20,000)
Potential gain (as before)	32,000

Actual proceeds of £18,000 are less than original cost
of £20,000 therefore the entire gain is eligible for GR.

	£
Less: Gain eligible to be held over	(32,000)
Chargeable gain	0

Regan – Base cost (for future disposal)

	£
Deemed acquisition cost	52,000
Less: Gain held over from Ronald	(32,000)
Base cost	20,000

Test your understanding 10

Alice bought an industrial storage unit, which she used in her trade in
May 2013 for £120,000. She gave it to her brother, Adam, on 29 June
2018 when the market value was £150,000. Alice and Adam made a
joint election to holdover any gain arising. Adam sold the unit on 1 May
2020 for £180,000.

(a) **Calculate the gain 'held over' and the chargeable gain arising
on the chargeable disposal by Adam in the tax year 2020/21.**

(b) **Calculate the gain eligible for gift relief and the base cost for
Adam if, instead of giving the asset to Adam, Alice had sold it
to him for £130,000.**

Assets not used wholly for trade purposes

The relief is restricted where either:

- only part of an asset is used for trading purposes, or

- an asset is used for trading purposes for only part of the donor's period of
  ownership.

Assets apart from shares

Only the gain relating to the period that the asset was used in the trade or the part of the asset used for trading purposes is eligible for GR.

The restriction to the relief operates in the same way as ROR where assets have not been wholly used in the trade.

Illustration 13 – Gift relief

Davina acquired a freehold commercial building in May 2012 for £160,000. She used 60% of the freehold building in her trade for business purposes.

In September 2020 she gave the building to her son, Ben, when its market value was £250,000. Davina and Ben signed an election to holdover the gain arising on the gift.

Calculate the gain held over and the chargeable gain arising on the gift of the building in September 2020.

Solution

Davina – Capital gains computation – 2020/21

	£
Market value at date of gift	250,000
Less: Acquisition cost	(160,000)
	———
Potential gain	90,000
As only 60% of the building has been used for the purposes of a trade, the gain eligible to be held over must also be restricted by the same %.	
Less: Gain eligible to be held over (60% × £90,000)	(54,000)
	———
Chargeable gain (40% of £90,000)	36,000

Note: This gain is taxed at 10% or 20% depending on the level of Davina's taxable income in the tax year 2020/21. The gain does not qualify for BADR. This is because this is the gift of an individual asset, not the disposal of a whole or substantial part of a business.

Shares in a personal trading company

Where the assets being gifted are shares; the gain eligible to be held over is restricted if:

- the shares are in the donor's personal company (i.e. at least 5% of the voting rights are owned by the donor) – whether quoted or unquoted, and

- the company owns chargeable non-business assets.

In this situation the gain eligible for GR is:

$$\text{Total gain} \times \frac{\text{MV of chargeable business assets (CBA)}}{\text{MV of chargeable assets (CA)}}$$

Note that where the donor holds less than 5% of the voting rights:

- for unquoted shares – the restriction does not apply; full relief is available

- for quoted shares – GR is not available at all.

 Chargeable assets (CA)

A chargeable asset is one that, if sold, would give rise to a chargeable gain or an allowable loss (i.e. capital assets that are chargeable).

Exempt assets such as motor cars are therefore excluded.

Inventory, receivables, cash, etc. are also excluded as they are not capital assets and therefore not chargeable.

 Chargeable business assets (CBA)

These are defined as chargeable assets (as defined above) that are used for the purposes of a trade.

Chargeable business assets therefore exclude shares, securities or other assets owned by the business but held for investment purposes.

Consequences of restricting GR

Note that if the individual disposes of shares in a personal trading company:

- GR is available:

    - subject to the (CBA/CA) restriction above

    - whether or not the individual works for the company

- a chargeable gain will arise at the time of the gift on the donor as not all of the gain can be deferred

- the chargeable gain will be taxed on the donor at 0%, 10% or 20% depending on:

    - the availability of the donor's AEA

    - the availability of BADR or IR from the donor's point of view and, if not available

    - the level of the donor's taxable income in that tax year.

Illustration 14 – Gift relief

Jin Ming has been a full time working director of Porcelain Products Ltd since 1 December 2001 and purchased 10% of the company's ordinary shares on 1 December 2005.

He resigned from the company in 2012 but kept the shares until 1 December 2020 when he gave his 10% shareholding, valued at £950,000, to his daughter Jun Ying.

The agreed capital gain on the disposal of the shares was £700,000. Jin and Jun signed an election to holdover the gain on the gift.

The market values of the assets held by the company at 1 December 2020 were:

	£
Land and buildings	550,000
Motor cars	80,000
Cash	45,000
Receivables	35,000
Inventory	50,000
Shares held as investments	60,000

Calculate Jin Ming's chargeable gain in the tax year 2020/21 and the base cost of the shares acquired by Jun Ying.

Solution

Jin Ming – Capital gains computation – 2020/21

	£
Total gain on disposal of shares	700,000
Less: GR (W) £700,000 × (£550,000/£610,000)	(631,148)
Chargeable gain	68,852

Working:

MV of CA = (£550,000 + £60,000) = £610,000 (Land and buildings and shares held as investments).

MV of CBA = £550,000 (Land and buildings).

Note: The gain will be taxed at 10% or 20% depending on the level of Jin Ming's taxable income in 2020/21. The gain does not qualify for BADR. This is because Jim Ming did not work for the company in the 2 years before the disposal. The gain does not qualify for IR as Jin purchased and did not subscribe for the shares on or after 17 March 2016.

Base cost for Jun Ying	£
MV at date of gift	950,000
Less: GR (held over gain)	(631,148)
Base cost	318,852

Test your understanding 11

Fred purchased 100% of the shares in Fred Ltd in June 2001. He worked for the company until he became unwell in October 2015, when his son stepped in and ran the company for Fred.

On 20 February 2021, Fred made a gift of his shares to his son, and this resulted in a chargeable gain of £420,000.

At the time of the gift the market value of the assets owned by Fred Ltd were as follows:

	£
Freehold trading premises	400,000
Investments – Shares in UK companies	100,000
Inventory and work in progress	130,000
Receivables	100,000
Cash	30,000
	760,000

Calculate the amount of Fred's chargeable gain and the amount that can be held over using gift relief.

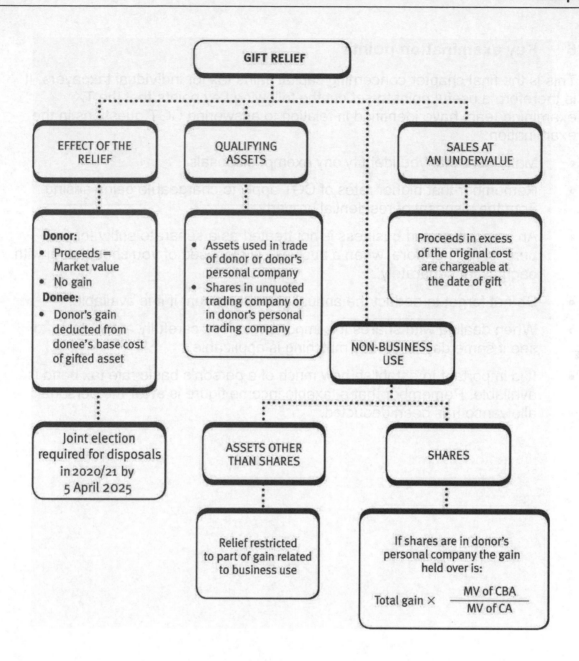

GIFT RELIEF

EFFECT OF THE RELIEF

QUALIFYING ASSETS

SALES AT AN UNDERVALUE

Donor:
- Proceeds = Market value
- No gain

Donee:
- Donor's gain deducted from donee's base cost of gifted asset

- Assets used in trade of donor or donor's personal company
- Shares in unquoted trading company or in donor's personal trading company

Proceeds in excess of the original cost are chargeable at the date of gift

NON-BUSINESS USE

Joint election required for disposals in 2020/21 by 5 April 2025

ASSETS OTHER THAN SHARES

SHARES

Relief restricted to part of gain related to business use

If shares are in donor's personal company the gain held over is:

$$\text{Total gain} \times \frac{\text{MV of CBA}}{\text{MV of CA}}$$

6 Key examination points

This is the final chapter concerning capital gains tax for individual taxpayers. It is therefore a useful point to set out the following key points that the TX examining team have identified in relation to answering CGT questions in the examination:

- Make sure that you identify any exempt disposals.

- Remember that higher rates of CGT apply to chargeable gains arising from the disposal of residential property.

- An unincorporated business is not treated as a separate entity for CGT purposes. Therefore, when a business is disposed of you should deal with each asset separately.

- Do not forget to deduct the annual exempt amount if it is available.

- When dealing with shares it is important to look carefully at the dates to see if same day or 30 day matching is applicable.

- It is important to establish how much of a person's basic rate tax band is available. Remember that a taxable income figure is **after** the personal allowance has been deducted.

7 Chapter summary

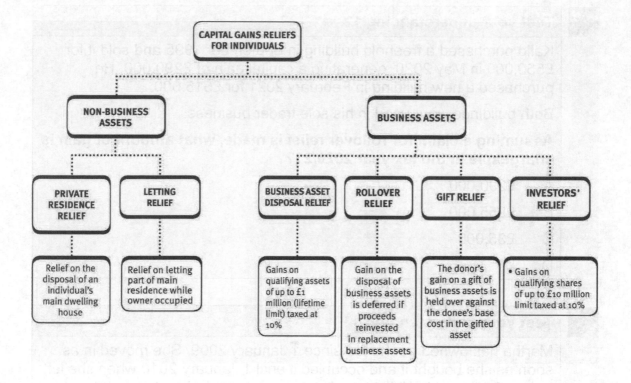

8 Practice objective test questions

Test your understanding 12

Kalid purchased a freehold building in September 1995 and sold it for £550,000 in May 2020, generating a capital gain of £290,000. He purchased a new building in February 2021 for £515,000.

Both buildings were used in his sole trader business.

Assuming a claim for rollover relief is made, what amount of gain is chargeable in the tax year 2020/21?

A   £290,000

B   £255,000

C   £35,000

D   £0

Test your understanding 13

Martha has owned her house since 1 January 2009. She moved in as soon as she bought it and occupied it until 1 January 2010 when she left to travel the world. Whilst travelling, she got married and moved to London and did not reoccupy the property. She sold the house on 1 January 2021.

In calculating the amount of private residence relief available to Martha, what is the period of her occupation?

Include periods of both actual and deemed occupation.

A   144 months

B   57 months

C   21 months

D   12 months

Test your understanding 14

Leon is a sole trader. He sold a factory in December 2020 which he had used in his business since 2005.

Leon can claim to rollover the gain on the factory against which of the following?

A   The purchase of a new factory in May 2020 which will be used in Leon's trade

B   The purchase of a commercial property in January 2021 which will be let to tenants for 7 years

C   The purchase of a shop in December 2020 which will be rented by his sister

D   The purchase of a new forklift truck in December 2020 for use in Leon's trade

Test your understanding 15

Josefine has taxable income of £18,000 for the tax year 2020/21. She also has capital gains of £26,300 on quoted shares not qualifying for business asset disposal (BADR) relief and £40,000 of gains qualifying for BADR relief.

What is her capital gains tax liability for the tax year 2020/21?

A   £5,400

B   £6,800

C   £7,310

D   £9,260

Test your understanding 16

Paul gives an antique vase to his son for his birthday. It has a market value of £7,000.

Which of the following reliefs are available, if any?

A   Rollover relief

B   Business asset disposal relief

C   Gift relief

D   None of the above

Test your understanding 17

On 5 July 2020 David subscribed for new ordinary shares in Gardening Ltd, an unquoted trading company. He works for the company and his shareholding represents 4% of the company's ordinary shares.

He intends to continue working for the company and to own the shares for the next 10 years when he will give the shares to his daughter.

Which of the following reliefs are available?

A   Investors' relief

B   Business asset disposal relief

C   Gift relief

D   None of the above

Test your understanding answers

Test your understanding 1

Andrea

Step 1 Calculate gain before reliefs (given) = £189,000.

Step 2 Identify – periods of ownership, actual occupation, and deemed occupation.

	Total	Exempt	Chargeable
Lived in house (actual occupation)	24	24	
Employed overseas (any period exempt)	78	78	
Travelling (3 years exempt for any reason)	66	36	
Rest of period chargeable			30
Lived in house (actual occupation)	93	93	
Number of months	261	231	30

The periods of occupation before and after deemed occupation do not need to be **immediately** before and after (for example the employment overseas is followed by actual occupation which did not start until Andrea had travelled the world).

Step 3 Deduct PRR.

	£
Gain before reliefs	189,000
Less: PRR (£189,000 × 231/261)	(167,276)
Chargeable gain after reliefs	21,724

CGT liability

	£
Chargeable gain	21,724
Less: AEA	(12,300)
Taxable gain	9,424

£		£
7,000 (W) ×18%		1,260
2,424 × 28%		679
9,424		1,939

Working:

Andrea's unused basic rate band is £7,000 (£37,500 – £30,500).

Test your understanding 2

Hessa

Hessa owned the house for nine years and used 1/7th of the house (one of the seven rooms) for business purposes.

The last nine months exemption does not apply to the business element of the gain as this part of the house has never been used for private purposes.

The chargeable gain after reliefs = (£60,000 × 1/7) = £8,571.

Test your understanding 3

Eleni

	£
Market value	140,000
Less: Cost	(45,000)
Enhancement expenditure	(10,600)
Chargeable gain before reliefs	84,400
Less: PRR (£84,400 × 86/157) (W)	(46,232)
	38,168

Less: Letting relief = lowest of:
(1) Maximum = £40,000
(2) PRR = £46,232
(3) Letting gain = £84,400 × 32/157 = 17,203   (17,203)

Chargeable gain after reliefs	20,965

Working: PRR and letting relief

	Total	Exempt	Chargeable after PRR	Letting relief
Lived in full house	13			
Actual occupation		13		
Lived in part of house	96			
2/3 actual occupation 1/3 let (Note)		64		
			32	32
Living with sister	48			
Last 9 months (Note)		9		
Rest of period – chargeable			39	
Number of months	157	86	71	32

Note: Letting relief is available for one third of the 96 month period when Eleni let part of the house to tenants. The last 9 months are exempt under the PRR rules.

Test your understanding 4

Paul

Capital gains tax

2020/21	Qualifying for BADR	Not qualifying for BADR
	£	£
Sale of warehouse (Note 1)		246,000
Sale of company shares	43,000	
Less: AEA (Note 2)	(0)	(12,300)
Taxable gains	43,000	233,700
Capital gains tax:		
Qualifying gains (£43,000 × 10%)		4,300
Non-qualifying gains (£233,700 × 20%) (Note 3)		46,740
		51,040

2021/22			
	£	£	£
Sale of antique table (Note 6)			6,225
Sales of trading business:			
Factory	649,500		
Goodwill	13,000		
	662,500		
Qualifying for BADR (W)	(607,000)	607,000	55,500
Chargeable gains		607,000	61,725
Less: AEA (Note 2)		(0)	(12,300)
Taxable gains		607,000	49,425
Capital gains tax:			£
Qualifying gains (£607,000 × 10%) (Note 4)			60,700
Non-qualifying gains (£49,425 × 20%) (Note 5)			9,885
			70,585

Working: Qualifying gains in 2021/22

	£
Lifetime limit	1,000,000
Claims prior to 2020/21	(350,000)
Claim in 2020/21	(43,000)
Qualifying gains in 2021/22	607,000

Notes:

1. The disposal of the warehouse in the tax year 2020/21 is the disposal of an individual business asset used for the purposes of a continuing trade. To qualify for BADR, there must be a disposal of the whole or part of the trading business. The sale of an asset in isolation does not qualify.

2. The AEA is set against gains not qualifying for BADR, and any remaining AEA is then set against gains qualifying for BADR.

3. The gains qualifying for BADR are deemed to utilise the BR band first. Paul's taxable income is £25,500 (£38,000 – £12,500 PA). Therefore the BR band remaining is £12,000 (£37,500 – £25,500). However, Paul's gains qualifying for BADR (£43,000) exceed £37,500. Therefore, there is no need to calculate the BR band remaining in this case because even if Paul had no taxable income, and all of his BR band was available, it would be matched against these qualifying gains. Therefore the gains not qualifying for BADR will be taxed at 20%.

4. After the first £1 million of gains qualifying for BADR have been taxed at 10%, any remaining qualifying gains are taxed at the appropriate rate depending on the individual's taxable income.

5. There is no BR band remaining in the tax year 2021/22 as Paul's taxable income of £38,850 (£51,350 – £12,500 PA) exceeds £37,500. Even if there were, the remaining BR band is set against gains qualifying for BADR first leaving remaining gains to be taxed at 20%.

6. It wasn't necessary to apply the chattels rules in this scenario. The question stated that the gain was chargeable and the amount of the gain was also given.

Test your understanding 5

Dwight

2020/21		Qualifying for IR £	Not Qualifying for IR £
Sale of Beta shares (W) (Note 1)			20,300
Sale of Dart shares (W)		55,000	
Less: AEA (Note 2)		(0)	(12,300)
		_____	_____
Taxable gains		55,000	8,000
		_____	_____
Capital gains tax:			
Qualifying gains	(£55,000 × 10%)		5,500
Non-qualifying gains	(£8,000 × 20%)		1,600
			_____
			7,100
			_____

Workings	£
Beta shares	
Sales proceeds	60,300
Less: Cost	(40,000)
	_____
	20,300
	_____
Dart shares	
Sales proceeds	150,000
Less: Cost – par value	(95,000)
	_____
	55,000
	_____

Notes:

1. As Dwight did not subscribe for newly issued shares in Beta Ltd the sale does not qualify for investors' relief. In addition, as Dwight did not work for Beta Ltd the sale does not qualify for business asset disposal relief.

2. The AEA has been set against the non-qualifying gains as they are subject to a higher rate of tax.

Test your understanding 6

Feng

Second building – November 2020 – 2020/21

	£	£
Sale proceeds		380,000
Less: Base cost		
Cost	140,000	
Less: ROR (Note)	(56,360)	
	————	(83,640)
Chargeable gain		296,360

The chargeable gain arising in 2020/21 will be taxed at 10% or 20% depending on the level of taxable income.

The disposal of an individual asset used for the purposes of a continuing business does not qualify for BADR. The business itself is not being disposed of.

Notes:

1   The full gain arising in May 2005 of £56,360 can be rolled over (i.e. deferred) as:

   –   the asset disposed of is a qualifying business asset and the replacement asset is a qualifying business asset

   –   the reinvestment has been made in August 2006 (i.e. within the qualifying period of May 2004 to May 2008)

   –   the amount reinvested exceeds the sale proceeds received (i.e. purchase price of new building of £140,000 exceeds the sale proceeds of £100,000).

2   The gain arising in the tax year 2020/21 of £296,360 can also be deferred, provided a qualifying business asset is purchased within the qualifying period (i.e. November 2019 to November 2023).

Test your understanding 7

Sherifa

	(a)	(b)
New factory purchased for	**£700,000**	**£550,000**
	£	£
Sale proceeds	750,000	750,000
Less: Cost	(635,000)	(635,000)
Gain before relief	115,000	115,000
Less:ROR (balancing figure)		
(£115,000 – £50,000)	(65,000)	
(£115,000 – £115,000)		(0)
Chargeable gain (W)	50,000	115,000

Working

Chargeable gain now = Lower of:	£	£
1 Sale proceeds not reinvested		
(£750,000 – £700,000)	50,000	
(£750,000 – £550,000)		200,000
2 Gain on disposal of original factory		
before relief	115,000	115,000
Therefore chargeable gain in 2020/21	**50,000**	**115,000**

Base cost of new replacement factory

Cost	700,000	550,000
Less: ROR	(65,000)	(0)
	635,000	550,000

Note: The chargeable gain arising in the tax year 2020/21 will be taxed at 10% or 20% depending on the level of taxable income.

The gain does not qualify for BADR as this is the disposal of an individual asset used for the purposes of a continuing business. The business itself is not being disposed of.

Test your understanding 8

Hadley

Disposal of factory – August 2020 – 2020/21

The asset disposed of is a qualifying business asset, but as only 85% of the building has been used for trade purposes, the gain must be split and only 85% is eligible for ROR.

	Business portion	Non-business portion
	£	£
Split of capital gain (85%:15%)	38,250	6,750
Less: ROR (Note)	(38,250)	(n/a)
Chargeable gain	0	6,750

Notes:
- the replacement asset is a qualifying business asset, used 100% for the purposes of the trade.
- the reinvestment has been made in October 2020 (i.e. within the qualifying period of August 2019 to August 2023).
- the amount reinvested for the purposes of the trade (i.e. purchase price of new factory of £500,000) exceeds the sale proceeds received on the first building relating to the trade use of the building (i.e. £560,000 × 85% = £476,000).
- therefore ROR is available on all of the business portion of the gain.
- the chargeable gain is taxed at 10% or 20% depending on the level of taxable income. The gain does not qualify for BADR. This is because the chargeable gain is in respect of an investment asset.

Base cost of replacement factory – October 2020

	£
Cost	500,000
Less: ROR	(38,250)
	461,750

Test your understanding 9

Amir

Freehold factory – May 2008 – 2008/09

	£
Capital gain	150,000
Less: Deferred gain (Held over gain) (see Note)	(150,000)
Chargeable gain	0

Note:
- the asset disposed of is a qualifying business asset
- the replacement asset is a qualifying business asset, but is a depreciating asset (fixed plant and machinery)
- the reinvestment has been made in July 2010 (i.e. within the qualifying period of May 2007 to May 2011)
- the amount reinvested (i.e. purchase price of new plant and machinery of £400,000) exceeds the sale proceeds received for the factory of £350,000
- therefore all of the gain can be deferred, but the deferred gain is not deducted from the base cost of the plant and machinery
- the gain of £150,000 is frozen and becomes chargeable on the earliest of:
  - the sale of the fixed plant and machinery (March 2022)
  - the date the plant and machinery ceases to be used in the trade (presumably March 2022)
  - ten years from the acquisition of the plant and machinery (July 2020).

Chargeable event – earliest date = July 2020 – 2020/21

Deferred gain (Held over gain) becomes chargeable	£150,000

This gain is taxable at 10% or 20% depending on the level of taxable income. The gain does not qualify for BADR. This is because it is the disposal of an individual asset used for the purposes of a continuing business.

Sale of plant and machinery – March 2022

	£
Sale proceeds	500,000
Less: Cost	(400,000)
Chargeable gain – 2021/22	100,000

Assuming that this asset is not replaced and the rates of CGT remain unchanged, this gain will be taxable at 10% or 20% depending on the level of taxable income. The gain does not qualify for BADR. This is because it is the disposal of an individual asset used for the purposes of a continuing business.

Test your understanding 10

Alice

(a) **Alice – Capital gains computation – 2018/19**

	£
MV at date of gift	150,000
Less: Acquisition cost	(120,000)
Chargeable gain	30,000
Less: GR	(30,000)
Chargeable gain	0

As Alice and Adam made a joint election this gain of £30,000 can be 'held over' from Alice to Adam (under the GR provisions).

Therefore there would be no chargeable gain on Alice in 2018/19.

Adam – Capital gains computation – 2020/21

	£	£
Sale proceeds		180,000
Less: Base cost		
MV at date of gift	150,000	
Less: Gain held over	(30,000)	
		(120,000)
Chargeable gain		60,000

Note: Assuming the rates of CGT remain unchanged, this gain will be taxable at 10% or 20% depending on the level of taxable income. The gain does not qualify for BADR. This is because it is the gift of an individual asset, not the disposal of a whole or substantial part of a business.

(b) **Alice – Capital gains computation – 2018/19**

	£	£
MV at date of gift		150,000
Less: Acquisition cost		(120,000)
Potential gain (as above)		30,000
Actual proceeds	130,000	
Less: Original cost	(120,000)	
Excess proceeds over cost	10,000	
Less: Gain eligible to be held over		(20,000)
Chargeable gain		10,000

This gain is taxable at 10% or 20% depending on the level of taxable income. The gain does not qualify for BADR. This is because it is the disposal of an individual asset used for the purposes of a continuing trade, not the disposal of a whole or substantial part of a business.

Adam – Base cost (for future disposal)

	£
Deemed acquisition cost (MV at date of gift)	150,000
Less: Gain held over from Alice	(20,000)
Base cost	130,000

Test your understanding 11

Fred

Fred Ltd's chargeable business assets total £400,000 (premises), whilst the chargeable assets total £500,000 (premises and shares held as investments).

Therefore £336,000 (£420,000 × £400,000/£500,000) of the capital gain can be held over.

Fred's chargeable gain in the tax year is therefore £84,000 (£420,000 – £336,000).

Note: This gain is taxable at 10% or 20% depending on the level of taxable income. The gain does not qualify for BADR. This is because Fred did not work for the company in the 2 years before he disposed of the shares. The gain does not qualify for IR as Fred did not subscribe for the shares.

Test your understanding 12

The correct answer is C.

The gain on the sale of the original building can be rolled over against the cost of the new building as follows:

	£
Gain on sale of building	290,000
Less: Rollover relief	(255,000)
Chargeable gain in 2020/21 = proceeds not reinvested (£550,000 – £515,000)	35,000

Test your understanding 13

The correct answer is C.

Martha's period of occupation includes actual occupations (i.e. 12 months from 1 January 2009 to 1 January 2010) plus any periods of deemed occupation as follows:

1 April 2020 – 1 January 2021 being the last 9 months of ownership. There is no requirement to reoccupy the property.

No part of Martha's absence can be a deemed period of occupation under the '3 years for any reason' rule as she did not reoccupy the property.

Test your understanding 14

The correct answer is A.

Rollover relief is available for the purchase of qualifying assets purchased within 12 months before and 3 years after the sale of the original factory.

However, property let out to tenants (i.e. not used in Leon's business) does not qualify for rollover relief, nor does movable (rather than fixed) plant and machinery (i.e. the forklift truck).

Test your understanding 15

The correct answer is B.

	Qualifying for BADR £	Not qualifying for BADR £
Gains	40,000	26,300
Less: AEA		(12,300)
	———	———
Taxable gains	40,000	14,000
	———	———
CGT rate	10%	20%
CGT	4,000	2,800
	———	———
Total tax		£6,800
		———

Note:

Gains not qualifying for BADR are taxed at 10% if they fall in the taxpayer's remaining basic rate band and 20% otherwise.

Gains qualifying for BADR are taxed at 10%. They are deemed to use up the taxpayer's basic rate band before the non-qualifying gains.

In this question the taxpayer has £18,000 of taxable income so she has £19,500 (£37,500 – £18,000) of unused basic rate band. As the gains qualifying for BADR exceed £19,500, there is no basic rate band left for the non-qualifying gains and they must be taxed at 20%.

The taxpayer can deduct the AEA (and any capital losses) from the non-qualifying gains in preference to qualifying gains.

Test your understanding 16

The correct answer is D.

A   Rollover relief is only available on disposals of qualifying business assets, not vases. It is also not available on gifts.

B   Business asset disposal relief is only available on the disposal of qualifying business assets, not antique vases.

C   Gift relief is only available on the disposal of qualifying business assets, not antique vases.

Test your understanding 17

The correct answer is C.

Gift relief is available on unquoted shares in a trading company.

Investors' relief is not available as David works for the company. Business asset disposal relief is not available as David does not own 5% of the shares.

Chargeable gains for companies

Chapter learning objectives

Upon completion of this chapter you will be able to:

- compute and explain the treatment of chargeable gains

- explain and compute the indexation allowance available using a given indexation factor

- explain and compute the treatment of capital losses

- understand the treatment of disposals of shares by companies and apply the identification rules including the same day and nine day matching rules

- explain and apply the pooling provisions

- explain and apply the treatment of bonus issues, rights issues, takeovers and reorganisations

- explain and apply rollover relief.

PER

One of the PER performance objectives (PO15) is to prepare computations of taxable amounts and tax liabilities according to legal requirements. Another objective (PO17) is to advise on mitigating and deferring tax liabilities through legitimate tax planning measures. Working through this chapter should help you understand how to demonstrate those objectives.

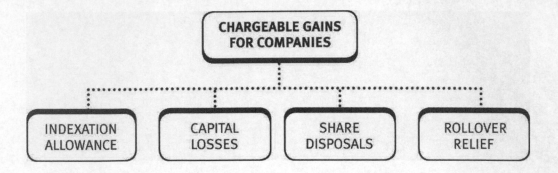

1   Introduction

The main principles of calculating chargeable gains for individuals were set out in Chapters 19 – 22.

Some of the content is applicable to companies, but there are some notable differences in the calculation of chargeable gains for companies.

Chargeable gains for a company

* The total net chargeable gains that a company makes during an **accounting period** (AP) are included in the taxable total profits computation.

* It is important to remember that companies pay **corporation tax** on chargeable gains, not capital gains tax.

Calculation of total net chargeable gains for a company

The following steps should be completed:

1   Calculate the chargeable gain/allowable loss arising on the disposal of each chargeable asset separately

2   Calculate the net chargeable gains arising in the AP = (chargeable gains less allowable losses)

3   Deduct capital losses brought forward = total net chargeable gains

4   Include in taxable total profits computation.

Note that there is no annual exempt amount available to companies. The total net chargeable gains are therefore simply included in the company's taxable total profits computation.

Pro forma – companies

	£
Disposal proceeds	X
Less: Incidental disposal costs	(X)
Net proceeds	X
Less: Allowable expenditure (as for individuals)	(X)
Unindexed gain	X
Less: Indexation allowance (section 2)	(X)
Chargeable gain/(allowable loss)	X/(X)

Note that:

- The calculation of chargeable gains is the same as for individuals except that companies are entitled to an indexation allowance for assets acquired prior to December 2017 (see section 2).

- There are a few other key differences when dealing with the disposal of assets by companies. These include

    - the treatment of capital losses (section 3)

    - the treatment of shares and securities (section 4), and

    - the availability of reliefs (section 7).

2 Indexation allowance

The indexation allowance (IA) gives a company some allowance for the effect of inflation in calculating a gain.

The rules for the IA are as follows:

- the IA applies to assets purchased prior to December 2017

- the IA is calculated as:

    cost of the asset × indexation factor

- the Indexation factor is the movement in the retail price index (RPI)

    - **from** the month of purchase

    - **to** the month of disposal (or December 2017 if earlier)

- the IA is calculated separately for each item of expenditure (e.g. calculate a different IA for the original acquisition cost and any subsequent enhancement expenditure because they have different purchase dates).

- the IA cannot create or increase a capital loss.

Note that the indexation factor will be provided in the TX examination.

Illustration 1 – Indexation Allowances

Pye Ltd bought a factory for £250,000, on 1 April 1998. On 15 August 2001, the company spent £70,000 on an extension to the factory. The factory was sold on 30 September 2020, for £950,000.

Assume the relevant indexation factors are as follows:

April 1998 to December 2017	0.710
April 1998 to September 2020	0.827
August 2001 to December 2017	0.598
August 2001 to September 2020	0.707

Calculate Pye Ltd's chargeable gain.

Solution

	£
Sale proceeds	950,000
Less: Cost	(250,000)
Enhancement expenditure	(70,000)
Unindexed gain	630,000
Less: Indexation allowance	
Cost (£250,000 × 0.710) Note	(177,500)
Enhancement expenditure (£70,000 × 0.598) Note	(41,860)
Chargeable gain	410,640

Note: Indexation allowance is frozen at December 2017.

Test your understanding 1

Hobbit Ltd bought a factory for £175,000 on 1 June 2000. On 15 January 2018, the company spent £62,000 on an extension to the factory. The factory was sold on 31 August 2020, for £680,000.

Assume the indexation factors are as follows:

June 2000 to December 2017	0.625
June 2000 to August 2020	0.731
January 2018 to August 2020	0.073

Calculate Hobbit Ltd's chargeable gain.

3 Capital losses

- A capital loss arises if the proceeds received for an asset are lower than the allowable expenditure.

- Remember that the indexation allowance cannot create or increase a capital loss.

Test your understanding 2

JNN Ltd is considering selling a field at auction in July 2020. It acquired the field in August 1992, for £10,000 and the sale proceeds are likely to be one of three figures:

(a) £25,000

(b) £12,000

(c) £8,000

Calculate the chargeable gain or loss under each alternative.

Assume the indexation factor from August 1992 to December 2017 is 1.002.

Utilisation of a capital loss

- Where allowable losses arise, they are set off against chargeable gains arising in the same accounting period.

- Any loss remaining, is carried forward against **chargeable gains** of future accounting periods, as soon as they arise.

- Capital losses **cannot** be:

  - set off against any other income of a company, nor

  - carried back against gains in previous accounting periods.

Illustration 2 – Capital losses

For the year ended 31 March 2021, Jump Ltd has a tax adjusted trading profit of £65,000, and a chargeable gain of £3,600.

At 1 April 2020, it had unused capital losses brought forward of £6,000.

Calculate Jump Ltd's corporation tax liability for the year ended 31 March 2021.

Solution

Corporation tax liability – y/e 31 March 2021

	£
Tax adjusted trading profit	65,000
Net chargeable gain (W)	0
Taxable total profits	65,000
Corporation tax (19% × £65,000)	12,350

Working: Net chargeable gain

	£
Chargeable gain	3,600
Less: Capital loss b/f	(6,000)
Capital loss c/f	(2,400)

Net chargeable gain in the accounting period is therefore £Nil.

The remaining capital losses cannot be set against the tax adjusted trading profit of the company in the year, they can only be carried forward and set against future chargeable gains.

Test your understanding 3

For the year ended 31 December 2020, High Ltd has a tax adjusted trading profit of £200,000, and a chargeable gain of £17,000.

At 1 January 2020, it had unused capital losses brought forward of £23,000.

Calculate High Ltd's corporation tax liability for the year ended 31 December 2020.

4 Shares and securities

The issues regarding the disposal of shares by a company are similar to those set out in Chapter 21 for disposals by individuals.

Remember that:

- Shares and securities present a particular problem for capital gains computations, because any two shares in a company (of a particular class) are indistinguishable.

- Matching rules are therefore needed, to solve the problem of identifying acquisitions with disposals. They apply when there has been more than one purchase of shares or securities, of the same class, in the same company.

Matching rules

The matching rules for shares disposed of by companies are different from those for an individual.

For a company, disposals are matched against acquisitions as follows:

- shares acquired on the same day (as the sale)

- shares acquired during the nine days before the sale (FIFO basis)

- shares in the share pool.

Illustration 3 – Disposal of shares and securities

Minnie Ltd sold 3,000 shares in Mickey plc for £15,000, on 15 February 2021. The shares in Mickey plc were purchased as follows:

Date	Number	Cost £
1 July 2006	1,000	2,000
1 September 2010	1,000	2,500
8 February 2021	500	1,200
15 February 2021	1,500	6,000

Explain which shares Minnie Ltd is deemed to have sold.

Solution

Using the matching rules, the 3,000 shares sold are as follows:

	Number
(1) Same day purchases: 15 February 2021	1,500
(2) Previous 9 days purchases: 8 February 2021	500
	2,000

(3) Share pool:

All other shares were purchased more than 9 days ago, therefore they must be in the share pool.

1 July 2006	1,000	
1 September 2010	1,000	
Total number of shares in pool	2,000	
Disposal from the pool	(1,000)	1,000
Left in share pool	1,000	
Shares disposed of		3,000

Calculation of gains on same day and previous 9 day purchases

There is no IA on either of these calculations.

Hence, the gain is calculated as:

	£
Sale proceeds	X
Less: Allowable cost	(X)
Chargeable gain	X

Illustration 4 – Disposal of shares and securities

From the above example (Minnie Ltd), calculate the gains on the shares purchased:

(a) **on the same day**

(b) **in the previous 9 days.**

Solution

Calculate sale proceeds per share:

3,000 shares are sold for £15,000, therefore 1 share is sold for £5.00 (£15,000/3,000).

Gain on same day purchases (1,500 shares):

	£
Sale proceeds (£5 × 1,500)	7,500
Less: Allowable cost	(6,000)
Chargeable gain	1,500

> ### Gain on previous 9 days purchases (500 shares):
>
> | | £ |
> |---|---|
> | Sale proceeds (£5 × 500) | 2,500 |
> | Less: Allowable cost | (1,200) |
> | Chargeable gain | 1,300 |

The share pool for companies is different from the share pool for individuals:

- It contains shares in the same company, of the same class, purchased **more than 9 days before** the date of disposal.

- The pool keeps a record of the:
    - number of shares acquired and sold
    - cost of the shares, and
    - indexed cost of the shares (i.e. cost plus IA).

- Each purchase and sale is recorded in the pool, but the indexed cost must be updated **before** recording the 'operative event' (i.e. a sale or purchase).

- When shares are disposed of out of the share pool, the appropriate proportion of the cost and indexed cost which relates to the shares disposed of is calculated on an average cost basis (as for individuals).

Pro forma for a company's share pool

	Number	Cost £	Indexed cost £
Purchase	X	X ⟶	X
IA to next operative event (December 2017 if earlier)			X
Purchase	X	X ⟶	X
	X	X	X
IA to next operative event (December 2017 if earlier)			X
	X	X	X
Disposal	(X)	(X) W1	(X) W2
Pool carried forward	X	X	X

Workings:

(W1) Calculates the average pool cost of shares disposed of

(W2) Calculates the average indexed cost of shares disposed of

Calculation of the gain on shares in the share pool

Workings 1 and 2 above feed into a normal gain computation, as follows:

	£
Sale proceeds	X
Less: Cost (W1)	(X)
	___
Unindexed gain	X
Less: Indexation allowance (W2 – W1)	(X)
	___
Chargeable gain	X
	___

It is important to show the cost (W1) and the indexation allowance (W2 – W1) separately in the gain computation, rather than simply deducting the indexed cost (W2) from sale proceeds, to ensure that the indexation allowance does not create/increase a loss.

Illustration 5 – Disposal of shares and securities

Continuing the example of Minnie Ltd (above), calculate the chargeable gain on the disposal from the share pool.

Assume the indexation factors are as follows:

July 2006 to September 2010	0.135
September 2010 to December 2017	0.234
September 2010 to February 2021	0.336

Solution

	£
Sale proceeds (£5 × 1,000)	5,000
Less: Allowable cost (W)	(2,250)
	___
	2,750
Less: Indexation allowance (£2,943 – £2,250) (W)	(693)
	___
Chargeable gain	2,057
	___

Working: Share pool

	Number	Cost	Indexed cost
		£	£
July 2006 purchase	1,000	2,000	2,000
IA to next operative event:			
(July 2006 to September 2010)			
0.135 × £2,000			270
September 2010 purchase	1,000	2,500	2,500
	2,000	4,500	4,770
IA to next operative event			
i.e. sale in February 2021 (use			
December 2017 as earlier)			
(September 2010 to December 2017)			
0.234 × £4,770			1,116
	2,000	4,500	5,886
February 2021 sale			
(1,000 out of 2,000) (Note)	(1,000)	(2,250)	(2,943)
Pool carried forward	1,000	2,250	2,943

Note: Half of the shares sold, therefore take out half of the cost and indexed cost.

Test your understanding 4

Braganza Ltd sold 10,000 ordinary shares in the FRP Co plc, a quoted company, on 20 December 2020, for £70,000.

The company had bought the ordinary shares on the following dates:

	Number of shares	Cost
		£
1 April 2003	8,000	25,250
22 December 2005	4,000	7,500

Calculate the chargeable gain arising on the disposal.

Assume indexation factors of:

April 2003 to December 2005	0.071
December 2005 to December 2017	0.433
December 2005 to December 2020	0.543

5   Bonus and rights issues

The key points to remember are as follows:

- A bonus issue is the distribution of free shares to shareholders, based on existing shareholdings.

- A rights issue involves shareholders paying for new shares, usually at a rate below market price and in proportion to their existing shareholdings.

- In both cases, the shareholder is making a new acquisition of shares.

- However, for matching purposes, such acquisitions arise out of the original holdings. They are not treated as a separate holding of shares.

- Bonus and rights issues therefore, attach to the original shareholdings, for the purposes of the identification rules.

Bonus issues

- As a bonus issue is free shares (i.e. no cost is involved), there is no indexation to be calculated.

- A bonus issue is not an operative event in the share pool.

- Simply, add the bonus issue shares to the share pool. When the next operative event occurs (e.g. next sale or purchase), index from the operative event before the date of the bonus issue.

Rights issues

- A rights issue is simply a purchase of shares (usually at a price below the market rate).

- Hence, it should be treated as an operative event, in the same way as a normal purchase in the share pool:

  - Index up to the date of the rights issue (or December 2017, if earlier), then

  - Add in the number of shares and their cost.

Illustration 6 – Bonus issue

Alpha Ltd acquired shares in S plc, a quoted company, as follows:

2,000 shares acquired in June 2003, for £11,500.

In October 2016, there was a 1 for 2 bonus issue.

Set up the share pool and deal with the events up to and including the bonus issue.

Solution

Share pool	Number	Cost	Indexed cost
		£	£
Purchase (June 2003)	2,000	11,500	11,500
Bonus issue (October 2016)			
(1 for 2) 1/2 × 2,000	1,000	0	0
	3,000	11,500	11,500

Note: Do not index up to the date of the bonus issue as no cost is involved. The next time there is an operative event, IA will be calculated from June 2003 (the last operative event).

 Test your understanding 5

Spencer Ltd sold 2,000 ordinary shares out of a holding of 5,000 shares in Plumb Ltd, on 30 September 2020, for £15,400.

Spencer Ltd prepares accounts every year to 31 March. The holding of shares in Plumb Ltd had been built up as follows:

Date acquired	Number of shares	Cost
		£
May 2000	4,000	7,000
March 2011 – Bonus issue 1 for 4	1,000	0

Compute the chargeable gain arising on the sale of shares, in the year ended 31 March 2021.

Assume the indexation factors are:

May 2000 to March 2011	0.362
May 2000 to December 2017	0.629
March 2011 to December 2017	0.196
May 2000 to September 2020	0.740
March 2011 to September 2020	0.277

Illustration 7 – Rights issue

Amber Ltd sold 2,600 shares in Pearl Ltd in December 2020 for £30,000.

Amber Ltd originally acquired 3,000 shares in Pearl Ltd in June 2002 for £11,500. In December 2009 Amber Ltd took up its entitlement to a 1 for 4 rights issue at £3 per share.

Calculate the chargeable gain arising on disposal of the shares, in December 2020.

Assume the following indexation factors apply:

June 2002 to December 2009	0.237
June 2002 to December 2017	0.578
June 2002 to December 2020	0.699
December 2009 to December 2017	0.276
December 2009 to December 2020	0.373

Solution

Chargeable gain

	£
Sale proceeds	30,000
Less: Cost (W)	(9,533)
Unindexed gain	20,467
Less: Indexation (£14,576 – £9,533) (W)	(5,043)
Chargeable gain	15,424

Working: Share pool	Number	Cost	Indexed cost
		£	£
Purchase – June 2002	3,000	11,500	11,500
IA to December 2009			
0.237 × £11,500			2,726
	3,000	11,500	14,226
December 2009			
– Rights issue (1 for 4) at £3	750	2,250	2,250
	3,750	13,750	16,476

IA to December 2017 (earlier than next operative event) 0.276 × £16,476			4,547
	3,750	13,750	21,023
Disposal – December 2020 (2,600/3,750) × £13,750/£21,023	(2,600)	(9,533)	(14,576)
Balance to c/f	1,150	4,217	6,447

Note: The indexed cost is updated prior to the rights issue, because it is a purchase which involves additional cost (i.e. it is an operative event).

Following the disposal, there are 1,150 shares in the pool, with a cost of £4,217 and an indexed cost of £6,447.

This will be used as the starting point, when dealing with the next operative event.

6 Takeovers/reorganisations

We have already looked at takeovers and reorganisations in relation to an individual taxpayer (see Chapter 21). The same principles apply to disposals by companies as summarised below.

Consideration: shares for shares

Where the consideration for the reorganisation or takeover only involves the issue of shares in the acquiring company, the tax consequences are:

- No chargeable gain arises at the time of the reorganisation or takeover.

- The cost of the original shares becomes the cost of the new shares.

- Where the shareholder receives more than one type of share, in exchange for the original shares:
    - the cost of the original shares is allocated to the new shares
    - by reference to the market values of the various new shares
    - on the first day of dealing in them after the reorganisation/takeover.

Mixed consideration

When both cash and shares are received on a takeover:

- There is a part disposal of the original shares.

- A chargeable gain arises on the cash element of the consideration.

- The calculation of the chargeable gain is the same as for individuals (see Chapter 21) except that indexation allowance must be taken into account.

Illustration 8 – Takeovers/reorganisations

In June 2002, Major Ltd purchased 2,000 ordinary shares in Blue plc, for £5,000.

In July 2017, Blue plc was taken over by Red plc, and Major Ltd received 2 ordinary shares and 1 preference share in Red plc, for each ordinary share in Blue plc.

Immediately after the takeover, the ordinary shares in Red plc, were quoted at £2 and the preference shares in Red plc, were quoted at £1.

In December 2020, Major Ltd sold all of its holding of ordinary shares in Red plc, for £8,000.

Calculate the chargeable gain arising in December 2020.

Indexation factors:

June 2002 to July 2017	0.549
July 2017 to December 2017	0.019
June 2002 to December 2017	0.578
July 2017 to December 2020	0.097
June 2002 to December 2020	0.699

Solution

	£
Sale proceeds	8,000
Less: Cost (W3)	(4,000)
Unindexed gain	4,000
Less: Indexation allowance (£6,314 – £4,000) (Note)	(2,314)
Chargeable gain	1,686

Workings:

(W1) Share pool – Blue plc

	Number	Cost	Indexed cost
		£	£
June 2002 – purchase	2,000	5,000	5,000
IA to takeover – July 2017			
(0.549 × £5,000)			2,745
Balance at takeover	2,000	5,000	7,745

(W2) Allocation of cost of shares in Blue plc

Major Ltd received:	MV	Cost	Indexed cost
	£	£	£
4,000 ordinary shares (valued at £2)	8,000	4,000	6,196
2,000 preference shares (valued at £1)	2,000	1,000	1,549
	10,000	5,000	7,745

The cost and indexed cost attributable to the ordinary shares is calculated as: (8,000/10,000) × £5,000/£7,745.

New share pools are then established for the new ordinary and preference shares received in Red plc.

(W3) Share pool in Red plc – ordinary shares

	Number	Cost	Indexed cost
		£	£
July 2017	4,000	4,000	6,196
IA to December 2017 as earlier than date of sale (£6,196 × 0.019)			118
December 2020	4,000	4,000	6,314
Disposal	(4,000)	(4,000)	(6,314)

Tutorial note:

Technically IA should be calculated up to the date of the takeover (i.e. from June 2002 to July 2017) on the original shares in the share pool. The new shares then inherit the indexed cost at the date of the takeover. On the disposal of the new shares, this indexed cost is indexed from July 2017 to December 2017 as shown above.

However, performing just one IA calculation from June 2002 to December 2017 will not give a materially different answer. This approach is therefore an acceptable short cut in the examination.

	£
Sale proceeds	8,000
Less: Cost	(4,000)
Unindexed gain	4,000
Less: IA from June 2002 to December 2017	
(£4,000 × 0.578)	(2,312)
Chargeable gain	1,688

Test your understanding 6

In July 2020, during its year ended 31 December 2020, Concert Ltd sold its entire holding of ordinary shares in Corus plc, for £75,000.

Concert Ltd had originally purchased 20,000 £1 ordinary shares in BNB plc, at a cost of £20,000, in April 2007.

In July 2013, BNB plc was taken over by Corus plc. Concert Ltd received one ordinary 50p share and one 50p 6% preference share in Corus plc, for each ordinary share it held in BNB plc.

Immediately after the takeover, the value of these new shares was:

50p ordinary share	£1.80 each
50p preference share	£0.80 each

(a) **Compute the chargeable gain arising in the year ended 31 December 2020.**

The relevant indexation factor to be used is 0.354.

(b) **Explain the consequences had Concert Ltd received cash of £16,000 rather than preference shares in July 2013.**

7 Reliefs available to companies

The **only** capital gains relief available to companies is rollover relief. The other reliefs covered in Chapter 22 are not applicable to companies.

Rollover relief for companies

Rollover relief (ROR) for companies operates, in general, in the same way as for individuals. The rules are summarised below.

Summary of rollover relief

- ROR allows a company to replace assets used in its trade, without incurring a corporation tax liability on the related chargeable gains.

- The gain arising on the disposal of the business asset, is deducted from (rolled over against), the acquisition cost of the new asset.

- Provided the proceeds are fully reinvested, no tax is payable at the time of the disposal.

- Common assets which qualify for ROR in the examination are:

  – Land and buildings that are both occupied and used for trading purposes.

  – Fixed plant and machinery ('fixed' means immovable).

- The acquisition of the replacement asset, must occur during a period that begins one year before the sale of the old asset and ends three years after the sale.

- The new asset must be brought into use in the trade when it is acquired.

- Where disposal proceeds of the old asset are not fully reinvested, the surplus retained, reduces the amount of chargeable gain that can be rolled over.

- When an asset has not been used entirely for business purposes throughout the company's period of ownership, ROR is scaled down in proportion to the non-business use.

- If reinvestment is in a depreciating asset, the chargeable gain is deferred until the earliest of:

  – disposal of the depreciating asset

  – depreciating asset ceases to be used for trading purposes

  – 10 years after the depreciating asset was acquired.

- Any asset with a predictable life of not more than 60 years, is a depreciating asset.

- If a new non-depreciating asset is acquired before the deferred gain becomes chargeable, ROR can be claimed and the deferred gain is deducted from the base cost of the new non-depreciating asset.

The key differences in the rules for companies are as follows:

- **goodwill is not a qualifying asset** for companies

- the gain deferred is the 'indexed gain' (i.e. the gain **after** IA)

- claim must be made within four years of the **later of** the end of the accounting period in which the asset is

  – sold, and

  – replaced.

Test your understanding 7

Medway Ltd has been offered £160,000 for a freehold factory that it owns, and is considering disposing of the factory in January 2021.

The company acquired the factory on 15 March 2009, for £45,000. The factory has always been used by Medway Ltd for business purposes.

Explain the chargeable gains implications of each of the following alternative courses of action that Medway Ltd is considering taking:

(a) **Acquiring a larger freehold factory in April 2021, for £170,000.**

(b) **Acquiring a smaller freehold factory in April 2021, for £155,000 and using the remainder of the proceeds as working capital.**

(c) **Using the proceeds to pay a premium of £180,000 in April 2021, for a 40 year lease of a new factory (it is possible that a freehold warehouse will be bought in the next two or three years for an estimated cost of £200,000).**

Assume the following indexation factors apply:

March 2009 to December 2017	0.316
March 2009 to January 2021	0.421

8 Summary of key differences between individuals and companies

	Individuals	Companies
Gains subject to	Capital gains tax – tax separately from income	Corporation tax – include in TTP – tax with income
Annual exempt amount (AEA)	✓	X
Indexation allowance to December 2017	X	✓
Matching rules	Shares purchased: 1 on the same day 2 in the **following 30 days** (FIFO) 3 in the share pool	Shares purchased: 1 on the same day 2 in the **previous 9 days** (FIFO) 3 in the share pool
Treatment of capital losses	• Offset against current year gains without restriction • Carry forward against future net gains after the AEA	• Offset against current year gains without restriction • Carry forward against future net gains without restriction
Business asset disposal relief, gift relief, PRR and investors' relief	✓	X
Rollover relief	✓	✓ (but not on goodwill)

9 Chapter summary

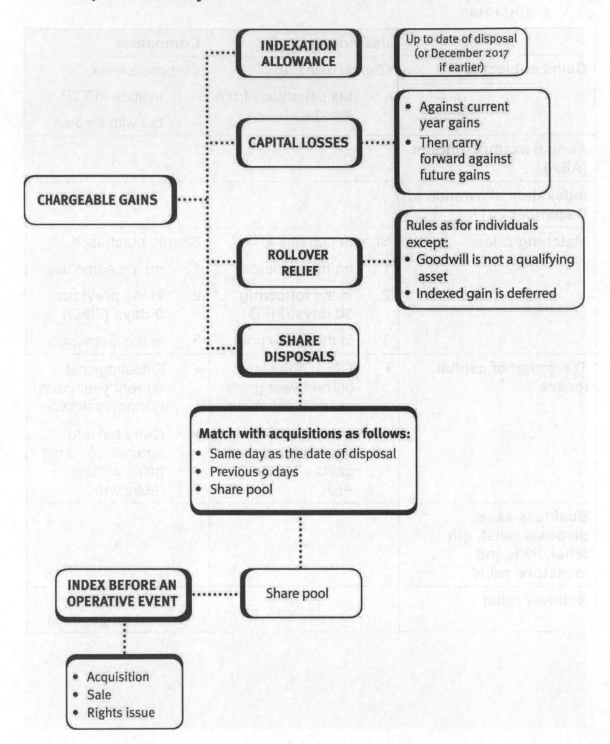

- **INDEXATION ALLOWANCE** — Up to date of disposal (or December 2017 if earlier)

- **CAPITAL LOSSES**
  - Against current year gains
  - Then carry forward against future gains

- **CHARGEABLE GAINS**

- **ROLLOVER RELIEF** — Rules as for individuals except:
  - Goodwill is not a qualifying asset
  - Indexed gain is deferred

- **SHARE DISPOSALS**

Match with acquisitions as follows:
- Same day as the date of disposal
- Previous 9 days
- Share pool

INDEX BEFORE AN OPERATIVE EVENT — Share pool
- Acquisition
- Sale
- Rights issue

10 Practice objective test questions

Test your understanding 8

X Ltd sold a building for proceeds of £330,000. The building cost £250,000. Surveyor and agents fees totalling £2,500 were also paid by X Ltd when the building was purchased.

What is the chargeable gain or allowable loss arising on this disposal?

Use an indexation factor of 0.316.

A   £1,000 gain

B   (£2,290) loss

C   £0

D   (£1,500) loss

Test your understanding 9

Walton Ltd bought 20 hectares of land on 13 January 2019 for £30,000. On 22 November 2020, the company sold 10 hectares for £60,000 and the market value of the remaining land at that time was £15,000.

The indexation factor from January 2019 to November 2020 is 0.055.

What is the chargeable gain arising on the disposal of the land in November 2020?

A   £44,175

B   £45,000

C   £34,680

D   £36,000

Test your understanding 10

In August 2020, Greengrass plc sold a property for £750,000 which it purchased in April 1999 for £125,000. In November 2010 the property was redecorated at a cost of £5,000.

What is the chargeable gain arising on the disposal? The indexation factors are:

April 1999 – August 2020	0.793
April 1999 – December 2017	0.683
November 2010 – August 2020	0.306
November 2010 – December 2017	0.226

A   £525,875

B   £519,345

C   £539,625

D   £533,495

Test your understanding 11

XYZ Ltd sold an unwanted factory for £634,000 on 15 March 2021. The company had paid £120,000 for the factory on 2 January 2012. XYZ Ltd had incurred expenses of £8,000 in buying the factory.

The relevant indexation factor is 0.168.

What is XYZ Ltd's chargeable gain arising on the above disposal?

A   £493,840

B   £484,496

C   £485,840

D   £506,000

Test your understanding answers

 Test your understanding 1

Hobbit Ltd

Chargeable gain computation

	£
Sale proceeds	680,000
Less: Cost	(175,000)
Enhancement expenditure	(62,000)
Unindexed gain	443,000
Less: Indexation allowance:	
Cost (£175,000 × 0.625) (Note)	(109,375)
Enhancement expenditure (Note)	0
Chargeable gain	333,625

Note: Indexation allowance is frozen at December 2017. There is therefore no indexation allowance on the extension which was added after December 2017.

 Test your understanding 2

JNN Ltd

	(a) £	(b) £	(c) £
Sale proceeds	25,000	12,000	8,000
Less: Cost	(10,000)	(10,000)	(10,000)
Unindexed gain/(loss)	15,000	2,000	(2,000)
Less: Indexation allowance			
£10,000 × 1.002	(10,020)		
Restricted (see note)		(2,000)	0
Chargeable gain/(allowable loss)	4,980	0	(2,000)

Note: Indexation is frozen at December 2017.

Part (b): IA is restricted as indexation cannot create a loss.

Part (c): no IA as indexation cannot increase a loss.

Test your understanding 3

High Ltd

Corporation tax liability – y/e 31 December 2020

	£
Tax adjusted trading profit	200,000
Net chargeable gain	0
Taxable total profits	200,000

		£
Corporation tax liability	(£200,000 × 19%)	38,000

Note: The corporation tax rate is 19% in FY 2019 and FY 2020

Working: Net chargeable gain

	£
Chargeable gain	17,000
Less: Capital loss b/f	(23,000)
Capital loss c/f	(6,000)

Therefore the net chargeable gain is £Nil.

Test your understanding 4

Braganza Ltd

Chargeable gain computation

	£
Sale proceeds	70,000
Less: Acquisition cost (W)	(27,292)
Unindexed gain	42,708
Less: Indexation allowance (£41,250 – £27,292) (W)	(13,958)
Chargeable gain	28,750

Working: Share pool

	Number	Cost £	Indexed cost £
1.4.03 acquisition	8,000	25,250	25,250
IA to December 2005			
0.071 × £25,250			1,793
December 2005 acquisition	4,000	7,500	7,500
	12,000	32,750	34,543
IA to December 2017 as earlier than next operative event			
0.433 × £34,543			14,957
	12,000	32,750	49,500
Disposal – December 2020	(10,000)	(27,292)	(41,250)
Balance c/f	2,000	5,458	8,250

Proportion of cost and indexed cost relating to the disposal:

Cost: (10,000/12,000) × £32,750 = £27,292

Indexed cost: (10,000/12,000) × £49,500 = £41,250

Test your understanding 5

Spencer Ltd

Chargeable gain computation – y/e 31 March 2021

	£
Sale proceeds	15,400
Less: Acquisition cost (W)	(2,800)
Unindexed gain	12,600
Less: Indexation allowance (£4,561 – £2,800) (W)	(1,761)
Chargeable gain	10,839

Working: Share pool

	Number	Cost	Indexed cost
		£	£
May 2000	4,000	7,000	7,000
March 2011 – bonus issue	1,000	0	0
	5,000	7,000	7,000
Index to December 2017 from May 2000			
0.629 × £7,000			4,403
	5,000	7,000	11,403
Disposal (Note)	(2,000)	(2,800)	(4,561)
Balance c/f	3,000	4,200	6,842

Note: The proportion of cost and indexed cost relating to the disposal is calculated as: (2,000/5,000) × £7,000 and £11,403 respectively.

Test your understanding 6

Concert Ltd

(a) **Chargeable gain computation – y/e 31 December 2020**

	£
Sales proceeds	75,000
Less: Deemed acquisition cost (W)	(13,846)
Unindexed gain	61,154
Less: Indexation allowance (£13,846 × 0.354) (Note)	(4,901)
Chargeable gain	56,253

Working: Deemed acquisition cost

Following the takeover in July 2013 of BNB plc by Corus plc, Concert Ltd now owns shares in Corus plc as per the terms of the takeover.

	Total M.V.	Original cost
	£	£
20,000 50p ordinary shares @ £1.80	36,000	13,846
20,000 50p preference shares @ £0.80	16,000	6,154
	52,000	20,000

Allocation of original cost incurred in April 2007, to the shares now owned in July 2013, using the average cost method.

To ordinary shares: (£36,000/£52,000) × £20,000 = £13,846

To preference shares: (£16,000/£52,000) × £20,000 = £6,154

Note: Technically IA should be calculated up to the date of the takeover (i.e. from April 2007 to July 2013) on the original shares in the share pool. The new shares then inherit the indexed cost at the date of the takeover. On the disposal of the new shares, this indexed cost is indexed from July 2013 to December 2017 (as earlier than date of sale of July 2020).

However, performing just one IA calculation from April 2007 to December 2017 will not give a materially different answer. This approach is therefore an acceptable short cut in the examination.

(b) **Mixed consideration on the takeover**

If Concert Ltd had received cash in July 2013, a chargeable gain would have arisen in the year ended 31 December 2013 calculated as follows:

	£
Cash received	X
Less: Cost	(X)
	X
Less: IA from April 2007 to July 2013	(X)
Chargeable gain	X

Test your understanding 7

Medway Ltd

Chargeable gain	£
Sales proceeds	160,000
Less: Cost	(45,000)
Unindexed gain	115,000
Less: Indexation allowance (0.316 × £45,000) =	(14,220)
Chargeable gain	100,780

(a) **Larger freehold factory**

As all the proceeds are reinvested, there will be no chargeable gain arising in January 2021 and the gain will be rolled over against the base cost of the new factory.

	£
Cost of factory	170,000
Less: ROR (deferred gain)	(100,780)
Base cost of new factory	69,220

(b) **Smaller freehold factory**

As only part of the proceeds are reinvested, the gain that cannot be rolled over will be £5,000 (£160,000 – £155,000). This will be immediately chargeable to corporation tax.

The balance of the gain will be rolled over as above:

	£
Cost of factory	155,000
Less: ROR (£100,780 – £5,000)	(95,780)
Base cost of new factory	59,220

(c) **Lease**

All of the proceeds are being used to acquire a depreciating asset (i.e. one with an expected life of not more than 60 years). The chargeable gain is therefore not rolled over, but is instead 'frozen'.

It will become chargeable to corporation tax on the earlier of:

– the date that the lease is sold

– the date the leased factory ceases to be used in the trade

– the expiry of ten years from April 2021.

Therefore, the base cost of the lease remains at £180,000.

If, before the 'frozen' gain becomes chargeable, a non-depreciating asset is acquired, the gain can be rolled over in the usual way.

In this question, if the freehold warehouse is acquired in the next two to three years, all the proceeds will be reinvested and so the rollover claim could be switched to the freehold warehouse.

The base cost of the freehold warehouse would be reduced to £99,220 (£200,000 – £100,780).

Test your understanding 8

The correct answer is C.

	£
Proceeds	330,000
Less: Cost (including incidental costs)	(252,500)
	77,500
Less: Indexation (0.316 × £252,500) (restricted)	(77,500)
Chargeable gain	0

Note: Indexation allowance cannot turn a gain into a loss.

Test your understanding 9

The correct answer is D.

	£
Proceeds	60,000
Less: Cost	
£30,000 × (£60,000/(£60,000 + £15,000))	(24,000)
	36,000
Less: Indexation allowance – land acquired after December 2017	(0)
Chargeable gain	36,000

Test your understanding 10

The correct answer is C.

	£
Proceeds	750,000
Cost	(125,000)
Unindexed gain	625,000
IA £125,000 × 0.683	(85,375)
Chargeable gain	539,625

Note: Redecoration is revenue expenditure and does not qualify as a capital improvement. Indexation is frozen at December 2017.

Test your understanding 11

The correct answer is B.

	£
Proceeds	634,000
Cost (£120,000 + £8,000)	(128,000)
	506,000
Less: Indexation allowance	
(0.168 × £128,000)	(21,504)
Chargeable gain	484,496

Selling costs are deducted from the sales proceeds. Buying costs can be added to the cost of purchase and indexed. Indexation allowance is calculated on the total acquisition costs of £128,000.

Inheritance tax

Chapter learning objectives

Upon completion of this chapter you will be able to:

- identify the persons chargeable

- understand and apply the meaning of transfer of value, chargeable transfer and potentially exempt transfer

- demonstrate the diminution in value principle

- demonstrate the seven year accumulation principle taking into account changes in the level of the nil rate band

- understand the tax implications of lifetime transfers and compute the relevant liabilities

- understand and compute the tax liability on a death estate

- understand and apply the transfer of any unused nil rate band between spouses

- understand and apply the residence nil rate band available when a residential property is inherited by direct descendants

- understand and apply the following exemptions: small gifts exemption; annual exemption; normal expenditure out of income; gifts in consideration of marriage; gifts between spouses

- basic inheritance tax planning

- identify who is responsible for the payment of inheritance tax and the due date for payment of inheritance tax.

PER

One of the PER performance objectives (PO15) is to prepare computations of taxable amounts and tax liabilities according to legal requirements. Another objective (PO17) is to advise on mitigating and deferring tax liabilities through legitimate tax planning measures. Working through this chapter should help you understand how to demonstrate those objectives.

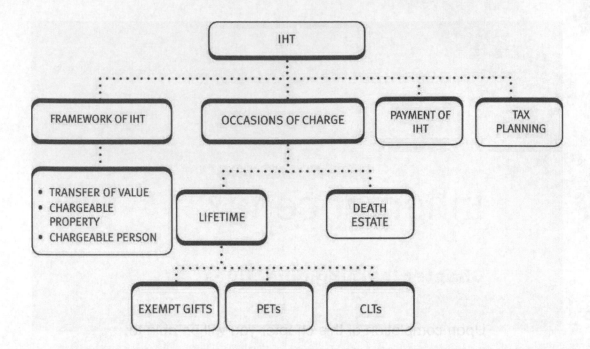

Introduction

Most inheritance tax (IHT) is collected on the death of an individual based on the value of his or her death estate. However, if IHT only applied on death, it would be an easy tax to avoid by giving away assets immediately before death. Therefore, there are IHT implications arising on some lifetime gifts as well as on death.

This chapter covers the principles that underpin IHT, deals with the way in which an individual is liable to IHT and considers the IHT payable on lifetime gifts. The detailed death estate computation is then covered, along with payment dates and some basic IHT planning.

Inheritance tax is an important topic. You should expect to be tested on this area in both sections A and B of your TX examination. Inheritance tax could also be the focus of the 10 mark question in section C.

1 The charge to inheritance tax (IHT)

Inheritance tax is charged on:

- a **transfer of value**
- of **chargeable property**
- by a **chargeable person**.

A charge to inheritance tax (IHT) arises:

- on the death of an individual
- on lifetime gifts where the donor dies within 7 years of the date of a gift
- on some lifetime gifts which are taxed at the date of the gift.

The donor is the person who makes the transfer of the asset, and the recipient is known as the donee.

Transfer of value

A transfer of value is **a gift of any asset** which results in a reduction in the value of the donor's estate.

To be treated as a transfer of value the transfer must be a 'gratuitous disposition'. This basically means a gift.

A bad business deal will therefore not be liable to inheritance tax, even though there is a fall in value of the estate, as it was not the donor's intention to give anything away.

To calculate the transfer of value for IHT purposes, the **loss to donor** principle is used (also referred to as the **diminution in value** concept).

 The loss to the donor, is the difference between the value of the donor's estate before and after the gift, and is the starting point for IHT calculations:

	£
Value of estate before gift	X
Less: Value of estate after gift	(X)
	——
Diminution in value or transfer of value	X
	——

The loss to the donor is usually the **open market value** of the asset gifted.

However, in some circumstances, the transfer of value from the donor's point of view is not necessarily the same as the value of the asset received from the donee's point of view.

This is most common with unquoted shares, where a controlling shareholding has a higher value per share than a minority shareholding.

Test your understanding 1

Linda owns 6,000 shares, which represents a 60% holding, in Loot Ltd. On 31 December 2020 she gave a 20% holding in the company to her friend, Bob.

The values of shareholdings in Loot Ltd on 31 December 2020 have been agreed for IHT purposes as follows:

Holding	Value per share
Up to 25%	£9
26% to 50%	£15
51% to 74%	£26
75% or more	£45

Calculate the transfer of value relating to the gift of unquoted shares for IHT purposes.

Chargeable property

All property to which a person is beneficially entitled is deemed to form part of his or her estate. Therefore, a gift of **any asset** is a transfer of value.

 For the purposes of the TX examination there is no such thing as an exempt asset for IHT purposes.

Chargeable persons

A chargeable person for the purposes of the TX examination will always be an **individual**.

All individuals are potentially liable to IHT.

An individual who is domiciled in the UK is liable to inheritance tax on his or her worldwide assets.

If not UK domiciled, he or she is generally only liable on UK assets only.

 However, for the purposes of the TX examination, all individuals will be UK domiciled.

Note that spouses and partners in a registered civil partnership are chargeable to IHT separately.

2 Occasions of charge

The main charge to IHT arises on the death of an individual as liability arises on the following:

- the value of all of the net assets in his or her estate at the date of death
- any lifetime gifts made in the seven years before his or her death, provided they are not exempt gifts.

However, an IHT charge also arises on certain lifetime gifts at the date of the gift.

3 Lifetime gifts

There are three categories of lifetime gifts that can be made by an individual and they are treated for IHT purposes as follows:

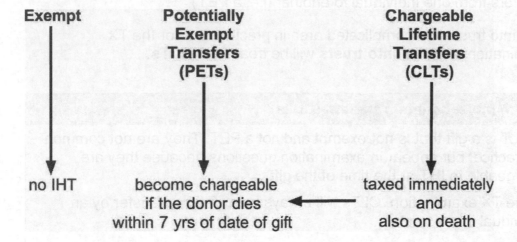

Types of lifetime gifts

The definition of each type of gift for the purpose of the TX examination and an overview of the way in which they are taxed is summarised in the table below:

Exempt transfers	Potentially Exempt Transfers (PETs)	Chargeable lifetime transfers (CLTs)
Definition		
A gift that is specifically deemed to be exempt from IHT (see below)	A gift by an individual to another individual	No definition = residual category (i.e. a gift which is not exempt nor a PET) For the TX examination, a CLT will be a gift into a trust
During lifetime		
No IHT payable	No IHT payable	IHT calculated using the lifetime rates of tax
If Donor lives 7 years		
No IHT payable	No IHT payable Gift becomes exempt	No further IHT payable
If Donor dies within 7 years		
No IHT payable	The PET becomes chargeable on death for the first time	Possibly extra IHT, calculated using the death rates of tax

It is important to note that in practice, the majority of lifetime transfers made by individuals are either:

* exempt transfers, or

* transfers from one individual to another (i.e. a PET).

 Gifts into trusts is a complicated area in practice, but for the TX examination, **all gifts into trusts** will be treated as **CLTs**.

 Chargeable lifetime transfers (CLTs)

A CLT is a gift that is not exempt and not a PET. They are not common in practice, but appear in examination questions because they are chargeable to IHT at the time of the gift.

In the TX examination, CLTs will always be a lifetime transfer by an individual into a trust.

Trusts

A trust is an arrangement where property (known as the trust assets or settled property) is transferred by a person (known as the settlor) to the trustees, to be held for the benefit of one or more specified persons (known as the beneficiaries) on terms specified in the trust deed.

The most common example of a trust is where parents wish to give assets to their children, but not until they are adults. The parents therefore put the assets into a trust with the children as beneficiaries, and the assets are controlled by the trustees until the children reach a specified age.

It is not necessary to understand the workings of trusts for the TX examination, only to learn that gifts into trusts are CLTs.

 Potentially exempt transfers (PETs)

PETs have derived their name from the fact that if the donor lives for seven years after making the gift, then the transfer is exempt (i.e. free from IHT). Therefore, at the time of transfer, it has the potential to be exempt.

However, if the donor dies within seven years of making the gift, then IHT may become chargeable on the gift.

Note that transfers on death can never be PETs.

4 Exemptions and reliefs for IHT

The following table summarises the exemptions and reliefs available for IHT that are examinable in TX.

Exemptions and reliefs available against:	
Lifetime gifts only	**Lifetime gifts and death estate**
• Small gifts exemption • Marriage exemption • Normal expenditure out of income • Annual exemption	• Inter spouse exemption

5 Exemptions available for lifetime gifts only

The following exemptions are available to reduce lifetime transfers only. They do not apply to the death estate.

 Note that the rules and limits for these exemptions are **not** included in the tax rates and allowances provided to you in the examination.

Small gifts exemption

Lifetime gifts are exempt if they are:

• an outright gift to an individual of no more than £250

• per recipient

• per tax year.

The small gift exemption does not apply if the gift is more than £250.

Therefore, a gift of £300 does not qualify. Similarly, if an individual makes a gift of £240 to a person followed by another gift of £100 to the same person in the same tax year, neither gift is exempt.

However, the donor can make gifts of up to £250 to any number of different recipients and they will all be exempt.

Marriage exemption

A lifetime transfer made 'in consideration of a marriage' (or registration of a civil partnership) is exempt up to the following maximum limits:

• £5,000 by a parent

• £2,500 by a grandparent or remoter ancestor

• £2,500 by a party to the marriage or civil partnership (e.g. from the groom to the bride)

• £1,000 by anyone else.

The exemption is conditional on the marriage taking place.

Normal expenditure out of income

IHT is levied on transfers of capital wealth.

Therefore, a lifetime transfer is exempt if it can be shown that the gift:

* is made as part of a person's normal expenditure out of income, and

* does not affect the donor's standard of living.

To be treated as 'normal', gifts must be habitual (i.e. there is a regular pattern of giving). For example, payment of school fees for a grandchild or annual payments into a life insurance policy for the benefit of a child are usually exempted under this rule.

The annual exemption

The annual exemption (AE) is an exemption available against **lifetime** transfers and operates as follows:

* The AE:

    – exempts the **first £3,000** of lifetime transfers in any one tax year

    – is applied chronologically to the first gift in the tax year, then (if there is any left) the second gift and so on

    – must be applied to the first gift each year, even if the first gift is a PET and never becomes chargeable.

* Any unused AE:

    – may be carried forward to the next year

    – however, it can be carried forward for one year only, and

    – can only be used after the current year's AE.

* The maximum AE in any one year is therefore £6,000 (£3,000 × 2).

* If other exemptions are available, they are given before the AE.

Test your understanding 2

Meron made the following lifetime gifts:

(a)   31 August 2018, £600, to her son

(b)   31 October 2018, £800, to a trust

(c)   31 May 2019, £2,100, to a trust

(d)   30 November 2019, £1,100, to a trust

(e)   30 April 2020, £5,000, to her daughter.

Calculate the chargeable amount after AEs for each of the gifts.

6 Exemptions available for lifetime transfers and the death estate

Inter spouse exemption

Transfers between spouses and partners in a registered civil partnership are exempt:

- regardless of the value of the transfer, and
- whether they are made during the individual's lifetime or on death.

Test your understanding 3

Felipe made the following lifetime transfers:

(a) Unquoted shares worth £525,000 in the family company to his husband on 1 June 2020.

(b) £15,000 to his son on 6 July 2020 as a wedding present.

(c) £20,000 to his nephew on 27 September 2020.

(d) £235 to a friend for her 40th birthday on 4 November 2020.

(e) £270,000 into a trust on 24 December 2020.

Calculate the chargeable amount for each of Felipe's lifetime gifts.

7 IHT payable during an individual's lifetime on CLTs

Lifetime IHT is payable when an individual makes a gift into a trust.

The procedure to calculate the lifetime IHT on a CLT

The chargeable amount for each lifetime gift (PETs and CLTs) is calculated on each gift separately, in chronological order.

Even though there is no lifetime tax on a PET, it is necessary to calculate its chargeable value as a PET uses the annual exemption, even if it never becomes chargeable. A PET may therefore reduce the amount of the annual exemption available to a CLT.

1 Calculate the chargeable amount of each CLT and PET:

	£
Value of estate before transfer	X
Less: Value of estate after transfer	(X)
Transfer of value	X
Less: (1) Wholly exempt transfers (i.e. to spouse/civil partner)	(X)
(2) Specific lifetime exemptions:	
– e.g. Marriage exemption	(X)
– Annual exemptions (applied last)	(X)
Chargeable amount	X

For a CLT (i.e. a transfer into a trust) the only exemption that is likely to be applicable is the annual exemption.

2 For CLT's only calculate the amount of nil rate band available after deducting gross chargeable transfers in the previous 7 years (see below).

3 Calculate the tax on the excess at either 20% or 25% depending on who has agreed to pay the tax; the donor or the donee (see below).

4 Calculate the gross amount of the gift to carry forward for future computations.

5 If required by the examination question, state the due date of payment of the IHT (see below).

The nil rate band

All individuals are entitled to a nil rate band (NRB) and are taxed on the chargeable value of CLTs in excess of the NRB at different rates depending on who has agreed to pay the lifetime tax.

The NRB has steadily increased each tax year in the past, although it has remained the same since the tax year 2009/10.

For lifetime tax calculations, the NRB applicable at the **time of the gift** is used.

 The current NRB of £325,000 is included in the tax rates and allowances provided to you in the examination.

However, where NRBs are required for previous years, these will be provided in the actual examination question to which they relate.

The appropriate rate of tax

The appropriate rate of tax to apply to lifetime gifts depends on who has agreed to pay the tax due.

Donee pays the tax

If the **trustees** of the trust (i.e. the donee) agree to pay the tax:

- the gift is referred to as a **gross gift**, and

- the appropriate rate of tax is 20%.

Donor pays the tax

If the donor agrees to pay the tax:

- The gift is referred to as a **net gift**.

- As a result of the gift, the donor's estate is reduced by:

  - the value of the gift, **and**

  - the associated tax payable on the gift.

- Accordingly the amount of the gift needs to be 'grossed up' to include the tax that the donor has to pay.

- The appropriate rate of tax is therefore 25% (i.e. 20/80ths of the net gift).

- The gross chargeable transfer value to carry forward is the net chargeable amount plus any IHT paid by the donor. This amount remains the same even if the nil rate band available at death differs from the amount available during the donor's lifetime.

In summary, the rate of tax on the value of CLTs in excess of the NRB is:

Payer:		Appropriate rate
Trustees of the trust	Gross gift	20%
Donor	Net gift	25% (or 20/80)

Note that the tax due on a CLT is primarily the responsibility of the donor.

Therefore, where an examination question does not specify who has agreed to pay the tax:

- always assume that the donor will pay and that the gift is therefore a net gift, and IHT is calculated at 25%.

  Note that the 25% tax rate is not included in the tax rates and allowances provided in the examination and therefore must be learnt.

The normal due date of payment of lifetime IHT

The date of payment of lifetime IHT depends on the date of the gift:

Date of CLT	Due date of payment
6 April to 30 September	30 April in the following year
1 October to 5 April	Six months after the end of the month of the CLT

Test your understanding 4

Charlotte makes a gift into a trust on 13 June 2020 of £366,000. She has made no previous lifetime gifts.

Calculate the amount of lifetime IHT due on the gift into the trust and state the gross chargeable amount of the gift to carry forward for future computations, assuming:

(a) **the trustees of the trust have agreed to pay any IHT due.**

(b) **Charlotte has agreed to pay any IHT due.**

State the due date for payment of tax in both cases.

The seven year cumulation period

In the TYU above, the individual had made no previous lifetime gifts and therefore all of the NRB was available to calculate the tax. However, the NRB is available for a 'seven year cumulation period'.

 Each time a CLT is made, in order to calculate the IHT liability, it is necessary to look back seven years and calculate how much NRB is available to set against that particular gift.

For lifetime calculations, to calculate the NRB available at any point in time, it is necessary to take account of the total of the **gross** amounts of all other **CLTs** made within the **previous seven years**.

- These CLTs in the seven year cumulation period are deemed to have utilised the NRB first.

- There will therefore only be NRB available to match against this latest gift if the total of the CLTs in the previous seven years is less than the NRB at the time of the gift.

- Note that although PETs may use the AE during the donor's lifetime, they do not affect the NRB available, as they are not yet chargeable.

Test your understanding 5

During his lifetime Alex had made the following gifts:

- 30 June 2010, £170,000 to a trust

- 12 June 2014, £150,000 to his daughter

- 30 June 2015, £191,000 to a trust

- 15 December 2020, £256,000 to a trust

The trustees of the first two trusts paid the IHT liabilities. Alex paid the tax on the last gift.

The nil rate bands for earlier years are as follows:

2010/11	£325,000
2014/15	£325,000
2015/16	£325,000

Calculate the IHT arising as a result of Alex's lifetime transfers.

State who will pay the tax, the due date for payment and the gross chargeable amount of each gift to carry forward to future computations.

Test your understanding 6

During his lifetime Yuuma had made the following cash gifts:

- 21 April 2008, £98,000 to a trust (trustees to pay tax)

- 15 April 2013, £140,000 to his son

- 19 March 2014, £234,000 to a trust (Yuuma to pay tax)

- 9 May 2019, £395,000 to a trust (trustees to pay tax)

The nil rate bands for earlier years are as follows:

2008/09	£312,000
2013/14	£325,000

Calculate the IHT arising as a result of Yuuma's lifetime transfers.

Summary of lifetime calculations

Remember to:

- only calculate IHT on CLTs

- consider the IHT position for each CLT separately and in chronological order

- use the NRB applicable for the tax year of the gift

- tax is due at 20% if the trustees pay, and 25% if the donor pays.

Also, remember that PETs are not chargeable at this stage, but you need to calculate the chargeable amount of the PETs as they may use the annual exemptions.

8 IHT payable on lifetime gifts as a result of death

On the death of an individual, an IHT charge could arise in relation to lifetime gifts **within seven years of death** as follows:

- PETs become chargeable for the first time.

- Additional tax may be due on a CLT.

The IHT payable on lifetime gifts as a result of death is **always** paid by the recipient of the gift:

Type of gift:	Paid by:
CLT	Trustees of the trust
PET	Donee

Calculating the death IHT on lifetime gifts

The death tax is calculated on each gift separately, in chronological order, as follows:

1   Identify all gifts within seven years of death.

2   Calculate the **gross chargeable amount** of each gift and any **lifetime tax paid**.

3   Calculate the amount of NRB available after deducting **gross chargeable transfers** in the 7 years before the gift:

      –   use the NRB for the tax year of **death** (rather than the tax year of the gift)

      –   **include PETs** which have become chargeable (but not those that have become completely exempt).

4   Calculate the death tax on the excess at 40%.

5   Calculate and deduct any taper relief available (see below).

6   For CLTs, deduct any lifetime IHT paid.

7   If required by the question, state who will pay the tax and the due date of payment (see below).

 Further points regarding death tax calculations on lifetime gifts

Chargeable amount

- The gross chargeable amount of each gift is taxed on death.

- The gross amount of CLTs will have already been calculated in the lifetime IHT calculations.

- Remember to use the grossed up value of any CLTs where the tax is paid by the donor.

- The chargeable amount of a PET is calculated using the values at the time of the gift and PETs may use up the AEs, even though they only become chargeable if the donor dies within 7 years.

The nil rate band

- The NRB for the tax year of the gift is used against the lifetime calculations as seen above.

- The NRB for the tax year of death is used to calculate the death tax but it is matched against **all** chargeable gifts in the 7 years prior to the date of the gift (i.e. CLTs and PETs that have become chargeable) in chronological order.

The seven year cumulation period

The seven year cumulation period for the NRB applies in a similar way as for the lifetime calculations.

However, note that:

- it is necessary to take into account the total of the **gross** amounts of **all chargeable gifts** made within the **previous seven years** (not just CLTs)

- therefore, to calculate the death IHT on each gift, it is necessary to look back seven years from the **date of each gift** and include the gross amount of:

  - all CLTs, **and**

  - PETs that have become chargeable due to the death of the individual.

This means that a CLT made more than 7 years before death may still affect the NRB when calculating death tax on lifetime gifts.

However, ignore any PETs made more than 7 years ago, as they are not taxable.

The death rate of tax

The death rate of IHT is 40% on the excess over the available NRB.

 Taper relief

Where IHT is chargeable on any lifetime transfer due to death, the amount of IHT payable on death is reduced by taper relief:

- where more than 3 years have elapsed since the date of the gift

- by a percentage reduction according to the length of time between

  - the date of the gift, and

  - the date of the donor's death.

Note that the relief applies to both CLTs and PETs.

The rates of taper relief are included in the tax rates and allowances provided to you in the examination, and are as follows:

Years before date of death:		Taper relief
Over	Less than	%
0	3	0
3	4	20
4	5	40
5	6	60
6	7	80

So for a chargeable transfer made more than 5 years but less than 6 years before death, the IHT due on death is calculated as normal and then 60% taper relief is applied such that only 40% of the death tax is payable.

For gifts made seven or more years before death there is no IHT payable on death, so taper relief is not relevant.

Deduction of lifetime IHT paid

For CLTs, any lifetime IHT already paid is deducted from the liability calculated on death.

However, no refund is made if the tax already paid is higher than the amount now due on death.

At best, the deduction of lifetime tax paid will bring the liability on death down to £Nil.

The normal due date of payment of IHT on death

IHT as a result of death is due **six months** after the **end of the month of death**.

Illustration 1 – Death tax payable on lifetime gifts

Fred had made the following lifetime transfers:

* 31 July 2011, £80,000, to his son

* 31 January 2014, £110,000, to his daughter

* 30 April 2014, £235,000, to his son.

He died on 31 December 2020.

The nil rate bands for earlier years are as follows:

2011/12	£325,000
2013/14	£325,000
2014/15	£325,000

Calculate the IHT arising as a result of Fred's death on 31 December 2020. State who will pay the tax and the due date of payment.

Solution

PET – 31 July 2011

- The PET made on 31 July 2011 to his son is more than seven years before 31 December 2020.

- It is therefore completely exempt. No IHT is payable during his lifetime and no IHT is due as a result of his death.

- The gift is ignored and is not accumulated for future calculations.

PETs – 31 January 2014 and 30 April 2014

The two gifts on 31 January 2014 and 30 April 2014 are PETs. Therefore no lifetime IHT is payable. However, both gifts will become chargeable as a result of Fred's death within seven years.

IHT payable during lifetime

	PET 31.7.2011		PET 31.1.2014		PET 30.4.2014	
		£		£		£
Transfer of value		80,000		110,000		235,000
Less: Annual exemption						
Current year	2011/12	(3,000)	2013/14	(3,000)	2014/15	(3,000)
Previous year	2010/11 b/f	(3,000)	2012/13 b/f	(3,000)	2013/14 b/f	(0)
Chargeable amount		74,000		104,000		232,000
IHT payable (as all PETs)		0		0		0
Gross chargeable amount c/f		74,000		104,000		232,000

All gifts are PETs, therefore there is no lifetime tax to pay. However the gross chargeable amount of the PETs must be established at the time of the gift.

Note that the earlier NRBs given in the question are not required, as they are only required if there is lifetime tax to pay.

IHT payable on death

Date of death: 31 December 2020

Seven years before: 31 December 2013

PET on 31.7.2011 is more than seven years before death – therefore no IHT payable on death.

	PET 31.1.2014		PET 30.4.2014	
	£	£	£	£
Gross chargeable amount b/f (as above)		104,000		232,000
NRB @ date of death – 2020/21	325,000		325,000	
Less:				
GCTs < 7 years before gift				
(31.1.2007 – 31.1.2014)				
(ignore 31.7.2011 PET as completely exempt)	(0)			
(30.4.2007 – 30.4.2014)			(104,000)	
(ignore 31.7.2011 PET as completely exempt, but include 31.1.2014 PET as became chargeable)				
NRB available		(325,000)		(221,000)
Taxable amount		0		11,000
IHT payable @ 40%		0		4,400
Less: Taper relief (30.4.2014 – 31.12.2020) (6 – 7 years before death) (80%)				(3,520)
Less: IHT paid in lifetime				(0)
IHT payable on death		0		880
Paid by (always the donee)				Son
Due date of payment (six months after end of month of death)				30.6.2021

Illustration 2 – Death tax payable on lifetime gifts

On 15 July 2013 Saanvi made a transfer of £365,000 into a trust. She had made no other lifetime transfers. The IHT due in respect of this gift was paid by Saanvi.

Saanvi died on 30 May 2020.

The nil rate band for 2013/14 is £325,000.

Calculate the IHT arising on Saanvi's lifetime gift, and the additional IHT arising as a result of her death.

State who will pay the tax and the due date of payment.

Solution

Lifetime IHT

15 July 2013 – CLT (2013/14)

	£	£
Transfer of value		365,000
Less: AE – 2013/14		(3,000)
– 2012/13 b/f		(3,000)
		———
Net chargeable amount		359,000
NRB at date of gift (2013/14)	325,000	
Less: GCTs in 7 yrs pre-gift (15.7.06 to 15.7.13)	(0)	
	———	
NRB available		(325,000)
		———
Taxable amount		34,000
		———
Lifetime IHT due (£34,000 × 25%)		
(= net gift as Saanvi paying the tax)		8,500
		———
Payable by		Saanvi
Due date (gift in first half of tax year)		30.4.14
Gross amount to carry forward for future computations		
(£359,000 + £8,500)		367,500
		———

IHT payable on death

15 July 2013 – CLT

	£	£
Gross chargeable amount (above)		367,500
NRB at death	325,000	
Less: GCTs in 7 yrs pre-gift (15.7.06 to 15.7.13)	(0)	
NRB available		(325,000)
Taxable amount		42,500
IHT due on death (£42,500 × 40%)		17,000
Less: Taper relief		
(15.07.13 to 30.05.20) (6 – 7 yrs) (80%)		(13,600)
Chargeable (20%)		3,400
Less: IHT paid in lifetime (CLT)		(8,500)
IHT payable on death		0

There is no repayment of lifetime IHT.

Illustration 3 – IHT payable on lifetime gifts as a result of death

Charbel made the following lifetime gifts:

	Nil rate band
1 September 2010, £315,000, to a trust.	£325,000
1 May 2014, £263,000, to his son Alexander.	£325,000
1 June 2015, £236,000, to a trust.	£325,000
1 July 2016, £21,000, to his daughter Jayne.	£325,000
1 August 2018, £103,000, to a trust.	£325,000

Charbel had agreed to pay any IHT due on CLTs. Charbel died on 1 December 2020.

Calculate the IHT payable on the lifetime transfers during Charbel's lifetime and on his death.

State who will pay the tax and the due date of payment.

Answer to illustration 3

IHT payable during lifetime

	CLT 1.9.2010	PET 1.5.2014	CLT 1.6.2015	PET 1.7.2017	CLT 1.8.2018
	£	£	£	£	£
Transfer of value	315,000	263,000	236,000	21,000	103,000
Annual exemption					
– Current year	(3,000)	(3,000)	(3,000)	(3,000)	(3,000)
– Previous year	(3,000)	(3,000)	(0)	(3,000)	(0)
Chargeable amount	309,000	257,000	233,000	15,000	100,000
	2010/11	2014/15	2015/16	2017/18	2018/19
	2009/10 b/f	2013/14 b/f	2014/15 b/f	2016/17 b/f	2017/18 b/f
NRB @ date of gift	Net £		Net £		Net £
– 2010/11	325,000		325,000		325,000
– 2015/16					
– 2018/19					
Less: GCTs < 7 years before gift					
(1.9.2003 – 1.9.2010)	(0)				
(1.6.2008 – 1.6.2015) (ignore PET)			(309,000)		
(1.8.2011 – 1.8.2018) (ignore both PETs and gift on 1.9.2010 drops out as too old)					(287,250)
NRB available	(325,000)		(16,000)		(37,250)
Taxable amount	0		217,000	0	62,250
IHT payable	0		54,250 @ 25%	0	15,562 @ 25%
Paid by			Matthew		Matthew
Due date of payment			30.4.2016		30.4.2019
Gross chargeable amount	(£309,000 net + £nil tax) 309,000	257,000	(£233,000 net + £54,250 tax) 287,250	15,000	(£100,000 net + £15,562 tax) 115,562

IHT payable on death

Date of death: 1 December 2020
7 years before: 1 December 2013

CLT on 1.9.2010 is more than 7 years before death – therefore no IHT payable on death

	PET 1.5.2014		CLT 1.6.2015		PET 1.7.2017		CLT 1.8.2018	
	£	£	£	£	£	£	£	£
Gross chargeable amount b/f (as above)		257,000		287,250		15,000		115,562
NRB @ date of death – 2020/21	325,000		325,000		325,000		325,000	
Less: GCTs < 7 years before gift								
(1.5.2007 – 1.5.2014) (always include CLTs)	309,000							
(1.6.2008 – 1.5.2015) (£309,000 + £257,000) (include 1.5.2012 PET as it became chargeable)			566,000					
(1.7.2010 – 1.7.2017) (£566,000 + £287,250) (include 1.5.2012 PET as it became chargeable)					853,250			
(1.8.2011 – 1.8.2018) (£287,250 + £15,000) (earliest CLT on 1.9.2010 drops out, include both PETs)							559,250	
NRB available		(16,000)		(0)		(0)		(0)
Taxable amount		241,000		287,250		15,000		115,562
IHT payable @ 40%		96,400		114,900		6,000		46,225
Less: Taper relief								
(1.5.2014 – 1.12.2020) (6 – 7 years before death)	(80%)	(77,120)						
(1.6.2015 – 1.12.2020) (5 – 6 years before death)			(60%)	(68,940)				
(1.7.2016 – 1.12.2020) (3 – 4 years before death)					(20%)	(1,200)		
(1.8.2018 – 1.12.2020) (< 3 years before death)								(0)
Less: IHT paid in lifetime		(0)		(54,250)		(0)		(15,562)
IHT payable on death		19,280	Lifetime tax not repaid	0		4,800		30,663
Paid by (always the donee)		Alexander				Jayne		Trustees
Due date of payment		30.6.2021				30.6.2021		30.6.2021

Test your understanding 7

Ximena made the following lifetime gifts:

1 May 2011	£182,000 to a trust; Ximena paid the IHT.
30 June 2013	£60,000 to her niece on her 21st birthday.
11 June 2014	£169,000 to her nephew on his wedding day.
11 November 2016	£159,000 to a trust; trustees paid the IHT.

The nil rate bands for earlier years are as follows:

2011/12	£325,000
2013/14	£325,000
2014/15	£325,000
2016/17	£325,000

(a) **Calculate the IHT liabilities arising as a result of the lifetime gifts and state who pays the tax and the due date.**

(b) **Assuming Ximena dies on 14 February 2021, calculate the additional IHT on the lifetime gifts as a result of Ximena's death and state who pays the tax and the due date.**

(c) **Calculate the nil rate band left to set against the death estate.**

9 IHT payable on the death estate

On the death of an individual, an inheritance tax charge arises on the value of his or her estate at the date of death.

The death estate includes all assets held at the date of death.

The value of assets brought into an individual's estate computation is normally the **open market value (OMV)** of the asset at the date of death (known as the probate value).

 The values to use will always be provided in the examination.

The death estate computation

The gross chargeable value of an individual's estate is calculated using the following pro forma:

Pro forma death estate computation

	£	£
Freehold property		x
Less: Mortgage (Note)		(x)
		___
		x
Business owned by sole trader/partnership		x
Stocks and shares (including ISAs)		x
Government securities		x
Insurance policy proceeds (Note)		x
Leasehold property		x
Motor cars		x
Personal chattels		x
Debts due to the deceased		x
Cash at bank and on deposit (including ISAs)		x
		___
		x
Less: Debts due by the deceased	(x)	
Outstanding taxes (e.g. IT, CGT due)	(x)	
Funeral expenses	(x)	
	___	
		(x)
		___
Estate value		x
Less: Exempt legacies to spouse or civil partner		(x)
		___
Gross chargeable estate		x
		___

Note:

- Endowment mortgages are not deductible from the property value as these are automatically repaid on the owner's death. Repayment and interest only mortgages are deductible.

- When the deceased has a life insurance policy on his or her own life, the proceeds of that policy are included in the death estate, rather than the market value of the policy at the date of death.

- Funds held in a pension scheme are outside of the estate for IHT purposes.

Allowable deductions in the death estate computation

Funeral expenses

The costs of the individual's funeral are allowable providing they are reasonable, even though the cost is incurred after the date of death.

Reasonable costs of mourning clothes for the family and the cost of a tombstone are also allowable.

Other allowable deductions

Debts are deductible if they:

- were outstanding at the date of death, and

- had been incurred for valuable consideration, or were imposed by law (i.e. legally enforceable debts).

This includes all outstanding taxes such as income tax, NICs and CGT, although not the IHT due on death itself.

Note that a 'promise' to pay a friend, for example, is not legally enforceable and therefore not deductible. Gambling debts are not incurred for valuable consideration and cannot be deducted.

If a debt is secured against specific property it is deducted from the value of that property. This is the case with a repayment or interest only mortgage secured against freehold property.

Note that endowment mortgages are not deducted from the value of the property as the endowment element of the policy should cover the repayment of the mortgage.

Exempt legacies

The only exempt legacies that are allowable in the death estate and examinable at TX are gifts to the spouse or civil partner (see section 6).

The procedure to calculate the IHT on the death estate

The procedure to calculate the IHT on the death estate is as follows.

1   Deal with the IHT on lifetime gifts within seven years of the date of death first **before** looking at the estate computation.

2   Calculate the gross chargeable estate value.

3   Calculate the available residence nil rate band (see below).

4   Calculate the amount of NRB available after deducting GCTs in the previous 7 years (i.e. CLTs and PETs).

5   Calculate the tax on the excess at 40%.

6   If required by the question, state who will pay the tax and the due date of payment (see below).

Further points regarding IHT payable on the death estate

The nil rate band (NRB)

The NRB available to an individual on death of £325,000 is first used to calculate the death tax on lifetime gifts, then the estate after the lifetime gifts have been dealt with.

Residence nil rate band (RNRB)

The RNRB applies when a dwelling house, which has been the deceased's residence, is inherited by direct descendants.

The seven year accumulation period

The seven year accumulation period applies in a similar way to the death calculations on lifetime gifts as follows:

- it is necessary to take into account the total of the gross amounts of
  all **chargeable gifts** made within the **previous seven years**

- therefore, look back seven years from the date of death and accumulate the gross amounts of:

  - **all** CLTs, **and**

  - **all** PETs (because all PETs within 7 years of death will have become chargeable on death).

The death rate of tax

The death rate of IHT is 40% on the excess over the NRB available.

The normal due date of payment of IHT on death estate

IHT as a result of death is due on the earlier of:

- **six months** after the end of the month of death, or

- on delivery of the account of the estate assets to HMRC.

Illustration 4 – IHT payable on the death estate

Sara died on 15 June 2020 leaving a gross chargeable estate valued at £427,000 which was bequeathed to her brother.

(a) **Calculate the IHT liability arising on Sara's estate assuming she made no lifetime transfers**

(b) **What if Sara had gross chargeable transfers of £147,000 in the seven years prior to her death?**

Solution

(a) No lifetime transfers

	£	£
Gross chargeable estate value		427,000
NRB at death	325,000	
Less: GCTs in 7 yrs pre-death	(0)	
NRB available		(325,000)
Taxable amount		102,000
IHT due on death (£102,000 × 40%)		40,800

(b) Lifetime transfers = £147,000

	£	£
Gross chargeable estate value		427,000
NRB at death	325,000	
Less: GCTs in 7 yrs pre-death	(147,000)	
NRB available		(178,000)
Taxable amount		249,000
IHT due on death (£249,000 × 40%)		99,600

Test your understanding 8

Timothy died on 23 April 2020 leaving a gross chargeable estate valued at £627,560 which was bequeathed to his girlfriend.

Timothy had made the following lifetime gifts:

	Nil rate band
1 June 2008, £180,000, to a trust	£312,000
16 March 2014, £228,000, to his cousin	£325,000

Calculate the IHT liability arising on Timothy's estate and state the due date of payment and who it is paid by.

Test your understanding 9

Bintou died on 30 June 2020 leaving the following assets:

	£
House	200,000
Boat	250,000
Bank account	75,000
Quoted shares	100,000
Car	15,000

At the date of Bintou's death she owed £2,000 on her credit card, and £3,000 of income tax and CGT.

In Bintou's will she left

- the house and shares to her wife
- the boat to her son
- the residue to her daughter.

Bintou made a lifetime gift of £115,000 in cash to her son in August 2013 (nil rate band is £325,000).

Compute the IHT payable on Bintou's death.

Additional residence nil rate band (RNRB)

An additional nil rate band, up to a maximum of £175,000 in 2020/21, is available when calculating the IHT on the death estate where a residential house, which has been the deceased's residence, is inherited on death by the deceased's direct descendants. This is known as the residence nil rate band (RNRB).

The RNRB applies when:

- calculating the tax on the **death estate**, and
- the date of death is **on or after 6 April 2017**, and
- the chargeable death estate includes a **residential property** (that the deceased has lived in at some time) that is inherited by the deceased's **direct descendants**.

  For the purpose of the TX examination, the deceased's **direct descendants** are either the **children** or **grandchildren**.

Unlike the normal NRB, the RNRB is not available when calculating the additional tax due on lifetime gifts as a result of death. So, if a house is given to a child during lifetime, the RNRB is not available when calculating any death tax due as a result of the PET becoming chargeable.

Note that the deceased must only have lived in the residential property at some time. It does not have to have been the deceased's main residence or be lived in by the deceased at the date of death. Also there are no minimum occupancy requirements.

In the TX examination a property that qualifies for the RNRB will always be referred to as the deceased's **main residence**. Therefore, you should assume that the RNRB is not available if there is no mention of a main residence.

The available RNRB is the lower of:

- **£175,000**, and

- The **value of the main residence**.

 The RNRB of £175,000 is included in the tax rates and allowances provided to you in the examination.

The **value** of the main residence is **after deducting** any repayment or interest only **mortgage secured on the property**.

If the value of the main residence in the death estate is less than £175,000 the balance (i.e. the unused amount) can be transferred to the deceased's spouse (see below).

In calculating the tax on the death estate the RNRB is applied before the normal NRB.

There are additional complex rules which deal with tapering for high value estates, individuals with more than one residential property and individuals who have moved into a smaller house, or have sold or given away their house before their death. These rules are not examinable at TX.

 Illustration 5 – Residence nil rate band

On 10 April 2020 the following individuals died, leaving their entire estates to their children. Set out below, for each individual, is the gross chargeable value of their estate together with the value of their main residence, which is included in their estate.

	Gross chargeable value of estate	Value of main residence
	£	£
Albert	850,000	300,000
Aroha	450,000	80,000

Calculate the available RNRB and the IHT liability on the death estate, for each individual, assuming that neither of them had made any lifetime gifts.

Solution

Each of the deceased is entitled to the RNRB as they died after 6 April 2017 and have left a main residence to a direct descendant (i.e. their children).

Albert

The available RNRB is the lower of £175,000 (the maximum) and the value of the main residence (£300,000) i.e. £175,000.

	£
Gross chargeable estate value	850,000
Less: RNRB	(175,000)
Less: NRB at death (no lifetime transfers)	(325,000)
Taxable amount	350,000
IHT liability (£350,000 × 40%)	140,000

Aroha

The available RNRB is the lower of £175,000 (maximum) and the value of the main residence (£80,000) i.e. £80,000.

	£
Gross chargeable estate value	450,000
Less: RNRB	(80,000)
Less: NRB at death (no lifetime transfers)	(325,000)
Taxable amount	45,000
IHT liability (£45,000 × 40%)	18,000

The unused RNRB is £95,000 (£175,000 – £80,000).

Test your understanding 10

On 1 December 2020 Ibha died, leaving the following assets and liabilities:

	£
Main residence	200,000
Bank account	100,000
Quoted shares	450,000
Value of estate	750,000

Ibha left the shares to her husband and the rest of the assets to her son.

On 1 May 2019 Ibha had made a lifetime gift to her daughter of £225,000 (after annual exemptions).

Calculate the IHT due as a result of Ibha's death.

Payment of inheritance tax on the death estate

IHT on the death estate is initially paid by the executors (personal representatives).

The tax is paid from the estate, and so it is effectively borne by the person who inherits the residue of the assets (known as the residual legatee) after the specific legacies have been paid.

A summary of the payment of tax is shown below:

Recipient/asset	Paid by	Suffered by
Spouse	N/A – exempt	N/A – exempt
Specific UK assets	Executors	Residual legatee
Residue of estate	Executors	Residual legatee

Summary

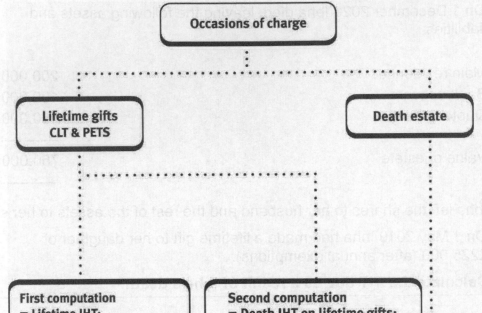

Occasions of charge

Lifetime gifts CLT & PETS

Death estate

First computation = Lifetime IHT:
1. Calculate the chargeable amount of the gift
   - use diminution in value principle if necessary
   - consider exemptions:
     - spouse
     - small gifts
     - normal expenditure from income
     - ME, AE
2. **CLTs only**
   Calculate the lifetime IHT at 20% or 25% after taking account of:
   - whether a gross or net gift
   - the NRB available during lifetime
   - gross CLTs in the 7-year cumulation period
3. Calculate the gross amount to carry forward for future computations

Second computation = Death IHT on lifetime gifts:
1. Calculate the gross chargeable amount of gifts in the seven years before death
2. Calculate the tax at 40% after taking account of
   - the NRB available on death
   - gross CLTs and PETs which have become chargeable in the 7-year cumulation period
3. Calculate and deduct taper relief
4. For CLTs, deduct lifetime IHT paid

Last computation = Death IHT on estate value:
1. Calculate the gross chargeable estate value
   - allowable deductions - funeral expenses, outstanding debts, including tax bills
   - legacies to spouse/civil partner are exempt
2. Calculate the tax at 40% after taking account of
   - the RNRB and NRB available on death
   - gross CLTs and PETs in the 7 years before death

10   Comprehensive example – death estate

> ### Test your understanding 11
>
> Wilma died in a car crash on 4 October 2020.
>
> Under the terms of her will, the estate was left as follows:
>
> - £170,000 to her husband
> - the residue of the estate (including her main residence) to her son Joe.
>
> At the date of her death, Wilma owned the following assets.
>
> - Her main residence valued at £268,000.
> - A flat in London valued at £175,000. An endowment mortgage of £70,000 was secured on this property.
> - Four shops valued at a total of £231,250.
> - A holiday cottage situated in Cornwall worth £120,000.
> - 20,000 shares in ZAM plc. The shares were valued at 200p each.
> - 8,000 units in the CBA unit trust, valued at 130p each.
> - Bank balances of £57,850.
> - Wilma has a life insurance policy which was valued at £100,000 on her death. The insurance proceeds paid to the executors of her estate were £260,000.
>
> Wilma's outstanding income tax liability was £7,500, and her funeral expenses amounted to £2,000. She had made no lifetime gifts.
>
> (a)   **Calculate the IHT that will be payable as a result of Wilma's death.**
>
> (b)   **Show who will pay and who will suffer the IHT liability and how the estate is distributed between the beneficiaries.**

11   Married couples/civil partners

Transfer of unused nil rate band (NRB)

Any amount of NRB that has not been utilised at the time of a person's death can be transferred to his or her spouse or civil partner.

As a result, each spouse or civil partner can leave the whole of his or her estate to the surviving spouse or civil partner with no adverse IHT consequences.

- The surviving spouse or civil partner will have the benefit of
  - his or her own NRB, **and**
  - any unused proportion of the spouse's or civil partner's NRB.

- This increased NRB can be used against any lifetime gifts taxable as a result of the donor's death and the death estate.

- The amount of the NRB that can be claimed is based on the proportion that was unused by the first spouse to die.

- The unused proportion is applied to the NRB available on the second spouse's death.

- The executors of the surviving spouse or civil partner must claim the transferred NRB by submitting the IHT return by the later of:

  – 2 years of the second death, or

  – 3 months of the executors starting to act.

Illustration 6 – Transfer of unused nil rate band

Winston died on 15 August 2006. Under the terms of his will £105,450 was left to his children, and the remainder of his estate to his wife, Florence.

Florence died on 24 February 2021.

The nil rate band in 2006/07 was £285,000.

Calculate the amount of nil rate band available against Florence's death estate.

Solution

On Winston's death the NRB available was £285,000 of which £105,450 was utilised. The remainder of the estate which was left to his wife was exempt.

The unused amount of £179,550 represents 63% (£179,550/£285,000) of his NRB on death.

The NRB available on Florence's death is therefore:

	£
Florence's NRB on her death	325,000
Winston's unused band transferred (£325,000 × 63%)	204,750
	———
	529,750
	———

Test your understanding 12

Marija is 67 years old, and was widowed on the death of her husband Zoran on 21 June 2007 (Nil rate band £300,000).

Zoran had a chargeable estate valued at £800,000, and this was left entirely to Marija.

Marija died on 23 May 2020 leaving an estate valued at £1 million, to her two children.

Marija has made no lifetime transfers.

Calculate the IHT liability due as a result of Marija's death assuming:

(a) **Zoran made no lifetime transfers**

(b) **Zoran gave £186,000 to his son on 16 March 2007.**

Transfer of unused residence nil rate band (RNRB)

An amount of RNRB that was not utilised at the time of a person's death can also be transferred to his or her spouse or civil partner.

There will be unused RNRB on the death of the first spouse/civil partner where:

- The maximum RNRB (£175,000 for 2020/21) exceeded the value of the main residence. In this case the balance can be transferred to the spouse/civil partner.

- On the death of the first spouse/civil partner:

    - there was no main residence in the estate, or

    - there was a main residence but it was not inherited by the deceased's direct descendants.

    In both these cases 100% of the RNRB is unused and can be transferred to the surviving spouse.

The transfer of the RNRB operates in a very similar way to the transfer of the NRB:

- The amount of the RNRB that can be claimed by the surviving spouse/civil partner is based on the **proportion that was unused** by the first spouse.

- The unused proportion is applied to the **RNRB available on the second** spouse/civil partner's death.

- The executors must claim the transferred RNRB within the same time limits as for the transferred NRB (see above).

The transfer is available even when the first spouse/civil partner died before 6 April 2017 (i.e. the date that the RNRB was introduced) provided the surviving spouse died on or after 6 April 2017. In this case, the unused proportion of the RNRB will always be 100% as the first spouse could not have used the RNRB on his or her death (as this was before the RNRB was introduced).

Illustration 7 – Transfer of unused residential nil rate band

Ezra died on 25 May 2020. He left an estate valued at £800,000, which included a main residence valued at £140,000. He left the main residence to his son and the rest of his estate to his wife, Elsa.

Frank died on 1 June 2020. His estate was valued at £1,000,000, which included a main residence, worth £175,000. He left the whole of his estate to his wife, Fleur.

Both Elsa and Fleur died on 1 February 2021.

For both Elsa and Fleur calculate the amount of unused RNRB which may be transferred from their husband to increase the RNRB available to them when calculating the IHT on their death estate.

Solution

Ezra and Elsa

Ezra died after 6 April 2017 and left a residential home to a direct descendant (i.e. his son). The maximum RNRB available to Ezra was £175,000 of which he used £140,000. £35,000 (i.e. 20%) of Ezra's RNRB is unused and can be transferred to Elsa. The unused % is applied to the RNRB available on Elsa's death and therefore £35,000 (20% × £175,000) will be added to Elsa's own RNRB.

Frank and Fleur

Frank died after 6 April 2017 and had a maximum RNRB of £175,000. He did not leave a main residence to a direct descendant therefore 100% of his RNRB was unused.

100% of Frank's RNRB can be transferred to Fleur. The unused % is applied to the RNRB available on Fleur's death and therefore £175,000 (100% × £175,000) will be added to Fleur's own RNRB.

12 Payment of IHT

Summary of normal dates of payment

IHT is payable as follows:

Transfer	Due Date
CLTs between 6 April and 30 September	30 April in the following year.
CLTs between 1 October and 5 April	6 months after the end of the month in which the transfer is made.
PETs chargeable as a result of death	6 months after the end of the month of death.
Additional tax due on CLTs within 7 years before the death	6 months after the end of the month of death.
Estate at death	On delivery of the estate accounts to HMRC. Interest runs from 6 months after the end of the month of death.

13 IHT Planning

It is important for an individual to plan his or her lifetime gifts to be tax efficient and to make a will so that his or her estate is distributed in a tax efficient way.

There are a number of tax planning measures that can reduce an individual's liability to IHT.

The overall objectives of all IHT tax planning measures are:

- to minimise the amount of tax payable
- to maximise the inheritance of the next generation.

Lifetime tax planning

IHT planning during an individual's lifetime involves making gifts of wealth as early as possible, as there are many advantages to making lifetime gifts.

Advantages of lifetime giving

- Lifetime giving reduces the IHT payable on death as the assets gifted will not be included in the donor's chargeable estate on death. Therefore, an individual should maximise the use of:
  - exemptions available (e.g. marriage, small gifts, annual exemption and normal expenditure out of income)
  - nil rate band every 7 years.

- Even if a lifetime gift becomes taxable, IHT on lifetime gifts is likely to be less than the IHT payable on the death estate because:

  - If the gift is a PET, no IHT will be payable if the donor survives seven years.

  - If the gift is a CLT, the tax is calculated at 20% and no additional IHT will be payable on death if the donor survives 7 years.

  - If the donor does not survive seven years, taper relief will be available after three years.

  - A lifetime gift is valued at the time of the gift and the value is 'frozen'. This locks in the value of an appreciating asset, so any increase in value up to the date of death will not be taxed.

  - Exemptions such as normal gifts out of income, small gifts, marriage and AEs may reduce or eliminate the value of a lifetime gift.

However, it is not necessarily advantageous to gift all assets pre-death, as:

- The donor will want to continue to enjoy a comfortable life in his or her old age, and

- IHT is not the only tax that needs to be considered in respect of lifetime gifts.

Disadvantages of lifetime giving

- The donor loses the use of the asset and any income that can be derived from the asset once given away.

- The residence nil rate band is not available for a lifetime gift of the main residence.

- Capital gains tax:

  - may be payable on lifetime gifts of chargeable assets (either immediately or later if deferred with a gift relief claim)

  - but is not payable on assets held at the date of death.

- Therefore, individuals should be advised not to gift assets during their lifetime that give rise to large CGT liabilities.

Death estate planning

Main residences should be left to direct descendants in priority to other assets.

A main residence left to anyone other than direct descendants is not eligible for the RNRB, resulting in more IHT being paid on the death estate.

Leaving a main residence to direct descendants could potentially save IHT of £70,000 (40% tax on £175,000 of RNRB), or as much as £140,000 (2 × £70,000) where an unused RNRB from a deceased spouse/civil partner is also available.

Skipping generations

When making lifetime gifts or leaving legacies on death, it may be beneficial for inheritance tax purposes if gifts and/or legacies are made to grandchildren rather than children. This avoids a further IHT charge when the children die, thus skipping a generation.

Gifts will then only be subject to IHT once before being inherited by the grandchildren (on the death of the grandparent), rather than twice (on the death of the parent and grandparent).

Such planning depends on the children being independently wealthy, so that they have no need for the inheritance.

14 Chapter summary

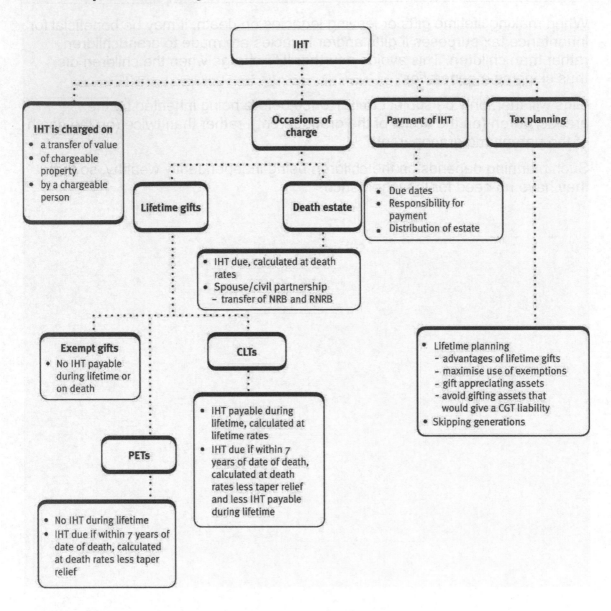

IHT

IHT is charged on
- a transfer of value
- of chargeable property
- by a chargeable person

Occasions of charge

Payment of IHT

Tax planning

Lifetime gifts

Death estate

- Due dates
- Responsibility for payment
- Distribution of estate

- IHT due, calculated at death rates
- Spouse/civil partnership
  - transfer of NRB and RNRB

Exempt gifts
- No IHT payable during lifetime or on death

CLTs

- IHT payable during lifetime, calculated at lifetime rates
- IHT due if within 7 years of date of death, calculated at death rates less taper relief and less IHT payable during lifetime

- Lifetime planning
  - advantages of lifetime gifts
  - maximise use of exemptions
  - gift appreciating assets
  - avoid gifting assets that would give a CGT liability
- Skipping generations

PETs

- No IHT during lifetime
- IHT due if within 7 years of date of death, calculated at death rates less taper relief

15 Practice objective test questions

Test your understanding 13

Nicholas, a bachelor, died on 20 February 2021. During his lifetime he made the following cash gifts:

		Gift to:	£
1	1 January 2014	A trust for his nephew	336,000
2	1 March 2015	His uncle	30,000
3	1 February 2017	His niece	25,000
4	1 March 2018	A trust for his aunt	28,000

Nicholas paid any tax due on the transfers.

On which gifts will inheritance tax be payable as a result of Nicholas' death?

A   1 and 4 only

B   2, 3 and 4 only

C   All of them

D   None of them

Test your understanding 14

Lucas made a gross chargeable transfer of £157,000 on 5 November 2018.

On 19 November 2020 he gave £200,000 to a trust, paying the tax himself.

How much lifetime IHT is payable on the gift in the tax year 2020/21?

A   £0

B   £5,200

C   £8,000

D   £6,500

Test your understanding 15

Chloe transferred £200 into a trust for her son Mathis in August 2020 and in the next month gave her daughter Clara £250 cash.

Which of the gifts will be covered by the small gifts exemption?

A   Neither

B   Son's trust only

C   Clara's only

D   Both gifts

Test your understanding 16

Eve made a chargeable lifetime transfer on 15 August 2017 on which £4,500 lifetime IHT was payable.

Eve died on 24 March 2021 and death tax is due on the chargeable lifetime transfer.

On what date is the related IHT payable?

	Lifetime IHT	Death IHT
A	28 February 2018	24 September 2021
B	30 April 2018	30 September 2021
C	28 February 2018	30 September 2021
D	30 April 2018	24 September 2021

KAPLAN PUBLISHING

Test your understanding answers

Test your understanding 1

Linda

	£
Value of estate before transfer (6,000 × £26)	156,000
Less: Value of estate after transfer (4,000 × £15)	(60,000)
Transfer of value	96,000

Note that a lifetime gift has both IHT and CGT consequences.

The diminution in value concept is very important but unique to IHT.

The value of the asset gifted; a 20% interest in these shares (i.e. 2,000 × £9 = £18,000):

- is not relevant for IHT purposes; it is the diminution in the value (i.e. £96,000) of the estate from the donor's point of view which is important, but

- is important for CGT purposes; the market value of the asset gifted is always the consideration used as the starting point of the chargeable gain computation.

Test your understanding 2

Meron

Chargeable amounts

	PET 31.8.18 2018/19	CLT 31.10.18 2018/19	CLT 31.5.19 2019/20	CLT 30.11.19 2019/20	PET 30.4.20 2020/21
Tax year of gift	£	£	£	£	£
Transfer of value	600	800	2,100	1,100	5,000
Less: Annual exemption					
2018/19	(600)	(800)			
2017/18 b/f (£3,000 avail) (all lost as not used and can only c/f for one year)	(–)	(–)			
2019/20			(2,100)	(900)	
2018/19 b/f (£1,600 avail) (remaining £1,400 lost as not used)			(–)	(200)	
2020/21					(3,000)
2019/20 b/f (none available – already used)					(0)
Chargeable amount	0	0	0	0	2,000

Test your understanding 3

Felipe

Exempt gifts

1.6.2020	Gift to husband = exempt inter-spouse transfer
4.11.2020	Gift to friend = small gift exemption applies as the gift is less than £250

Remaining gifts – chargeable amount

	PET 6.7.2020	PET 27.9.2020	CLT 24.12.2020
Tax year of gift	2020/21	2020/21	2020/21
	£	£	£
Transfer of value	15,000	20,000	270,000
Less: Marriage exemption	(5,000)		
Less: Annual exemption			
2020/21	(3,000)	(0)	(0)
2019/20 b/f	(3,000)	(0)	(0)
Chargeable amount	4,000	20,000	270,000

The gifts to the son and nephew are PETs – therefore no tax is payable unless Felipe dies within seven years.

The gift into trust is a CLT and is chargeable during Felipe's lifetime. However, as she has no chargeable gifts in the preceding seven years, there will be no IHT to pay as the gift is covered by the NRB of £325,000 (see later).

Test your understanding 4

Charlotte

	(a) Trustees to pay IHT	(b) Charlotte to pay IHT
	CLT	**CLT**
	13.6.2020	**13.6.2020**
	£	£
Transfer of value	366,000	366,000
Annual exemption		
– Current year 2020/21	(3,000)	(3,000)
– Previous year 2019/20 b/f	(3,000)	(3,000)
Chargeable amount	Gross 360,000	Net 360,000
NRB @ date of gift 2020/21	(325,000)	(325,000)
Taxable amount	35,000	35,000
IHT payable	@ 20% 7,000	@ 25% 8,750
Paid by	Trustees	Charlotte
Due date	30.4.2021	30.4.2021
Gross chargeable amount c/f	360,000	368,750 (£360,000 net + £8,750 tax)

Test your understanding 5

Alex

	CLT 30.6.2010	PET 12.6.2014	CLT 30.6.2015	CLT 15.12.2020
	Gross £	£	Gross £	Net £
Transfer of value	170,000	150,000	191,000	256,000
Annual exemption				
– Current year	(3,000) [2010/11]	(3,000) [2014/15]	(3,000) [2015/16]	(3,000) [2020/21]
– Previous year	(3,000) [2009/10 b/f]	(3,000) [2013/14 b/f]	(0) [2014/15 b/f]	(3,000) [2019/20 b/f]
Chargeable amount	164,000	144,000	188,000	250,000
NRB @ date of gift	£		£	£
– 2010/11	325,000			
– 2015/16			325,000	
– 2020/21				325,000
Less: GCTs < 7 years before gift				
(30.6.2003 – 30.6.2010)	(0)			
(30.6.2008 – 30.6. 2015) (ignore PET)			(164,000)	
(15.12. 2013 – 15.12.2020) (ignore PET and gift on 30.6.2010 drops out as too old)				(188,000)
NRB available	(325,000)		(161,000)	(137,000)
Taxable amount	0	0	27,000	113,000
IHT payable	0	0	5,400 @ 20%	28,250 @ 25%
Paid by			Trustees	Alex
Due date of payment			30.4.2016	30.6.2021
Gross chargeable amount c/f	164,000	144,000	188,000	278,250 (£250,000 net + £28,250 tax)

Test your understanding 6

Yuuma

	CLT 21.4.2008		PET 15.4.2014		CLT 19.3.2015		CLT 9.5.2020	
		£		£		£		£
Transfer of value		98,000		140,000		234,000		395,000
Annual exemption								
– Current year	2008/09	(3,000)	2014/15	(3,000)	2014/15	(0)	2020/21	(3,000)
– Previous year	2007/08 b/f	(3,000)	2013/14 b/f	(3,000)	2013/14 b/f	(0)	2019/20 b/f	(3,000)
Chargeable amount	Gross	92,000		134,000	Net	234,000	Gross	389,000
		£				£		£
NRB @ date of gift								
– 2008/09		312,000						
– 2014/15						325,000		
– 2020/21								325,000
Less: GCTs < 7 years before gift								
(21.4.2001 – 21.4.2008)		(0)						
(19.3.2008 – 19.3.2015) (ignore PET)						(92,000)		
(9.5.2013 – 9.5.2020)								(234,250)
(ignore PET and gift on 21.4.2008 drops out as too old)								
NRB available		312,000				(233,000)		(90,750)
Taxable amount		0		0		1,000		298,250
IHT payable		0		0	@ 25%	250	@ 20%	59,650
Paid by					Sidney		Trustees	
Due date of payment					30.9.2015		30.4.2021	
Gross chargeable amount		92,000		134,000	(£234,000 net + £250 tax)	234,250		389,000

Test your understanding 7

Ximena

(a) IHT payable during lifetime

	CLT 1.5.2011	PET 30.6.2013	PET 11.6.2014	CLT 11.11.2016
	£	£	£	£
Transfer of value	182,000	60,000	169,000	159,000
Less: Marriage exemption			(1,000)	
Less: Annual exemption				
– Current year	(3,000)	(3,000)	(3,000)	(3,000)
– Previous year	(3,000)	(3,000)	(0)	(3,000)
Chargeable amount	176,000	54,000	165,000	153,000
	Net			Gross
NRB @ date of gift	£			£
– 2011/12	325,000			
– 2016/17				325,000
Less: GCTs < 7 years before gift				
(1.5.2004 – 1.5.2011)	(0)			
(11.11.2009 – 11.11.2016) (ignore PETs)				(176,000)
NRB available	(325,000)			(149,000)
Taxable amount	0	0	0	4,000
IHT payable	0	0	0	@ 20% 800
Paid by	(£176,000 net + £Nil tax)			Trustees
Due date of payment				31.5.2017
Gross chargeable amount	176,000	54,000	165,000	153,000

(b) IHT payable on death

| Date of death: | 14 February 2021 |
| 7 years before: | 14 February 2014 |

CLT on 1.5.2011 and PET on 30.6.2013 are more than 7 years before death – therefore no IHT payable on death

	PET 11.6.2014		CLT 11.11.2016	
	£	£	£	£
Gross chargeable amount b/f (as above)		165,000		153,000
NRB @ date of death – 2020/21	325,000		325,000	
Less: GCTs < 7 years before gift				
(11.6.2007 – 11.6.2014)				
(exclude PET on 30.6.2013 as it became completely exempt)	(176,000)			
(11.11.2009 – 11.11.2016) (£176,000 + £165,000)			(341,000)	
(exclude PET on 30.6.2013 as it became completely exempt, but include 11.6. 2014 PET as it became chargeable)				
NRB available		(149,000)		(0)
Taxable amount		16,000		153,000
IHT payable @ 40%		6,400		61,200
Less: Taper relief				
(11.6.2014 – 14.2.2021) (6 – 7 years before death)	(80%)			
(11.11.2016 – 14.2.2021) (4 – 5 years before death)			(40%)	
		(5,120)		(24,480)
Less: IHT paid in lifetime		(0)		(800)
IHT payable on death		1,280		35,920
Paid by (always the donee)		Nephew		Trustees
Due date of payment		31.8.2021		31.8.2021

(c) **Nil rate band left to set against the death estate**

	£
NRB at death	325,000
Less: GCTs in 7 years pre-death	
(14.2.2014 to 14.2.2021) (£165,000 + £153,000)	(318,000)
(first two gifts = too old, include PET on 11.6.2014 as became chargeable on death)	
NRB available against death estate	7,000

Test your understanding 8

Timothy

IHT payable during lifetime

		CLT 1.6.2008		PET 16.3.2014
		£		£
Transfer of value		180,000		228,000
Less: Annual exemption				
Current year	2008/09	(3,000)	2013/14	(3,000)
Previous year	2007/08 b/f	(3,000)	2012/13 b/f	(3,000)
Chargeable amount	Net	174,000		222,000

	£		
NRB @ date of gift – 2008/09	312,000		
Less:			
GCTs < 7 years before gift (1.6.2001 – 1.6.2008)	(0)		
NRB available		(312,000)	
Taxable amount		0	0
IHT payable		0	0
Gross chargeable amount c/f		174,000	222,000

Note: the earlier NRBs given in the question are not required as they are only required if there is lifetime tax to pay.

IHT payable on death

Date of death: 23 April 2020

Seven years before: 23 April 2013

CLT on 1.6.2008 is more than seven years before death – therefore no IHT payable on death

	PET 16.3.2014		Estate value 23.4.2020	
	£	£	£	£
Gross chargeable amount		222,000		627,560
NRB @ date of death 2020/21	325,000		325,000	
Less: GCTs < 7 years before gift (16.3.2007 – 16.3.2014)	(174,000)			
Less: GCTs < 7 years before death (23.4.2013 – 23.4.2020) (earliest CLT on 1.6.2008 drops out, include PET on 16.3.2014 as it became chargeable)			(222,000)	
NRB available		(151,000)		(103,000)
Taxable amount		71,000		524,560
IHT payable @ 40%		28,400		209,824
Less: Taper relief (16.3.2014 – 23.4.2020) (6 – 7 years before death)	(80%)	(22,720)		
Less: IHT paid in lifetime		(0)		
IHT payable on death		5,680		
Paid by		Cousin		Executors
Due date of payment		31.10.2020		31.10.2020

Test your understanding 9

Bintou

Death estate – date of death 30 June 2020

	£	£
House		200,000
Boat		250,000
Bank account		75,000
Quoted shares		100,000
Car		15,000
Allowable expenses – Credit card		(2,000)
– Income tax and CGT		(3,000)
		———
		635,000
Exempt legacy to wife – house		(200,000)
– quoted shares		(100,000)
		———
Gross chargeable estate		335,000
NRB at death	325,000	
Less: GCTs in 7 yrs pre-death		
(30.6.13 – 30.6.20) (W)	(109,000)	
	———	
NRB available		(216,000)
		———
Taxable amount		119,000
		———
IHT on chargeable estate (£119,000 × 40%)		47,600
		———

Working: Lifetime gift to son

	£
Transfer of value	115,000
Less: AE – 2013/14	(3,000)
– 2012/13 b/f	(3,000)
	———
Chargeable amount	109,000
	———

Notes:

1   No lifetime tax was payable on the gift as it was a PET.

2   At death, the current NRB of £325,000 is applied to the gift. The NRB in 2013/14 given in the question is therefore not relevant.

Test your understanding 10

Ibha

The gift on 1 May 2019 is a PET which is now chargeable. The value of the gift (£225,000) is below the NRB of £325,000 and so no IHT liability arises on death.

Ibha is entitled to the RNRB as she died after 6 April 2017 and has left a main residence to a direct descendant (i.e. her son).

The available RNRB is the lower of £175,000 (maximum) and the value of the main residence (£200,000) i.e. £175,000.

	£	£
Estate value		750,000
Less: Exempt legacy to husband (shares)		(450,000)
		————
Gross chargeable estate		300,000
Less: RNRB		(175,000)
NRB at death	325,000	
Less: GCTs in 7 years prior to death	(225,000)	
	————	(100,000)
		————
Taxable amount		25,000
		————
IHT liability (£25,000 × 40%)		10,000
		————

Test your understanding 11

Wilma

Death estate – date of death 4 October 2020

	£	£
Main residence		268,000
Flat (Note 1)		175,000
Shops		231,250
Holiday cottage		120,000
Shares in ZAM plc (20,000 @ 200p)		40,000
Units in CBA unit trust (8,000 @ 130p)		10,400
Bank balances		57,850
Life insurance policy proceeds		260,000
		————
		1,162,500
Less: Income tax due	(7,500)	
Funeral expenses	(2,000)	
	————	(9,500)
		————
Estate value		1,153,000
Less: Exempt legacies – Husband		(170,000)
		————
Gross chargeable estate		983,000
RNRB (Note 2)		(175,000)
NRB at death	325,000	
Less: GCTs in 7 yrs pre-death (4.10.13 to 4.10.20)	(0)	
	————	(325,000)
		————
Taxable amount		483,000
		————
IHT due on Wilma's death (£483,000 × 40%)		193,200
		————

Allocation of the IHT liability on the estate

The executors will pay the IHT out of the estate.

The tax is suffered by Wilma's son, Joe (the residual legatee).

Distribution of the estate

	£
Wilma's husband	170,000
Joe (residual legatee) (Note 3)	789,800
HMRC	193,200
Total estate to distribute	1,153,000

Notes:

1 Since the endowment mortgage would have been repaid upon Wilma's death, it is not deducted from the value of the flat.

2 Wilma is entitled to the RNRB as she died after 6 April 2017 and has left a main residence to a direct descendant (i.e. her son).

 The available RNRB is the lower of £175,000 (maximum) and the value of the main residence (£268,000) i.e. £175,000.

3 Residual legatee Joe will receive the residue of the estate calculated as follows:

	£
Value of estate (before specific legacies)	1,153,000
Less: Legacy to husband	(170,000)
IHT to HMRC	(193,200)
Residue of estate	789,800

Test your understanding 12

(a) **Zoran made no lifetime transfers**

On Zoran's death:

- no lifetime gifts, so all NRB available for his death estate
- the transfer of his estate to Marija is an exempt legacy
- so, no IHT was due on his estate, and
- therefore none of his NRB was utilised (i.e. 100% unutilised).

Marija – Death estate

	£
Gross chargeable estate	1,000,000
Less: NRB at date of Marija's death	(325,000)
Less: NRB transferred from Zoran (Note) (£325,000 × 100%)	(325,000)
Taxable amount	350,000
IHT payable on death (£350,000 × 40%)	140,000

This IHT is paid by the executors, but borne by Marija's children.

Note:

- Although the NRB available on Zoran's death was only £300,000, the amount unused was 100% of the NRB. This percentage is applied to the current NRB of £325,000 to calculate the amount that can be transferred.

- Marija's executors must claim the transferred NRB on the submission of her IHT return within 2 years from her death, or 3 months after they start to act if later.

(b) **Zoran made a lifetime gift to his son**

On Zoran's death:

- Lifetime gift to son is a PET; therefore no lifetime IHT is due but the gift becomes chargeable on his death

- The PET is covered by the nil rate band available at death, therefore no death IHT is due

- However, the PET utilises £180,000 (£186,000 – (£3,000 × 2) AEs) of his nil rate band available at death

- The transfer of his estate to Marija is an exempt legacy

- Therefore, after taking account of his lifetime gifts, £120,000 (£300,000 – £180,000) of his nil rate band is unutilised

- The unutilised proportion is 40% ((£120,000/£300,000) × 100).

On Marija's death:

	$
Gross chargeable estate	1,000,000
Less: NRB at date of Marija's death	(325,000)
Less: NRB transferred from Zoran (£325,000 × 40%)	(130,000)
Taxable amount	545,000
IHT payable on death (£545,000 × 40%)	218,000

Test your understanding 13

The correct answer is B.

Gift (1) is more than seven years before death and therefore no death tax is due.

Gifts (2), (3) and (4) are within seven years of death and are chargeable on death.

To calculate the death tax, for each gift, the nil rate band on death is compared to gross chargeable transfers in the previous seven years. In all cases, this includes the CLT on 1 January 2013 which exceeds £325,000.

Therefore, the gifts are not covered by the nil rate band and death tax is payable in all cases.

Test your understanding 14

The correct answer is D.

	£	£
Transfer of value		200,000
Less: Annual exemption 2020/21		(3,000)
2019/20 b/f		(3,000)
		194,000
Nil rate band – 2020/21	325,000	
GCTs in previous seven years (19.11.2013 to 19.11.2020)	(157,000)	
		(168,000)
Taxable amount		26,000
IHT @ 25% (Lucas to pay tax)		6,500

Note: The question gives the GCT for 5 November 2018 which, by definition, means after the deduction of annual exemptions.

Test your understanding 15

The correct answer is C.

The gift into the trust does not qualify as it is not an outright gift to an individual.

The gift to Clara qualifies.

Test your understanding 16

The correct answer is B.

If the gift is in the first half of the tax year, lifetime IHT is due on the following 30 April.

Death tax on lifetime gifts is due six months after the end of the month of death.

VAT: Outline

Chapter learning objectives

Upon completion of this chapter you will be able to:

- recognise the circumstances in which a person must register or deregister for VAT (compulsory) and when a person may register or deregister for VAT (voluntary)

- recognise the circumstances in which pre-registration input VAT can be recovered

- explain the conditions that must be met for two or more companies to be treated as a group for VAT purposes, and the consequences of being so treated

- calculate the amount of VAT payable/recoverable

- recognise the tax point when goods or services are supplied

- explain and apply the principles regarding the valuation of supplies

- recognise the principal zero rated and exempt supplies

- recognise the circumstances in which input VAT is non-deductible

- recognise the relief that is available for impairment losses on trade debts

- understand the treatment of the sale of a business as a going concern.

One of the PER performance objectives (PO15) is to prepare computations of taxable amounts and tax liabilities according to legal requirements. Another objective (PO17) is to advise on mitigating and deferring tax liabilities through legitimate tax planning measures. Working through this chapter should help you understand how to demonstrate those objectives.

PER

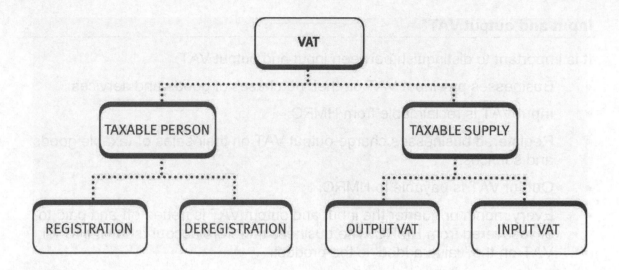

Within the Financial Accounting unit you had an introduction to VAT from an accounting perspective; this chapter will introduce how VAT works as an indirect tax on expenditure. VAT will be explored in further detail in ATX.

1 Introduction

VAT is:

- an indirect tax on consumer spending

- charged on most goods and services supplied within the UK

- suffered by the final consumer, and

- collected by businesses on behalf of HMRC.

2 The scope and nature of VAT

There are three essentials needed before VAT can be charged.

A **taxable person** is one who is or should be registered for VAT, because they make taxable supplies (see registration section 4).

- A person can be an individual or a legal person, such as a company.

A **taxable supply** is everything which is not exempt or outside the scope of VAT. It includes sales and purchases of most goods or services.

- For VAT to apply the taxable supply must be made in the course or furtherance of a business carried on by a taxable person.

Input and output VAT

It is important to distinguish between input and output VAT:

- Businesses pay input VAT on their purchases of goods and services.

- Input VAT is reclaimable from HMRC.

- Registered businesses charge output VAT on their sales of taxable goods and services.

- Output VAT is payable to HMRC.

- Every month or quarter the input and output VAT is netted off and paid to or recovered from HMRC. The business therefore accounts to HMRC for VAT on the 'value added' to the product.

How VAT works

Assume that the rate of VAT throughout is 20%.

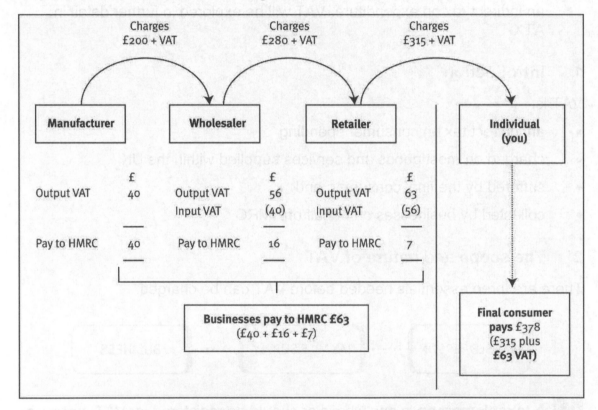

| Test your understanding 1 |

Which of the following statements is/are correct?

1   VAT is an indirect tax.

2   Lucy, an accountancy student, who sells some of her spare CDs to a friend, should charge the friend VAT on the sale.

3   Businesses may keep all the output VAT they charge to customers.

3 Types of supply

Supplies can be taxable, exempt or outside the scope of VAT.

Taxable supplies

- VAT is charged on taxable supplies but not on exempt supplies or supplies which are outside the scope of VAT.

  It is therefore important to be able to correctly classify supplies in order to determine whether VAT should be charged.

- It is also important to correctly classify supplies because:

  – only taxable supplies are taken into account in determining whether a trader needs to register for VAT

  – input VAT related to exempt supplies is not recoverable.

- Taxable supplies are charged to VAT at one of three rates:

  – **zero rate:** This is a tax rate of nil.

    No VAT is charged but it is classed as a taxable supply. It is therefore taken into account in determining whether a trader should register for VAT and whether input VAT is recoverable.

  – **reduced rate:** Some supplies, mainly for domestic or charitable use are charged at the reduced rate.

    Note the reduced rate is not important for the examination and the temporary reduced rate for hospitality in 2020–21 is not examinable.

  – **standard rate:** Any taxable supply which is not charged at the zero or reduced rates is charged at the standard rate of 20%.

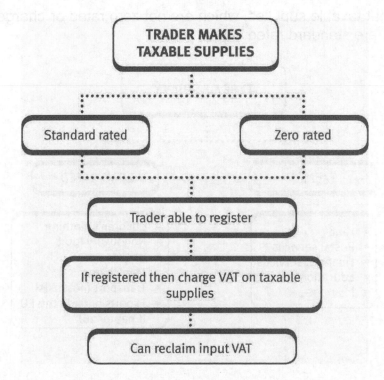

Zero rated and exempt supplies

 You must understand the important difference between zero rated and exempt supplies.

Trader making:	Exempt supplies	Zero rated supplies
Can charge VAT?	X	✓ at 0%
Can reclaim input VAT?	X	✓
Can register for VAT?	X	✓

Test your understanding 2

Fill in the blanks in the following statements:

1   Traders making wholly exempt supplies .... register for VAT.

2   The standard rate of VAT is ....

3   Traders who are registered for VAT must charge VAT on all their taxable ....

4   The difference between zero rated and exempt traders is that zero rated traders .... recover input VAT, whereas exempt traders .... recover input VAT.

You do not need to remember the rates of VAT which apply to different goods and services. However, it is useful to know the treatment of some of the more common types of supply.

For example, items such as wages and dividends are outside the scope of VAT.

Remember that taxable supplies, which are not zero rated or chargeable at the reduced rate, are standard rated.

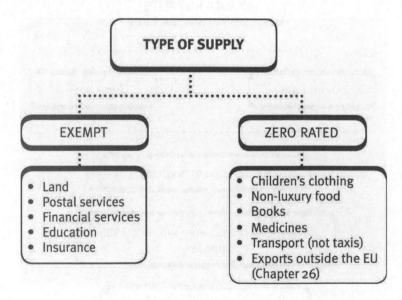

Zero rated and exempt supplies

The most important **zero rated items** are briefly described below.

- Food: Food used for human consumption unless it is either a supply in the course of catering (e.g. in a restaurant) or is classed as a luxury item, such as alcohol or confectionery.

- Books and other printed matter (e.g. newspapers, books, maps and sheet music).

- Construction of dwellings, etc.: This includes new buildings for residential or charitable use, but not the reconstruction of an existing building.

- Transport: Transporting passengers by road, rail, sea or air, but excluding smaller vehicles (e.g. not taxis).

- Drugs, medicines and appliances: Drugs supplied on prescription and certain supplies to the disabled.

- Charities: Gifts to charities are zero rated.

- Clothing and footwear: Young children's clothing and footwear.

The most important **exempt supplies** are briefly described below.

- Land: Transfers of land and rights over land, but not buildings.

- Insurance: premiums.

- Financial services, including making loans, hire purchase, share dealing and banking services.

- Education: If provided by schools and universities.

- Health: The services of registered doctors, dentists, opticians, chemists and hospitals (but not health farms).

- Sports: Entry fees to sports competitions used to provide prizes or charged by non-profit-making sporting bodies.

4 VAT registration – compulsory

Registration threshold

If a person's taxable supplies (excluding sales of capital assets) exceed the registration threshold, then registration is compulsory.

There are two separate tests for compulsory registration:

- Historic turnover test

- Future prospects test.

Historic turnover test

At the end of each month, the trader must look at the cumulative total of taxable supplies for the last 12 months, or since commencing trade, whichever is the shorter.

If the total exceeds the registration threshold, currently £85,000, then the trader must register as follows:

- Notify HMRC **within 30 days** of the end of the month in which the registration threshold is exceeded, by completing form VAT1, or via HMRC's online services.

- Registration is effective from the **first day of the second month** after the taxable supplies exceed the threshold.

- A trader need not register if his/her taxable supplies for the next 12 months are expected to be less than the deregistration threshold (see below) currently £83,000.

- A trader need not register if his/her supplies are wholly zero rated.

 The registration and deregistration thresholds are provided in the tax rates and allowances in the examination.

 Illustration 1 – VAT registration – compulsory

Hill Ltd commenced trading on 1 January 2019. Its monthly taxable supplies are as follows:

	2019 £	2020 £
January	3,500	5,090
February	3,600	5,160
March	3,700	5,780
April	3,800	5,850
May	3,840	5,970
June	3,910	6,440
July	3,980	7,260
August	4,050	8,730
September	4,120	9,900
October	4,490	9,750
November	4,550	10,500
December	4,630	10,050

In addition, in May 2020 the company sold surplus plant for £3,450.

State from what date Hill Ltd is liable to register for VAT.

Solution

At the end of November 2020, Hill Ltd's taxable turnover for the previous 12 months is:

	£
Value of supplies for registration purposes:	
Supplies to customers	85,060
Supply of plant (disregarded)	0
	———
	85,060
	———

Hill Ltd is therefore liable to register on 30 November 2020, and must notify HMRC by 30 December 2020.

The company will be registered from 1 January 2021, or such earlier date as may jointly be agreed.

Test your understanding 3

Jana owns a shop selling newspapers (zero rated) and stationery (standard rated). In her first year of trading to 31 July 2020, her sales of newspapers were £3,050 per month and of stationery £2,250 per month. In her second year of trading, these figures increased to £5,400 and £4,280, respectively.

State from what date Jana is liable to register for VAT.

Future prospects test

This test is considered at any time, when taxable supplies in the next 30 days in isolation are expected to exceed £85,000.

- HMRC must be notified before the end of the 30 days, by completing form VAT1, or using HMRC's online services.

- Registration will be effective from the beginning of the 30 day period.

Illustration 2 – VAT registration – compulsory

Cat Ltd signs a lease for new business premises on 1 May 2020 and opens for business on 20 July 2020. The company estimates, from the outset, that taxable supplies will be in the region of £85,500 per month.

State when, if at all, Cat Ltd is liable to register for VAT.

Solution

Cat Ltd is liable to register on 20 July 2020 because supplies for the 30 days to 18 August 2020, are expected to exceed £85,000.

> The company must notify HMRC of its liability to registration by 18 August 2020 and is registered with effect from 20 July 2020.
>
> **Note:** Cat Ltd does not make any taxable supplies during the period 1 May 2020 to 19 July 2020, so the liability to register under the future prospects test cannot arise during that period.

Test your understanding 4

State which of the following unregistered traders are liable to register for VAT and the effective date of registration.

Name	Supplies	Details
Majid	Accountancy services (standard rated)	Started in business 1 November 2020. Estimated fees £17,100 per month.
Jane	Baby wear (zero rated)	Established the business 1 March 2021 when Jane signed a contract to supply a national retail store. Sales for March 2021 are expected to be £86,000.
Sayso Ltd	Insurance (exempt)	Commenced trading 2 January 2021. Sales are £100,000 per month.

Consequences of registration

Once registered, a certificate of registration is issued and the taxable person must start accounting for VAT:

- Output tax must be charged on taxable supplies.

- Each registered trader is allocated a VAT registration number, which must be quoted on all invoices.

- Each registered trader is allocated a tax period for filing returns, which is normally every three months.

- Input tax (subject to some restrictions) is recoverable on business purchases and expenses.

- Appropriate VAT records must be maintained.

There are penalties for late registration. In addition, the trader must pay over the VAT they should have collected in the period that they should have been registered.

5 Voluntary registration

Actual or intending traders

Even if not required to register, a person may register voluntarily provided he/she is making, or intending to make, taxable supplies.

HMRC will register the trader from the date of the request for voluntary registration, or a mutually agreed earlier date.

Advantages and disadvantages of voluntary registration

Advantages	Disadvantages
• Avoids penalties for late registration. • Can recover input VAT on purchases. • Can disguise the small size of the business.	• Business will suffer the burden of compliance with all VAT administration rules. • Business must charge VAT. This makes their goods comparatively more expensive than an unregistered business, for customers who cannot recover the VAT (i.e. final consumers).

Voluntary registration is therefore beneficial where the business is making:

• zero rated supplies and has input VAT that it can recover, or

• supplies to VAT registered customers

but is probably not beneficial where the business is making:

• supplies to non-VAT registered customers (e.g. the general public).

Illustration 3 – Voluntary registration

Alfred sells goods, which would be standard rated if he were registered for VAT. All of his sales are to members of the public. His current annual turnover is £40,000. He incurs input VAT of £5,000 on purchases each year.

Assuming that, due to the competitive nature of his business, Alfred is unable to increase his prices to the public advise him whether it would be beneficial to register voluntarily for VAT.

Solution

If Alfred registered for VAT he would be required to charge his customers output VAT. As he is unable to increase his prices his VAT inclusive turnover would be £40,000 and he would have to account for output VAT to HMRC of £6,667 (£40,000 × 20/120). His profits would therefore decrease by £6,667.

He would however be able to reclaim input VAT of £5,000 p.a. The net cost to Alfred of registering for VAT would be £1,667 (£6,667 – £5,000) and it is therefore not beneficial for him to register voluntarily.

If Alfred's sales were to other VAT registered businesses, he would be able to charge VAT in addition to his normal selling price, as his customers would be able to recover the VAT charged.

In this situation it would be beneficial for Alfred to register for VAT voluntarily. He would be able to recover the input tax, on his purchases and, as a result his profits would increase by £5,000.

Accepting additional new business

Accepting additional new work may increase the taxable supplies of the business above the compulsory registration threshold.

The VAT status of the customers of the business is therefore very important in deciding whether or not taking on the new business is beneficial.

- If customers are VAT registered:
    - they can recover the output VAT charged, and
    - it will be advantageous to accept the new work.

- If customers are not VAT registered:
    - they cannot recover the output VAT charged, and
    - if the selling price cannot be increased, the output VAT will become an additional cost to the business.

    This may make the additional new work unattractive:
    - it may be beneficial to decide to not accept the work, and
    - maintain taxable supplies below the VAT registration threshold.

6 VAT Groups

 Companies that are under common control can elect for a group VAT registration, provided that all the companies have a place of business in the UK.

A VAT group is treated as if it is a single company for the purposes of VAT. Group registration is optional; not all members of the group have to join the VAT group.

The effect of a group VAT registration is as follows:

- Goods and services supplied by one group company to another within the group registration are disregarded for the purposes of VAT. Therefore there is no need to account for VAT on intra-group supplies.

- The VAT group appoints a representative member which is responsible for accounting for all input and output VAT for the group.

- The representative member submits a single VAT return covering all group members, but all companies are jointly and severally liable for the VAT payable.

- The normal time limits apply for submission of VAT returns.

Advantages and disadvantages of group VAT registration

Advantages	Disadvantages
• VAT on intra-group supplies eliminated. • Only one VAT return required, which should save administration costs.	• All members remain jointly and severally liable. • A single return may cause administrative difficulties collecting and collating information.

7 Recovery of pre-registration input VAT

Normally, VAT incurred before registration cannot be accounted for as input VAT. If the conditions below are satisfied, however, then it can be treated as input tax and reclaimed accordingly.

Goods	Services
• The goods must be acquired for business purposes and should not be sold or consumed prior to registration (e.g. should still be in inventory). • The goods have not been acquired more than **four years** prior to registration.	• The services must be supplied for business purposes. • The services should not have been supplied more than **six months** prior to registration.

Note that the term goods includes both current (e.g. inventory) and noncurrent (e.g. machinery) assets for VAT purposes.

Test your understanding 5

X Ltd registered for VAT with effect from 1 January 2021. The company incurred the following expenditure prior to registration:

1. 12.2.2020   Paid accountancy fees of £500 plus VAT for preparing cash flow forecasts.

2. 14.8.2020   Paid rent of £1,500 to a landlord. This was an exempt supply hence no VAT paid.

3. 15.10.2020   Bought headed stationery, paying £1,150 including VAT.

> 4   1.11.2020   Bought inventory intended for resale, costing £5,000 plus VAT.
>
> 5   14.11.2020   Bought machine, costing £6,500 plus VAT.
>
> At the date of registration, 60% of the inventory intended for resale had already been sold. The stationery was unused and the company still owned the machine.
>
> **State the amounts of pre-registration input VAT that can be claimed.**

8   Deregistration

Compulsory deregistration

A person must deregister when he/she ceases to make taxable supplies.

- HMRC should be notified **within 30 days** of ceasing to make taxable supplies.

- VAT registration is cancelled from the date of cessation.

Voluntary deregistration

A person may voluntarily deregister, even if the business continues, if there is evidence that taxable supplies in the next 12 months, will not exceed £83,000.

- The 12 month period is measured starting at any time.

- The onus is on the trader to satisfy HMRC that they qualify.

- VAT registration is cancelled from the date of request or an agreed later date.

Effect of deregistration

On deregistration, VAT output tax must be accounted for on the value of non-current assets and inventory held at the date of deregistration, on which a deduction for input tax has been claimed.

However, this final tax liability is waived if it is £1,000 or less.

> **Test your understanding 6**
>
> 1   Jig Ltd closes down its business on 10 January 2021.
>
> 2   At 1 January 2021, Elk Ltd forecasts taxable turnover for the year to 31 December 2021, will be £40,000. It immediately decides to apply for deregistration.
>
> **State when Jig Ltd should notify HMRC of the business cessation and from when the company will be deregistered.**
>
> **State when Elk Ltd will be deregistered.**

9 VAT on sale of a business

Alternative treatments

Compulsory deregistration applies where a business is sold or otherwise transferred as a going concern to new owners.

The sale may be treated in one of two ways:

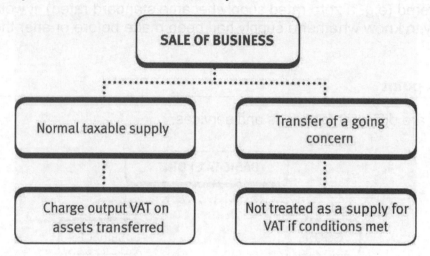

Conditions for transfer of business as a going concern

If certain conditions are satisfied, then the sale/transfer:

*   is not treated as a taxable supply

*   no output tax is therefore charged on the assets transferred by the seller, and

*   no input tax is recoverable by the purchaser.

Conditions:

*   The business is transferred as a going concern.

*   There is no significant break in the trading.

*   The same type of trade is carried on after the transfer.

*   The new owner is or is liable to be registered for VAT, immediately after the transfer.

Note that **all** these conditions **must** be met.

Transfer of registration

On the sale of a business it is normally compulsory to deregister. However, instead of doing so, both the transferor and the transferee may make a joint election, for the transferor's registration to be transferred to the transferee.

Where this is done, the transferee assumes all rights and obligations in respect of the registration, including the liability to pay any outstanding VAT. Therefore, this may not be a good commercial decision.

10 The time of supply (the tax point)

Importance of tax point

VAT is normally accounted for to HMRC on a quarterly basis, so it is important to know the time of a supply, to identify the quarter in which it falls.

Also, if the standard rate of VAT were to change or if the classification of a supply altered (e.g. a zero rated supply became standard rated), it would be necessary to know whether a supply had been made before or after the date of change.

Basic tax point

The rules are different for goods and services.

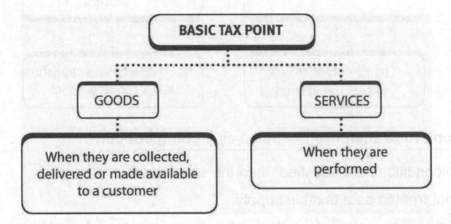

 Illustration 4 – The time of supply (the tax point)

Queue Ltd received an order for goods from a customer on 14 August 2020. The goods were despatched on 18 August 2020 and the customer paid on 15 September 2020 when they received their invoice, which was dated 14 September 2020.

What is the basic tax point date?

Solution

The basic tax point date is 18 August 2020 (i.e. the date of despatch).

Actual tax point

The basic tax point (BTP) may be overridden by the actual tax point as follows:

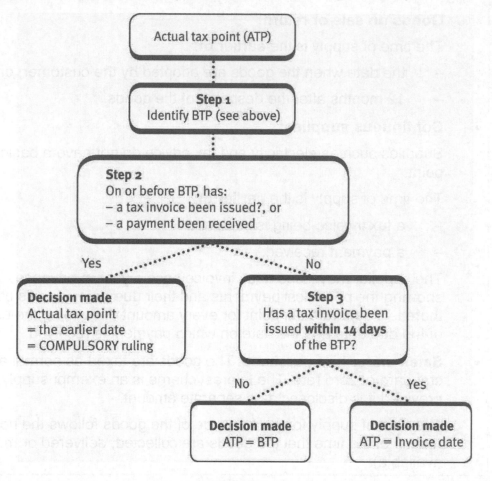

Note that traders can agree an extension to the 14 day invoicing rule with HMRC, to fit in with their invoicing routines.

 Illustration 5 – The time of supply (the tax point)

Explain the effect if Queue Ltd, in illustration 4 above, were to issue an invoice for the goods dated 30 August 2020.

Solution

The tax point would become 30 August 2020 as an invoice is issued within 14 days after the basic tax point date.

Tax point – special rules

Certain supplies of goods do not fit naturally into the above scheme:

- **Goods on sale or return:**

  The time of supply is the **earlier of**:

  - the date when the goods are adopted by the customer, or

  - 12 months after the despatch of the goods.

- **Continuous supplies:**

  Supplies such as electricity and tax advice do not have a basic tax point.

  The time of supply is the **earlier of**:

  - a tax invoice being issued, and

  - a payment received.

  The supplier may issue a tax invoice once a year in advance, showing the periodical payments and their due dates. In this case, there is a separate tax point for every amount due, being the earlier of the due date and the date on which payment is received.

- **Sales under hire purchase.** The goods are taxed as normal at the standard or zero rate. The interest charge is an exempt supply, provided it is disclosed as a separate amount.

  The time of supply for the full value of the goods follows the normal rules (i.e. the time that the goods are collected, delivered or made available).

Test your understanding 7

On 30 April 2020, Oak Ltd ordered a new felling machine, and on 16 May 2020, paid a deposit of £25,000. The machine was despatched to Oak Ltd, on 31 May 2020. On 12 June 2020, an invoice was issued to Oak Ltd for the balance due of £75,000. This was paid on 20 June 2020.

State the tax point for:

(a)   the £25,000 deposit

(b)   the balance of £75,000.

11 The value of a supply

Basic rule

The value of a taxable supply is the amount on which the VAT charge is based. This is normally the price (before VAT) charged by the supplier.

VAT fraction for standard rated goods

The price of goods before VAT is the VAT exclusive amount. If the price includes VAT, then this is the VAT inclusive amount.

- VAT is 20% of the VAT exclusive amount.
  If a standard rated supply is made at a price of (£2,000 + VAT), then the value of the supply is £2,000 and the total consideration given for the supply is £2,400.

- If the VAT inclusive amount is given, then the VAT element is (20/120) of the gross amount. The fraction of (1/6) gives the same result and is more commonly used.

Discounts

If a discount is offered, then VAT must be calculated on the amount that the customer actually pays.

Customers may be offered:

- trade discounts – a reduced price for being a loyal customer or for buying large quantities of goods

- prompt payment discounts – a reduced price for paying within an agreed timescale.

In both cases VAT is charged on the price paid by the customer.

For prompt payment discounts, the supplier may not know when the invoice is raised whether the customer will qualify for the discount. The supplier must therefore charge VAT on the invoice on the full price and either:

- issue a credit note if the discount is taken, or

- show full details of the terms of the prompt payment discount and include a statement that the customer can only recover input tax based on the amount paid to the supplier. If the discount is taken, the supplier must then adjust their records to account for output tax on the amount received.

Illustration 6 – The value of a supply

Gurminder sells standard rated goods for £4,000, excluding VAT on 1 December 2020 and issues an invoice on the same day. He includes the following statement on the invoice:

'A discount of 5% of the full price applies if payment is made within 14 days of the invoice date. No credit note will be issued. Following payment you must ensure that you have only recovered the VAT actually paid.'

State the amount of VAT that Gurminder should show on the VAT invoice and explain what Gurminder should do if the customer pays within 10 days of the invoice date.

Solution

VAT shown on the invoice must be based on the full price i.e. £800 (£4,000 × 20%).

If the customer pays within 10 days of the invoice date, Gurminder must adjust his VAT records to ensure that output tax of £760 (£4,000 × 20% × 95%) is paid to HMRC.

Gurminder is not required to issue a credit note to the customer but must retain evidence that the invoice was paid within the terms of the discount arrangement (e.g. a bank statement).

Goods for own use

The treatment of goods taken for the trader's own use depends on the purpose for which the goods were purchased.

- Where the trader withdraws goods which were purchased for business purposes, input VAT can be recovered and output VAT must be accounted for on the **replacement** value of the supplies.

- Where the trader initially purchased the goods for private purposes, no input VAT can be reclaimed and there is no output VAT charge.

Gifts

Gifts of inventory or non-current assets are treated as taxable supplies at replacement cost, except gifts of:

- goods to the same person which cost the trader £50 (excluding VAT) or less in a 12 month period.

- business samples, regardless of the number of same samples given to the recipient.

Gifts of services, whether to employees or customers, are not taxable supplies.

Test your understanding 8

State the amount of VAT due in each of the following cases:

Description	Output VAT
Sale of standard rated goods for £500, excluding VAT. A trade discount of 3% is then applied.	
Sales of standard rated goods for £5,500, including VAT.	
Gifts of 10 calendars costing £5 each, including VAT.	
Removal of standard rated goods by the owner. The goods cost £200 and would cost £220 to replace, both figures exclude VAT.	

Assume that all transactions are in the quarter to 30 June 2020.

12 Recovery of input VAT

Conditions for recovery of input VAT

Input VAT is recoverable by taxable persons on goods and services that are supplied to them for business purposes.

A VAT invoice (see Chapter 26) is needed to support the claim.

Capital and revenue expenditure

Unlike other taxes, there is **no distinction** between capital and revenue expenditure for VAT.

Provided the assets are used for the purposes of the trade, the related input VAT is recoverable on both capital assets (i.e. purchase of plant and machinery, delivery vans, equipment, etc.) and revenue expenditure.

If capital assets are subsequently sold, output VAT must be charged as a taxable supply of goods.

However, the exception to this rule is the purchase of motor cars (see below).

Irrecoverable input VAT

Input VAT on the following goods and services cannot be recovered:

*   Business entertaining (e.g. entertaining suppliers and **U.K.** customers)
    *   although VAT incurred on staff entertaining and entertaining overseas customers is recoverable.

- Motor cars, unless they are:
  - used 100% for business purposes (e.g. driving school cars), in which case 100% recovery available, or
  - leased, in which case 50% of input VAT is recoverable where the car has some private use.

Note that where input VAT cannot be recovered on the purchase of a motor car, no output VAT will be due on its disposal.

Illustration 7 – Recovery of input VAT

Riker plc makes standard rated supplies and is registered for VAT. It incurs the following costs during 2020.

1 £5,400 on business entertaining (UK customers) and £2,400 on staff entertaining.

2 £30,000 on a new car for the managing director and £72,000 on new delivery lorries.

The managing director's car is used partly for private purposes.

All figures are VAT exclusive.

State the amount of input tax the business can claim and the figures that should be included in the financial statements in respect of these items. Explain how they will be treated for corporation tax purposes.

Solution

1 **Entertaining UK customers**

No VAT recoverable on business entertaining of UK customers. The VAT inclusive figure of (£5,400 × 120%) = £6,480, charged against profit will be a disallowed expense for the purpose of the tax adjusted trading profit computation.

VAT of £480 (20% × £2,400), will be recoverable on staff entertaining. The VAT exclusive amount of £2,400 will be charged against profits and is an allowable expense for tax purposes.

2 **Car and lorries**

No VAT recoverable on cars with private use. The VAT inclusive figure of (£30,000 × 120%) = £36,000, will be capitalised in the accounts and will be eligible for capital allowances.

VAT of £14,400 (20% × £72,000) is recoverable on the lorries. The VAT exclusive figure of £72,000 will be capitalised in the accounts and will be eligible for capital allowances.

Private use

Input VAT cannot be claimed for goods or services that are not used for business purposes.

Where goods or services are used partly for private and partly for business purposes (e.g. use of telephone/mobile phone), an appropriate apportionment is made to calculate the recoverable input VAT.

The exception to this rule is the recoverability of input VAT on motor expenses (see below).

Motor expenses

A business can recover **all** input VAT incurred on the running costs of a car, such as fuel and repairs, even when there is some private use.

Note that VAT is not charged on the insurance and road fund licence.

When a business pays for fuel costs for an employee, sole trader or partner and there is some private use of the vehicle, a VAT charge will be payable:

- where the full cost of the private fuel is reimbursed by the employee/owner, output VAT is payable on the cost of fuel reimbursed.

- if the employee does not reimburse the employer, output VAT is due based on a prescribed scale charge.

The scale charge depends on the CO_2 emissions of the car. The scale charges will be provided in the examination if necessary.

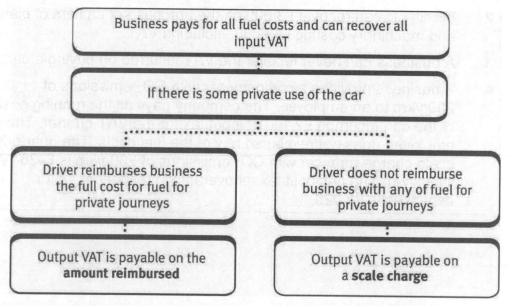

Note that partial reimbursement of fuel costs is not examinable.

Illustration 8 – Recovery of input VAT

Forge Ltd provides a company car with CO_2 emissions of 205 g/km for the managing director for business and private use. The company pays for all running costs including petrol, with no reimbursement by the employee. The relevant VAT fuel scale charge is £450.

State the value of the output tax in respect of the running costs for this car for the quarter to 31 December 2020.

Solution

The scale charge for a petrol-powered car with CO_2 emissions of 205 g/km is £450. This is the VAT inclusive output amount.

The output VAT charge is £75 (£450 × 1/6).

Note that the scale charge will be given in the question in the examination.

Test your understanding 9

For each of the following situations state whether the statement concerning the recovery of input tax is true or false. Assume all the businesses in the question are VAT registered traders and the transactions occur in the quarter to 30 September 2020.

1   VAT incurred by a business on entertaining overseas customers is recoverable.

2   Firmin plc can recover £3,000 on the purchase of an item of plant and machinery costing £15,000, including VAT.

3   A business can never recover the VAT incurred on buying a car.

4   A business provides a company car with CO_2 emissions of 200g/km to an employee. The company pays all the running costs of the car, incurring £2,100 of input tax for the VAT quarter. The employee does not reimburse any of the fuel costs. The quarterly scale charge for a car with CO_2 emissions of 200g/km is £436 (VAT inclusive). The net input tax recoverable in respect of motor expenses is £2,026.

13 Relief for impairment losses

Normally, VAT output tax is accounted for when an invoice is issued. If the debt becomes irrecoverable, the seller has paid VAT to HMRC and never recovers this from the customer. This position is addressed by the seller being able to claim VAT relief for impairment losses.

The following conditions apply:

- At least **six months** must have elapsed from the time that payment was due (or the date of supply if later).

- The debt must have been written off in the seller's VAT account.

- Claims for relief for irrecoverable debts must be made within four years and six months of the payment being due.

Relief is obtained by adding the VAT element of the irrecoverable debt to the input tax claimed.

Illustration 9 – Relief for impairment losses

Fox Ltd made sales to X Ltd as follows: £3,500 due for payment on 1 August 2020 and £2,260 due for payment on 1 September 2020. Fox Ltd wrote off the debts in January 2021.

All figures are VAT inclusive.

State the amount of relief available to Fox Ltd for irrecoverable debts in the quarter to 31 March 2021.

Solution

At 31 March 2021, both invoices are unpaid more than 6 months from the due date of payment.

The total debt to be written off is £5,760, including VAT. A claim for relief can be made for the VAT element of £960 (£5,760 × 1/6).

This claim can be made by adding £960 to the input tax claimed for the quarter.

Note that VAT is recovered at the rate at which it was originally charged, not at the rate at the time of the VAT recovery.

Test your understanding 10

On 1 December 2020, Berry Ltd wrote off two debts. The first was a debt of £2,456, due for payment on 1 May 2020 and the second a debt of £3,100, due for payment on 31 August 2020.

All figures are VAT inclusive.

State the amount of relief for impaired debts available to the company in the return for the quarter ended 31 December 2020.

14 Comprehensive example

Dynamo Ltd commenced trading as a wholesaler on 1 November 2019. Its sales have been as follows:

		£			£
2019	November	4,150	2020	June	5,950
	December	4,750		July	5,850
2020	January	5,250		August	6,500
	February	5,050		September	8,650
	March	4,450		October	10,800
	April	4,650		November	11,250
	May	4,850		December	12,200

The company's sales are all standard rated, and the above figures are exclusive of VAT.

(a) **Explain from what date Dynamo Ltd will be required to compulsorily register for VAT, and what action the company must then take.**

(b) **Explain the circumstances in which Dynamo Ltd will be allowed to recover input VAT incurred on goods purchased and services incurred prior to the date of VAT registration.**

(c) **Advise Dynamo Ltd of the VAT rules that determine the tax point in respect of a supply of goods.**

15 Chapter summary

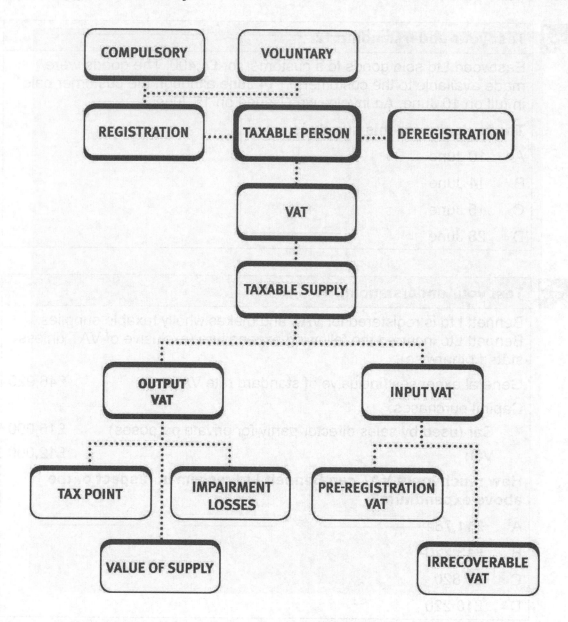

16 Practice objective test questions

Test your understanding 12

Eastwood Ltd sold goods to a customer for £4,400. The goods were made available to the customer on 14 June although the customer paid in full on 10 June. An invoice was issued on 15 June.

The tax point for this supply is:

A   10 June

B   14 June

C   15 June

D   28 June

Test your understanding 13

Bennett Ltd is registered for VAT and makes wholly taxable supplies. Bennett Ltd incurred the following expenditure (exclusive of VAT unless stated otherwise).

General expenses (inclusive of standard rate VAT)	£46,920
Capital purchases:	
Car (used by sales director partly for private purposes)	£15,000
Van	£12,000

How much input VAT can Bennett Ltd reclaim in respect of the above expenditure?

A   £11,784

B   £13,220

C   £9,820

D   £10,220

Test your understanding 14

Banana plc is registered for VAT. In the quarter to 31 December 2020 it made the following standard rated supplies (all VAT exclusive):

1 Cash sales to non-VAT registered members of the public of £40,000.

2 Credit sales to two VAT registered companies on 1 November 2020 for £1,200 each. Banana plc offered both companies a 5% discount for paying within 14 days. Only one of the companies paid within the discount period.

How much output VAT must Banana plc pay to HMRC in respect of the quarter to 31 December 2020?

A £8,468

B £7,135

C £8,456

D £7,147

Test your understanding 15

J Ltd received an order for 18,000 widgets on 14 December 2020. J Ltd despatched these to the customer on 18 December 2020. An invoice was sent on 31 December 2020 and full payment was received on 15 January 2021.

What is the tax point (i.e. the deemed date of sale for VAT purposes) for the sale of the widgets?

A 18 December 2020

B 31 December 2020

C 15 January 2021

D 14 December 2020

Test your understanding 16

Which of the following VAT registration statements are true?

1 A business making wholly zero rated supplies cannot register for VAT.

2 A business which has a taxable turnover of £60,000 in its first year of trading cannot register for VAT.

3 A business making only exempt supplies can register for VAT.

A 1 and 2 only

B 2 and 3 only

C None of them

D All of them

Test your understanding answers

Test your understanding 1

Correct or incorrect

1   Correct.

2   Incorrect. Lucy is not a taxable person and is not making a supply in the course of a business.

3   Incorrect. Businesses must pay output VAT over to HMRC after deducting any input VAT they have suffered for the period.

Test your understanding 2

Missing words

1   cannot

2   20%

3   supplies

4   can, cannot

Test your understanding 3

Jana

Both newspapers and stationery are taxable supplies, so Jana must register when her sales for the previous 12 months exceed the registration threshold of £85,000.

In her first year, sales are £5,300 per month, so her turnover for the year ended 31 July 2020, is £63,600. Thereafter, her sales are £9,680 per month, so each month she sells £4,380 more than one year ago.

Her cumulative turnover for the previous 12 months at each month end thereafter is as follows:

Month end	£
31 August 2020	67,980
30 September 2020	72,360
31 October 2020	76,740
30 November 2020	81,120
31 December 2020	85,500

Jana is liable to register at the end of December 2020 and she must notify HMRC by 30 January 2021 and will be registered with effect from 1 February 2021, or an earlier date agreed with HMRC.

Test your understanding 4

Name	Supplies	Details
Majid	Accountancy services	Taxable turnover will exceed £85,000 at the end of March 2021. Notify HMRC by 30 April 2021 and registered with effect from 1 May 2021.
Jane	Baby wear	Sales for the next 30 days are expected to exceed £85,000 on 1 March 2021, so Jane must notify HMRC by the end of the 30 days, i.e. by 30 March 2021 and will be registered with effect from 1 March 2021. Note that Jane could apply for exemption from registration as she is making wholly zero rated supplies, but then she would not be able to reclaim any input tax. Jane must complete a VAT registration form in accordance with the compulsory registration rules. However she can claim exemption from registration on that form.
Sayso Ltd	Insurance	Making wholly exempt supplies so cannot register.

Test your understanding 5

X Ltd

1   Accountancy is a service. It is supplied more than six months prior to registration, hence, no input VAT can be reclaimed.

2   Rent is exempt so no VAT paid and no VAT reclaimable.

3   VAT of £192 (£1,150 × 20/120) is included in the cost of stationery. This can be recovered as the stationery had not been used prior to registration.

4   40% of the inventory is unsold at registration, so 40% of the VAT on the goods can be recovered. This is £400 (40% × 20% × £5,000).

5   The machinery is still owned by the company, so the VAT of £1,300 (£6,500 × 20%) can be recovered.

Test your understanding 6

Jig Ltd and Elk Ltd

If Jig Ltd closes down its business on 10 January 2021, the company must notify HMRC on or before 9 February 2021 and is then deregistered from 10 January 2021.

If Elk Ltd forecasts taxable turnover for the year to 31 December 2021 will be £40,000, and applies for deregistration on 1 January 2021, the company can be deregistered with effect from 1 January 2021 or an agreed later date.

Test your understanding 7

(a) **£25,000 deposit**

The basic tax point is the date of despatch, 31 May 2020.

As the deposit was paid before the basic tax point (BTP), the BTP is overridden and the actual tax point is the date the deposit was paid (i.e. 16 May 2020).

(b) **The balance of £75,000**

As an invoice was issued within 14 days of the basic tax point; the date of the invoice is the actual tax point (i.e. 12 June 2020).

Test your understanding 8

Description	Output VAT
Sale of standard rated goods for £500, excluding VAT. A trade discount of 3% is then applied.	(20% × £500 × 97%) = £97
Sales of standard rated goods for £5,500, including VAT.	(1/6 × £5,500) = £917
Gifts of 10 calendars costing £5 each, including VAT.	As less than £50 each, no output VAT
Removal of standard rated goods by the owner. The goods cost £200 and would cost £220 to replace, both figures excluding VAT.	(20% × £220) = £44

Note that calculations in the examination are to the nearest £.

Test your understanding 9

True or false

1   True.

2   False. (1/6 of £15,000) = £2,500.

3   False. Input VAT can be recovered for cars with 100% business use.

4   True. The business can recover £2,100 input tax but must account for £73 (£436 × 1/6) of output tax on the fuel scale charge. The net input tax recoverable is £2,027 (£2,100 – £73).

Test your understanding 10

Berry Ltd

The second debt is less than six months old, so no relief is available yet.

On the first debt the VAT included of (1/6 × £2,456) = £409, can be recovered.

Test your understanding 11

Dynamo Ltd

(a)   **Compulsory registration**

–   Dynamo Ltd will become liable to compulsory VAT registration when its taxable supplies during any 12 month period exceed £85,000.

–   This will happen on 31 December 2020 when taxable supplies will amount to £85,450 (£5,250 + £5,050 + £4,450 + £4,650 + £4,850 + £5,950 + £5,850 + £6,500 + £8,650 + £10,800 + £11,250 + £12,200).

–   Dynamo Ltd will have to notify HMRC by 30 January 2021, being 30 days after the end of the period.

–   The company will be registered from 1 February 2021 or from an agreed earlier date.

(b)   Recovery of input VAT on goods and services purchased prior to registration

- The goods must be acquired for business purposes, and not be sold or consumed prior to registration.

- The goods were not acquired more than four years prior to registration.

- The services must be supplied for business purposes.

- The services were not supplied more than six months prior to registration.

(c)   The supply of goods

- The basic tax point is the date goods are made available to the customer.

- If an invoice is issued or payment received before the basic tax point, then this becomes the actual tax point.

- If an invoice is issued within 14 days of the basic tax point, the invoice date will replace the basic tax point date provided an actual tax point has not already arisen as above.

Test your understanding 12

The correct answer is A.

The normal tax point of 14 June (i.e. the date the goods are made available to the customer) is overridden as payment was made earlier (on 10 June).

As the payment was made earlier, the 14 day invoice rule is irrelevant.

Test your understanding 13

The correct answer is D.

Input VAT	£
£46,920 × 1/6	7,820
£12,000 × 20%	2,400
	———
Reclaimable	10,220
	———

Note: VAT on the purchase of the car is blocked and cannot be reclaimed as the car is used for private purposes.

When figures are quoted as VAT exclusive, the VAT on standard rated items is found by multiplying by 20%.

If the figure is quoted as VAT inclusive the VAT element is calculated by multiplying by 20/120, usually simplified to 1/6. This is often referred to as the VAT fraction.

Test your understanding 14

The correct answer is A.

	£
Cash sales (£40,000 × 20%)	8,000
Discounted sales (£1,200 × 20%) + (£1,200 × 95% × 20%)	468
Output tax payable	8,468

Where a prompt payment discount is offered output VAT is charged on the amount received.

Test your understanding 15

The correct answer is B.

The basic tax point is the date of delivery i.e. 18 December 2020. However, as the invoice is issued within 14 days of the basic tax point, then the invoice date i.e. 31 December 2020 becomes the actual tax point.

Test your understanding 16

The correct answer is C.

A business which makes any level of taxable supplies (which includes zero rated supplies), can register for VAT. They do not have to wait until their turnover exceeds the registration threshold.

A business which only makes exempt supplies cannot register for VAT.

VAT: Administration and overseas aspects

Chapter learning objectives

Upon completion of this chapter you will be able to:

- understand how VAT is accounted for and administered

- list the information that must be given on a VAT invoice

- understand when the default surcharge, a penalty for an incorrect VAT return, and default interest will be applied

- understand the treatment of imports, exports and trade within the European Union

- understand the operation of, and when it will be advantageous to use the VAT special schemes:

  (i) Cash accounting scheme

  (ii) Annual accounting scheme

  (iii) Flat rate scheme.

PER

One of the PER performance objectives (PO15) is to prepare computations of taxable amounts and tax liabilities according to legal requirements. Another objective (PO16) is to make sure that individuals and entities comply with their tax obligations on time, and in the spirit and letter of the law. Working through this chapter should help you understand how to demonstrate those objectives.

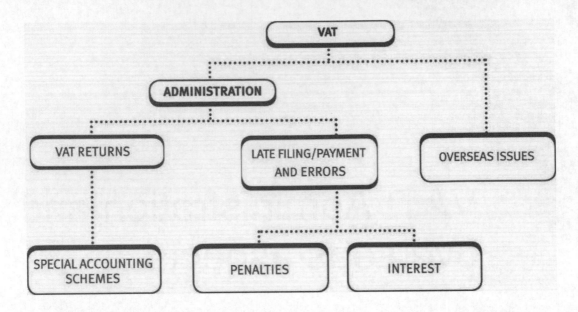

1 VAT computation

All registered traders have to:

- complete a VAT return every return period (see below), and
- pay net VAT due to HMRC or reclaim net VAT repayable from HMRC.

Details of output and input VAT must be included, together with claims for relief for impairment losses and any errors made on earlier returns below a de minimis limit (see section 7).

Illustration 1 – VAT computation

Cart Ltd is registered for VAT, and its sales are all standard rated.

The following information relates to the company's VAT return for the quarter ended 31 December 2020:

(1) Standard rated sales amounted to £240,000.

(2) In addition to the above Cart Ltd issued a sales invoice for £25,000 on 1 December 2020. The customer was offered a 5% discount if the invoice was paid within 14 days. The customer paid within the 14 day period.

(3) Standard rated purchases and expenses amounted to £71,280. This figure includes £960 for entertaining UK customers.

(4) On 15 December 2020, the company wrote off irrecoverable debts of £4,000 and £1,680, in respect of invoices due for payment on 10 May and 5 August 2020 respectively.

(5) On 30 December 2020, the company purchased a motor car at a cost of £32,900, for the use of a director, and machinery at a cost of £42,300. Both these figures are inclusive of VAT. The motor car is used for both business and private mileage.

Unless stated otherwise, all of the above figures are exclusive of VAT.

Calculate the amount of VAT payable by Cart Ltd for the quarter.

Solution

	£	£
Output VAT		
Sales (£240,000 × 20%)		48,000
Discounted sale (£25,000 × 95% × 20%)		4,750
Input VAT		
Purchases and expenses		
(£71,280 – £960) = (£70,320 × 20%)	14,064	
Relief for irrecoverable debts (£4,000 × 20%)	800	
Machinery (£42,300 × 1/6)	7,050	
		(21,914)
VAT payable		30,836

Notes:

(1) Output VAT is charged on the amount received when a prompt payment discount is offered.

(2) Input VAT on business entertaining (for UK customers) cannot be reclaimed.

(3) Relief for an irrecoverable debt is not given until six months from the time that payment is due. Relief is given on the discounted amount.

(4) Input VAT on motor cars not used wholly for business purposes cannot be reclaimed.

Test your understanding 1

Hairby Ltd has provided the following information for the quarter to 31 March 2021. All figures exclude VAT.

(1) Sales consisted of £45,000 of standard rated sales and £15,000 of zero rated sales.

(2) Purchases for resale were all standard rated and totalled £31,000.

(3) Standard rated expenses were £7,600, including £350 for entertaining UK customers.

(4) One gift to a customer out of inventory costing £250 was made. The replacement cost of the goods was £300.

(5) A photocopier costing £6,400 was purchased.

Calculate the amount of VAT payable by Hairby Ltd for the quarter ended 31 March 2021.

2 VAT return and payment procedures

Normal VAT accounting

VAT return periods are normally three months long, but traders who regularly receive repayments, can opt to have monthly return periods to receive their repayments earlier.

- VAT returns show total output VAT and total input VAT for the period.

- All businesses must file their VAT return and pay VAT electronically.

- The deadline for filing and payment online is:

  - **One month and seven** days after the end of the quarter.

Under the Government's Making Tax Digital (MTD) project businesses with taxable turnover above the VAT threshold of £85,000 are required to keep VAT records digitally. These digital records of supplies, purchases, output VAT payable and input VAT recoverable must be used, in conjunction with MTD compatible software, to automatically compile a digital VAT return. The business is then required to review the digital VAT return and confirm that it is correct and can be submitted to HMRC.

There are temporary Covid-19 tax deferral options available regarding VAT payments due between 30 March and 30 June 2020. However, for any question relating to this period, you should assume that the taxpayer has not deferred any payments.

VAT refunds

- VAT refunds are normally made within 10 days.

- Where it is discovered that VAT has been overpaid in the past, the time limit for claiming a refund is four years from the date by which the return for the accounting period was due.

 Substantial traders

Substantial traders are those with a VAT liability exceeding £2.3 million p.a.

- Monthly payments on account are required.

- Payments at the end of months 2 and 3 in every quarter are 1/24th of the annual liability for the previous year.

- Any additional amounts are paid with the normal VAT return.

Other methods can be agreed with HMRC for calculating the payments on account.

3 VAT records

Records must be kept of all goods and services received and supplied in the course of a business. Records must be kept up-to-date and must be preserved for **six years**.

In practice, the main records that must be kept are as follows:

- Copies of all VAT invoices issued.

- A record of all outputs (e.g. a sales day book).

- Evidence supporting claims for the recovery of input VAT (e.g. invoices).

- A record of all inputs (e.g. purchase day book).

- VAT account.

Businesses with taxable turnover above the VAT threshold of £85,000 are required to keep the records required to complete the VAT return digitally.

Other businesses, such as those with taxable turnover below the VAT threshold that are registered voluntarily, no particular form is specified, but they must be sufficient to allow the VAT return to be completed and to allow HMRC to check the return.

4 Normal VAT invoices

- A VAT invoice must be issued when a standard rated supply is made to a VAT registered business.

- The invoice can be sent electronically provided the customer agrees.

- No invoice is required if the supply is exempt, zero rated or to a non- VAT registered customer (however, see below regarding simplified invoices).

A VAT invoice should be issued within 30 days of the date that the taxable supply is treated as being made.

The original VAT invoice is sent to the customer and forms their evidence for reclaiming input VAT, and a copy must be kept by the supplier to support the calculation of output VAT.

A VAT invoice must contain the following particulars

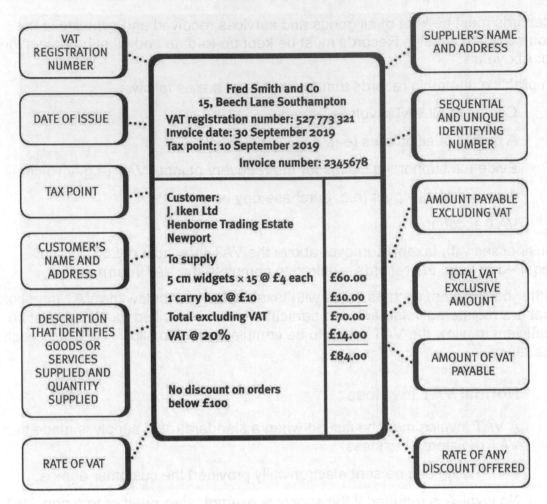

5 Less detailed VAT invoices

VAT registered businesses can provide UK customers with an invoice which is less detailed than normal, if the consideration for the supply is £250 (VAT inclusive) or less.

This less detailed invoice must show the following information:

- The supplier's name, address and VAT registration number.

- The date of supply.

- A description of the goods or services supplied.

- The consideration for the supply.

- The rate of VAT in force at the time of supply.

Test your understanding 2

For each of the following statements, state whether they are true or false:

(1)   All VAT invoices must show the rate of VAT on the supply.

(2)   A VAT invoice should show the customer's VAT registration number.

(3)   All VAT registered businesses must always supply a full VAT invoice to their customers when requested.

(4)   Where the value of a supply is more than £250, a business must always issue a detailed VAT invoice.

6   The default surcharge

A default occurs if a VAT return is not submitted on time or a payment of VAT is made late. The sequence of events is as follows:

On the first default, HMRC will serve a surcharge liability notice on the trader.

- The notice specifies a surcharge period, starting on the date of the notice and ending on the 12 month anniversary of the end of the VAT period to which the default relates.

- If the trader has a further default during the surcharge period, there are two consequences:

    - The surcharge period is extended to the 12 month anniversary of the VAT period to which the new default relates.

    - If the default involves the late payment of VAT, then the trader will be subject to a surcharge penalty.

- There is no surcharge penalty where a late VAT return involves the repayment of VAT, or if the VAT payable is £Nil.

Calculating the surcharge penalty

The rate of surcharge penalty depends on the number of defaults in the surcharge period:

Default in the surcharge period	Surcharge as a percentage of the unpaid VAT due
First	2%
Second	5%
Third	10%
Fourth	15%

- Surcharge penalties at the rates of 2% and 5% are not made for amounts less than £400.

- Where the rate of surcharge is 10% or 15%, a surcharge penalty is the higher of:

  (i) £30, or

  (ii) the actual amount of the calculated surcharge.

- The surcharge liability period will only end when a trader submits four consecutive quarterly VAT returns on time, and also pays any VAT due on time.

Illustration 2 – The default surcharge

Mole Ltd's VAT return for the quarter ended 30 June 2020, was submitted late, and the VAT due of £14,500 was not paid until 16 August 2020.

The company's VAT return for the following quarter to 30 September 2020, was also submitted late and the VAT due of £26,200, was not paid until 9 November 2020.

State the consequences for Mole Ltd.

Solution

VAT return period for the quarter ended 30 June 2020	VAT return period for the quarter ended 30 September 2020
• First default • Surcharge liability notice issued • Surcharge period ends 30 June 2021	• First default within the surcharge period • Surcharge penalty 2% of £26,200 = £524 • Surcharge period extended to 30 September 2021

Test your understanding 3

Fill in the missing words in the following statements:

(1) If a business submits its VAT return late then HMRC will issue a . . . . (3 words).

(2) The . . . . default within a surcharge period will attract a penalty of 5%.

(3) In order to avoid further surcharges, a business must submit all VAT returns and pay all VAT due, on time for a period of . . . . months.

(4) If a trader's first default produces a penalty of £300, then HMRC . . . . collect it.

7 Errors on VAT returns

Self-assessment

VAT is a self-assessed tax. Traders calculate their own liability or repayment.

- HMRC make occasional control visits to check that returns are correct.

- HMRC have the power to enter business premises, inspect documents, including statements of profit or loss and statements of financial position, take samples, and inspect computers records.

Errors found on earlier VAT returns

If a trader realises that there is an error, this may lead to a standard penalty as there has been a submission of an incorrect VAT return.

The calculation of the standard penalty is covered in Chapter 13.

However, if the error is below the de minimis level and voluntarily disclosed, no default interest will be charged.

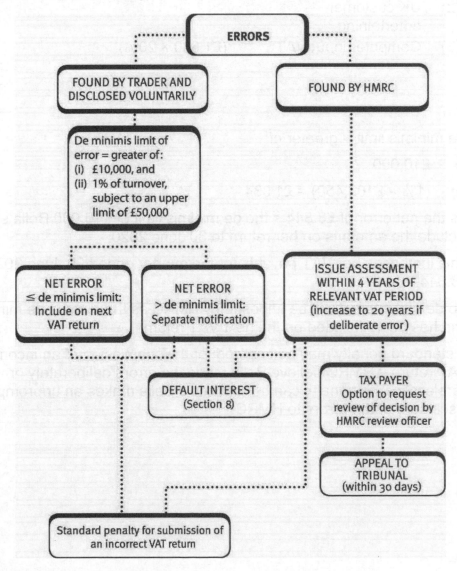

Illustration 3 – Errors on VAT returns

Bella is a registered trader who prepares VAT returns quarterly. In the quarter to 30 June 2020, she has a turnover of £103,450 and she discovers the following errors in earlier returns:

(1) Bella incorrectly recorded the total of output VAT for the previous quarter as £45,590, when it should have been £54,590.

(2) Input VAT on UK customer entertaining of £180, was wrongly reclaimed as input tax in the same quarter.

(3) No input tax was reclaimed on the purchase of a computer in September 2019, costing £1,680 plus VAT.

State the action Bella should take to correct these errors.

Solution

			£
(1)	Output VAT	(£54,590 – £45,590)	9,000
(2)	UK customer entertaining		180
(3)	Computer input VAT	(£1,680 × 20%)	(336)
			8,844

De minimis limit = greater of:

(i) £10,000

(ii) (1% × £103,450) = £1,034

As the net error of £8,844 < the de minimis limit of £10,000 Bella should include the amounts on her return to 30 June 2020.

This increases her VAT payable for the quarter ended 30 June 2020 by £8,844.

No default interest will be imposed by HMRC as the error is de minimis and has been included on the next VAT return.

A standard penalty may be charged for the submission of an incorrect VAT return if HMRC believe Bella made the errors deliberately or carelessly. The penalty can be reduced if Bella makes an unprompted disclosure of the errors to HMRC.

8 Default interest

Default interest (also known as penalty interest) is charged, if HMRC raise an assessment, or an error is voluntarily disclosed by the trader, and the net value of errors exceeds the de minimis limit.

Interest is charged from the date that the outstanding VAT should have been paid, to the actual date of payment.

Any interest charged by HMRC is limited to a maximum of three years, prior to the date of the assessment or voluntary disclosure.

Illustration 4 – Default interest

Hem Ltd discovers that in the quarter ended 31 May 2020, it made an error on its VAT return and output VAT of £12,800 was under declared. This was in excess of the de minimis limit.

The company voluntarily disclosed the amount to HMRC, paying the VAT due on 7 October 2020.

Assuming the rate of default interest is 2.75%, calculate the charge made on Hem Ltd.

Solution

The under declared VAT should have been paid on 7 July 2020.

Default interest will be charged from 7 July to 7 October 2020. This will be (£12,800 × 2.75% × 3/12) = £88.

Test your understanding 4

HMRC issue an assessment on 30 April 2021 showing £4,100 VAT payable, for the quarter ended 31 May 2020. Grab Ltd paid the outstanding sum on 7 May 2021.

Assume the rate of interest is 2.75%.

Calculate the default interest charged on Grab Ltd.

9 The cash accounting scheme

Purpose of the scheme

Normally VAT is accounted for on the basis of invoices issued and received in a return period. Accordingly:

- output VAT is paid to HMRC by reference to the period in which the invoice is issued regardless of whether payment has been received from the customer.

- input VAT is reclaimed from HMRC by reference to the invoices received in the return period, even if payment has not been made to the supplier.

This can give cash flow and impaired debt problems, particularly in the case of smaller businesses. As a result:

- 'Smaller' businesses may optionally use the cash accounting scheme if the conditions, set out below, are met.

- Under the cash accounting scheme VAT is accounted for on the basis of cash receipts and payments, rather than on the basis of the dates of invoices issued and received.

- The tax point becomes the time of receipt or payment.

Advantages	Disadvantages
• Businesses selling on credit do not have to pay output VAT to HMRC until they receive it from customers. • This gives automatic relief for impaired debts.	• Input tax cannot be claimed until the invoice is paid. This delays recovery of input VAT. • Not suitable for businesses with a lot of cash sales or zero rated supplies which would simply suffer a delay in the recovery of input VAT.

Conditions

The scheme is aimed at smaller businesses, hence, there are a number of conditions.

- The trader must be up-to-date with VAT returns and must have committed no VAT offences in the previous 12 months.

- Taxable turnover, including zero rated sales, but excluding sales of capital assets, must not exceed £1,350,000 p.a.

- A trader must leave the scheme once taxable turnover (excluding VAT) exceeds £1,600,000 p.a.

- The cash accounting scheme cannot be used for goods that are invoiced more than six months in advance of the payment date, or where an invoice is issued prior to the supply actually taking place.

Test your understanding 5

State which of the following businesses would benefit from joining the cash accounting scheme:

(1) JB Ltd, which operates a retail shop selling directly to the public (standard rated supplies). All sales are for cash.

(2) Amber and Co, which manufactures and sells computer printers to other businesses (standard rated supplies) on credit terms.

(3) Janet, who manufactures children's shoes and sells them to retailers (zero rated supplies).

10 Annual accounting

Purpose of the scheme

Smaller businesses may find it costly or inconvenient to submit (the normal) four quarterly VAT returns.

An 'annual' accounting scheme is available, whereby, a single VAT return is filed for a 12 month period (normally, the accounting period of the business). This helps relieve the burden of administration.

How the scheme works

Only one VAT return is submitted each year, but VAT payments must still be made regularly. The scheme works as follows:

- The annual return must be filed **within two months** of the end of the annual return period.

- Normally, nine payments on account of the VAT liability for the year, are made at the end of months 4 to 12 of the year. Each payment represents 10% of the VAT liability for the previous year.

- Regular payments aid budgeting and possibly cash flow if the VAT liability is increasing year on year.

- A new business will base its payments on an estimate of the VAT liability for the year.

- A balancing payment (or repayment) is made when the return is filed.

- Businesses may apply to HMRC to agree quarterly payments on account instead of the normal nine monthly payments.

Conditions

As with cash accounting the scheme is aimed at smaller businesses:

- Businesses can join the scheme provided their taxable turnover (excluding the sale of capital assets) does not exceed £1,350,000 p.a.

- The business must be up-to-date with its VAT returns.

- Businesses must leave the scheme once taxable turnover exceeds £1,600,000 p.a.

Test your understanding 6

Jump Ltd applied to use the annual accounting scheme from 1 February 2020. The company's net VAT liability for the year ended 31 January 2020, was £3,600. The actual net VAT liability for the year ended 31 January 2021, is £3,821.

Explain the returns and payments Jump Ltd must make for the year ended 31 January 2021.

11 The flat rate scheme

Purpose of the scheme

The optional flat rate scheme simplifies the way in which very small businesses calculate their VAT liability.

Under the flat rate scheme, a business calculates its VAT liability by simply applying a flat rate percentage to total turnover.

This removes the need to calculate and record output VAT and input VAT and can save the business money.

How the scheme works

- The flat rate percentage is applied to the gross (VAT inclusive) total turnover figure (inclusive of zero rated and exempt supplies); with no input VAT being recovered.

- The percentage varies according to the type of trade that the business is involved in, and will be given to you in the examination.

- A higher flat rate of 16.5% applies to all types of business with limited, or no purchases of goods. You will not be expected to identify when to use this percentage but it could be provided to you in a question in the examination.

- The flat rate scheme percentage is only used to calculate the VAT due to HMRC.

In other respects, VAT is dealt with in the same way:

- A VAT invoice must still be issued to customers and VAT at the rate of 20% is still charged on standard rated supplies.

- A VAT account must still be maintained.

Conditions

- Like the cash accounting and annual accounting schemes, the flat rate scheme is aimed at small businesses. However, the turnover thresholds applied to determine eligibility for the flat rate scheme are much lower than those for the other two schemes.

- To join the scheme the expected taxable turnover (excluding VAT) for the next twelve months must not exceed £150,000.

- A business has to leave the scheme if total VAT inclusive turnover (including taxable and exempt supplies) exceeds £230,000.

- The business must have committed no VAT offences in the previous 12 months.

- The flat rate scheme can be used with the annual accounting scheme.

- It is not possible to join both the flat rate scheme and the cash accounting scheme. However, it is possible for a trader to request to apply the flat rate percentage to the cash amount actually received in relation to VAT inclusive supplies during the period, rather than applying it to the VAT inclusive turnover in the period.

Test your understanding 7

In the year ended 31 December 2020, Apple Ltd has annual sales of £90,500, all of which are standard rated and to the general public. The company incurs standard rated expenses of £4,500 p.a. These figures are inclusive of VAT.

Calculate Apple Ltd's VAT liability using:

(1) **The normal method.**

(2) **The flat rate scheme.**

Assume a relevant flat rate percentage for Apple Ltd's trade of 10%.

12 Overseas aspects of VAT

VAT is a tax levied within the European Union (EU) only. It is therefore necessary to distinguish imports and exports from outside the EU from transactions within the EU.

Note that, although the UK officially left the EU prior to the Financial Year 2020, the VAT treatment of transactions within the EU will not change during the Brexit transition period. This period is due to end on 31 December 2020, however for exams between June 2021 and March 2022, it is assumed that the EU rules will continue to apply.

Imports from outside the EU

Goods

VAT is charged on goods imported from outside the EU as if it were a customs duty. It is normally collected direct from the importer at the place of importation, such as a port or airport.

- Approved traders can pay all of their VAT on imports through the duty deferment system. In order to set up an account with HMRC the trader must arrange a bank guarantee. This allows all VAT on imports to be paid on the 15th of the month following the month of importation. This assists the trader's cash flow and is more convenient than having to pay the VAT at the point of import.

- The VAT paid on importation can be reclaimed as input VAT on the VAT return for the period during which the goods were imported.

- The net effect of importing goods is therefore the same as if the goods were bought within the UK.

Services

The treatment of services purchased from outside the EU is generally the same as the treatment of services purchased from within the EU, and is discussed later in this section.

Exports outside the EU

Goods

The export of goods outside the EU is a zero rated supply.

This is a favourable treatment for the exporter as it allows them to recover input tax. It also means the customer is not charged VAT.

Services

The supply of services outside the EU is outside the scope of VAT.

Transactions within the EU

Goods

The following table summarises the VAT treatment when trading goods between EU countries where both supplier and customer are VAT registered (i.e. business to business transactions (B2B)).

Transactions
Supply is zero rated in country of origin
VAT chargeable at the appropriate rate in force in country of destination (reverse charge procedure)
Accounting for VAT
(a) Supplier does not account for output VAT – supply zero rated
(b) Customer must account for output VAT on their VAT return at the rate in force in customer's country
(c) VAT suffered by customer may be reclaimed by them as input VAT in the appropriate quarter

The output VAT on purchases from the EU must be accounted for by the customer in their VAT return for the date of acquisition.

The date of acquisition is the earlier of the date of the VAT invoice, and the 15th day of the month following the month in which the goods came into the UK.

Both the output VAT and input VAT are therefore likely to be on the same VAT return and will cancel out, unless the business makes exempt supplies and therefore cannot reclaim input VAT.

VAT on purchases from within the EU and outside the EU is collected via different systems. However, both leave the UK business in the same overall financial position.

Services

The rules governing VAT on the supply of services are complex. These notes just cover the basic principles needed for the TX examination.

For services, VAT is generally charged at the place of supply. For business customers the place of supply is where the customer is established.

These rules can be applied to B2B transactions involving a UK business as follows:

UK business	Accounting for VAT
Supplies services to overseas business customer	• Place of supply is overseas (i.e. where customer established). • Outside the scope of UK VAT.
Receives services from overseas business	• Place of supply is UK. • Reverse charge procedure: UK business accounts for 'output VAT' at standard UK rate on VAT return. This VAT can then be reclaimed as input VAT.

Time of supply for cross border supplies of services

For single supplies, the tax point will occur on the earlier of:

• when the service is completed, or

• when it is paid for.

Test your understanding 8

Overseas Ltd is a UK resident company and is VAT registered. It has been importing computers from Ruritania since 1 January 2021.

Ruritania is not currently a member of the European Union but is expected to join in the near future.

Overseas Ltd makes only taxable supplies. For the quarter ended 31 March 2021 imports of £100,000 have been made. This amount excludes any VAT or duties.

Explain how Overseas Ltd will have to account for VAT on the computers imported from Ruritania.

State how this will change if Ruritania becomes a member of the European Union and show the entries required on Overseas Ltd's VAT return in this case.

Test your understanding 9

Foreign Ltd, a UK resident company registered for VAT, has the following international transactions.

(a)   Sale of children's toys to a customer in Germany, who is VAT registered.

(b)   Sale of ladies' handbags to Venezuela.

(c)   Purchase of silk fabric from Hong Kong.

Outline the VAT treatment in each case for Foreign Ltd.

Note that Germany is in the EU, but Venezuela and Hong Kong are not.

13 Chapter summary

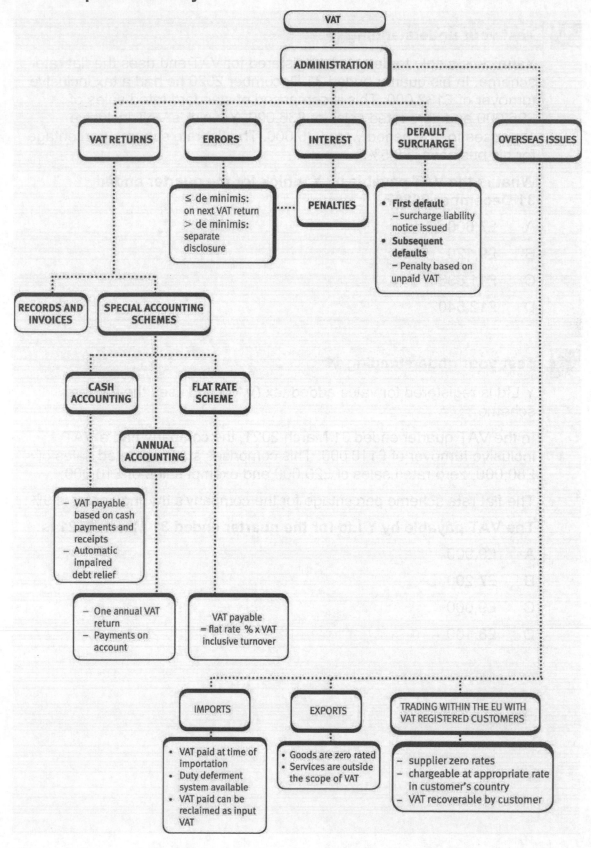

14   Practice objective test questions

Test your understanding 10

Yannick is a sole trader. He is registered for VAT and uses the flat rate scheme. In his quarter ended 31 December 2020 he had a tax inclusive turnover of £132,000. This is comprised of standard rated sales of £96,000 and zero rated sales of £36,000. Yannick's VAT inclusive expenses for the period were £25,000. The flat rate scheme percentage for his business is 9.5%.

What is the VAT payable by Yannick for the quarter ended 31 December 2020?

A   £7,600

B   £9,120

C   £11,833

D   £12,540

Test your understanding 11

Y Ltd is registered for value added tax (VAT) and uses the flat rate scheme.

In the VAT quarter ended 31 March 2021, the company had a VAT inclusive turnover of £110,000. This comprises standard rated sales of £80,000, zero rated sales of £20,000 and exempt sales of £10,000.

The flat rate scheme percentage for the company's trading sector is 9%.

The VAT payable by Y Ltd for the quarter ended 31 March 2021 is:

A   £9,900

B   £7,200

C   £9,000

D   £8,100

Test your understanding 12

X Ltd is a VAT registered trader that prepares quarterly VAT returns.

When should the VAT for the quarter ending 30 April 2020 be paid to HM Revenue and Customs (HMRC)?

A   31 May 2020

B   7 June 2020

C   7 July 2020

D   7 August 2020

Test your understanding 13

Meurig runs a UK VAT registered business. He exports a large amount of goods overseas. His UK sales and purchases are all standard rated.

In the quarter ended 31 December 2020 he makes the following sales and purchases (all figures are stated exclusive of VAT):

	£
Sales to UK businesses	70,000
Export sales outside the EU	12,400
Sales to EU businesses (all VAT registered)	10,000
Purchases from UK businesses	38,500

What is Meurig's output VAT and input VAT for the quarter?

	Output VAT	Input VAT
A	£14,000	£7,700
B	£16,480	£7,700
C	£14,000	£9,700
D	£18,480	£9,700

Test your understanding 14

Which of the following must be shown on a simplified (or less detailed) VAT invoice where the supply is entirely standard rated?

(1)   Supplier's name and address

(2)   A unique and sequential invoice number

(3)   Customer's name and address

(4)   Description of goods or services supplied

A   (2) and (4)

B   (1) and (4)

C   (2) and (3)

D   (1) and (3)

Test your understanding 15

Which of the following statements concerning the VAT cash accounting scheme is/are correct?

(1)   The business calculates its output tax on sales for a VAT return period by applying the VAT fraction (20/120) to gross (VAT inclusive) total cash receipts (inclusive of zero rated and exempt supplies).

(2)   The scheme would not be beneficial for a business that makes wholly zero rated sales and standard rated purchases on credit terms.

(3)   The tax point for output tax is always determined by the date of payment.

A   (1) and (3)

B   (2) and (3)

C   (1) and (2)

D   (2) only

Test your understanding answers

Test your understanding 1

VAT return

	£	£
Output VAT		
Sales (£45,000 × 20%)		9,000
Gift to customer (£300 × 20%)		60
		9,060
Input VAT		
Purchases (£31,000 × 20%)	6,200	
Expenses (£7,600 – £350) = £7,250 × 20%	1,450	
Photocopier (£6,400 × 20%)	1,280	
		(8,930)
VAT payable		130

Notes:

(1) Output VAT due on gifts over £50 is based on the replacement cost.

(2) VAT on business entertaining (of UK customers) is not reclaimable. Only staff entertaining and entertaining overseas customers is allowed.

Test your understanding 2

True or false

(1) True.

(2) False – it should show the **supplier's** VAT registration number.

(3) False – for supplies of £250 or less they need only issue a less detailed invoice to UK customers.

(4) False – VAT invoices are not required if the supply is to a non-VAT registered customer.

Test your understanding 3

Missing words

(1)   Surcharge liability notice

(2)   Second

(3)   Twelve

(4)   Will not

Test your understanding 4

Grab Ltd

Interest runs from 7 July 2020 to 7 May 2021.

Default interest at 2.75% for 10 months will be charged:

(£4,100 × 2.75% × 10/12) = £94.

Test your understanding 5

Cash accounting scheme

Amber and Co would benefit from joining the cash accounting scheme as it will not be required to account for output VAT to HMRC until it receives payment from the customer.

JB Ltd makes cash sales, and Janet zero rated sales, so neither of them have a problem with VAT on impaired debts.

Joining the scheme may also delay the recovery of input VAT on supplies.

They are therefore unlikely to benefit from joining the cash accounting scheme.

Test your understanding 6

Jump Ltd

Jump Ltd's annual VAT return must be submitted by 31 March 2021.

Payments of VAT will be made as follows:

	£
Monthly payments: 31 May 2020 to 31 January 2021	
9 at £360 (£3,600 × 10%)	3,240
Final payment due on 31 March 2021	
(£3,821 – £3,240)	581
	———
	3,821
	———

Test your understanding 7

Apple Ltd

(1) Using the normal method, Apple Ltd has a VAT liability as follows:

		£
Output VAT	(£90,500 × 1/6)	15,083
Input VAT	(£4,500 × 1/6)	(750)
		———
VAT payable		14,333
		———

(2) Using the flat rate method Apple Ltd, has the following VAT liability:

(£90,500 × 10%) = £9,050

By using the flat rate scheme:

- there is a VAT saving of £5,283 (£14,333 – £9,050).

- Administration is also simplified; Apple Ltd will not have to keep records of input or output VAT. It will not have to issue VAT invoices anyway, as none of its customers are VAT registered.

Test your understanding 8

Overseas Ltd

(1) **Ruritania is not in the EU**

Overseas Ltd will have to account for VAT on the value of the computers (including any carriage and import charges) at the point of importation. This will amount to £20,000 (£100,000 × 20%). Overseas Ltd will therefore pay £100,000 to the Ruritanian suppliers and £20,000 to HMRC. Overseas Ltd can then claim input tax relief of £20,000 on its next VAT return.

Overseas Ltd may be able to defer the payment of VAT on import under the duty deferment scheme and pay monthly on the 15th of the month following the month of importation.

(2) **Ruritania is in the EU**

The goods will be zero rated supplies in Ruritania and Overseas Ltd will be responsible for paying over the output VAT on the computers at the rate in force in the UK. This is essentially the same as if Ruritania were not in the EU, except that the VAT does not have to be paid over immediately at the date of importation.

The output VAT must be accounted for in the VAT return in which the date of acquisition arises, i.e. the earlier of the date the invoice is issued and the 15th of the month following that in which the goods are supplied.

As before, Overseas Ltd will be able to reclaim the VAT as input VAT on its next VAT return. It will therefore pay £100,000 to the Ruritanian supplier and include the following on its VAT return:

Output tax

On acquisition from Ruritania	£20,000

Input tax

On acquisition from Ruritania	£20,000

Test your understanding 9

Foreign Ltd

(a) Foreign Ltd will charge VAT at the zero rate because it is an EU transaction, and the customer is VAT registered.

(b) The transaction is zero rated as an export outside the EU.

(c) VAT will be paid at the point of entry into the UK. Foreign Ltd will then recover the VAT through its VAT return.

Test your understanding 10

The correct answer is D.

The flat rate scheme percentage is applied to the total tax inclusive turnover, including all standard, zero rated and exempt supplies. Expenses are not taken into account in calculating the VAT under this scheme.

£132,000 × 9.5% = £12,540

Test your understanding 11

The correct answer is A.

The flat rate percentage is applied to the total tax inclusive turnover including all standard, zero and exempt supplies (i.e. £110,000 × 9% = £9,900).

Test your understanding 12

The correct answer is B.

The value added tax payment is due one month and seven days following the related quarter.

Test your understanding 13

The correct answer is A.

Output VAT = (£70,000 × 20%) = £14,000

Sales outside the EU are zero rated and therefore there is no output VAT on exports.

Sales within the EU to other VAT registered businesses are also zero rated and therefore there is also no output VAT on these.

Input VAT = (£38,500 × 20%) = £7,700

Test your understanding 14

The correct answer is B.

A simplified (or less detailed) VAT invoice can be issued where the VAT inclusive total of the invoice is less than £250. Such an invoice should be issued when a customer requests a VAT invoice.

A simplified VAT invoice must show the following information:

- The supplier's name and address
- The supplier's VAT registration number
- The date of supply (the tax point)
- A description of the goods or services supplied
- The VAT inclusive total
- The rate of VAT.

Test your understanding 15

The correct answer is B.

Output tax for a VAT return period is calculated as 20/120 × cash receipts in respect of standard rated supplies.

It would not be beneficial for a business that makes wholly zero rated sales and standard rated purchases on credit terms to use the cash accounting scheme as this would delay the repayment of input tax (until the date of payment of the invoice).

Under the cash accounting scheme the tax point for the output and input tax is the time of the payment for the supply.

Questions & Answers

1 The UK tax system

There are no questions for this chapter.

2 Basic income tax computation

There are no questions for this chapter.

3 & 4 Property and investment income

Amos

Question 1

Amos owns four houses that he lets out to tenants. Details of the income and expenditure incurred in respect of the houses in the year to 5 April 2021 are as follows:

House 1

Amos purchased this house on 1 June 2020. He immediately undertook repair work to the leaking roof that cost £5,000 and redecorated the house at a cost of £800. The house was rented out, unfurnished, from 1 September 2020 on a six-year lease at an annual rental of £4,500, payable quarterly in advance. The incoming tenant was charged a premium of £2,500.

House 2

This house was let furnished throughout the year at a monthly rent of £650, payable monthly in advance. Amos paid the following amounts during the year; water rates £300, council tax £850, property insurance £500, purchase of a replacement cooker £400. He also incurred loan interest of £3,750 on a loan taken out to purchase the property.

The old cooker was scrapped for nil proceeds.

House 3

The tenants left this unfurnished house on 30 November 2020. Monthly rent of £500 was payable on the first day of the month in advance. The tenants left owing two month's rent totalling £1,000, which Amos was unable to recover.

Decoration work was carried out in January 2021 at a cost of £2,500 and advertising costs of £450 were paid when looking for new tenants. Other allowable costs paid in the year amounted to £1,175. The property was re-let on 1 April 2021, again unfurnished, at a monthly rent of £600, payable in advance.

House 4

This house was let out unfurnished to tenants throughout the year at a monthly rent of £450, payable in advance. Amos replaced a broken window at a cost of £100 during the year. The property was insured at a cost of £400 for the year ended 30 June 2021 on 12 May 2020. Other allowable costs paid were £200 for the year.

Other income

Amos received income from a part time employment of £10,300 during the year to 5 April 2021. In addition he received interest of £1,625 on a bank deposit account and dividends of £500 from UK quoted companies during the year. No PAYE was deducted from his employment income.

(a) **Calculate Amos' property income assessment for the tax year 2020/21.**

(b) **Calculate the income tax payable by Amos for the tax year 2020/21.**

5 Employment income

Gabriel

Question 1

Gabriel is employed as the sales director of Drakemain Ltd at a salary of £20,000 p.a.

Details of expenses paid by his employer for the year ended 5 April 2021, are as follows:

	£
Entertainment expenses reimbursed	683
Travelling and subsistence expenses reimbursed (including £385 rail fares home to office)	826
Private medical insurance paid to insurer	409
Company flat telephone calls reimbursed (Note 3)	160

You are given the following further information.

(1) A petrol driven motor car and private fuel were provided throughout the year (CO_2 emissions of 106g/km, list price £20,900). £10 per month is deducted from Gabriel's net salary to cover his private use of the motor car. The car was first registered on 6 April 2020.

(2) Gabriel is provided with the use of a company flat that was acquired for £70,000 in 2019. The flat has an annual value of £650. Gabriel pays rent of £40 per month to the company. Gabriel paid the council tax on the company flat in the tax year 2020/21 which amounted to £325.

> (3)   The telephone installed in the company flat is used for both business and private calls. Only 40% of the £160 of calls relate to business.
>
> (4)   Unless otherwise indicated, all expenses reimbursed to Gabriel were incurred for business purposes.
>
> (5)   The company purchased a TV on 6 April 2019 and allowed Gabriel the use of it for the whole of the tax years ended 5 April 2020 and 2021. The set was then given to him on 5 April 2021. The set cost £500 and was worth £150 in April 2021.
>
> **Calculate Gabriel's taxable employment income for the tax year 2020/21.**

6   Pensions

There are no questions for this chapter.

7 Income from self-employment

Parson

Question 1

For the past five years Parson has run a business importing electrical goods from the Far East, which he then sells to wholesalers in the UK.

His statement of profit or loss for the y/e 31 December 2020 shows:

	£	£
Sales revenue		325,000
Less: Cost of goods sold		(172,500)
Gross profit		152,500
Rent received (Note 1)		9,500
		162,000
Wages and salaries	50,200	
Rent and rates (Note 1)	12,900	
Light and heat (Note 1)	5,250	
Depreciation of fixtures and fittings	1,500	
Insurance	3,550	
Travelling and entertaining (Note 2)	10,750	
Impairment losses (Note 3)	6,750	
Depreciation of vehicles	7,500	
Motor car expenses (Note 4)	4,500	
Sundry expenses (Note 5)	750	
Legal and professional charges (Note 6)	4,750	
Interest on bank overdraft	1,500	
Van expenses	9,300	
Telephone	3,350	
Repairs and renewals (Note 7)	3,500	
		(126,050)
Net profit		35,950

Notes:

(1) **Rent received**

Rent received is in respect of a flat above Parson's business premises that is rented out. Parson estimates that a tenth of the rent and rates, and a seventh of the light and heat expenses relate to the flat.

(2) **Travelling and entertaining expenses:**

	£
Parson's business travelling expenses	5,175
Christmas presents for staff	250
Entertaining overseas suppliers	2,750
Entertaining UK customers	2,300
Gifts to customers that carry the business name	
Boxes of chocolates costing £5.00 each	125
Calendars costing £1.50 each	150
	————
	10,750
	————

(3) **Impairment losses**

	£
Trading debts written off	3,750
Increase in allowance for receivables	1,750
Supplier loan written off	1,700
Trade debt recovered (written off last year)	(450)
	————
	6,750
	————

(4) **Motor car expenses**

	£
Parson's motor car expenses	3,300
Salesman's motor car expenses	1,200
	————
	4,500
	————

Parson's total mileage for the year was 12,000 miles. During the year he drove 2,000 miles on a touring holiday and estimates that the balance of his mileage is 20% private and 80% business.

(5)   **Sundry expenses**

	£
Donation to national charity	50
Donation to local political party	100
Subscription to Chamber of Commerce	25
Wedding gift to a member of staff	45
Parson's squash club subscription	250
Advertising in trade press	280
	750

Parson often uses the squash club as a place to take customers since several of them are keen squash players.

(6)   **Legal and professional charges**

	£
Cost of renewing a 21-year lease on business premises	250
Accountancy	3,050
Debt collection	300
Legal fees in connection with an action by an employee for unfair dismissal	1,150
	4,750

Included in Parson's accountancy fee is £950 for taxation services. Of this, £200 is for the normal taxation work involved in submitting accounts to HMRC. The balance is in respect of calculating Parson's capital gains tax liability following the disposal of some shares that he had owned.

(7)   **Repairs and renewals**

	£
Repairs to the office photocopier	175
New printer for the office computer	650
Installation of new central heating for the office	2,200
Decorating the office	475
	3,500

(8)   During the year ended 31 December 2020 Parson took various electrical goods out of inventory for his own and his family's use without paying for them. These goods cost £450 and would have normally been sold at a mark-up of 30%. No adjustments have been recorded in Parson's statement of profit or loss to reflect this.

(9)   Parson has a room in his house that he uses as an office as he often works at home. The allowable amount for the use of the office is £250 and appears to be a fair estimate. Also, Parson makes business calls from his home telephone and he estimates the business use as two fifths. The total cost of his calls from his home telephone for the year was £450.

Calculate Parson's tax adjusted trading profit (before capital allowances) for the year ended 31 December 2020. Your computation should start with the net profit figure of £35,950 and should list all the items referred to in notes (1) to (9) indicating by the use of a zero (0) any items that do not require adjustment.

Angela

Question 2

Angela opened a guest house on 1 July 2020. She lives at the guest house with her dog. Her business records for the year ended 30 June 2021 have been summarised for you as follows:

	£
Revenue	
This is the amount of invoices billed, however, at 30 June 2021 she is still owed £4,560 from customers.	57,640
Guest house furniture	
Payments for furniture purchased.	5,300
Food and household expenses (cleaning and utilities)	
All paid at 30 June 2021. Personal living costs account for 40% of the food and household expenses.	16,200
Motor car	
On 20 July 2020 Angela purchased a car (paid for by cheque) with CO_2 emissions of 100g/km. She uses the car approximately 80% for business purposes.	18,500
Motor expenses	
During the year ended 30 June 2021 she incurred petrol, servicing and MOT costs (all paid at 30 June 2021). She drove 10,800 business miles.	5,720
Other expenses (all allowable)	
This is the amount of bills payable, however, she has not paid £850 of them by 30 June 2021.	4,960

The cash basis private use adjustment for one occupant in a business premises for 12 months is £4,200.

Under the accruals basis capital allowances of £7,964 are available.

Calculate Angela's tax adjusted trading profit for the year ended 30 June 2021 assuming she:

(a) Uses the cash basis

(b) Uses the accruals basis.

8 Capital allowances – plant and machinery

Austin

Question 1

Austin commenced business as a self-employed decorator on 1 June 2020.

His tax adjusted trading profits before capital allowances, have been

10 months ended 31 March 2021	£1,488,514
Year ended 31 March 2022	£1,502,891

The following capital transactions took place:

		£
15 May 2020	Purchased equipment	834,760
1 June 2020	Purchased a short life asset	2,400
1 June 2020	Purchased a van	16,500
15 June 2020	Purchased a motor car	15,600
1 May 2021	Sold equipment (original cost £600)	500
12 May 2021	Purchased equipment	20,200
20 August 2021	Purchased furniture	18,020
18 January 2022	Sold the short life asset	550

The motor car purchased on 15 June 2020 is used by Austin, and 15% of the mileage is for business purposes. The car has CO_2 emissions of 138g/km.

Compute the tax adjusted trading profits (after capital allowances) for the two periods of account ended 31 March 2022.

Assume the rules for the tax year 2020/21 apply throughout.

9 Sole traders: Basis of assessment

Abiya

Question 1

Abiya commenced in business as a fashion designer on 1 July 2019, and prepared her first accounts to 30 April 2021. Her profit for the period, adjusted for taxation, was £33,000.

(a) **Calculate the tax adjusted trading profits assessable on Abiya for the first three tax years, and the amount of overlap profits.**

(b) **State how Abiya could have avoided the creation of overlap profits, supporting your statement with a relevant example.**

Maggie

Question 2

Maggie commenced in business on 1 November 2017 manufacturing ladies clothing. Her tax adjusted trading profits (before capital allowances) were:

	£
Period to 31 December 2018	32,000
Year ended 31 December 2019	38,000
Year ended 31 December 2020	45,000

Capital allowances were as follows:

	£
Period to 31 December 2018	18,000
Year ended 31 December 2019	15,675
Year ended 31 December 2020	17,550

Calculate the trading profits assessable on Maggie for the tax years 2017/18 to 2020/21 inclusive and the amount of any overlap profits.

10 Partnerships

Roger, Brigitte and Xavier

Question 1

Roger and Brigitte commenced in business on 1 October 2016 as hotel proprietors, sharing profits equally.

On 1 October 2018 their son, Xavier, joined the partnership and from that date each of the partners, was entitled to one third, of the profits.

The profits of the partnership adjusted for income tax are:

		£
Period ended	30 June 2017	30,000
Year ended	30 June 2018	45,000
Year ended	30 June 2019	50,000
Year ended	30 June 2020	60,000

(a) **Calculate the assessable profits for each of the partners for all relevant tax years from 2016/17 to 2020/21.**

(b) **State the amount of the overlap profits for each of the partners.**

11 Trading losses for individuals

Lucifer

Question 1

Lucifer commenced trading as a second hand car dealer on 6 April 2018. He had no taxable income prior to the tax year 2018/19.

Trading results, adjusted for income tax and capital allowances, were:

		£	
Period ended	30 September 2018	(20,000)	loss
Year ended	30 September 2019	(10,000)	loss
Year ended	30 September 2020	11,000	profit

He received dividend income as follows:

Tax year	£
2018/19	3,750
2019/20	2,778
2020/21	2,000

In the tax year 2018/19 he had also realised a chargeable gain (before deducting the annual exempt amount) of £15,000 on the sale of quoted shares.

(a) **State the ways in which the trading losses may be relieved.**

(b) **Show how the trading losses can be utilised most effectively by Lucifer, giving your reasoning.**

Oprah

Question 2

Oprah has been a sole trader for many years and has recent adjusted trading results as follows:

	£
Year ended 30 September 2019	72,000
Year ended 30 September 2020	(151,000)

She has property income of £80,000 each tax year but no other income. She makes £20,000 of charitable donations under the gift aid scheme each year.

Calculate Oprah's taxable income for the tax years 2019/20 and 2020/21 assuming that she wishes to take relief for the loss as soon as possible.

Assume that the rates and allowances for the tax year 2020/21 apply throughout.

12 National Insurance

There are no questions for this chapter.

13 Tax administration for individuals

Sadiq

Question 1

Sadiq has been a self-employed interior designer for a number of years, preparing his accounts to 30 April each year. His income for the tax year 2020/21 was as follows:

	£
Tax adjusted trading profit	59,900
Property business income	5,200
Building society interest	2,625
Dividends received	1,556

During the tax year 2020/21 Sadiq paid £12,000 into his registered personal pension.

Sadiq's payments on account for the tax year 2020/21 totalled £10,255. Sadiq has a capital gains tax liability for the tax year 2020/21 of £2,090.

(a) **Calculate Sadiq's income tax and class 4 NIC payable for the tax year 2020/21.**

(b) **Calculate Sadiq's balancing payment for the tax year 2020/21 and his payments on account for the tax year 2021/22 and state the relevant payment dates.**

(c) **State:**

  (i) **the consequences of Sadiq not paying the balancing payment for the tax year 2020/21 by the due date.**

  (ii) **the due date by which Sadiq should file his tax return for the tax year 2020/21 assuming he wishes to file a paper return.**

  (iii) **how long Sadiq should retain his accounting records for the year to 30 April 2020.**

BM Ltd

Question 2

BM Ltd manufactures bike components. It has ten employees. The managing director is paid an annual salary of £50,000, payable monthly on the last day of each month. The remaining employees are paid £385 per week, on Friday each week.

In addition to his salary the managing director had the use of a company car for private purposes throughout the tax year 2020/21. The petrol powered car has a list price of £18,000, but the company acquired it second hand for £16,000. It has CO_2 emissions of 166g/km.

The other nine employees were given non-cash vouchers by the company in December 2020 for use in the local department store. Each employee received vouchers which could be redeemed for goods worth £200 but the company purchased them at a discount for £180.

(a) **Explain when the company is required to submit details of income tax and NIC deducted from the employees' earnings to HM Revenue & Customs under the RTI PAYE system. Include details of both in year and end of year reporting.**

(b) **State the date that the income tax and NIC deducted under the PAYE system from the employees' earnings in the final tax month of the tax year 2020/21 should be paid to HM Revenue & Customs, assuming the company pays electronically.**

(c) **Calculate the taxable value of the benefits provided to the employees in the tax year 2020/21 and explain how and by when they should be reported to HM Revenue & Customs.**

(d) **Calculate the company's class 1A national insurance liability for the tax year 2020/21 and state the date that it must be paid to HM Revenue & Customs if the company pays electronically.**

Olive – Comprehensive income tax question

Question 3

Olive is self-employed running a health food shop. Her statement of profit and loss for the year ended 31 December 2020 is as follows:

	£
Gross profit	134,200
Expenses	
Depreciation	2,350
Light and heat (note 1)	1,980
Motor expenses (note 2)	4,700
Rent and rates (note 1)	5,920
Sundry expenses (note 3)	2,230
Wages and salaries (note 4)	78,520
	(95,700)
Net profit	38,500

Note 1 – Private accommodation

Olive lives in a flat that is situated above the health food shop. 30% of the expenditure included in the accounts for light, heat, rent and rates relates to the flat.

Note 2 – Motor expenses

During the year ended 31 December 2020 Olive drove a total of 20,000 miles, of which 8,000 were for business purposes.

Note 3 – Sundry expenses

The figure of £2,230 for sundry expenses includes £220 for a fine in respect of health and safety regulations, £180 for the theft of cash by an employee, £100 for a donation to a political party, and £140 for a trade subscription to the Health and Organic Association.

Note 4 – Wages and salaries

The figure of £78,520 for wages and salaries includes an annual salary of £14,000 paid to Olive's daughter. She works in the health food shop as a sales assistant. The other sales assistants doing the same job are paid an annual salary of £10,500.

Note 5 – Goods for own use

Each week Olive takes health food from the shop for her personal use without paying for it. The weekly cost of this food is £30, and it has a selling price of £45. No entry has been made in the accounts for these drawings.

Note 6 – Plant and machinery

The only item of plant and machinery is Olive's motor car, which has CO_2 emissions of 108g/km. The tax written down value of this vehicle at 1 January 2020 was £16,667.

Note 7 – Patent royalties

Olive pays a patent royalty of £150 (gross) every quarter for the use of equipment that allows her to make organic breakfast cereal to sell in the shop. This has not been accounted for in arriving at the net profit of £38,500.

Other income

(1) Olive has a part-time employment for which she was paid a salary of £6,000 during the tax year 2020/21. Income tax of £1,200 has been deducted from this figure under PAYE.

(2) During the tax year 2020/21 Olive received building society interest of £1,800 and dividends of £1,200.

Other information

(1) During the tax year 2020/21 Olive paid interest of £220 on a loan taken out on 1 January 2019 to purchase equipment for use in her part-time employment.

(2) Olive contributed £5,000 (gross) into a personal pension scheme during the tax year 2020/21.

(3) Olive's payments on account of income tax in respect of the tax year 2020/21 totalled £4,559.

(4) Olive's capital gains tax liability for the tax year 2020/21 was £392.

(a) **Calculate Olive's tax adjusted trading profit for the year ended 31 December 2020.**

(b) **Calculate:**

   (i) **the income tax payable by Olive for the tax year 2020/21**

   (ii) **Olive's balancing payment for the tax year 2020/21 and her payments on account for the tax year 2021/22, stating the relevant due dates. Ignore national insurance contributions.**

(c) **Advise Olive of the consequences of not making the balancing payment for the tax year 2020/21 until 30 April 2022.**

14 Introduction to corporation tax

There are no questions for this chapter.

15 Taxable total profits

There are no questions for this chapter.

16 Losses for companies

Ball Ltd

Question 1

Ball Ltd has the following results

Year ended 31 December:	2018 £	2019 £	2020 £	2021 £
Tax adjusted trading profit/(loss)	42,000	19,000	(67,000)	16,000
Bank interest received	3,000	2,000	1,000	2,000
Chargeable gains	4,000	4,000	4,000	4,000
Qualifying charitable donations	(10,000)	(10,000)	–	(2,500)

Calculate the taxable total profits, for all of the accounting periods shown above, clearly indicating how you would deal with the trading loss, to obtain relief as soon as possible with the minimum possible wastage of reliefs.

17 Groups of companies

Gold Ltd

Question 1

Gold Ltd owns 100% of the ordinary share capital of Silver Ltd. Gold Ltd has an accounting date of 30 September, whilst Silver Ltd has an accounting date of 31 March.

The results of Gold Ltd are as follows

Year ended	30.9.20	30.9.21
	£	£
Tax adjusted trading profit	141,000	90,000
Property income	5,000	–
Chargeable gains	–	12,000
QCD	(2,000)	(2,000)

For the year ended 31 March 2020 Silver Ltd had total profits of £149,000 and paid qualifying charitable donations of £50,000. The company made a tax adjusted trading loss of £140,000 for the year ended 31 March 2021. No information is available regarding the year ended 31 March 2022.

(a) **Assuming that the tax rate for FY2020 continues into the future and that the maximum possible claim for group relief is made in respect of Silver Ltd's tax adjusted trading loss of £140,000, calculate Gold Ltd's corporation tax liabilities for the year ended 30 September 2020 and the year ended 30 September 2021.**

(b) **Explain the factors that should be considered within a group of companies when determining how to utilise losses within the group.**

(c) **Based on the information available, advise Silver Ltd of the most beneficial way of relieving its trading loss of £140,000, assuming that Silver Ltd is experiencing cash flow problems.**

Apple Group

Question 2

Apple Ltd owns 100% of the ordinary share capital of Banana Ltd.

The results of each company for the year ended 31 March 2021 are

	Apple Ltd £	Banana Ltd £
Tax adjusted trading profit/(loss)	(125,000)	650,000
Chargeable gain/(loss)	180,000	(8,000)
Qualifying charitable donations	(40,000)	

Apple Ltd's chargeable gain arose from the sale of a freehold warehouse on 15 April 2020 for £418,000. Banana Ltd purchased a freehold office building for £370,000 on 10 January 2021.

(a) **Explain the group relationship that must exist in order that group relief can be claimed.**

(b) **Assuming that reliefs are claimed in the most favourable manner, calculate the corporation tax liabilities of Apple Ltd and Banana Ltd for the year ended 31 March 2021.**

18 Tax administration for a company

Ramble Ltd

Question 1

Ramble Ltd's taxable total profits for the two years to 31 March 2020 and 31 March 2021 were £2,150,000 and £2,780,000 respectively.

The company filed its tax return for the year ended 31 March 2020 on 15 October 2021 and on the same date made a payment of the tax outstanding.

Ramble Ltd made the following payments on account of its corporation tax liability for the year ended 31 March 2021:

	£
1 May 2021	389,150
1 January 2022	139,050

(a) **State the date that the company's self-assessment corporation tax return for the year ended 31 March 2020 was due and advise the company of the penalties that will apply as a result of filing the return and making the payment of tax on 15 October 2021.**

(b) **State the due date(s) for the payment of the company's corporation tax liability for the year ended 31 March 2021 and advise the company of any late payment interest that will be payable in respect of this year (interest calculations are not required).**

19 Computation of gains and tax payable

Amina

Question 1

Amina disposed of the following assets during the tax year 2020/21:

(1) On 30 June 2020, Amina sold a freehold warehouse for £140,000. The warehouse was purchased, as an investment property, on 1 September 2012 for £95,000.

(2) On 30 November 2020, Amina sold a motor car for £25,000. The motor car was purchased in November 2012 for £23,500.

(3) On 15 February 2021, Amina sold a factory for £320,000. The factory had been purchased on 14 October 2003 for £194,000, and was extended at a cost of £58,000 during March 2006. During May 2008, the roof of the factory was replaced at a cost of £44,000 following a fire. The building was not insured.

Amina had incurred legal fees of £3,300 in connection with the purchase of the factory, and £6,200 in connection with the disposal.

Amina had always used the factory for business purposes in her trade since it was bought in 2003. The factory is a small insignificant part of her business which she continues to operate.

Amina incurred a capital loss of £17,100 during the tax year 2018/19 and made a chargeable gain of £12,700 during the tax year 2019/20.

Amina's taxable income for the tax year 2020/21 was £33,500.

Calculate Amina's CGT liability for the tax year 2020/21 and advise her by when this should be paid. Assume that the AEA for the tax year 2020/21 applies throughout.

20 Computation of gains: Special rules

Lethabo and Faith

Question 1

Lethabo and Faith had the following capital transactions in the tax year 2020/21.

Lethabo

(1) Sold a house on 1 July 2020, which had been bought for £4,000 on 3 April 2001 and let to tenants thereafter. On 2 April 2002 an extension costing £2,000 was built, and on 12 June 2014 the loft was converted into a bedroom at a cost of £3,000. The net proceeds of sale were £63,850.

(2) Sold a piece of sculpture for £6,500 on 30 August 2020, which he had bought for £5,500 on 31 May 2012.

(3) Sold a one-tenth share in a racehorse on 31 August 2020 for £6,200. The interest had cost £1,340 in November 2002.

(4) Sold a vintage Alfa Romeo motor car for £76,500 on 19 December 2020. The car had cost £17,400 on 31 March 2011. During his period of ownership Steel had never used the car on the road.

Lethabo's taxable income for the tax year 2020/21 was £55,000.

Faith

(1) Sold a rare Russian icon on 24 July 2020 for £5,600 which had cost £6,300 on 20 June 2012.

(2) Sold three hectares out of a 12 hectare plot of land on 14 December 2020 for £15,000. The whole plot had been purchased for £4,500 on 15 June 2012. On 14 December 2020 the unsold hectares had an agreed market value of £25,000.

(3) Sold a piece of Chinese jade for £11,800 on 1 September 2020. This was purchased at auction in March 2005 for £6,500.

(4) Sold a plot of land for £12,300 on 1 October 2020. Lethabo acquired the land for £2,000 in April 2012 and gave it to his wife in June 2015 when it was worth £5,000.

Faith has no taxable income in the tax year 2020/21.

Calculate the CGT liability of both Lethabo and Faith for the tax year 2020/21.

21   CGT: Shares and securities for individuals

Jasper

Question 1

Jasper had the following transactions during the tax year 2020/21:

(1)   Sold 2,145 ordinary shares in Carrot plc on 19 November 2020 for net sale proceeds of £8,580.

His previous dealings in these shares were as follows:

July 2012   purchased 1,750 shares for £2,625

May 2013   purchased 200 shares for £640

June 2014   took up 1 for 10 rights issue at £3.40 per share

(2)   Sold 400 £1 ordinary shares in Grasp plc for £3,600 on 31 March 2021. Jasper had acquired these Grasp plc shares as a result of a takeover bid by Grasp plc of Cawte plc on 5 December 2020.

Prior to the takeover Jasper had owned 12,000 £1 ordinary shares in Cawte plc, which he had acquired for £15,700 on 3 May 2013.

The terms of the takeover bid were:

–   one £1 ordinary share in Grasp plc, plus

–   two 10% preference shares in Grasp plc, plus

–   40p in cash

for every £1 ordinary share in Cawte plc.

The quoted prices for Grasp plc shares at 5 December 2020 were:

£1 ordinary shares	350p
10% preference shares	110p

Calculate the total chargeable gains arising in the tax year 2020/21.

22   CGT: Reliefs for individuals

Takunda

Question 1

Takunda has been in business as a sole trader since 1 May 2004. On 28 February 2021 he transferred the business to his daughter Sienna, at which time the following assets were sold to her:

(1)   Goodwill with a market value of £60,000. The goodwill has been built up since 1 May 2004, and has a nil cost. Sienna paid Takunda £50,000 for the goodwill.

(2)   A freehold office building with a market value of £130,000. The office building was purchased on 1 July 2014 for £110,000, and has always been used by Takunda for business purposes. Sienna paid Takunda £105,000 for the office building.

(3)   A freehold warehouse with a market value of £140,000. The warehouse was purchased on 1 September 2010 for £95,000 and has never been used by Takunda for business purposes. Sienna paid Takunda £135,000 for the warehouse.

(4)   A motor car with a market value of £25,000. The car was purchased on 1 November 2014 for £23,500, and has always been used by Takunda for business purposes. Sienna paid Takunda £20,000 for the car.

Takunda and Sienna have elected to hold over any gains where possible.

Takunda has unused capital losses of £5,500 brought forward from the tax year 2019/20.

Takunda has taxable income in the tax year 2020/21 of £59,000.

Calculate Takunda's capital gains tax liability for the tax year 2020/21, and advise him by when this should be paid.

Ignore business asset disposal relief.

23 Chargeable gains for companies

Earth Ltd

Question 1

Earth Ltd sold the following shareholdings during the year ended 31 March 2021:

(1) On 20 November 2020 Earth Ltd sold 25,000 £1 ordinary shares in Venus plc for £115,000. Earth Ltd had originally purchased 40,000 shares in Venus plc on 19 June 2001 for £34,000. On 11 October 2011 Venus plc made a 1 for 4 bonus issue.

Assume the indexation factors are as follows:

June 2001 to October 2011	0.365
October 2011 to December 2017	0.168
June 2001 to December 2017	0.595
June 2001 to November 2020	0.712
October 2011 to November 2020	0.255

(2) On 22 January 2021 Earth Ltd sold 30,000 £1 ordinary shares in Saturn plc for £52,500. Earth Ltd purchased 30,000 shares in Saturn plc on 9 February 2006 for £97,500.

The indexed value of the share pool on 3 January 2021 was £139,623.

On 3 January 2021 Saturn plc made a 1 for 2 rights issue. Earth Ltd took up its allocation under the rights issue in full, paying £1.50 for each new share issued.

(3) On 28 March 2021 Earth Ltd sold its entire holding of £1 ordinary shares in Jupiter plc for £55,000. Earth Ltd had originally purchased 10,000 shares in Mercury plc on 5 May 2009 for £14,000.

The indexed value of the share pool on 7 March 2021 was £18,296.

On 7 March 2021 Mercury plc was taken over by Jupiter plc. Earth Ltd received two £1 ordinary shares and one £1 preference share in Jupiter plc for each share held in Mercury plc. Immediately after the takeover £1 ordinary shares in Jupiter plc were quoted at £2.50 and £1 preference shares were quoted at £1.25

Earth Ltd has never held more than a 1% shareholding in any of the above companies.

Calculate the chargeable gain or capital loss arising from each of Earth Ltd's disposals during the year ended 31 March 2021.

24 Inheritance tax

Gerry

Question 1

Gerry has made the following gifts during his lifetime. Gerry agreed that he would pay any inheritance tax arising on these gifts.

		Nil rate band
4 June 2013	£368,000 cash gift to a trust.	£325,000
4 March 2015	£10,000 cash as a wedding gift to his son Takunda.	£325,000
4 June 2020	A further £100,000 cash gift to the trust.	£325,000

Explain the IHT implications arising from Gerry's lifetime gifts.

Your answer should include a calculation of any IHT payable, an explanation of any exemptions available and the date the tax is payable.

Tareq

Question 2

Tareq died on 31 July 2020. At the time of his death, Tareq owned the following assets:

(1)   100,000 £1 ordinary shares in ABC plc, a quoted trading company with an issued share capital of 20,000,000 shares. ABC plc's shares were valued at 242.5p for that day.

(2)   A holiday cottage that he never lived in, valued at £120,000.

(3)   Bank and cash balances of £150,000.

(4)   Other assets valued for IHT purposes at £208,000.

(5)   Tareq had a life insurance policy, which provided proceeds of £88,000 to his estate on his death.

Under the terms of his will, Tareq left £55,000 in cash to his wife, and the residue of his estate to his daughter.

Tareq made no lifetime gifts.

Calculate the IHT liability arising as a result of Tareq's death.

State who will pay the tax due, the due date and who suffers the burden of the tax.

Nur

Question 3

Nur died on 20 November 2020. At the date of her death Nur owned the following assets:

(1)   A main residence valued at £235,000. This had an outstanding repayment mortgage of £40,000.

(2)   Building society deposits of £100,000.

(3)   10,000 £1 ordinary shares (a 4% shareholding) in Banquo plc. On 20 November 2020 the shares were valued at £9.48 per share.

(4)   A life assurance policy on her own life. Immediately prior to the date of Nur's death, the policy had an open market value of £86,000. Proceeds of £91,000 were received following her death.

(5)   A plot of land valued at £108,000.

Nur made the following gifts during her lifetime (any IHT arising was paid by Nur):

(1)   On 28 November 2008 she made a cash gift of £93,000 into a trust.

(2)   On 15 April 2014 she made a gift of 50,000 shares (a 2% shareholding) in Shakespeare plc, to her son as a wedding gift. The shares were valued at £71,000.

(3)   On 10 March 2015 she made a cash gift of £268,000 into a trust.

Nur's husband Omri is wealthy in his own right. Under the terms of her will Nur has therefore left a specific gift of the building society deposits of £100,000 to her brother, with the residue of the estate being left to her children.

(a)   **Calculate the IHT that will be payable as a result of Nur's death.**

   The nil rate bands for earlier years are as follows:

   2008/09   £312,000

   2014/15   £325,000

(b)   **State who is primarily liable for the tax, the due dates of the IHT liabilities, and the amount of inheritance that will be received by Nur's children.**

Michaela

Question 4

Michaela died on 15 October 2020, leaving a chargeable estate of £1,000,000 to her daughter, Natalia. The estate included Michaela's main residence valued at £330,000.

Michaela's husband died in June 2008, having fully utilised his nil rate band.

Michaela made the following gifts during her lifetime:

(1)   A gross chargeable transfer of £340,000 into a trust on 2 November 2016. Lifetime tax of £3,000 was paid by the trustees in respect of this gift.

(2)   A gift of £190,000 cash to her daughter on 7 July 2019, the date of her wedding.

(a)   **Calculate the IHT that will be payable as a result of Michaela's death.**

The nil rate band for 2016/17 and 2019/20 was £325.000.

(b)   **State who is primarily liable for the tax and the due dates of the IHT liabilities.**

25   VAT: Outline

Wilf

Question 1

(1)   Wilf is a systems analyst who has recently started his own business. He has supplied you with the following information:

(a)   His sales revenue for his first year ending 31 December 2020 is estimated to be £113,580 accruing evenly over the year. All Wilf's customers are VAT registered businesses and all Wilf's turnover is of taxable supplies.

(b)   He purchased computer equipment for the business for £3,150 including VAT on 14 January 2020.

(c)   His business telephone bills are £360 per quarter including VAT.

(d)   He uses a room at his home as his office. His house has five main rooms and the electricity bill for the whole house for the year is estimated as £1,500 including VAT of £71.

(e) He has a petrol engine car which he uses 75% for business. Wilf bought the car in October 2020 for £15,000 including VAT. It was valued at £13,500 when he started his business on 1 January 2020. The car emits 190 g/km of CO_2 and annual running costs excluding petrol are £1,100 per year which includes £183 of VAT. He charges all his petrol costs through the business which amounts to £150 (VAT inclusive) per month.

(f) Prior to starting in business, Wilf paid his accountant £350 plus VAT on 1 December 2018 for drawing up cash flow projections.

For this part of the question assume that today's date is 1 February 2019.

Wilf has not yet registered for VAT. He wishes you to advise him when he will have to register compulsorily for VAT and whether it would be beneficial to register immediately. The VAT scale charge for a car with 190 g/km of CO2 emissions is £406 per quarter (inclusive of VAT).

For the remaining parts of the question assume that Wilf has registered for VAT and that he has been trading for a few years.

(2) In his second year Wilf had problems collecting a debt from XYZ Ltd. He invoiced the company £3,500 including VAT, which was due for payment on 15 March 2021. In September 2021 he received £1,000 from XYZ Ltd in partial settlement of the debt but in October 2021 he wrote off the rest of the debt as irrecoverable.

Advise Wilf of the VAT position on this debt.

(3) In his third year of trading, Wilf decided to offer a discount for prompt payment to try to improve his cash flow. The discount offered is 5% if invoices are paid within 14 days.

Explain to Wilf what action he should take for VAT purposes when invoicing his customers.

(4) In his fourth year of business Wilf receives an offer for his business of £450,000.

Wilf wants you to advise him whether VAT needs to be charged on this amount and whether there are any other actions he should take. The projected sale date for the business is 31 May 2024.

Assume the VAT rules for the VAT year to 31 March 2021 apply throughout.

26   VAT: Administration and overseas aspects

 Mary

Question 1

You are provided with the following information for the quarter ended 31 March 2020 relating to your client Mary who is registered for VAT.

	£
Sales (all VAT exclusive):	
Standard rated supplies	
– Sales invoices	230,000
– Sales invoice (before 2.5% discount) (Note 1)	40,000
Zero rated supplies	50,000
Purchases and expenses	
Standard rated purchases (excluding VAT)	102,440
Standard rated expenses (excluding VAT)	18,000
(includes £5,000 for entertaining UK customers)	
Exempt purchases	14,350
Car (excluding VAT and bought on 1 February 2020) (Note 2)	16,200

Notes:

(1)   Mary offered a prompt payment discount on a large sale as an incentive for the customer to pay before 31 March 2020. The invoice was paid on 28 March 2020.

(2)   The car bought on 1 February 2020 was used 60% for business and has CO_2 emissions of 210 g/km. Petrol for both private and business mileage was paid for by the business. The quarterly scale charge figure is £473 (inclusive of VAT).

(3)   Impaired debts of £3,000 (exclusive of VAT) were written off in March 2020 in respect of three separate invoices, each of £1,000 for goods supplied on 1 May 2019, 1 August 2019 and 1 November 2019, payment for which was due on 1 June 2019, 1 September 2019 and 1 December 2019 respectively.

Calculate the VAT payable for the quarter ended 31 March 2020 and state when this is payable to HMRC.

27   Practice section B questions

Section B questions by their nature require knowledge from more than one chapter to answer well. You are therefore advised to only attempt each practice question once you have fully studied the area of the syllabus that it relates to.

Amber and Sonya

Question B1: Income tax

Amber and Sonya are friends. The following information is available for the tax year 2020/21:

Amber

Amber has been employed by Startling Architects Ltd for a number of years. On 6 April 2020 she received a promotion which entitled her to the following benefits from that date:

(1)   A petrol driven car with a list price of £21,000. The company paid the car dealer £19,800 for the car. Amber was required to pay £400 to Startling Architects Ltd as a contribution towards the capital cost of the car. Amber was not provided with fuel for private mileage. The appropriate percentage of the car for the purposes of calculating the car benefit is 30%.

(2)   Private medical insurance which cost the company £450 in the tax year 2020/21. The insurance company paid £800 for Amber to have medical treatment during the tax year 2020/21.

During the tax year 2020/21 Amber's total salary and benefits from her employment was £123,000 and she contributed £1,000 to her employer's occupational pension scheme. She also made a donation to charity of £480 under the gift aid scheme. She had no other income or outgoings.

Sonya

Sonya commenced self-employment as an architect on 1 June 2019. She prepared her first set of accounts for the 16 months to 30 September 2020 and annually thereafter. Prior to 1 June 2019 Sonya had been in employment.

Sonya's total taxable income (after the personal allowance) for the tax year 2020/21 was £45,500 (trading income of £31,900 and dividend income of £13,600. In the tax year 2020/21 Sonya made a personal pension contribution of £1,200 (net).

In the tax year 2021/22 Sonya is expecting to make a trading loss due to investment in specialised design equipment. In the tax year 2021/22 she will have dividend income of £15,000 and realise a capital gain of £20,000.

Required (Each question is worth 2 marks):

(1) **What is Amber's taxable employment income in respect of the car and the private medical insurance for the tax year 2020/21?**

    A   £6,350

    B   £6,630

    C   £7,430

    D   £6,270

(2) **What amount of personal allowance is available to Amber for the tax year 2020/21?**

    A   £1,740

    B   £1,300

    C   £1,500

    D   £1,800

(3) **What is the basis period for Sonya's trading income assessment for the tax year 2020/21?**

    A   1 October 2019 to 30 September 2020

    B   1 June 2019 to 31 May 2020

    C   1 June 2019 to 30 September 2020

    D   6 April 2020 to 5 April 2021

(4) **How much of Sonya's dividend income in the tax year 2020/21 is subject to the higher rate of income tax?**

    A   £6,500

    B   £6,800

    C   £4,500

    D   £8,000

(5) **Which of the following statements concerning the loss relief available to Sonya is correct?**

A   In the tax year 2021/22 Sonya could claim to offset the trading loss against either the dividend income or the capital gain.

B   If Sonya makes a claim to offset the loss in the previous tax year it will be offset against her trading income only.

C   The trading loss can be offset against total income in the tax years 2018/19, 2019/20 and 2020/21 in that order.

D   If Sonya does not make a loss relief claim the trading loss will automatically be carried forward and offset against the first available total income.

Nim and Mae Lom

Question B2: Capital gains tax

Nim and Mae Lom are a married couple. They disposed of the following assets during the tax year 2002/21:

Mae Lom

(1) On 30 September 2020 Mae sold a house for £186,000. The house had been purchased on 1 October 2010 for £122,000.

Throughout the period of ownership the house was occupied by Nim and Mae as their main residence, but one of the house's eight rooms was always used exclusively for business purposes by Mae.

(2) On 30 November 2020 Mae sold a business that she had run as a sole trader since 1 December 2011. The sale resulted in the following capital gains:

	£
Goodwill	80,000
Freehold office building	136,000
Investment property	34,000

The investment property has always been rented out.

Also on 30 November 2020 Mae realised a gain of £45,000 on the sale of a 10% shareholding in W Ltd, which she had owned for 5 years. W Ltd is a trading company which Mae has worked in part time for the last three years.

Nim Lom

On 20 July 2020 Nim sold 10,000 £1 ordinary shares in Kapook plc. Nim had made the following purchases of shares in Kapook plc:

19 February 2012	8,000 shares for £16,200
6 June 2017	6,000 shares for £14,600
24 July 2020	2,000 shares for £5,800

Other information

Nim's total chargeable gains, including the gain arising on the sale of Kapook plc shares in the tax year 2020/21 was £450,300, £200,000 of which qualified for business asset disposal relief. None of the gains were in respect of residential property.

Nim does not have any taxable income for the tax year 2020/21. He has unused capital losses of £16,000 brought forward from the tax year 2019/20.

Required (Each question is worth 2 marks):

(1) **What is the chargeable gain, after exemptions, arising on the sale of the house by Mae?**

   A   £8,000

   B   £64,000

   C   £0

   D   £7,400

(2) **How much of the gains arising on the disposal of the business and shares by Mae on 30 November 2020 qualifies for** business asset disposal **relief?**

   A   £216,000

   B   £250,000

   C   £261,000

   D   £181,000

(3) **What is the total cost of the shares in Kapook plc that will be used in Nim's capital gains computation in respect of the sale of 10,000 shares on 20 July 2020?**

   A   £19,000

   B   £21,067

   C   £23,400

   D   £22,875

(4) **What is Nim's capital gains tax liability for the tax year 2020/21?**

   A   £60,650

   B   £67,230

   C   £66,860

   D   £64,400

(5) **Nim has a number of assets which he is considering disposing of in the tax year 2021/22. Which of the following statements are INCORRECT?**

(1) The transfer of a 2% shareholding in an unquoted trading company to his wife, which is valued at £80,000 and which was purchased for £30,000, will not give rise to a chargeable gain.

(2) The sale of an antique table for £5,200, which Nim acquired for £5,900 will result in a capital loss of £700.

(3) The gain on the sale of a copyright for £7,000, which was acquired for £5,500 will be restricted to 5/3rds of £1,000 i.e. the excess proceeds above £6,000.

A (1) and (2) only

B (2) and (3) only

C (1) and (3) only

D All of them

Jamal

Question B3: Inheritance tax

Jamal died on 1 July 2020.

Jamal had made a gift of cash of £520,000 (after all available exemptions) to a trust on 4 May 2014. Jamal paid the tax arising on the gift. Jamal had made no previous gifts.

The value of Jamal's estate at the date of death included the following assets:

(1) An antique brooch, worth £200, which he bequeathed to his goddaughter. He had not made any other gifts to his goddaughter in the tax year 2020/21.

(2) Quoted shares worth £50,000, held in an ISA account.

(3) A life assurance policy on Jamal's life which was valued at death at £150,000. The proceeds paid to the executors were £158,000.

His estate does not include any residential property.

Jamal's wife died on 1 August 2007. Her chargeable estate for IHT purposes was £890,000. She left £75,000 to her son and the rest to Jamal. She had made no lifetime transfers.

The nil rate band in the tax year 2014/15 was £325,000 and in the tax year 2007/08 it was £300,000.

Required (Each question is worth 2 marks):

(1) **What is the gross chargeable value of the chargeable lifetime transfer made to the trust on 4 May 2014 that is accumulated in future IHT computations?**

    A   £568,750

    B   £243,750

    C   £559,000

    D   £520,000

(2) **If Jamal had also made cash gifts of £800 to his daughter on 8 April 2013 and £2,000 to his granddaughter on 1 May 2013, in consideration of her marriage, what would have been the amount of annual exemption available on the gift into the trust on 4 May 2014?**

    A   £3,000

    B   £5,200

    C   £6,000

    D   £3,200

(3) **In respect of the IHT due on the gift to the trust on 4 May 2014 as a result of Jamal's death, what rate of taper relief reduces the tax payable and what date is the tax payable?**

	Taper relief	Due date
A	80%	30 April 2021
B	20%	31 January 2021
C	80%	31 January 2021
D	20%	30 April 2021

(4) **What is the total value of the three assets listed above that will be included in Jamal's chargeable death estate for IHT purposes?**

    A   £208,200

    B   £208,000

    C   £200,000

    D   £158,200

(5) **By how much can Jamal's nil rate band available on death be increased as a result of his wife's death?**

    A   £225,000

    B   £300,000

    C   £250,000

    D   £243,750

Cherry Ltd

Question B4: Corporation tax

Cherry Ltd is a UK resident trading company. The following information is available in respect of the year ended 31 March 2021.

Trading profits

In the company's statement of profit or loss for the year ended 31 March 2021 the following expenses have been deducted:

	£
Motor expenses for the Managing Director's car, which has 40% private use	5,720
Staff Christmas party (costing £200 per head)	48,000
Legal fees in connection with the acquisition of land for use as a staff car park	15,000
	68,720

During the year ended 31 March 2021 Cherry Ltd had the following capital transactions.

		Cost/ (proceeds) £	CO$_2$ emission rate
New motor car (1)	Purchase	14,000	50 grams per kilometre
Motor car (2)	Disposal	(5,200)	170 grams per kilometre

The original cost of motor car (2) was £4,500.

The balance on the special rate pool as at 1 April 2020 was £4,000 and on the main pool it was £Nil.

Property income

On 1 January 2021 Cherry Ltd received a premium of £50,000 and annual rent of £6,000 in consideration for the grant of a 20 year lease over one of the three floors of its office premises. The purchase of the office premises in 2017 had been financed by a loan on which interest of £10,000 was payable in the year to 31 March 2021.

Related companies

During the year ended 31 March 2021 Cherry Ltd had taxable total profits of £1,800,000. It owned the following shareholdings in and received the following dividends from other companies.

	Shareholding	Dividends received £
Pear Ltd	80%	100,000
Grape Ltd	50%	50,000
Apricot Ltd	45%	35,000

In addition Pear Ltd owns 75% of the ordinary shares of Damson Ltd.

Required (Each question is worth 2 marks):

(1) **What amount must be added back in the adjustment of trading profits computation in respect of the expenses of £68,720 set out above?**

    A   £17,288

    B   £65,288

    C   £15,000

    D   £63,000

(2) **Assuming that Cherry Ltd claims the maximum capital allowances, what capital allowances would be claimed for the year ended 31 March 2021?**

    A   £13,500

    B   £12,800

    C   £2,020

    D   £3,020

(3) **What amount of property income must Cherry Ltd include in its corporation tax computation for the year ended 31 March 2021?**

    A   £29,167

    B   £22,500

    C   £20,500

    D   £32,500

(4) **What is the amount of Cherry Ltd's augmented profits for the year ended 31 March 2021?**

A   £1,985,000

B   £1,835,000

C   £1,900,000

D   £1,885,000

(5) **Which of the companies in which Cherry Ltd has a direct or indirect interest are members of Cherry Ltd's capital gains group?**

A   Pear Ltd, Damson Ltd and Apricot Ltd

B   Pear Ltd only

C   Pear Ltd, Damson Ltd and Grape Ltd

D   Pear Ltd and Damson Ltd only

Guys and Dolls

Question B5: VAT

Amanda runs 'Guys and Dolls' a business selling adult and children's clothing and footwear. Amanda started trading on 1 April 2020. Her sales since the commencement of trading have been as follows:

	Standard rated sales	Zero rated sales
1 April to 30 June 2020	£6,500 per month	£3,500 per month
1 July to 30 September 2020	£7,000 per month	£6,000 per month
1 October to 31 December 2020	£9,200 per month	£3,500 per month
1 January to 31 March 2021	£10,100 per month	£3,500 per month

These figures are stated exclusive of value added tax (VAT).

Amanda voluntarily registered for VAT from 1 April 2020 and prepared her first return for the quarter to 30 June 2020.

Quarter to 30 June 2020

In the quarter to 30 June 2020 she incurred input VAT of £5,500 in respect of sundry expenses as follows:

	£
Legal fees in connection with purchase of business premises	2,000
Entertaining overseas customers	500
Stationery (half of which was still on hand at 30 June 2020)	3,000

Quarter to 30 September 2020

In the quarter to 30 September 2020 Amanda incurred recoverable input tax of £1,800 in respect of goods and services purchased for the business.

Quarter to 30 June 2021

On 1 June 2021 Amanda received a large order of £25,000 (VAT inclusive) for the supply of standard rated clothing. As the order was from a new customer she asked for a deposit of £5,000, which she received on 5 June 2021. On 30 June 2021 the clothing was delivered to the customer. Amanda sent an invoice to the customer on 6 July 2021, which was paid on 31 July 2021.

Required (Each question is worth 2 marks):

(1) **If Amanda had not registered for VAT voluntarily by what date would Amanda have been required to inform HM Revenue and Customs that she was liable to be compulsorily registered for VAT?**

　　A　　30 March 2021

　　B　　31 March 2021

　　C　　30 December 2020

　　D　　31 December 2020

(2) **How much input tax incurred on sundry expenses can Amanda recover in the VAT return for the quarter to 30 June 2020?**

　　A　　£3,000

　　B　　£3,500

　　C　　£5,500

　　D　　£4,000

(3) **Assuming that the flat rate percentage for Amanda's business is 9% by how much would Amanda's VAT liability differ if she had claimed to use the flat rate scheme for the quarter to 30 September 2020?**

    A   £312 lower

    B   £132 lower

    C   £1,812 higher

    D   £1,488 higher

(4) **Amanda submitted the VAT returns and VAT payments for the two VAT quarters ended 30 September 2020 and 31 December 2020 late. If Amanda submits the VAT return and VAT payment for the quarter ended 31 March 2021 on 14 May 2021 which of the following statements is/are CORRECT?**

    (1)   Default interest will be charged from 7 May 2021 to 14 May 2021.

    (2)   A default surcharge liability period will run until 31 March 2022.

    (3)   A default surcharge penalty of 10% of the late paid VAT will be charged.

    (4)   A late filing penalty of £100 will be charged.

    A   (1) and (2)

    B   (2) only

    C   (3) and (4) only

    D   (1), (3) and (4)

(5) **How much output VAT should be included in the VAT return for the quarter to 30 June 2021 in respect of the large order of clothing from the new customer?**

    A   £833

    B   £1,000

    C   £4,167

    D   £5,000

Test your understanding answers

Amos

Answer 1 – Chapters 3 & 4

(a) **Property business income – y/e 5 April 2021**

	£	£
Rent received		
(£3,375 (W1) + £7,800 (W2) + £2,500 (W3) + £600 (W3) + £5,400 (W4))		19,675
Premium assessable (W1)		2,250
		21,925
Repairs and decorating (£800 + £2,500 + £100)	3,400	
Expenses (£2,050 + £1,625 + £600)	4,275	
Loan interest re. House 2	0	
		(7,675)
Property business income		14,250

Workings

(W1) **House 1**

(i) Rent received in period 1 September 2020 to 5 April 2021: (£4,500 × 3/4) = £3,375

(ii) Lease premium

	£
Premium	2,500
Less: (6 – 1) × 2% × £2,500	(250)
Assessable premium	2,250

(iii) Roof repairs are not allowable as they were making good a deficiency on purchase, and are therefore capital expenditure.

(W2) House 2

(i)   Rent: (£650 × 12) = £7,800.

(ii) Allowable expenses = (£300 + £850 + £500 + £400) = £2,050.

(iii) The cost of replacing the cooker is an allowable deduction as it is a domestic item provided for use by the tenant.

(iv) Relief for finance costs incurred in relation to residential properties is restricted to basic rata tax relief. No deduction is given in the property income calculation; instead, a tax reducer is given in the income tax computation.

(W3) House 3

(i)   Rent from expired lease: Received on 1 May to 1 September 2020 inclusive (£500 × 5) = £2,500. Rent due on 1 October and 1 November 2020 never received and is therefore not taxable under cash basis.

(ii) Rent from new lease: £600 (include rent received on 1 April 2021).

(iii) Allowable expenses = (£450 + £1,175) = £1,625.

(W4) House 4

(i)   Rent: (£450 × 12) = £5,400.

(ii) Insurance for the year to 5 April 2021 paid during the year £400.

(iii) Allowable expenses = (£400 + £200) = £600.

(b)   Income tax computation – 2020/21

	Non-savings income	Savings income	Dividend income	Total
	£	£	£	£
Employment income	10,300			10,300
Property income (part a)	14,250			14,250
Interest income		1,625		1,625
Dividend income			500	500
Total income	24,550	1,625	500	26,675
Less: PA	(12,500)			(12,500)
Taxable income	12,050	1,625	500	14,175

	£		£
Income tax:			
Non-savings income – basic rate	12,050	× 20%	2,410
Savings income – nil rate	1,000	× 0%	0
Savings income – basic rate	625	× 20%	125
Dividend income – nil rate	500	× 0%	0
	———		
	14,175		
Income tax liability			2,535
Less: Property interest (£3,750 × 20%)			(750)
			———
Income tax payable			1,785
			———

Gabriel

Answer 1 – Chapter 5

Taxable employment income

	£	£
Salary		20,000
Expenses reimbursed: (Note 1)		
Entertainment expenses – exempt	0	
Travelling and subsistence expenses	385	
Telephone (£160 × 60%)	96	
	——	481
Benefits:		
Private medical insurance		409
Company car (24% × £20,900) (W)	5,016	
Less: Employee contribution (£10 × 12)	(120)	
	——	4,896
Private fuel (24% × £24,500)		5,880
Annual value of flat	650	
Less: Employee contribution (£40 × 12) (Note 2)	(480)	
	——	170
Benefit for use of TV (20% × £500)		100
Benefit for gift of TV (£500 – £100 – £100)		
(Note 3)		300
		——
Employment income assessment		32,236

Working: Appropriate percentage

101g/km	Basic % for petrol	14%
	Plus (105 – 55) × 1/5	10%
		——
		24%

Notes:

(1) The reimbursed expenses for which Gabriel could claim a deduction are exempt.

(2) The council tax is the personal liability of Gabriel. If his employer met the cost, it would be taxed on Gabriel as a benefit.

(3) The market value of the TV at the time of the gift is £150, therefore the £300 benefit calculation is used as it is higher.

Parson

Answer 1 – Chapter 7

Tax adjusted trading profit – y/e 31 December 2020

	£	£
Profit per accounts	35,950	
Rent received		9,500
Wages and salaries	0	
Rent and rates (£12,900 × 1/10)	1,290	
Light and heat (£5,250 × 1/7)	750	
Depreciation of fixtures and fittings	1,500	
Insurance	0	
Business travel expenses	0	
Christmas presents for staff	0	
Entertaining suppliers	2,750	
Entertaining customers	2,300	
Gifts of food	125	
Gifts of calendars	0	
Trading debts written off	0	
Increase in allowances for receivables	0	
Supplier loan written off	1,700	
Trade debt recovered		0
Depreciation of vehicles	7,500	
Private motor expenses (£3,300 × 4,000/12,000)	1,100	
Salesman's motor expense	0	
Donation to national charity	50	
Political donation	100	
Subscription to Chamber of Commerce	0	
Wedding gift to member of staff	0	
Squash club subscription	250	
Advertising in trade press	0	
Cost of renewing 21 year lease	0	
Taxation services re capital gains tax	750	
Debt collection	0	
Legal fees re unfair dismissal of employee	0	
Interest on bank overdraft	0	
Van expenses	0	
Telephone	0	
Repairs to office photocopier	0	
New printer – capital	650	
Central heating – capital	2,200	
Decorating the office	0	
Own consumption (£450 × 130/100)	585	
Use of office		250
Private telephone (£450 × 2/5)		180
	———	———
	59,550	9,930
	(9,930)	———
	———	
Tax adjusted trading profit (before capital allowances)	49,620	
	———	

Note: It is unlikely that there will be such a long question solely on the adjustment of profits in the examination. It is included here as it is a good practice question, which tests a wide range of expenses.

Angela

Answer 2 – Chapter 7

(a) **Cash basis – year ended 30 June 2021**

	£	£
Revenue (£57,640 – £4,560)		53,080
Less: Guest house furniture	5,300	
Food and household expenses (£16,200 – £4,200)	12,000	
Motor expenses (W) (Note)	4,700	
Other expenses (£4,960 – £850)	4,110	
	———	(26,110)
		———
Tax adjusted trading profit		26,970
		———

Note: The cost of the car is not allowable under the cash basis. Capital allowances are available instead for expenditure on cars, but are not available where the flat rate mileage allowance is claimed.

The TX examining team has stated that where the cash basis is used, you should assume that flat rate expenses will also be claimed.

Working: Motor expenses – cash basis

	£
10,000 × 45p	4,500
800 × 25p	200
	———
	4,700
	———

(b) **Accruals basis – year ended 30 June 2021**

	£	£
Revenue		57,640
Less: Food and household expenses		
(£16,200 × 60%)	9,720	
Motor expenses (£5,720 × 80%)	4,576	
Other expenses	4,960	
Capital allowances (per question)(Note)	7,964	
		(27,220)
Tax adjusted trading profit		30,420

Note: In the TX examination you may be required to calculate the available capital allowances (see Chapter 8).

The following working sets out how the figure given in the question has been calculated. You may wish to revisit this once you have studied Chapter 8.

Working: Capital allowances

	£	Private use car £	Allowances £
Additions – no AIA or FYA			
Private use car (CO_2 emissions < 110g/km)		18,500	
Additions – with AIA			
Furniture	5,300		
AIA	(5,300)		5,300
	———	0	
		18,500	
WDA (18% × £18,500)		(3,330) × 80%	2,664
TWDV c/f		15,170	
Total allowances			7,964

Austin

Answer 1 – Chapter 8

Tax adjusted trading profits

	Adjusted profit before CAs £	Capital allowances (W) £	Tax adjusted trading profits £
10 m/e 31.3.2021	1,488,514	(836,499)	652,015
y/e 31.3. 2022	1,502,891	(42,496)	1,460,395

Working: Capital allowances computation

	Main pool £	Short life asset £	Private use car £	B.U. %	Allowances £
10 m/e 31 March 2021					
Additions (no AIA or FYA):					
PU car (CO$_2$ emissions > 110 g/km)			15,600		
Additions (eligible for AIA):					
Equipment (Note 1)	834,760	2,400			
Van	16,500				
	851,260				
AIA (Max) (Note 2)	(833,333)	(0)			833,333
		17,927			
	17,927	2,400	15,600		
WDA (18% × 10/12)	(2,689)				2,689
WDA (6% × 10/12)			(780)	× 15%	117
WDA (18% × 10/12)		(360)			360
TWDV c/f	15,238	2,040	14,820		
Total allowances					836,499
y/e 31 March 2022					
Additions (eligible for AIA):					
Equipment	20,200				
Furniture	18,020				
	38,220				
AIA	(38,220)				38,220
	0				
Less: Disposal	(500)	(550)			
	14,738	1,490	14,820		
Balancing allowance		(1,490)			1,490
WDA (18%)	(2,653)		0		2,653
WDA (6%)			(889)	× 15%	133
TWDV c/f	12,085	0	13,931		
Total allowances					42,496

Notes:

1. Expenditure incurred pre-trading is treated as if incurred on the first day of trading.

2. Maximum AIA for a 10 month period is £833,333 (£1,000,000 x 10/12). This is allocated to general plant and machinery in preference to the short life asset.

3. It is unlikely that you will get such a long question in the examination solely on capital allowances. It is included here as it is a good practice question which tests a number of issues.

Abiya

Answer 1 – Chapter 9

(a) **Assessable tax adjusted trading profits**

Tax year	Basis period		Assessable profits £
2019/20	(1 July 2019 – 5 April 2020)		
	Actual basis	9/22 × £33,000	13,500
2020/21	(6 April 2020 – 5 April 2021)		
	Actual basis	12/22 × £33,000	18,000
2021/22	(1 May 2020 – 30 April 2021)		
	CYB	12/22 × £33,000	18,000

Overlap profits

The profits assessed twice are those for the period 1 May 2020 to 5 April 2021 = (11/22 × £33,000) = £16,500.

(b) **Avoidance of overlap profits**

By choosing an accounting date coterminous with the tax year it is possible to avoid the creation of overlap profits.

If Abiya had chosen 5 April as her accounting date instead of 30 April the assessments for the first three tax years would have been based on the following basis periods with a consequent absence of overlap profits.

Tax year	Basis period
2019/20	1.7.19 – 5.4.20
2020/21	6.4.20 – 5.4.21
2021/22	6.4.21 – 5.4.22

Tutorial note:

Using a 5 April and not a 30 April year end may make a significant difference to assessable amounts in the year of cessation.

If Abiya ceases on 31 December 2026, for example, her 2026/27 basis period is nine months from 6 April 2026 in the first instance, but is 20 months from 1 May 2025 in the second instance, albeit with 11 months of overlap relief brought forward. In terms of 2026 values, the overlap relief created seven years earlier may not be sufficient to give a 'fair' nine months of assessable profits.

Maggie

Answer 2 – Chapter 9

Tax adjusted trading profit assessments

Tax year	Basis period		Assessable profits
			£
2017/18	Actual (1.11.17 – 5.4.18)	£14,000 (W) × 5/14	5,000
2018/19	Y/e 31.12.18	£14,000 (W) × 12/14	12,000
2019/20	Y/e 31.12.19	(W)	22,325
2020/21	Y/e 31.12.20	(W)	27,450

Overlap profits (1.1.18 – 5.4.18): (£14,000 × 3/14) = £3,000.

Working: Adjusted profit after capital allowances

	Adjusted profit	CAs	Tax adjusted trading profit
	£	£	£
14 m/e 31.12.18	32,000	(18,000)	14,000
Y/e 31.12.19	38,000	(15,675)	22,325
Y/e 31.12.20	45,000	(17,550)	27,450

Roger, Brigitte and Xavier

Answer 1 – Chapter 10

(a) **Assessable profits for each partner**

Profits are allocated between the partners as follows:

	Total	Roger	Brigitte	Xavier
	£	£	£	£
9 m/e 30 June 2017	30,000	15,000	15,000	
Y/e 30 June 2018	45,000	22,500	22,500	
Y/e 30 June 2019				
1.7.18 – 30.9.18 £50,000 × 3/12 (1/2:1/2)	12,500	6,250	6,250	
1.10.18 – 30.6.19 £50,000 × 9/12 (1/3:1/3:1/3)	37,500	12,500	12,500	12,500
Total	50,000	18,750	18,750	12,500
Y/e 30 June 2020	60,000	20,000	20,000	20,000

Roger and Brigitte are assessed under the opening year rules commencing in the tax year 2016/17:

Tax year	Basis period	Assessable profits £
2016/17	1.10.16 – 5.4.17: Actual (£15,000 × 6/9)	10,000
2017/18	1.10.16 – 30.9.17: First 12 months (£15,000 + (£22,500 × 3/12)	20,625
2018/19	Y/e 30.6.18: CYB	22,500
2019/20	Y/e 30.6.19: CYB	18,750
2020/21	Y/e 30.6.20: CYB	20,000

Xavier is assessed using the commencement rules starting in the tax year 2018/19:

Tax year	Basis period	Assessable profits £
2018/19	1.10.18 – 5.4.19: Actual (£12,500 × 6/9)	8,333
2019/20	1.10.18 – 30.9.19: First 12 months £12,500 + (£20,000 × 3/12)	17,500
2020/21	Y/e 30.6.20: CYB	20,000

(b) Overlap profits

	Roger £	Brigitte £
1.10.16 – 5.4.17 (£15,000 × 6/9)	10,000	10,000
1.7.17 – 30.9.17 (£22,500 × 3/12)	5,625	5,625
	15,625	15,625

	Xavier £
1.10.18 – 5.4.19 (£12,500 × 6/9)	8,333
1.7.19 – 30.9.19 (£20,000 × 3/12)	5,000
	13,333

Lucifer

Answer 1 – Chapter 11

(a) **Utilisation of trading losses**

The losses may be relieved in three ways:

(1) The losses may be set off against total income of the tax year of the loss and/or against total income of the preceding year.

(2) The losses may be carried forward against the first available tax adjusted trading profits of the same trade.

(3) Where a claim is made to set off the loss against total income for the tax year, any remaining loss may be set off against chargeable gains of the same tax year.

Note that the special opening year loss relief option is not available as Lucifer has no taxable income prior to the tax year 2018/19.

(b) **Most effective utilisation of the trading losses**

(i) **Calculation of losses**

	£
2018/19 – Actual basis	
6.4.18 to 5.4.19	
Period ended 30.9.18	20,000
Year ended 30.9.19 (1.10.18 – 5.4.19)	
(6/12 × £10,000)	5,000
	25,000
2019/20 – CYB	
Year ended 30.9.19	10,000
Less: Used in 2018/19	(5,000)
	5,000

(ii)   Income tax computations after loss relief

	2018/19	2019/20	2020/21
	£	£	£
Tax adjusted trading profit	0	0	11,000
Less: Loss relief b/f	–	–	(W)(6,250)
	–	–	(W)(4,750)
	0	0	0
Dividend income	3,750	2,778	2,000
Less: Loss relief			
– Current year	(3,750)		
Net income	0	2,778	2,000

(iii)   Chargeable gain computation – 2018/19

	£
Chargeable gain	15,000
Less: Trading loss relief	(15,000)
	0

(iv)   Explanation of optimum use of loss

Although the method of loss utilisation chosen results in the PA for the tax year 2018/19 being wasted it is considered the best of the several options available, as relief can be given against chargeable gains in that year.

There is rarely a guarantee of future profits and in view of the poor trading results it is thought the maximisation of cash flow and claiming relief as early as possible is the critical factor.

The dividend income in the tax year 2019/20 is covered by the PA. A claim against total income is not therefore made in this year.

> **Working: Loss working**
>
> | **2018/19** | **£** |
> |---|---|
> | Loss (part (b) (i)) | 25,000 |
> | Less: Used in 2018/19 – Total income | (3,750) |
> | Used in 2018/19 – Chargeable gains | (15,000) |
> | | |
> | Loss to carry forward | 6,250 |
> | Less: Used in 2020/21 | (6,250) |
> | | |
> | Loss to carry forward | 0 |
> | | |
> | **2019/20** | **£** |
> | Loss (part (b) (i)) | 5,000 |
> | Less: Used in 2020/21 | (4,750) |
> | | |
> | Loss to carry forward to 2021/22 | 250 |
>
> **Key answer tips**
>
> Loss questions should be answered by following a few simple rules:
>
> * Firstly, calculate the loss of the tax year, and
>
> * Secondly, deal with each loss separately and in chronological order.
>
> The choice is usually to relieve total income in the tax year of loss and/or the previous year.
>
> If there is a chargeable gain, it may be worthwhile making a claim against it.
>
> Any loss remaining is carried forward against future trading profits from the same trade.

Oprah

Answer 2 – Chapter 11

Loss relief offset

If Oprah wishes to take relief for the loss as soon as possible she will offset the loss against total income in 2019/20 and then 2020/21.

	2019/20 £	2020/21 £
Trade profits	72,000	0
Property income	80,000	80,000
Total income	152,000	80,000
Less: Loss relief		
(i) Against 2019/20 total income		
– No restriction against profits of same trade	(72,000)	
– Against other income (W1)	(50,000)	
(ii) Against 2020/21 total income – balance of loss (no restriction as < £50,000)		(29,000)
Net income	30,000	51,000
Less: Personal allowance	(12,500)	(12,500)
Taxable income	17,500	38,500

Working: Maximum loss relief against other income for 2019/20

	£
Total income/Adjusted net income	152,000
25% thereof	38,000

Maximum set off is £50,000 as it is greater than £38,000

Note that gift aid payments do not reduce total income for the purposes of calculating the maximum loss relief.

Sadiq

Answer 1 – Chapter 13

(a) Income tax and NIC payable – 2020/21

	£
Tax adjusted trading profit	59,900
Property business income	5,200
Building society interest	2,625
Dividend income	1,556
Total income	69,281
Less: PA	(12,500)
	56,781
Taxable income	

Income tax:	£		£
Non-savings income – basic rate (Note)	52,500	× 20%	10,500
Non-savings income – higher rate	100	× 40%	40
	52,600		
Savings income – nil rate band	500	× 0%	0
Savings income – higher rate	2,125	× 40%	850
Dividends – nil rate band	1,556	× 0%	0
Income tax liability	56,781		
			11,390

		£
Class 4 NIC		
(£50,000 – £9,500) × 9%	3,645	
(£59,900 – £50,000) × 2%	198	3,843
Total income tax and NIC payable		15,233

Note: The basic rate band is extended by the gross amount of the personal pension contributions of £15,000 (£12,000 × 100/80). The extended basic rate band is therefore £52,500 (£37,500 + £15,000).

(b) **Tax payments**

(i) **Balancing payment – 2020/21**

	£
Total income tax and NIC payable (part (a))	15,233
Capital gains tax liability	2,090
	———
Total tax payable	17,323
Less: POAs	(10,255)
	———
Balancing payment due 31 January 2022	7,068
	———

(ii) **Payments on account – 2021/22**

	£
POAs for 2021/22 are based on the total income tax and class 4 NIC payable of the previous tax year:	
Total income tax and NIC payable in 2020/21	15,233
	———
POAs for 2021/22:	
– 31 January 2022 (50% × £15,233)	7,617
– 31 July 2022 (50% × £15,233)	7,616
	———

Note that POAs are not required for CGT.

(c) **(i)** **Paying tax late**

If Sadiq does not pay the balancing payment for 2020/21 by the due date, interest will be charged from 31 January 2022 until the date of payment.

In addition, a 5% penalty of £353 (£7,068 at 5%) will be imposed if the balancing payment is not made within 30 days of the due date.

A further 5% penalty will be imposed if the payment has still not been made six months after the due date, and a further 5% if it has still not been made after 12 months.

(ii) **Filing date**

If Sadiq wishes to submit a paper return he should file his 2020/21 tax return by 31 October 2021.

(iii) **Retention of records**

The accounting records for the year to 30 April 2020 form the basis of the tax return for 2020/21.

Business records should be retained for five years after the normal filing date.

The accounting records for the year to 30 April 2020 should therefore be retained until 31 January 2027 (i.e. 5 years after 31 January 2022).

BM Ltd

Answer 2 – Chapter 13

(a) Under the RTI PAYE system the company is required to submit payroll information to HM Revenue & Customs each time a payment is made to an employee, on or before the date of the payment. Thus, the company must submit details of the managing director's salary on or before the last day of each month and the payroll information for the other employees must be submitted on or before Friday each week.

The last RTI submission for the tax year should be indicated as such and should include a year end summary of the total income tax and NICs deducted for each of the employees during the tax year.

(b) The company must pay the income tax and national insurance in respect of the employees' earnings in the tax month to 5 April 2021 by 22 April 2021.

(c) **Taxable benefits 2020/21**

   (i)   Car benefit

       £18,000 × 36% (W) = £6,480

       Note: The taxable benefit is based on the list price of the car when new. The price paid by the employer is irrelevant even when it was acquired second hand.

   (ii) Non-cash vouchers

       The taxable benefit per employee is based on the cost to the employer of providing the voucher, i.e. £180 per employee.

The car and the vouchers should be reported to HM Revenue & Customs on a P11D for each employee unless BM Ltd has applied to HMRC to tax the benefits through the PAYE system. A P11D must be submitted by 6 July 2021.

Working – Car %

13% + ((165 – 50)/5) = 36%

(d) **Class 1A NIC 2020/21**

Class 1A is only due on the car benefit. The non-cash vouchers are subject to class 1 NICs.

Class 1A liability: £6,480 × 13.8% = £894

The due payment date for an electronic payment is 22 July 2021.

Olive – Comprehensive income tax question

Answer 3 – Chapter 13

(a) **Tax adjusted trading profit – year ended 31 December 2020**

	£
Net profit	38,500
Depreciation	2,350
Private accommodation (£1,980 + £5,920 = £7,900 × 30%)	2,370
Motor expenses (£4,700 × 12,000/20,000)	2,820
Fine (Note 1)	220
Donation to political party	100
Excessive salary (Note 3) (£14,000 – £10,500)	3,500
Own consumption (Note 4) (52 × £45)	2,340
Less: Patent royalties (£150 × 4) (Note 5)	(600)
Capital allowances (Note 6)	(1,200)
Tax adjusted trading profit	50,400

Notes:

(1) Fines are not allowable except for parking fines incurred by an employee.

(2) Theft is an allowable expense provided it is by an employee rather than the business owner.

(3) A salary to a family member must not be excessive. Since Olive's daughter is paid £3,500 more than the other sales assistants, this amount is not allowable.

(4) Goods for own consumption are valued at selling price as no entries have been made in the accounts.

(5) The patent royalties have been paid wholly and exclusively for the purposes of the trade and are therefore deductible from trading profits.

(6) Capital allowances for Olive's motor car are £3,000 (£16,667 × 18%), with the business proportion being £1,200 (£3,000 × 8,000/20,000).

(b) **Income tax computation – 2020/21**

	Total	Non-savings	Savings	Dividends
	£	£	£	£
Trading income	50,400	50,400		
Employment income	6,000	6,000		
Building society interest	1,800		1,800	
Dividends	1,200			1,200
Total income	59,400	56,400	1,800	1,200
Less: Reliefs				
Loan interest (Note 1)	(220)	(220)		
Net income	59,180	56,180	1,800	1,200
Less: PA	(12,500)	(12,500)		
Taxable income	46,680	43,680	1,800	1,200

Income tax:			£
Non-savings income – basic rate (Note 2)	42,500	× 20%	8,500
Non-savings income – higher rate	1,180	× 40%	472
Savings income – nil rate band (Note 3)	500	× 0%	0
Savings income – higher rate	1,300	× 40%	520
Dividends – nil rate band	1,200	× 0%	0
	46,680		
Income tax liability			9,492
Less: PAYE			(1,200)
Income tax payable			8,292

Notes:

(1) The loan interest qualifies as a relief deductible from total income since the loan was used by Olive to finance expenditure for a qualifying purpose.

(2) The personal pension contribution results in Olive's basic rate tax band threshold being extended to £42,500 (£37,500 + £5,000).

(3) As Olive is a higher rate taxpayer, her savings income nil rate band is £500.

Balancing payment for 2020/21 due on 31 January 2022

(£8,292 + £392 – £4,559) = £4,125

Note: The balancing payment includes the CGT liability for the year (given in the question).

Payments on account for 2021/22

Payments on account are not required for CGT, so the payments on account for 2021/22 will be £4,146 (£8,292 × 50%).

These are due on 31 January 2022 and 31 July 2022.

Consequences of paying balancing payment late

(1) Interest is charged where a balancing payment is paid late. This will run from 1 February 2022 to 30 April 2022.

(2) The interest charge will be £27 (£4,125 × 2.6% × 3/12).

(3) In addition, a 5% penalty of £206 (£4,125 × 5%) will be imposed as the balancing payment is not made within one month of the due date.

Ball Ltd

Answer 1 – Chapter 16

Ball Ltd

Year ended 31 December	2018 £	2019 £	2020 £	2021 £
Tax adjusted trading profit	42,000	19,000	0	16,000
Interest income	3,000	2,000	1,000	2,000
Chargeable gains	4,000	4,000	4,000	4,000
Total profits	49,000	25,000	5,000	22,000
Less: Loss relief				
– Current year			(5,000)	
– 12 month carry back		(25,000)		
	49,000	0	0	22,000
Less: Trading loss b/f	–	–	–	(19,500)
Less: QCD relief (Note)	(10,000)	Wasted	–	(2,500)
Taxable total profits	39,000	0	0	0

Loss memorandum

	£
Loss in y/e 31 December 2020	67,000
Less: Used in current year – y/e 31.12.20	(5,000)
Used in 12 month carry back – y/e 31.12.19	(25,000)
Loss carried forward	37,000
Less: Used in y/e 31.12.21	(19,500)
Loss carried forward at 31.12.21	17,500

Notes:

(1) The QCD of £10,000 paid in the y/e 31 December 2019 is wasted. Note that the amount of the loss offset cannot be restricted to leave sufficient profits to be covered by the QCD.

(2) The unrelieved loss of £37,000 as at 31 December 2020 is carried forward for offset against total profits but can be restricted to preserve relief for the QCD. Therefore, £19,500 will be used against profits in the y/e 31 December 2021.

Gold Ltd

Answer 1 – Chapter 17

(a) **Gold Ltd – Corporation tax liabilities**

Year ended	30.9.20	30.9.21
	£	£
Tax adjusted trading profit	141,000	90,000
Property income	5,000	0
Chargeable gain	0	12,000
Total profits	146,000	102,000
Less: QCD relief	(2,000)	(2,000)
	144,000	100,000
Less: Group relief (see notes)	(70,000)	(50,000)
TTP	74,000	50,000
Corporation tax liability (£74,000/£50,000 × 19%)	14,060	9,500

Notes:

(1) The APs are not coterminous, so both Gold Ltd's taxable total profits and Silver Ltd's tax adjusted trading loss must be time apportioned.

(2) For the year ended 30 September 2020 group relief is the lower of Gold Ltd's available profits of £72,000 (£144,000 × 6/12) and Silver Ltd's available loss of £70,000 (£140,000 × 6/12) i.e. £70,000.

(3) For the year ended 30 September 2021 group relief is the lower of Gold Ltd's available profits of £50,000 (£100,000 × 6/12) and Silver Ltd's available loss of £70,000 (£140,000 × 6/12) i.e. £50,000.

(b) **Factors to consider**

– Maximising the tax saving.

– Obtaining relief as soon as possible.

– The extent to which QCD relief will be lost if loss relief is set against the loss making company's total profits in the current and previous accounting period.

(c) **Most beneficial way to relieve Silver Ltd's trading loss**

– To obtain relief as soon as possible Silver Ltd should make a claim to offset the loss against its total profits in the year ended 31 March 2020. So that the carry back claim does not result in the wastage of the QCDs the loss offset should be restricted to £99,000, leaving total profits of £50,000, which the QCDs will reduce to £nil. This will result in a repayment of the tax paid in respect of this year and improve the company's cash flow position.

– A loss carryback claim itself cannot be restricted (i.e. it is an all or nothing claim against total profits before QCDs). However, making a group relief claim first will reduce the loss available for carry back.

– A group relief claim should therefore be made to offset £41,000 of the losses against the taxable total profits of Gold Ltd for the year ended 30 September 2020. This leaves losses of £99,000 (£140,000 – £41,000) in Silver Ltd which it can carry back to the year ended 31 March 2020 (there are no profits in the year ended 31 March 2021 to set the losses against).

– No group relief claim can be made in respect of the year ended 30 September 2021 as Silver Ltd's loss has been fully utilised.

Apple Group

Answer 2 – Chapter 17

(a) **Group relationship – Group relief**

One company must be a 75% subsidiary of the other, or both companies must be 75% subsidiaries of the holding company.

The parent company must have an effective interest of at least 75% of the subsidiary's ordinary share capital.

The parent company must also have the right to receive at least 75% of the subsidiary's distributable profits and net assets (were it to be wound up).

(b) **Corporation tax liabilities – y/e 31 March 2021**

	Apple Ltd £	Banana Ltd £
Tax adjusted trading profit	–	650,000
Chargeable gain (£48,000 – £8,000) (see note)	40,000	–
Total profits	40,000	650,000
Less: QCD's	(40,000)	
TTP before group relief	0	650,000
Less: Group relief		(125,000)
TTP	0	525,000
CT @ 19%	0	99,750

Note:

Some of Apple Ltd's chargeable gain can be rolled over against the reinvestment by Banana Ltd. The proceeds not reinvested of £48,000 (£418,000 – £370,000) remain chargeable in the year ended 31 March 2021. The balance can be deferred.

Banana Ltd and Apple Ltd should make a joint election to transfer the capital loss realised by Banana Ltd to Apple Ltd to be set against Apple Ltd's gain.

Net chargeable gain = (£48,000 – £8,000) = £40,000.

Apple Ltd's total profits of £40,000 are reduced to £Nil by the QCDs. The trading loss of £125,000 is surrendered to Banana Ltd.

Ramble Ltd

Answer 1 – Chapter 18

(a) **Self-assessment tax return**

Ramble Ltd's self-assessment corporation tax return for the year ended 31 March 2020 was due by 31 March 2021.

As the company did not submit the return until 15 October 2021 there will be a late filing penalty of £200 as the return was submitted more than three months late.

As the outstanding tax was also made on 15 October 2021 there will also be a tax geared penalty of 10% of the tax unpaid more than six months after the filing date.

(b) **Corporation tax payments**

As Ramble Ltd's TTP in each of the two years ended 31 March 2021 exceeds £1,500,000 it is a large company for the purposes of paying its corporation tax liability for the year ended 31 March 2021. The company is therefore required to pay by quarterly instalments as follows:

– 14 October 2020 (month 7) (£2,780,000 × 19% × 1/4)	£132,050
– 14 January 2021	£132,050
– 14 April 2021	£132,050
– 14 July 2021	£132,050

Interest will be due on the late payment of corporation tax as follows:

– £132,050	– from 14 October 2020 to 1 May 2021
– £132,050	– from 14 January 2021 to 1 May 2021
– £132,050	– from 14 April 2021 to 1 May 2021
– £7,000 (W)	– from 1 May 2021 to 1 January 2022
– £132,050	– from 14 July 2021 to 1 January 2022

Working: underpayment

	£
Outstanding payments (3 × £132,050)	396,150
Less: Payment on 1 May 2021	(389,150)
Underpayment as at 1 May 2021	7,000

Amina

Answer 1 – Chapter 19

Capital gains computation – 2020/21

Warehouse	£	£
Sale proceeds	140,000	
Less: Cost	(95,000)	
Chargeable gain		45,000
Motor car		Exempt
Factory	£	
Sale proceeds	320,000	
Less: Incidental costs of disposal	(6,200)	
Net sale proceeds	313,800	
Less: Cost	(194,000)	
Incidental costs of acquisition	(3,300)	
Enhancement expenditure	(58,000)	
Chargeable gain (Note)		58,500
Net chargeable gains for the year		103,500
Less: Annual exempt amount		(12,300)
Less: Capital loss b/f (W)		(16,700)
Taxable gains		74,500

Capital gains tax

	£		£
Basic rate (£37,500 – £33,500)	4,000	× 10%	400
Higher rate	70,500	× 20%	14,100
	74,500		
Capital gains tax liability			14,500
Due date			31.1.2022

Note: The expenditure incurred in May 2008 for replacing the roof does not enhance the value of the factory and is not an allowable deduction – as it is replacing a roof that was already there!

The factory is an insignificant part of Amina's business and the disposal is not associated with the disposal of the entire business. Therefore business asset disposal relief is not applicable (see Chapter 22).

Working: Capital losses

In the tax year 2019/20, £400 (£12,700 – £12,300) of the capital loss brought forward is used to reduce that year's gains to zero.

The remaining capital loss of £16,700 (£17,100 – £400) is available to carry forward to the tax year 2020/21.

Lethabo and Faith

Answer 1 – Chapter 20

Lethabo – Capital gains tax computation – 2020/21

	Other £	Other £	Residential property £
House			
Net sale proceeds	63,850		
Less: Cost	(4,000)		
Extension	(2,000)		
Loft	(3,000)		
Chargeable gain	54,850		54,850
Sculpture			
Sale proceeds	6,500		
Less: Cost	(5,500)		
	1,000		
Gain cannot exceed (£6,500 – £6,000) × 5/3	833	833	
One tenth interest in racehorse			
Exempt as a chattel which is also a wasting asset		0	
Alfa Romeo vintage car			
Cars are exempt assets		0	
Chargeable gains		833	54,850
Less: AEA			(12,300)
Taxable gain		833	42,550
Capital gains tax			
£833 × 20%		167	
£42,550 × 28%		11,914	
			12,081

Note: Lethabo has no basic rate band remaining in 2020/21, therefore all his gains are taxed at 28% (residential property) and 20% (non-residential property).

Faith – Capital gains tax computation – 2020/21

	£	£
Icon		
Deemed sale proceeds	6,000	
Less: Cost	(6,300)	
Allowable loss		(300)
Plot of land		
Sale proceeds (3 hectares)	15,000	
Less: Cost (3 hectares)		
£4,500 × £15,000/(£15,000 + £25,000)	(1,688)	
Chargeable gain		13,312
Jade		
Sale proceeds	11,800	
Less: Cost	(6,500)	
Chargeable gain		5,300
Land		
Disposal proceeds	12,300	
Less: Deemed acquisition cost	(2,000)	
Chargeable gain		10,300
Net chargeable gain		28,612
Less: AEA		(12,300)
Taxable gain		16,312
Capital gains tax (£16,312 × 10%)		1,631

Notes: All of Faith's gains are non-residential property and fall within her basic rate band and are therefore taxed at 10%.

There will not be such a long question on CGT tax in the examination. It is included here as it provides good practice for a number of CGT issues.

Jasper

Answer 1 – Chapter 21

Total chargeable gains – 2020/21

		£	£
Shares in Carrot plc			
Net sale proceeds		8,580	
Less: Cost (W1)		(3,928)	
			4,652
Takeover			
Cash received (W2)		4,800	
Less: Cost (W2)		(1,030)	
			3,770
Shares in Grasp plc			
Sale proceeds		3,600	
Less: Cost (W2) £9,008 × 400/12,000		(300)	
			3,300
Total chargeable gains			11,722

Workings

(W1) **Carrot plc**

		Number	Cost £
July 2012	Purchase	1,750	2,625
May 2013	Purchase	200	640
		1,950	3,265
June 2014	Rights issue (1:10) @ £3.40	195	663
		2,145	3,928
November 2020	Sale	(2,145)	(3,928)

(W2) Grasp plc

Apportionment of cost of Cawte plc shares to new shares and cash acquired at date of takeover.

	Market value £	Cost allocation £
For 12,000 Cawte plc ord shares:		
12,000 Grasp £1 ord shares at 350p	42,000	9,008
24,000 Grasp 10% pref shares at 110p	26,400	5,662
Cash (12,000 × 40p)	4,800	1,030
	73,200	15,700

Takunda

Answer 1 – Chapter 22

CGT computation – 2020/21

	£	£
Goodwill		
Market value (Note 1)	60,000	
Less: Cost	(0)	
	60,000	
Less: Gift relief (£60,000 – £50,000) (Note 2)	(10,000)	
		50,000
Freehold office building		
Market value	130,000	
Less: Cost	(110,000)	
	20,000	
Less: Gift relief (Note 3)	(20,000)	
		0

Freehold warehouse (Note 4)

	£	£
Market value	140,000	
Less: Cost	(95,000)	
		45,000
Motor car (Note 5)		0
Net chargeable gains for the tax year		95,000
Less: Annual exempt amount		(12,300)
		82,700
Less: Capital loss brought forward		(5,500)
Taxable gains		77,200

	£
Capital gains tax (£77,200 × 20%) (Note 6 and 7)	15,440

Due date for CGT liability	31 January 2022

Notes:

(1) Takunda and Sienna are connected persons, and therefore the market values of the assets sold are used.

(2) The consideration paid for the goodwill exceeds the original cost by £50,000 (£50,000 – Nil). This amount is immediately chargeable to CGT.

(3) The consideration paid for the office building does not exceed the original cost, so full gift relief is available. Gift relief is not restricted.

(4) The warehouse does not qualify for gift relief as it has never been used for business purposes.

(5) Motor cars are exempt from CGT.

(6) Takunda does not have any basic rate band remaining, therefore all his gains are taxed at 20%.

(7) The gain on the goodwill left after gift relief would also qualify for business asset disposal relief as the whole of the business is disposed of. Therefore £50,000 of the gain should be taxed at 10% and the remaining £27,200 relating to the warehouse is taxed at 20%. However, the question says that business asset disposal relief should be ignored.

Earth Ltd

Answer 1 – Chapter 23

(1) **Venus plc – sale of 25,000 shares**

	£
Sale proceeds	115,000
Less: Cost (W)	(17,000)
Unindexed gain	98,000
Less: IA (£27,115 – £17,000) (W)	(10,115)
Chargeable gain	87,885

Share pool	Number	Cost	Indexed cost
		£	£
Purchase – June 2001	40,000	34,000	34,000
Bonus issue – October 2011 (40,000 × ¼)	10,000	0	0
	50,000	34,000	34,000
Indexation to December 2017 £34,000 × 0.595			20,230
	50,000	34,000	54,230
Disposal – November 2020 Cost/Indexed cost × (25,000/50,000)	(25,000)	(17,000)	(27,115)
Balance c/f	25,000	17,000	27,115

(2) **Saturn plc**

	£
Sale proceeds	52,500
Less: Cost (W)	(80,000)
Allowable capital loss	(27,500)

Share pool	Number	Cost	Indexed cost
		£	£
3 January 2021	30,000	97,500	139,623
Rights issue (1 : 2) @ £1.50	15,000	22,500	22,500
	45,000	120,000	162,123
Disposal – 22 January 2021	(30,000)	(80,000)	(108,082)
Balance c/f	15,000	40,000	54,041

Note: Indexation cannot be used to increase a capital loss.

(3) **Jupiter plc**

	£
Sale proceeds	55,000
Less: Cost (W)	(11,200)
Unindexed gain	43,800
Less: IA (£14,637 – £11,200)	(3,437)
Chargeable gain	40,363

Share pool	Number	Cost	Indexed cost
		£	£
7 March 2021	10,000	14,000	18,296

Takeover consideration

	Value
	£
20,000 Ordinary shares @ £2.50	50,000
10,000 Preference shares @ £1.25	12,500
	62,500

Allocation of cost and indexed cost

	Cost	Indexed cost
	£	£
Ordinary shares		
(50,000/62,500) × £14,000/£18,296	11,200	14,637
Preference shares		
(12,500/62,500) × £14,000/£18,296	2,800	3,659
	14,000	18,296

Note: It is unlikely that there will be such a long question on company chargeable gains in the examination. It is included here as it provides good practice for a number of areas.

Gerry

Answer 1 – Chapter 24

IHT payable during lifetime

	CLT 4.6.2013 £	PET 4.3.2015 £	CLT 4.6.2020 £
Transfer of value	368,000	10,000	100,000
Less: Marriage exemption		(5,000)	
Less: Annual exemption			
Current year	(3,000)	(3,000)	(3,000)
Previous year	(3,000)	(0)	(3,000)
Chargeable amount	**362,000**	**2,000**	**94,000**
NRB @ date of gift	£		£
– 2013/14 (2012/13 b/f) Net	325,000		
– 2020/21 (2019/20 b/f) Net			325,000
Less: GCTs < 7 years before gift			
(4.6.2006 – 4.6.2013)	(0)		
(4.6.2013 – 4.6.2020) (ignore PET)			(371,250)
NRB available	(325,000)		(0)
Taxable amount	**37,000**	0	**94,000**
IHT payable @ 25%	9,250	0	23,500
Paid by	Gerry		Gerry
Due date of payment	30.4.2014		30.4.2020
Gross chargeable amount c/f	(£362,000 net + £9,250 tax) **371,250**	**2,000**	(£94,000 net + £23,500 tax) **117,500**

(Annual exemption current year: 2013/14, 2014/15, 2020/21 respectively)

Notes:

1 No further IHT will be due in respect of the first CLT as Gerry will have survived the gift by more than 7 years.

2 The wedding gift to Jack is a PET. There is no IHT payable during Gerry's lifetime and providing Gerry survives until 4 March 2022, no IHT will arise in relation to this gift at all. However, if Gerry dies before 4 March 2021, the PET will become chargeable. The £2,000 chargeable amount will be liable at 40%, but taper relief will reduce the IHT by 20% per annum if Gerry survives for more than three years.

3 Should Gerry die before 4 June 2026, additional IHT at death rates of 40% may become payable on the last CLT. Taper relief may be available and the lifetime tax paid is an allowable deduction.

Tareq

Answer 2 – Chapter 24

Estate computation – Death on 31 July 2020

	£	£
Shares in ABC plc (100,000 × 242.5p)		242,500
Holiday cottage		120,000
Bank and cash balances		150,000
Other assets		208,000
Insurance policy proceeds		88,000
Estate value		808,500
Less: Exempt legacy – wife		(55,000)
Gross chargeable estate		753,500
NRB at death	325,000	
Less: GCTs in 7 yrs pre-death (31.7.13 – 31.7.20)	(0)	
NRB available		(325,000)
Taxable amount		428,500
IHT due on death (£428,500 × 40%)		171,400

The tax is payable by the executors of Tareq's estate, and is due by 31 January 2021 or on submission of the estate accounts to HMRC if earlier.

The tax will be paid out of the estate and is therefore borne by Tareq's daughter, who inherited the residue of the estate.

Nur

Answer 3 – Chapter 24

Nur

(a) IHT payable during lifetime

	CLT 28.11.2008 £	PET 15.4.2014 £	CLT 10.3.2015 £
Transfer of value	93,000	71,000	268,000
Less: Marriage exemption		(5,000)	
Less: Annual exemption			
Current year	(3,000) 2008/09	(3,000) 2014/15	(0) 2014/15
Previous year	(3,000) 2007/08 b/f	(3,000) 2013/14 b/f	(0) 2013/14 b/f
Chargeable amount	87,000 Net	60,000	268,000 Net
NRB @ date of gift	£		£
– 2008/09	300,000		
– 2014/15			325,000
Less: GCTs < 7 years before gift			
(28.11.2002 – 28.11.2008)	(0)		
(10.3.2008 – 10.3.2015) (ignore PET)			(87,000)
NRB available	(300,000)		(238,000)
Taxable amount	0	0	30,000
IHT payable	0	0	7,500 @ 25%
Paid by			Jane
Due date of payment	(£87,000 net + £Nil tax)		30.9.2015 (£268,000 net + £7,500 tax)
Gross chargeable amount	87,000	60,000	275,500

IHT payable on death

Date of death: 20 November 2020
7 years before: 20 November 2013

CLT on 28.11.2008 is more than 7 years before death – therefore no IHT payable on death

	PET 15.4.2013		CLT 10.3.2014	
	£		£	
Gross chargeable amount b/f (as above)		60,000		275,500
NRB @ date of death – 2020/21	325,000		325,000	
Less: GCTs < 7 years before gift				
(15.4.2007 – 15.4.2014)	(87,000)			
(10.3.2008 – 10.3.2015) (£87,000 + £60,000)			(147,000)	
(include 15.4.2014 PET as it became chargeable)	-------		-------	
NRB available		(238,000)		(178,000)
		-------		-------
Taxable amount		0		97,500
		-------		-------
IHT payable @ 40%		0		39,000
Less: Taper relief				
(10.3.2015 – 20.11.2020) (5 – 6 years before death)	(0)		(60%)	(23,400)
Less: IHT paid in lifetime				(7,500)
		-------		-------
IHT payable on death		0		8,100
		-------		-------
Paid by (always the donee)				Trustees
Due date of payment				31.5.2021

IHT on Estate at death – 20 November 2020

	£	£
Main residence		235,000
Mortgage		(40,000)
		———
		195,000
Building society deposits		100,000
Ordinary shares in Banquo plc (10,000 × £9.48)		94,800
Life assurance policy		91,000
Land		108,000
		———
Gross chargeable estate		588,800
RNRB (Note)		(175,000)
		———
NRB at death	325,000	
Less: GCTs in 7 yrs pre-death		
(20.11.12 – 20.11.19)		
(£60,000 + £275,500)		
(first gift is too old,		
Include PET as chargeable on death)	(335,500)	
	———	
NRB available		(0)
		———
Taxable amount		413,800
		———
IHT due on death (£413,800 × 40%)		165,520
		———

Note:

Nur died after 6 April 2017 and left a main residence to her children. She is entitled to a RNRB of the lower of £175,000 and £195,000 (the net value of the property).

(b) **Payment of IHT liability**

The additional IHT in respect of the gift made on 10 March 2015 is payable by the trustees of the trust by 31 May 2021.

The IHT liability of the estate will, (in practice), be payable by the executors of Nur's estate on the earlier of 31 May 2021 or the delivery of their account to HMRC.

Inheritance received by Nur's children

Nur's children will inherit £298,280 (W).

Working:

Inheritance to children

	£
Chargeable estate	588,800
Less: Specific gift to brother	(100,000)
IHT payable on the estate (Note)	(165,520)
Estate value to be shared between the children	323,280

Note:

The IHT payable on the whole estate comes out of the residue of the estate and is therefore borne by the residual legatees (i.e. the children). This is because specific gifts (e.g. £100,000 to the brother) do not normally carry their own tax.

Michaela

Answer 4 – Chapter 24

Michaela

(a) IHT payable on death

Date of death: 15 October 2020
7 years before: 15 October 2013

	CLT 2.11.2016		PET 7.7.2019		Death estate 15.10.2020	
	£	£	£	£	£	£
Transfer of value				190,000		
Less: Marriage exemption				(5,000)		
Less: Annual exemption						
Current year 2019/20				(3,000)		
Previous year 2018/19 b/f				(3,000)		
Gross chargeable amount		340,000		179,000		1,050,000
RNRB						(175,000)
RNRB transferred from spouse						(175,000)
NRB @ date of death						
– 2020/21	325,000		325,000		325,000	
Less: GCTs < 7 years before gift						
(2.11.2009 – 2.11.2016)	(0)					
(7.7.2012 – 7.7.2019)			(340,000)			
(15.10. 2013 – 15.10.2020)						
(340,000 + 179,000)					(519,000)	
NRB available	(325,000)		(0)		(0)	
Taxable amount		15,000		179,000		700,000
IHT payable @ 40%		6,000		71,600		280,000
Less: Taper relief						
(2.11.2016 – 15.10.2020)	(20%)(1,200)		(0)		(0)	
Less: IHT paid in lifetime		(3,000)		(0)		(0)
IHT payable on death		1,800		71,600		280,000

(b)		Trustees	Natalia	Executors
	Payable by			
	Due date	30.4.2021	30.4.2021	30.4.2021
	(6 months from end of month of death)			

Wilf

Answer 1 – Chapter 25

(1) Registration

- Wilf will become liable to compulsory registration for VAT when his taxable supplies for any 12 month period exceed £85,000. His turnover is £9,465 per month starting on 1 January 2019 so he will exceed £85,000 after 9 months i.e. at the end of September 2019.

- He will need to notify HMRC by 30 October 2019 and will be registered with effect from 1 November 2019 or an earlier agreed date.

- As Wilf is selling to VAT registered traders, there should be no disadvantage to registering for VAT voluntarily before 1 November 2019. His customers will be able to reclaim any VAT charged by Wilf.

- It would therefore be beneficial to register immediately as Wilf will be able to reclaim input VAT as follows:

(i) Computer equipment – even if purchased before registration, the VAT can be recovered provided Wilf still owns the computer at the date of registration. Reclaim £525 (£3,150 × 1/6).

(ii) Business telephone – reclaim £60 per quarter (£360 × 1/6).

(iii) Use of home as office – Wilf can reclaim VAT on the business proportion of his electricity bills £14 (£71 × 1/5) for the year.

(iv) Wilf cannot recover VAT on his car purchase. He can recover VAT on the running expenses of £183 and VAT on his petrol of £25 per month (£150 × 1/6). However, if he recovers input tax on the petrol, he will have to account for a VAT fuel charge. For a car with CO_2 emissions of 190 g/km, the VAT scale charge is £414 per quarter, which represents £69 of VAT (£414 × 1/6). This must be added to the output tax for each quarter.

(v) If Wilf registers by 1 June 2019 he will be able to reclaim the input VAT on his accountant's fee for preparing his cash flow projections. This is because he can recover input VAT on services supplied in the six months prior to registration.

(2) **Irrecoverable debts**

In the quarter which includes October 2020 Wilf could make a claim for the VAT on his outstanding debt.

The recoverable VAT is £417 (£2,500 × 1/6). This is permitted because Wilf has written off the debt in his books and it is more than 6 months since the date payment was due.

(3) **Discounts**

Where a discount is offered, then VAT must be calculated on the amount that the customer actually pays.

When Wilf raises the invoice, he will not know whether the customer will qualify for the discount by paying within the required timescale. He must therefore charge VAT on the invoice on the full price and either:

– issue a credit note if the discount is taken, or

– show full details of the terms of the prompt payment discount and include a statement that the customer can only recover input tax based on the amount paid. If the discount is taken then Wilf must then adjust his records to account for output tax on the amount received.

(4) **Sale of business**

There are two issues to consider here:

(i) No VAT needs to be charged if Wilf sells his business as a going concern provided:

– the new owner is or is liable to be VAT registered

– the assets sold are used in the same trade in the future, and

– there is no significant break in the trading.

Note that all of the above conditions must apply to avoid VAT otherwise VAT must be charged on the assets that are being sold.

(ii) Wilf must

– deregister unless his registration is transferred to the new owner. This is unlikely if they are unconnected third parties.

– notify HMRC that he has ceased to make taxable supplies. This notification must be within 30 days of cessation.

– account for VAT on the replacement values of his inventory (if any) and tangible non-current assets on hand at the date of deregistration, unless the business is sold as a going concern as above. However there will be no charge where the VAT due is below £1,000.

Mary

Answer 1 – Chapter 26

VAT return – quarter ended 31 March 2021

	£
Output tax	
Standard rated supplies:	
(£230,000 × 20%)	46,000
(£40,000 × 97.5% × 20%)	7,800
Zero rated sales (£50,000 × 0%)	0
Car fuel charge (2/3 × £406 × 1/6) (Note)	45
	———
	53,845
Input tax	
Standard rated purchases (£102,440 × 20%)	(20,488)
Standard rated expenses (£18,000 – £5,000) × 20%	(2,600)
Relief for impaired debts (£1,000 + £1,000) × 20% (Note)	(400)
	———
VAT payable	30,357
	———

Due and payable date is 7 May 2021 (filed and paid electronically).

Notes:

When a prompt payment discount is offered VAT is charged on the amount paid by the customer.

The car was bought on 1 February 2021 – therefore, in this quarter there are only two months of private use. The scale rates are VAT inclusive amounts, therefore the VAT element is (20/120) or (1/6).

Relief for impaired debts is available for the sales invoices issued on 1 May 2020 and 1 August 2020 as:

- the payments for these invoices were due on 1 June 2020 and 1 September 2020
- the debts are written off, and
- are more than six months overdue.

Relief for the invoice issued on 1 November 2020, the payment for which was due on 1 December 2020 is not available in this quarter as the debt is not over six months old.

Amber and Sonya

Answer B1: Income tax

(1) **B**

	£	£
List price of car	21,000	
Less: Capital contribution	(400)	
	———	
	20,600	
	———	
Car benefit (£20,600 × 30%)		6,180
Private medical insurance (cost to the employer)		450
		———
Taxable employment income		6,630
		———

(2) **D**

	£	£
Personal allowance		12,500
Total income = net income (£123,000 – £1,000)	122,000	
Less: Gross gift aid (£480 × 100/80)	(600)	
	———	
ANI	121,400	
Less: Limit	(100,000)	
	———	
	21,400 × 50%	(10,700)
		———
Adjusted PA		1,800
		———

Notes:

(1) Occupational pension scheme contributions are an allowable deduction from employment income.

(2) Charitable donations under gift aid are grossed up by 100/80 before being used in the adjusted personal allowance computation.

(3) As the adjusted net income exceeds £100,000 the allowance is reduced by £1 for every £2 it exceeds the limit. Net income for these purposes is adjusted (i.e. reduced) for both gross gift aid and gross personal pension contributions (PPCs) made in the year.

(3) **A**

Note: The tax year 2020/21 is the second tax year of trading. The period of account ending in 2020/21 is the 16 month period to 30 September 2020. As this period of account exceeds 12 months the basis period is the 12 months to the accounting date ending in the tax year, i.e. the 12 months to 30 September 2020.

(4) **A**

	Dividend income
	£
Taxable income	13,600
Less: Dividend nil rate band	(2,000)
Basic rate band	(5,100)
Income taxed at higher rate	6,500

Working: Basic rate band

	£
Basic rate band	37,500
Extended by gross PPCs (£1,200 × 100/80)	1,500
	39,000
Less: Non-savings income	(31,900)
Remaining BRB	7,100
Used by dividend NRB	(2,000)
Available	5,100

(5) **C**

Notes:

(1) A current year loss relief claim must be made against total income before any remaining loss can be offset against a capital gain.

(2) A prior year loss relief claim is against total income and not just trading income.

(3) A loss carried forward is offset against the first available trading profits from the same trade.

Nim and Mae Lom

Answer B2: Capital gains tax

(1) **A**

	£
Main private residence	
Disposal proceeds	186,000
Less: Cost	(122,000)
	64,000
Less: PRR (W)	(56,000)
Chargeable gain	8,000

Working: Private residence relief

One of the eight rooms in Mae's house was always used exclusively for business purposes, so the private residence exemption is restricted to £56,000 (£64,000 × 7/8).

Note: The final nine months exemption does not apply to any part of a property used for business purposes throughout the whole period of ownership.

(2) **C**

	£	£
Gains qualifying for business asset disposal relief:		
Business		
Goodwill	80,000	
Freehold office building	136,000	
		216,000
Shares		45,000
		261,000

Notes:

(1) The investment property does not qualify for business asset disposal relief because it was never used for business purposes.

(2) The shares qualify for business asset disposal relief as they are in Mae's personal trading company (i.e. she owns at least 5% of the shares) and she has been employed by the company and owned the shares for the previous 24 months.

(3) C

The disposal is first matched against the purchase on 24 July 2020 of 2,000 shares (this is within the following 30 days), and then against the shares in the share pool.

The cost of the shares in the share pool is calculated as:

Share pool – Kapook plc

		Number of shares	Cost
		£	£
Purchase	19 February 2012	8,000	16,200
Purchase	6 June 2017	6,000	14,600
		14,000	30,800
Disposal	20 July 2020		
	(£30,800 × 8,000/14,000)	(8,000)	(17,600)
Balance carried forward		6,000	13,200

Total cost is £23,400 (£5,800 + £17,600)

(4) D

Nim's capital gains tax liability – 2020/21

	Qualifying for BADR	Not qualifying
	£	£
Chargeable gains	200,000	250,300
Less: AEA		(12,300)
Less: Capital loss brought forward		
(see below)		(16,000)
Taxable gain	200,000	222,000
Capital gains tax		
£200,000 × 10%	20,000	
£222,000 × 20%	44,400	
	64,400	

Note: The annual exempt amount and capital losses brought forward can be deducted in the most advantageous way. Therefore, they are deducted from the gains not eligible for business asset disposal relief, leaving the whole £200,000 to be taxed at 10%.

Although Nim has no taxable income, gains qualifying for business asset disposal relief are deemed to utilise the basic rate band before non-qualifying gains. Therefore all of the non-qualifying gains are taxed at 20%.

(5) **B**

Notes:

(1) The transfer of any asset between spouses never gives rise to a gain or loss.

(2) An antique table is a non-wasting chattel. However, as it is bought and sold for less than £6,000 it is an exempt disposal and therefore an allowable loss does not arise.

(3) The copyright is a wasting asset (it has a useful life of less than 50 years), however it is not a chattel so the special £6,000 chattels rules do not apply. Instead the cost must be reduced on a straight line basis for the period of time that the asset has been held by Nim.

 Jamal

Answer B3: Inheritance tax

(1) **A**

	£	£
Value transferred (after exemptions)		520,000
NRB at date of gift (2014/15)	325,000	
Less: GCTs < 7 years before gift	(0)	
	———	
NRB available		(325,000)
		———
Taxable amount		195,000
		———
IHT payable × 25%		48,750
		———
Gross chargeable transfer accumulated (£520,000 + £48,750)		568,750
		———

Note: The inheritance tax is charged at 25% if it is paid by the donor as it is a net gift. This tax must then be added to the value transferred after exemptions (the net chargeable amount) to calculate the gross chargeable amount to carry forward.

(2) **B**

	PET 8 April 2013 £	PET 1 May 2013 £	CLT May 2014 £
Transfer of value	800	2,000	
Less: ME (max £2,500)		(2,000)	
Less: AE – 2013/14	(800)		
Less: AE – 2014/15			(3,000)
– 2013/14 b/f			
(£3,000 – £800)			(2,200)
	0	0	5,200

Notes:

The AE

- exempts the first £3,000 of lifetime transfers in any one tax year

- is applied chronologically to the first gift in the tax year, then (if there is any left) the second gift and so on

- must be applied to the first gift each year, even if the first gift is a PET and never becomes chargeable.

Any unused AE can only be carried forward one tax year.

The small gifts exemption only applies to gifts of £250 or less.

The marriage exemption (i.e. £2,500 for a grandparent) is used before the annual exemption.

(3) **C**

Note: The date of death is more than six years but less than seven years since the CLT on 4 May 2014. The rate of taper relief is 80%.

IHT as a result of death is due six months after the end of the month of death, i.e. 31 January 2021.

(4) **A**

	£
Brooch	200
Quoted shares	50,000
Life assurance policy	158,000
	208,200

Notes: The small gifts exemption (£250 per recipient per year) only applies to lifetime transfers.

Assets held in an ISA are chargeable assets for IHT purposes.

Life assurance policies on the deceased's own life are included at the value of the proceeds received, not the market value at the date of death.

(5) **D**

	£
Nil rate band on death of wife	300,000
Used on bequest to son	(75,000)
Unused NRB	225,000
Proportion of available NRB (£225,000/£300,000)	75%
Amount transferred to Jamal £325,000 × 75%	243,750

Notes: The unused proportion of the nil rate band on the death of a spouse is transferred, not the unused amount.

 Cherry Ltd

Answer B4: Corporation tax

(1) **C**

	£
Motor expenses	0
Staff Christmas party	0
Legal fees (capital)	15,000
Amount added to trading profit	15,000

Notes:

(1) There are no private use adjustments for a company. The Managing Director will have an employment income benefit for the private use of the car.

(2) Staff entertaining is always an allowable deduction for the employer. As the cost per head exceeded £150 the employees will have a taxable employment benefit of £200.

(2) **A**

	Special rate pool	Allowances
	£	£	£
TWDV b/f		4,000	
Proceeds – Motor car (2)		(4,500)	
– restricted to cost			
		(500)	
Balancing charge		500	(500)
New low emission car			
($CO_2 \leq 50g/km$)	14,000		
FYA (100%)	(14,000)		14,000
TWDV c/f		0	
			13,500

Notes:

(1) Motor car (1) is a new car and has CO_2 emissions up to 50 grams per kilometre and therefore qualifies for the 100% first year allowance (FYA).

(2) The proceeds for motor car (2) are restricted to the original cost figure of £4,500. The car has CO_2 emissions of 170 grams per kilometre and the proceeds are therefore deducted from the special rate pool, resulting in a balancing charge.

(3) **D**

	£
Premium received	50,000
Less: 2% × £50,000 × (20 – 1)	(19,000)
Assessable as property income	31,000
Plus: Rent (£6,000 × 3/12)	1,500
Property income	32,500

Note: Alternative calculation of the assessment on the landlord:

£50,000 × (51 − 20)/50 = £31,000

Interest payable on a loan to acquire a property which is rented out (i.e. not used for trading purposes) is not allowed as a deduction from property income. Instead, it is taxed under the loan relationship rules and is deducted from interest income.

(4) **D**

	£
TTP	1,800,000
Dividends received from:	
Grape Ltd	50,000
Apricot Ltd	35,000
Augmented profits	1,885,000

Note: Augmented profits is taxable total profits plus dividends received excluding those received from related 51% group companies.

Two companies are related 51% group companies if one is a 51% subsidiary of the other or both are 51% subsidiaries of a third company.

A 51% subsidiary is one where more than 50% of the ordinary share capital is directly or indirectly owned.

Thus Pear Ltd (60% direct ownership) and Damson Ltd (60% indirect ownership (80% × 75%)) are related 51% group companies.

(5) **D**

Note: A capital gains group comprises the parent company and its 75% (direct or indirect) subsidiaries and also, the 75% subsidiaries of the first subsidiaries and so on.

The parent company must have an effective interest of over 50%, in ALL companies.

Damson Ltd is a member of Cherry Ltd's gains group as Pear Ltd owns 75% of the company, and Cherry Ltd's effective interest is over 50% (i.e. 80% × 75% = 60%).

Guys and Dolls

Answer B5: VAT

(1) **C**

Amanda would be liable to compulsory VAT registration when her taxable supplies (i.e. standard rated and zero rated sales) during any 12 month period exceeded £85,000.

This would have happened on 30 November 2020 when taxable supplies amounted to £94,400 (((£6,500 + £3,500) × 3) + ((£7,000 + £6,000) × 3)) + ((£9,200 + £3,500) × 2)).

Amanda would have been required to inform HM Revenue & Customs that she was liable to be registered for VAT within 30 days of the end of the month in which the VAT registration threshold was exceeded, i.e. by 30 December 2020.

(2) **C**

Note: There is no distinction between capital and revenue expenses for VAT purposes. Thus the input tax on the legal fees in connection with the purchase of business premises is recoverable.

Input tax on entertaining overseas customers is specifically recoverable. Input tax on other entertaining (apart from entertaining staff) is irrecoverable.

Stationery is a business expenses and the input tax is recoverable in the return period in which the date of supply (i.e. tax point) arises. The fact that some of the stationery has not been used is irrelevant.

Note however, that if the stationery had been bought prior to the date of VAT registration then under the special rules for pre-registration VAT only input tax on goods still on hand at the date of registration would be recoverable.

(3) **D**

Using the flat rate scheme Amanda's VAT liability for the quarter to 30 September 2020 would be £3,888 (((£7,000 × 120%) + £6,000) × 3 × 9%).

Under the normal accounting method Amanda's VAT liability for the quarter to 30 September 2020 would be £2,400 ((£7,000 × 20% × 3) − £1,800).

Amanda's VAT liability would therefore have been £1,488 higher if she had used the flat rate scheme.

Note: Under the flat rate scheme, VAT is calculated by applying a fixed percentage to the sales figure (standard and zero rated) inclusive of VAT.

(4) **B**

Note: The late payment and filing of VAT returns is dealt with under the default surcharge provisions.

Default interest is charged on HMRC assessments and on errors voluntarily disclosed which are above the de minimis limits, but not on late payments of VAT shown on a VAT return.

The late submission for the quarter ended 31 March 2021 is the second default while under a surcharge liability notice. It will result in a penalty of 5% of the late paid VAT and an extension of the surcharge liability period to the 12 month anniversary of the end of the VAT period to which the default relates, i.e. to 31 March 2022.

(5) **A**

Note: The tax point determines the VAT return in which a transaction should be included.

The basic tax point for the order is the date the goods were delivered to the customer, i.e. 30 June 2021. However, the basic tax point (BTP) is overridden by an actual tax point (ATP) if prior to the BTP payment is received or an invoice is issued.

The actual tax point for the deposit is therefore the date of payment, i.e. 5 June 2021. The payment is VAT inclusive and the output tax is £833 (£5,000 × 1/6) which should be included in the VAT return for the quarter to 30 June 2021.

Provided the BTP has not already been overridden by a payment it is overridden if an invoice is issued within 14 days of the BTP. The ATP for the balance of the contract value of £20,000 is therefore 6 July 2021 and the output tax should be included in the VAT return for the quarter to 30 September 2021.

KAPLAN PUBLISHING